Table of Contents

THERAPEUTIC ACT WITH PERSONS D... BY ALZHEIMER'S DISEASE AND RELATED DISORDERS

Carol Bowlby, BA, BScOT, ODH

Occupational Therapist Geriatric Assessment Team
Victoria General Hospital
Halifax, Nova Scotia, Canada

pro·ed
An International Publisher
8700 Shoal Creek Boulevard
Austin, Texas 78757-6897
800/897-3202 Fax 800/397-7633
www.proedinc.com

© 1993 by PRO-ED, Inc.
8700 Shoal Creek Boulevard
Austin, Texas 78757-6897
www.proedinc.com

Illustrations copyright © 1992 by Michael Stowe

ISBN-13: 978-089079900-0
ISBN-10: 0-89079-900-8

Previously printed under ISBN 0-8342-1162-9.

Printed in the United States of America

5   6   7   8   9   10   11   12   13   17   16   15   14   13   12   11   10

To my husband Paul, and my parents Muriel and Russell Sifton.

Paul, the precious gifts of our love and growing older together bless every day; your unflagging belief in me and this project, and the countless hours of editorial and technical assistance made this book a reality.

Mom and Dad, your boundless love and confidence nurtured my creativity and independence. To Mom, my dearest friend, who has grown older in years and richer in wisdom, with energy and enthusiasm for new challenges—like learning to use a computer to type this manuscript. To Dad, who taught me about a knowledge that passes beyond words—that springs from the land—and about the importance of a hearty laugh.

The author gratefully acknowledges the
contribution of

Judith S. Bloomer, PhD, OTR/L
Director and Associate Professor
Department of Occupational Therapy
Xavier University
Cincinnati, Ohio

The mind . . . is not the heart.
I may yet live, as I know others live,
To wish in vain to let go with the mind—
Of cares, at night, to sleep; but nothing tells me
That I need to learn to let go with the heart.

—Robert Frost

VOICES FROM THE HEART

Let me introduce you to a very important person: His name is Robert.* He is the reason I wrote this book. Looking back, it seems that Robert's charm had its way with me from our first meeting. From the end of the corridor, I saw a frail bent figure, his gaunt frame contained by a geriatric chair. As I approached, I extended my hand in greeting. With great difficulty, but tremendous dignity, he attempted to rise to return my greeting. Gently taking my hand, he kissed it with a gallant flourish and said he was charmed to make my acquaintance. It was immediately obvious why Robert had been the loving center of his family for his entire 86 years! He was retired from his career as a professional engineer, but he continued to be enthusiastically engaged in living every day to its fullest. His step was somewhat unsteady, but with a partner for balance, his feet still moved lightly through his favorite step dances. His eyes twinkled, and he always had energy for a tease or a joke. Robert seemed to have achieved an enviable old age: he was loved and respected, active and enthusiastic, and financially secure.

There is, however, one more thing you should know about Robert. He is severely demented (probable Alzheimer's type). As his disease progressed, first his family and then the nursing home found it impossible

---

*The clinical anecdotes throughout this book are based on actual occurrences; however, the names of the patients have been changed.

to manage his severe behavioral and care difficulties. Frequent periods of loud and repetitive clapping and banging and indiscriminate urination and defecation were the most difficult of these problems. In this light, perhaps Robert's old age does not seem so enviable, but more likely a great tragedy.

Despite his severe impairments, Robert was an enthusiastic and responsive participant in sensory stimulation groups conducted on the specialty unit of the provincial psychiatric hospital. He told me with pride about the things he had grown in his garden, as he admired and arranged flowers for the dining table. He spoke eloquently, without words, about his managerial skill as he made calculations and arranged papers and documents on his tray. He shook with laughter as he hid the exercise materials from me. Robert was suffering from a devastating, dementing illness, but supported by the reassurance and structure of the group, he was once more enabled to affirm the value of his life experiences and, indeed, his own personhood.

Over the months, Robert's response to the group became less animated and less frequent, but it always occasioned some enlivenment and served to calm his often agitated behavior. One day a few months before his death, despite my frequent approaches by voice and touch, Robert failed even to open his eyes. My heart was in my shoes. It seemed that Robert's deterioration had progressed to a stage where he could not be reached. Nonetheless, when I returned Robert to the day room, I persisted with our ritual group ending. I took his hand in mine and put my other hand on his shoulder. I wished him a good day and told him I would see him tomorrow. His thin fingers came alive again and grasped my hand. He lifted his head and his sparking blue eyes opened wide. His face was aglow with what could only be called a beatific smile. With a clear voice, he said, "You have a good heart."

Somehow, my words and actions had made their way through to Robert's deteriorated senses and enabled him to express himself and experience some personal peace and happiness. I had been amazed to learn, while caring for my own father as he died of cancer, that engagement in living continues to the very end. I now learned the same lesson about Alzheimer's disease from Robert. As Yogi Berra said about the game of baseball, "It ain't over till it's over."

The point of this vignette is not so much to tell you about how Robert's words encouraged me, which indeed they continue to do. It is rather to demonstrate that beneath his severe impairments, which had devastated his capacity to think, to communicate, to do, and even to be as he once was, the essential self—Robert—was still so much alive and so desperate to get out, to find expression, to be part of life, and to be recognized and affirmed by others. His attempts to be active and engaged were often inappropriate and frustrating. His communication was frequently garbled and incomprehensible to the listener. Robert was coming to the end of his life. And yet, like everyone who ages, he had a tremendous need to reaffirm the value of his life, to put the events of his years in perspective. The great tragedy of his illness was that the devastation of his mental capacities prevented him from proceeding with this task on his own. Robert and the millions of others who suffer from Alzheimer's disease and related disorders (ADRD) require the facilitation and support of friends, family, and caregivers to accomplish their essential and final life task.

At the time of writing, there were an estimated 4.7 million "Roberts," people with ADRD in Canada and the United States (Evans et al. 1989). As the population ages, these numbers will increase to epidemic proportions. The search for a cure or preventive action is of enormous importance, but of importance equal to a cure for the disease is treatment for the millions presently affected. It is commonly stated that just as there is no cure there is no treatment. Such a narrow definition of treatment is a great injustice. Although in a classic sense there may be no treatment—that is, an intervention that will halt or reverse the progress of the disease—there are indeed treatments that serve the humanistic and holistic purposes of maximizing function and minimizing suffering and dysfunction. As yet, there is no cure for Alzheimer's disease, but there are treatments for *Robert*, the *person* with Alzheimer's disease.

The word *treatment* has been chosen deliberately. The intent is to emphasize that everyone who comes in contact with persons with ADRD has the potential to use a conversation, an activity, or an approach that can positively affect the individual's self-image. In their excellent book, *The Loss of Self*, Cohen and Eisdorfer (1986) describe the importance of these treatments as follows: "As the disease progresses, there is little or no hope of recovery of memory, but people do not exist of memory alone. People have feelings, imagination, desires, drives, will and moral being. It is in these realms that there are ways to touch patients and let them touch us" (p. 22). They continue: "Our patients and families have taught us that there is life that transcends ADRD" (p. 24). The ways in which we speak, act, and relate to ("treat") people with ADRD allow us as caregivers to get in touch with this life.

The focus of this book is on treatments for persons with ADRD who require part-time (e.g., day programs, acute hospitalization) or full-time residential care. The broad goal of these treatments is to enable such individuals to accomplish their final life tasks, to affirm their personhood, to reaffirm the value of their previous life experiences. Thus affirmed, individuals with ADRD are encouraged to respond to their environment and to participate in their own care. The progression of the disease is inevitable, but with treatment the devastation of the individual's self-esteem and capacity to function can be lessened. The course of ADRD may run 15 or more years. In the absence of a cure, enhancing the quality of these years must be a priority for all caregivers—family, paid staff, and volunteers. Just as essential as quality physical care is quality emotional care. Indeed, there can and should be no separation of these two elements. ADRD profoundly affects the functioning of the whole person. Effective treatment is holistic.

Providing for the physical care and safety of individuals with severe ADRD is a superhuman task. The reader may rightly wonder how the caregiver can possibly do more. This book is not about the amount of doing, but about the way of doing. For those whose primary responsibility is nursing care, the treatments outlined in this book include practical approaches incorporated within daily activities, such as ways of structuring the conversation while assisting with morning dressing. There are also treatments that will help family visits be less stressful for family members and of great benefit to the affected relative. For activity specialists charged with the difficult task of engaging persons with ADRD in meaningful activities, there are guidelines for client assessment; activity analysis; planning and leading groups; basic and adapted techniques; and activities in the modalities of music, horticulture, pets, cooking, handicrafts, and other areas. In addition, there are specific plans for yearlong sensory stimulation and reminiscence group activities. For all caregivers, there are guidelines for enabling independence, compensating for the sensory changes that accompany normal aging, and enhancing communication with persons with ADRD, as well as background information on ADRD and therapeutic models and methods.

Reliable research is just beginning to document officially the positive effects of these interventions. Reference to this research is found throughout the book. Research is affirming my ongoing experience, and that of many others, that treatment for ADRD is effective in enhancing the self-esteem of the individual and can in fact reduce care needs by enabling functioning (e.g., Calkins 1988; Cohen 1988; Cohen & Eisdorfer 1986; Coons 1991a, 1991b; David 1991; Davis & Kirkland 1988; Edelson & Lyons 1985; Fernie et al. 1990; Freeman 1987; Glickstein 1988; Holden & Woods 1982; Johnson 1989; Judd 1983; Karlinski & Sutherland 1990; Leverett 1991; Mace 1990; Paire & Karney 1984; Reichenback & Kirchman 1991; Rogers et al. 1989; Williams et al. 1987; Zgola 1987).

The book is specifically targeted for those working with individuals with ADRD, but many of the techniques (e.g., communication, compensation for sensory losses) and group modalities (e.g., reminiscence) are equally applicable to the cognitively well elderly.

This material is based on my experience as an occupational therapist working with the many severely demented individuals who were patients of the Nova Scotia Hospital Geriatric Organic Disorders Assessment Unit from 1986 to 1989. It is also based on the experience of caring for my mother-in-law during the long course of Alzheimer's disease. It is supplemented by the independent reading and research that I have done during and since that time.

The impetus to write this book was promoted by the many requests from caregivers, students, and other professionals for the approaches and ideas I had used. These requests persuaded me that a manual on sensory stimulation techniques would be useful. As I began accumulating and organizing my resources and ideas the project, like Topsy, "just growed" (Stowe 1852). The manual format has remained, hopefully making this a convenient working document. Resource information for supplies, equipment, and free materials is also included. There is an extensive bibliography for those who may wish to read the original sources.

It is my hope that this manual will be of assistance in the gargantuan tasks of those who are caregivers for persons with ADRD. It is even more my hope that, through sharing this information, some of the 4.7 million "Roberts" in Canada, the United States, and elsewhere will find their final years enriched, enlivened, and fulfilled through the treatment and facilitation of their caregivers. This hope is best expressed by an individual in the early stages of Alzheimer's disease:

> I am hungry for the life that is being taken away from me. I am a human being. I still exist. I have a family. I hunger for friendship, happiness, and the touch of a loved hand. What I ask for is that what is left of my life shall have some meaning. Give me something to die for! Help me to be strong and free until my self no longer exists. J. T. (Cohen & Eisdorfer 1986, 21)

Acknowledgments

This book is a gift of love, with appreciation and thanks to the many people who have enriched and touched my life. As I write, the paper is flooded with faces and moments, each precious and special, which have surrounded me with love, inspiration, and encouragement. Out of so many, I can identify only a few by name.

First of all, I thank the countless relatives, friends, and patients who have shown me, each in his or her own unique way, the beauty of growing older. Many have struggled with failing physical and mental health, yet all have embraced life with an inspiring dynamism. By sharing their life stories and their days with me, they have inspired me to write this book.

In particular, I am grateful to my parents-in-law, John and Alice Bowlby. Dad B. helped me to glory in the present moment and to strive to make every day a happy day. Mom B. faced the devastation of Alzheimer's disease with strength, dignity, and enduring love for her family.

Friends and colleagues have offered encouragement and hours of assistance in preparing the many drafts of this manuscript. Thank you "sunshine," Gayle Manley, for your encouragement and that bus driver's holiday, editing the original proposals for the book. Thank you to a special family friend, Phil Street, whose incisive

commentary on the first chapters were an essential source of inspiration.

I shall be forever indebted to Judith Bloomer, friend, colleague, and teacher, who not only dedicated hours of time she didn't have to the research and writing of Chapter 8, but since student days, has inspired and nurtured my involvement in program development, research, and publishing.

Michael Stowe, artist and colleague, has immeasurably improved this book with his art. Thank you, Michael, for dedicating so much of your time and creative energies to bring the human stories in this book so wonderfully alive in your linocuts and drawings.

The Center on Aging at the University of California at Berkeley very generously provided me with access to their materials and expertise which was invaluable while researching the book.

Thank you to the many colleagues who have read all or part of the manuscript and made many helpful suggestions. In particular I thank Susan Hare, Jo-Anne MacQueen, Ken Rockwood, Susan Vidito, and Zitka Zgola.

To my many colleagues who encouraged me throughout the long process of planning, research, and writing, a heartfelt thanks. Staff of the psychogeriatric units and the occupational therapy department of the

Nova Scotia Hospital supported me and this project with affection, appreciation, and tolerance of my eccentricities, and in doing so, provided the creative environment for the development of the programs and ideas that ended up in this book. I also thank my current colleagues in the occupational therapy department of the Victoria General Hospital for your tremendous moral support, good humor, and indulgence of my preoccupation with "The Book."

External financial support for manuscript preparation was gratefully received from the Canadian Occupational Therapy Foundation.

The enthusiasm of the staff of Aspen Publishers for this project and their patient and painstaking assistance allowed me to complete the book while working full-time, and still have enough time to restore my soul in the garden. Thank you in particular to Martha Sasser, Loretta Stock, and Barbara Priest.

My final thank you is for my children, Joseph, Miriam, and Nathaniel. There were many times in the past three years that time with you has come second to the book. Thank you for understanding your true place in my heart, despite letters that didn't get written, prom dresses finished minutes before the dance, and bicycle races I never saw. Most of all, thank you for surrounding me with rich experiences of love and joy to reminisce about as I age.

Halifax, Nova Scotia
October 15, 1992

For age is opportunity no less
Than youth itself, though in another dress.
And as the evening twilight fades away
The sky is filled with stars, invisible by day.

—Henry Wadsworth Longfellow

Normal Aging

1.0 NORMAL AGING AND ALZHEIMER'S DISEASE AND RELATED DISORDERS (ADRD)

Why discuss normal aging in a book on ADRD? There are two major reasons. First of all, it is absolutely essential to know as much as possible about normal age-related changes in order to be able to distinguish them from changes caused by diseases such as ADRD. Until very recently the classic symptoms of ADRD—disorientation, memory loss, and personality changes—were incorrectly assumed to be a normal part of aging. There has been, and continues to be, untold suffering because of this kind of grievous error.

Second, the vast majority of those with ADRD are over 65. The individual with ADRD is experiencing, to a greater or lesser degree, the changes in vision, hearing, and other senses that are associated with "normal" aging. They are also subject to the negative attitudes toward aging, which are discussed under section 2.0 below, as well as the considerable negative associations with their disease. This situation has been described as "double jeopardy" for the individual with ADRD (Davis & Kirkland 1988). Knowledge about normal aging can assist the caregiver to alleviate this problem.

1.1 Introduction: Four Friends, Four Stories

Sarah and Elizabeth, now both in their 90s, had been friends since they were in their teens. They shared over 75 years of friendship. The intervening years had been full of countless joys and sorrows, and so much change. Their first times together had seen evenings lit by coal oil lamps and heated by wood-burning stoves. Now the wonders of electricity provided light, heat, and even television.

The two women had met through Elizabeth's husband, Avery. Orphaned as a boy of 12, Avery had been indentured to a local farmer and worked long hours to earn his keep. During those lonely and hard years, Avery had few comforts. When he dropped into his bed at night the mournful whistle of the ten o'clock train at the local station provided a peculiar solace. There was, in fact, a life beyond his daily drudgery on the farm, but his greatest reassurance came from Sarah's family, who befriended him and provided human warmth and companionship during those years. He was their guest for Sunday dinners after church and other such occasions.

When he came of age at 18, Avery was finally able to take over the farm. Sarah followed her older sister to "the States," where she found work as a seamstress. For the remainder of their lives the homes of Sarah and Avery were separated by hundreds of miles, but the bond of their friendship remained strong. It stretched to a circle to include, first, Avery's wife, Elizabeth, and then Sarah's husband, William. The four friends were busy during those early years, struggling to survive and make a go of it through the depression and the war years. There was little time or money for personal visits. They shared their news through letters exchanged between Sarah and Elizabeth.

Sarah kept on at outside work, gaining a responsible position in the dry goods store in a nearby town. In her late 30s she gave birth to a daughter, the delight of her life. More taciturn than the exuberant Sarah, William too took great pride in their daughter. Eventually, the daughter went away to college and stayed on to work at some distance from Sarah and William. William struggled to manage their small farm, and worked away at other jobs to keep things going. Sarah continued to work in town. In her own time she used her amazing energy, enthusiasm, and talent with a needle to turn their home into a welcoming gathering spot for the many Canadian friends of her youth. They now came to visit with husbands, wives, children, and grandchildren. Sarah retired at 65 and turned her enthusiasm full time to her many interests of sewing, cooking, preserving, gardening, and reading. Undaunted by limited money, an increasingly cantankerous husband, changing life circumstances, and failing eyesight, Sarah embraced life with a contagious optimism. Sarah was almost 70 when the Beatles revolutionized music and, it seemed, the entire younger generation. Unlike most of her peers, including her husband William and her friend Elizabeth, Sarah thought the Beatles were cute! No one who knew Sarah will forget the particular energy with which she welcomed life, saying with her acquired midwestern drawl, "I think that's *real* pretty" or "I hope I'll see you *real* soon."

Circumstances fell out rather differently in the lives of Avery and Elizabeth. Through hard work their farm prospered. In their late 30s they too had a child. Their son stayed on to farm with Avery and eventually was the prosperous owner of several other nearby farms. As Avery aged, his son and grandsons took over the work and management of the home farm. To avoid the tax collector, Elizabeth and Avery turned their property entirely over to their only son. During those years of hard work Elizabeth had her own struggles. There were a few times when she became overwhelmed and withdrew from friends and activities. However, she had an amazing strength and resilience. She worked long hours preparing fabulous feasts for gangs of men who came to do the haying or threshing or fill the silo. She worked at church bazaars, prepared the garden, and lovingly decorated her own home—and homes of friends—with her paintings.

In their old age the four friends, Sarah and William and Avery and Elizabeth, at last had the time and money to visit each other. For a decade, once or twice a year, they visited each other's homes. They shared in the news of farm prices and new wonders in equipment, enjoyed Sarah's and Elizabeth's toothsome home cooking, and played endless hands of euchre, with much laughter and conversation, long into the night.

When they were in their 80s, the health of both William and Avery began to deteriorate. Visits among the four friends became less frequent and were usually organized by younger friends. Elizabeth struggled on with determination, caring for Avery after two hip replacement surgeries. Avery continued to check on the crops, trudging the rows of corn with his walker. Despite her own heavy load in caring for William, Elizabeth carried on in the wonderful country way of caring for neighbors and friends. She was known for doing things such as picking her way up a country lane coated with ice, carrying a fresh raisin pie for an old friend dying of cancer.

At age 89 Avery had a stroke, and Elizabeth could no longer manage alone. Assuming entire control, their son and daughter-in-law arranged for the immediate placement of Avery and Elizabeth in a dingy, local nursing home. They stopped to pick up Elizabeth, who had been warned by a phone call 45 minutes earlier, to be packed and ready to leave her home of 65 years. Avery sat in the car, tears streaming down his face onto his gnarled farmer's hands. He was forbidden even the opportunity to say goodbye to his home or his beloved land. Elizabeth accepted the move as fate, signing over not only financial control, but submitting her will and independence to that of her son and daughter-in-law.

Elizabeth and Avery passed their 65th wedding anniversary in the nursing home. The staff arranged for a cake, which one longtime friend shared with them. Afterward they returned to their separate rooms, Avery seemingly to endless tears and the few sad words that were left to him after his stroke, Elizabeth to a stony and resigned silence. A room they could share did become available but the family refused it, feeling that the couple would adjust better if they were separated.

Eventually Avery and Elizabeth were moved to a much happier, brighter, more active home. Avery died a few months later. Elizabeth carries on in her resigned fashion. Despite continuing good health, she refuses involvement in any of the activities or outings in the home, spending the majority of her days in bed. She brightens when a friend visits, but persists in refusing to leave her bed. She is delighted, still, to receive letters from Sarah, but insists that she is unable to reply, even when a friend offers to help. How, one wonders, has Elizabeth's loving attention to friendship vanished? This is the same lady who, only a few years earlier, had been arranging a welcoming party of friends for William and Sarah. She felt unable to prepare the whole meal and decided to "go modern" and order fried chicken from the takeout restaurant in town. However, she added her own delightful personal touch, in order to be assured that her role as hostess was perfectly accomplished. She went directly to the manager to request that extra special attention be given to her order, as she was expecting very important company from "the States."

The circumstances of Sarah's life had also changed. Seeing only shadows, she had become legally blind. William's health was very poor and his temperament worse. They moved to a smaller house in town, leaving behind Sarah's loving decorative touches. Sarah, like Elizabeth, struggled along doing her housework, entertaining friends, and preparing meals. She, however, continued to embrace life with an astounding vitality. When William died, Sarah was unable to maintain their home. With the help of her daughter and a niece she gathered together her most precious possessions and moved several hundred miles to a bed-sitting room in her daughter's home.

Now 96 and unable to see or move with ease, Sarah continues to greet each new day or old friend with *real* enthusiasm. She writes letters only by the memory of how the words are shaped. Energy and vibrancy radiate from her diminutive five-foot frame to everyone who meets her. She was recently visited by a longtime friend and her friend's son. The son was astounded to see that neither her energy nor her wit had diminished one iota in the 25 years since he had last seen her. He asked in amazement, "Sarah, what are you going to be like when you are old?" Sarah did not hesitate a moment. Her face broadened into her engaging smile and she replied, "You know, I've often wondered that myself!"

Four friends, four stories—four unique stories of growing old.

2.0 WHAT DOES IT MEAN TO GROW OLD? ATTITUDES AND AGING

The life stories of Sarah, Avery, William, and Elizabeth are but snapshots of the incredible diversity of personalities and life circumstances of millions of older adults. Every aging person has his or her own particular story. Aging is, in fact, a lifelong process that begins at birth. We humans are more alike at this initial point in our existence than we ever will be again. Every individual is as unique in old age as her or his astounding variety of life experiences would predict. The "typical" 65-year-old is even more elusive than the "typical" 15 year-old. The diverse experiences of the intervening 50 years have created a vast and magnificent array of creativities, personalities, and ways of being. What, then, does it mean to grow old? There are as many specific answers to this question as there are old people. Aging is a highly personal experience. What does it mean to grow old? It means many different things to many people—in a word, diversity.

So, having begun with the premise that there is an infinitude of specific answers to the question, "What does it mean to grow old?" why even attempt to describe normal aging? Perhaps the sane person would now abandon the task. This might be expedient, but not prudent. Why not?

First of all, the process of normal aging is something that affects each of us. We are growing older this very minute! What it means physically, mentally, and socially to grow older in North American society has tremendous implications for our lives. What do we wish from our friends, our family, the health care system, the media, etc., in our old age? In order to develop informed responses to these issues we need to learn about both normal aging and attitudes toward aging.

For those who work with the elderly in a professional or personal capacity, learning as much as possible about "normal" aging and what it means to grow old is absolutely vital. We can be truly effective and therapeutic only if we develop empathy, coming as nearly as possible to stand in the shoes of the other.

Finally, whether or not it is based on truth, "they"— that elusive group of people who determine public feelings and standards but never stand and identify themselves—are saying a great deal about "normal" aging. And, although there are encouraging signs of improvement, much of what "they" are saying about old age is negative and *wrong*. Being old in western society is all too often viewed as being sick, disabled, feeble, nonproductive, dependent, poor, confused, or worthless.

Despite advances, this negative stereotype of old age persists through all levels of society, from the media to health care professionals. Aging is seen as something to be avoided, beaten back, defeated: "erase those wrinkles," "get that tummy tuck," "wash away that gray," "exercise away that fatigue." And when one finally succumbs to some particular ache, pain, or disease, an older person may be told that little can be done because "after all, you are getting older!" Such a response is not a diagnosis, but a failure to diagnose. Old age is not a disease, nor is it an explanation for deteriorating function. It is amazing how much things have changed and yet how much they have stayed the same since 165 B.C., when Terrence said that "old age is a disease" (Lonergrin 1990).

The most immediate and most serious effect of these negative attitudes is found among the elderly themselves. Schulz and Fritz (1987) studied 120 community-dwelling, well elderly who, despite positive self-evaluations, reported negative evaluations of aging. These negative results were related to the negative societal and media attitudes toward aging. The frail elderly are particularly vulnerable. With limited physical, social, or emotional resources to support them, they are at great risk of simply accepting society's negative attitudes. This in turn has disastrous effects on self-esteem, motivation, creativity, and health. Such resignation becomes its own self-fulfilling prophecy. When the old are expected to be dependent, ill, and in decline they become so. They learn to be helpless (see Chapter 4).

The contention that the predominant societal attitude toward aging is negative is supported in both academic and popular literature. Although the majority of studies report more negative attitudes toward the aged than toward the young, a few studies contradict this finding (Gekoski & Knox 1990, Kite & Johnson 1988). Resolution of these contradictions involves complicated issues, far beyond the scope of this book. However, taken on the whole, surveys of attitudes report more negative attitudes toward the old than toward the young (Becker & Kaufman 1988; Cohen 1988; Davis & Kirkland 1988; Erber 1989; Kite & Johnson 1988; Lonergrin 1990; Rosenbloom & Morgan 1986). Kite and Johnson (1988) conducted a meta-analysis (considering many variables) of 43 empirical studies of attitudes toward the elderly. Thirty of these studies demonstrated more negative attitudes toward the elderly than toward younger people.

Negative attitudes toward the elderly have been identified by the Canadian Medical Association's Committee on Delivery of Health Care to the Elderly as the single greatest problem facing Canadians over 65 (CMA 1988). Research studies have found a frightening lack of knowledge about some basics of geriatric medicine, such as how long valium remains in the system (Goodwin 1989), and the signs, symptoms, assessment, and treatment of depression in the elderly (Rapp & Davis 1989).

There is solid evidence that valid health problems of the elderly are frequently ignored or not actively treated because of the patient's age (Becker & Kaufman 1988; Braun et al. 1988; Estes & Binney 1989; Goodwin 1989; Henig 1988; Jarvik & Winograd 1988; Lipowski 1987; Lonergrin 1990; Rapp & Davis 1989; Robins & Wolf 1989; Rubenstein 1987; Tarbox 1983; VanHorn 1987; Wells 1979; Winnett 1989; Wright 1988). For example, mental disorders are frequently untreated, even when diagnosed (Rapp & Davis 1989; Tarbox 1983; Winnett 1989), and even cancer tends to be under-rated (Goodwin 1989).

The negative attitudes of long-term care staff are often cited as affecting the care of nursing home residents (Davis & Kirkland 1988; Edelson & Lyons 1985; Tarbox 1983; Wright 1988) and possibly contributing to premature death by playing a part in the "failure to thrive" syndrome observed in some residents (Braun et al. 1988). Failure to thrive also contributes to functional

decline and premature institutionalization among the hospitalized and community-dwelling elderly (Berkman et aL 1989; Palmer 1990). The negative attitudes of health care staff play an important role in the exclusion of a great majority of the disabled elderly from adequate rehabilitation (Becker & Kaufman 1988).

On another, but equally important, level the popular press and media often convey negative attitudes toward aging. Consider the portrayal of old people in advertising, who are shown to be in need of pepping up, de-wrinkling, and de-graying; or in popular shows and movies, such as *Cocoon,* in which the central characters escape old age and find happiness by "leaving this world."

Of countless possibilities, the following are two examples of the often covert, but nevertheless negative, attitude in the popular press toward aging. The June 5, 1990 edition of *Family Circle* included an article entitled "Can Your Diet Prevent Wrinkles? Foods That Fight Aging" (Rinzler 1990). Some quotations from this article are "Another age give away you can minimize is dryness" (p. 42); "Another symptom of aging you can offset with diet is lowered resistance to illness" (p. 42); "Whether you are 30, 40, 50 or older no doubt you want to do all you can to slow down the clock" (p. 40). There is a powerful negative message here, and in the many other articles of its kind: getting old is bad news and to look old is very bad news, to be avoided at all costs. And cost it does; one estimate suggests that Americans spend $2 billion a year on various "potions" to fight off aging, plus several billion more to mask its physical signs (Rinzler 1990).

An article with a more scientific focus, but much the same message, appeared in the March 5, 1990 edition of *Newsweek* (Begley et al. 1990). The very title, "The Search for the Fountain of Youth," is an indication of the attitude toward aging. The article goes on to say, "Ponce de Leon was looking in all the wrong places. With the benefit of time, brainstorms and biochemistry, scientists are on the verge of finding the true fountain of youth" (Begley et al. 1990, 44). This hope is contrasted with the "percentages" for the decline in heart rate, muscle strength, etc. from age 25 to age 85. Most of these data on the so-called "inevitable physical decline of aging" are now being challenged by current, more rigorous, research. This research is discussed in the following sections.

Fortunately, these negative attitudes are slowly being eroded as more and more people live to enjoy a healthy old age. As more groups like the Gray Panthers, the American Association of Retired Persons, and Canadian Pensioners Concerned make themselves seen and heard, the public image of old age is improving (Estes & Binney 1989; Gekoski & Knox 1990; Kite & Johnson 1988; Mitchell 1990; Robins & Wolfe 1989; Scott et al. 1991; Wright 1988).

The research literature also indicates that attitudes toward aging are improving. In the previously cited review, Kite and Johnson (1988) found that the more recent studies report less pronounced negative attitudes. They also found that negative attitudes were less pronounced when study subjects knew more about the person. This finding is related to the opening comments of this section. It is very important to understand that "the old" are not at all a homogeneous, one-dimensional group, but a diverse and wonderful group of individuals whose largest common denominator is their chronological age.

One controlled study examined the effects of a very simple intervention with and without the inclusion of a one-page personal history in the resident's medical chart. Staff who read this brief history and learned something more about the person viewed the resident in a more positive light, i.e., as being more personally acceptable, more independent, and more capable of adapting, than did staff who read the chart without the history (Pietrukowicz & Johnson 1991).

Another interesting study, which measured the attitudes of 120 college undergraduates, found that health status and not age in and of itself was related to negative attitudes (Gekoski & Knox 1990). Indeed, there is evidence that older people themselves experience a sense of "aging" in association with the occurrence of health problems (Keller et al. 1989). This raises a current and vital issue, what Estes and Binney (1989) have called the "bio-medicalization of aging." They present a convincing argument that with the current focus on the biological and disease-centered characteristics of aging, important social issues (e.g., inadequate finances) are sidetracked and old age becomes more and more synonymous with disease and decline. There is valid concern, both within the health care system (e.g., Becker & Kaufman 1988; Lyman 1989; Mitchell 1990) and outside of it, that a system that has focused on "cure" can cope neither with the chronic nature of many of the diseases (e.g., arthritis or Alzheimer's disease) that are more common in old age nor with the more crucial issue of quality of life in old age.

In this regard, consider the results of one interesting study that examined the experience of aging among 32 healthy, active, community-dwelling elderly (Keller et al. 1989). These individuals had a very positive attitude toward their own aging, despite negative views of the changes they associated with aging in both themselves and others. A further aspect of this study examined cop-

ing strategies for dealing with age-associated changes. The results are consistent with those of Rodin (1986), which indicate that when aging persons have a sense of control, of coping satisfactorily with associated changes, their aging is viewed as a positive experience. Caregivers and the community at large have a responsibility to enable and support the development of a sense of control by providing informed knowledge about the aging process, by providing health and social supports as necessary, and by promoting positive attitudes about the life stage toward which aging persons are growing.

To end this section on a positive note, there is hopeful evidence that negative attitudes and the associated lack of knowledge can be altered. For example, a controlled study of 197 medical students found that a five-week training program had a significant positive effect on the students' therapeutic responses to elderly patients (Robins & Wolf 1989). This and other such projects are a good beginning on what is needed in North American society, a complete reversal of our attitude toward aging. Consider that the very sight of an infant or a small child brings a smile to most faces. It seems that the essence of innocence, joy, and wonderment that they embody lifts our hearts. Most people do not recoil from them, overwhelmed by the thought of the unpleasant associations of teething, toileting, teenage rebellion, etc. Would it not be fine if the very sight of an aged person—the absolute wonder of all that they have seen, experienced, accomplished, and known—also lifted our hearts? Perhaps, since we have already been children, we can overlook the tears of childhood because we have experienced the joy. Not having been there yet, we need to stretch ourselves to stand in the shoes of the aged person: to appreciate not only the trials but the joys of growing old, so we can be free to experience it with them.

2.1 What Does It Mean To Grow Old? Advantages of Aging

In traditional Chinese society, the reversal of attitudes envisioned above is in fact the case. Elders are respected and revered because of their advanced years. For example, it is considered a compliment to be mistaken for older than you are! This is the polar opposite of the present situation in modern western society. It is hard to imagine that most of us would smile in appreciation if an acquaintance remarked, "My, you look wonderful. You look 30 years older than when I saw you 10 years ago." We would much rather hear remarks such as "You look younger every time I see you" or "You haven't changed a bit in the last 20 years." Certainly it is neither realistic nor sensible to imagine that our cultural and social values could take such a 180-degree turn. It is, however, realistic and desirable that we learn to appreciate the positive aspects of aging in the context of our contemporary society.

In the following pages you will find descriptions of many age-associated changes. Although these changes are much less disconcerting than has long been assumed, in the face of losses in vision, hearing, etc., one may wonder whether there are any advantages associated with aging.

The most convincing argument for the positive aspects of aging is made by older people themselves. One example is the previously cited study of 32 community-dwelling seniors who had overwhelmingly positive associations with aging. Only seven subjects described any negative aspects of getting old, but these individuals also described positive aspects (Keller et al. 1989). What follows is a brief overview of some positive aspects of aging.

First, the most phenomenal advantage associated with aging in contemporary society is a gain in time, a commodity of which younger people simply never seem to have enough. In most cases, retirement from paid work and the absence of responsibility for child or parent care affords older persons more discretionary time than ever before in their life spans. This extra time can be richly used to pursue lifelong leisure interests, to travel, to reflect on and recall life experiences, to enjoy children and grandchildren, and even to develop a second career. For a minority, this extra time can become a burden, and they may need assistance to develop meaningful avocational activities. The person with ADRD particularly requires this assistance, which is the purpose of the following chapters of this book.

Older persons have the advantage of years of accumulated life experiences to guide them, an expertise in living. These life experiences guide and ease day-to-day decisions. Wisdom, based on years of life experience, has long been associated with aging. Unfortunately, in our contemporary technological society, the wisdom of life experiences may be discounted, and aging may instead be equated with technological obsolescence. Maintaining technological expertise in the face of the whirlwind pace of technological change is a daunting undertaking. Human nature, however, remains constant, and in this regard the older person has an expertise based on years of living. On the one hand, there can be a danger in oversentimentalizing the wisdom of old age. On the other hand, there is a tendency to undervalue insights and knowledge gained from years of life experience. Just one example of many such insights from older patients came from an 80-year-old

gentleman. In a discussion about the ever-increasing cost of food, he commented, "The way I see it, the only way to get the value out of a bushel of potatoes is to eat 'em!"

In a more concrete expression of this expertise or wisdom, there is widespread evidence that there are age-related gains in crystallized intelligence, i.e., knowledge based on information acquired over a lifetime, such as vocabulary (Birren & Schaie 1990; Clarkson-Smith & Hartley 1990; Cohen 1988; Dippel & Hutton 1988; Finch & Schneider 1985; Henig 1988; Jarvik 1988; Lonergrin 1990, Rosenbloom & Morgan 1986; Schaie 1989; Stankov 1988; Woodruff-Pak 1989). Research on aging and "intelligence" is changing focus, from measuring what is lost, via intelligence tests, to assessing what is gained, via assessments that are meaningful to adult life experiences and that examine experiential and practical skills. These assessments are finding not only gains in measures of "crystallized intelligence" but also a more integrative, reflective style of thought (Woodruff-Pak 1989). This is closely related to the concept of wisdom. This new focus suggests that older adult "intelligence" continues to grow and develop.

In summary, old age has the advantage of increased discretionary time and enhanced knowledge based on life experience, two dimensions that have great potential to enhance the quality of life in old age. In addition, improved health care, better diet, and an awareness of the importance of continued physical and cognitive activity are eliminating many of the long-assumed "inevitable losses" associated with aging.

3.0 DESCRIBING "NORMAL" AGING

After the preceding lengthy discussion, it is time to begin where angels fear to tread, to describe the "normal" aging processes. It is essential, however, to consider the following qualifiers when interpreting this information.

Keep the whole person at the forefront. As so eloquently stated by Robert Frost, "the mind . . . is not the heart" (quoted in Salber 1989, ix); nor is the person represented by his or her ability to hear or to see or to move, nor even the sum of all these bodily systems. We need to keep firmly fixed on the message, repeated time and again from so many old people, in life and in literature, "I may look different but I still feel like the same person inside." This echoes, in a personal way, what Erikson et al. (1986) describe as the old-age task of achieving integrity, of coming to terms with who you are (see Chapter 4). Indeed, there is some cause for concern that those who struggle so hard to maintain the exterior "look" are in fact having an internal struggle to maintain this sense of personal integrity.

Remember that each person is unique. There are two important considerations here. The percentages reported from the literature are averages; not every older person experiences these changes. For example, if 50 percent of people over 65 experience hearing loss, it must also be emphasized that 50 percent do not experience hearing loss. We must change our perspective, to see the half-full glass instead of the half-empty glass. Second, individuals do not respond to age-related changes in the same way. One person may be totally demoralized by a slight vision loss, and another may cope admirably with near blindness.

Keep in mind that there is considerable variability in changes between bodily systems and between people. There is by no means change in every system in every person. Some older people may experience, for example, a significant hearing loss while every other bodily function continues as when they were 50.

Remember that aging changes do not necessarily mean changes in function. The human body is absolutely amazing. Unlike the workings of our modern miracle the computer, when there is some change or loss in the human body, there is still tremendous adaptability and reserve to draw upon, allowing the system to continue to function very well. One glitch (error or dysfunction) does not bring the whole system down. This is particularly true of the brain and the central nervous system. Most changes, especially in the sensory systems, have happened gradually and the individual makes a gradual adjustment. In addition, some changes have positive effects on function. For example, for the person who has been farsighted, the usual age-related changes in vision mean that he or she will be able to read without glasses for the first time in years.

Distinguish between "normal" aging changes and those caused by disease and/or environmental insult. The following pages outline some of the physiological changes that may occur during aging. Distinguishing these changes from those actually caused by disease requires a full, multidisciplinary health assessment. Anyone who is told that a particular problem is due to old age, without a proper investigation, should seek a new practitioner immediately. The practice of failing to distinguish between aging changes and disease has been compounded by poor-quality research (see the next section) and not enough consideration of the effects of damage from the environment and of a decreased level of activity.

It is interesting, for instance, to speculate on how much of the hearing loss experienced during aging may be due to environmental factors, rather than to aging as

such. For example, without the noisy insult of modern industrial society, the bushmen in the Kalahari experience no such loss (Lonergrin 1990). Many other long-accepted "inevitabilities" are being challenged by more careful research. For example, in healthy older adults, heart output, kidney filtration, and oxygen utilization have shown little significant change with age (Larson & Bruce 1986; Lindeman et al. 1985; Rodeheffer 1984). Losses in strength and flexibility are now understood to be related more to a decrease in physical activity than to actual age-related loss.

Be aware that the empirical research on aging has limitations. First of all, there are many flaws in the existing research. This is discussed in more detail in the section on cognition. Many early studies were based on small sample size. Consider one example: One study that reported that age spots (melanocytes) increase by 20 percent every decade past young adulthood has been widely accepted as a standard (Finch & Schneider 1985). However, this study consisted of only 12 people, with 1 60-year-old and 1 65-year-old representing the aging population.

Much research on aging employs grossly unequal comparison groups. The majority of the "young" subjects have been undergraduate college students, while most of the older subjects have been sedentary nursing home residents or older people who have not been screened for existing disease. This type of research, which compares two different groups of different ages, is called cross-sectional research. Cross-sectional research is problematic because the effects of age cannot be separated from other differences in education, social experience, diet, etc. (cohort effects). This is a particular problem in research on aging and intelligence, where cohort effects have been found to be greater than age effects (Woodruff-Pak 1989).

Longitudinal studies examine changes in one group of people over an extended period of time. These studies have found fewer age-related changes. However, these findings are specific to the particular (cohort) group studied. The other disadvantage of longitudinal studies is the difficulty and expense of studying a large group of people for a long period of time.

Beyond these particular difficulties, there is the more general difficulty of relying on empirical research, which results in group measures, for information about individual performance. How can we be guided in our work with particular individuals by empirical research, which seeks to average or level out individuality? Indeed, the exception, the unusual case, the particular can be said to be the enemy of multiple-subject empirical research; whereas our concern as clinicians is with the parlicular, the individual person (Ottenbacher 1984), especially since the aging population is characterized by diversity. Over-reliance on research that sets out to water down or eliminate this diversity is problematic. Social science rightly advises that we cannot make conclusions about the general from the particular. Conversely, we cannot make conclusions about particular individuals on the basis of averages or general characteristics. A scientist from the Institute of Food Technology reminds us that

> . . . science is not fact. It is not truth. It is not holy scripture. It's a compendium of information. You try to put all the research together and come to a consensus. Just because somebody runs a study that comes to a particular conclusion doesn't change everything that's gone before. (Schmitz 1991, 42)

The noted neurologist, Oliver Sacks, echoes this view: "There has always, seemingly, been a split between science and life, between the apparent poverty of scientific formulation and the manifest richness of phenomenal experience" (Sacks 1990, 44).

This is excellent advice for reading the research literature on "normal" aging. The reader is cautioned to be mindful of the ever-present gap between the performance of research subjects in test situations and the actions, affections, and motivations of older persons in their own homes and communities. Our interest is in that community, specifically in creating a caring community in which older adults are treated with dignity and respect. Although careful empirical research can provide cues and suggestions for our work, what is true or proper for Mrs. Jones or Mr. Smith or anyone comes from our assessment and understanding of the person and the community. Ultimately, such understanding comes more from the heart than the head. Science should guide and clarify our thinking by providing information; caring should guide our heart and enable our understanding.

Introduce suggested environmental changes and individual compensations with care and sensitivity. Some guidelines for introducing change are found at the end of this chapter. On the other hand, many suggested adaptations are beneficial to all ages and should be advocated (for example, lighting changes).

Remember that it is never too late to change, to improve health and functioning. As discussed in previous sections, it is now evident that many changes that have long been associated with "normal" aging are in reality due to other factors. There is ample evidence that life style changes in diet, exercise, stopping smoking, etc., can have a positive effect at any age (Cohen 1988;

Davis & Kirkland 1988; Finch & Sehneider 1985; Henig 1988; Leitner & Leitner 1985; Lonergrin 1990; Rogers et al. 1990; Shepherd 1987; Short & Leonardelli 1987; Tager 1990; Timiras 1988). For instance, when the older person stops smoking there is considerable recovery of lung function, even after decades of heavy tobaceo use (Tager 1990).

Beware of stereotypes, positive or negative. There is ample good news in the pages that follow. Many changes that have been incorreetly assumed to be the inevitable consequence of old age are now being disclaimed. However, this good news, combined with our youth-oriented society's obsession with avoiding signs of aging, is giving rise to still another stereotype—the "super elder." Through conscientious attention to a proper diet, judicious financial planning, and a disciplined program of exercise, this "stereotypical" old person manages to remain forever young. While there is no question that attention to a healthy life style contributes greatly to healthy aging, there is also no question that growing older is the inevitable, and natural, conclusion of the life cycle. The most worrisome consequence of the super elder stereotype is blaming the disabled elderly for their frailties. Being enticed by this mythical "super elder" is as dangerous and detestable, and as much to be avoided, as the mythical "decrepit old geezer." Like all stereotypes, they serve no useful purpose.

The purpose here is to discover ways to enable and enhanee the quality of life of all older adults, most particularly the 15 to 25 percent who are mentally and/or physically frail. To accomplish this purpose, all older adults must be treated with dignity and respect while nurturing their particular qualities or assets and compensating for their particular limitations or liabilities.

The following sections provide a brief overview of what is now known about "normal" aging. This summary is by no means comprehensive, as there are volumes on this topic alone. There are references for those who wish to read further. This overview includes only those areas most pertinent to activities—cognition, sensory systems, and the musculoskeletal system. There are, of course, important changes in the internal organ systems, although not to the extent that has long been assumed.

4.0 COGNITION

What are the "normal" changes in cognition that accompany aging? No other area of function, in relation to age, has caused such controversy among scientists, clinicians, and the lay public alike. The debate continues and the arguments and counterarguments could fill volumes, far beyond the intent or scope of this brief section. After a careful review of a considerable portion of this literature, my conclusion is that there is no substantial loss, associated with age alone, in overall cognitive function that significantly interferes with daily function. In fact, there is widespread evidence that there are gains in crystallized intelligence (i.e., knowledge based on information acquired over a lifetime, such as vocabulary) with aging. Although evidence also suggests that there may be some decrease in fluid intelligence skills, such as problem solving and the speed of doing cognitive activities, given enough time healthy older individuals perform cognitive activities just as well as do younger ones. This conclusion also applies to learning. As Cohen (1988) points out, the old saw that "you can't teach an old dog new tricks" is true of neither humans nor dogs. The potential for learning and for the effective functioning of the human brain is lifelong (Birren & Schaie 1990; Clarkson-Smith & Hartley 1990; Cohen 1988; Dippel & Hutton 1988; Finch & Schneider 1985; Henig 1988; Jarvik 1988; Lonergrin 1990; Rapoport 1983; Rosenbloom & Morgan 1986; Schaie 1989; Stankov 1988; Woodruff-Pak 1989).

Perhaps the cognitive change most commonly attributed to old age is memory loss. This is a false and dangerous belief. Healthy older adults do not have significant memory loss, i.e., a forgetfulness that significantly interferes with daily living. There may be a slight increase in absent-mindedness, what some have called "benign senescent forgetfulness" (Kral 1978). Even this, however, is open to question because of the experimental methods used to measure memory and the prevailing negative assumptions about old age and forgetfulness. Problems in the experimental measurement of memory and other cognitive functions are discussed later in this section. Suffice it to say here that older adults may be less motivated to recall lists of meaningless numbers or words, and they may be significantly more anxious in test situations than younger adults.

The setting of the test also influences performance. One study of 116 elderly persons found that test scores on the 30-point Mini-Mental State examination were an average of 1.5 points higher when tested at home. The authors conclude that in-home assessment may give the best measure of cognitive function (Ward et al. 1990).

A study by West (1988) on prospective memory—remembering to do something in the future—found no significant difference between the performances of young and old subjects when testing was done at home. However, in a laboratory test situation younger subjects performed better than older subjects on the tasks of remembering to make a phone call or mail a card.

Another study of 94 community-dwelling subjects between the ages of 70 and 93 investigated the relationship among everyday memory, measured by the Rivermead Behavioural Memory Test, and age, activity involvement, and fluid intelligence, measured by the Raven Colored Progressive Matrices (Cockburn & Smith 1991). In this study, increasing age was found to be associated with poorer performance on three prospective memory tasks. However, some features of the study design may have influenced the outcome. First of all, the subjects were not screened for the presence of dementia. Since the incidence of dementia also increases markedly with advancing age, these results may, in fact, reflect the presence of dementia and not the memory of healthy, older adults. In addition, some subjects were tested in the laboratory and some at home. The investigators did not separate the scores of these subjects, and this may have had an influence on performance, as in the study by West (1988). The authors concluded that assessing cognitive decline during aging is much more complicated than taking measures of fluid intelligence. In addition, they questioned the use of the Raven Matrices to measure fluid intelligence in an elderly population. Of the 119 original subjects, 15 were unable to do the test because of visual problems, and 8 refused to attempt it at all. This test requires good vision and good lighting. In the test manual, Raven himself disclaims it as a good overall "intelligence" measure.

Another important variable in the forgetfulness of older adults is expectation, both of themselves and by society at large. Because seniors are expected to become more forgetful, there is a much more negative and fearful association with misplacing keys at age 75 than at age 25. Samuel Johnson, the British scholar, expressed this very well:

> There is a wicked inclination in most people to suppose an old man decayed in his intellect. If a young or middle-aged man, when leaving a company, does not recollect where he has laid his hat, it is nothing. But if the same inattention is discovered in an old man, people will shrug their shoulders and say "his memory is going." (Cited in Hening 1988, 45)

These types of expectations are dangerous because some old people believe them and, in effect, come to live the myth and deteriorate in function. These expectations are also dangerous because significant memory loss is a sign of disease that may be reversible (e.g., depression or chemical imbalance) or irreversible, yet may be ameliorated by the proper environment (e.g., Alzheimer's disease).

What are the sources of the myth of cognitive decline? There are several:

There is negative stereotyping of the old. Negative stereotyping has already been discussed in the introduction to this chapter. A very interesting illustration of this is found in a study wherein 115 young adults rated the memory loss vignette of Mrs. X more seriously when she was 70 than when she was 30, regardless of how serious the incident was (Erber 1989).

There is a failure to distinguish between disease and normal aging. When an older person becomes ill, not just with brain disease but with other illnesses, cognitive performance tends to decline. No one, at any age, is able to reason, think, or remember as well when ill. During illness, the reserves of the brain are stressed, particularly the center for memory, as the central nervous system focuses on healing the affected structures. The older adult, because of the loss of neurons associated with aging, has fewer reserves and thus there is a greater likelihood of cognitive impairment during times of illness and stress (Moore 1991).

Since the elderly are more likely to have a chronic or serious illness, there is also a greater likelihood of cognitive decline related to illness (Birren & Schaie 1990; Cohen 1988; Henig 1988; Jarvik 1988; Moore 1991). Until very recently, both these illnesses and cognitive decline have been accepted as "normal" in old age. Old age itself has been used as a diagnosis, a reason for decline, without benefit of a genuine investigation.

Basic methods of testing intelligence and cognitive function may be flawed. This is a very complex and controversial issue. The debate about the significance and meaning of intelligence tests is likely to continue for some time to come and could fill volumes. Becoming embroiled in the technicalities of this debate has little relevance to the purpose of this book, to enhance and enliven the cognitive and other capacities of older adults. However, the issues themselves are relevant in that the content and context of standard intelligence tests have been biased against the older adult. Fortunately, a more holistic understanding of cognition, as it relates to actual life skills, is emerging. Unfortunately, narrow interpretations, which equate performance in test situations with performance on real-life tasks, persist (Woodruff-Pak 1989). The reader must be aware of the issues in order to interpret both the research literature and the test scores of a particular client.

What follows is a brief overview of these issues. Some pertinent, current research has been cited. These citations are used to illustrate the issues, not as an attempt to make definitive statements on aging and cog-

nition. The reader is reminded, again, that research findings are not "holy scripture" (Schnitz 1991). Woodruff-Pak (1989) has conducted an excellent review of the topic of intelligence testing and the aged that should be consulted for more detail. The critical issues are as follows:

1. Intelligence tests were developed and intended for use with young adults. Woodruff-Pak (1989) describes this approach as follows: "Old people are assessed with the yardstick designed to measure the young, and if they deviate from the young pattern, they are labelled deficient. . . . What intelligence tests measure may not relate to the context of older adults' lives" (p. 106). Initially, there were no standard scores beyond age 59. As Jarvik (1988) points out, the addition of standard scores to the Wechsler Adult Intelligence Scale to age 74 has simply resulted in "under-ground ageism." These standard scores have determined, in advance, that a "normal" score for an older person is considerably lower than that for a younger person.

This model accepts a decline in intelligence with age as normal instead of investigating *why* it has happened. This is indeed a critical issue, as numerous longitudinal studies have found that, even between identical twins, a drop in measured intelligence predicts death (Birren & Schaie 1990; Jarvik 1988; Maddox & Busse 1987; Schaie 1989). This is described as the "terminal drop" in intelligence.

2. Comparison groups are uneven. The first studies comparing intelligence between younger and older adults were the United States Army screening tests used during World War I. Younger recruits consistently performed better than older recruits on these tests. Common sense suggests that this would be true, since the young recruits were that much closer to having been in school and doing paper and pencil type tests. This effect is further exaggerated when college students are used as the comparison group. The social and educational experiences of this particular group are very different, not only from their peers, but especially from those of most older adults. Consider just one very important illustration of these differences: In the United States, for those over 75, less than 75 percent have completed high school and more than one in seven had fewer than five years of schooling. In the younger population today, 75 percent and fewer than one out of forty has had fewer than five years of education (Lonergrin 1990). This fact alone, without even considering all of the other differences, such as social, cultural, health, and diet, has a tremendous impact on intelligence test performance. Studies have consistently found that there are very large differences in test performance between generations, with each younger genera-

tion having improved average scores (Shaie 1989). The whole practice of basing social psychological research so heavily on the testing of undagraduate college students is being seriously questioned (Schaie & Schooler 1989).

The effect of education on cognitive test performance is well illustrated by a study of the performance of 358 elderly persons on the Mini-Mental State examination (Murden et al. 1991). The authors found that persons with eighth-grade or lower education had significantly lower scores than those with more education.

With regard to the selection of older adult study participants, a matter of great concern is the incidence of ADRD. Changes in intelligence test performance can occur very early in the disease, well before simple objective measures detect it (Jarvik 1988). Since the incidence of ADRD in the population over 65 is now thought to be as high as 15 percent, it is quite likely that a number of older adult subjects in cross-sectional studies had early, undetected, ADRD that lowered average test scores.

The findings described above were based on cross-sectional studies. The first longitudinal studies, comparing the performance of the same individuals over a period of years, contradicted findings of the early cross-sectional studies (Birren & Schaie 1990; Cohen 1988; Schaie 1989). The 1984 Washington longitudinal study of over 1400 adults reported that even at age 81 less than half of all observed individuals had shown reliable, decremental change over the preceding seven years. Further, it is stated that "maintenance of functioning on one or more abilities is characteristic for most individuals, well into advanced old age" (Schaie 1989, 486).

Unfortunately, cross-sectional studies continue to be carried out, without adequate regard for the enormous differences in life experiences between generations and the equally enormous effect these differences have on test performance. But fortunately, as Cohen (1988) states, "the findings of stable over-all intellectual functioning in later life are being replicated in different ways in an increasing number of studies" (p. 25).

3. The format and content of tests and assessments have been biased against the older adult. As previously mentioned, the younger adult is much more likely to be familiar and comfortable with the paper and pencil tests used in many studies (Woodruff-Pak 1989). In addition, most of these test materials are based on visual skills. There is a much greater likelihood that an older adult will have visual deficits (see the following section in this chapter).

For many older adults the content of tests may be not only unfamiliar, but downright frivolous in terms of their everyday lives (Birren & Schaie 1990; Cockburn & Smith 1991; Cohen 1988; Erber 1989; Rosenbloom & Morgan 1986; Woodruff-Pak 1989). Numerous studies have reported that the use of materials with which older adults have prior knowledge and that are part of their life experiences can eliminate age differences in memory performance (Backman & Herlitz 1990; Backman et al. 1987; Barret & Wright 1981; Erber et al. 1985; Hanley-Dunn & McIntosh 1984; Hultsch & Dixon 1983; Worden & Sherman-Brown 1983). This concept is referred to as "ecological validity."

In skill areas based on accumulated life experiences ("crystallized intelligence," such as vocabulary skills), older adults perform better than do younger adults. Reduced performance speed is commonly attributed to older adults. Given enough time, healthy older adults perform just as well as or better than younger adults (Dippel & Hutton 1988). For instance, older bridge players were quicker at a card selection task than younger ones (Lonergrin 1990). Studies examining specific work skills or productivity are finding either no difference (clerical workers) or improved skill (proofreaders) in older workers compared with younger workers (Cohen 1988). There is a poor correlation between standardized measures of intelligence and the actual competence of older workers (Birren & Schaie 1990).

The reliance on the results of standardized test scores in measuring actual competency is being questioned for persons of all age groups. The report of the Ford Foundation's National Commission on Testing and Public Policy recommends that tests be used to promote human talents, rather than to inhibit them (Gifford 1990). Findings may be summarized as follows: ". . . recent work using familiar materials, some specifically defined to be cohort relevant, indicates much less and in some cases no age-related decline in memory tasks similar to those encountered in everyday life" (Erber 1989, 170).

Information about the capacity of the human brain for development well into old age has only recently become available. Until very recently, the brain had been assumed to be hard-wired and fixed at a vay young age and to remain so for the rest of life. The large number of neurons that die daily in the human brain is frequently cited as support for an inevitable cognitive decline during aging. Both of these commonly accepted ideas are now known to be false.

Although the *number* of neurons is fixed at a relatively young age, the communication structures (dendrites) of these neurons do grow in response to injury, and most probably in response to environmental stimulation (Birren & Schaie 1990; Cohen 1988; Diamond

1984; Finch & Schneider 1985; Moore 1991; Rapoport 1983; Timiras 1988; Woodruff-Pak 1989). The human brain has tremendous potential for growth and development.

Second, although many neurons may die daily, this must be kept in perspective. There are approximately as many neurons in the human brain as there are stars in the Milky Way, 15 billion. The loss of even 1 million by the seventh decade still leaves a great reserve of neurons. There must be a much more substantial loss before function is seriously affected (Cohen 1988; Robertson 1987). In addition, some investigators believe that the previously assumed loss and shrinkage of the human brain may be due, at least in part, to laboratory methods used during postmortem examinations (Cohen 1988; Lonergrin 1990).

The evidence in support of brain plasticity, and hence the continued potential for cognitive development in old age, is supported by animal studies (see Chapter 7) and by the increasing number of recent experiments that demonstrate the potential for older adults to continue learning. Consider the longitudinal studies of 134 sets of older twins by Jarvik (as reported in Henig 1988). Those persons who aged most successfully were those who participated in mental (which seemed to be particularly important), physical, and emotional activities. In addition, activities in later years were even more important than those engaged in as a young adult. Cohen (1988) also stresses the importance of continuing mental activities for successful aging.

A study of subjects between the ages of 70 and 93 years used a memory assessment based on everyday activities, called the Rivermead Behavioural Memory Test (Cockburn & Smith 1991). Performance on verbal, visual, and spatial memory tasks correlated with the level of involvement in social and daily living tasks, whereas crystallized intelligence and years of formal education showed little correlation with test performance. Another study compared the performances of 50 bridge players and 50 non-bridge players between the ages of 55 and 91 on tests of working memory, reasoning, reaction time, and vocabulary (Clarkson-Smith & Hartley 1990). Players performed better than nonplayers on measures of working memory and reasoning.

Other studies have found that continued involvement in the activities of daily life promotes continued cognitive function (Arbuckle et al. 1986; Birren & Schaie 1990; Butler & Gleason 1985; Cockburn & Smith 1991; Craik et al. 1987; Heacock et al. 1991; Hill et al. 1989; Henig 1988; Winocur et al. 1987). Studies showed, for example, improved performance on standardized tests with training and practice (Woodruff-Pak

1989), improved memory skills with training (Birren & Schaie 1990; Clarkson-Smith & Hartley 1990, Scoggin et al. 1985), and the important concept of the development of a more integrative, holistic pattern of thinking and problem solving that is associated with increasing age (Woodruff-Pak 1989).

This concept is closely related to Erikson's eighth stage of development, which he describes as seeking "integrity versus despair" (Erikson et al. 1986). This, in turn, is related to what has traditionally been called the "wisdom of old age," the integration of thought and feeling. Questions of cognitive function in old age have been too much tied to the narrow concept of "intelligence," ignoring the broader and more significant concept of "wisdom." The large numbers of old people who have made dynamic and "wise" contributions to the world of thought (e.g., Erik Erikson published a book, *Vital Involvement in Old Age* [1986] at age 85), art (e.g., Monet painted his masterpiece panel of the water lilies at age 82), music (e.g., Verdi composed the opera *Falstaff* at age 80), and literature have been dismissed too often as exceptions, rather than used to illustrate the tremendous continued potential for cognitive development and learning in old age. As one final, concrete illustration, the text you are reading was originally typed by my dynamic and devoted 74-year-old mother, who learned word processing and typing in order to do this project.

Although this view is increasingly expressed in the literature, earlier views unfortunately persist. The reader must constantly question the methods and assumptions of research regarding aging and cognition. Woodruff-Pak (1989) reviewed 209 articles on aging and intelligence and was surprised that the incorrect assumption of inevitable cognitive decline continued to be used for the interpretation of studies in the 1970s and 1980s. Indeed, this *misinformation* seems to be self-perpetuating. As one illustration, consider a 1987 book by Shepherd, *Physical Activity and Aging*. The author states, without qualification, that "normal aging leads to a slow and orderly deterioration of cognitive function" (p. 248). This assertion is supported by a single reference, from 1962.

Negative stereotyping of the cognitive capacity of the elderly is pervasive, persistent, and WRONG. It is particularly essential to counteract this stereotyping because the predominant assumption in modern western society is that "you are what you think."

4.1 Interventions That Enhance Cognitive Functioning

Tear down the negative stereotype of the reduced cognitive function of the aged. Use examples from research, personal experiences, and famous people to counter this in conversation, writing, public speaking, research, and every facet of personal and professional life. In work settings with seniors, post newspaper and biographical accounts of the accomplishments of other seniors, excerpts from research, etc.

Reinforce the self-esteem and competence of older people through emphasizing and encouraging their skills and wisdom. Create a positive self-fulfilling prophecy. Use research findings that suggest that older individuals have particular skills in the areas of crystallized intelligence (e.g., accumulated life skills, such as vocabulary) and for organization or "chunking" of information.

Provide a stimulating and encouraging environment. This is particularly important in institutional settings. Encourage and enhance lifelong learning. Provide learning experiences that are of interest; draw on life experiences and hence stimulate participation. Allow adequate time to integrate and reflect on the information. Provide encouragement and positive feedback.

Provide opportunities for learning and practice in cognitive skills in areas that are personally meaningful (e.g., memory improvement classes). There is evidence that the specific techniques of memory improvement are effective and that participation in cognitive and daily activities has a positive effect on maintaining cognitive functioning in old age (Birren & Schaie 1990; Butler & Gleason 1985; Cockburn & Smith 1991; Cohen 1988). Training in specific memory techniques, such as mnemonics (word strategies), is enhanced by pretraining in imagery and relaxation (Hill et al. 1989).

Ensure assessment and treatment of diseases that interfere with maximum cognitive performance.

Provide conducive learning situations and environments. These are the general principles of learning, which apply at all ages:

- Keep in mind that learning should be interactive.
- Eliminate unnecessary confusion and distraction.
- Remember that multi-modal learning, using several sensory systems, is most effective. There is some evidence that older adults learn better using auditory, rather than visual, systems.
- Use the principles of cues, practice, and motivation.

4.2 ADRD and Cognitive Function

Wlhen considering ADRD and cognitive function, it is essential, above all else, to understand that the mind and cognitive function do not equal the person. Because of the obvious deterioration in cognitive function

associated with ADRD, there is a tendency to assume that deterioration is all-encompassing, even to assume that the person no longer exists. One author eloquently described this dilemma as follows:

> These residents are capable of much more than we facilely imagine and assiduously expect. We limit them by our own doubts and dark expectations. Our technological society highly values mature cognition, that secondary mental process which involves categories, figures, facts and manipulation of empirical data. But much wealth of human experience occurs at the primary level of creative arts. (Greenblatt 1988,1 15)

With this introduction in mind, it must be stated that there is little evidence that the kinds of cognitive and memory retraining that are successful with the well elderly are effective with persons with ADRD, even those who are mildly impaired (Beck et al. 1988; Carroll & Gray 1981; Davis & Kirkland 1988; Yesavage et al. 1981; Zarit et al. 1982). This, however, should not be mistaken for inability of the person with ADRD to learn. There are many types of learning and memory and many methods, using, for example, communication techniques, relevant cuing, or visual imagery (Byrd 1990), which make it possible for the person with ADRD to learn (Arkin 1991).

By making use of communication techniques (Chapter 3) and group guidelines (Chapter 4), in combination with the guidelines to enabling independence (this chapter) and recognition of the importance of a supportive environment, it is possible to maximize daily functioning and practical cognition.

The case below is one of many possible illustrations of the potential of the person with ADRD for learning.

> About three years after the initial symptoms, the effects of Alzheimer's disease caused Alice to have increasing difficulty with her ability to remain in her own home. As a result, her son and his family helped her to move to an apartment near their home, in a city several hundred miles from where she had lived for more than 50 years. Although Alice had visited many times, living in this new environment was a different matter. Her daughter-in-law's mother, Muriel, came to stay for three weeks and to help get her settled. With Muriel's help, the furniture and other treasures collected over a lifetime were arranged and displayed in her new home. She even entertained family and Halifax friends,

familiar from many visits. During this time Muriel was also going with her on daily walks to the neighborhood stores, the bank, and the post office, subtly pointing out cues for way-finding. She was very happy, but the family was concerned about how she would manage after Muriel left. She showed no signs of being able to find her way to the store, or of taking any initiative to prepare meals, or to state her new address, despite repeated prompting from her son and daughter-in-law.

Her son was astounded when he dropped Alice off at the apartment, after taking Muriel to the airport, to hear her say, "I think I'll walk over to the store now. I need a few things." And he was even more amazed when she made it there and back with her purchases, with no trouble whatsoever. Alice was able to live in her apartment, with support from her family and eventually a homemaker a few hours a week, for almost two years. She walked to the store, her son's home, and the hairdresser, and entertained family and friends. She learned to manage happily in her new environment (concrete visual–spatial learning). She never did learn her new address or telephone number (verbal learning).

Indeed, Alice continued to learn when she moved to a nearby long-term care facility. Despite now-progressed Alzheimer's disease she learned to find her way to the dining room and the chapel in this large facility, and, although at some risk to her safety, she learned to find her way to her son's house, a few blocks away.

Persons with ADRD are capable of learning. Suggestions for enhancing this learning are found in Chapter 4.

5.0 THE SPECIAL SENSES

Sensory losses are widespread among the old, with nearly 75 percent of those over 65 suffering from a significant impairment of one or more functions. Most of these changes have been gradual, beginning as early as age 35, and the older person has made a gradual accommodation. Nonetheless, the interactive effects of sensory losses with emotional well-being (e.g., being isolated from others because of decreased hearing) and physical well-being (e.g., increased likelihood of falls because of poor vision) are profound. Sensory changes, perhaps more than any other aspect of psychobiological change, have a pervasive effect because of the detri-

mental impact on receiving information. This in turn affects not only the activities of daily living but relationships with others. There are both individual changes (e.g., using hearing aids) and environmental changes (e.g., improving lighting and removing obstacles from walkways) that can lessen the effects of these sensory losses.

The changes described in the following pages are the usual age-related changes. However, it must be stressed again that not every older person experiences them. In addition, it is absolutely essential that every older person have thorough and regular physical examinations to identify the presence of diseases (e.g., cataracts or glaucoma) that can cause sensory impairment beyond the usual changes associated with age. Many of these diseases are treatable. Such examinations are particularly important for the person with ADRD. Sensory losses, combined with the effects of the disease, can cause an even greater level of disability. Unfortunately, it may be assumed that, since the degree of disorientation and confusion is already so great, interventions such as improved hearing or vision will make little difference. Nothing could be further from the truth; in fact, they are most particularly in need of these treatments.

> Because of cataracts on both eyes, Alice had great difficulty threading a needle. Despite having been an avid seamstress, as her Alzheimer's disease progressed, she gave up sewing completely. Approximately four years after the first signs of Alzheimer's disease she had successful cataract surgery on both eyes. After this she was able not only to thread a needle but to do simple mending for the first time in years.

The information in the following sections is based on the following references: Christenson (1990), Crepeau (1986), Davis and Kirkland (1988), Finch and Schneider (1985), Rosenbloom and Morgan (1986), Shore (1976), and Timiras (1988). Other references used in the specific sections are listed in the text body.

6.0 VISION

Changes in vision are numerous and begin early in life with, for instance, a decreased ability to accommodate, to focus on an object at varying distances, beginning at age 10 (Cristarella 1977). Interference with activities such as driving and reading because of changes in vision is 20 times more likely for the older adult than for someone who is middle-aged. When adjustments are not made, limitations in vision can lead to decreased motivation and attention, increased anxiety, and a lowered self-esteem. Even minor vision loss requires some changes in activities of daily living routines. It also has an effect on the level and nature of leisure activities (Heinemann et al. 1988). Some areas in which visual changes may occur are described below.

Acuity. Acuity is the ability to distinguish fine details in the visual field. This change usually becomes most noticeable after age 40. However, with proper glasses 80 percent of the elderly have adequate acuity to age 90 and beyond.

Accommodation. Accommodation is the ability to adapt the focus of the eye to objects at different distances. This also begins to deteriorate most noticeably in the mid-40s, with most people requiring glasses for near vision by the mid-5Os, although to a lesser degree there is also deterioration of the ability to see far objects. As we age, objects that are either too close or too far are difficult to see.

Visual field. Visual field is the area of vision and is sharpest in the center. After age 60 the visual field begins to decrease in size.

Light sensitivity. The older eye requires increasing levels of illumination for good vision. The average 70-year-old requires three times as much light as the average 20-year-old (e.g., a 300-watt bulb as compared with a 100-watt bulb).

Dark adaptation. Dark adaptation is the adjustment of vision when moving from bright light to dim light or darkness. This takes longer as we age. This increased period of decreased vision is particularly problematic in adjusting to the light of oncoming cars during night driving and when moving from a brightly lit room to a darkened hallway. The ability to recover from glare (excessive reflection of light into an individual's eyes) also decreases with age because of the opacity of the lens and changes within the eyeball. Direct glare is caused by light shining directly into the eye. Indirect glare is caused by light bouncing off surfaces, such as floors or furniture.

Color sensitivity. Color sensitivity is the ability to distinguish between colors. This decreases with age, with women less affected than men. Colors of shorter wave-length, in the blue-green spectrum, are the most affected. Changes in the perception of the blue color range occur in the 40- and 50-age range, and problems in distinguishing the green colors begin in the 60s. Colors in the longer wave-lengths (red/orange) are more easily distinguished.

Perception. Perception is the awareness of the physical environment. There are many different types of perception. Research on perceptual changes in the elderly is problematic; for example, the tests used in the research studies may be particularly affected by the older subject's test anxiety and slowed reaction time. However, there is some evidence to suggest that as people age there is more difficulty with figure-ground distinctions (e.g., seeing a green toothbrush lying on a green and gold bathroom counter); with visual-spatial ability (determining the relative size, position, and distance of various objects); with the persistence of a visual image; and with susceptibility to visual illusion (perceiving objects differently than they are).

Visual memory. Visual memory is the pictorial or symbolic storage of information and is much more effective at all ages than pure auditory memory. At least four times as much visual material can be stored as verbal material. There is some evidence that this capacity deteriorates with age.

Response time to visual stimulus. There is evidence of an age-associated increase in response time to visual stimuli, but this is complicated by the presence of decreased visual acuity.

The above changes, when present, are made worse by the presence of eye disease such as glaucoma, cataracts, and macular degeneration, which are much more common in old age.

6.1 Environmental Interventions for Visual Changes

There is much that can be done with the environment to compensate for visual changes. Figure 1-1 illustrates some of these changes, such as use of contrast, spot lighting, glare-reducing curtains, and furniture with rounded edges.

Increase light intensity. Increase light in such important areas as stairs, hallways, closets, and bathrooms. Use spot lighting for work areas and reading. The light should be directly on the reading or work material, not on the person's face. Shade or focus bulbs to avoid glare.

Make sure glasses are clean. This may seem obvious but is frequently overlooked, especially for older individuals who may not be physically or cognitively able to clean their own glasses.

Avoid glare. Use mat or dull finishes on floors, walls, reading materials, signs, art supplies, bathroom fixtures, counters, and furniture. Use sheer curtains to avoid sun glare through windows, and shades to avoid glare from light bulbs. Recessed lighting also reduces glare. Outdoor areas should be shaded with umbrellas, latticework, awnings, foliage, etc. Do not wax floors. The glare causes visual difficulties and distortion, which results in a hesitance to move. This, combined with the polished surface, may also lead to falls.

Use large print and large focal points for symbols. This is especially important on medication bottles, but also for directional signs in institutions, reading materials, and the telephone book. The telephone dial and

Figure 1-1 Environmental Compensations for Visual Changes

thermostat dial should have enlarged numbers. Type sizes larger than 12 points do not seem to improve visibility (Rosenbloom & Morgan 1986). Lettering on signs should be at least five-eighths of an inch high. The older adult with recent vision loss usually finds raised letters or signs more manageable than Braille.

Use contrast (Cooper 1985). There are several different types of contrasts that can be used to enhance visibility: intensity (brightness), complementary colors, and warm and cool colors. The most effective contrast in brightness is light on dark, for example, white letters on a red background for a calendar. Some complementary color combinations are yellow/violet, orange/blue, and red/green. Warm colors are those from the red end of the spectrum (red, orange, and yellow) and cool colors are those from the blue end of the spectrum (green, violet, and blue). The strongest contrast is between red/orange and blue/green. Use of two types of contrast (e.g., brightness and color) further enhances visibility. A narrow border contrast also enhances visibility (e.g., a sign for the bathroom door would be more visible with white letters on a red background with a border of green). Contrast is useful to distinguish

- floors from walls
- doorways from doors
- bathroom fixtures from the background walls
- plate, tray, cutlery from the table
- food from the plate surface
- the edge of the step from the other steps (This is an especially important safety consideration. A painted strip or a well-secured, nonskid tape about five centimeters wide, with a high contrast in color and brightness to the step itself, should be added to the edge of the step and the riser.)
- craft and games materials from the table surface
- appliance dial indicators from the background (use bright reflector tape or stick-on marker dots)
- toilet articles from bathroom counter or bureau
- sliding glass doors (mark with decals)

If fluorescent lights are used, use full-spectrum bulbs to avoid fatigue. Fluorescent lights reduce glare, but they should be checked regularly to eliminate a subtle flicker, which is disturbing to the older eye. They are best used in combination with incandescent lights.

Avoid pastels. Pastels (e.g., light pinks, beige), dark colors (e.g., black, brown), and colors in the blue-green spectrum are difficult for the aging eye to distinguish.

Make a safety check.

- Tack down or remove scatter rugs.
- Remove glass-topped tables (invisible to someone with low vision).
- Keep doors closed, or all the way open, to avoid accidentally running into the door edge.
- Place cutlery in the drain rack sharp edge down.
- Keep main traffic ways (e.g., bathroom and kitchen) clear of clutter.
- As much as possible, remove all sharp-edged furniture, especially that near walking routes.

Position reading and work material for maximal vision. This should include placement

- in the center of the visual field
- at optimum for near vision
- with excellent illumination
- supported with a reading stand or lap tray to prevent fatigue

Use other sensory cues to compensate for lost vision.

- Use well-positioned handrails along hallways leading to the dining room or bathrooms; use textural changes around doorways, such as wallpapered to painted surface). Contour or change the shape of handrails to cue for coming corners or changes in direction.
- Put raised numbers on telephone dials.
- Make notches to distinguish front and back door keys.

Arrange the environment consistently. Avoid rearranging furniture and changing the placement of kitchen tools, toilet articles, and clothing.

- Arrange different clothing types in separate sections in drawers.
- Coordinate clothing according to color, and place on separate hangers.
- Arrange denominations of paper money by using a series of paper clips or by folding each denomination differently.

Avoid competing and confusing stimuli. Avoid confusing patterns in flooring, tablecloths, place mats, counter tops, wallpaper and craft materials, wallpaper, and in other interior decoration.

6.2 Individual Interventions for Visual Changes

First and foremost, every aging person should have regular examinations by a qualified optician or ophthal-

mologist. Unfortunately, this tends to be ignored, particularly if the person lives in an institution. As many as 80 to 95 percent of the elderly living in institutions may not have regular eye examinations (Rosenbloom & Morgan 1986). The need for a change in prescribed lenses and for other assistive devices (e.g., telescopes and magnifiers) and adaptations to standard eyeglass frames (e.g., special bridges and nosepieces to reduce pressure on sensitive skin) should be professionally assessed.

Numerous assistive devices designed for persons with limited vision may assist in daily living. Local branches of the Canadian National Institute for the Blind or the American Foundation for the Blind can provide information about what is available and may also sell them. Most larger centers have a visual aids center or clinic where the individual can try out devices such as illuminated magnifiers to decide whether they will be useful. An excellent guide to these devices, *Aids and Appliances for the Visually Impaired*, is available from the American Foundation for the Blind. Some examples of these devices are

- enlarged dial numbers or enlarged Touch-Tone pad (These and other devices are usually available from the telephone company, often free of charge for the disabled.)
- a typoscope reading guide (a mat frame that focuses on a few lines at a time and reduces glare from the rest of the page)
- large-print checks (often free of charge from banks)
- talking books available from the National Library Service, many local libraries, and the Canadian National Institute for the Blind or the American Foundation for the Blind
- special syringes to assist the visually impaired diabetic

Other helpful ideas include the following:

- Wear sun visors or peaked hats, even indoors, if glare is a particular problem.
- Apply training in eye relaxation to reduce strain (see Hiatt et al. 1982).
- Use other senses (sound, touch, smell), as well as counting and way finding, to supplement vision.

6.3 ADRD and Visual Impairment

Early intervention to compensate for visual changes (e.g., prescription lenses, environmental changes) is particularly important for the person with ADRD because the perceptual changes that accompany the disease make distinguishing objects difficult. If the individual has difficulty in communicating, a caregiver who is very familiar should accompany the individual for reassurance and guidance during an eye examination.

- Be aware that because of memory impairment eyeglasses are often lost, traded, or left behind. This may be overcome by attaching a snug elastic strap or, if that is not tolerated, a chain or string to eyeglasses.
- Be particularly cautious about visual stimuli that may be misinterpreted.

Perception is affected not only by age-associated visual changes but also by perceptual deficits associated with the disease. Avoid designs in floor patterns that may appear as if there is something on the floor or may even look as if there is a change in height. Remove wall coverings that are too realistic and too distracting. For example, some ADRD patients were disoriented by a beautiful, full-wall mural of the woods in autumn. These visual deficits can be turned to advantage for the caregiver by disguising doorways that should not be used. Such doors can be painted the same color as the surrounding walls or disguised with other visual barriers such as screens, blinds, and room dividers. As the disease progresses, mirrors, especially large decorative ones, should be removed. Persons with ADRD are often alarmed or frightened by their own reflections, which they no longer recognize.

7.0 HEARING

Hearing loss, even slight, is frequently considered to have an even greater impact on the individual than vision loss, because it causes isolation from people and the environment. Isolation from environmental sounds can be both physically dangerous (e.g., inability to hear sirens or car horns) and psychologically devastating (e.g., inability to hear bird songs in spring, music, or the laughter of children) (Voeks et al. 1990). Lack of conversation with people can have profound effects on the individual's self-esteem, thinking, and orientation and can even lead to paranoia. If what people are saying cannot be heard the individual may assume that he or she is being talked about.

It is also frequently stated that, compared with persons who are visually impaired, persons who are hearing impaired are treated with less empathy and may even be the butt of jokes (Crepeau 1986). Perhaps this lack of empathy is the result of the extra effort and frustration involved in communicating with the hearing impaired. This frustration is probably related to the

common loss of the ability to hear high-frequency sound. Speech can still be heard, but not understood, and may lead people to believe falsely that individuals "hear what they want to hear" (Voeks et al. 1990). So much of social and leisure activity is based on hearing that persons with hearing loss, particularly late-life hearing loss, may become culturally and socially isolated. Hearing loss is widespread in persons over 65, with 40 to 70 percent having a hearing loss that interferes with conversation (Davis & Kirkland 1988). Twenty percent more men than women have hearing loss. This is thought to be related to the greater effect of damaging environmental sounds that older men have experienced in the course of their jobs. Twenty percent of all individuals over 65 are profoundly deaf (Glass 1990). Frequently, loss is more pronounced in one ear than in the other.

7.1 Auditory Changes

Decreased ability to hear high-frequency (high-pitched) sounds. This is the most common type of hearing loss and has a devastating effect on the ability to understand speech. Consonants are high frequency; thus, although the individual may hear, he or she can hear only lower-frequency vowel sounds (e.g., *car* is heard as *ar*, *dog* as *og*, etc.). Consonants make speech understandable. Although music, because of its vibrating characteristics, can be used to reach the hearing impaired, high-frequency music can be very irritating.

Decreased sound localization capacity. The ability to locate where a sound is coming from generally decreases, particularly high-frequency sounds.

Decreased ability to mask background sound. With aging, it becomes increasingly difficult to filter out background sounds (e.g., conversations, radio, traffic noise, even the ringing in one's own ears). This further increases difficulty in understanding conversation.

Decreased ability to comprehend when speech is repeatedly interrupted. This may be subtle and unconscious, such as the eight-times-per-second interruptions of modern telephone systems (Timiras 1988). For those with a particular type of metabolic hearing loss related to a deterioration of blood vessels, there is the difficult problem of "recruitment." As a sound becomes more intense, there is an abnormally large increase in loudness.

7.2 Environmental Interventions for Hearing Changes

- Reduce or eliminate background noise. This is particularly important in dining and other group conversation areas. Close windows to block out traffic noise and shut doors to reduce hum (e.g., from the kitchen refrigerator).

- Have speakers use a microphone, as this lowers the pitch of the sound.
- Turn up the bass and turn down the treble on stereo systems and speakers.
- Turn off the radio, television, etc., during conversation. Televisions and radios should not be left on constantly, as they become one more part of distracting background sounds.
- Use acoustic tiles.
- Enhance other sensory cues (e.g., color, texture).
- Ensure proper lighting to support lip reading and other nonverbal communication (which should be emphasized).
- Write key words for those who can read.
- Enhance hearing through "looping" a room used for meetings and groups. This system enables individuals with hearing aids to receive sound directly from the loop to their hearing aids. In some localities this service is provided free of charge to public institutions.
- Use headphones for stereo systems or portable cassette players.

7.3 Individual Interventions for Hearing Loss

As with visual loss, it is absolutely essential that the individual experiencing hearing loss be examined by a qualified professional. Some hearing loss can be alleviated by surgery or by something as simple as the removal of a buildup of excess wax. Other types of hearing loss can be improved with the use of hearing aids. It is important to check the batteries regularly. In addition, a comprehensive medical review should include a drug review. Many common medications (e.g., the diuretic Lasix [furosemide], aspirin, and antibiotics) can worsen or cause hearing loss.

A recent study underlined the importance of screening and environmental interventions in settings used by large numbers of older people. A screening for hearing loss among 192 persons recently admitted to a nursing home revealed that only 24 percent had normal hearing thresholds, 54 percent had loss of higher frequency sounds, and 22 percent had moderate or greater losses. Of those with significant loss, 66 percent had not been identified by the routine admission screening and ~0 percent overall reported that they had difficulty in hearing normal conversation (Voeks et al. 1990).

7.4 Tips for Talking to the Hearing Impaired

- Face the person, preferably at eye level, when you speak. Never say something while walking by or calling from another room. Make sure the light on your face is clear, to enhance lip reading.

- Pronounce words carefully, using good lip movements. Do not chew gum, eat, or smoke while speaking.
- Lower the pitch of your voice, because high-frequency sounds are harder to hear.

- Do not shout, as this distorts word formation and makes lip reading more difficult.
- If your message is not understood, rephrase and try again.
- Many people with hearing impairment hear better with one ear than the other. Direct conversation to this ear or speak directly into the ear.

- Gain attention (e.g., by touching the hand) before speaking.

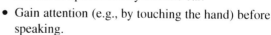

- Supplement conversation with nonverbal cues (e.g., hand gestures and facial expressions).
- Make extra associations with names to clarify them (e.g., "Joe, my friend who makes the delicious wine, is coming for dinner").
- Use round tables for group situations (to make it easier to see the other person's face).

- Avoid "long row seating," as this makes conversation difficult for the hearing impaired. Have small conversation areas in lounges, seat at small tables for meals.
- Appreciate that hearing loss will be worse when the person is sick.

7.5 Technical Services

Hearing aids. For some, hearing aids may help and should be prescribed by a qualified audiologist. They should be kept in good working order. The prescription of hearing aids is becoming more precise. There are, for example, new models that can screen out extraneous noises. It is very important to be patient. Adjustment to hearing aid use is slow and difficult, on the same scale as adjusting to an artificial limb. In addition to hearing aids, there are other technical devices that may assist in daily living. There are also Hearing dogs, specially trained like Seeing Eye dogs.

Telephone aids. Telephone conversation is particularly difficult for the hearing-impaired person, as the nonverbal cues are missing and the telephone distorts sound. In addition to the excellent—but expensive—TDD (telecommunication device for the deaf) system, many telephone companies have a service center for assessing and supplying telephone devices for the hearing impaired. Many are free to the hearing impaired. Some examples are:

- different bells or flashing lights to indicate a call
- devices that amplify the sound
- devices that replace the conventional earpiece with one that is "looped" and will function with an existing hearing aid

Alarms, doorbells, and smoke alarms. These devices can be adapted with various systems, using flashing lights, vibrating systems, and low-tone sounds. Amplifiers and headphones are available for radio and television.

Two-way communication systems. The two-way aspect is *essential;* otherwise it is not communication. Much progress has been made beyond the cumbersome writing of notes, which may be particularly difficult for elderly individuals with other diseases, such as arthritis. Inexpensive amplification systems are readily available from electronic stores. Technology that will project spoken words onto a screen or change them into print will soon be available to the public. Signing is a highly complex communication system, which some with late-life hearing loss may find difficult to learn. However, learning even a few signs may be helpful. Discussion of the differences between American Sign Language and signed English is beyond the scope of this book. An excellent overview of this topic is found in *Seeing Voices,* by Oliver Sacks (1989).

7.6 ADRD and Hearing Loss

More detailed information on communicating with persons with ADRD is found in Chapter 3.

- Do repeat the same words over, more clearly and distinctly, when they have not been heard the first time. This is in contrast to the usual approach with the hearing impaired. For persons with ADRD, rephrasing would cause confusion. If the message still is not being understood after two or three attempts, change the topic and focus attention on something else to avoid frustration. Try again later, using different phrasing.
- Be especially careful not to shout, as persons with ADRD may interpret this as anger.

8.0 OLFACTION (SENSE OF SMELL)

The importance of the sense of smell is often underrated, and yet this system occupies a larger area of the brain than any other sensory system (Rosenbloom & Morgan 1986). Perhaps because, more than any other sensory system, the olfactory neurons are exposed to environmental hazards (e.g., cigarette smoke), the sense of smell begins to show a marked decline at about age 60. According to one study of 2,000 subjects, the deterioration in the seventh and eighth decade is staggering. For example, 80 percent of those over 80 years of age had impaired function and 50 percent were unable to smell at all. This impaired ability to smell involves both an increasing inability to identify different smells and the need for a greater concentration of a particular smell before it can be detected (Timiras 1988). The deterioration in the sense of smell is greater for men than for women.

These changes are important from at least three perspectives. First, there are safety concerns. Several studies have reported that the elderly have a much higher threshold (up to ten times) for detecting the smell of warning substances added to natural gas, as well as a higher proportion of accidents as a result of household gas poisoning. Another major concern is the decreased ability to detect the smell of smoke and the smell of spoiled or burning food.

Second, because of its relation to taste and appetite, a decreased sense of smell can have a major effect on appetite and nutrition. As much as two-thirds of taste sensations are, in fact, dependent on the sense of smell (Shore 1976). Recall the bland taste of food when you have a cold. Third, a deteriorated sense of smell can mean that the elderly are unaware of offensive personal and environmental odors. This could have a negative effect on social contacts, both at home and in the community.

8.1 Environmental Interventions for Changes in the Sense of Smell

- Check smoke and gas detectors frequently to make sure that they are working.
- If safety spring caps cannot be installed on gas stoves, consider switching to an electric stove.
- Check frequently for leaks in containers of ammonia and other toxic agents.
- Enhance other sensory cues and social activities with meals (see Chapter 7) to improve appetite.
- Serve heated foods, as they have more aroma than cold foods.
- Offer aromatic, premeal appetizers.

- Use slow-simmering foods and pleasant but pervasive food smells (e.g., perked coffee, fresh-baked bread, simmering soups). See Appendix 5A for short-cut methods such as quick breads and dried, packaged soups.
- Encourage and support habitual grooming and hygiene. For example, perhaps the person is not bathing because getting in and out of the tub is too difficult and frightening. Sturdy grab rails and no-skid decals in the tub could overcome this problem.

8.2 ADRD and the Sense of Smell

The deterioration of the sense of smell is even greater for persons with Alzheimer's disease than for other older adults as well as in comparison to the deterioration of other sensory systems during the course of ADRD (Serby 1986; Timiras 1988). Therefore, extra attention should be paid to the preceding suggestions as well as to the other suggestions for enhancing pleasant environmental smells, which are found in Chapter 7.

9.0 TASTE

The sense of smell is closely related to the sense of taste. Although earlier studies reported a marked decrease in the sense of taste with aging, more recent studies suggest that the amount of loss is considerably less than the loss in the sense of smell. There are also recent studies that report no significant age-related changes in taste perception (Lonergrin 1990). There is no difference in the degree of loss between men and women. Taste acuities for salt and sweet deteriorate considerably more with age than those for bitter or sour. This may account for the fact that some older people describe food as either bland or bitter. A lifetime of smoking, as well as the likelihood that the elderly will be taking more medications than younger people, may account for part of the losses in taste. In addition to the loss of the sensory pleasure of eating, decreased taste may have an effect on nutritional and health status, particularly the risk of an increased use of salt. There is also a decrease in the amount of saliva in the mouth.

9.1 Interventions To Counteract the Loss of Taste

- Do not mix food together when feeding.
- Enhance the gustatory aspects of food with extra herbs and seasonings, different cooking methods, tasty sauces, ethnic and local food specialties, and the use of flavor-fresh products.

- Enhance other sensory properties of food (color, texture, smell).
- Make ample use of natural appetite stimulants, such as social gatherings, exercise, and appetizers. Unless prohibited for medical or social reasons or because of interaction with medications, moderate amounts of premeal alcoholic beverages can be an appetite stimulus.
- Serve favorite and familiar traditional foods.
- Facilitate pleasant mealtime experiences by improving the environment (e.g., flowers on the table and attractive table settings) and enhance the social aspects of mealtime.
- Ensure proper oral hygiene.

9.2 ADRD and Decreased Taste

The above considerations become especially important. The inclusion of familiar foods in the diet is a particularly important consideration. See Chapter 7 for more suggestions.

10.0 SOMATIC ("FEELING") SENSATIONS

There is a wide array of somatic sensations, such as pain, temperature, vibration, pressure, touch, two-point discrimination, stereognosis (the ability to distinguish objects by touch), proprioception (the awareness of the location of body parts in space), and kinesthesia (the awareness of body parts moving through space). These sensations have, from the very beginning of life, played a vital role in how we understand and respond to objects and people in our world. The importance of exploring, understanding, and appreciating the world through touch sensations begins in infancy and continues through to old age. Survival, physical and emotional, is dependent on them. The baby finds food and nurture in the arms of its parents; the elder finds reassurance and love in the touch of a caregiver.

With the rather pronounced loss of other vital senses, such as hearing and vision, it is most fortunate that the deterioration of these sensations is much less common. Although there is a great need for further careful research, the somatic senses, particularly touch, appear to be relatively spared during aging. Not all of these sensations are discussed here, but only those most relevant to work with individuals with ADRD.

10.1 Touch

The receptors for touch are located in the body's largest organ, the skin. There is some age-related loss of touch sensitivity, particularly in the palm of the hand, the finger tips and the soles of the feet. However these areas, especially the finger tips, are so richly endowed with sensory nerves that remaining sensation usually continues to allow for normal function, with some loss of fine discrimination. Balance may be affected by the changes in touch sensation on the soles of the feet. There is some evidence that touch is best preserved on hairy body surfaces, as well as on the lips. The importance of touch and capitalizing on the preserved sensation of touch for communication is discussed in more detail in Chapter 3.

10.2 Pain

Although there are numerous studies dealing with changes in pain sensation with aging, the results are inconclusive. This is probably due to the fact that, as with any age group, the perception of pain is highly individual and based on complex personality factors, past experiences, and cognition. Although the issue is a long way from settled, current research indicates that the elderly are less sensitive to pain (Finch & Schneider 1985; Timiras 1988). At first blush this may appear to be an entirely good thing, requiring, for example, less pain medication and involving less personal suffering due to chronic conditions. However, pain is also a vital warning system. This deficient warning system, combined with dry and fragile skin and the possibility of decreased mobility, means that the elderly are particularly vulnerable to skin breakdown, especially in the buttocks. Skin damage and potential ulceration can begin in only two hours. Decreased pain sensation, combined with a slowed reaction time, means that touching a hot pot, for example, could result in severe burns.

Finch and Schneider (1985) state that "We have established beyond reasonable doubt that acute inflammatory reactions of all kinds are muted and reduced in the aged" (p. 835). Consequently, a particular danger from the decreased sense of pain is that the elderly individual can be seriously ill and not even be aware of it.

10.3 Temperature

Current evidence indicates that the sensation of temperature (e.g., skin sensitivity to hot and cold) as such does not deteriorate with age. Rather, other factors interfere with the perception of temperature. As already mentioned, reduced pain sensation interferes with feelings of extreme heat (such as too-hot bath water). There is decreased surface blood circulation in the skin, especially skin that has been exposed to sunlight. Blood circulation serves to cool the skin as well as to warm it, making the elderly much more sensitive to extremes in temperature. There is a decrease in the number of sweat glands in the skin, which in turn decreases the cooling effect, making the elderly more vulnerable to heat stroke. On the other hand, there is also a great danger of hypothermia (dangerously lowered body temperature). This is the result of the factors described above, plus a generally lower core body temperature, a decreased shiver response (which is warming), and a deficiency in the body thermostat (the ability to adjust the internal body temperature to various environmental conditions). For many older people, a comfortable room temperature is 10 to 15 degrees F higher than for younger people. Hypothermia can occur even under "normal" room temperature conditions and can cause apathy and a decrease in responsiveness. Also related to problems with lower body temperature is the reduced likelihood of developing a fever in response to an infection (Davis Kirkland 1988).

10.4 Proprioception (Body Position Sense) and Kinesthesia (Body Movement Sense)

There is some evidence that there is a decrease in body position sense (static and moving) with aging (Davis & Kirkland 1988). This evidence, however, is far from conclusive. There is inadequate information on how a decrease in mobility and the general sensory deprivation associated with poor health and/or institutionalization affects these senses. It seems likely that as activity level decreases and the brain receives less stimulation and feedback the sensations of body position would deteriorate further. One study compared the body image of inactive nursing home residents with that of community-dwelling elderly. The nursing home residents were found to have a significantly impaired body image (Bruneau et al. 1981). As is obvious with the pronounced deficits in proprioception and kinesthesia associated with ADRD, these senses have a profound effect on every aspect of function. How can we feed ourselves when our brain is unaware of where our hand is in relation to our mouth? How can we walk when our brain is unaware of how our feet are moving in relation to the floor and each other? How can we sit down in a chair when we are unable to perceive where our body is in relation to the chair?

10.5 Environmental Interventions for Somatosensory Loss

- Check on settings for water heaters and be careful of the temperatures of such things as bath water and hot fluids. Protect from contact with hot water pipes and hot radiators.

- For independent elders at risk, train to carefully monitor risk areas (e.g., buttocks, elbows, ankles) for skin breakdown and redness, to maintain adequate liquid intake, and to change positions frequently.

- For dependent elders, change sitting and lying positions frequently (at least every 2 hours); monitor carefully for skin breakdown during bathing and dressing; and check cushions, bed sheets, and clothing for wrinkles and rough areas. Avoid shearing forces on fragile older skin during changes in position or transfers. Provide special cushions that distribute weight evenly while seated. Ensure that elders drink plenty of liquids and eat a high-protein diet.

- Make sure that elders living alone, and at risk, have adequate heat during winter months.

- Check the body temperature of sedentary patients.

- Keep the room temperature warmer by eight to ten degrees F.

- Follow safety procedures to prevent falls (as described in Section 15.1 below).

- Enhance tactile stimuli by using a variety of textures and surface shapes in clothing, bedding, furnishings, etc., and introducing other tactile-rich materials, including pets and plants (see Chapters 5 and 7). However, avoid the overuse of too many different textures, especially in a small area

- Monitor carefully for signs of illness in addition to increased temperature (e.g., agitation, decreased alertness, poor appetite, increased or decreased sleep, incontinence).

- Use frequent, reassuring personal touch—to the extent that this is acceptable to the individual—to communicate (see Chapter 3).

- Use regular eating utensils (not plastic), or even weighted ones, to increase awareness of hand position during eating.

- Provide opportunities for movement and activity to ensure continued stimulation of body position sense.

11.0 VESTIBULAR FUNCTION

The vestibular system, located in the inner ear, assists in maintaining balance during changes of position. The vestibular system is stimulated during changes in head position by motion through space. There is gentle vestibular stimulation, such as during rocking, or more sudden vestibular stimulation such as during circus rides. Vestibular stimulation is thought to play a vital role not only in maintaining normal movement but also as a foundation for the organization of thought processes (Yack 1989). As with most other areas, the evidence is not conclusive, but there is a suggestion that vestibular function declines with age. This could have the effect of decreasing balance and play a role in falls. This important topic of falls and the elderly is discussed in more detail in Section 15.1. Some elderly individuals, especially those with ADRD, can be observed rocking back and forth. This may be an indication of a need for vestibular stimulation. Rocking chairs, outdoor swings, and other forms of vestibular stimulation should always be available.

12.0 BONES, JOINTS, AND SKELETAL MUSCLE

Perhaps more than any other area, the traditionally accepted deterioration in these systems is being challenged by new, more thorough, research. Earlier studies that compared the musculoskeletal function of young adults with that of older adults did not control adequately for health status and the level of physical fitness. When these factors are controlled, the previously assumed age-related loss of muscle and bone is much less, and in some cases disappears altogether. In their comprehensive text, *Handbook of the Biology of Aging,* Finch and Schneider (1985) state, "Physical inactivity no doubt plays a role, for when sedentary people become active or active people remain active, their body composition tends to resemble that of younger people" (p. 898). In most studies of neuromuscular response time, the older adult subjects were inactive, long-term care residents, which undoubtedly biased the results. One very interesting illustration of this point is the absence of age-associated change in the speed of muscle contraction and the weight and the size of the diaphragm, the muscle involved with breathing. It is highly likely that the constant use of this muscle has maintained its function (Finch & Schneider 1985; Timiras 1988).

It is also important to consider how musculoskeletal changes actually affect function. Consider osteoarthritis as an example. In this disease, changes in both the cartilage of the joint and the bones themselves reduce the space in the joint and result in the "creaking and grinding" of joints as bone rubs on bone, often associated with aging. More than 75 percent of those over 65 have these osteoarthritic changes in their joints. However, only 30 percent have any symptoms at all and only 10 percent have a significant disability as a result (Timiras 1988).

In general, in comparing age-associated changes in various musculoskeletal systems, the greatest changes

in strength occur in cartilage, followed by muscle, then bone, and then tendon. In comparison with other body tissues, bone tissue declines more slowly than, for example, intestinal tissue.

12.1 Bones

It has long been assumed that bone mass decreases considerably with age and that older people have "thin" bones, making them more susceptible to fracture. The topic is not as straightforward as it seems. Bone is living tissue that continues to grow throughout life. Thinness of bones is related to a slowing down of the growth in the internal part of bone. This, in turn, is related to calcium needs elsewhere in the body (e.g., to balance the acidity of body fluids), calcium absorption, and many other variables.

Although all the evidence is by no means in, current studies indicate that even a moderate level of physical activity greatly reduces bone loss by building up the mineralization of the outer layers of bone (Finch & Schneider 1985). In addition, diet is believed to play an important role. This is now thought to be not so much related to the calcium content of the diet, as increased calcium intake has not been proven to improve calcium absorption by the body. Current research is focusing on excess acid associated with a high-protein diet, which is balanced by calcium resorption from the bone. Attempts are being made to balance the acid instead with other sources (e.g., bicarbonate of soda). This interesting research is currently under way at the University of California at San Francisco (Sebastion 1992). It is of particular relevance to women, as postmenopausal hormone changes negatively affect calcium absorption; hence women are more at risk than men for thin bones. There is a great need for more research using larger numbers of healthy older women.

12.2 Joints

The major and most common joint changes during aging are the osteoarthritic changes mentioned in the introduction to this section. More than 75 percent of persons over 65 experience these changes. It is important to stress again that, although these joint changes appear to be inevitable, they are not inevitably disabling. In addition, new information on the nature of these osteoarthritic changes suggests that it is not just a matter of wear and tear on the joints, as has been assumed. In fact, thickening of cartilage, which is associated with aging, is opposite to thinning of cartilage, which occurs with osteoarthritis (Knowlton et al. 1990). There are many unanswered questions in this area. It is clear, however, that exercise, particularly to strengthen muscles around the joints, plays an important role in preventing disability.

12.3 Muscles

Body muscles do change with age. The general decrease in strength and changes in body muscle mass with aging are particularly noticeable because of the large number of muscles. However, it is not clear how such changes are affected by the level of physical activity. If the levels of physical activity at various ages are the same, muscular changes are much less than has long been assumed. There is overwhelming evidence that even modest physical activity greatly improves muscle strength and endurance for the elderly, as it does for all age groups (Finch & Schneider 1985). In addition, there is some evidence that endurance, the length of time a muscular contraction is held, actually increases with age (Finch & Schneider 1985; Timiras 1988).

12.4 Interventions To Compensate for Bone, Joint, and Muscle Changes

The most important intervention can be summed up in one word—*exercise*. It is as essential during old age, if not more so, as it is in any life stage. Since job- and home care-related physical activities are likely to decrease with age, supplemental activity is crucial. A review of the research literature on exercise and aging by Schilke (1991) found evidence in the literature that

> Exercise reduces the age-related decline in VO$_2$ max [maximum oxygen consumption], reduces mean blood pressure and systemic vascular resistance, preserves lean body mass and decreases fat deposits, increases HDL [high-density lipoproteins] and decreases triglycerides, increases bone mineral content, improves basal metabolic rate, increases muscle strength, and increases cognitive functioning. (p. 7)

The effects of physical activity on community-dwelling elderly are illustrated by a study of 90 neurologically normal older adults. One group continued to work, another group retired but remained physically active, and the third group retired but did not participate in regular physical activities. This inactive group showed a significant decline in cerebral blood flow and scored worse on cognitive tests than the active groups (Rogers et al. 1990).

These effects have also been noted in studies of older frail adults. The researchers at Tufts Research Center on Aging, in Boston, have conducted several interesting studies on the effects of exercise and resistance training on muscle mass and strength (National Resource Center on Health Promotion and Aging 1991a, 1991b). A study of men between 60 and 70 found a dramatic increase in strength and mobility after an eight-week training program. Another study introduced an eight-week (three sessions per week), adapted weight-resistance training program to ten persons over the age of 90. These individuals were living in institutions and had multiple chronic conditions such as heart disease, hypertension, and arthritis. After the sessions, these frail elderly persons had 61 to 374 percent increases in strength, a striking demonstration that it is never too late to exercise. In another study, 166 community-dwelling, well seniors, with a mean age of 68, were introduced to a 16-week, low-to-moderate intensity exercise program. Compared with the matched control group who attended weekly talks, the exercise group demonstrated a significant improvement in oxygen uptake and ventilatory thresholds.

Introduction of any significant increase in physical activity should always be preceded by a medical examination. Introduce exercise gradually, slowly increasing the length of time. Develop exercise programs that are related to individual interests. For example, for some people providing an opportunity for continued involvement in a lifelong interest, such as gardening, is the most motivating form of exercise. Walking is one of the best forms of exercise; development of a walking group, with social aspects, encourages participation. For others, chair exercises are appropriate. See Chapter 5 for more information.

Safety equipment. Install grab bars and other safety equipment for the bathtub and toilet. The best handrail is 1½ to 1½ inches in diameter and cylindrical in shape (Christenson 1990).

Proper seating. Whether or not they are independently mobile, frail old people spend a great deal of time sitting. Attention to the design of chairs makes it easier for persons to get up independently and also helps to prevent problems with skin breakdown (Christenson 1990). One study of 92 nursing home residents found that 77 percent of those who previously had needed assistance were able to get up independently from a properly designed chair (Finlay et al. 1983). This chair was 16 to 17 inches from the floor and had arms that were at least 10 inches above the seat height. Frail older individuals depend not only on leg muscles but also on arm muscles to rise from a chair. The interaction between seat height and arm height is important.

The seat should be firm, not a sling type, but with adequately firm foam to be comfortable and prevent skin breakdown. Breathable upholstery prevents problems with moisture buildup.

Full-length arms—preferably padded—that slope slightly to the back of the chair are comfortable and assist with rising. The back should support the natural curve of the back but still allow for weight shift. Legs should be stable and sturdy and not have a bar or brace across the front, which prevents positioning the feet under the body's center of gravity for ease in rising. Make sure that there is adequate space under the front of the chair to allow for the "nose-over-your-toes-while-rising" rule.

Easy chairs that are too low can be raised with the addition of a firm piece of foam under the cushion.

Individuals who require long-term seating should be properly fitted with a chair by an occupational therapist.

12.5 ADRD and Exercise

See the section on exercise in Chapter 5.

13.0 SKIN

Skin is the body's largest organ, making up approximately 16 percent of body weight. Perhaps more than any other single factor, the appearance of the skin affects the perception of having "aged," or looking old. The profound psychological effect of wrinkled skin is often underestimated. The skin serves many important functions, such as regulating temperature; providing a barrier to harmful environmental substances; and receiving sensory informational in regard to pain, touch, and temperature. Unfortunately, there is really little known about the degree and exact nature of the changes in the skin that occur with aging. For instance, the anatomy of the wrinkle is still not understood. Furthermore, many changes that had been accepted as absolute were based on studies with very small sample sizes, which are now being called into question. It is essential to distinguish between normal aging changes and those caused by disease. Many of the skin diseases (e.g., cancers) of the elderly are due to environmental stress (e.g., exposure to ultraviolet light) and are preventable.

The following are some general age-associated changes in the skin, but the degree to which they are present is not clear:

- decreased sweat and oil production, leading to dry skin and a reduced cooling effect (but also less need for deodorants)
- slower growth of the outer skin layer, thinner skin, and less elastic inner skin, leading to skin that is more susceptible to tearing and pressure sores
- decreased fine blood circulation, decreased immune response and clearance of foreign materials

by cells, which means an increased time for skin wound healing, less temperature control, and less absorption of external creams or salves

13.1 Interventions for Skin Changes

- Guard against overexposure to the sun. This is important at all ages, but it is particularly so for the elderly, as they do not show the usual reddening of the skin with overexposure to the sun.
- Exercise facial muscles to help reduce sagging.
- Take temperature and pressure sore precautions, which are described in the somatic sensations section.
- Take extra precautions to avoid shearing forces on the skin, for example, during transfers.
- Avoid using bath oils for dry skin, as this may increase the risk of falls.

14.0 SLEEP

Although sleep is easily recognized as essential to mental and physical health, surprisingly little is known about the nature of the restorative mechanism of sleep and about how sleep patterns may change with aging. Once again statements about these changes must be interpreted, bearing in mind the following factors:

- Laboratory studies of sleep are difficult because of the "abnormal" nature of the setting.
- There is a tremendous need for more research.
- Most studies of sleep in the elderly are based on rules developed for a younger population.
- The level of physical activity and fitness also plays a role in sleep and has not always been accounted for.
- Distinctions between sleep pathologies and actual aging changes are not clearly understood.

In regard to the last point, there seems to be an increasing frequency of sleep disturbances in older people, which are actually called sleep disorders when they occur in younger people. More attention should be given to treating these sleep problems of the elderly as disorders (Timiras 1988). There is, for example, an amazing similarity between symptoms of disruption of the day-night rhythm (circadian rhythm) of the elderly and those of depression. It bears considering what relationship this has to the high prevalence of depression among the elderly.

Furthermore, studies have found that prolonged sleep deprivation has a negative, and often permanent, effect on the bioelectrical functioning of the brain.

Sleep plays an important role in maintaining brain function. The connection between sleep disturbances, which are more frequent among the elderly, and level of alertness during the day must be considered.

Bearing the preceding limitations in mind, the following sleep disturbances occur in a significant proportion of the elderly:

- Stage IV sleep (slow-wave sleep, when the restorative function of sleep is thought to be greatest) is absent altogether in at least 25 percent of older people and significantly reduced in others, especially men.
- Sleep of older people is disrupted by periods of wakefulness more often.
- Older people experience an increased level of disordered breathing (e.g., 60 percent of men over 60 snore (Finch & Schneider 1985), and snoring appears to be related to an increased risk of cardiovascular disease.
- Older people take longer to fall asleep.
- Disruption of normal circadian rhythms due to daytime naps and less sleep at night may become a pattern. Older people seem to require progressively less sleep during the night.

For persons with ADRD, these sleep disturbances are exaggerated, resulting in more frequent night-time awakenings and very much reduced rapid-eye-movement (REM) sleep. As ADRD progresses, REM sleep becomes less and less (Cohen-Mansfield & Marx 1990).

14.1 Interventions to Promote Adequate Sleep

- Encourage exercise and physical fitness activities during the day.
- Maintain a consistent and familiar bedtime routine. This becomes especially important for the individual living temporarily or permanently in an institution. Lifelong rituals at bedtime are an important part of triggering sleep.
- Encourage relaxing bedtime activities (e.g., a warm bath, listening to calming music, progressive relaxation exercises, a back rub, reading in bed, a cup of hot milk,) and avoid stimulating ones (e.g., caffeine drinks, vigorous activity).
- Discourage use of the bedroom or the bed for non-sleep activities such as exercise, eating, paperwork, etc. The bedroom then becomes associated with being awake and alert as opposed to associated with sleep and rest.

- Educate older persons about the reduced need for sleep that is associated with aging. Bedtimes may need to be altered, or earlier awakening accepted.

14.2 Sleep and ADRD

The sleep-wake cycle is often seriously disturbed as dementia progresses. Attention to the above suggestions takes on a special significance. Usual bedtime routines should be a part of the history obtained from family or significant others. A reasonable level of activity during the daytime is also very important. Research indicates that awakening persons with ADRD during the night for toileting is significantly associated with increased daytime agitation (Cohen-Mansfield & Marx 1990).

15.0 NEUROMUSCULAR CONTROL

This complex function is concerned with the control of organized, purposeful movement, such as walking. It involves the coordination, by the central nervous system, of a variety of information from the sensory systems (e.g., vision); vestibular, muscle, and joint systems; and brain function. It is a vital area, affecting every facet of an individual's ability to function—from brushing teeth, to walking, to going to the bathroom. One particularly important aspect is the relationship of neuromuscular control to the high incidence of falls among the elderly. Many more factors play a part in this problem, such as decreased sensory input (especially vision), vestibular malfunction, adverse drug reactions, blood pressure irregularities, etc. However, there is no doubt that disturbances in neuromuscular control are also important. The study of the gait (walking pattern) of the elderly is the most common area of neuromuscular research and investigation. It has been stated that it is rare for the individual over age 75 or 80 to walk without the associated gait pattern of the aged: shorter step length, wider walking base, and a longer time in the stance (support) phase compared with the swing phase. Evidence suggests that changes in the muscles and joints alone do not account for this different way of walking but are more likely due to changes in the central nervous system (Timiras 1988). The central processing of information appears to be slowed.

It is absolutely essential, however, that the cause of falls (e.g., disease, poor vision, dangerous environment, drug reactions) be investigated and that falls not be assumed to be inevitable. The issue of falls and the elderly is a major health concern, and one for which there are preventative measures. The National Resource Center on Health Promotion and Aging (1991 b) reports that injury is the sixth leading cause of death for people over 65. Most of these injuries are related to falls. More than 75 percent of all fatal falls are accounted for by people over 65, but they make up only 12 percent of the population (Rubenstein et al. 1988). For adults aged 65 to 74, 25 percent report one fall each year; for those over 75, this rises to 33 percent.

Falls can lead to death, but they also lead to other problems that have a major impact on the well-being of the elderly. Older persons who develop a fear of falling may become less active, leading to a cycle of physical deterioration and reduced social contacts.

In 40 percent of cases, falls are at least one of the reasons leading to nursing home admissions. In dollars and cents, measured in 1980 medical costs for falls by persons over 65 in the United States, it cost $3.5 billion (National Resource Center on Health Promotion and Aging 1991b).

As already mentioned, there are many causes of falls among the elderly. Fortunately, there are also things that can be done to prevent falls.

I5.1 Interventions To Prevent Falls

- Provide an exercise program to maintain or improve muscle strength.

- Focus health care team assessment on a medication review, postural training, walking aids, and home safety equipment, as required.

- Provide a safe environment that is well lit and free of obstacles in main thoroughfares; avoid scatter rugs and clutter; use contrast as described in the vision section. The vast majority of falls occur in the home, at the head or landing of a stairway, especially if the landing is well lit and the stairs are less so. This is probably due to the age-associated increase in the time required to adapt to changes in light intensity. Areas should be evenly lit, particularly areas around entrances, exits, and stairs.

- Install sturdy rails and other safety equipment along hallways. Remove towel racks and other nonsturdy items that might be used for support.

- Allow plenty of time for moving from one place to another.

- Make sure footwear fits well and is safe.

- Remember that carpeting is the easiest and safest walking surface.

- Avoid positioning signs, pictures, television, or entertainment in such a way that the older person must tip the head back. This can lead to dizziness and a fall.

16.0 ENABLING INDEPENDENCE

The preceding sections of this chapter have presented evidence that the losses associated with aging are neither as inevitable nor as great as has long been assumed. This is demonstrated concretely by the fact that 95 percent of those over 65 in the United States and 92 percent of those over 65 in Canada continue to live in the community; 70 percent remain in their own homes (Davis & Kirkland 1988; McPherson 1983).

Continued and maximal independence in all aspects of living, self-care, leisure, and work is a widely cherished value in North American society (Lowy 1989; Viney et al. 1989). This is particularly true in old age, when independence is more likely to be threatened by the negative attitudes of others, social circumstances, increased risk of chronic and disabling disease, and changes in sensory and motor functioning. The lifelong values and goals of elderly individuals persist. Their capacity to accomplish these goals, such as independence, may change. Decreasing independence is closely associated with a decrease in self-esteem or self-worth, particularly among the elderly (Aitken 1982; Burnside 1988; Clark 1989; Davis & Kirkland 1988; Fabiano 1984; Hegeman & Tobin 1988; Judd 1983; Teitelman 1982; Zgola 1987).

There has been an unfortunate tendency among family and professionals working with the elderly to assume total control during illness or at the time of a crisis in independence. This is illustrated by a randomized, controlled study that examined the effects of staff expectations on the status of 63 newly admitted nursing home residents. At a three months post-test, residents whom nurses and aides were told were expected to do better than most persons with these difficulties had significantly fewer depressive symptoms but they also had significant losses in functional independence (Learman et al. 1990). It seems likely, as the authors suggest, that nursing staff expressed their interest and encouragement for these high-expectation residents by doing more for them, rather than encouraging independence. This tendency to take control, to create dependence, has further disastrous effects on self-esteem. It may well create a situation of self-fulfilling prophecy, wherein the elderly are thought to be dependent and thus become so (Learman et al. 1990). Excess disability, disability beyond that caused by the disease alone, is the result (Brody et al. 1971; Brody et al. 1974). Also important here is the concept of "learned helplessness" (Seligman 1975; Teitelman 1982), which is discussed further in Chapter 4.

Fortunately, there is a growing awareness of the need to avoid these pitfalls and enable the maximal independence of the elderly. This awareness not only stems from an empathetic and caring therapeutic approach but also results from financial practicalities. It is much less expensive to support the growing number of seniors in the community than to pay the cost of institutional care. In an institution, it is more cost-effective to provide supervision as opposed to full care. In order to encourage and enable maximal independence, it may be necessary to introduce changes in the environment and/or in ways of doing activities.

The preceding sections of this chapter offer many suggestions for environmental or individual adaptations to compensate for the changes associated with aging. However, just as there is a danger in making the frail older adult overly dependent, there is also a danger in introducing these changes in a "command performance" manner. The caregiver who gives orders for change, without considering the wishes and needs of the older adult, will meet with failure. The following pointers are offered as a guideline to enhance success when introducing change. These pointers apply equally to persons with ADRD and are expanded on in Chapter 4. Since persons with ADRD are likely to have difficulty in changing their personal habits and behaviors, it is essential that the emphasis be placed on changes in the environment and in the behavior of caregivers.

Appreciate that most elderly individuals are experiencing an enormous number of changes and are coping with them very well. The changes in social circumstance (e.g., retirement), environment (e.g., moving to an apartment), and possibly physical capacity (e.g., reduced visual acuity) that frequently accompany aging are wide ranging. Adjusting to these major life changes while reaffirming the value of previous life experiences is the primary task of aging. For some, adjusting to these major changes is enough, and the idea of some seemingly minor change, suggested in order to enable independence, may be just too much. It becomes the straw that breaks the camel's back. So, for example, instead of replacing the favorite chair that is now too difficult to get out of, add a wedge cushion to the chair.

Respect the right of the individual to live at risk. It is particularly difficult, for both professional and family caregivers, to accept a situation in which loved ones or clients seem to be putting themselves at risk of injury, or even death. However, if the person is mentally competent and has been informed about the risks involved and about possible alternatives, his or her decision must be respected. For instance, many frail older adults would rather risk a fall or other problems at home than move to a supervised setting. The most striking example from my practice is the case of Mrs. Archibald:

This charming and wildly eccentric 90-year-old lady lived in her own home in a rural

area. Her dilapidated house was shared with several dogs and cats and sometimes an errant grandson, whom she had raised. About once a year, one of her many health problems—high blood pressure, heart disease, or diabetes—resulted in a hospital admission. On each admission, the hospital staff would join with her family in expressing grave concern about this lady's continuing to live on her own. I joined the chorus of concern during a two-week admission one January. She described to me her fine home and how she managed to prepare excellent meals there. In fact, she demonstrated her cooking skills in the occupational therapy kitchen. She welcomed the suggestion that I visit her when she was discharged.

When I arrived, she smothered me in a great hug and exclaimed, "See, I told you I had a fine house." I was at a loss for words. The house was in total disarray. Clothes, garbage, excrement from untended animals, and food were strewn everywhere. The hot water pipes were frozen and the furnace wasn't working. A wood-burning stove, standing on the tattered carpet covering the wooden floor, was struggling to dent the minus 20-degree outdoor temperatures.

Listing the ways in which Mrs. Archibald's health and safety were gravely at risk in her home environment would fill columns. But this was where she vehemently stated she wished to remain, and to remain without others meddling in her affairs. She was delighted with the loan of a wheelchair, the offer of assistance to fix her furnace, and the offer of a homemaker to help clean up. She was furious at family members who continued to insist that she be placed in a nursing home.

As a professional, I found it hard to argue with Mrs. Archibald. She had, after all, lived this way all of her 90 years. She had surpassed the average life expectancy by more than a decade, this in spite of breaking every rule in the book! She was living at known risk, and she was succeeding!

Plan change with the individual. The caregiver may know from experience or study just which changes will make things easier for the person. This knowledge is useless unless it is combined with the person's own knowledge about what is important to him or her. The most logical, rational plan for change will fail unless it is developed with the older person concerned. This ensures that the plan is based on the individual's own values, goals, and priorities as well as on practical information about alternatives. Successful change is not made for or to the person, but with the person. The individual is much more motivated to work toward personal goals.

Introduce changes that are consistent with the individual's values and beliefs. In order to develop a successful plan for change, one must stand in the shoes of the other. This is particularly difficult when our personal values differ. For persons with impairments that may limit their ability to participate in planning changes, caregivers and family members have a particular responsibility in this regard.

> Mr. Green was a veteran of both world wars, having served in the medical corp. He was certainly eligible for assistance with homemaking and equipment from the Department of Veterans Affairs. When this was suggested, he refused to apply, and paid the expenses out of his own pocket. The social worker and Mr. Green's son saw this as a right he had earned through valiant and dangerous service. He viewed receiving such assistance as charity, akin to welfare and social assistance, and a threat to his ferociously defended independence.

Incorporate change into the pattern of lifelong habits. We all become comfortable with certain ways of doing things. Even though there may be no particular reason for doing it a particular way, it becomes comfortable. This includes not only inconsequential habits, such as the way you fold your arms when seated or whether you dress before or after breakfast, but other more fundamental habits, such as the hand you eat with or the type of shoes you like to wear. In order to appreciate how difficult it may be to change these lifelong habits, try folding your arms with other than the accustomed hand on top, or holding the telephone receiver to your other ear, or eating with your other hand. The frustration you experience in making these simple (temporary) changes will help you to appreciate how difficult it can be to learn to walk with a cane or to eat with your other hand or, indeed, to get dressed when someone else says you must.

There is ample evidence that offering opportunities for choice overcomes feelings of helplessness, enhances self-esteem, and improves motivation (Avorn & Langer 1982; Davis & Kirkland 1988; Foy & Mitchell 1990; Le Sage et al. 1990; Lowy 1989; Morganti et al. 1990; Rodin & Langer 1977; Seligman 1975; Teitelman 1982). Even the most severely disabled person can participate in decision making (for example, when to have a bath or which shirt to wear).

Put the emphasis on strengths rather than deficits. For example, Mrs. MacDonald knits beautifully and wishes to make an afghan for her church bazaar. However, because of a combination of failing eyesight and decreased sensation it is difficult. Her strengths are her skill and motivation. Capitalize on these to introduce changes such as visual aids, improved lighting, and working with larger needles and coarser yarn. This issue, with respect to persons with ADRD, is discussed in detail in Chapter 2.

Focus on enhancing the quality of life. Being independent, despite disabilities or difficulties, is usually going to mean it takes more time for self-care or home maintenance activities. Some would rather spend this extra time and effort to maintain independence. Others may prefer to get assistance with, for example, meals and shopping in order to have more time for hobbies and socialization. These decisions are based on personal values, and priorities and must be considered in order to ensure an optimal quality of life. Everyone needs a balance of involvement in the activities of work, rest, and play. The focus on enabling independence and the increasing attention to supporting the elderly in their own homes may be centered too much on basic physiological needs (food, shelter, hygiene) and not enough on the need for personal recognition, self-esteem, and belonging (see Chapter 4 for further discussion of Maslow's Hierarchy of Needs).

17.0 CONCLUSION

Consideration of the quality-of-life issue is a fitting theme for the end of this chapter. Gerontologists often refer to the problem generated by the modern health care system. Years have been added to life, but we must also be very sure we are adding life, a quality of life, to these years. The remainder of this book seeks to illuminate ways in which the quality of life for individuals with ADRD can be enhanced.

Alzheimer's Disease and Related Disorders

And so the mind is quieted, slowly by some, rapidly by others. The body can slouch, the mouth hang open, the eyes wander, and thoughts come and go without conscious recognition. Released, at last, from the confines of the tightly controlling intellect, the heart can soar.

—P. Rodegast and J. Stanton

Alzheimer's Disease and Related Disorders

1.0 WHAT IS DEMENTIA?

Alzheimer's disease is the most common of many disorders that cause dementia. Dementia itself is neither a disease nor a diagnosis but a syndrome, a descriptive term for a collection of symptoms. These symptoms are all part of a large picture of global, progressive, cognitive impairment that is severe enough to interfere with independent functioning. The cognitive deterioration associated with dementia is acquired later in life, not present since birth as in mental retardation. The symptoms of dementia are primarily behavioral, not physical. These changes in behavior are

- not part of normal aging
- not irreversible (10 to 20 percent of the causes of dementia are treatable, e.g., caused by depression, thyroid imbalance)
- not universal (not every person with dementia has every symptom)
- not unilateral (for a particular individual some symptoms may be severe and others barely noticeable)
- not consistent (at one time of the day or week the symptoms may be present and at other times not)

Although there are certain common characteristics that describe the syndrome of dementia, there is no one description of a "typical" person with dementia. Each person is unique, and the severity and range of the symptoms depend on many factors:

- cause of the dementia
- stage of the disease
- pre-existing personality factors
- environmental supports
- social supports
- presence of other diseases (e.g., Parkinson's or heart disease) or an acute infection
- area of the brain affected
- level of fatigue or stress

Bearing the above qualifications in mind, dementia is defined as follows:

- a decline in intellectual function
- a global cognitive impairment, i.e., memory impairment and at least one of the following:
  1. impairment of abstract thinking
  2. impairment of judgment
  3. impairment of other complex capabilities such as language use, ability to perform complex physical tasks, ability to recognize objects or people, or ability to construct objects
  4. personality change
- a state of being *in* clear consciousness, i.e., awake and alert (OTA 1987, 60)

The above definition is found in the report of the Office of Technology Assessment to the United States Congress. It combines the criteria of the *Diagnostic and Statistical Manual of Mental Disorders* (American Psychiatric Association 1987) and the joint effort of the National Institute of Neurological and Communicative Disorders and Stroke and the Alzheimer's Disease and Related Disorders Association (McKhann et al. 1984). These are the standard definitions used in clinical and research settings.

Particular features of this definition should be noted. Intellectual function must *decline*. This implies some understanding of the previous level of functioning, not just poor or even adequate performance currently. Highly intelligent individuals may perform "normally" on tests, but may have declined considerably from their usual skilled level of performance. Conversely, others may have always been more forgetful or disorganized than most people their age, so poor performance may be a lifelong pattern, not a symptom of dementia.

The change in intellectual function must be global, that is, affecting more than one area, not just memory or just communication. Finally, these changes must take place when the person is in a state of clear consciousness; that is, even when the person is awake and alert, mental impairment persists. This distinguishes dementia from delirium, which is a temporary cognitive dysfunction with clouded consciousness and often involves sleep and psychomotor disturbances. In the aged, delirium is frequently associated with acute physical illness, particularly during hospitalization. The onset of delirium is usually rapid and after a fluctuating course lasts a relatively brief time. Usually the primary cause of delirium is not in the central nervous system itself; rather, the delirium is due to the effect of such problems as acute illness, vitamin deficiencies, dehydration, electrolyte imbalance, or substance withdrawal on the brain's metabolic function (Gregory & Smeltzer 1983; Lipowski 1987; Mace 1990).

1.1 Disorders Causing Dementia

More than 70 disorders or diseases can cause dementia (Advisory Panel on Alzheimer's Disease 1989; Aronson 1988; Cohen 1988; Katzman & Jackson 1991). A thorough interdisciplinary evaluation is essential to determine the cause of the dementia. This is particularly important, as in 10 to 20 percent of cases the cause may be treatable and the dementia reversible (Dippel & Hutton 1988; Rapoport 1983). The following is a partial list of the potentially reversible causes of dementia or dementia-like behavior (Aronson 1988;

Cohen 1988; Dippel & Hutton 1988; Mace 1990; Rapoport 1983; Van Horn 1987; Volicer et al. 1988):

- alcoholism
- acute physical illness
- brain tumor
- chemical intoxication
- depression
- drug toxicity
- electrolyte imbalance
- hormone imbalance
- hypothermia
- hypothyroidism or hyperthyroidism
- infections of the central nervous system
- liver or kidney dysfunction
- metabolic imbalance
- normal pressure hydrocephalus
- pernicious anemia
- psychotic state
- sensory deprivation
- sensory losses (e.g., vision and hearing)
- vitamin deficiency

Alzheimer's disease (AD) is the most common cause of dementia. Since AD and other dementias result in symptoms that are more or less similar, the dementias are referred to throughout the text as AD and related disorders (ADRD). A definitive diagnosis of AD can be made only by a postmortem examination. Since studies of the distribution of the causes of dementia are based—at least in part—on clinical diagnosis, the following percentages can be considered only approximations. In addition, most studies are based on patients referred to hospital clinics. One study based on the community-dwelling elderly reports that 84.1 percent of those with ADRD had AD (Evans et al. 1989).

AD alone accounts for 50 percent of cases of dementia. Another 20 percent of cases have a combination of AD and multi-infarct dementia. Multi-infarct dementia, without coexisting AD, accounts for another 15 to 20 percent of cases of dementia. The remaining 10 to 15 percent of cases of dementia are accounted for by the potentially reversible causes listed above, plus those associated with other disease processes in which dementia is a primary (e.g., Parkinson's disease, Pick's disease, Creutzfeldt-Jakob disease) or secondary (e.g., Huntington's disease, multiple sclerosis, acquired immunodeficiency syndrome [AIDS]) feature of the disease (Aronson 1988; Cohen 1988; Mace 1990; OTA 1987; Rapoport 1983; Volicer et al. 1988).

1.2 Epidemiology of Dementia

Epidemiology is the study of the occurrence of disease. A 1989 study of a large number of community-dwelling elderly concluded that the number of persons with ADRD was even higher than had been previously assumed (Evans et al. 1989). It is estimated that 4.7 million North Americans are presently affected, comprising 10 to 15 percent of those over 65. With increasing age, an even higher percentage is affected (Aronson et al. 1992; Aronson 1988; Advisory Panel on Alzheimer's Disease 1989; Evans et al. 1989; Pfeffer et. al. 1987; Robertson et al. 1989; Volicer et al. 1988). The study by Evans et al. (1989) revealed the following prevalence rates among 3,623 community-dwelling elderly:

Age (yr)	Prevalence (%)
65–74	3.0
75–84	18.7
85 and older	47.2

The study did not include the elderly living in institutions, so these figures may in fact be low. Since those over 65, and particularly the group over 85, are the most rapidly growing segment of the population, the number of persons with ADRD in the near future is likely to reach epidemic proportions. The incidence of ADRD may more than triple in the next 50 years.

For persons over 65, ADRD constitutes the primary cause of admission to institutional care and affects 50 to 75 percent of the institutionalized elderly (Advisory Panel on Alzheimer's Disease 1989; Alzheimer's Association 1990; Aronson 1988; Carnes 1984; Davis & Kirkland 1988; Dippel & Hutton 1988; Jazwiecki 1988; OTA 1987; Sloane & Mathew 1991). Some suggest that this figure may be as high as 70 to 90 percent (Aronson et al. 1992). AD is the fourth or fifth leading cause of death in Canada and the United States (Alzheimer's Association 1990; Cohen 1988; Jarvik & Winograd 1988; Volicer et al. 1988). It is estimated that the direct and indirect costs (e.g., lost hours of caregiver work time) of ADRD of the United States in 1985 was $88 billion (Huang et al. 1988). Currently in North America, ADRD represents the highest morbidity (affected by disease) cost of any single disease.

2.0 ALZHEIMER'S DISEASE

AD was first described in 1906 by a German physician, Alois Alzheimer. This first case involved a woman in her 50s, who had the classic symptoms of dementia just described. Unfortunately, for many years after this time Alzheimer's disease was thought to be a rare disease, with onset before age 65 (presenile dementia). Dementia with onset after age 65 (senile dementia) was thought to be unrelated and due either to aging or arteriosclerotic disease (hardening of the arteries). Fortunately, in recent years this classification and the understanding of AD has been greatly altered. Work begun in the 1960s has clearly established the following:

- Dementia (of any type) is not caused by "normal" aging.
- Arteriosclerotic changes alone account for only about 20 percent of cases of dementia.

AD accounts for about half of the cases of dementia. There is no difference in either the pathological changes in the brain or the behavioral symptoms of AD with onset before and after age 65. What were previously called presenile dementia and senile dementia are the same disease entity (Aronson 1988; Cohen 1988; Fox 1989; Van Horn 1987). So, although Dr. Alzheimer identified the neurological changes of AD at the turn of the century, only in recent decades has it been recognized as a major disease. The time elapsed from the first identification of AD until it became recognized as a major public health problem is most unfortunate. First, major research efforts into the cause, cure, and treatment of AD were undertaken only when it became clear that AD was not rare, but a relatively common disease. Second, the system of describing dementia as presenile or senile stages has contributed to a widespread and harmful misunderstanding that dementia, particularly memory loss, is a normal part of aging. The term *senility* has been widely and incorrectly used to describe dementia and/or confusion and memory loss in the elderly. In fact, *senile* simply means old or aging. If the aging person becomes forgetful or shows another sign of dementia, it is not "normal" aging but a signal for a thorough investigation into the cause. All who work with the elderly must do their part to inform the elderly, themselves, and the general public about these distinctions in order to counteract years of misinformation.

2.1 What Is Alzheimer's Disease?

AD is a progressive neurological disease characterized by the following pathological changes in the brain, which are greater than those associated with normal aging:

- *neurofibrillar tangles*—accumulation, within the nerve cell, of nerve filaments that are abnormally coarse and thick

- *senile plaques*—abnormal deposits, outside the cell, of products from neuronal breakdown. At the core of these plaques is a protein fragment, amyloid beta-protein
- *brain atrophy*—abnormal shrinkage of the brain

These brain changes can be absolutely identified only by an autopsy. Consequently, the diagnosis of AD in a living patient is a clinical one, based on a detailed history, current behavioral symptoms, and exclusion of all other possible causes of these symptoms. AD is a neurological disease, but the primary symptoms, particularly in the early and middle stages, are behavioral, not physical.

At the present time there is no cure for AD. It must be emphasized, however, that there are indeed numerous treatments, primarily social and environmental, that enhance the quality of life, alleviate the symptoms, and enable the maintenance of function. These treatments are the subject of succeeding chapters.

2.2 Progression of Alzheimer's Disease

The progression of AD is variable, with the course running anywhere from 3 to 20 years from the first symptoms until death. The average course is 7 or 8 years, characterized by a progressive decline. However, in some cases the course may be very rapid (2 to 3 years) or excessively long (Burns et al. 1991b; Cohen 1988; Katzman & Jackson 1991; NIHCD 1987; Volicer et al. 1987).

As with all dementias, there is much individual variation in the course and the symptoms of the disease. It is not possible to give a precise description of a "typical" presentation of AD or to define in detail the symptoms at various stages of the disease. This variability was recognized in the revised edition of the DSM-III (American Psychiatric Association 1987), where the phrase *generally progressive* was substituted for *uniformly progressive*, found in the earlier edition (American Psychiatric Association 1980, 126). The course is one of progressive impairment in cognitive and functional abilities, until death. The overwhelming consensus among clinicians and in the literature is that staging instruments are not very useful for education, care planning, and research because of the extreme variability in onset, presentation, and severity of the symptoms from person to person (Baum et al. 1988; Cohen 1988; Dippel & Hutton 1988; Goldman & Lazarus 1988; Mayeux et al. 1985; NIHCD 1987; OTA 1987; Sloane & Mathew 1991; Teri et al. 1990; Volicer et al. 1987; Volicer et al. 1988).

This variability was illustrated by a study that followed the course of 88 institutionalized patients with AD (Volicer et al. 1987). The study investigated the time period from date of onset until half of the patients were unable to carry out independently a particular functional activity such as walking, eating, or bathing. Within the context of these time periods the authors point out that there was extreme individual variation. This was particularly noticeable with regard to motor skills. Although 50 percent of the patients had lost their ability to ambulate independently 8 years after onset, some were still able to walk independently more than 14 years after onset and others were nonambulatory after a few years.

In addition to the variability in symptoms among different individuals with AD, there is also great variability from hour to hour and day to day for the same person. As already described in relation to all dementias, actual performance depends on the available environmental and social supports, level of fatigue or stress, and the presence of other diseases (for example, a urinary tract infection).

It is absolutely essential for family and professional caregivers to appreciate the variable nature of AD, and indeed of all dementias. Otherwise the performance of the person with AD is limited by the assumption that, for example, because the person is in the end stage he or she is unable to speak. These assumptions can become a self-fulfilling prophecy. In addition, the person's performance may be limited not by AD but by an unsupportive environment, a case of excess disabilities. For example, persons with advanced AD may be able to feed themselves if the sights, sounds, and smells of the dining room provide cues that it is lunch time. Each person must have individual assessment and care planning according to particular assets and liabilities. Avoid assumptions and hard-and-fast rules.

With these important considerations in mind, it is necessary for caregivers to have a generalized framework of disease progression in order to plan for future care needs. A very general guiding principle is that the degenerative process follows the reverse order of the way development occurred during infancy and childhood; for example, it follows the reverse of the old axiom that one must learn to sit before one learns to stand. Individuals with AD lose the ability to stand and walk before they lose the ability to sit independently. Fine motor control becomes difficult before gross motor control. This rule of thumb is, of course, greatly tempered by the persistence of overlearned skills, such as feeding oneself. Reisberg (1983) has developed a seven-stage Global Deterioration Scale for age-associated cognitive disorders and AD. This scale describes the progression of losses from normal functioning to advanced dementia. Volicer et al. (1988) divide the progression into four stages. The format of Volicer et al. (1988) is followed in this text. Again, bearing in mind that there is great individual variability and that no definitive assessment or symptom indicates progression from one stage to the next, the general symptoms of each stage are described below.

2.3 Early Stage of Alzheimer's Disease (Mildly Impaired)

In the early stages of AD the changes are so subtle that neither the individual nor significant others may take particular note of the changes. The hallmark symptom of AD, memory loss, appears at this stage. This memory loss is periodic and inconsistent and occurs particularly in unfamiliar surroundings. The individual may forget how to get home, be unable to recall a particular word or name, be unable to locate personal items, or find himself or herself at times unable to carry out a familiar but complex activity, such as writing a check. Initially, these difficulties may be dismissed by the individual as being due to fatigue or other stresses. The frequency of these incidents increases, and the individual begins having regular and noticeable difficulty with complex work or leisure activities. Individuals react very differently to these losses. Some may attempt to carry on as usual. Others may gradually withdraw from familiar activities with which they can no longer cope; they may appear apathetic and may in fact be depressed. Still others may express frustration at their incapacities and seek assistance from their physician or counseling from friends. Depression is quite common in this early stage and may make the symptoms appear worse than they actually are.

2.4 Middle Stage of Alzheimer's Disease (Moderately Impaired)

The difficulties with memory loss become much more pronounced in the middle stage, such that they interfere with day-to-day living. The individual begins to need cuing and prompting for activities such as dressing and hygiene. More complex activities, such as meal preparation, shopping, and financial management, require the direct assistance of others. Safe driving becomes impossible and should be discontinued. The individual becomes less and less able to cope in unfamiliar settings and experiences frequent disorientation as to place and time. Difficulties with communication,

written and verbal, become more apparent. For some, language difficulties become very marked during this stage. The physical ability to speak and use words persists, but the content may be hollow or have other pathologies such as perseveration (getting stuck on a particular word or phrase). Motor coordination problems appear, and are more pronounced for some than for others. Apraxia (the inability to carry out complex motor activities) may interfere with dressing, eating, and walking. Walking may be further impaired by other perceptual problems. On the other hand, motor restlessness (frequent pacing and wandering) also often occurs during this stage. Although it is unclear why, for many these problems become much worse at the end of day, when the unexplained restlessness and agitation is known as "sundowning." These symptoms are undoubtedly related to the individual's increasing inability to remember, and hence to locate, familiar places or people.

Frustration with the progressive losses may lead to extreme emotional reactions, or catastrophic reactions, to seemingly minor events. These outbursts may also be accompanied by physical aggression. Alternately, the individual may be apathetic and disoriented because of an overwhelming sense of the inability to cope. Some may express paranoia and blame others for misplaced items or misperformed activities.

Cognitive function is greatly impaired, and the learning of new material, especially verbal material, is very difficult. Concentration, attention, reasoning, and judgment are all noticeably deficient. Loved ones will be recognized, but frequently they cannot be named. Urinary incontinence may occur.

2.5 Advanced Stage of Alzheimer's Disease (Severely Impaired)

In the advanced stage, verbal cues alone usually are not sufficient, and the individual requires constant supervision and physical assistance for personal activities such as toileting and personal hygiene. Incontinence—both fecal and urinary—is common. Language skills have greatly deteriorated and only simple phrases or familiar expressions persist. Language comprehension is limited. There is widespread loss of fine and gross motor skills, and assistance is required for ambulation. Support is frequently required to maintain a normal sitting posture. Disorientation is constant. Some may develop seizures. Some may also tend to put all objects in their mouth (hyperoralia). The return of primitive reflexes, particularly the grasp reflex, may occur (see Chapter 3).

2.6 Terminal Stage of Alzheimer's Disease

In the terminal stage, the Alzheimer's patient is totally dependent on others. The patient may be unable to move, speak, or swallow. Particular attention must be given to maintaining comfort and preventing such complications as bed sores, dehydration, aspiration pneumonia, and painful contractures. In this stage, the family and professional caregivers often must make painful decisions about such issues as the initiation of tube feedings. The complications of AD in this stage lead to death.

3.0 CAUSES OF ALZHEIMER'S DISEASE

Since the time of Dr. Alzheimer, great advances have been made in understanding the nature of the pathology of AD; however, the cause remains unknown. Numerous theories currently are being studied. All of these theories attempt to explain the trigger that leads to the formation of the senile plaques, which is the central pathological characteristic of AD. Much of the current investigation of the biology of AD is focused on the precursor protein of amyloid beta-protein, which is at the core of these plaques (Katzman & Jackson 1991; Selkoe 1991). The degree of plaque formation at death correlates well with premorbid functioning (Cohen 1988; Jagust et al. 1989; Katzman & Jackson 1991; Samuel et al. 1991). Unfortunately, as Cohen (1988) states, "the clues are myriad and mounting, but the solution as to its etiology is still elusive" (p. 137). Many now believe that there are, in fact, several types of Alzheimer's disease, each of which may have a different cause (Burns et al. 1991b; Katzman & Jackson 1991; Mayeux et al. 1985).

The following are the most prominent theories under investigation (Aronson 1988; Cohen 1988; Cole & Scheibel 1989; Dippel & Hutton 1988; Katzman & Jackson 1991; Van Horn 1987).

3.1 Neurotransmitter Irregularities

Neurotransmitters are chemicals that enable the sending of messages through the neurons of the brain. It is known that the levels of certain neurotransmitters, particularly acetylcholine and noradrenaline, are decreased in the brains of patients with AD. The areas of the brain that produce these chemicals are speculated to be the source of the problem.

3.2 Cerebral Blood Flow

Although "hardening of the arteries" (arteriosclerosis) has long been discounted as the cause of AD, recent research has focused on blood flow to the brain. There is reduced blood flow to parts of the brain in individuals with AD, but which is cause and which is effect is not clear. In addition, there is now evidence of abnormalities in the capillaries of the brains of those with AD. These vessels appear to become more and more porous with AD, and some investigators speculate that this porosity may compromise the blood-brain barrier, leading to the amyloid beta-protein deposits of the senile plaques.

3.3 Infection

A small number of researchers still support the theory that a slow virus or another unusual infection triggers a reaction that eventually causes AD.

3.4 Genetic Theories

In a small percentage of cases of AD, there is believed to be a genetic link. Familial AD is characterized by a relatively young age of onset. A genetic marker for AD has been located on chromosome 21, which is also the site of the marker for Down's syndrome. If individuals with Down's syndrome live long enough they do develop AD. However, the genetic nature of AD is far from clear.

3.5 Autoimmune Reaction

In autoimmune diseases, the body is fooled into attacking its own cells, as, for example, in rheumatoid arthritis. The plaques associated with AD do contain antibodies (immunoglobulin). However, again, the cause-and-effect nature of the presence of the antibodies is unknown.

3.6 Toxins

The toxin most often mentioned, especially by the popular press, as a potential cause of AD is aluminum. Although there is an excess accumulation of aluminum in the senile plaques associated with AD, there is no evidence that this is the cause of the plaques.

4.0 OTHER IRREVERSIBLE CAUSES OF DEMENTIA

4.1 Multi-Infarct Dementia

Multi-infarct dementia (MID) alone (15 to 20 percent) or in combination with AD (20 percent) accounts for 35 to 40 percent of cases of dementia. An infarct is an area of body tissue that dies because of loss of blood supply. In the case of MID, the dead tissue is in the brain. The loss of blood supply may be due to a clot or to a buildup of deposits in blood vessels caused by arteriosclerotic disease. These infarcts occur at various areas throughout the brain and are the result of several events, not one major event such as a stroke. If the cause of the infarct can be determined and treated, MID is potentially treatable but the already existing dementia is not reversible. With MID, the onset of the dementia symptoms is abrupt and the progression of the symptoms is steplike rather than gradual. These two characteristics are the major distinctions between MID and AD. Van Horn (1987) and Aronson (1988) cited other criteria for the diagnosis of MID as variability of impairment, a history of brain infarcts, specific neurological signs, and specific neurological symptoms. Hachinski (1983) and colleagues have developed a scale for use by a trained clinician that is helpful in distinguishing between MID and AD.

Unfortunately, little work has been undertaken to document differences in behavioral characteristics between persons with MID and AD. A study of 25 individuals with AD and MID reported that persons with MID are more likely than those with AD to display a fluctuating mood, loss of emotional control, somatic complaints, depression, night-time confusion, patchy cognitive impairment, and sudden reduction of speech. On the other hand, individuals with AD are more likely than those with MID to display an early loss of insight, spatial disorientation, memory loss, diminished emotional expression, irritability, and personality change (Maddox & Busse 1987). Much more work in this regard is needed in order to assist those working with individuals with MID.

4.2 Acquired Immunodeficiency Syndrome

AIDS is a relatively recently appearing cause of dementia. Van Horn (1987) estimated that up to 65 percent of patients with AIDS will develop dementia that is accompanied by motor problems. In most cases, AIDS will have already been diagnosed, but there are some cases in which a dementia syndrome developed before the systemic infections associated with AIDS. There is little information on the frequency of AIDS among the elderly. One study reported the following age breakdown for AIDS-positive cases (Moss & Miles 1987):

Age (yr.)	Prevalence (%)
50+	10
60+	2.5
70	0.4

The majority of AIDS-related dementia is due to brain infection with the human immunodeficiency virus (HIV), but in some cases it is related to an opportunistic infection.

4.3 Creutzfeldt-Jakob Disease

Creutzfeldt-Jakob disease is extremely rare, with an incidence of one per million per year (Aronson 1988; Cohen 1988). It is a progressive neurological disease caused by a slow virus with an unconventional form of transmission. Age at onset is usually in the 50s or 60s. Over 80 percent die within one year, but some may live as long as eight years (Cohen 1988). The disease is characterized by dementia, pronounced motor problems such as poor coordination and jerkiness during walking, and unpredictable jerks caused by muscle spasms.

4.4 Chronic Alcoholism

It must be stressed that if alcohol abuse is treated in the early stages, before permanent brain damage occurs, alcoholism is a potentially reversible cause of dementia. However, chronic alcoholism can and does lead to dementia. Korsakoff's syndrome is caused by thiamine deficiency due to chronic alcoholism. These individuals have a somewhat different form of dementia, with marked recent memory loss and, as a result, severe difficulty in learning new information. Early in the disease, other cognitive functions are usually quite well preserved. The person tends to confabulate to compensate for memory loss, and to demonstrate a lack of insight about deficits. Other signs may include disorientation, muttering, delirium, insomnia, illusions, and hallucinations, as well as disorders in the peripheral nerves that may cause a condition such as foot drop (Gregory & Smeltzer 1983; Thomas 1981; Van Horn 1987).

In addition to Korsakoff's syndrome, there is a dementia associated with alcoholism. In this case, impairment of cognitive function is more generalized and associated with widespread cerebral atrophy and variable clinical signs (Gregory & Smeltzer 1983; Van Horn 1987).

4.5 Huntington's Disease

Huntington's disease is a rare, hereditary, neurological disease. Huntington's disease involves the deterioration of the cerebral cortex and always leads to dementia. Prominent features of Huntington's dementia are pronounced memory loss, slowed cognitive function, and involuntary twitching and jerking movements of the limbs (choreiform movements). The disease is also accompanied by personality changes, irritability, depression, and apathy, which may occur before the chorea. In the early stages of the disease, patients are frequently suicidal. The disease progresses relentlessly until death, 5 to 20 years after onset, which usually occurs in the fourth or fifth decade (Aronson 1988; Gregory & Smeltzer 1983; Van Horn 1987).

4.6 Multiple Sclerosis

Multiple sclerosis is a disease of the central nervous system that is characterized by periodic and sporadic loss of the nerve fiber sheaths. The patient may experience scattered sensory and motor loss, poor gait, visual disturbances, and general weakness, depending on the nerves affected. The course of the disease is unpredictable, with periodic flare-ups and remissions. In the advanced stages, most patients experience memory loss and/or mild to moderate dementia.

4.7 Parkinson's Disease

Parkinson's disease is a degenerative neurological disease with prominent motor characteristics that include tremor (at rest), bradykinesia (slowness of movement), rigidity, and loss of normal postural reflexes. Dementia has been associated with Parkinson's disease ever since Dr. Parkinson's original description in 1817 (Van Horn 1987). However, in recent decades, the percentage of those with Parkinson's disease who also have dementia has been recognized as much higher than the incidence of dementia in the general population. Of those with Parkinson's disease 40 to 80 percent have dementia (Gregory & Smeltzer 1983; Hutton & Kenny 1985; Van Horn 1987). The dementia associated with Parkinson's disease is progressive. Both the clinical symptoms and the brain changes found at autopsy are similar to those associated with AD. The neurological source of the dementia associated with Parkinson's disease is unclear, but some investigators speculate that there are in fact different types of Parkinson's disease, one that is associated with dementia and one that is not (Hutton & Kenny 1985).

4.8 Pick's Disease

Along with AD, Pick's disease is known as a primary degenerative dementia. That is, it has a slow onset and a progressive course, and after complete examinations, no other cause of the dementia can be determined. Pick's disease is relatively rare and is thought to have an inheritable component. It is very difficult to distinguish between Pick's disease and AD on the basis of clinical signs. An autopsy reveals localized neurological losses with Pick's disease as opposed to the more generalized losses of AD. Positron emission tomography (PET) scans reveal more damage to the frontal lobes in Pick's disease. These areas affect social behavior, which is consistent with the frequent reports of disinhibition and social inappropriateness with Pick's disease (Aronson 1988). The presence of "Pick bodies" in nerve cells and the absence of plaques and tangles at autopsy confirm a diagnosis of Pick's disease (Aronson 1988).

5.0 DIAGNOSIS OF ADRD

There are two absolutely crucial points that must be made about diagnosis:

1. It is essential in order to identify and treat potentially reversible causes of dementia.
2. The assessment must be carried out by a qualified medical practitioner who is experienced in working with the elderly.

Family and professional caregivers must insist on a comprehensive assessment before a diagnosis of AD or other dementia is made. Under no circumstances are consistent problems with memory, which significantly interfere with normal daily function, to be dismissed as a "normal part of growing old." They are not! In addition to identifying potentially treatable causes of dementia the assessment and diagnostic process is important in order to

- assist the family and other caregivers to develop an individualized treatment and management plan that will maximize remaining abilities
- identify coexisting diseases, which may make the symptoms of dementia worse (e.g., urinary tract infection or depression)
- enable the family and the patient to make future plans for finances, care, guardianship, etc.
- help the family and other caregivers to understand the source of changes in behavior, personality, and abilities

5.1 The Diagnostic Process

The conclusive diagnosis of AD and most other irreversible dementias is possible only with a postmortem examination of brain tissue. No single test or procedure can diagnose ADRD in a living patient. The clinical diagnosis of AD is based on assessment of current symptoms and the elimination of other possible causes of dementia. Clinical diagnosis of AD is 80 to 90 percent accurate (Aronson 1988; Dippel & Hutton 1988; Katzman & Jackson 1991; Mayeux et al. 1985; McKhann et al. 1984; Volicer et al. 1988).

The assessment process can be initiated and coordinated by the family physician, a geriatrician, a neurologist, a psychiatrist, or other medical practitioner. The physician is responsible for coordinating essential information from other medical practitioners, laboratories, and other health care professionals involved with social, functional, and physical assessment. Determining the final diagnosis is the responsibility of the physician, but the information necessary to make the diagnosis comes from many health care professionals, as well as from family and significant others. Assessment is not a one-time-only occurrence. Because of the progressive nature and variability of the disease and the hampered communication skills of persons with ADRD, assessment must be ongoing (Mace 1990).

Since ADRD are progressive diseases, an essential part of the assessment and diagnostic process is a complete history. This history must come not only from the patient, who because of memory loss may not be a reliable source, but also from family members, friends, and other caregivers. Only through documenting changes in behavior, over time, can ADRD be clinically diagnosed. An important part of this history is information about previous personal coping styles and personality factors (e.g., how the person reacted to stress, style of sociability, temperament, self-image, etc.). This information is invaluable in explaining behavior and responses during the course of the disease, as well as indicating important areas of personal strengths and related treatments. It is essential for treatment planning purposes that an assessment identify not only deficits, but persisting strengths and abilities.

The assessment must include the following (Aronson 1988; Carnes 1984; Dippel & Hutton 1988; Mace 1990; McKhann et al. 1984; NIHCD 1987):

- a complete history
- a neurological examination to identify possible neurological causes of the dementia
- a psychiatric screen for the presence of coexisting depression or depression presenting as pseudo-dementia
- a social/behavioral evaluation, which must include the availability of family and social support systems and be based on actual functional performance as observed by the evaluator or a reliable caregiver source
- an evaluation of functional performance in the activities of daily living and leisure pursuits

- cognitive functioning based on clinical observation and standardized assessment
- a comprehensive physical examination
- laboratory investigations (While testing for testing's sake must be avoided, it is important that the patient receive a thorough investigation, especially in cases where the diagnosis is unclear, based on clinical investigation.)

Standard investigations should include the following:

- full blood count and differential
- serum electrolytes
- tests of hepatic and renal function
- serum calcium
- thyroid function studies
- syphilis serology and, depending on history, screening for HIV antibodies
- serum vitamin B_{12} and other folate levels
- urine analysis
- chest X-ray
- electrocardiogram
- electroencephalogram
- computed axial tomography (CAT scan) of the brain

6.0   PERSISTING ASSETS OF INDIVIDUALS WITH ADRD

> As the disease progresses, there is little or no hope of recovery of memory, but people do not exist of memory alone. People have feelings, imagination, desires, drives, will and moral being. It is in these realms that there are ways to touch our patients and let them touch us. (Cohen & Eisdorfer 1986, 22)

The above quotation is a poignant reminder, from the great neuropsychologist Luria, that individuals with ADRD have continuing strengths despite their many deficits. It is important to understand the nature of these deficits, and they are discussed in detail in the following section. For family and professional caregivers who are involved in "treatment," an understanding of the persisting assets of individuals with ADRD is particularly vital. By accenting these assets during activities, self-care, and indeed during all aspects of daily life they can be utilized to compensate for deficits and thus enable maximal functioning. These persisting assets are

- emotional awareness and emotional memory
- sensory appreciation

- primary motor function
- sociability and social skills
- procedural memory/habitual skills
- long-term memory
- sense of humor

6.1 Emotional Awareness and Memory

The persisting capacity and need for emotional expression, for giving and receiving affection, are identified throughout literature; for example, the poem by Robert Frost quoted at the beginning of this book embodies such emotions. The clinical literature also emphasizes the capacity for, and the importance of, emotional expression: "Moreover, throughout much of the course of the illness those with AD remain very capable of giving and receiving love, of sharing warm interpersonal relationships, and of participating in a variety of meaningful activities with family and friends" (Cohen 1988, 149).

The capacity to experience the full range of emotions—love, joy, fear, anger, and sorrow—persists (Mace 1990; OTA 1987; Zgola 1987). The deficit is in the ability to express these emotions, particularly verbally, as well as in the ability to interpret the environment and make an appropriate emotional response. The onus is on caregivers to facilitate the expression of emotion, especially through nonverbal methods (see Chapter 3). Activities involving modalities such as music, pets, plants, and children are excellent for stimulating emotional expression (see Chapter 5). Simplifying and clarifying the environment also help to facilitate appropriate emotional expression (see Chapter 4).

Emotional memory is the memory of the feelings associated with an event, as opposed to the facts of the event. Emotional memory is a persisting asset of persons with ADRD. This asset can be capitalized on by ensuring that activities and self-care routines have positive emotional associations, and thus future participation is encouraged. A good example is bath time. This is often a negative and frightening experience for persons with ADRD. Increasing the positive and pleasant stimuli during bath time (for example, music, colorful and soft towels and robes, scented soaps and talc, even candlelight) help to create a positive emotional memory about baths. Previous happy emotional experiences can be triggered by using reminiscence materials and other positive emotional cues such as favorite songs, pieces of clothing, pictures, or foods (see Chapter 6).

Alice was in the advanced stage of Alzheimer's disease. She required 24-hour care and assistance with all activities of daily living, which was provided in a nursing home. In spite of these severe deficits, every Sunday Alice went to church with her son and his family and afterward to their house for Sunday dinner. Usually she sang along and smiled happily during the hymns at church. Afterward, at dinner, she was sometimes able to help set the table or mix the salad. Whatever she was able to do or not do, surrounded by her family, she smiled happily and was free of the restlessness that so often disturbed her at the nursing home. During the Easter church service, Alice didn't smile or hum during the music and had to be fed the communion bread. She dozed through much of the service and during the car ride home. Her family decided that Easter dinner would be just too much and drove back to the nursing home. When the car stopped at the entry doors, Alice sat up with a start and opened her eyes wide. In a clear voice she demanded, "What am I doing back here already?" Alice was not able to articulate the factual order of what she did on Sundays, but she had a strong emotional memory of a pleasant family time after church.

6.2 Sensory Appreciation

The primary sensory areas of the brain remain relatively untouched by the processes of AD (Aronson 1988; Jagust et al. 1989; Van Horn 1987; Zgola 1987). Experiencing the touches, smells, movement, sights, sounds, and tastes of everyday life can serve as an ongoing source of pleasure, stimulation, and method of communication.

John Angus had spent his life working with the soil and plants. It was both his life work and his joy. He had been an innovative farmer, developing one of the province's first commercial blueberry farms from wild bushes, and had a thriving greenhouse business. This lifework had been shared, both in pleasure and labor, with his wife. In their lifetime, John Angus and his wife had launched millions of seedlings and plants into the gardens and homes of Nova Scotia.

As familiar as these activities were, as his Alzheimer's disease progressed, he could no longer independently do even the simplest of plant care duties such as watering or pruning.

However, with hand-over-hand guidance and cuing, he derived enormous pleasure from such activities as potting up cuttings.

One day we were going to work together on some geranium cuttings. John Angus's reaction when I placed the large mother plant on the table in front of him was quite amazing. First of all his face wrinkled up in disgust as he said "Whew, I know what that is by the terrible smell. It's a geranium. I never could stand the smell of geraniums." Then, as he moved his hands over the leaves and stems his expression gradually changed to one of mirth and delight.

He said, "Mother, now, she liked geraniums. When we were working together in the greenhouses, she used to tease me by putting geranium leaves around my face. Of course, I would make a big fuss, and then she would laugh even harder. It was one of our special jokes. That was how it was. We shared the work and the fun. It was a good life we had together."

The flood of happy memories and feelings of accomplishment left John Angus smiling, content, and satisfied. All of this because of the smell of a geranium!

Chapter 7 is devoted to methods that make use of this persisting asset. Compensations for the sensory deficits that accompany normal aging are found in Chapter 1. Information on the use of caring touch is found in Chapter 3.

6.3 Primary Motor Function

Particularly in the early stages, primary motor control areas of the brain also remain relatively untouched by the processes of AD (Aronson 1988; Jagust et al. 1989; Van Horn 1987; Zgola 1987).

Although some persons with AD may experience gait disturbance early in the disease, strength, dexterity, and muscle control usually persist until the late stages. At all stages, the innate pleasure associated with movement brings not only enjoyment but improved health through positive effects on range of motion, circulation, respiration, and body sense. More information on the use of movement is found in Chapter 5.

6.4 Sociability and Social Skills

For almost all individuals with ADRD, ingrained overlearned social skills persist until death (Carnes 1984; Mace 1990; Reisburg 1983; Zgola 1987). The handshake is an excellent example. With proper cuing, even individuals in the advanced stages respond by shaking an outstretched hand held out in greeting. If the greeter smiles warmly and asks, "How are you?" there is more often than not a smile and a "Fine, thank you" in return.

The simple handshake is a wonderful way to accomplish many ends. Through touch, perhaps clasping the outside of the hand as well, the greeter communicates caring. It serves to bring the individual to attention, to increase alertness in an adult, socially appropriate, and familiar way. It causes the person to initiate movement and perhaps speech.

By supporting and encouraging sociability in groups and with individuals, this persisting skill can help to compensate for losses in memory, reasoning, and language. Returning a standard greeting with a generic social response does not require remembering the person's name and, because the phrase is an overlearned one, it does not require more complex verbal and reasoning skills.

Family member: "Mom, this is our old friend, Wayne, visiting from Hamilton, Ontario." Mom: "I am so glad to see you again. How are you?" The family member provided the cues, so the person was not struggling for the name, and standard social responses were made. The mother was happy to be able to participate in welcoming the old friend and was saved the embarrassment of admitting that she did not recognize him. Dignity and adult function were preserved.

While these skills must be encouraged, it is also important that family and professional caregivers not mistake social skills for the persistence of higher skills, such as memory. Many individuals with ADRD, especially in the early and middle stages, cover their losses by relying on social skills. This is an excellent coping mechanism in social situations, but it should not be mistaken for actual skill in vital areas of self-maintenance such as nutrition (e.g., "No thank you, I already had a delicious supper"), taking medication, or safety.

In the preceding illustration, the visitor was impressed to have been remembered and thought that the mother's memory must be quite good. After he left the room she quietly asked, "Who is that nice man?" Be aware of the potential for great cover-ups!

Groups are a particularly good setting for encouraging social skills. Social groups and parties inspire all of these long-practiced skills (David 1991; Fernie et al. 1990). Using a social group setting for treatment-directed goals such as exercise, reminiscence, sensory stimulation, or eating facilitates maximal function. More information on groups is found in the remaining chapters.

6.5 Procedural Memory/Habitual Skills

Since memory loss is one of the hallmark features of ADRD, it may seem peculiar to list procedural memory as an asset. However, it must be understood that there are different types of memory, which are affected differently by the disease process (Dippel & Hutton 1988).

Episodic memory. Episodic memory is the recollection of the circumstances—the where, what, when, who, and how—surrounding a particular event or occurrence. "What did you have for breakfast today?" "How did you spend Christmas last year?" "What do you remember about your first day of school?" These questions are all directed at tapping episodic memory, the memory of events that may be recent or remote. Individuals with ADRD demonstrate impaired episodic memory, which becomes much worse as the disease progresses. In general, the memory for remote events, long-term memory, is less affected than that for more recent events. However, even long-term memory has noticeable gaps, especially as the disease progresses (Backman & Herlitz 1990; Dippel & Hutton 1988; Fromholt & Larsen 1991).

Semantic memory. Semantic memory stores general knowledge, which is not specific to particular events. "What sorts of foods are eaten at breakfast?" "What date is Christmas?" "What elementary school did you go to?" Semantic memory is not affected by normal aging and, in fact, there is much evidence that the fund of knowledge actually increases with age (see Chapter 1). However, with ADRD there are measurable decreases on semantic memory tests and observable clinical changes in semantic memory performance. Since persons with ADRD also have perceptual and language impairment, these further contribute to semantic memory losses.

Difficulty in naming things and people is one of the first symptoms of ADRD that are noted by family members. Frequently, category names are substituted (e.g., *fruit* for *apple*), or the item is described by its use (e.g., a pen is a "writing thing"). On the basis of his research and that of others, Mitchell (1988) concluded that the naming errors associated with ADRD are based more on semantic memory problems than on perceptual problems. A very important point from this research is that recognition remains much more intact than does recall. That is, the person may not be able to name his or her daughter but a nonverbal response, such as a smile, indicates recognition. The person may not be able to state his or her address, but recognizes the house. In a recent study comparing the recognition and recall of photographs of faces among college students, healthy older adults, and older adults with mild cognitive impairment, both sets of older adults showed better recognition for dated (1940s) personalities than for contemporary personalities (Backman & Herlitz 1990). Of particular interest was the finding that there was no difference between the healthy and the cognitively impaired elderly in their ability to recognize dated photographs.

Procedural memory. Procedural memory is remembering how; it is the most basic memory system. Procedural memory is triggered by a familiar cue associated with the action. Being seated at a dining room table with prepared food triggers the response to begin to eat. Being handed a bowl with partially mixed batter and a spoon triggers the response to stir the batter. Responses based on procedural memory are rather rigid, stereotyped responses, not usually adaptable to particular circumstances. They are habitual skills such as brushing teeth, riding a bicycle (for some), playing the piano, knitting, drying dishes, etc. Calling forth these habitual skills depends upon the presence of a familiar cue, but it does not depend on a conscious recollection.

The limited research available indicates that persons with AD retain procedural memory skills (Mitchell 1988). Clinical experiences also include many accounts of the preservation of procedural memory (e.g., familiar dance steps enacted when cued with music and the invitation of a partner, sweeping the floor when handed a broom) (Cohen & Eisdorfer 1986; Dippel & Hutton 1988; Edelson & Lyons 1985; Mace 1990; Zgola 1987). In order to facilitate this persisting skill the following are essential:

- The cues must be familiar.
- The action is not amenable to different methods of carrying it out.
- The cues should be presented so as to encourage a subcortical response (i.e., without conscious processing). Do not say, "Can you put on your sweater?" Instead, hand the person the sweater.

The following is an illustration of the differences between the types of memory:

> Alice had always been a prolific seamstress. She made all of her own clothes and was conscientious about doing the family mending. In the early stages of her Alzheimer's disease she continued to sew, but she had difficulty with fine work because of developing cataracts. Finally, she abandoned her sewing altogether. Four years after the first symptoms of AD, she had cataract surgery and lens implants in both eyes. The day

after her first surgery, she looked in the mirror and was startled by all the bruising around her eye. She asked "What on earth could I have done to make my eye such a mess?" Even after repeated explanations she couldn't seem to retain the information about her surgery. This was particularly remarkable because Alice was a registered nurse.

A year after her second cataract surgery, Alice required care in a nursing home. However, she was still a regular part of family gatherings. One such occasion was a backyard barbecue, during an older grandson's visit home. Alice was predictably offended at the ragged state of his "cutoffs." She requested a "sewing thing" (a needle) so that she could hem them. Needle, thread, and ragged shorts were produced. To everyone's amazement she threaded the needle and hemmed the shorts beautifully!

Although Alice could not remember her surgery (episodic memory) or the name of a needle or that of her grandson (semantic memory), she did remember how to thread the needle and sew a hem (procedural memory).

6.6 Long-Term Memory

As outlined in the preceding section, there are several different types of memory. Episodic memory for long-term events is less impaired than that for more recent events. Events of particular personal significance, such as the first day of school, marriage, the birth of a child, the first car, or outstanding personal accomplishments are those most usually recalled. As the disease progresses, the details about these events may become spotty, but with familiar verbal and nonverbal cues, even persons with advanced ADRD can usually recall some fragments. Stimulating these long-term memories encourages verbalization, improves mood by recalling happy previous experiences, and enhances self-esteem by reaffirming the value of previous life experiences. For more details see Chapter 6 on reminiscence.

6.7 Sense of Humor

Many consider humor to be a method of nonverbal communication (Williams 1986). For persons with ADRD, sense of humor persists despite increasing difficulties with communication (Green 1991). Frequently jokes are used to cover embarrassment about memory or functional loss. These subtle ways of protecting

adult dignity should be supported, being careful, of course, not to be fooled about the actual capacity to perform.

A good laugh is therapeutic, relieving tension and bringing pleasant feelings. Laughter has positive physiological effects on respiration, circulation, and musculature. It releases neurotransmitters in the brain that increase alertness (catecholamine) and give sensations of pleasure and reduction of pain (endorphins) (Cousins 1979; Peter & Dana 1982; Stone 1992; Tennant 1990; Williams 1986). Encourage laughter and gentle humor by example while working with individuals with ADRD. Pick up on personal jokes and mimes by encouraging and supporting a lighthearted, playful tone during activities and communication.

Gentle humor is also a good way to divert an individual who is becoming upset or agitated.

Humor used therapeutically is never laughing *at*, but rather *with* the person. It implies an understanding of the person, for example, the particular types of humor that appeal, longstanding family jokes, favorite stories and anecdotes, pleasant activities, and age-appropriate entertainers and comedians. For persons who are moderately impaired, old-time favorite performers on film (e.g., Charlie Chaplin, Buster Keaton, Laurel and Hardy, Abbott and Costello, the Marx Brothers) or on radio (e.g., Jack Benny) provide interest and an opportunity for laughter. An experiment with 31 community-dwelling elderly presented a six-session humor program. It consisted of situation comedies such as "I Love Lucy" and a live performance. Compared with a control group, those who participated were found to have a significant decrease in agitation and demonstrated a trend toward improved morale scores (Tennant 1990).

It is essential to appreciate limitations in language and understanding. Complex verbal jokes usually are not understood; but accenting the humor in a situation by mime or exaggeration is a good, nonverbal source of humor and communication.

7.0 DEFICITS OF INDIVIDUALS WITH ADRD

Although ADRD are neurological diseases, it is important to appreciate that the symptoms, until the later stages, are primarily behavioral. This frequently causes frustration for family members and other caregivers because the person looks well, may carry on a normal conversation, and yet put the garbage in the refrigerator. It is essential to understand that these symptoms are based on neurological losses. The caregiver can be frustrated further by the variability in functioning from day to day and by the uniqueness of the array of symptoms of each individual. The following is only a very general outline of possible symptoms. Their presentation at various stages of the disease is unique to the individual.

There are numerous ways of classifying symptoms. The format used in the report to the United States Congress by the Office of Technology Assessment is followed here. In that report, symptoms are classified as follows: cognitive or neurological symptoms; functional symptoms, or impairment of the ability to carry out normal daily activities; behavioral or psychiatric symptoms; and excess disabilities brought about by outside factors (OTA 1987, p. 68). There are obvious overlaps between these categories, and many symptoms could be classified under more than one of these headings. The additional category of physical symptoms is also discussed here.

8.0 COGNITIVE OR NEUROLOGICAL SYMPTOMS

8.1 Memory loss

Memory loss is the hallmark symptom of ADRD. It is usually the first symptom to be noticed by family and significant others (Carnes 1984; McKhann et al. 1984; NIHCD 1987; OTA 1987). At first, this memory loss is sporadic and little different from ordinary forgetfulness, such as misplacing keys or being temporarily unable to recall a name. However, the frequency of these occurrences increases. In addition, familiar but more complex routines such as writing a check or getting home from the store will be sporadically forgotten. As the disease progresses, these memory losses become more and more pronounced. The individual will forget appointments, forget the answer just given to a question, and eventually forget what day it is and where he or she is.

Throughout the progression of ADRD, short-term memory is more impaired than is memory for remote events. However, as the disease progresses there are obvious gaps in long-term memory. In addition, verbal recall is complicated by language difficulties.

As noted in the previous section, procedural memory is much less affected than are other types of memory. Making use of procedural memory, along with targeting and multisensory cuing for recognition, rather than recall, can help to compensate for losses in episodic and semantic memory.

8.2 Aphasia

Difficulty with spoken language is undoubtedly related to memory loss, for example, forgetting the name of an item. However, with ADRD there are impairments in the use of language that are not related to memory or sensory or motor losses. These language impairments are called *aphasia*. These impairments take many forms:

- *receptive aphasia*—difficulty with understanding written or spoken language
- *expressive aphasia*—difficulty with expressing written or spoken language
- *anomia*—difficulty with naming people and things
- *agraphia*—difficulty with writing
- *alexia*—difficulty with reading
- *paraphasia*—substitution of words that sound the same or are from the same class (e.g., *bill* for *pill* or *clock* for *watch*)

For some, language impairments may occur early in the disease (Bayles & Tomoeda 1991; OTA 1987; Van Horn 1987; Zgola 1987). The language loss may be quite specific, for example, difficulties with understanding written language. A written message, such as "Doctor's appointment at 10 A.M.," can be read but the individual is unable to understand it and act accordingly. Anomia is commonly the first noticeable language deficit, but there is enormous variation between individuals in language capabilities. As the disease progresses, language losses become more and more pronounced. In the advanced stage many with ADRD are mute. Communication depends more and more on nonverbal methods, and verbalization depends on external cues. See Chapter 3 for more details.

8.3 Apraxia

Apraxia is impairment in the ability to use objects properly or to plan and carry out purposeful movement, despite adequate sensory and motor skills. Apraxia greatly interferes with daily activities such as getting dressed, toileting, eating, walking, or changing from standing to sitting, as well as with more complex activities such as driving or engaging in sports and hobbies.

As with other symptoms, apraxia may be present to a great degree in some individuals and hardly at all in others. Some may demonstrate significant gait impairment early in the disease (Van Horn 1987). Usually, apraxia first appears as a general clumsiness and progresses to an extreme disorganization of movement and subsequent falls. Initially, the person may have difficulty doing buttons or zippers, and this will progress to an inability to dress oneself at all. At first, during meals, the person may have difficulty using the proper utensil and may progress to eating only finger foods (OTA 1987; Volicer et al. 1987, 1988; Zgola 1987). A study of 274 healthy and demented subjects found that the occurrence of apraxia and other deficits, such as memory and language, was highly individualized, with apraxia causing significant dysfunction for some persons (Baum et al. 1988). Another study also reported great variability in the appearance of apraxia. The study found that some individuals had symptoms of constructional apraxia, even in the early stages, and others were severely demented with no apraxic symptoms (Edwards et. al. 1991).

8.4 Perceptual Problems

Perception is the awareness and sensory impression of the environment. Individuals with ADRD frequently have difficulty in accurately perceiving their environment, difficulties that are added to those caused by memory loss or sensory impairment. The presentation of perceptual problems has a particularly high variability from person to person throughout the course of ADRD. These perceptual problems take many forms (OTA 1987; Zgola 1987).

Visual-spatial deficits. Visual-spatial deficits cause difficulties in the ability to perceive objects in relation to each other or in relation to one's own body or in regard to distance and direction. For example, persons may bump into furniture because they cannot perceive where the furniture is in relation to themselves. Or they may attempt to step over cracks in the sidewalk, which appear to them to be changes in height. Visual-spatial deficits undoubtedly contribute to persons with ADRD getting lost, even in familiar surroundings. One study found that functional spatial tasks of persons with AD were impaired in unfamiliar surroundings but not in familiar surroundings (Liu et al. 1991). Another very significant problem arises when the person cannot distinguish between an object and the background, (figure-ground perception), especially when colors are similar. For example, if the toilet, the floor, and the walls are all about the same color, the toilet may simply not be visible to the person with ADRD.

Agnosia. Agnosia is impairment in the ability to recognize familiar objects and people. Agnosia may be very specific to a particular sense, for example, visual agnosia may prevent a person from recognizing a spoon until he or she can pick it up and feel it. Others may have tactile agnosia, which may cause them to be startled when touched, unless they see or hear the person coming. Agnosia may cause a person not to recognize a spouse of 50 years. For example, every day after supper, in his home of 30 years, one man with advanced AD would thank his wife for the lovely meal and say that he had better be getting back home.

Body perception. Body perception (proprioception) difficulties may prevent the person from being able to relate body position to that of a chair, in order to sit in it.

9.0 HIGHER COGNITIVE FUNCTION

The processes of higher cognitive function, judgment, attention, problem solving, abstract thought, and reasoning are all progressively affected as ADRD itself progresses (Mace 1990; OTA 1987; Van Horn 1987; Volicer et al. 1988; Zgola 1987). Other associated symptoms of memory loss and perceptual deficits compound the difficulties with higher cognitive function. All of these symptoms add together to make new learning difficult, but not impossible, if proper attention is paid to using persisting abilities and premorbid interests and skills. These cognitive deficits also contribute to the frequently observed personality changes of persons with ADRD.

9.1 Attention

All levels of attention are affected by ADRD. Early in the disease, caregivers may observe a certain apathy, which is in large part related to difficulties with initiative, getting started. This difficulty becomes more and more pronounced until, in the final stages, direct hand-over-hand guidance is needed for such basic activities as eating. Unfortunately, this apathy and lack of initiative often are mistaken for disinterest, poor motivation, or inability to be active.

9.2 Abstract Thought

Difficulties with abstract thought may also be observed, with the person having difficulty understanding abstract concepts involved in an activity such as financial planning. As the disease progresses, common figures of speech may become confusing because they are taken too literally; for example, a person with moderate ADRD would probably be totally perplexed by the expression "It's raining cats and dogs."

9.3 Judgment

Difficulties with judgment may cause the person to leave the house on a winter's day wearing only a sweater. Making decisions, even about such a minor matter as ordering food in a restaurant, becomes difficult. As the disease progresses, problems with judgment become more pronounced. Social conventions may be disregarded, and the person may do such things as undress in public. Decision making becomes extremely difficult, and choices are important but must be limited to two options.

9.4 Problem Solving (Reasoning)

Individuals with ADRD are still capable of reasoning but, because of accompanying deficits in memory, perception, and judgment, their reasoning often ends with a faulty conclusion. Problem solving is a complex higher cognitive skill. It requires integrating information about the nature of the problem, coming up with possible solutions, making a judgment about what solution is best, and implementing the plan. It can easily be deduced that the person with ADRD has associated deficits that will interfere with every step of this process. In the early stages, solving the problem of a lamp that will not work may be too difficult. By the late stages, solving the problem of the feeling of a full bladder may be too difficult.

10.0 BEHAVIORAL OR PSYCHIATRIC SYMPTOMS

The division between the symptoms presented here and those in the preceding section is somewhat arbitrary. The neurological losses associated with ADRD are obviously at the root of the following behavioral symptoms.

A recent study of 127 patients with AD type dementia found that the number of behavioral problems (e.g., incontinence, poor hygiene, wandering, falling, suspiciousness, restlessness) increased significantly with the level of cognitive impairment (Teri et al. 1988). Another study of 3,351 Rhode Island nursing home residents found that the highest rates of disruptive behavior were associated with the greatest level of cognitive impairment (Jackson et al. 1989). Suggestions for managing difficult behaviors are found in Chapter 4.

10.1 Catastrophic Reactions

A catastrophic reaction is a reaction that is in excess of the usual response to apparently minor situations. The reaction may be emotional (anger, verbal abuse, crying, agitation) or physical (hitting or other forms of physical aggression), or both. These excessive reactions occur most often in the middle stages of the disease as the person becomes overwhelmed by his or her incapacities. These reactions are not inevitable and may occur infrequently, or never, in a supportive environment.

10.2 Depression

In the early stages of the disease, insight into increasing impairment frequently causes depression. Some investigators suggest that as many as 30 percent of those with ADRD are also depressed (Cohen 1988; Reifler et al. 1986). Untreated depression not only causes personal distress but has the effect of making the dementia symptoms appear much worse than they really are.

10.3 Delusion

A delusion is a fixed false belief. Delusions may accompany ADRD and can be remarkably persistent, despite marked memory loss for recent events.

10.4 Disruption of Sleep/Wake Cycle

This is a common symptom during the middle stages of the disease. It is particularly distressing to caregivers because of concern about the person's safety. This disruption is probably due both to particular difficulty in interpreting the environment at night and to actual neurological damage to the sleep/wake centers of the brain (Cohen-Mansfield & Marx 1990; Jarvik & Winograd 1988; OTA 1987). Frequently another contributing factor is a lack of exercise or stimulation during the day.

10.5 Hallucinations

Hallucinations are experiences of particular sounds, sights, smells, feels, or tastes that are uniquely experienced by the individual. This is not a common symptom, but it may occur in the middle stages of the disease. Hallucinations are frightening to the caregiver and may be dangerous to the person if acted upon. Hallucinations are usually responsive to pharmacological treatment (OTA 1987).

10.6 Perseveration

The individual with ADRD may "get stuck" and perpetually repeat a particular phrase or action. This is known as perseveration. Although actions such as repetitive banging or clapping can be a problem, the deficit can be used as an asset to encourage a necessary repetitive activity (e.g., spoon to mouth), exercise, or functional activity (e.g., stirring batter).

10.7 Restlessness

Pacing, fidgeting with clothing, and other restless behaviors often become a problem during the middle stages of the disease. This restlessness is sometimes a side effect of psychotropic medication. More often it is due to the frustration of increasing difficulties in managing day-to-day living. Restlessness may become particularly pronounced at the end of the day and has been termed *sundowning*. This behavior is little understood, but it is probably related to several factors: the increased activity of caregivers at this time of day (especially the change of shift in institutions), fatigue, lack of meaningful activity, and more difficulty in interpreting the environment as it becomes dark (Dippel & Hutton 1988; Mace 1990; OTA 1987). In the later stages, a certain amount of repetitive, restless behavior is undoubtedly an attempt to provide self-stimulation (e.g., perpetually rubbing chair arms or wheelchair trays).

10.8 Suspiciousness

This symptom is particularly prominent during the middle stages of the disease. Increasing problems with memory cause the person to suspect others of hiding their things. Similarly, increasing difficulty in interpreting the environment may cause the person to be suspicious of others, even to the point of paranoia.

10.9 Wandering

This is a particularly difficult problem for caregivers during the middle stage of the disease, as cognitive function deteriorates more and more and the environment looks less and less familiar. If institutional care becomes necessary, the problem of unfamiliarity is even greater. The individual, whether or not at home, may wander in a fruitless search for the familiar.

11.0 PHYSICAL SYMPTOMS

Aside from gait disturbance, the individual with Alzheimer's type dementia is usually relatively free of physical symptoms in the early and even the middle stages of the disease. Other types of dementia, particularly Huntington's chorea, have particular physical symptoms very early on. However, as AD progresses to the middle and late stages, physical symptoms appear. Approximately 10 percent of those with advanced AD experience generalized seizures (Volicer et al. 1988). There is a loss of muscle control, progressing from fine to gross movements and peripheral motor control (e.g., hands and feet) to central control (e.g., torso muscles controlling posture and balance). In the terminal stages of the disease, the person with AD may be bedfast and contracted into a fetal position. He or she may also experience difficulty in swallowing. Some in the middle and advanced stages develop hyperoralia, the tendency to put everything in the mouth.

Although it is far from universally present, a common physical symptom is the return of primitive reflexes. The most commonly observed reflexes are the snout reflex, the grasp reflex, hypersensitive startle reflex, the sucking reflex, and the gegenhalten response (Altman 1987; Burns et al. 1991a; Volicer et al. 1988). Further information about primitive reflexes is found in Chapter 3.

12.0 IMPAIRMENTS IN FUNCTIONAL ABILITY

The preceding neurological, behavioral, and physical symptoms have a profound effect on the ability of the individual to carry out the functional activities required for daily living. It is estimated that one-third of persons with dementia require assistance with daily activities such as toileting, eating, grooming, and dressing (Carnes 1984; OTA 1987; Reisburg 1983; Volicer et al. 1988; Zgola 1987). The degree to which function is affected depends on the complexity of the task, the stage of the disease, and the degree to which the environment supports function. It is not possible to state categorically at which stage a particular function is lost. One study of 88 patients with AD recorded the time from onset until 50 percent of the patients had lost a particular function (Volicer et al. 1987). The researchers reported that:

> Half of the patients were unable to dress themselves five years after onset of symptoms and unable to sleep regularly six years after onset. By seven years 50% had developed rigidity on passive movement, and by eight years half were unable to feed themselves and walk without assistance. By nine to ten years, 50% had developed contractures of the limbs and were mute. (p. 83)

However, they continued, emphasizing variability: "Our clinical observations indicate that the time from onset of symptoms of DAT to institutionalization varies widely. . . . Moreover, even in our institutionalized patient population, there was considerable variability of disease progression" (p. 87). A study of 127 cognitively well older adults and 108 persons with mild, moderate, or severe dementia found that the subjects with dementia had more difficulty with dressing than with any other daily living task. These problems appeared early (mild dementia) and worsened as the dementia progressed (Edwards et al. 1991).

The following is a very general outline of the effect of ADRD on functional abilities as the disease progresses.

In the very early stages the individual can manage most functions, except the more complex demands of work or daily function (the instrumental activities of daily living) that require problem solving and high levels of judgment. In the home, areas such as financial planning and driving are the first with which difficulty is experienced. Driving can be particularly difficult because the person may not be able to understand that he or she can no longer drive safely. Family members may need to involve the family physician in arranging for a driving retest. Other functional problems during the early stages occur in unfamiliar settings or when a novel situation arises that requires the person to use judgment and problem-solving skills.

In the middle stages, the person begins to have difficulty even in familiar surroundings. More complex daily functions such as shopping, meal preparation, and laundry require supervision and cuing or full assistance. Self-care activities such as hygiene and dressing can still be carried out but require cuing, and careful attention must be given to providing a maximally supportive environment. Loss of coordination, perceptual problems, and restlessness contribute further to problems in daily activity and usually interfere with ambulation and the sleep/wake cycle. Tasks can be carried out, but much cuing and prompting are required to compensate for reduced initiative and other deficits. Difficulties with independent bathing appear at this stage. The person can usually feed himself or herself but requires assistance to ensure proper nutrition. Because of difficulties with such functions as communication and locating the bathroom, urinary incontinence may occur at this stage.

By the advanced stage, verbal cuing and prompting usually are no longer sufficient. The person frequently requires hand-over-hand guidance to initiate self-feeding, tooth brushing, and washing. Only portions of self-dressing may be possible. Urinary and fecal incontinence occur. Difficulties with ambulation increase, and the person may no longer be able to walk. At this stage the person requires 24-hour care.

13.0 EXCESS DISABILITY BROUGHT ABOUT BY OUTSIDE FACTORS

Excess disability (Figure 2-1) is disability beyond that caused by the disease process itself (Brody et al. 1971; Brody et al. 1974). For persons with ADRD, this is an essential consideration. Cohen (1988) states, "Overall, the treatment of excess disability states offers one of the most important intervention opportunities available for Alzheimer's disease" (p. 148). While it is the case that as yet there is no effective pharmacologi-

cal treatment or cure for ADRD, there is much potential for family and professional caregivers to provide treatments that eliminate excess disability. Excess disability can be caused by many factors:

- other diseases
- medication toxicity
- level of fatigue/stress
- decreased expectation of caregivers
- sensory deprivation
- inadequate environmental supports
- inadequate social supports

13.1 Other Disease Processes

Since the reserve, physical and mental, of the person with ADRD is limited, the presence of other disease processes frequently has the effect of appearing to increase the severity of the dementia. Problems with cognition and communication make it difficult for the person to let others know when he or she is in pain or unwell. Coexisting mental illness, especially depression, is common and greatly decreases function (Cohen 1988; OTA 1987). Thorough and regular medical assessment is essential. Caregivers have a very important role in detecting these diseases by observing carefully for unusual or sudden changes in behavior, which frequently indicate the presence of other diseases.

13.2 Medication Toxicity

The side effects of some medications, particularly psychotropic medications, can have a negative effect on some individuals with ADRD (Cohen 1988; Eimer 1989; Knopman & Sawyer-DeMaris 1990; OTA 1987; Taft & Barkin 1990). The caregiver also has a vital role in alerting the physician about behavioral changes after a change in medication. The physician and the caregiver should discuss possible side effects and drug interactions so that the caregiver knows what to look for.

13.3 Level of Fatigue/Stress

At least part of the variability in function of persons with ADRD can be accounted for by fatigue. The person is trying very hard to cope in an increasingly complicated environment, using decreasing skills (Mace 1990). The extra effort required to perform normal daily activities greatly increases fatigue. Ensuring proper rest and postponing demanding activities until

Figure 2-1 Excess Disability

the person is rested can contribute greatly to improved function. Proper attention to the social and personal environment can reduce the level of stress. Good nutrition is also important. More information on these areas is found throughout this book.

13.4 Decreased Expectations of Caregivers

It is an unfortunate, but understandable, tendency to anticipate that individuals with cognitive impairment are unilaterally impaired. However, as has been discussed throughout this chapter, impairment in function for individuals with ADRD is not unilateral. A person may be unable to prepare a grocery list but can prepare a meal for a friend. A person may be unable to judge the need for a bath but play the piano beautifully. Unfortunately, if caregivers expect disability in all areas, the individual frequently fulfills this expectation. This can be a potent factor in creating excess disability. For more information see Chapter 4.

13.5 Sensory Deprivation

Sensory deprivation due to sensory losses, the effects of ADRD itself, and/or a deprived environment can greatly increase the dysfunction of individuals with ADRD. This issue is dealt with extensively in Chapters 1 and 7.

13.6 Inadequate Environmental and Social Supports

The person with ADRD is particularly dependent on the human and non–human environment to cue behavior and promote function. More information on these important areas is found throughout the book.

14.0 WHY TREAT PERSONS WITH ADRD?

Having detailed the devastating array of symptoms that accompany ADRD, it is necessary at this point to refocus attention on the purposes of treatment. Given the facts that the disease process itself is progressive and at present irreversible and that the symptoms are multidimensional, one may indeed feel defeated and wonder, Why treat?

Unfortunately, this air of "therapeutic nihilism" continues to be all too present among the general public and even in health care settings. There is a false, widespread belief that nothing can be done for persons with ADRD (Calkins 1988; Cohen 1988; Cohen & Eisdorfer 1986; Davis & Kirkland 1988; Edelson & Lyons 1985;

Freeman 1987; Glickstein 1988; Greenblatt 1988; Heacock et al. 1991; Jarvik & Winograd 1988; Mace 1990; OTA 1987; Volicer et al. 1988). This pervasive misperception presents itself in conversations with family and friends, in the popular press, and even in therapeutic and health education settings. Three of many personal examples include (1) a 1985 lecture by a neurologist who stated that Alzheimer's patients will be our most difficult clients as therapists because "you can't teach them anything"; (2) a 1988 music therapy workshop where the more than 50 participants were told by the leader that it was impossible to work in groups with persons with Alzheimer's disease; and (3) a statement in 1991, by a registered nurse, that I might as well give up on an 84-year-old woman, who was disoriented and confused ten days after hip surgery, because the woman was senile.

This attitude is graphically reflected in the allocation of funds for research on AD. In the United States, this is a tragic one-tenth per patient of that spent on AIDS, cancer, or cardiovascular disease (Alzheimer's Association 1990). Currently, in the United States, 90 percent of this limited funding is directed toward search for a cure and 10 percent toward family needs. These areas of investigation are indeed crucial. However, it is also crucial to research answers to the questions Why treat? and more specifically How to treat? Dr. Kevin Namazi, Director of Research at the Corinne Dolan Alzheimer Research Center at Heather Hill, Ohio, states, "Figuring out the how to make the patient's daily life easier is completely forgotten" (Lewis 1990).

Consideration of these questions leads me to recall my early clinical and personal experiences with persons with ADRD:

> My first day on the dementia unit was a memorable one, to say the least. On the one hand, I was convinced of the value and need for therapy. On the other hand, I was overwhelmed by the enormity of the task and how to begin to answer the question of How to treat, for these 25 persons with advanced dementia, the most disabled, cognitively impaired, elderly persons in the province. Being a concrete person, I decided that the first thing to do was to read four charts and then to meet these four people. In this way I could gradually do a needs assessment of everyone on the unit. The chart reading went well, indeed very well. I met the first person, Amanda B. So far so good. I decided to begin my assessment by getting Amanda to show me her room. From here on things went

downhill. Amanda was mobile but was in the very advanced stages of AD. She was dysphasic, uttering only a few disconnected words; had an attention span of 30 seconds; was constantly disoriented to time and place; required full assistance for all activities of daily living; and, at times, when the severity of her impairments overwhelmed her, she struck out unpredictably at staff and her fellow residents. Do I need to add that Amanda was unable to show me where her room was?

With the help of staff we did, however, find her room. To my surprise the bed was already occupied by a very frail old gentleman. I suggested to him that this was Amanda's room. He sat part way up in bed, saying, "I'm so sorry," then lay down again! This little scenario was repeated four times until on the fifth rising I took his arm and escorted him down the hall to his room. When I returned Amanda had returned to the day room, where she sat on the floor, rocking slowly back and forth. I went back to another chart and to think further on How to treat.

After working with hundreds of dementia patients and doing much reading and research, I have a much better idea of How to treat? although there is certainly no concrete formula. Amanda was a "founding member" of my first sensory stimulation group, as well as receiving one-to-one sensory stimulation. In group she was able to attend for longer and longer periods, verbalized more, and was less agitated and restless. This, together with the treatments provided by other team members, eventually made it possible for Amanda to be transferred to a nursing home.

Beyond learning more about the "how to's," my experience has greatly strengthened my conviction that there is a staggering need for treatment for persons with ADRD.

14.1 So, why treat?

While there is no cure for the disease, it is vital to appreciate that there are effective approaches and interventions for the *person* with ADRD. The symptoms of ADRD and the factors causing excess disability are amenable to treatment. Specialized treatment and care regimens maximize the self-esteem and functioning and minimize the suffering and dependence of the mil-

lions of affected individuals during the long course of their illness. Whatever the devastation of their capacity to think, remember, communicate, and do, persons with ADRD remain unique and special individuals who require and benefit from the same opportunities for human expression and quality of life as those who are well or those who are disabled as a result of other fatal diseases such as AIDS, cancer, or heart disease. This need is most poignantly expressed by an individual in the early stages of AD:

> I am hungry for the life that is being taken away from me. I am a human being. I still exist. I have a family. I hunger for friendship, happiness and the touch of a loved hand. What I ask for is that what is left of my life shall have some meaning. Give me something to die for! Help me to be strong and free until my self no longer exists. J. T. (Cohen & Eisdorfer, 1986, 21)

Without treatment, the progressive disabilities associated with ADRD will result in a precipitous downward spiral in function. Since part of the symptomatology of ADRD includes such characteristics as decreased initiative, difficulties with planning and problem solving, problems with interpreting the environment, and decreasing communication skills, the person has difficulty acting independently to maintain his or her own health and functional status. This lack of action leads to a further decline in function. Like persons with diabetes, persons with ADRD require ongoing treatment to be as healthy and functional as possible. Unlike persons with diabetes, persons with ADRD have a limited capacity to initiate and organize their own treatment.

Treatment reduces the burden of care for family, friends, and paid caregivers. Studies of family caregivers have shown that the care of a relative with AD is among the most stressful and demanding of family responsibilities (Advisory Panel on Alzheimer's Disease 1989; Mace 1990). Treatments that enhance the functioning and self-esteem of individuals with ADRD also support their millions of caregivers.

Treatment promotes maximal function and hence reduces the financial burden of care. The direct and indirect costs (e.g., lost hours of caregiver work time) of ADRD in the United States in 1985 was estimated to be $88 billion (Huang et al. 1988). As the numbers of those with ADRD increase with the increasing aging population, the financial costs will become even more staggering. One carefully considered estimate suggests that, unless innovations are made, by the year 2000 the total American health care budget for the elderly will be consumed by the cost of institutional care for persons with ADRD (Pfeffer 1989).

In conclusion, in neither human nor financial terms can we afford not to study, apply, and develop treatment for the millions of individuals with ADRD. It is a major public health problem of epidemic proportions, with urgent and compelling needs for treatment. Not to treat is to invite a public health catastrophe. ADRD is, as some have stated, the disease of the century (Advisory Panel on Alzheimer's Disease 1989; Aronson 1988; Cohen 1988; OTA 1987).

Michael, don't forget that I am still in here.

—Anonymous Alzheimer patient to her spouse

Communication

1.0 ADRD AND COMMUNICATION PROBLEMS

Difficulties with communication begin very early in ADRD. As they progress, they become, perhaps, the most distressing symptom of the disease for family and other caregivers. The decreasing ability to communicate, at least in usual ways, underlines deterioration and gives a sense that the person is "lost" to you. Ways of maintaining communication are vital, particularly to overcome the danger of depersonalization—treating the person with ADRD as if he or she were not there. Skills and abilities may vanish; the person does not. Vulnerable, disabled people who are treated impersonally, with negative expectations, most often act to fulfill the negative expectations. Maintaining communication short-circuits this vicious cycle. It is also essential for reasons of safety and monitoring other illnesses.

For the person with ADRD, the frustration of not being able to express needs and feelings is enormous.

Edith had moved to another province, to be near her son and his family. This move had been suggested by family members when they noticed Edith's increasing problems with managing her own household. She settled happily into a retirement home where meals were provided, but she did all of her own personal care. She was thrilled to be close enough to attend sports and school events with her grandchildren. Unfortu-

nately, six months after the move, Edith fell and broke her hip. She had surgery to put in a new hip joint. Normally, after this surgery, the person is up and about, with some restrictions, and functioning at home within ten days. However, because Edith couldn't remember the restrictions on her movement, she dislocated her new hip joint three times and required three more surgeries.

This is when I met Edith. She was in a four-bed room on an orthopedic ward of a large, acute care hospital. Both she and the medical staff were frustrated with the weeks she had spent in bed and with her slow progress. Edith was supremely embarrassed that she didn't know what day or month it was, and sadly shook her head that she had come to such a circumstance. She tried to tell me what had happened to cause her to spend so long in bed. What was understandable was her constant repetition of "pain" and "I can't move." Edith looked at me with tear-filled, hopeless eyes and shrugged her shoulders, saying, "Well, that's that." Edith's physiotherapist was equally discouraged with her lack of progress. Supported by a cumbersome brace, so she wouldn't dislocate her hip yet again, she was able to walk a few feet once a day, but the distance hadn't increased for weeks. She never remembered, from one day to the next, the ways in which she should move in order to assist with putting on the brace. She always screamed with pain when moving to the side of the bed. She was termed a poor rehabilitation candidate because of her lack of motivation. Nursing staff reported that Edith became very agitated at night, calling for her long-dead husband, and disturbing other patients so much that she had to be moved out of the room. To Edith's humiliation, she was regularly incontinent of urine, but always apologized for the accident, saying she couldn't move to take care of herself. When the nurses reminded her to use the call bell she said, "Oh, thank you very much, I didn't know that was there. I will use it the next time."

Although Edith was only in the early to middle stages of Alzheimer's disease, her communication deficits, in this unfamiliar environment, had imprisoned her. After the pain of so many dislocations and surgeries she was imprisoned by the fear of moving, because of the pain it had caused in the past. She couldn't say, "Help me, I'm afraid to move." Instead, she said, "I can't move," "I can't walk any farther today." She couldn't move to get to the bathroom or remember how to use the call bell, so she was incontinent. She couldn't say that she was frightened and nothing looked familiar in the dark hospital room, so she called out for her lifelong companion and comforter.

Edith's deteriorating ability to express her needs and fears, and the medical staff's unfamiliarity with special communication techniques, had resulted in Edith's being far more disabled and dependent than either her dementia or her broken hip should account for. And even more important, Edith herself felt completely hopeless, discouraged, and defeated.

There is another side of the picture of Edith and her deteriorating ability to communicate. One day, while I was working with her to improve her sitting balance, an old friend appeared. Without hesitating a moment, she introduced her friend, Sister Mary Rose, calling her by name. Unable to remember my name or role, she introduced me as her helper. Although she couldn't say the date or my name, Edith's capacity to perform lifelong social skills was entirely intact.

In this case, there was a happy ending to the story. Edith was assessed by the hospital's geriatric assessment team, who were able to communicate with her, and they determined that she had potential for rehabilitation. She was transferred to a geriatric rehabilitation service, where she did learn to walk again. Without this opportunity to meet with someone who could communicate with her, the story wouldn't have ended so happily.

As with other symptoms of ADRD, communication losses do not follow a predictable course. The losses vary from (1) person to person, even in the same stage of the disease; (2) one type of communication skill to another, for the same person; (3) one time to the next, depending on the person's mood, health status, and environment.

At the most basic level, communication is the sharing of thoughts, information and feelings. Without shared meaning there is no communication. Persons with ADRD have difficulty both in understanding what others are saying to them and in expressing themselves to others. Because some portions of language skills are preserved while others are seriously affected, it is very easy to be frustrated in attempts to communicate. It is very common, for instance, for the person to be able to read but be unable to understand what the written message says.

Alice always amazed the members of her Bible study group with her oral reading of the scripture passages, in spite of quite progressed Alzheimer's disease. What they didn't see was her difficulty with understanding even simple written language. After a major disaster with a plugged sink drain, her son had posted a sign above the kitchen sink that read "DO NOT PUT ANY GREASE DOWN THIS SINK." Alice frustrated visiting family and her homemaker by insisting that absolutely nothing, not even water, was allowed to be put down the sink drain.

Bayles and Tomoeda (1991) investigated the order of appearance of linguistic symptoms in 99 AD patients. Based upon caregiver reports, they found that the "prevalence of linguistic symptoms was strongly correlated with order of symptom appearance, a finding suggestive of relative homogeneity in linguistic symptomatology in AD patients (Bayles & Tomoeda 1991, 214). The most prevalent linguistic symptoms were difficulty with word finding, difficulty in thinking of names, and difficulty in writing a meaningful letter. These, and the other 13 linguistic symptoms, generally occurred after the nonlinguistic symptoms of memory loss. However, even in this sample there was variability, with all of these linguistic symptoms occurring before nonlinguistic symptoms at an average frequency of 10 percent. It is also interesting to note that the performance of the AD patients on linguistic tests of naming, reading, defining, and comprehending was related to the prevalence of linguistic symptoms as reported by caregivers, except for the symptom of using meaningless sentences. This symptom and the symptoms of difficulty with reading, inappropriate conversation content, failure to recognize humor, and failure to complete sentences were the only 5 of the 16 symptoms that were significantly correlated with the severity of the dementia.

This study underlines a persistent theme with regard to ADRD symptomatology: although general characteristics at various stages can be described, these symptoms cannot be precisely assigned to a particular stage of the disease. As a result, approaches must be adapted to suit the person involved and be flexible according to the circumstances. What follows are some general guidelines that have been derived from my clinical experience and the literature (Age Wave Inc. 1990; Alzheimer's Association 1988; Bayles & Kaszniak 1987; Dippel & Hutton 1988; Glickstein 1988; Gross 1990; Gwyther 1985; Hoffman et al. 1988; Jarvik & Winograd 1988; Lee 1991).

The following is a brief overview of the general effects on communication and language through the stages of ADRD. Usually, language and communication skills are lost in reverse order to the way they were acquired in childhood.

2.0 COMMUNICATION SKILLS PRESERVED

2.1 Nonverbal Communication

The ability to interpret the emotional message of tone of voice, facial expression, eye contact, body posture, and touch remains. This has been verified by countless clinical observations and by a well-controlled experiment. In that study, there was no difference in the ability of nondemented and moderately and severely demented subjects to distinguish between pleasant and unpleasant nonverbal messages (Hoffman et al. 1985). This persisting skill can, and should, be widely used. The person with ADRD also continues to communicate nonverbally with facial expressions, tone of voice, touch, gestures, and other behaviors such as fidgeting, pacing, singing, crying, laughing, and shouting.

2.2 Standard Conversational Structure

Even though the content may be difficult to understand, the person continues to follow normal, adult patterns of turn taking in conversation; changes in voice inflection to end a sentence or ask a question; most social proprieties of conversation; the rhythmic quality of language; and lifelong patterns of pronunciation, syntax, and grammar. These are the more automatic, unconscious components of verbal communication, which are better preserved than semantic (factual) and pragmatic (understanding) linguistic skills (Emery & Breslau 1988).

2.3 The Need To Communicate

The need to communicate is obvious and of paramount importance. What may not be so obvious is that part of this need can be fulfilled just by having someone else pay attention. Even though you may not understand what the person is trying to say, he or she understands that you are listening, and this is reassuring. Although communication loss is inevitable, use of the suggestions in the following sections to encourage and maintain skills will make the loss less devastating to the person and to the caregiver.

3.0 COMMUNICATION LOSSES

3.1 Early Stage

In the early stage of AD, memory loss is the greatest source of communication problems. Frequently individuals attempt to cover the loss by using several techniques.

Standard conversational responses and social skills. Standard conversational responses are exemplified by bland, cocktail party phrases such as: "Isn't that interesting," "I'm so glad to hear that," and "Really, no one ever told me that before." For example, one patient in the early stages of AD who was unable to name what she wanted for lunch smiled coquettishly and said, "Surprise me."

Confabulation. Confabulation is the making up of a response or explanation that it is totally fictitious.

> Roseanne had been functioning in her own apartment, with the support of family. One relative did grocery shopping, but recently even that didn't seem necessary, as Roseanne would say that she had just picked up a few things herself. However, when this relative was unable to reach her by telephone after several hours she became alarmed. The su-

perintendent opened the door and found Roseanne unconscious on the floor. She was taken to the hospital and rehydrated, and a huge pressure sore was discovered on her lower back. After several days, she became much more alert, was able to feed herself and wash herself, and eventually began to walk again. When asked by her therapist if she had any visitors, she would often give elaborate, logical accounts of visiting nephews and nieces, complete with details of what they were doing and what they had brought her. When asked by her family if she had been for a walk, she would describe a long and tiring route traversing the hospital corridors and sometimes including adjacent outdoor areas.

Although they were completely plausible because they incorporated so many factual details, none of Roseanne's accounts was true. In all probability, neither were her earlier grocery shopping trips. Aside from dehydration and poor nutrition, the actual cause of Roseanne's loss of consciousness was never discovered. She was clinically diagnosed with possible Alzheimer's disease.

Flattery. By complimenting or charming another person, the person with ADRD very skillfully throws the other off guard and his or her communication deficits may be overlooked. As I was describing how I would be working with him, I asked one gentleman in the middle stages of AD whether he had ever met an occupational therapist. He smiled his most engaging smile, took my hand, and said, "Well yes, of course, my dear, and a very charming one—you!"

Humor. One patient very cleverly covered her deficits in abstract thinking by using her sense of humor. In reply to a question from the expanded Folstein Mini-Mental State examination, asking how an arm and a leg were similar, she said, "Well, sometimes I've paid an arm and a leg for something."

Social conversation remains well preserved, but those who know the person well may begin to notice peculiar things, such as more than normal difficulty in recalling names. The main difficulties, at this stage, are in recalling names and in communicating information about plans, events, appointments, taking pills, etc. At this stage, it is usually possible to make use of calendars, charts, written reminders, and "talking" watches or clocks, as long as these are consistent with the methods the person used before the disease began.

Alice, my mother-in-law, had always described herself as having a poor memory and kept track of appointments, important names and telephone numbers, and her grocery lists on scraps of paper from old envelopes, fastened together with a paper clip. As she progressed into the middle stages of Alzheimer's disease, she could no longer manage this system and was having increasing difficulty in keeping track of appointments, visit times, etc. As a therapist, I was sure that there had to be a way to support her with an organized system of calendar reminders and a daily diary notebook. Unfortunately, this system did not work. After trying it for several weeks, Alice's purse still contained her jumbled, paper-clipped notes, and her beautifully illustrated diary was carefully preserved in her drawer with only my messages inscribed. Finally, the lights went on and I realized that it would be more beneficial to spend time helping her to organize her scraps of paper so that they were useful to her.

At this stage, the person is usually very aware of the difficulties, tries to cover up mistakes, and appreciates tactful suggestions on how to overcome the problems.

Other problems that may begin to appear at this stage are the following:

- The person uses longer pauses in order to digest the information or to think of a response. Be sure to be patient with this need for more time.

- The person has a tendency to wander off the topic. If the topic has some urgency, gentle redirection is helpful.

- The person is beginning to have difficulties in recalling the names of people, places, and things. Words that sound the same (e.g., *mouse* for *house*), words of the same category (e.g., *daughter* for *son*) or a description of the object (e.g., "the lock thing" for key) may be substituted. Attempt to interpret these substitutions and, unless it is upsetting to the person, supply the missing word. Encourage the person to use other words or gestures to describe what he or she wants to say.

3.2 Middle Stages

- Naming losses become more pronounced and obvious. More complex, less frequently used words disappear first; e.g., the name of the color cerise will be forgotten before the name of the color red.

- Nouns and proper names are replaced by pronouns (e.g., it, he, she, they) or generic terms (e.g., the thing, the whatchamacallit).

- Requests to repeat questions or directions are frequent.
- The person has great difficulty in following verbal directions.
- Language becomes increasingly "hollow." Vocabulary and structure may be present, but what is said does not make much sense.
- There is increasing reliance on standard social phrases.
- The person has difficulty in understanding figures of speech and expressions.
- The person has difficulty in interpreting written directions.
- The person has difficulty concentrating.
- The person has difficulty in initiating conversation.
- The person may forget some of the accepted rules of social conversation (e.g., accepted distance from another person).

3.3 Advanced Stage

- The person has extreme difficulty with verbal communication.
- The person may be primarily mute, speaking, if at all, in short phrases or single words.
- The person requires much prompting to speak.
- The person may get stuck (perseverate) on a single word, phrase, or sound.
- The person may "babble" a great deal, using real or invented words, but conversation has no easily understood meaning.
- The person has great difficulty understanding even simple words.

4.0 SUGGESTIONS FOR ENHANCING VERBAL COMMUNICATION

Speak to the person as an adult. The person with ADRD remains acutely aware that he or she is an adult. Show recognition of the individual as a worthwhile adult by making eye contact, addressing by proper name, and commenting on personal attributes such as eye color or an attractive item of clothing. Speaking to persons with AD

What a lovely shawl Mrs. Comeau!

other than with the dignity and respect they deserve causes them either to withdraw or to become understandably agitated. Never, never use condescending terms or unfamiliar nicknames (e.g., "pops," "babes," "gramps," "grannie") or baby talk (e.g., "Are we ready to go wee-wee now?").

Although he was unable to dress himself or find the bathroom because of advanced AD, Reverend Donald Jamison still retained the personal dignity and decorum of his profession. It was hard to imagine what could suddenly cause the transformation of this genteel, polite gentleman into a cursing, arm-waving, out-of-control individual. However, with further investigation, it was discovered that some staff had developed the habit of referring to Reverend Jamison as "Donnie Boy." When they told "Donnie Boy" to go to the bathroom or shave or go to lunch he rebelled against this insult to his dignity with the only means available to him.

Address a person by proper title and use the first name only with permission. Many older adults are not comfortable with or accustomed to being addressed by their first name, except by close friends. It is important to find out from family or significant others how the person wishes to be called. A nickname is fine, if this was how the person was most commonly known. A man may have been known as "Sonny" all his adult life, and this is the best way to address him. For someone else, this nickname would be very insulting. It is also essential to know the proper pronunciation of names. Otherwise, there may be an incorrect assumption that the person does not respond to his or her own name. The following is just one example of such a case:

Mrs. Watson was in the advanced stages of AD. For many years, previous to her AD, she had also experienced a significant hearing loss. Friends and family members were able to communicate with her by using familiar expressions and long-practiced techniques. However, the staff in the nursing home were especially concerned and frustrated because they couldn't get her to respond even when they tried to communicate that it was meal time. They had to resort to feeding her the few bites she would take. A dear friend was visiting one day at lunch time and was astounded to hear the staff calling loudly, "Lois, eat your lunch," and being very frustrated when they got no response at all. The friend gently suggested that she wouldn't answer to "Lois" because that wasn't the proper pronunciation of her name. She had always been called "Loise" (pronounced like *noise*). When her friend addressed her this way she lifted her head and smiled.

Unfortunately, despite the friend's mentioning the proper pronunciation of the name to the charge nurse, and the family's doing the same, the staff continued to call "Lois" and get no response.

Reassure by confirming the emotional message of a communication, even if you cannot understand what the person is saying. Even if the words are not making any sense to you, attend to the non-verbal parts (e.g., voice tone, facial expression, body posture, gestures). This, combined  with any understandable words, should give an indication of the feeling the person is trying to express, for example, happiness, frustration, embarrassment, anger, fear. Check your interpretation out with the person by saying something like, "Mary do you feel frustrated?" If you get agreement, acknowledge the feeling by caring touch and saying something like, "I'm sorry you feel frustrated. Is it because you can't explain what you need?" Continue to reassure and explore the reasons for the feeling. Sometimes the source can never be uncovered, but just acknowledging that you are aware of the person's feelings is calming and reassuring. It is particularly important to discover whether the person has pain or is feeling unwell, since as ADRD progresses even these expressions become impaired.

Mr. Cormier's mother tongue was French, but he had learned to speak English quite well in the small fishing village where he had lived all his life. As his dementia progressed, Mr. Cormier could no longer safely live independently and was placed in the only available facility that could provide the care he required. Unfortunately, this was an English-language facility in a city a hundred miles from his lifelong home. Mr. Cormier didn't do well in this unfamiliar setting. The bathroom didn't look like the outdoor john he was used to, so he urinated in corners, doorways, and potted plants around the unit. He missed the fresh air and his active life in the village

and was constantly pacing the unit, moving furniture, and rummaging in drawers. As his disease progressed, the once-familiar English words of his caregivers lost their meaning.

One day, the laundry cart was late and there were no clean pants for Mr. Cormier. At 11:30 A.M. he was still wearing his pajamas and pacing the corridor in great agitation. He approached me full of distress, pointing to his pajamas saying "*Ce ce non, non, terrible, this, this jacket.*"

His words, taken at face value, made absolutely no sense whatsoever. However, by including the nonverbal context, I was able, this time at least, to know exactly what he meant. I replied "Yes, I agree it is terrible that there are no pants for you to wear yet. I'm sure it's very upsetting for you to be still in your pajamas long after breakfast. I will help you to change as soon as the clean pants come from the laundry."

Never argue, disagree with, or embarrass a person who has expressed incorrect information or ideas. This is particularly important if these ideas are expressions of paranoia. As inaccurate as the information may be, the person has arrived at it independently, if through deteriorated reasoning and perception processes. Direct attempts to correct the faulty information will be threatening and will probably cause agitation. Instead, try to identify with the feelings associated with these statements and make positive connections with the people or things mentioned. For instance, a person may say that his or her daughter never comes to visit, when in fact she was just there yesterday. DON'T SAY, "That's not true, she was just here yesterday." DO SAY something like, "Your daughter is a very wonderful person. You must miss her a lot and it must seem like a long time since you have seen her." Gradually, begin to make positive associations with the person's daughter and slowly work around to talking about yesterday's visit.

Early in my career both as a professional and as a family caregiver, my mother-in-law, Alice, stayed with us after cataract surgery. This coincided with Christmas vacation and many social and family activities. After one such happy occasion, during which Alice was an accomplished co-hostess, she was wearily heading off to bed. I told her she hadn't taken her pills yet. She insisted that she had. I attempted to disagree with her, at which point she became very angry, insisting that she had taken her own pills for years and couldn't possibly have made such a mistake. At this point her agitation was so great that she threw the pills across the room, an act that was completely out of character. The situation was resolved by my husband, sitting and reassuring her for some time, and finally gently giving her the pills, saying that he was very concerned about her health. The longer-term solution was discussing dosages with her doctor, so that she took medication only once a day. We took over dispensing the pills, giving her a week's supply of daily doses so it was easily determined whether that day's dose had been taken.

My mistakes in this situation were many. I should have begun by thanking her for all her help, saying calmly that I had her evening pills, and handed her the actual pills. In all likelihood, this would have prevented the problem altogether. If she still insisted, rather than disagree, I should have diverted the topic by talking about what a busy and happy day we had had, and then gradually changed the conversation to how easy it was to forget things (like pills) when it gets busy. Another example, from a conversation in a nursing home elevator:

It was Sunday afternoon and the lobby and elevator were full of visitors. A frail elderly lady, accompanied by her caregiver, got on the elevator after us. Both were wearing their coats, and it seemed as if they had just come back from a visit to the hospital emergency department. One visitor politely asked the lady which floor she wanted. She replied, "Six please." Her caregiver said abruptly "No, we're going to three." The lady looked puzzled and said to her nurse, in a very perplexed manner, "How come?" Instead of saying something like, "I know it's hard to keep track of things after all the rushing around this afternoon, and especially since you aren't feeling well, but your room is on the third floor." She, in fact, patted the lady on the head and said "Because you're 90 years old and you're all confused." The lady was needlessly humiliated and embarrassed in front of strangers, and she still hadn't been provided with reassuring orienting information.

Emphasize recognition, not recall. Never begin a conversation with a person with ADRD by saying, "Do you know who I am?" This is done over and over again by every level of staff and by family members. It is natural for us to want personal recognition from our patient or loved one. It is also natural for the person with ADRD to be unable to remember your name, as difficulty with names begins very early in the disease. Furthermore, these types of questions put the person on the spot, confront the disability, and set a negative tone for the whole conversation. Look for recognition, instead, in nonverbal responses such as a smile, a warm embrace, and other comments. Try to imagine the person's embarrassment at not being able to name a son, daughter, spouse, or dear friend. Perhaps you have experienced something of this when you have temporarily forgotten the name of a colleague or an acquaintance in a social situation. How would you appreciate having someone rub it in by saying, "Don't you know me? It's your daughter, Carol." This same principle applies in all aspects of conversation with the person with ADRD. You provide the orienting cues, the prompts, and they help him or her to follow through.

Henry was in the advanced stages of Alzheimer's disease. He could no longer walk independently and frequently had great difficulty settling to sleep at night. During the day, he would often doze in his chair. At other times, his booming lumberjack's voice would echo through the corridors of the dementia unit. Most often his voice was calling his hearing-impaired sister, Emily, to fetch over his supper or help with some chore. Emily and her husband lived up the hill, and for years before his illness, she had provided meals for her bachelor brother. Given that Henry was so frequently calling for Emily it was curious that when she did visit, he didn't recognize her—or did he?

One winter's day Emily came, with two grandchildren and her sister-in-law, to visit her brother. Eager to see a favorite uncle, the family, still wearing their coats and hats, crowded around Henry in the busy unit day room. Even more eager to be recognized, Emily stood above Henry and said, "Do you know me?" Henry boomed out, "No, who are ye?"

Arriving partway through this scene, I suggested that the family move their visit to a quieter room and that Emily try another approach. At that, Emily took off her coat and hat, bent down to Henry's level, took him by the hand, and said his name. In response, Henry boomed out "Why Emily, how are ye?"

Staff also want and need personal recognition, but they must appreciate that sorting out the comings and goings of the many institutional staff is difficult for the healthy person, and an enormous task for the person with ADRD.

For several months, John Angus had been a regular participant in reminiscence and other occupational therapy groups on the dementia unit. In spite of his progressed AD, which prevented him from, for instance, dressing himself or sitting in a chair without assistance, he was always an enthusiastic and eager participant in my groups. On one occasion, I was busy preparing for the group and welcoming two new patients to it. Knowing that John Angus always came happily and eagerly to this group, I asked one of the nursing staff to escort him.

When his nurse reported to me that he wasn't coming, I was puzzled, and went to investigate. When I came to his room his nurse was still suggesting that he come to the group with Carol: the time in the kitchen where we talked about and looked at old things. The expression on his face was one of mixed puzzlement and dismay. However, when he glanced up and saw me in the doorway, his face broke into a broad smile. He rose from his bed saying "Oh, oh yes, so you're the one." He walked to the door, put his hand warmly in mine and came to the group.

On another occasion, after a sensory stimulation group on the theme of spring, featuring our favorite Nova Scotia mayflowers, John Angus showed his recognition and appreciation in another touching way. I had remained in the kitchen cleaning up after the group. When I looked up to see who was knocking at the door, I was surprised to see John Angus's beaming face through the glass. I must also confess to feeling somewhat aggravated as I walked to the door, thinking "I just don't have any more time for him today, I have to prepare for the next group."

How humbling and absolutely overwhelming to open the door and be greeted not only by John Angus's beaming face, but by his outstretched arm giving me the rather tattered, but very precious, bouquet of mayflowers that his daughter had brought a few days earlier.

Just one more anecdote, one of particular personal significance:

When my mother-in-law, Alice, was in the later stages of AD, our family made a very difficult decision to move to California for 14 months of study and research. During that time, Alice remained in the nursing home where she had lived for more than a year. Over the period of these 14 months, her abilities had deteriorated greatly. She no longer walked independently, was incontinent, and was restrained in a chair most of the day. She spoke very little to staff, but they reported that her face always brightened at the mention of her son, Paul. She amazed staff at her ability to carry on a conversation of her favorite responses, such as "It's so wonderful to hear from you," and "How are the kids?" during calls from California. Eight months after leaving, my husband returned for a short visit. When he took her hand and said, "Hi, Mom," her entire body came alive in recognition. Her face broadened to a wide smile, her eyes sparkled, and her arms reached out for a hug. Six months later, when the whole family returned, this scene was repeated with every family member, even our teenaged son and daughter, who had grown considerably during this time.

Although we all wept tears at the frail, demented figure who was all that was left of our mother and grandmother, we had no doubt that she knew, without need for naming, who we were. And that our visits were happy and reassuring occasions for her.

These simple, but eloquent, expressions of recognition are the ways in which our family members and patients with ADRD let us know that our efforts, and ourselves, are recognized.

Hello Alice,
I am John. ~ Why John, how are you?
Fine thanks – and you?
It's time for ~ Just fine.
our group, where we share tea.
~ That would be lovely.

Be aware of every aspect of how you present yourself: voice tone, posture, facial expression. These nonverbal methods of communication are very powerful (see following sections) and set the mood for communication. Speak calmly, with a warm voice tone, a welcoming facial expression, and a relaxed posture.

Alert the person to your presence by touching a hand and saying his or her name. Perceptual deficits may prevent the person from recognizing that you are addressing him or her, unless you give extra cues.

Always introduce yourself, state your relationship to the person, and provide other orienting information. Say, for example, "Hello, Mrs. Comeau. I am your therapist. It is time for our group, where we share tea together. It is a beautiful Monday in June, a good time for a cup of tea."

Eliminate background noise and confusion. For example, avoid distraction caused by radios, TVs, other conversations, traffic noise from an open window.

Face the person when you speak, being sure to make eye contact. Never say something as you are passing in

the hall or shout from another room. Persons with ADRD need every possible nonverbal cue to interpret the message. For this reason, telephone communication may also be difficult. If the person is seated, squat down or bend over so that you are on the same level. On the other hand, do not get too close because this is never

socially acceptable and may be either thought to be threatening or interpreted as a sexual gesture.

Speak slowly and clearly.

Do not use abstract language, confusing figures of speech or sayings, or sarcasm.

> Doris was a severely demented woman with remarkably well-preserved social skills, which charmed everyone. These skills often made it appear as if her language skills were more intact than they actually were. One day, during group, I offered Doris assistance to get up from a chair in the following way: "Can I give you a hand?" She replied, "Well now, wouldn't I look silly with three hands?" Although socially skilled, Doris couldn't understand figures of speech or abstract language.

Use short, simple (but adult) sentences.

Use full names and other descriptors, not pronouns. Say, for example, "Tom, you and I are going to eat at the Red Star restaurant, the place where you always like the clam chowder."

Use the phrases and mannerisms the person frequently uses or used. The observant caregiver will be able to pick up these expressions from fragments overheard and reinforce their use by repetition. Family and significant others are important sources for favorite expressions and phrases.

> Alice was in the advanced stage of Alzheimer's disease. Verbal communication was reduced to a few singular words and occasional short phrases. A few weeks before her death, family members were talking with her about her upcoming birthday. She barely opened her eyes when the type of cake and other arrangements were being discussed. It had been a long-standing joke between Alice

and her family that she had remained age 39 for the past 43 years. Suddenly inspired, her daughter-in-law asked, "How old are you going to be on your birthday, Mom—39 again?" Alice was instantly present, eyes open, face wreathed in a mischievous grin. She replied, "Well, yes, of course," and joined in the full spirit of the joke.

Use the name or term that is most familiar to the person. Avoid technical or professional jargon. It is important to appreciate the subtle meanings of language as they have been understood and used by the person.

There are amazing differences in names for everyday items, even within the English language itself. Although a person may have lived most of her adult life in North America, if she learned to speak English elsewhere, those original terms or names will have the most meaning. For instance, the person who grew up in Britain would be more likely to understand "terry" for face cloth or "petrol" for gas.

There are also amazing regional variations with regard to commonly used phrases or terms. The following are but two examples:

A Russian-born and -trained psychiatrist was having great difficulty understanding the source of her demented patient's agitation at bedtime. He kept insisting that he had to be "tucked in." It required several minutes of team meeting, with everyone adding a personal account, to explain the many nuances of security and comfort that were associated with these two simple words.

At three in the afternoon, a severely demented lady asked a fellow resident's out-of-province visitor, "Have we had our dinner yet?" Understanding "dinner" to be the evening meal, as it was in his province, he said, "No, not yet. Dinner will be in two hours, at five o'clock." The lady was very distressed and muttered that she had never heard of waiting until five o'clock for her dinner. Another visitor, who was local, attempted to calm her agitation by reinterpreting her question about dinner, according to local use, which means the noontime meal. "Yes, you had your dinner at noon. You will have supper in two hours." Unfortunately, it was too late to relieve her agitation entirely. She continued muttering, saying, "One person says yes, one says something else." To the next person she passed in the hall she asked, "Have we had our dinner yet?"

It is essential to familiarize yourself with these local and personal language differences in order to enhance communication with the person with ADRD.

Lower your voice tone and speak somewhat more loudly, but do not shout. Shouting conveys anger and irritation and will cause the person to become upset.

Allow ample time for a response. Be comfortable with silences. It takes the person with ADRD longer to process information and organize a response.

One day, while striding hurriedly down the hall, I waved and said, "Hi, Mr. Fraser, how are you?" Several minutes later, on my way back, I was embarrassed to hear Mr. Fraser call out, "Fine, thank you."

If repeating seems necessary, repeat the question or comment using the same words and phrasing. Changing the wording will add to the cognitively impaired person's confusion. The problem is not so much in hearing, but in understanding and processing. This is in contrast to the approach with the hearing impaired, where the wording should be changed. If the person does not understand after two or three repetitions, it is best to change the subject and try again later with different phrasing.

Supply the words the person is trying to recall. Some persons may be upset by this; if so, discontinue.

Encourage the use of gestures and demonstration to get the message across. This is addressed in more detail in a following section.

Use frequent turn-taking, the normal structure of adult conversation. To help maintain the train of thought, repeat the last words the person said. If the person becomes frustrated, reassure and distract; do not keep trying to get the message across.

Speak positively and avoid using "don'ts" and commands. For example, if a resident is found rummaging in another resident's possessions, gently take the

person's arm and say, "Mabel, would you come with me, please? I want to show you a pretty blouse in your closet." *Not*, "Mabel, get out of here right now. This is not your room!" This response inevitably causes the person to become more upset and resistant to leaving.

Cue or prompt over-learned behaviors, based on procedural memory, with concrete cues and limited or no verbal instruction. For example, handing a person a dish towel as he or she is standing beside the just-washed dishes is a cue to begin the familiar activity of drying dishes. Asking the person verbally, without the dishes or dish towel in sight, requires cortical processing that may be too difficult.

Give instructions one step at a time, breaking activities into several steps. For example, the instruction, "Put the sugar in your coffee," involves many steps. For the person who cannot follow this, it is better to give directions for each step: "Take the spoon. Now put the spoon in the sugar. Fill the spoon with sugar. Add the spoonful of sugar to your coffee. Stir the coffee with the spoon. Take the spoon out of the coffee. Put the spoon on the table. Drink your coffee."

Offer only two choices or options at a time. Too many choices overwhelm the person and make understanding difficult.

If you do not understand, say so. Never use pretense, as this does not lead to good rapport.

Give immediate rewards and feedback for attempts at conversation. Even if the words are not understandable to you, acknowledge the attempt with a smile, a touch, or a greeting.

Use familiar, favorite music to provide an avenue for expression of emotions and to encourage verbalization. See "Music" in Chapter 5. Music is a powerful nonverbal language.

Never speak in front of the person as if the person is not there. The words may not be understood, but there is a clear message that the person is a nonperson, not to

be considered or included. And in many cases, the words are understood much more than we will ever imagine.

Use ample nonverbal communication and interpret and attend to this from the individual. See the next section.

5.0 NONVERBAL COMMUNICATION

In North American society, words—spoken language—have come to mean the same thing as communication. We rejoice at the infant's first words and celebrate as these are strung into phrases and sentences. Through all stages of life, words—written and spoken—describe life's happy and sad occasions: the toast to the bride and the eulogy. Speaking and writing skills are the focus of language arts courses through years of schooling and fill the shelves of bookstores and libraries, and drawer upon drawer of files. From the first early utterances, humans have developed the art of speaking and writing what they feel, know, understand, and wonder about to a high level.

With this strong emphasis on spoken and written language, elaboration of the unspoken language of touch, gesture, facial expression, tone of voice, and body posture has gone almost unnoticed. Aside from a flurry of interest when encounter groups were popular during the 1960s and 1970s, the whole area of "body language" has been little discussed and even less researched.

And yet, if we stop to consider it, nonverbal language was our first way of communicating, before words were available to us. It remains a vital part of verbal communication, comprising from 55 to 97 percent of the message (Gross 1990). We announce happy news with a face wreathed in smiles and an excited tone of voice; we welcome one another with a warm handshake or a hug. With a look that "shoots daggers," we mothers give stern messages of disapproval to our offspring for poor manners at a guest table. The list can go on and on. We can understand something of how important this unspoken language is by our reluctance to deliver by telephone the news of the death of a dear friend, or by our preference for delivering criticism by letter—perhaps even a letter written in the sometimes inaccessible language of the law.

The senses of touch, smell, and sound become even more vital for the blind person; and sight, touch, and smell are a lifeline for the deaf person. Similarly, for persons with ADRD, the first language—the unspoken language of the body—becomes again the most important one. As ADRD progresses, the person becomes less and less able to speak and understand the spoken word. In order to continue communication, the sharing and understanding of thoughts, needs, and feelings, the caregiver must also make nonverbal language the first language. In this way, the person with ADRD is reassured of his or her self-worth, understands what is expected, and has a channel for self-expression. Developing the first language relieves the anxiety and frustration caused by not being able to communicate verbally and often opens up the path of verbal communication. The patient and the caregiver are able to communicate person to person, using the eloquent voices of the heart.

Our lifelong focus on verbal communication makes return to the first language difficult. It may be easier for some, whose personal style has always included much language of touch and gesture. For others, the first language requires more practice and conscious thought before it becomes automatic. But it is possible; even more to the point, it is essential.

Before exploring the first language modalities of touch, facial expressions, voice tone, body posture, and gestures, the following points must be appreciated:

- Know that a return to first language is *not* a return to childhood and childish ways. The person with ADRD is an adult and must be spoken to and treated as an adult. Patting on the head, as one would a child, is nonverbal communication that very clearly tells the older person that you regard him or her as a child.

- Respect and understand personal and cultural traditions. For some older people, touching is an invasion of personal space, a privilege given only to intimates. In communal living situations, such as nursing homes, protection of personal space becomes even more important.

- Observe the types and combinations of the first language and the verbal language to which particular individuals respond.

5.1 Touch

We first understand, experience, and explore the world through touch: the security of mother's womb; the comfort of cuddling in daddy's lap; the feel of warm blankets, a wet diaper, our own hands. The fetus first responds to touch at eight weeks (Huss 1976). Although we develop other, more sophisticated, ways of communicating, touch remains a powerful medium of communication throughout life. In North American society, touch has become reserved for the most intimate of personal relationships: parents and children, lovers, spouses, dear friends. For other relationships, we distance ourselves by touching from "arm's length," with

a handshake. And yet how eloquently this handshake speaks: the warmth of caring from a lingering firm grasp; dominance or anger from the too-firm grip; anxiety and fear in the weak, hesitant offering of a limp hand.

The T word comes up everywhere in conversation: "Let's keep in Touch"; "Your comments Touched me"; "We need to Touch base"; "That's a Touchy subject." As Mary Judd (1983) says so eloquently, "Touch is a language seen by the blind, heard by the deaf and felt by everyone" (p. 13).

The need to be touched, and to touch another, continues up to and including death. At times of sorrow, illness, or fear, we especially need a warm and caring touch. I am sure that everyone carries a comforting and vibrant memory of a loving touch, offered in the time of need. For me, this comes from a time in my childhood, when I was very sick with an illness that would keep me from my playmates and school for several weeks:

> Late one winter afternoon, when the fever, aches, and nausea were at their worst, my father came quietly to my bedside before going to the barn for his evening chores. He sat down beside me and without saying a word lay his massive, roughened hand across my forehead. My father was not a person to talk about his feelings, then or ever, but this gentle touch from his powerful hand was so loving, reassuring, and calming, it returns to me still, in full vivid detail, sensation, and comfort.

As we age, and experience losses and sickness, we especially need this touch. People whom we have touched so intimately all our lives—spouses and children—may well not be there. Paid caregivers are often reluctant to touch an old person, recoiling at the wrinkled, sagging skin. Often the physical fences erected because of frailty—gerichairs, wheelchairs, bed rails—prevent touch. And so those who are most in need of a caring touch, ill old persons, especially those in an institution, are the least likely to receive it. There are numerous accounts in the clinical literature that support this. Nurses, for instance, touch elderly patients much less frequently than they touch younger patients (Burnside 1988).

On the other hand, evidence of the powerful reassuring effect of touch is overwhelming. Infants, especially premature infants, deprived of touch in a sterile nursery fail to thrive (Brown 1984). Some have argued convincingly that the same failure to thrive syndrome can describe some withdrawn old people in nursing homes (Berkman et al. 1989; Braun et al. 1988; Palmer 1990).

Others have found that a brief, simple touch on the hand during meals significantly improved the nutrition of older persons with organic brain disease (Eaton et al. 1986). Another investigator found improved self-appraisal in nursing home residents who were frequently touched while getting medication, compared with those who were not touched (Copstead 1980). The nursing profession has developed a program of therapeutic touch, initiated by Doris Kreiger, which emphasizes the healing and restorative nature of centered, caring touch. Although accounts of effectiveness are anecdotal, the reports of the effects on seriously ill and dying patients are remarkable (Brown 1984).

For persons with ADRD, the need for, and the effect of, caring personal touch is profound. Those in institutions are separated from the touch of loved ones, often cut off from the touch of their environment because of sensory deprivation (see Chapter 7), and deprived of fluent verbal communication because of their disease. We see many illustrations of this need for touch in the reaching hands and clinging behavior to passersby, and in some self-stimulating behaviors such as rubbing the chair tray, clothing, pieces of fabric, or stuffed animals. A clasp of the hand or an arm around the shoulder can frequently calm a frightened and agitated patient, this touch providing reassurance that can be understood without words.

Roberta was in the advanced stages of dementia, probable multiinfarct type. In addition to the ravages of this disease, she had had a stroke that had left her with significant right-sided weakness and severe expressive aphasia. Her appetite and fluid intake were poor, and she had frequent urinary tract infections. Roberta was understandably frustrated. Her anger often boiled over, and she swung out physically with her remaining functional limb and verbally with an onslaught of the remaining words left to her, swear words. On one occasion, she grabbed out at the unit psychiatrist as he walked by. A person of infinite patience and gentleness, he wrapped her arm through his and began speaking calmly as he walked her toward her room. He was telling her that he was sure she must feel terrible, having an infection on top of everything else, and that perhaps a rest in bed would help her to feel better. He helped her to her bed, carefully tucked the covers around her, and, just before leaving, ever so gently caressed her cheek. Comforted by this healing touch, Roberta was able to rest calmly.

As marvelous as it is, touch is not universally good. If used inappropriately, it can add to agitation by, for example, arousing sexual feelings, stimulating primitive reflexes, or offending dignity. In fact, since they are often unconscious, the messages communicated by touch are even more prone to misinterpretation (Vortherms 1991). The following are some pointers to help touch become a useful and caring therapeutic tool.

Respect the dignity and cultural and social background of the individual. Touching with dignity means touching as one adult to another; it means respecting the need for privacy; it means getting permission to touch during necessary procedures that may invade privacy. Use information gathered during assessment to understand the social and cultural background of the person and what this says about his or her lifelong use of touch. For example, in some European cultures touching between adults is common and accepted. (I will never forget my surprise when my university friend's Russian landlady greeted me on our first meeting with a smothering kiss on both cheeks!) On the other hand, in India, strangers greet each other with a respectful bow with palms pressed together at the forehead. Understanding these cultural differences becomes particularly important as persons with ADRD preserve these familiar habits, long after verbal language becomes difficult.

Begin the use of touch gradually, constantly assessing the person's reaction. For most who have lived in Western culture for any length of time a handshake is an acceptable and familiar greeting. Use it frequently. It is amazing how even those with the most advanced ADRD respond to this familiar, over-learned action. Watch how the person responds to this; if the response is positive, add a double handshake, with the person's hand comfortably between your two hands. Remain at what is usually the acceptable distance for social conversation, about three to four feet, and gradually move closer as the person feels comfortable. Watch for facial expression, muscle response in areas touched (relaxed muscles mean that the person is comfortable, tight muscles mean that the person is not comfortable), and body posture (leaning back in withdrawal or forward in acceptance).

Be aware of the emotional component of touch. Touch gently, but not hesitantly, and above all, touch with compassion and caring. As with verbal communication, how you communicate by touch is as important as what you say, perhaps more so.

Be aware of where you touch. The most socially acceptable area of touch is the hand, with the least threatening being the handshake. Other acceptable areas for touch are the back of the hand, the upper back, the arm, and the shoulder. Touching the head is much more personal, and many older people find this uncomfortable—especially from those whom they do not know well. There is some loss of the sensation of touch with aging, especially the finer discrimination in the finger tips and palms. Touch seems to be best preserved on hairy body surfaces (e.g., the lower arms).

Use conventional approaches and activities that involve touch:

- handshaking
- double handshaking
- taking an arm while walking to group
- grooming activities (e.g., manicure; washing, setting, and brushing hair)
- rubbing in hand cream or after-shave lotion
- massaging of feet, hands, arms, and shoulders
- dusting with talcum powder
- dancing

Encourage the appropriate use of touch between peers. Use activities which encourage touch, such as shaking hands, rubbing on hand cream, dancing and other music activities which incorporate hand holding.

Remember that light touch is stimulating and arousing (e.g., gently touching with finger tips, the brush of soft fabric or fur). Firm or pressure touch is reassuring or calming (e.g., a firm handshake, arms around the shoulder, being snugly tucked under the blankets). Use the different types of touch to calm or stimulate as necessary.

Make sure that the person is aware of your presence before you touch. Never approach from behind or to the sides; because of hearing and visual loss, the person may well be startled by this touch from out of nowhere. If the person has better vision, hearing, or hand function on one side than on the other, approach from that side.

Be careful of fragile older skin, which may tear or shear much more easily.

Be sensitive and responsive to appropriate touch from the client or patient to you. We assume our right and need to touch our patients. However, the usual social order does not approve of patients touching those in authority, such as nurses, physicians, or therapists. There may be an additional concern because of the sometimes unpredictable behavior of persons with ADRD. However, the offer of a touch to us as caregivers is a gift that we must learn to accept. Patients also have needs to nurture and care for others and to express their thanks. Touch is a way for them to express these feelings to others. Some time and good rapport are required to become comfortable with this expression. However, the rewards are wonderful. Some of my most precious moments have involved a patient's

touch: the gentle caress of a frail old hand on my cheek; a compliment on my long hair and a smile of appreciation while a patient's fingers moved over my braids. As caregivers, we need these expressions of appreciation, but we often must learn to find them outside of verbal language.

Be extremely careful that caring touch will not take on a sexual interpretation. Because of difficulties with interpreting the environment, persons with ADRD may misinterpret touch. If the person's response, in any way, suggests that the touch was interpreted as a sexual overture, DO NOT USE that approach. For example, caregivers should not sit on a bed beside a patient with hips touching. Putting an arm around the waist is more likely to arouse sexual feelings than is a hand on the shoulder or arm. It is very unfair to the patient to arouse sexual feelings, as such feelings inevitably will lead to disappointment and frustration and probably agitation. Sometimes the uninhibited or confused behavior of a few persons with ADRD becomes a source of teasing and is even encouraged by staff. I have, for instance, observed a staff member caressing the hair and sitting in the lap of a confused, agitated elderly man, who sometimes made verbal sexual overtures. This is touch in its least therapeutic form and is NEVER appropriate.

Be aware that touching in certain areas may stimulate primitive reflexes (Altman 1987 Burns et al. 1991; Volicer et al. 1987).

5.2 Primitive Reflexes

Primitive reflexes (e.g., rooting and sucking reflexes in search of food) were essential for survival and development during the first months of life. Gradually, they became integrated into more sophisticated and planned motor patterns. Because ADRD are neurological diseases, they can cause a deterioration of some of these motor patterns, and the early reflexes may appear again, especially in the advanced stages of disease. One study of 103 candidates for a dementia day treatment program found a significant association between positive snout and grasp reflexes and the degree of cognitive impairment (Tweedy et al. 1982). Another study of 178 patients with probable or possible AD, as assessed at a psychiatric hospital, found that 46 percent demonstrated primitive reflexes. Most common were the snout reflex (46 percent) and the grasp reflex (7 percent). There was a strong association between the presence of a grasp reflex and severe cognitive impairment (Burns et al. 1991a).

If you are aware of them, these reflexes can again be used for survival. Most important of all, remember that these responses are not deliberate but are involuntary.

The person who clasps too tightly onto your hand and will not let go is most likely locked into this pattern by the grasp reflex.

Some of the more commonly appearing primitive reflexes are described as follows:

Grasp reflex. The grasp reflex is the tight closing of the fingers, locked into flexion around an object. The stimulus is a light touch on the central area of the palm. To release the grasp reflex, do not struggle to pull the item or your hand away or try to unbend the fingers. This tends to increase the tightness of the grasp. Better approaches are to offer another interesting object to hold onto instead, or gently to rub or tap on the muscle bulk on the underside of the forearm, next to the body and just below the elbow. These are the muscle bodies that extend the fingers. Locate this area on your own body by laying your forearm on a table, with fingers bent, and feeling the change as you push your fingers straight out.

If these approaches fail and you absolutely must release a firm grasp on a person or a dangerous object, gently bend the wrist down toward the forearm; this action automatically releases the fixed fingers. This should be done with extreme caution with fragile bones and skin, and only if absolutely crucial. The best approach is not to stimulate this response unless you wish to use it. Some ways in which the grasp reflex can be useful are for

- holding on firmly during transfers or while rising from lying to sitting or standing
- grasping a spoon for eating
- grasping safe, interesting objects for self-directed activity

Suck reflex. The stimulus for the suck reflex is a light stroking of the lips; the response is the closing of the lips around the object. If this reflex is present, it can greatly interfere with eating. There are methods that can overcome the problem, but feeding people who have a positive suck reflex should be done only by skilled professionals or those who have been properly trained. Others should be very careful to avoid stimulating this reflex. Particular care must also be taken to limit access to inedible or dangerous objects that may be put in the mouth. The suck reflex can be used to assist the drinking of fluids through a straw or a special cup. Providing the agitated person who has a positive suck reflex with a safe, long-lasting food on which to suck (e.g., a bread stick) may be calming. Be very careful to guard against choking.

Rooting reflex. The stimulus for the rooting reflex is a light touch on the cheek or the corners of the mouth. When the rooting reflex is present, the response is a movement of the corner of the mouth toward the stimulus. Again, this reflex can interfere with eating and feeding, unless it is used carefully by a skilled clinician.

Snout reflex. The stimulus for the snout reflex is firm pressure (e.g., from a finger tip) in the midline groove of the upper lip. When the reflex is present the lips respond with a pursing/pouting movement. This reflex makes eating and feeding with a utensil very difficult, and care should be taken to avoid it in persons who have a positive response.

Gegenhalten response. The stimulus for the Gegenhalten response is passively moving the forearm from a flexed (bent) position to an extended (straight out) position. When the reflex is present there will be resistance to extension or a tightening of the muscles. This reflex can interfere with offering hand-over-hand guidance during dressing and exercise activities, such as throwing a ball or a beanbag. Avoid stimulating this reflex during care and other activities. Offer the object and encourage the person to extend his or her arms. Putting on blouses, shirts, and sweaters will be easier when the person is standing and the arms are already extended.

Positive supporting reaction. The stimulus for the positive supporting reaction is firm pressure on the bottom of the feet. If the positive supporting reaction is present, the response is the locking of the legs in full extension. This response is helpful in being able to move from sitting to standing; but it can be problematic when changing from standing to sitting, for instance, while being seated for a meal or a group. The person may remain standing and as rigid as a board. The best way to break up this reflex is to provide a stimulus that will encourage an automatic response to bend the knees and sit down. For persons who exhibit this reflex, having the table prepared and others seated around it is a help. Gently guide the person to the chair by placing your hands on the person's hips and his or her hands on the chair arms or the table. Use gentle downward pressure on the hips. Do not force, and above all, do not push on the head and shoulders.

Startle reflex. The stimulus for the startle reflex is a sudden, sharp noise or a sudden, unanticipated change in position. If the reflex is present, the person will fling arms and legs outward into extension and throw the head back, while extending the neck and back. Everyone jumps at the unexpected slamming of a door. However, the startle reflex is an extreme exaggeration of this response and can be stimulated by what may seem to be only a slight, sudden sound, such as a sneeze. It is *very* distressing to the person and may lead to agitation and/or a catastrophic reaction. Special care should be taken to provide a calm and quiet environment for all persons with ADRD. *Never* move the chair of a dependent person without telling him or her first.

5.3 Touch from the Non–Human Environment

Every effort should be made to provide stimulating, appropriate materials and furnishings that offer a variety of pleasing touch experiences. The touch of the environment also communicates caring and reassurance. Upholstery on furniture, in addition to being sturdy and stain-resistant, should be warm, soft, and comfortable. The feel of vinyl and other plastics is not pleasant, increases moisture buildup, and may contribute to skin breakdown. Breathable, washable fabric is safer and more pleasing. If plastics cannot be avoided, covering with a sheet increases comfort.

Sturdy, industrial-grade carpet is durable; is stain-resistant; is safer for walking; does not cause dangerous glare; dampens environmental sound, making conversation easier; and provides pleasing touch stimulation. It may not be practical to have an entire residential facility carpeted, but carpeting a sitting room or a living room makes the room a much more welcoming place and eases communication. Textures can be used in interior design in other ways, for both stimulation and touch communication.

- Place strips of interestingly textured carpet along walls to provide a tactile directional path to areas such as bathrooms and dining rooms.
- Outline doorways with differently textured paint, wallpaper, fabric, or carpet to help distinguish them from the corridor wall and provide a textured cue to room location.
- Use a textured daily calendar (e.g., made with fabric of various textures, wood strips, etc.).
- Install textured room/name plates. These can be made very simply, even with coffee stirrers painted in bright colors.
- Decorate walls with textured murals or wall hangings.
- Make use of textured state or provincial maps (see Chapter 6).

Provide individualized touch materials and experiences for stimulation and encouraging communication. These materials are described in more detail in Chapters 6 and 7, but some suggestions are listed below:

- Encourage pet visitation, which provides a living responsive touch experience, communication, and a nonthreatening opportunity for the person to express affection and nurturing.

- Provide plants that are nontoxic, withstand handling, and provide a variety of textures. For more information see the horticulture section in Chapter 5. Some suggestions are pothos, philodendron, Chinese evergreen, sansevieria, rubber plant, and scented geraniums.
- Provide adult textured books, balls, and tray covers.
- Ensure that clothing is comfortable, soft, and welcoming and has a variety of textures.
- Use decorator items of various textures (e.g., pillows, afghans, quilts, bedspreads, wallpaper, tablecloths, place mats).
- Make use of age appropriate, high-quality stuffed animals. I offer this suggestion with considerable hesitation. Soft, stuffed animals can be very comforting for some people with ADRD to hold and caress. However, the risk is that these animals are presented or talked about with the person in a childlike manner or to encourage the confused reality that these animals are, in fact, real. Such responses destroy the dignity of the person with ADRD and add to agitation. If the stuffed animal encourages even one person to talk to or treat the person as a child, a soft fabric handbag, book, or quilt should be substituted immediately. The self-esteem of the person with ADRD is under constant assault. If giving stuffed animals further diminishes adult dignity, they do more harm than good.

6.0 GESTURES

Gestures are a three-dimensional language that can be effective when words fail to get the point across. These include commonly accepted gestures, as well as demonstration using exaggerated movements, as in mime. Before using gestures, be very aware of any cultural differences in the meaning of these gestures. In addition to the many other cultural differences I discovered while living in India, I found that a slight variation on our North American wave actually signaled Come here! Gestures that were familiar in childhood will be best understood by the person with ADRD. When using gestures, as with verbal communication, make sure to face the person, alert him or her to your presence, and use slow, exaggerated movements. Moving too quickly may cause the message to be lost and may also cause agitation. Accompany gestures with the associated verbal cue and appropriate facial expression, to strengthen the impact of the message.

Encourage persons with ADRD to use gestures when they are unable to say what they want to say. Through modeling the use of gesture, they will get the idea. Some useful common gestures are:

- waving hello or goodbye
- beckoning (outstretching a hand and bringing it back to yourself)
- indicating a chair or place at the table with an outstretched hand
- mimicking and exaggerating movements to indicate functional activities such as washing hands and face, eating, brushing teeth, combing hair, using the telephone (To avoid confusion, be sure to use these movements only in the appropriate context.)
- pointing or indicating with the whole hand toward yourself or others as you identify yourself or others by name
- sliding your arm gently under the person's elbow, to indicate that you want the person to come with you

7.0 PERSONAL PRESENTATION

There is a great deal of truth to the expression "It's not so much what you say but how you say it." This is particularly true when communicating with persons with ADRD. While verbal language deteriorates, the nonverbal messages found in facial expression, voice tone, and body posture are very powerful methods of communication. By attending to these factors, we can develop an essential window on thoughts and feelings that can no longer be communicated with words. Of equal importance is how we put together our vocabulary of nonverbal language to get our message across to the person with ADRD. Words of welcome or instruction will be entirely lost if our faces are tense and frowning, our voice tone angry, and our body posture stiff and aloof. On the other hand, the invitation to "come with me" will be welcomed if we are smiling, speak in a warm voice tone, and lean respectfully toward the person as we speak. Volicer et al. (1988) have developed an excellent checklist of nonverbal behaviors to assist direct caregivers in monitoring comfort, pain, mood, etc.

7.1 Facial Expression

The expressions on our faces instantly convey a thousand words about what we are thinking or feeling. Some people have become very skilled at hiding their feelings and present a "good face" no matter what turmoil may be going on inside. When working with individuals with ADRD we must learn to be careful that our facial expressions match the messages we wish to send. Exaggerated facial expressions can be used very effectively to convey surprise, pleasure, concern, interest, caring, and other emotions.

Facial expression is also an excellent way for persons with ADRD to communicate with us. The social inhibitions of "keeping a straight face" are usually lost, and facial expression can become a window on thoughts or feelings that can no longer be communicated with words. While speaking and working, watch their faces. You will find there messages not only of pleasure, interest, and enjoyment, but also of bewilderment, anxiety, concern, fear, anger, distress, pain, embarrassment, and frustration. Watch carefully for these communications. Helping persons to communicate their concerns or distresses can reduce agitation and perhaps prevent a catastrophic reaction. It can also give an indication of developing illness or infection.

Central to communication through facial expression are the eyes. Consider that people often hide their eyes in order to hide feelings. Also consider how disconcerting it is to talk with someone or listen to a speaker who avoids making eye contact. For this reason, it is particularly essential to make eye contact when communicating. The person with ADRD usually has perceptual deficits and difficulties in understanding the environment, which require extra cues in order to get their attention and establish eye contact. Follow the suggestions in the verbal communication guidelines in order to gain attention, using gentle touch to alert the person to your presence. It is particularly important to face the person directly, in order to establish eye contact.

Voice tone should be warm, quiet, and calm. To compensate for hearing loss, lower the pitch of your voice. Body posture should be relaxed, leaning toward the person in acceptance and anticipation, but without interfering with personal space.

8.0 CONCLUSION

Through maximizing verbal communication and developing "first language" communication techniques of gestures, facial expression, voice tone, and body posture, the caregiver is able to share thoughts and feelings with the person with ADRD. The adult person retains his or her dignity and individuality, and does not become merely the "Alzheimer's patient" or the "demented patient."

As the disease progresses, there is little or no
hope of recovery of memory, but people do not
exist of memory alone. People have feelings,
imagination, desires, drives, will and moral being.
It is in these realms that there are ways to touch
our patients and let them touch us.

—D. Cohen and C. Eisdorfer

Group Work

1.0 THEORETICAL MODELS AND THERAPEUTIC METHODS: IMPLICATIONS FOR GROUP WORK

The information in the preceding three chapters has emphasized that there is no magic formula or secret recipe for working with individuals with ADRD, just as with any population. The unique nature of individual life experiences and the inherent variability of the disease make exacting specification of technique particularly useless. As in previous sections, general guidelines or premises for group work are offered.

A lack of specificity or precision should not, however, be mistaken for a haphazard or "anything goes" approach. In fact, order and consistency are of particular importance in working with individuals with ADRD. A focus, or unifying approach, is essential in order to transform a confusing conglomeration of approaches into a creative and adaptable mélange. One needs to develop an awareness of how the components of various approaches will best fit together to serve the needs and strengths of the population and the setting. What follows is a survey of some of the available ingredients (approaches) from which you can develop your own "recipes," judging amounts as experienced cooks do, not by formula, but "by the feel."

The nature of this eclectic approach is well illustrated by a favorite Nova Scotian specialty. Around Lunenberg, Nova Scotia, folks make a delectable dish called hodgepodge. It consists of the finest and freshest of summer vegetables, gently cooked to preserve their freshness and flavor, melded together with a delicate sauce of sweet cream, butter, and seasonings. Each presentation is unique to the cook and the ingredients available, but still recognizable as that fine local dish. Therapeutic group work with persons with ADRD does not have as long a history as hodgepodge. However, in my work I attempt to put together the best combination of various approaches, the approaches most suited to the particular individuals in my groups and those with which I personally feel most comfortable. Readers are invited to use the suggestions found in this book and elsewhere to develop their own unique hodgepodge. The following is a brief outline of the approaches from which I have drawn. Further reading is suggested in the bibliography.

1.1 The Developmental View of the Human Life Span

Reference was made in Chapter 1 to aging as a life-long process that begins at birth. Erik Erikson is a developmental psychologist who, along with his colleagues, has done a masterful job of researching and detailing the developmental and emotional tasks of each life stage. In Erikson's model, the emotional task of each life stage is depicted as one of resolving the conflict between two opposing tendencies. He describes the task of older adults as one of resolving the conflict of integrity versus despair (Erikson et al.

1986). Older adults struggle to put the events and experiences of their lives in order; to come to a clearer understanding of who they are and where they have been; to reaffirm the value of previous life experiences; to sum up their lives and to arrive at a wisdom, an understanding of their lives and the world around them. While the tasks of other life stages continue to a lesser or greater degree, depending on the individual, this focus on summing up, putting things in perspective, predominates.

Erikson and his colleagues (1986) have written an excellent book on this stage of life, *Vital Involvement in Old Age.* Both Eriksons were in their 80s at the time of writing, adding the weight of personal insight to their years of study and research. Their book is highly recommended to those who wish to learn more about this important aspect of growing old.

It is particularly vital that those who work with individuals with ADRD have an understanding of the emotional tasks of aging. The need to accomplish these tasks remains, whatever the nature of one's neurological deficits. Victims of ADRD, like all aging people, struggle to bring their lives into perspective. Their struggle is more difficult, more in need of facilitation, because of the ravages of the disease on their cognitive (e.g., memory, judgment, reasoning) and language capacities. In addition, they may be separated from the support and assistance of family members and friends by disease-associated changes in personality and behavior.

It is the responsibility of all caregivers to reaffirm the sense of self of persons with ADRD, to validate who they are and have been through caring, nonverbal interaction, guided reminiscence, and other techniques. This is the central and most essential goal of all activities with persons with ADRD. The need for and benefit from emotional expression and nurture continues even though—and especially because—other capacities deteriorate (Akerlund & Norberg 1986; Carnes 1984; Cohen 1988; Cohen & Eisdorfer 1986; David 1991; Davis 1986; Davis & Kirkland 1988; Edelson & Lyons 1985; Freeman 1987; Judd 1983; Mace 1990; Mace & Rabins 1981; Tarbox 1983; Volicer et al. 1988; Zgola 1987). It is important to recall here that the retention of emotional capacity and a relatively intact emotional memory are assets of persons with ADRD. The role of caregivers is to facilitate and nurture this emotional expression, which is so often made difficult by the deficits that accompany the disease.

The problem of negative attitudes toward aging has particular relevance in the context of developmental theories. In our youth-oriented society, aging is all too often perceived only as a time of loss, decline, and decay (Birren & Renner 1980; Butler 1975; Davis & Kirkland 1988; Greenblatt 1988; Henig 1988; Kite & Johnson 1988; Lonergrin 1990; Tarbox 1983).

Whether or not one has read all the right books, there tends to be a general understanding of what normal development is for a two-year-old child. This includes something about their physical capabilities (e.g., walking, beginning to talk in sentences) as well as emotional development (e.g., there would be few who have not heard about or experienced the terrible twos). This culturally accepted understanding continues throughout childhood and the various stages of adulthood. It is thought to be "normal," for instance, that someone in their 30s is preoccupied with work and household responsibilities and is generally physically capable of carrying out these activities.

So it goes until approximately age 65, when our cultural understanding runs aground. It becomes, instead, a negative stereotype that runs something like the following: life is finished; there is nothing further that can be accomplished or hoped for; it is all down hill from here, etc. Tragically, there is not a common appreciation of old age as the grand finale of the developmental life process; as a time of dynamic and meaningful personal growth, a time for integrating all that has been experienced and accomplished. The two-year-old's temper tantrums are an attempt at self-definition over and against his or her parents. The midlife crisis finds a middle-aged adult struggling with personal accomplishments to date. The older adult's struggle to put the events of life into perspective is little understood.

As has already been discussed, individuals with ADRD are in double jeopardy, because they suffer not only the stigmas and general misunderstandings associated with old age, but also those associated with mental illness. There is a widespread lack of understanding about ADRD in general. There is an even greater absence of appreciation for the emotional needs of the person with ADRD.

False and destructive views of persons with ADRD are widespread among both the general public and the health care community (Goodwin 1989; Greenblatt 1988; Tarbox 1983). Those who work with people with ADRD must strive to rid themselves of these popular, but false, stereotypes. The losses during the course of ADRD are many, but we must appreciate, above all, that these individuals are feeling human beings with emotional and developmental needs and that they do retain their capacity to respond to the care and nurturing of another. Perhaps the greatest danger to the well-being of individuals with ADRD is the tendency to treat them as nonpersons (Berdes 1988; Cohen & Eisdorfer 1986; Edelson & Lyons 1985; Jarvik & Winograd

1988; Lyman 1989; Reichenback & Kirchman 1991; Volicer et al. 1988).

The following clinical example is offered as one illustration of the need for, and response to, interventions that facilitate the aging person's need to sum up, to reflect on life.

> Although his language was less affected than other functions, John Angus was severely demented. He required full assistance to get dressed and frequently to eat his meals. He particularly enjoyed and benefited from an eating stimulation group. This group not only helped him to eat more independently, but it also improved his mood. He would sing along with the music, comment on how good the food was, help to make the biscuits, make jokes, and encourage other participants. On other occasions, the homelike setting at mealtime would trigger great sadness. He would weep as he recalled the happy meals with his wife and their years and times together. On one such occasion, he had been a happy and appreciative participant in the group, but also shed many tears for his much-loved and missed wife. He was consoled in his loss by me and other group members, and eventually resumed his happy disposition. As the meal came to a close, I began clearing up and helping the participants back to their rooms. John Angus said, with a contented smile on his face, "You take it easy now, I'll do the dishes. That's what I always did for Mom and it was a big help to her."
>
> Helped to re-experience emotionally both the joy of their lives together and his great sorrow at her death, John Angus was able to be at peace. He seemed to be saying, "I did my best to be a helpmate and I feel my wife appreciated it. I was a good husband and deserving of my wife's devotion." The group assisted him to work through his emotions and experiences. John Angus left the group feeling that his life, in this aspect, was affirmed.

1.2 Hierarchy of Needs

Another psychologist, Maslow, has also developed an interesting and useful theory for understanding basic human needs. Maslow's hierarchy of needs is traditionally depicted as a pyramid. However, this may not be the most descriptive representation. First, Maslow describes the need for feelings of self-esteem, usually found in the narrower portion of the pyramid, as virtually limitless. Second, and most pertinent to the focus of this book, Maslow states that the fulfilment of higher needs and self-actualization is particularly prominent during old age. In this light, the depiction of the hierarchy of needs in Figure 4-1 is suggested. In this illustration the basic needs form the foundation, with higher level needs expanding out from this and leading to self actualization (Maslow 1970; Munroe 1988).

Maslow understands human motivation as the drive to satisfy progressively more complex needs. As the most basic needs are satisfied, the individual is motivated to fulfil higher needs. This model has particular relevance for those working with the frail elderly, especially the mentally frail. The most basic human needs are physiological, the requirement for essentials such as food, water, shelter, and personal hygiene. For individuals severely disabled by ADRD, the focus of care so often is on meeting these most basic needs. Since these individuals often are unable to meet these needs independently, there is an undeniable necessity for caregivers to do so. The danger, however, is in assuming that when these basic needs are met, all their human needs are met. Nothing could be further from the truth. For the individual with ADRD, it is particularly urgent that needs for security, belonging, and self-esteem be addressed, in order that they too can strive toward accomplishing the highest level of need satisfaction, what Maslow calls self-actualization. Maslow describes individuals who have achieved self-actualization as having a clear, *integrated* understanding of who they are. This is akin to Erikson's final life goal of achieving *integrity*, of summing up. Maslow brings another perspective to this goal, what I see as the ultimate goal of all work with individuals with ADRD, the perspective of needs fulfilment and motivation. As the more basic needs are met, the individual is motivated or driven to fulfil higher-level, more complex needs, and finally to achieve an integrated sense of self.

As caregivers of persons with ADRD, our task is to enable and assist in the fulfilment of these needs. This is the purpose of the therapeutic interventions outlined in this book. This process can be illuminated by specifically examining Maslow's hierarchy of needs in relation to persons with ADRD.

The level of needs above physiological needs is described as security needs. These needs go beyond the mere availability of shelter and physical resources and encompass the need for predictability and stability in the environment, as well as the need for a sense of personal control over the environment. These issues are central in promoting function for individuals with

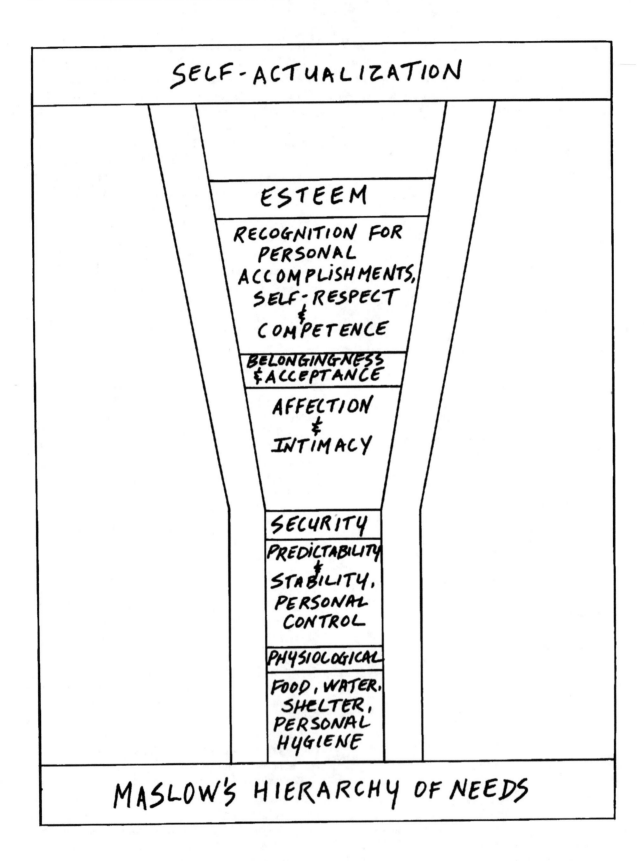

Figure 4-1 Hierarchy of Needs

ADRD, and are discussed in more detail in the environmental section of this chapter. Providing an opportunity for manageable, personal choice is also integral to meeting security needs.

Maslow describes the next level as the need for belonging and acceptance. Essential to this concept is acceptance of the person as himself or herself at the present moment. This is particularly crucial for the individual with ADRD, whose ability to accomplish complex—and often even simple tasks—is severely impaired by the disease. Here Maslow underlines the essential human need for what Rogers (1977) calls unconditional positive regard, irrespective of personal abilities or disabilities. Despite the limitations imposed by the disease, the person persists. Sadly, this personhood is often overshadowed or masked by the symptoms of the disease. Personnel in activities programs have a vital role to play in affirming and accepting the person as himself or herself. First and foremost, it is essential to treat the individual with ADRD as an adult with a unique and special personal life story. Activities programs should enable the expression of personal interests, values, talents, and wisdom. Sharing these expressions with other caregivers encourages others in meeting belonging needs. It is important to use projects from activities groups, as well as personal mementoes, pictures, furnishings, etc., to provide a concrete expression of personhood in residential rooms of long-term care settings. Personal space is particularly essential in communal living situations.

The next level of needs described by Maslow is esteem needs. At this level, the person has needs for recognition for personal accomplishments. It is here that the person with ADRD is most at risk of having unmet needs. The many disabilities related to the disease process severely interfere with the accomplishment of both complex and daily life tasks. It is here also that the role of the activity specialist is critical. On the basis of a careful assessment of persisting skills, the activities program encourages and enables continued accomplishments in leisure and daily activities, and reinforces the value of previous life experiences through reminiscence techniques.

Thus supported and enabled, the individual with ADRD can also achieve Maslow's highest level of need fulfilment, self-actualization.

2.0 ACTIVITY THEORY

Activity theory includes a diverse, and often contradictory, number of theories or ways of viewing the relationship between aging and involvement in activities. There is, however, agreement that involvement in meaningful, purposeful activity is an essential part of what it is to be human (Birren & Schaie 1990; Burgener & Barton 1991; Cohen & Eisdorfer 1986; Crabtree et al. 1990; Crepeau 1986; Dannefer 1989; Davis & Kirkland 1988; Duellman et al. 1986; Erikson et al. 1986; Greenblatt 1988; Hastings 1986; Hatter & Nelson 1987; Heacock et al. 1991; Kane & Kane 1987; Kirchman et al. 1982; Lawton 1985; Levy 1990; Mace 1990; OTA 1987; Ray & Heppe 1986; Sloane & Mathew 1991; Steinkamp & Kelly 1987; Trace & Howell 1991; Zgola 1987). Whether activities be related to work (e.g., paid jobs, volunteer efforts, babysitting), leisure (e.g., knitting, gardening, golf, reading), or activities of daily living (e.g., brushing teeth, visiting grandchildren, cooking supper), we all define who we are with reference to these activities and the roles associated with them (e.g., mother, friend, carpenter, Red Cross volunteer). The centrality of doing is so deep in our culture that it forms a part of the usual formal (How DO you DO?) and informal greeting (How are you DOING?). Lawton (1985) describes the powerful human need to do as follows: ". . . empirical evidence overwhelmingly supports the idea that both animals and people will create activity where none exists, as if the void of doing nothing or the same thing for too long was as aversive as having too many demands" (p. 131).

Four main theories have been proposed as a way of understanding the relationship between activity and aging. *Disengagement theory* proposes that there is a gradual withdrawal from engagement in activities as people age, and that this pattern is necessary for the health of the individual and society (Cumming & Henry 1961). By contrast, *activity theory* proposes that the more active a person is while aging (i.e., the greater the number of activities engaged in), the healthier and happier he or she is (Kart & Manard 1981). Neither theory is strongly supported by research measuring the life satisfaction of older adults (Crepeau 1986; Howe 1988; Steinkamp & Kelly 1987). Both theories are now commonly regarded as too simplistic (Howe 1988). Just as there is no formula for living at any life stage, common sense suggests that there is no formula for a satisfying and happy old age; e.g., as activity theory suggests, do more and you will be happier. Indeed, there is valid concern that the popular acceptance of activity theory is promoting still another dangerous misperception about aging. That is, if the aging person just keeps active enough and puts mind and body to it, he or she does not need to experience the effects of aging! Enter the era of the "super elder" and all of its attendant problems! This is just as destructive as the negative stereotype associated with disengagement theory: the old are withdrawn, incompetent, and disinterested.

Neither activity theory nor disengagement theory takes adequate account of the effect of purposeful human activity on the life course (Dannefer 1989) or the uniqueness of an individual. These theories are, however, part of both the popular belief system and the foundation for much social science research. Both must be considered carefully by those working with the elderly.

The third theory, *continuity theory* (Atchley 1980, 1989) attempts to incorporate not just the simplistic quantity of activity, but also the quality of activity. This theory proposes that those who are most satisfied with life, as they age, are those who are able to continue life-long activities or find appropriate adaptations or substitutes. This view of activity sits most comfortably with my experience, personal and professional, with aging persons as well as with the information in the literature (Crepeau 1986; Butler & Gleason 1985; Dannefer 1989; Davis & Kirkland 1988; Duellman et al. 1986; Greenblatt 1988; Hastings 1986; Hatter & Nelson 1977; Howe 1988; Kirchman et al. 1982; Mace 1990; OTA 1987; Ray & Heppe 1986; Steinkamp & Kelly 1987; Zgola 1987). It takes account of unique individual values, habits, and roles (Kielhofner 1983) and allows for the need to alter activity patterns because of age-related or other life changes.

A fourth theory, the *socioenvironmental theory* of aging, places these individual expectations for activity within the context of the social environment. This theory, developed by Jaber Gubrium, proposes that life satisfaction in old age is dependent on a balance between the personal and environmental resources available for activity and individual expectations (Crepeau 1986). Socioenvironmental theory rounds out our understanding of the relationship between aging and activity by including not only individual goals and abilities, but also those of the social environment.

As an occupational therapist, my colleagues and I have come to appreciate the profound importance of activity not only in maintaining health and life satisfaction but as a therapeutic medium to restore, develop, or maintain function in all realms and enhance associated life satisfaction (Arnetz 1982; Birren & Schaie 1990; Crepeau 1986; Davis & Kirkland 1988; Fernie et al. 1990; Judd 1983; Kielhofner 1983; Kirchman et al. 1982; Levy 1990; Lilley & Jackson 1990; Munson 1991; Mace 1990; Reichenback & Kirchman 1991; Sloane & Mathew 1991; Smith et al. 1986; Szekias 1986; Trace & Howell 1991; Zgola 1987). Longitudinal studies (including Jarvik's study of 134 pairs of aging twins and other time-limited studies) support the

importance of continued involvement in the activities of daily life, as well as physical, cognitive, and emotional activities, to successful aging (Arbuckle et al. 1986; Birren & Schaie 1990; Butler & Gleason 1985; Cohen 1988; Crabtree et al. 1990; Craik et al. 1987; Heacock et al.1991; Henig 1988; Kane & Kane 1987; Winocur et al. 1987). There is strong evidence that continued cognitive activities may be especially important to successful aging (Cohen 1988; Henig 1988).

The importance of activities to the quality of life has also been recognized by a federal law, the nursing home reform section of the Omnibus Budget Reconciliation Act of 1987 (OBRA), commonly referred to as OBRA87. As part of the assurance of quality of life under this law, nursing facilities certified by Medicare and Medicaid must conduct a comprehensive assessment of each resident's functional capacities, including activities potential (Perschbacher 1991). Kane and Kane (1987) conducted a review of long-term care, including a review of the empirical literature on various activity programs. They conclude as follows:

> The implications of the material we have reviewed seem inescapable. The preponderance of the evidence is that in a nursing home little things mean a lot, and that the choices and control that are so important to Americans throughout their lifespan actually sustain health and well-being in long term care facilities. (p. 244)

Illness, disease, and/or a change in life circumstance can greatly interfere with an individual's capacity "to do," or to participate in activities. The effect of ADRD on the capacity to do is staggering. During the course of the disease there is hardly a facet of life that is not affected. Initially, the person with ADRD experiences difficulty with complex functional and leisure activities such as writing a check or following a knitting pattern. As the disease progresses, difficulties arise in carrying out the most fundamental of human activities, such as feeding oneself or going to the bathroom. Without the support and facilitation of others, the experience of persons with ADRD is one of ever-increasing failure in their attempts to do. The effect on self-esteem is devastating. For example, there is a strong association between lack of activities and the presence of depression in persons with ADRD (Teri & Logsdon 1991). And yet, the observed need to do, to be actively engaged in life, persists. Even in the severely demented we continue to see activity—what may appear from the outside to be totally purposeless and repetitive activity: ceaselessly rubbing the chair tray; wringing the hands, over and over, hour after hour; perpetually pacing the same route over and over; refolding the same worn tissue again and again; repeating the same, apparently meaningless, phrase so many times that those around are driven to distraction.

This speaks to me of the persisting need to do; the desperation to continue activity, even when neurological and physical deficits stand in the way of independent adult activity. The basic human need to find pleasure and satisfaction in purposeful activity, to exert mastery over the environment, persists. This need is spoken of by Cohen and Eisdorfer (1986) as follows:

> Perhaps the most important concern of many patients is the need to participate as actively as possible for as long as possible. (p. 64)

> Even the most impaired patients can be active if the tasks are simple enough. (p. 235)

> . . . dementia is not a hopeless condition for which nothing can be done. Patients are human beings—first, last and always. They usually live for years with the disease, and those are long and difficult years. The challenge during that time is to maximize an individual's ability to function at the highest possible level. (p. 221)

Disease-associated defects in initiation, planning, problem solving, motor ability, etc. make it progressively more difficult for the person with ADRD to organize his or her own activities. However, by adapting the environment—using nonverbal communication, breaking activities down into manageable steps, and other specialized techniques detailed in this book—involvement in the essential activities of self-care, work, and leisure can become a source of satisfaction rather than one of frustration. It can and should be the role of an activities program to reconnect the individual with meaningful activities that will support self-definition as an adult who is capable of acting in a purposeful and personally satisfying way.

3.0 LEARNED HELPLESSNESS

At some point in our lives we have all felt totally helpless, completely vulnerable to events around us; there are times when it seems as if no matter what we do, there is no way to change how things turn out. This feeling might overcome us while watching a loved one die of a fatal illness or as the result of an accident. The feeling might be triggered even by something less personally traumatic, such as seeing the newly sprouted garden laid low by a freak snowstorm. For most people these experiences are devastating, but they do eventually pick themselves up and start again. On the other hand, we also may have met someone who seems to have been rendered totally inactive and apathetic by difficulties, be they large or small. It is perplexing to observe these individuals, who, as seems plain to almost everyone else, could remedy their own problems; instead they simply fold their hands.

When Martin Seligman was a graduate student in psychology, he happened to observe the same pattern in laboratory dogs. This observation triggered Seligman's curiosity. He and his colleagues began a series of laboratory and clinical investigations into the phenomenon of learned helplessness, using both animal and human subjects. Based on these extensive investigations in the laboratory and the "real" world, Seligman developed his theory of learned helplessness (Seligman 1975). There is persuasive evidence that if an individual learns, through repeated experience, that his or her actions have little effect on the outcome of a situation, whether the outcome is positive or negative, the individual will be rendered helpless in situations in which actions could make a difference. Seligman stresses that it is not so much that events do not have positive outcomes, but that the individuals feel that they have no control over what happens. This state of helplessness includes a loss of motivation, a negative mind set, and emotional distress.

Those who wish to read further in this fascinating area are referred to the works of Abramson et al. 1978; Avorn and Langer 1982; Foy and Mitchell 1990; Garber and Seligman 1980; Hunt 1988; Langer and Benevento 1978; Langer and Rodin 1976; LeSage et al. 1989; Rodin 1986; Solomon 1982, 1990; Teitelman 1982.

Learned helplessness has great relevance for those who work with individuals with ADRD. All older people are prone to its effects as the physical and psychosocial losses associated with aging confront them (Foy & Mitchell 1990; Teitelman 1982). For individuals with ADRD these losses are compounded by the progressive loss of memory and other cognitive abilities. Surely it is difficult to imagine a situation in which an individual would be more likely to feel that outcomes were beyond their control. Unable to manage their daily routines independently; rendered incapable of interpreting, and hence predicting, much of what goes on around them; undermined in their ability to communicate and remember, the individual with ADRD may rage to assert control, or as is often observed, they may simply give up.

Consider, for example, mealtime in an institutional setting. Whether the residents are hungry or not, whether they like corned beef hash or not, whether they prefer white bread or whole wheat is frequently of no consequence. Whatever their wishes or actions, the meal trays appear three times a day, 365 days a year. Is it puzzling that some with ADRD may stare apathetically into space and make no attempt to eat when reminded? And yet, they readily consume that same meal when it is fed to them. Obviously, there are many factors involved here, but learned helplessness is surely one of them. Their actions or desires about meals have no effect on the outcome. They will be fed anyway.

Despite impaired memory and difficulty with conventional learning, the person with ADRD is particularly prone to learned helplessness. It is important to distinguish between learning facts, such as the day of the week, or actions, such as putting on a shirt, and other learning that takes place at an emotional or "gut" level. Learned helplessness is primarily emotional learning about the feeling of not being in control (Seligman 1975). As was discussed in Chapter 2, persons with ADRD retain the capacity for emotional memory and emotional experience (Cohen and Eisdorfer 1986; Greenblatt 1988; Volicer et al. 1988; Zgola 1987).

What are the implications of learned helplessness for working with persons with ADRD? Briefly stated, they are as follows:

Encourage positive action. Demonstrate constantly, by verbal and nonverbal responses, that the individual's actions (e.g., a smile, a hand extended, a gift of a shared snack offered) do have an effect on outcomes (e.g., a smile returned, a hand warmly clasped, a gift accepted). "Forced exposure to the fact that responding produces reinforcement is the most effective way of breaking up learned helplessness" (Seligman 1975, 99).

Offer as much personal control and choice as possible. It is important that the choices offered be manageable, that is, within the individual's capability. Too much choice can be overwhelming. Some suggestions of choices are whether to have coffee or tea, which dress or shirt to wear, what flowers to select for a bouquet. For the most impaired individuals, choices should be limited to two items; more choices become overwhelming. The positive effect of offering choice on alertness and affect has been demonstrated (Keller et al. 1989; Rodin 1986; Rodin & Langer 1977, 1980; Solomon 1990).

Provide a reassuring and predictable order to the events of the day and each particular activity. This may seem, at first, to contradict offering choice. However, a predictable order of general events is reassuring.

Everyone requires a context, a certain routine, in order to function. Within this context, choice about individual and personal matters such as the kind of eggs for breakfast, the music for exercise class, or the kind of cookie for break provides an opportunity for personal choice. As Seligman (1975) notes, when events are predictable anxiety is removed and the sense of personal control is increased. Consistency and structure are particularly important for persons with ADRD, since their deficits interfere with their ability to provide structure for themselves.

Provide success experiences. Because of their disabilities, persons with ADRD are continuously confronting situations in which their actions meet with no success. Involvement in purposeful activities at which they can succeed gives them a sense of control. Choosing suitable activities requires ongoing assessment of capabilities by staff. Success experiences help to immunize the individual against helplessness and improve self-esteem (Davis & Kirkland 1988; Foy & Mitchell 1990; Seligman 1975; Teitelman 1982).

4.0 ENVIRONMENTAL THEORIES

We are all profoundly affected by our physical and social environment; we can feel uplifted and encouraged by the bright, welcoming furnishings and decor of a friend's home or threatened and intimidated by the formality and intensity of a corporate cocktail party. Lawton has made a particular study of the impact of the environment on the elderly (1980, 1981, 1982, 1983, 1985). On the basis of his extensive research, he developed his theory of "environmental docility." Lawton proposes that an individual becomes increasingly dependent on and affected by the environment as his or her capabilities decrease. This theory is well supported by theorists and clinicians (Calkins 1988; Carnes 1984; Coons 1991a, 1991b; Davis 1986; Davis & Kirkland 1988; Edelson & Lyons 1985; Greenblatt 1988; Henig 1988; Mace 1990; Munson 1991; Skolaski-Pellitteri 1985; Sloane and Mathew 1990; Tarbox 1983; Volicer et al. 1988; Wister 1989; Zgola 1987).

A supportive or prosthetic environment is particularly crucial for individuals with ADRD, since the disease process results not only in decreasing mental and physical capabilities but a decreasing ability to adapt their behavior to the environment. Consequently it is essential that the environment, both physical and psychosocial, be adapted to their needs. Chapter 1 contains some specific suggestions for adapting the physical environment to compensate for the physical changes associated with aging.

Environmental interventions that support remaining function and/or compensate for the deficits associated with ADRD are among the most effective treatments currently available to us (Calkins 1988; Coons 1991b; Corcoran & Gitlin 1991; Davis & Kirkland 1988; Edelson & Lyons 1985; Hiatt 1987a; Hyde 1989; Johnson 1989; Karlinsky & Sutherland 1990; Mace 1990; Munson 1991; OTA 1987; Sloane & Mathew 1990; Volicer et al. 1988; Zgola 1987). Since ADRD results in progressive disability, treatment to maintain function must be ongoing. The environment is a constant feature; if adapted to become a prosthetic or therapeutic environment, it becomes a potent source of ongoing treatment. Interventions such as reducing the level of unnecessary stimulation have resulted in increasing nutrient intake and reducing the use of restraints (Cleary et al. 1988). Redesigning the dining room has resulted in a decrease in aggressive behavior (Negley & Manley 1990). Environmental camouflage of unlocked exits reduced the number of attempts to leave a specialty unit (Namazi et al. 1989). The introduction of stimulus objects for manipulation resulted in a calmer mood and reduced agitation among persons with dementia who had severe behavioral problems (Mayers & Griffin 1990).

A one-year study of 12 residents of a dementia specialty unit that paid particular attention to the environment found improved functional performance for 11 of these residents in the areas of language/conversation, social interaction, attention/awareness, and spatial orientation (McCracken & Fitzwater 1990). In addition, 6 persons improved in bowel and bladder continence, and there was a reduction in the number of catastrophic reactions during toileting.

Empirical research, such as that in the examples just cited, has begun to detail and document the types of environmental interventions that are most effective for individuals with ADRD. Although there is agreement that the proper environment is crucial, there is, as yet, only limited research to help to define precisely the nature of this environment. There is some very interesting work currently in progress at the Corrine Dolan Alzheimer's Center in Cardon, Ohio, a facility with two identical special care units specifically intended for applied environmental research (Carey 1991; Namazi et al. 1989).

The following general guidelines are based on the clinical literature and the available empirical research on ADRD and the environment (Calkins 1988; Cleary et al. 1988; Coons 1991a, 1991b; Davis & Kirkland 1988; Edelson & Lyons 1985; Heacock et al. 1991; Hiatt 1987a; Hyde 1989; Johnson 1989; Karlinsky & Sutherland 1990; Mace 1990; Munson 1991; Namazi et al. 1989; Negley & Manley 1990; OTA 1987; Volicer et al. 1988; Zgola 1987).

The variability of both the symptoms and the capabilities of the patients make developing precise guidelines impractical. As a result, the following suggested guidelines fall into two main categories. First, there are those which prompt or encourage functional behavior and secondly, those which compensate for disabilities. In addition, in some variables, such as the appropriate level of stimulation, there are apparent paradoxes which can only be resolved by careful evaluation of the particular residents, the setting, and the available resources in staff and materials.

4.1 Environments That Promote Functional Behavior

Environments that promote functional behavior must have certain characteristics.

The environment should be familiar. A familiar, homelike environment provides cues for functional behavior (such as feeding oneself) and sociability, thus making use of persisting skills in procedural and emotional memory. One study of fifteen persons with AD found that their functional spatial skills were the same as cognitively well seniors in a familiar environment. In an unfamiliar environment the persons with AD did not perform as well (Liu et al. 1991). Kirasic (1989) reported that older adults solved spatial problems as well as did younger adults when the environment was familiar. An institutional environment can be made more homelike by

- using comfortable, noninstitutional furnishings and familiar furniture arrangements (e.g., a kitchen table for conversation)
- adding plants, pictures, pets, wall hangings
- eliminating institutional features, such as the nursing station
- using decor and design like those of a home (e.g., wallpaper and/or warm colors on the walls, meals served family style in the dining room)

To promote functional behavior in self-care and eating, it is especially important that bathrooms and dining rooms be as much like those in a normal home as possible. Toilet stalls in institutional bathrooms may not look at all like places to urinate and may lead to indiscriminate urination. One must sometimes trade off the greater physical ease of adapted bathroom equipment, such as lever taps or bath benches, for familiarity, which promotes function.

The dining area and the food service should look, sound, and smell as much like a home as possible. Food cooked in institutional kitchens, isolating the appetizing aromas, and served on multicourse trays does not provide familiar cues to stimulate the procedural memory for eating.

The environment should be appropriate for adults. The setting should look as much like a regular community home as possible, making use of good-quality pictures, photos, and other types of interior decorations. Well-meaning efforts to compensate for a bland institutional environment with construction-paper decorations, juvenile craft projects, and cuddly infant toys can make an adult residence look like a nursery school. A helpful question to ask is "Would you put this up in your home?"

The residents themselves should be dressed appropriately for their age and the time of day. The wearing of pajamas or hospital gowns in the daytime conveys a very powerful message of dependence and illness to the person, the caregivers, and visitors. The environment for individuals with ADRD must facilitate wellness and function by focusing on a social, as opposed to a medical, model of care (Leverett 1991). Indeed, this is consistent with the fact that, until the late stages, the symptoms of ADRD are primarily behavioral.

The environment should provide opportunities for reminiscence. Because persons with ADRD have disease-associated deficits in language and cognitive function, actual objects cue memories better than do verbal cues. The use of vintage (or reproduction) furnishings and pictures related to familiar local scenes and the display of familiar vintage items (e.g., kerosene lamps, an old-fashioned apple peeler) provide such opportunities. The items can also be displayed in hutches or plexiglass cases, if safety is a concern. It is essential to include such items during group activities and to make an opportunity to provide access on a regular basis.

The environment should provide opportunities for familiar activity. In addition to group activities, the focus of this book, it is important that the environment itself allow for familiar, independent activity. Household and kitchen activities such as preparing vegetables, mopping, sweeping, vacuuming, washing and drying dishes, and folding laundry are all familiar adult activities with an obvious purpose that can be done by the individual with ADRD. Other activity opportunities can be provided by having available plants or gardens to tend; wood to sand or polish; interactive artwork or a safe wall gym (made up of various textures and moving parts); books, magazines, and newspapers to look at; paper, envelopes, and pens for writing or folding; and such things as a telephone and a piano. Opportunities for exercise and movement can be provided by having a safe wandering path (indoors and/or outdoors), rocking chairs, and exercise bikes. Pacing and wandering can be good outlets for energy and in one study were associated with better physical health (Cohen-Mansfield et al. 1991). In that study, pacing was more likely when the environment was well lit and the noise level was low.

4.2 Paradoxical Variables

The level of sensory stimulation, opportunity for manageable choice, and the need for privacy are paradoxical variables. It is important to achieve the appropriate balance between the extremes of excess and insufficiency in these paradoxical variables. Determining the appropriate level is very much dependent on the particular setting and the individuals involved, and is arrived at only by careful assessment.

Determine the appropriate level of sensory stimulation. Sensory stimulation is essential and should include an array of the colors, smells, textures, and sounds that comprise any home environment. Since some of these materials may be restricted for reasons of safety or institutional policy, an extra effort must be made to provide self-directed, individual, or group opportunities for sensory stimulation. Inappropriate sensory stimulation is an overabundance of these stimuli, which is overwhelming and incomprehensible to the person. The extra stimulation of the comings and goings of staff, smell of institutional cleansers, disruptive intercoms, blaring radio or television, and other such institutional noises are inappropriate. The key is to arrive at an appropriate level of stimulation to avoid sensory deprivation, but not so much stimulation that there is sensory overload. Sensory overload can be caused by too much stimulation (e.g., too many people or too much noise) or sensory input that is incomprehensible (e.g., the two-dimensional stimulation of TV). Sensory overload causes additional problems with attention and may lead to agitation and distress (further information on this topic is found in Chapter 7).

Colors in walls, furnishings, and draperies can do a great deal to enhance environmental stimulation (Christenson 1990; Cooper 1985; Mace 1990), but some colors should be avoided. White sets a cold, sterile tone and also increases glare. Black and brown are somber and difficult to distinguish; pastels are also difficult to distinguish. Colors in the blue-green wavelength should be avoided because they are difficult for the older eye to distinguish. Because the lens of the eye yellows with age, all colors will appear more muddy. To overcome this effect, some have advocated the use of bright, primary colors in environments for the elderly. Naturally, this is not a general principle and the use must be appropriate to the context. Too much would be overwhelming, such as an entire room painted brilliant blue, and serve little useful purpose.

Primary colors are probably most useful as a way to identify smaller, important objects, such as self-care equipment (e.g., toothbrushes, combs), or to accentuate doorways, stair risers, etc. In fact, these objects are more visible not so much because of the color itself, but because of the contrast it creates. When using contrast, objects or signs are more visible when the background is significantly darker or lighter than the featured item. Lack of contrast can also be used as a safety measure to make exit doorways, cupboards, etc., less visible to the person with ADRD.

There is no body of research that confirms that particular colors set a mood or tone (Mace 1990). The effect of a color scheme is determined by a range of other features such as how it can be combined with textures, furniture arrangement, and lighting as well as the individual's associations with those colors. Some commonly accepted associations with particular colors (Christenson 1990) are that light oranges, yellows, and corals are lively and cheerful; mid-reds and light greens (not blue-greens but in the yellow-green spectrum) are calming and relaxing; pale coral and peach are warm, and encourage socialization.

One can overcome the sometimes antiseptic smells in an institution by using scented plants, natural air fresheners such as potpourri, simmering cinnamon sticks, essential oils, baking and, of course, fresh air where possible.

Provide opportunities for manageable choice. Because of cognitive losses in such skills as judgment, decision making, and reasoning, the individual with ADRD requires a consistent environment. To avoid confusion there needs to be a reassuring structure to the routine of the day, the arrangement of furniture, and other constant aspects of the environment. However, within this structure, it is essential that the person have opportunities for manageable choice, which reduces frustration by giving a sense of personal competency and control. Opportunities for choice can be made in areas such as which shirt to wear, whether to have coffee or tea, whether to dress before or after breakfast, etc. For the severely impaired, choice between more than two options is unmanageable. Groups provide an excellent opportunity for offering choice.

Provide for privacy as well as encouraging socialization. One of the most difficult adjustments for the person in long-term care is the loss of privacy. This is especially true in the case of shared bedrooms. The resident requires, at the least, a place for safely storing personal possessions and a curtain for privacy.

The issue of personal space and privacy is particularly crucial for persons with ADRD. They may well feel a need for a privacy but be unable to move to create it or to express these feelings. Consequently, when they feel overcrowded or that their privacy has been invaded, they may become agitated, restless, and upset. Caregivers must be sure to protect privacy and respect personal space. Oftentimes personal space is identified with a particular chair or place at the table. This attachment may seem irrational and rigid, and unfortunately is sometimes not respected by staff. Persons with ADRD, particularly those living in communal situations, need these concrete expressions of personal space. They define something secure and familiar in a larger environment that becomes less and less understandable.

Protecting personal space is further complicated by the tendency of some persons with ADRD to rummage in others' possessions. This is undoubtedly related to orientation and perceptual difficulties. They are searching for familiar possessions, which they are not able to find or recognize. Other residents require a secure storage space for personal possessions. Residents with ADRD may benefit from portable personal storage space, such as a purse, large bag, briefcase, or "fanny pack."

Providing maximal orienting and way-finding cues to identify individual rooms is especially important. For some, using a half-door or Dutch door to bedrooms satisfies the need for a sense of privacy but still allows for interaction with the rest of the unit. Privacy during bathing and toileting is particularly essential. When physical assistance is required for these activities, staff must also be sure to protect individual dignity. Communal bathrooms must have doors that close.

On the other hand, the individual with ADRD continues to have a need to socialize and to spend time with peers and family. Disease-associated deficits often make it difficult for the person to take the initiative in socialization. The environment should support socialization by providing comfortable and cozy conversation areas of manageable size, such as small groupings in a larger living room and seating in hallways and alcoves. Private, quiet areas for socialization and family visits are essential, as the daily comings and goings of the facility are too disruptive for the person with ADRD. Use of a table as a focal point for visiting and conversation is a helpful cue for socialization.

4.3 Environmental Characteristics That Assist Persons with ADRD To Compensate for Deficits

The environment should be unambiguous and understandable. The physical environment should avoid abstract designs in wallpaper, flooring, pictures, and fabrics. Because of cognitive deficits, persons with ADRD may be confused and even frightened by such designs.

Patterns on the floor can be particularly troublesome as they may appear to be a change in depth or look like objects that should be picked up. Avoid using objects that look like something with another use. For example, some patients may try to eat table shuffleboard pieces because they look like cookies. Others may urinate in a wastebasket placed too near the toilet. Use color and texture to distinguish between objects and the background, especially to distinguish the handrail from the wall, dishes from the table, food from the plate, self-care equipment from the counter, and the toilet from the floor and walls. Many with ADRD are confused and frightened by mirrors because they no longer recognize their own reflections.

The environment should provide cues for prompting and way finding (Figure 4-2). Label the doors for important rooms such as the bathroom and the dining room. Use contrast in color and intensity. Light lettering on a darker background provides the greatest contrast. Signs should be at eye level, to avoid having to tip the head back. Multimodal or redundant cuing is helpful. For example, the dining room can be identified by a lettered sign, a picture of food or eating, a canopy over the door, signs with arrows pointing to the dining room, a textured or colored path on the wall, and a distinguishing color or texture separating the door itself from the surrounding wall. Label dresser drawers and kitchen cupboards with words and/or pictures.

Cues must also be provided to assist the individual to locate his or her own room. It may require considerable individualized problem solving to arrive at a meaningful, identifying feature for a particular person. However, this is especially important in a setting in which there are long corridors with rooms that all look the same. As with other areas, doorways and doors should be distinguished from the corridor walls by using contrast and differences in color and texture. There should be a clear, large-print nameplate at eye level. This can

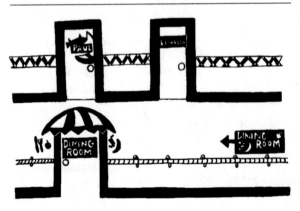

Figure 4-2 Cues for Prompting and Way Finding

be textured using fabric, popsicle sticks, quick clay, or other materials. Making these personalized name plates is an excellent group activity.

Every effort should be made to personalize rooms and the environment with color schemes, personal furniture, and pictures. Important pictures or items of particular significance, displayed near the door, may also help with way finding (for example, a collage of fabric and sewing materials for a seamstress). Family and caregivers should collaborate to develop a pictorial autobiography, which helps staff to know the whole person and reinforces the value of previous life experiences. Tapes of favorite music are reassuring, and provide an opportunity for emotional expression as well as helping to personalize the environment. Opportunities for creative self-expression in familiar activities, guided by the group leader's knowledge of the person, should be provided in activity groups and on a one-to-one basis. Concrete products from these activities should be displayed.

The environment should provide reality assurance. In addition to the importance of familiarity, environmental cues should provide reassuring, orienting information. Clocks should be easy-to-read numerical ones hung at eye level or set in familiar places such as the bedside table. Clocks that tick or chime not only call attention to the time of day but also are familiar and provide auditory stimulation. It is essential that all clocks be set at the same time. Colorful and easily read calendars should have the days marked off to aid orientation. Larger calendars using textural and visual (e.g., fabric) numbers and letters are stimulating. Plants should be real, not plastic. Wall murals (e.g., of outdoor scenes) that are too realistic can be disorienting if, for example, they show a spring scene and it is autumn outside. Accessible windows and outdoor spaces provide the most understandable cues for orientation to season and to time of day. Familiar, adult, seasonal decorations (e.g., Christmas decorations or a pumpkin at Halloween) aid in orientation. This was strikingly demonstrated by an elderly woman in the middle stage of ADRD during her hospitalization for pneumonia. She was unable to say the year, the day of the week, or what building she was in, but she stated—without hesitation—that it was December. Undoubtedly, she was cued by the poinsettia on her bedside table and by the hospital corridors, which were brightly decorated for Christmas.

The environment should be free of hazards. Remove or lock up all hazardous materials such as medications, sharp tools and knives, cleaning supplies, and poisonous plants. Many common house plants such as poinsettia, dieffenbachia, and the Jerusalem cherry are in fact toxic. Avoid sharp-cornered furniture. Limit access to hot water, electrical outlets, appliances, and other potential hazards. Avoid clutter and items such as scatter rugs, which may cause falls. Provide a security system or camouflage exits for those who may wander from the premises. Painting doorways the same color as the surrounding walls or disguising them with cloth strips are effective camouflage techniques (Namazi et al. 1989). For an individual who falls while climbing out of bed, placing the mattress on the floor is a safer option.

The environment should compensate for physical deficits. In the later stages of the disease, the person with ADRD will require seating and positioning assistance to maintain an upright posture for comfort, promoting maximal respiratory function, and safe and comfortable eating. Seating needs should be assessed and prescribed by a qualified occupational therapist. At all stages, it is essential to provide chairs of a proper height for easy rising and access to tables used for eating and other activities (see Chapter 1). Knees and hips should be bent at approximately 90 degrees, and feet should be flat on the floor. Chairs should have arms to make getting up easier.

4.4 The Psychosocial Environment

For all older people, the psychosocial environment has a particularly potent effect on behavior and function. The destructive consequence of negative attitudes and stereotyping of the aged was discussed in Chapter 1.

When we work with persons with ADRD, we come with ourselves and our attitudes. These attitudes and the actions they inform have a powerful impact on the psychosocial environment and hence the performance of the persons with whom we are working. If individuals with ADRD are expected by those around them to be unilaterally incompetent and to be unable to exert control in any aspect of their lives, it is virtually guaranteed that, vulnerable as they are, this is how they will perform (Cohen & Eisdorfer 1986; Davis & Kirkland 1988; Greenblatt 1988; Libow 1978; Rodin 1986; Rodin & Langer 1980; Ruskin 1983; Solomon 1990; Winnet 1989). If, on the other hand, they are treated with dignity as adult individuals with unique capabilities and personal experiences and with the same basic human needs as you and I, the door to potential is opened: potential for them to be the best they can be and hence to understand themselves as worthwhile and capable; potential for you and me to share in the beauty of seeing others' lives come to fulfilment.

In order for this to take place the caregiver of persons with ADRD must first come to a personal understanding of how it feels to be ill, what it means to grow old, and how to deal with death. These are hard questions with very personal answers, which are fuzzy at that. Nonetheless they are essential considerations. Unless these issues are faced, precious time with persons with ADRD will be wasted, or worse still, will be damaging, as caregivers displace personal fears of illness, aging, infirmity, and death with negative attitudes toward the elderly themselves.

A psychosocial environment that conveys unconditional positive regard and a supportive physical environment provides a milieu that supports an optimal quality of life and the maximal functioning of individuals with ADRD.

5.0 REALITY ORIENTATION*

Reality orientation (RO) was the first comprehensive attempt at group work with the disoriented, institutionalized elderly. Thirty years ago, the prevalent mood of both patients and staff on the long-term geriatric units of American psychiatric hospitals was one of hopelessness and despair. The approach to care was custodial, with an emphasis on physical maintenance. There was no sustained belief in, or effort at, rehabilitation with these disabled elderly patients. Patients spent most of their days sitting, staring into space, doing nothing for themselves, disengaged from both each other and their environment. Staff morale on these units was extremely low. It was described by one employee as a "waiting room for hell" (Folsom 1968, 294).

The psychogeriatric unit at Winter Veterans Administration Hospital, Topeka, Kansas, was typical of its time. It was on this unit that Dr. James Folsom initiated a pilot rehabilitation project. This project was not a singular introduction of a weekly treatment group, but a 24-hour-a-day comprehensive and innovative restructuring of the approach to care for patients who had, up to this point, been assumed to be beyond rehabilitation. The program was based on a total team rehabilitation approach and included not only what later became known as reality orientation therapy but also recreational, occupational, and physical therapy. Existing nursing staff served as the primary agents to reactivate, reorient, and promote independence. For these patients, who had been passive recipients of care for 20 years or more, this new approach, at least by anecdotal ac-

Source: From "Reality Orientation Thirty Years Later: Are We Still Confused?" by C. Bowlby, 1991, *Canadian Journal of Occupational Therapy, 58,* pp. 114–122. Copyright 1991 by COAT Publications ACE. Adapted by permission.

counts, led to phenomenal changes in their ability to interact with the environment. The general atmosphere changed from one of "hopelessness to one of hopefulness" (Holden & Woods 1982, 60), and there was a corresponding improvement in staff morale.

Building on this apparent success, programs were introduced at other hospitals. Gradually, the approach became more defined, and the title "reality orientation," used first in an Iowa hospital, took hold. As it was originally designed, RO included three components.

1. Twenty-four-hour RO: All staff in the facility were trained to orient patients/residents to person, place, and time with every interaction. Verbal prompts were given, when necessary, and appropriate responses were rewarded with praise and attention. Rambling and confused talk was discouraged. To serve as a cue for appropriate behavior, RO was carried out during the course of normal daily activities. Folsom considered the 24-hour component (also known as informal or basic) RO to be the most crucial.

2. Classroom RO: These were intensive, small group sessions designed as a supplement to 24-hour RO. Small groups of patients (usually four to six) were instructed, as in a classroom, usually by nursing staff, in basic orientation information. The information was constantly repeated, making use of calendars, clocks, and blackboards and involving the patients in the activity. Groups met once or twice a day, usually in 30-minute sessions, 5 to 7 days a week. In some cases advanced classes were also developed.

3. Attitude therapy: A consistent approach (e.g., "active" or "passive friendliness" or "matter-of-fact") to a patient was to be adhered to by the whole team. All staff were to enhance the milieu for the patients by developing and encouraging participation in recreational and functional activities, both on and off the unit.

5.1 Implementation of Reality Orientation

RO quickly became widely adopted in psychogeriatric units and nursing homes in North America and Britain. There is no quantitative statement in the literature about the prevalence of RO therapy. It is commonly described as "the most widely accepted and researched technique" (Baines et al. 1987, 222) and "the most typical treatment for elderly mentally impaired nursing home residents" (Carroll & Gray 1981, 28). Over a 12-year period, some 23,000 staff were trained in RO at the center at Tuscaloosa, Alabama (Folsom 1985). However, the first book detailing the RO approach was not published until 1982 (Holden & Woods). Outside of the formal literature, it is my per-

sonal experience that RO is assumed by clinicians of various backgrounds to be an important therapeutic approach for the confused elderly. It also continues to be noted as a valid group intervention in current nursing and social work texts (Burnside 1988; Hancock 1987) as well as in activity books (Beisgen 1989). It is not surprising that RO has become so widely accepted. The confused, disoriented elderly individual was, and continues to be, an extremely challenging rehabilitation candidate. The introduction of RO was a breath of hope in what was described by Powell-Proctor and Miller (1982), as an "air of therapeutic nihilism" (p. 458) that surrounded psychogeriatrics. In a climate in which there had been assumed to be no hope of rehabilitation, one wonders whether the reported successes were in response to RO or simply a response to an organized intervention where previously there was none.

The RO classroom group became the most commonly applied component. However, careful examination of the research and clinical practice literature reveals many difficulties with this approach. Reliable research is limited and weakly supports a modest, temporary gain in verbal orientation only, after involvement in conventional classroom RO (Baines et al. 1987; Burton 1982; Campos 1984; Gropper-Katz 1987; Holden & Woods 1982; Powell-Proctor & Miller 1982; Zepelin et al. 1981). The actual significance of these gains for severely disabled elderly persons and their caregivers is doubtful. Does it really matter whether the person can recite that it is "Friday, January 5, 1990, and my name is Carol," if he or she cannot find the way to the bathroom? Constantly confronting persons with ADRD with their inability to recall where, when, who is bound to be threatening to the participants and frustrating for the staff. Carrying out such activities with adults in a classroom setting contradicts an emphasis on "reality" or "normalcy."

RO is now much more widely understood, both by the rearticulation of RO itself (Holden & Woods 1982) and by other, more holistic, approaches (Cohen & Eisdorfer 1986; Davis & Kirkland 1988; Edelson & Lyons 1985; Greenblatt 1988; Judd 1983; Reichenback & Kirchman 1991; Zgola 1987), as being important for reassurance, not for the repetition of the facts themselves. The approach that I and many others have found to be more therapeutic is to say, "Good morning, Mrs. MacDonald, how are you this snowy Friday in January? It is time to get dressed and go to breakfast in the dining room here at Sunshine Manor." Orienting information is provided for reassurance, not for repetition and recall. In the light of current research findings and knowledge about ADRD, reality *orientation* should now be more properly known and implemented as reality *reassurance*. It is essential neither to confront disoriented individuals nor to encourage their disorientation by playing along with their misperceptions; do not lie to them.

How does one respond to someone who feels that she must get home to prepare supper for her husband, who has in fact been dead for 20 years? Usually, connecting with some of her ideas, the person named, or the feelings expressed in her statement is helpful; for example: "I'll bet you are a wonderful cook. What is your specialty?" or "You must miss your husband a lot," and then gently assist the woman to reminisce about him. These responses reassure the individual that her concerns and her feelings have been heard, without confronting her with a sometimes incomprehensible reality and without furthering her confusion by agreeing. As the conversation progresses, it is a good idea to include some reorienting information. For example: "The cooks here at Sunshine Manor, where you live, will soon have supper ready. After all the meals you have made, isn't it good to have someone else do the work?" For a more detailed discussion and illustration of this approach see the excellent book, *Institutional Care of the Mentally Impaired Elderly*, by Edelson and Lyons (1985).

Naomi Feil, a social worker, gives many workshops and has self-published a book on her formulation of this approach, which she has called "validation" (Feil 1988). While there are worthwhile aspects to Feil's therapeutic approach, her book must be viewed critically. The diagnostic and clinical information she presents, particularly on persons with ADRD, is grossly inaccurate and very misleading. For example, consider some of her characterizations of those with Alzheimer's disease: "Becomes unaware of angry or sad feelings; cannot grieve, Denies feelings; Unaware of losses in later stage; does not respond to touch, eye-contact, voice tone" (Feil 1988, pp. 64, 66, 68, 70). The research and clinical practice literature on ADRD unanimously rejects the blatant inaccuracy of these characterizations (Allison & Bowlby 1992).

6.0 REMINISCENCE

Like activity, reminiscence, or looking back over past experiences, is an essential human need (Baines et al. 1987; Berghorn & Schafer 1987; Boylin et al. 1976; Buechel 1986; Froehlich & Nelson 1986; Goldwasser et al. 1987; Haight 1991; Kiernat 1979; Merriam 1989; Molinari & Reichlin 1984–85). There was, and to some extent continues to be, a popular mistaken belief that as people age they spend more and more of their time dwelling in the past. Butler (1975) was the first to take a

public stand against this negative view of the elderly and reminiscing. Butler saw the process as a healthy and natural one, enabling the aging individual to come to terms with life in relation to approaching death. This is very closely connected to the developmental task of summing up (Erikson et al. 1986), already discussed.

Reminiscence and its particular importance and use with persons with ADRD, is discussed in detail in Chapter 6. Suffice it to say here, with Butler, that it is a natural and universal need. An appreciation of its importance and integration into all activities is central to working with individuals with ADRD.

7.0 SENSORY STIMULATION

This section serves as a brief introduction only. Further details are found in Chapter 7. An overview is included here because of the centrality of sensory stimulation to all work with individuals with ADRD.

We all enjoy and understand the world around us through our senses: the sound of the alarm beginning the day, the rich aroma of stew signaling dinner, the sight of smoke warning us of fire and so forth. We take the world in through our senses, interpret what it means on the basis of our experience, and then act accordingly. For persons with ADRD, this whole chain of action and pleasure is interrupted at every stage. Since they are elderly, there is an increased likelihood that their basic sensory systems are not as sharp as they used to be. Because of the effects of their disease, both their ability to understand or recognize what their senses tell them and their ability to decide what action to take are impaired. In addition, the physical capacity to act is impaired because of the effects of their disease and possibly those of age-associated changes. And, as if that were not enough, the understimulation (e.g., bland colors and textures, food preparation isolated from the living quarters) or overstimulation (e.g., announcements made over blaring sound systems, chatter of staff, the clanging of meal carts and trays) characteristic of institutional life combine to interfere further with the ability to interpret their sense stimulations and to act on them.

The purpose of sensory stimulation is to enable the person to overcome these obstacles and to experience the pleasures of life through the senses. In turn, this stimulation is the cue for an active response. By presenting sensory-rich materials in a manageable way (for example, with a verbal cue such as "It's time to get washed up for lunch," hands are gently placed in a basin of warm water; a soft, colorful washcloth is close at hand; and scented soap is within sight and smell), the individual is stimulated to wash his or her own hands and face before a meal and enabled to experience the sensory pleasures and personal satisfaction associated with this activity. I have seen many individuals termed "total care" who competently, and with great satisfaction, washed their own hands and faces when cued by the smell of the soap, the feel of the warm water, the sight of the washcloth, and verbal reminders. Every opportunity should be taken to enliven the senses and thus make use of a strength, the ability to derive pleasure from sensory experiences.

8.0 BEHAVIORAL APPROACHES

The use of planned, environmental changes and cues or planned systems of rewards and punishments in order to increase certain positive behaviors (e.g., socialization) or decrease negative behaviors (e.g., aggressive behavior), has its roots in the work of the psychologist B. F. Skinner and his colleagues. These concepts have been successfully applied in many areas, most particularly with children. Existing research studies of elderly people have also documented the effectiveness of behavioral principles in areas such as increasing socialization (McEvoy & Patterson 1986; O'Quinn et al. 1982), increasing activity (MacDonald et al. 1986; O'Quinn et al. 1982), increasing exercise (Perkins et al. 1986), improving continence (Schnelle et al. 1983; Spangler et al. 1984), and reducing disruptive and aggressive behavior (Hussian 1988; Rosberger & MacLean 1983; Vaccaro 1988a, 1988b). Unfortunately, as with so many areas of intervention with the elderly, although the effectiveness of these techniques has been demonstrated there is a great need for further study and clinical application. Although successful, most studies have consisted of short-term research or demonstration projects (Hussian 1984; Mosher-Ashley 1987; Williamson & Ascione 1983).

There are also strong indications that behavioral approaches for the secondary symptoms of ADRD (e.g., wandering, decreased self-care skills, disruptive behavior, incontinence) can have significant positive effects on functioning and quality of life (Birren & Schaie 1990; Dippel & Hutton 1988; Heacock et al. 1991; Hussian 1984; Namazi et al. 1989; Vaccaro 1988a, 1988b; Williamson & Ascione 1983). Unfortunately, these techniques have scarcely been applied outside of research situations. This situation is due to several factors: the general lack of training of care staff in behavioral approaches; the difficulty in developing approaches that are absolutely consistent among various caregivers; the false perception that persons with ADRD are unable to learn or change their behavior; a general lack of interest in the professional, therapeutic, and research communities in therapeutic applications

for persons with ADRD; and the tendency of institutions to reward dependent behavior and discourage initiative (Baltes 1988; Baltes & Baltes 1986; Burgener & Barton 1991; Heacock et al. 1991).

Whether or not behavioral approaches are intentionally applied, there is ample evidence in the research literature cited above, and from my own clinical experience, that persons with ADRD do shape their behavior according to the rewards they receive. Individuals do learn that dependent behavior (e.g., needing assistance with dressing or eating) gets the attention that they so desperately need. They learn that, in the absence of other stimulation, self-stimulating behaviors are rewarding, pleasant, and immediately available (e.g., repetitive noises, clapping, rubbing the chair tray, masturbation). Most unfortunate of all, they learn that what is called "negative attention" (attention for negative behaviors such as striking out, swearing, or throwing food) is better than no attention at all. My clinical experience includes two striking illustrations of this type of learning:

Gwen was in the advanced stages of Alzheimer's disease. She had recently been admitted to our unit because of disruptive and seemingly uncontrollable noise-making in the nursing home. She was referred to occupational therapy for eating stimulation group. Nursing staff reported that although she was physically and cognitively capable of self-feeding, she refused to do so. On her first day in the group she was an ideal participant. She fed herself entirely after a few physical and verbal prompts. She expressed appreciation for the group, socialized with her peers, and was generally pleasant and cheerful. The subsequent group was another matter altogether. She refused to feed herself, struck out physically, was verbally abusive when attempts were made to provide hand-over-hand guidance for feeding, and was extremely loud and disruptive, insisting that she be fed. This behavior was very disturbing to other participants, and Gwen was not involved in the group for about three weeks. Two further attempts were made to involve Gwen in the group. Her responses are an absolutely astounding demonstration of this severely demented woman's capacity to learn. On the first occasion, I found Gwen in her room. She was in a very pleasant and quiet mood and we chatted amiably as I pushed her wheelchair down the hall to the group. What an incredible, instantaneous reaction as soon as we entered the group room! Gwen began shouting and hollering, flailing her arms about and shrieking "Take me out! I hate you! You're the one who won't feed me! I want to be fed!" She was removed, and one week later we made one final attempt. Gwen was brought by nursing staff to the group, which, on this particular day, was in another room. Again, she was pleasant and quiet, but as soon as she came into the group setting and saw me working with another patient, she again began shouting that she wanted to be fed. Gwen had learned that she liked the attention of being fed, and exactly where and with whom she didn't get that attention. In other groups, such as sensory stimulation, located in another room, she responded favorably both to me and to the group!

Shaughn was a feisty Irishman with a devilish grin and a lifelong penchant for hell-raising. He had been a hard-drinking, hard-working miner. Years of drinking finally took its toll on Shaughn's brain, and he developed Korsakoff's syndrome dementia. Shaughn continued his lifelong rowdy behavior, which in spite of his undeniable *joie de vivre* didn't endear him to nursing home staff. He was eventually admitted to our unit, bearing the label of "totally incorrigible." His reputation continued to build. He threw his food trays, cursed, hollered, pounded his chair, and struck out at staff, visitors, and other patients. In spite of his now frail and immobile body, sometimes three or four male staff were required to do his self-care. And yet, there was an undeniable appeal and wit in his wild behavior and outrageous comments. Some staff would laugh and encourage his verbal onslaughts, from a distance. Whether it was this positive attention, or more negative responses, there was no doubt that Shaughn got lots of attention for being the bad actor of the unit.

I honestly have to say that I was not enthusiastic when I received a referral to assess Shaughn for involvement in groups. But, putting on my best therapeutic face, I welcomed him to sensory stimulation group. The first few minutes were great. Shaughn loved the attention and poured forth his Irish charm, his blue eyes twinkling in his smiling face. However, the honeymoon was soon over. While I was working with another patient, Shaughn began cursing and hollering, flailing his arms threateningly toward his fellow patients. I made several attempts to get him settled, but as soon as I went to someone else he started up again. Finally, I firmly reminded him that he was disturbing others, not least of all me, and told him he would have to leave if he didn't settle down. And leave he did! After five minutes in the hall, Shaughn returned; then a few more minutes calm, and then ejected again. And so began a seesaw of exits and entrances. After about 6 weeks, Shaughn was usually able to stay for the whole group, participate appropriately, and apparently enjoy it enormously. Observing this new side of Shaughn, nursing staff also began to give Shaughn "time outs" for disruptive behavior and the same effects were observed. He no longer required large numbers of staff for personal care and only occasionally dumped his food tray. Eventually, he was able to be transferred to a long-term care facility.

There is an addendum to Shaughn's story, which leaves no doubt that behavioral approaches have limits. Shaughn continued to be a hell-raiser, as he had been all his life. This should be no surprise. It is just that behavioral techniques were, for the most part, able to contain this behavior within more appropriate limits, not an immodest accomplishment. I learned this in a most graphic way:

> Once, after several days of lively good humor and relative calm, Shaughn seemed to find things a little too dull in group. He wasn't responding to praise and attention, but he was finding ways to disturb—throwing the exercise ball at his peers, demanding tea immediately. It was early spring and I had brought some fresh flowers to the group. When I showed them to Shaughn and asked him what they were, he hollered "horseshit" at the top of his lungs. The effect was great, and aided by his tendency to perseverate, he continued repetitively hollering "horseshit." Nothing I could do would calm him down. Exit Shaughn to the corridor.

8.1 Implementing Behavioral Approaches

For persons with ADRD, approaches that manipulate the environment to promote or discourage certain behaviors are the most effective (Dippel & Hutton 1988;

Heacock et al. 1991; Williamson & Ascione 1983). Implementation of large-scale environmental and milieu changes requires the input and cooperation of the whole staff team. Even if this is not entirely manageable, it is possible for those running an activities program to apply these principles in the smaller "environment" of the activities group. Environments that promote optimal functional behavior should

- be as normal and homelike as possible
- avoid both overstimulation and understimulation
- provide maximal cues as to expected behavior (e.g., a table set with teacups for a social group) and orientation (e.g., prominently displayed clocks and calendars)
- avoid clutter and confusion
- provide reassurance and positive feedback for every positive behavior
- contain no safety hazards or block access (e.g., poisonous plants, electrical cords)

Programs to target specific, individual behaviors should be designed by a qualified professional with knowledge of behavioral principles. However, it is also essential that direct care staff and—as far as possible— the individual concerned have input (e.g., in deciding the monitoring schedule and suitable rewards). Without consistency any program is doomed to fail. Although the professional staff or an external consultant may be the expert in behavior programs, the direct care staff are the experts who know the individual best and who will implement the program.

A detailed description of behavioral principles is well beyond the scope of this brief section. However, it is possible to use simple and effective behavioral techniques, such as positive feedback or "time outs" for unacceptable behavior in day-to-day work with people with ADRD. The following points, based on the literature and my clinical experience, can serve as a guide in implementing some simple, behavioral techniques:

- Analyze the what, where, why, and when surrounding an undesirable behavior (e.g., physical aggression, shouting, incontinence) to determine what may have caused it. Keeping a checklist or chart is essential. Often, the frequency or the environment surrounding a behavior is not accurately understood by subjective observation alone.
- Keep careful records. Document with a checklist the frequency of occurrence before and after introducing any changes.
- Target one behavior at a time. There is an understandable desire to solve everything at once. This

is neither reasonable nor possible. Rather, pick the behavior that is most problematic and work at it.

- Remember that consistency is of the utmost importance. Even one "reward" for negative behavior is enough to keep it going (for example, the laughter of staff at Shaughn's carryings on).
- If an approach is not working, be adaptable and try something else. Despite the overall need for consistency, because of the degenerative nature of the disease and the fluctuating nature of performance, it is necessary to constantly re-evaluate the effectiveness of an approach. Behavior also varies from day to day and hour to hour. What works one day may not work the next.
- Remember that rewards are the most effective reinforcement for desirable behavior. For persons with ADRD the use of touch, a hug, a smile, or a brief conversation can be very rewarding. As far as possible, eliminate negative behavior by ignoring it; that is, do not reward it with attention.
- Be aware that although traditional cognitive learning is impaired, the capacity for procedural memory (recognizing and repeating previous nonverbal behavior) and for emotional learning and memory persist. The individual may not remember what he or she had for lunch (or when) but will remember the positive or negative experience of eating and socializing.
- Never use punishment in any form. Time out is not punishment, but the loss of the positive reward of being in the group or the setting.
- Focus on increasing positive behaviors rather than decreasing negative ones. If the target behavior is loud, repetitive clapping, the best approach is to encourage positive behaviors that conflict with this behavior (e.g., sanding a stationary block, looking at a book or magazine, using a safe wall gym, folding towels).

Some specific suggestions for managing the challenging behaviors which can accompany ADRD are found at the end of this chapter.

9.0 THERAPEUTIC GROUPS

9.1 Why Group Work with the Cognitively Impaired Elderly?

People have been gathering together in groups since the beginning of time. Family and community groups were essential for physical survival in a harsh world. But more than that, groups became vital for passing on knowledge, sharing customs and ritual, worship, play, and the sheer comfort of being with others—for emotional survival. Our modern society abounds with organized and informal groups with purposes as varied as the human imagination. They range from the wildly unconventional, such as the Flat Earth Society, to the more staid, such as the Imperial Order of the Daughters of the Empire and the Daughters of the American Revolution. There are groups for fun, fellowship, fitness, and foolishness; and, beginning from the time of World War II, groups especially for healing and personal growth.

Therapeutic groups are equally diverse in nature and purpose, from self-help groups, such as the Alzheimer Society, to professionally led groups for abused children. Whatever the specific focus, all therapeutic groups fit under an umbrella of working toward some sort of personal change. The success of personal-growth groups is dependent on many factors: the support of the other members of the group; the guidance of the leader; the conscious will of the individual to work toward change.

The associated deficits in reasoning, language, initiative, judgment, and memory make it difficult for individuals with moderate and advanced ADRD to participate in conventional, therapeutic groups. Unfortunately, rather than adapt the group structure to compensate for deficits, the overwhelming response has been to suggest that individuals with ADRD, particularly in the advanced stages, are incapable of participating in groups. In fact, the persisting assets of sociability, emotional memory, and awareness and sensory appreciation DO make a specially structured group an ideal therapeutic setting for the individual with ADRD. It is a place to restore and repair a self-concept ravaged by disease and disability, for emotional survival in an often incomprehensible world. These groups provide essential opportunities for socializing, nurturing of others, fun, hobbies, exercise, self-expression, and most of all for success experiences that enhance self-esteem and promote functional performance (David 1991; Fernie et al. 1990; Reichenback & Kirchman 1991; Trace & Howell 1991).

9.2 What Is a Group for Persons with ADRD?

Like any group, a group for persons with ADRD is a coming together with others with similar interests, needs, and capabilities. It is a normal and essential human activity. However, individuals with ADRD do require structures, formats, and a style of leadership that is different from that of traditional community groups. These important differences make it possible to build on their strengths and compensate for their disabilities.

With these adaptations, individuals with ADRD are also able to make gains in self-esteem and self-awareness and to realize personal growth. The importance of opportunities for supportive social involvement and their positive contribution to individual functioning cannot be underestimated.

In their excellent book on ADRD, Cohen and Eisdorfer (1986) stress the importance of interaction with others as follows:

> Since other people affect our feelings about ourself, our life satisfaction, and even our health, working with the patient's social network is often an effective means of reinforcing feelings of independence and self worth. Friends help us believe in ourselves when we see ourselves as less valuable. Other people are thus important resources for rehabilitating the patient's motivation to continue to live and feel wanted. (p. 233)

There is no doubt that organized community groups and less formal social and family groups have always served important therapeutic purposes for their members. However, around the time of World War II, groups whose singular purpose was therapeutic began to develop. The impetus to develop group treatment was a practical one—economics—with the goal of spreading out the limited resources of trained personnel in order to provide treatment for the many war veterans. In the intervening years, groups have proven not only to be economical, but also to be a unique treatment setting in which to provide opportunities for improved health and personal growth that are different from those provided by individual treatment. Therapeutic groups are valued by both participants and therapists because of their ability to develop group cohesiveness, improve self-esteem, provide a sense of hope, and develop interpersonal skills (David 1991; Falk-Kessler et al. 1991; Fernie et al. 1990). While some have floundered, many self-help and therapeutic groups, such as Alcoholics Anonymous, have met with incredible success. Therapeutic groups are now so commonplace that they even form the setting for a popular situation comedy, "Dear John." In fact, it is no wonder that therapeutic groups have grown by leaps and bounds. How often is it that a solution is not only the most effective but the least expensive?

For individuals with ADRD, there are several particular advantages to working in groups.

Groups fill a basic human need for belonging and togetherness. This is particularly true for individuals with ADRD, who are frequently isolated from peers, friends, and family by difficulties in communication and comprehension. Specialized group structures and formats compensate for these difficulties and help to decrease isolation. They are a place where persons with ADRD can find acceptance by their peers.

Both Helen and Frank were in the advanced stage of Alzheimer's disease. Language comprehension was minimal, but both had very-well-preserved language structure and vocabulary, deeply ingrained social behaviors, and a great sense of humor. Both sat in the same day room, vacantly staring straight ahead or alternately pacing the corridors or perpetually rearranging the furniture. They didn't speak to each other. Gathered around the table in sensory stimulation group one day, they happened to be side by side. Frank winked and made one of his animated mime jokes with me as he displayed the fresh flowers placed decoratively behind his ears. Helen caught his joke, laughed, and touched his hand in appreciation. And so began a beautiful friendship of shared jokes and gentle reassurance, as they sat side by side holding hands and enjoying conversation and music. The factual content of what transpired between Frank and Helen was unintelligible to everyone else. The emotional content was transparent. Although this friendship flourished most obviously in the group, with the encouragement of staff it also continued outside of group time and had an obvious calming and reassuring effect on both Frank and Helen.

Groups are a natural, normal, and adult setting for socialization and activities that make use of the persisting asset of sociability. The aim is to develop a group atmosphere that, as much as possible, resembles a community gathering or a coffee klatch. Participants have described groups to me as a party, a class, or a club. I felt I had succeeded when they thanked me for the lovely time or insisted that I also sit down and share in the tea at the table. The highest compliment for successfully achieving this kind of atmosphere was given by one charming lady who suggested to the "girls" that they had better go and let Carol get back to work!

The social atmosphere of a group encourages social behavior, participation, and normal adult function. The group serves as an assistive or prosthetic environment to enable normal social functioning (Lawton 1980, 1983). This was most obvious in my practice in an adaptation of sensory stimulation designed to encourage independent eating. The group was designed to resemble, as much as possible, a normal dining situation. Many participants showed marked improvement in independent eating, sociability, and other positive mealtime behaviors (Rogers et al. 1989).

Mary's usual pattern was to spend most of her day slumped in her chair, interrupted only by periods of agitated pacing, during which she insisted that she had to get home to fix supper. By contrast, in sensory stimulation group, she was a charming hostess. She engaged and entertained her peers with stories and witty comments. She was alert to their needs, for example, for more tea and attention. She was transformed.

The more disabled members of the group pattern their behavior on that of more highly functioning members. This is most obvious during rhythmic, overlearned activities. One member may toss the exercise ball or beanbag to another and stimulate a game of catch; one may begin to sing a familiar tune, and others will join in; one may smile and wave at a staff member or a peer, and others will follow suit.

Group members, enabled by staff, provide support and encouragement for each other. The old adage that the whole is greater than the sum of the parts is particularly true of group work with the cognitively impaired elderly.

10.0 GUIDELINES FOR LEADING GROUPS WITH INDIVIDUALS WITH ADRD

In the preceding sections, the reader has been offered a selection of basic ingredients (approaches) for group work with individuals with ADRD. The following sections can be viewed as basic methods with which to develop a personal "hodgepodge" for special groups. The group leader is reminded, once again, that the most essential guideline is to be able to stand in the shoes of the participant, to have empathy. In working with persons with ADRD this means coming to terms, personally, with the very difficult issues of aging, loss, disability, and death. It means confronting our own aging with its many emotional colors, both the joys and the sorrows.

A good understanding of general group work principles is a helpful foundation for these special groups (Crepeau 1986; Kaplan 1988; Posthuma 1989). However, because of the particular strengths and deficits of these individuals, there are also some important additions and differences. It must be emphasized that what follows are pointers only. There are no "recipes" for successful group work with any population. Owing to the fluctuating nature of each person's ability to participate, this is particularly true of groups with persons with ADRD. It is absolutely essential to be adaptable, to cultivate the art of thinking on your feet. Successful group leaders must accomplish a delicate balance between encouraging maximal participation and avoiding confronting participants with their disabilities.

The following guidelines are based on my clinical experience and information in the literature (Beisgen 1989; Burgener & Barton 1991; Cohen & Eisdorfer 1986; Crepeau 1986; David 1991; Davis & Kirkland 1988; Edelson & Lyons 1985; Fernie et al. 1990; Freeman 1987; Greenblatt 1988; Heacock et al. 1991; Judd 1983; Kaplan 1988; Mace 1990; Reichenback & Kirchman 1991; Volicer et al. 1988; Zgola 1987).

Have fun. As demanding as it is, the rewards of the work are many. To see a person with ADRD come alive with enthusiasm, beam with self-satisfaction, or move and act in ways thought to be long-forgotten is an amazing experience. Relish it. Do activities that are fun for you as well as for the participants. This is important for the effectiveness of the group as well as for your continued mental health. Your enjoyment will communicate to group members and set a happy and positive atmosphere that will encourage participation and facilitate enjoyment.

Keep in mind that normality and naturalness are essential. Everything about the group—your voice, your manner, the setting, the activities, and the conversation—should be as much like a normal community club, coffee group, or work "bee" of older adults as possible. Remember, above all else, that whatever their current disabilities, individuals with ADRD are adults who remain acutely aware of their adult status.

> Mary was a highly educated, well-read woman who had traveled widely and found great satisfaction in her life as an artist. As her dementia progressed, she was enormously frustrated by her pervasive inability to continue lifelong pleasures. She withdrew in arrogance and anger from the assistance that she so much needed for bathing and other daily activities. She spent her days wandering the halls, inquiring after her daughter. In time, with short interactions during activities such as walking to see the flowers or looking at travel pictures, she and I developed a rapport. Perhaps now Mary would be able to be part of my group, centering on simple sensory, adult-oriented activities. Mary walked calmly beside me to the group and sat at the table. On the first day, she was unwilling to participate and sat in stony silence until the closing teatime, when she was pleasant and sociable. Thinking that she would participate as she became more comfortable with the group, I invited her on three more occasions. Never will I forget the scene that unfolded on her fourth, and last, visit to the group. I gently approached Mary, suggesting that some throwing and catching of the beanbag would be good exercise for her hands. She gave me a scorching look, folded her arms defiantly, and said No! I tried my best to reassure her and moved to another participant. The reassurance, the adult approach, the struggle to empathize were to no avail, in Mary's case. The next thing I knew, Mary had moved to the floor. The painful image of this accomplished, severely demented woman sitting on the floor, pounding her feet, and screaming, "Baby, baby, baby, it's all just baby, baby, baby" will never leave my mind.

Sometimes even our best efforts to present activities in an adult manner are just not enough. But anything less than the most sincere efforts are damaging beyond belief. There is no doubt in my mind that Mary, and every one of the many other individuals with ADRD with whom I have worked, although perhaps unable to find expression in conventional ways, are acutely aware of their status as adults with diminishing abilities to function in adult ways.

The most effective leadership style is caring and compassionate, but directive. Persons with ADRD almost always have difficulty in taking initiative or getting started on their own. They also have difficulty in making choices and decisions. Unfortunately, these difficulties are often interpreted as an inability or unwillingness to participate. However, when the group leader compensates for these deficits, the person with ADRD is enabled to participate in activities, to become a "doer." The group leader must supply the needed direction while encouraging maximal individual dignity and freedom. It is not enough to gather people together in one place for an activity. The leader must take more than the usual role in encouraging and facilitating conversation and participation.

Except for persons who are only mildly impaired, one of the more difficult areas is getting people to the group itself. The usual approach of posting activities, or even personally asking people if they would like to come, generally does not work, except for those who are only moderately impaired. "Would you like to come to group or to the garden?" is most often met with

No! Unable to understand or remember exactly what the group is about, or where it is, or what is going to be expected of them, persons with ADRD, fearing the unknown, have a natural tendency to refuse to go along with any suggestion. Approaches that assume a positive response are the most successful.

After a warm greeting, using the person's name, some examples of useful verbal approaches are:

"Let's go and have a cup of tea together."

"I'd like you to come with me to chat for a while."

"It's time to come to the kitchen for coffee."

"I have an interesting old camera I'd like to show you."

"I need your help to make some cookies."

These types of invitations should be accompanied by gentle physical cues such as taking the person's arm or hand or assisting him or her to rise from a chair. Recall from Chapter 3 other important nonverbal cues such as voice tone, facial expression, and use of caring touch. On the way to the group, continue talking, reassuring, and orienting to the day's activities. As the individual comes to recognize you (do not confuse being able to name a person with recognition) and to have positive associations with the group, his or her response to your invitation will become more immediate. This approach also applies to the presentation of activities and the flow of the group. Because of their deficits, group members will not necessarily be spontaneous in suggesting ideas, in doing what comes next independently, or even in participating in the activity. It is important to avoid ambiguous or vague suggestions and too many choices.

The following is a brief outline of some leader invitations for a reminiscence group on cameras/photos for moderately impaired individuals:

- "Today I brought in an old camera for you to see." (Hand the individual the camera.)

- "Try to take a picture with it." (Guide gently with your hands, if necessary.)

- "Did you ever use a camera like this?"

- "Did you ever take pictures? Of whom? Where?"

- "Does this old photo remind you of anyone you know?"

- "Do you recall a favorite photo of yours?" (Be more specific if necessary; e.g., name baby photo, wedding picture, picture of parents.)

- "This is a new-fashioned camera, a Polaroid, which makes pictures very fast. I'd like to take your picture now. Ready, say 'cheese.' Here is your picture already! I think it turned out very well. You have beautiful eyes. Do you like the picture?"

- "Would you like to keep the picture yourself or give it to someone? Who would you like to give it to? Would you like it mounted on red or black paper?" (Illustrate the choices with actual pieces of paper.)

- "Let's put your name and today's date on the paper." (Assist if necessary.)

- Show or assist the individual to display the photo to other group members. Invite positive comments, such as, "Doesn't Joe have a wonderful smile?" Post the photo or see that it gets to its desired destination.

See Chapter 6 for more details on this group plan. See Chapter 7 for suggestions on groups for individuals with lower functioning.

The camera theme for a group represents an abbreviated sample of interactions during a group. The leader is constantly providing positive feedback, reassurance, and direction while encouraging as much choice and response as the individual is capable of. Achieving a balance between enabling individual choice and providing necessary direction is essential. This rests on ongoing observation and assessment of individual capabilities, so that neither too little nor too much is expected of group members.

Avoid direct commands and confrontation. A directive approach, mediated by empathy, does not mean giving orders. It does mean offering concrete suggestions based on knowledge of the individual. No one likes to be told what to do. For persons with ADRD, being ordered about is another assault on self-esteem. Because of their difficulties in understanding and communicating, persons with ADRD often react particularly negatively to being told what to do. Orders may, in fact, be necessary in the case of safety, but even under such circumstances it is best to approach the individual calmly and warmly. The person with ADRD may not be able to interpret the words, but he or she can interpret the emotion behind orders or commands. Direct confrontation may lead to a catastrophic reaction. At the very least, because of the persistence of emotional memory, the group may become associated with a time of unpleasant and unhappy feelings. Distracting attention, changing the topic, or using gentle humor are all good ways to avoid confrontation. For those who are used to more traditional therapeutic groups in which some confrontation may be necessary to help the group members grow or work something through, this approach may take some adjustment.

Provide opportunities for manageable choice. Providing choice contributes to the sense of personal control and adult competence, which is so important to self-esteem and preventing learned helplessness. However, cognitive deficits (e.g., in decision making and judgment) make too much choice overwhelming and unmanageable for the person with ADRD. For the most severely impaired, the choice should be limited to two alternatives (for example, "Would you like tea or coffee?"). Be sure to find opportunities to offer choice, even in seemingly minor matters such as which cookie to take or whether teeth should be brushed before or after washing.

Prepare, prepare, prepare; adapt, adapt, adapt. In order to give full attention to group members and be comfortable, personable, and appropriately directive, it is essential to have made preparations for the group in advance. For example, have supplies laid out in order, tea and coffee preparations under way, the order of activities and discussion ideas clearly in mind, and a list of possible questions ready as well as invitations to participate. This level of preparation is especially important because group members have difficulty sequencing activities for themselves. It is part of this preparation, however, to be prepared to adapt your plan. Be spontaneous if members do not respond, get sidetracked onto another topic, or take longer than anticipated. The importance of the group is the process itself, not necessarily to get through the whole plan. For persons with ADRD the most important moment is the present one. Adapt the group in accordance with its responses and present needs or capabilities.

For example, on one occasion during a reminiscence group session on boats, we had come to the topic of the Nova Scotia Bluenose. Just before showing a film on the building of the ship itself, I reached into my pocket and pulled out a Canadian dime, illustrated with the Bluenose. This spun off a discussion of how much a dime would buy when the participants were young compared with the present. Before we knew it, the time for the film had passed, but everyone was smacking lips and recalling the penny candy of youth. Returning to the present time, one member said a dime today would not even buy the smell of such candy. Another said it would not even pay the tax. Everyone had a good laugh at the humor and truth of these observations.

Planning and organizing will be time-consuming at first. As you become more familiar with this special group work and your individual participants, it will become almost second nature.

The most successful group format, especially as individuals become more disabled, is one of parallel presentation (Figure 4-3). Because of deficits in skills such as concentration/attention, communication, and initiation of activity, the individual with ADRD would have great difficulty following a standard group format in which everyone follows the group leader and does the same thing at the same time. Parallel presentation makes group activities possible. In this format, each participant is presented with a particular step of the activity in turn. The next step is then presented to everyone in turn. In a discussion type of activity this means asking, in a nonthreatening manner, each person in turn to respond ("What do you like best about spring, Mary?"). It also means frequent recapping of what has been said and clarification of the topic of a person's response. However, the excitement of these particular groups is that the participants are enabled to perform at the top level of their capacity, and there are times when the conversation becomes spontaneous. As this happens, structuring may not be necessary.

For activity-based groups, unless the members are highly functioning or there is a very low staff to resident ratio, it is best to present activities in distinct steps and to one person at a time. This format has several advantages:

- Repetition with each participant reinforces the information.

- By beginning with a more highly functioning, more verbal individual, the response can serve as a model or cue for others.

- The format compensates for memory loss, reduced attention span, and spontaneity.

- The format allows adapting the presentation and cuing to individual interests, needs, and capabilities.

- The format provides for individual attention and feedback within a group setting.

Provide immediate, but not excessive, positive feedback. The individual with ADRD has learned to expect to fail. Attempts to take initiative or to respond should be rewarded, and thus further response encouraged. For example, attempts to communicate should be rewarded with a greeting, a smile, a touch; successfully completing an activity such as putting flowers in water should be praised. One must be careful, however, not to overdo. Giving excessive praise for completing ordinary tasks can be an affront to adult dignity.

Do not confront the individual with his or her disabilities. It is essential that no individual be put in a situation of being asked to do something beyond his or her abilities, such as writing a name or stating the date. Although more subtle, it is also important to avoid phrasing questions in ways that require a precise answer, such as "What color is this?" There are numerous ways of encouraging a response, with cues or information-seeking questions, that are less threatening. Everyone can offer an opinion. For example, "What color would you say this scarf is?" or "Does the color of this

Figure 4-3 Parallel Presentation

scarf remind you of anything?" or "Does this scarf feel rough or soft to you?"

Always allow an option for not answering. Supply hints from background information that you know. *Never* tell the person that a response is wrong or demonstrate impatience with his or her inability to answer or remember what was just said. The personal approach emphasized is one of unconditional positive regard for each participant. If someone whose wife has been dead for ten years says that she just died last week, support his "feeling" by saying something like, "You must have many wonderful memories of your wife" or "You must miss your wife a lot." Gently draw out these memories and assist the individual to grieve the loss of his wife and recollect and reaffirm his role as a husband.

Plan and run groups that focus on the residual strengths of persons with ADRD. See Chapter 2 for a discussion of strengths.

Learn as much as possible about individual group members. While good observations about preferences can be made during a group, it is also important to remember that, because of memory loss and communication problems, individuals with ADRD are not good self-historians. Read the chart; talk to family, friends, and other staff; and discover as much as possible about individual interests, work, family, preferences, significant personal accomplishments, habits, life experiences, approaches that work, etc. This is essential to being an effective group leader. This information is necessary both for using cues to draw out and involve the person as much as possible and for reaffirming the value of previous life experiences. Most of us have difficulty keeping all of this information straight. Quick notes on file cards or in a small three-ring binder are a handy reminder.

In this way we can come to know the group member as a whole person, not just as someone with a dementing illness but as someone who is still a daughter or son, husband or wife, worker, lover, friend, reader, knitter, etc. Each person has a rich history of life experiences that continue to be very much part of the personal identity. Each individual is a treasure chest of experiences waiting to be discovered and explored.

Allow as much time as possible. Rushing or hurrying participants with ADRD causes confusion and emotional distress. Reassure and encourage, but do not rush. Because it takes longer for persons with ADRD to process information and to respond, the whole group process will take longer.

Be consistent. For persons with memory loss, a daily routine, a constant ritual in the group format, is reassuring since it helps to make their surroundings more predictable. Although the content can and should be varied, the group should meet at the same time and at the same place and should use the same general format. Introduce changes gradually and allow participants time to adjust. Consistency in the personal approach by all staff members is also important. Since persons with ADRD have difficulty structuring their own behavior, structure in their environment is essential.

Groups must have a definite purpose or goal for those participating. Whatever the capabilities of the individual, groups or activities that merely fill time do not develop self-confidence. Furthermore, they are demeaning to the individual and promote a negative image of the elderly as dependent, helpless, and incapable. The activities must be meaningful to the individual, call for his or her involvement at some level, and have a goal. The general group goal is always to enhance the individuals' self-esteem, to make them feel better about themselves. Successful group activities for persons with ADRD are those that enliven and enrich the present time, not just pass the time. Constant evaluation is essential. Does the group meet this and other more specific goals, such as increasing alertness, enhancing socialization, maintaining communication skills, stimulating gross motor movements? Individual goals need not be grandiose. For persons severely disabled by ADRD, responding to the greeting of another is a most worthwhile and achievable goal.

Maintenance of existing abilities for as long as possible is an important goal of groups. With progressive illnesses like ADRD, just staying in one place in terms of, for example, verbal skills, is in itself a good outcome. Although there may also be improvements, such as a calmer mood or increased alertness, the absence of positive change does not mean that the group is ineffective.

Above all, do not be discouraged. Although you may not be seeing or hearing the effects of a group with a particular individual, this does not mean that the activity is failing. Because of communication deficits and the fluctuating abilities of the participants, these effects may not be obvious or immediate. (Recall the account of Robert in the preface.)

Seek out a support group. There is no doubt that working with persons with ADRD is an exhausting and demanding job. Find a group of peers, such as other activity workers, nursing personnel, recreationists, and occupational therapists, with whom you can share tragedies and triumphs, trade ideas, and do mutual problem solving. This may be a formal group or just a get-together over coffee.

Be in constant communication with other staff. It takes time, but building a team or total staff approach to general care and individual treatment is essential. For persons with ADRD, consistency of approach is absolutely critical. By sharing information, everyone gains an insight into approaches that are most successful with particular individuals. Without communication, individual staff are likely to be undoing the work of others.

11.0 SELECTING AND PLANNING ACTIVITIES

Do you know the children's story about Bonnie, a little girl who seemed to drive her mother and other adults "blithery-blathery out of their mind" (Alderson 1977)? Our dementia unit also had a Bonnie, and she, too, often caused staff to shake their heads and wonder, "Bonnie McSwithers, whatever are we going to do with you?"

Our Bonnie had recently come to us from her home, which she had shared with her husband of more than 60 years. As her Alzheimer's disease progressed her loving husband found it more and more difficult to care for her at home. She did, however, keep very busy tidying up her house, cooking meals she forgot to eat, and trying the best she could to maintain her lifelong routines and activities, which sometimes resulted in bathing and dressing in the middle of the night. One night Bonnie was terrified to find a "strange man" in bed with her, and, brandishing the garden shears, she chased her husband out into the village street. After this upsetting incident, Bonnie's family sought outside help and she was admitted to our dementia unit.

On the unit, her disorientation and agitation worsened. She couldn't find the kitchen to get supper, she would not eat the meals provided because she had to get home to eat the supper she had prepared, she couldn't sit down to read the paper because she hadn't done her sweeping yet, and furthermore, she couldn't even find the broom. She had so much she needed to do and she was so frustrated not to be able to get at it.

Bonnie joined the eating stimulation group. In this homelike setting not only was she more content, but she also ate more—although she still didn't eat her full meal, as she was so happily involved in making sure that everyone else got their dinner! On one particularly memorable day, Bonnie put on an apron, washed her hands, and went to work mixing and cutting the biscuits, with hardly a word of direction. When the biscuits were in the oven she washed up, removed the apron, and spontaneously picked up the newspaper. What a picture of contentment she made, sitting on the sofa in the sunshine with the newspaper spread out in her lap. To an outsider, this scene would appear quite unremarkable in its normalcy. To those of us who were familiar with Bonnie's constant pacing and agitation, or had seen her throw the newspaper across the room in frustration, it was miraculous.

What we needed to do with Bonnie was to enable her to do what she had done all of her adult life. Without having accomplished these duties first, it was simply unthinkable for any self-respecting homemaker to sit down for a leisurely read of the paper!

Bonnie reminds us that the most meaningful and successful activities are those that enable the continuation of lifelong roles (Coons 1991a, 1991b; Davis & Kirkland 1988; Edelson & Lyons 1985; Levy 1990; Mace 1990; Munson 1991; Sloane & Mathew 1991; Smith et al. 1986; Trace & Howell 1991; Watts et al. 1989; Zgola 1987). The role of homemaker is supported by providing opportunities for such activities as doing dishes, baking, dusting, sweeping, and folding laundry. The availability of a safe workshop that includes a variety of woods, sandpaper, small tools such as screwdrivers and wrenches, and mounted objects to "fix" supports the role of the handyman or woodworker. The gardening hobbyist needs plants to mist, water, and prune. Organizing the environment, providing special equipment and appropriate cuing, supports the essential role of an adult who washes and dresses independently. Viewed from this perspective, the role of planning activities changes from finding ways to fill up the day, to occupy the person, to finding ways to facilitate, support, and enable the continuation of activities that had always filled the person's daily life, his or her traditional daily occupations in self-care, work, and leisure. Maintaining these familiar roles and the associated activities is particularly essential for the person with ADRD because of their difficulty in learning new activities.

Self-care activities are the most fundamental of human activities. Unfortunately, under the guise of efficiency, these activities tend to be done for older persons requiring institutional care. This is so efficient that staff are then obliged to create new activities to keep the residents busy!

Work activities have been the central focus of daily routines for most older adults (Marino-Schorn 1985/86). These activities can be continued by providing opportunities for the homemaker to cook and tidy up, the retired office manager to organize books and papers, the grandparent to play with children, etc. These work-associated activities have much more intrinsic value to the older adult, and hence hold much more interest, as has been demonstrated by the research study of MacDonald & Settin (1978). A Wisconsin veterans' home has a paid work therapy program for its residents (Voeks & Drinka 1990). Approximately 250 residents per month participate in the program, with an annual payroll of $20,000. Residents are paid half of the hourly minimum wage. A survey of the residents involved found that 91 percent thought the work program improved their sense of self-worth and 80 percent felt that their work was of value. Sixty-three percent of the residents thought the program was important because it gave them something to do. This is particularly interesting in relation to the comprehensive therapeutic recreation and activities program that is also available at this facility. It seems that the opportunity to do work is a particularly valued activity.

During retirement, voluntary activities are important for many, and, with support, this role can also be continued by the person with ADRD. Stuffing envelopes for a daycare center, arranging flowers for the dining room, and folding napkins for the table are but a few of many possibilities. Activities that have the purpose of helping others are motivating and meaningful. For example, one study found that a significantly larger number of nursing home residents volunteered to participate in decorating cookies when they were to be given as a gift to a preschool than when there was no stated purpose (Hatter & Nelson 1987).

For many older adults, the work role was so central to their lives that there was little opportunity to develop leisure or avocational roles. However, the skilled activities programmer can take advantage of the time now available to develop and/or maintain meaningful leisure activities.

For the long-term care resident, as for the community-dwelling older adult, leisure activities enrich the daily routine by providing opportunities for meeting such important needs as creativity and self-expression. Appropriately planned, introduced, and facilitated, they form a vital component of the essential balance of daily occupation in self-care, work, and leisure. Involvement in a normal balance of activities promotes maximal occupational function, and thus these activities are therapeutic. Inappropriately planned leisure activities are merely busy work, diversions to fill long days devoid of meaningful occupation. These activities do little to promote function and are not therapeutic. One study of 20 healthy young adults demonstrated a significant increase in heart rate and perceived exertion during nonpurposeful activity, as compared with purposeful activity (Bakshi et al. 1991).

In order to select and plan activities that support the continuation of lifelong roles, it is essential to learn as much as possible about your participants. In addition to assessing current individual capabilities, discover as much as possible about their backgrounds, interests, and hobbies and their personal, family, and work histories. An activity survey developed by Teri and Logsdon (1991) provides a helpful beginning for exploring activity interests. Learn about the community context of activities incorporated into local customs, traditions, festivals, and folklore.

Careful selection and planning are the keys to enabling success experiences in doing and thus to enhance the self-esteem of the person with ADRD. We must be sure, however, that success is measured by the participant's yardstick, not our own. For the person with ADRD, the experiences of the present moment are the ones that matter the most. Consequently success in the process of the activity is just as important, if not more so, as a successful outcome. For example, although both the person who was fed lunch and the person who ate finger food independently had a "successful" intake of calories, the person who was fed was denied the success experience of the process of feeding himself or herself.

11.1 Guidelines for Selecting Activities

The most successful activities are those that

- recall overlearned, very familiar activities, such as shaking hands, playing catch, adding milk and sugar to tea and coffee
- are simple, repetitive, but ADULT activities, such as bowling, putting flowers in a vase, winding yarn, looking at the newspaper (a good activity even if the person does not read it)
- emphasize the ability to appreciate sensory experiences, such as feeling a fur muff or a felt hat; lifting, commenting on, cutting, and tasting a watermelon; looking at colorful photographs of familiar local sights
- emphasize overlearned and persistent social skills, such as greeting one another, gathering around a table to share a snack and a drink
- emphasize the ability to participate in gross motor activities, such as dancing, moving to music, walking, simple exercises, digging in the garden

- emphasize remote memory, especially childhood and young-adult memories, and provide an opportunity for reminiscence; for example, looking at, trying on, or using vintage objects such as cameras, a crank telephone, kitchen equipment, clothing, schoolbooks

- provide opportunities for manageable choice; for example, of color of yarn for the Eye of God, of which flower to wear for a boutonniere, of which cookie to take, of what color background for a greeting card

- provide an opportunity for active participation, such as watering plants; grooming pets; signing a greeting card; singing, humming, or clapping with music (in contrast to passive activities such as looking at pets or listening passively to music).

- tie into positive, nondisruptive, repetitive activities, such as polishing shoes, sweeping the floor, wiping the tables, dusting, churning ice cream, stirring or mixing dough, or preparing potting mix for plants

- have an obvious or identifiable purpose, such as making ornaments for the Christmas tree, folding towels for the laundry, baking for visitors

- emphasize nonverbal skills, such as responding to music, stuffing envelopes, or cuddling children

- can be broken down into several steps, such as making greeting cards or fruit cakes, potting plants

- provide immediate positive feedback, such as baking, arranging flowers, and tasting foods

- do not require immediate memory skills, verbal skills, or fine motor skills, such as singing familiar songs; misting plants; polishing silver, shoes, or apples

- do not confront the individual with his or her disability, such as attempting to persuade someone with advanced dementia to play an instrument on which he or she used to be very skilled

- are related to familiar and seasonal life activities, including putting up Christmas decorations, painting Easter eggs, setting the table, raking the leaves (Involvement in one's own personal care is the most familiar and most essential of activities.)

- are meaningful, such as making a birthday card for a loved one, planting a garden, or brushing one's own hair

- are rhythmic, such as moving or clapping to music, playing catch, shuffling cards, sanding wood

- are related to acceptable work activities for that generation (Many older people are unaccustomed to the concept of leisure activities, as their busy working lives did not allow for it. Select activities related to work, such as baking, woodworking, gardening, and self-care.)

11.2 Guidelines for Planning Activities

Plan around a theme that is related to the season, holidays, popular local events. See Chapters 6 and 7 for suggested themes.

Use ample familiar, concrete physical cues and memorabilia. Such materials cue participants to the topic and trigger both verbal and nonverbal participation. For example, during a summer group on beaches and the seashore I used a plastic bucket of sand. I gently placed the hands of a participant, who was usually nonverbal, into the sand. She smiled broadly, ran her fingers through the sand, and said, "Beach, beach, Malmerby beach—lots of sun and water."

Use multisensory cues. For example, in a group about horses, use a horseshoe, which feels cold, smooth, and heavy and may even have the smell of horses; pictures of horses; ceramic or stuffed horses; the sound of a horse race commentator; films, slides, and movies about horses; and other equipment, such as a harness, saddle, bit, collar, blanket, and curry comb.

Begin the activity with a step in which you are sure the participants can be successful. Prepare more intricate steps in advance. For example, measure out ingredients for baking or do intricate cutting for craft projects in advance of the group.

Include one or two participants who are high functioning and will respond well to the group. These individuals serve as a model and as a stimulus for others to participate.

Make an agenda and a written plan. Include a list of supplies and keep revising, adding and subtracting ideas that work and those that do not.

Break activities into simple steps and do one step at a time with each participant. Finishing an activity may take several days, but it should not be hurried.

Keep supplies on hand for self-directed activities for those who will benefit while you are working with others. See Chapter 7 for suggestions.

Plan to take the initiative throughout the group, as most persons with ADRD are unable to do so for themselves.

Always be ready to adapt. If the group is not going well or participants seem interested in pursuing a different agenda, try something else.

Do not expect to be able to run a traditional group, with everyone following the group leader and doing the same thing at the same time.

Schedule demanding verbal activities for the times of day when participants are most alert, usually in the morning, or most in need of releasing energy, usually in the late afternoon.

Provide a bridge from the general milieu of the day room or unit to the group and back again (Figure 4-4). Greet the person individually, orient him or her to the planned activity, and move slowly to the group. Use ample nonverbal cues such as a touch, a welcoming tone of voice, and a smile, and repeat this orientation when introducing the first activity or cue. Repeat the process when returning the person to the unit. Say a personal goodbye, using a handshake, reorient the person to their location; and leave them with a concrete memento of the group, such as a picture, a book, or a magazine. If the person has a difficult time resettling into the general milieu, connect him or her with a direct care staff person, who will give reassurance.

If other staff assist in bringing participants to and from groups, it is essential that they also follow this procedure. Always inform transportation helpers of the group theme. The best way to establish this routine is to model the behavior yourself. It is better to begin with fewer participants than to have people herded in a rush, completely confused about where they are and why they are there. Post lists of participants for particular groups, along with the times and themes of the groups. Some facilities schedule direct-care staff to bring participants to groups as part of their work duties. This can be a wonderful help to an activities leader if the staff are

Figure 4-4 Build a Bridge

good at helping the participant make a bridge to and from the group.

12.0 SETTING GOALS

What do you hope to achieve by involving a particular individual in a group or activity? This question is not asked enough, but it is absolutely essential. Groups and activities, in themselves, are not necessarily good. They are only good if they serve some purpose. The outcome is only as good as the goals and expectations of the leader.

Activity leaders become demoralized when direct-care staff see their work only as a means to keep the residents "busy," a pure diversion. In order to counteract this attitude, activity leaders themselves must be very clear about their goals for the group. Communicate this information to others and take every possible opportunity to demonstrate the positive effects of the group and other purposeful activity. Leaders should be able to articulate clearly the vital importance of activities with persons with ADRD. Since it is so central, the goal statement from the activity section is mentioned again here: It can and should be the role of an activities program to reconnect the individual with meaningful activities that will support self-definition as an adult who is capable of acting in a purposeful and personally satisfying way.

Some ideas for communicating this information to others are the following:

- Seek the advice of direct-care staff on who would do best in a particular group or on the best approaches with a particular individual.
- Prepare one-page outlines of group descriptions and goals.
- Prepare a small manual of group programs and related success stories, photos, and research articles. This is an excellent resource for orienting new staff.
- Share your successes by writing them up for newsletters and newspapers. All the staff will appreciate the positive publicity.
- Offer frequent in-services when starting new groups. An experiential component during an orientation is particularly effective. Include activities that assist others to understand both the frustration associated with being unable to do activities and the satisfaction associated with the successful completion of activities. Some suggestions are writing with the nondominant hand; buttoning a garment while wearing socks on your hands; drawing the lines in a maze, guided only by a mirror; being fed (preferably puréed food) while blindfolded; counting out change while wearing rubber gloves; walking with a walker while wearing Vaseline-smeared glasses.
- Offer orientation to your program to new staff, new residents, and their families.
- Share vignettes of individual responses with other staff.
- Invite staff, individually, to observe a group.
- Post photos (labeled), artwork, and other projects done by participants and encourage staff, by example, to give participants positive feedback on their efforts.

12.1 What Are the Goals?

Goals for the group are set forth in a general statement of purpose for the group as a whole. As has been emphasized, the central goal of all groups is to enhance self-esteem. Individual goals are called objectives and are specific to the person. They may be as simple as having the person respond to the greeting of another. These personal goals and objectives are based on individual assessments.

Since persons with ADRD live most fully in the present moment, goals and expectations for groups should be focused on the present moment. At the most important and fundamental level, the overall goal is to enrich the present moment by providing pleasurable, rewarding experiences. These positive experiences are essential to the self-esteem of the person with ADRD. Enhancement of self-esteem is particularly crucial, as the effects of ADRD are so devastating to the individual's sense of competence and self-worth. Although the facts or experiences in the group may be forgotten, the feelings of pleasure and satisfaction remain. This is what counts.

Some other group goals include the following:

- Encourage the continuation of lifelong roles.
- Encourage socialization.
- Improve level of alertness.
- Assist with reality reassurance.
- Provide success experiences.
- Maintain motor skills and/or stimulate motor responses.
- Maintain verbal skills and/or stimulate verbal responses.
- Provide pleasurable sensory experiences.
- Provide an outlet for creativity and self-expression.

- Encourage self-directed activity by providing both the structure and the encouragement for an activity that can replace lost skills.
- Promote awareness of the surroundings.
- Provide opportunities for reminiscence.
- Provide an opportunity for the expression of feelings.

Specific goals are given for the therapeutic activities in Chapters 5, 6, and 7.

12.2 Evaluating Goals

Having determined the goals for a group, it is also essential to ask constantly if the group or the activity is achieving its particular goal(s). In terms of the general goal of improving self-esteem (first two questions) and evaluating effectiveness, some questions to ask are the following:

- Does the person appear calm and happy in the group?
- After a period of involvement, does the person appear pleased when seeing you and/or the group setting?
- Does the person respond verbally and/or nonverbally?
- How long does the activity hold attention?
- Does the activity create social exchange between participants?
- Do the participants appear content?
- Do the participants become restless?
- Is it difficult to return participants to the general milieu? If so, is the activity overstimulating?

A simple checklist, such as that included for sensory stimulation and reminiscence groups, is a quick and easy way to evaluate group and individual responses.

13.0 THE GROUP MILIEU

The importance of the proper environment during groups was discussed earlier in this chapter. Consideration must be given to both the social milieu and the physical setting.

Social Milieu

The social atmosphere of a group should be welcoming, reassuring, and nonthreatening, a setting in which the individual will feel and experience unconditional positive regard. The individual is accepted as important and worthwhile, for who he or she is now and what he

or she can accomplish at the present time. The leader sets a tone of positive expectation, within the limits of present capabilities, and offers opportunities for the individual to experience success. The leader uses knowledge of the participant's history to reaffirm the value of previous life experiences and the participant's self-worth. The milieu of the group provides an atmosphere in which the participant is able to grow in self-esteem. A supportive group milieu should:

- be reassuring, warm, accepting
- have positive expectations
- be good-humored, caring, enthusiastic
- treat each person as an individual
- enable the expression of feelings
- be adult-oriented
- encourage socialization
- preserve dignity
- provide reality reassurance

Physical Setting

The physical setting of a group should not only contribute to the atmosphere but also promote physical and social function. Environmental compensations for the sensory changes associated with aging are found in Chapter 1. The environmental section earlier in this chapter describes important environmental compensations for persons with ADRD. The following are suggested features of the physical environment specific to groups.

The setting should be free of distractions. It should be isolated in some way from the comings and goings of the facility as a whole. It is very difficult, if not impossible, to run groups for individuals with ADRD in the common living room or day room, as there are too many distractions. A large activity room should be partitioned off with dividers or furniture to make a manageable, reassuring space.

The setting should be homelike (Figure 4-5). It should contain comfortable furnishings and use warm colors with appropriate contrast for poor vision. Even a standard institutional room can be made much more inviting by adding a cloth and flowers to the table, plants in the window, afghans or throws for the chairs, attractive posters or pictures on the wall, and welcoming, age-appropriate background music.

The setting should avoid clutter and confusing or ambiguous materials. Abstract designs in fabric, wallpaper, or floor coverings are too difficult for individuals with ADRD to understand and may increase confusion.

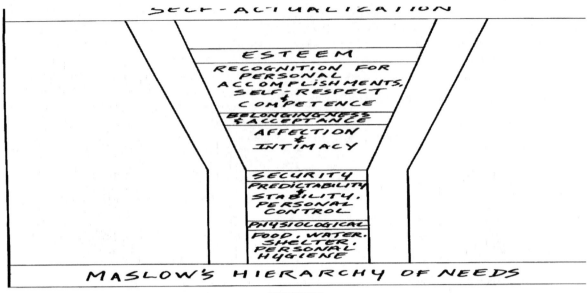

BEFORE

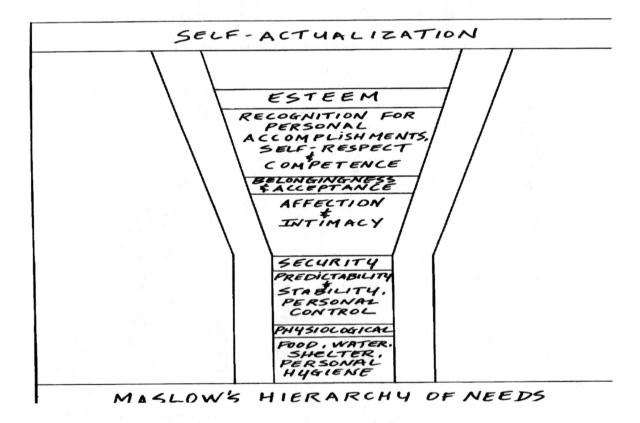

AFTER

Figure 4-5 A Homelike Setting

The setting should have a table as a central focus. This, in my experience, is essential. In traditional, verbal, "therapeutic" groups the presence of a table is viewed by some as a barrier to communication. However, for persons with ADRD the table provides a focus for the group and enhances socialization. It is like sitting around the kitchen or dining room table, so familiar as a center for socializing. The table is a concrete expression of being gathered together. It is a familiar cue to the expected social behavior, triggering procedural memory. Adding a colored, textured cloth and flowers or other seasonal table centerpieces provides a further focus as well as sensory stimulation and reality reassurance. In addition, the table serves the practical purpose of a place to put props, cues, and refreshments. The table should be accessible to persons seated in wheelchairs and gerichairs. However, one must always adapt. Even if large gerichairs do not fit under the table, it is important to bring them as close as possible to the others. My groups took place in the unit kitchen, where I pushed together two square dining tables.

The seating arrangement should be planned. Position those who are compatible beside each other and those who tend to be disruptive at the ends of the table.

Name tags should be used, as appropriate. For the moderately impaired, these may be a helpful cue. The more severely impaired are usually unable to make use of this cue and the attempt to focus on names is too much for them. Be sure not to use name tags fastened with pins or dangerous materials. For my severely impaired participants, I emphasized their individual names during conversation but de-emphasized learning the names of their peers, as it was too challenging. I also did not emphasize my name, as recall of names is difficult from the earliest stages of the disease, and learning my name would serve little useful purpose. We all like to be remembered and recognized. We must learn to look for this recognition and appreciation in facial expression and other non-verbal responses.

The setting should provide orientation cues such as calendars, clocks, windows to the outside, and seasonal centerpieces.

14.0 ACTIVITY ANALYSIS

Activity analysis is breaking an activity into its component parts. It considers the steps involved in the activity, the skills required for each step, and the value of participation in each step. With this information, it becomes possible to take the activity apart in several useful ways.

14.1 Grade the Activity

The level of participation in an activity is selected according to present abilities and skills. As skills deteriorate or improve, the level of participation is adjusted accordingly. For example, the person may not be able to stir a whole batch of cookie dough, but he or she may be able to mix the liquid ingredients. As strength increases, the person may become able to mix a stiffer and stiffer dough.

Activities may be graded according to particular skills. Cognitive skills are especially pertinent with regard to persons with ADRD. The cognitively well person or someone in the early stages of ADRD will probably be able to carry out the whole activity of baking cookies—shopping for ingredients, following the recipe, baking the cookies, and serving and eating them. The moderately impaired individual will require assistance with selecting and measuring the ingredients but will be able to mix, shape, and serve the cookies, as well as help to clean up. The severely impaired person, perhaps with hand-over-hand guidance, will be able to mix the dough, drop spoonfuls on a cookie sheet, appreciate the aroma of baking cookies, and eat them.

Most activities can be graded to account for different skill levels, and thus provide a greater opportunity for success. Consider, for example, sanding, graded from the highest skill level to the lowest skill level.

1. Prepare all materials, cut wood in the desired shape, and sand it; decide when the wood is smooth enough.

2. Select a precut object and sand it, using coarse and then fine sandpaper.

3. Given a precut, partially sanded object, sand it with fine sandpaper until it is smooth.

14.2 Adapt the Activity

Changes are made in the materials, equipment, or method to enable the participation of persons with disabilities. There are literally thousands of examples, many of which are given in the activity modality sections. For persons with poor vision, use larger letters, coarser yarn, and outline guides. For persons with poor grasp, use larger handles and fatter pens, and stabilize with clamps or nonskid material. For persons with memory loss, do one step at a time, post a chart of steps, and use concrete cues.

14.3 Backward Chaining

An often-repeated activity is broken into steps. The person is first assisted to do the last step independently, then progresses backward to the previous step until it is mastered. Continue in this fashion until the whole activity can be done. This works very well with self-feeding, where the last step is bringing food to the mouth. Providing hand-over-hand guidance for this step often serves as a cue that triggers procedural memory for the whole activity of eating. This also works well with an activity such as playing catch. The last step is the release of the beanbag to another's hand. The person is physically guided, as necessary, to do only this step. As this step is mastered the person progresses to the previous steps, pick up and toss the beanbag, catch it, etc.

14.4 Spreading the Steps of an Activity over Several Sessions or Days

Spreading out the steps allows the completion of very complex activities, even with the very severely impaired. For example, it took us five days, but my severely impaired patients and I made pumpkin pies for Thanksgiving.

- Day 1: Examine and appreciate the pumpkin and prepare for cooking. (I did the cutting and cooking.)
- Day 2: Sieve the pumpkin and refrigerate.
- Day 3: Mix the ingredients for pie dough and refrigerate. (Cutouts of baked dough are tasty treats!)
- Day 4: Appreciate the aroma of the spices, mix the pumpkin filling, and refrigerate.
- Day 5: Spoon prepared filling into tart and pie shells. (Some were able to roll their own, others used dough already rolled.) Bake and enjoy the wonderful smells, along with the delicious taste.

14.5 Doing an Activity Analysis

Someone running an activities program simply does not have time to do a detailed analysis of every activity. However, a basic understanding of the many parts of an activity is essential. It is highly recommended that you do this process in detail with at least one activity, perhaps most usefully one that has not been successful. It will help to explain why it failed. You may discover, for example, that the person does not have adequate fine motor coordination and concentration to do stenciling.

14.6 Sample Outline for Activity Analysis

Sample Activity: Peeling and Eating an Orange

Steps

1. Wash hands.
2. Select an orange and put on plate.
3. Start removing peels with thumbnail or spoon.
4. Remove peels and white membrane.
5. Divide orange into sections.
6. Eat sections, removing seeds as necessary.
7. Wash hands.
8. Dispose of peels.

Skills Required

- *motor:* fine (e.g., to pinch the pieces of peel between thumb and finger), gross (e.g., to hold the orange), coordination (e.g., to hold the orange in one hand and peel with the other), strength (e.g., to pull off the peels), endurance (e.g., to continue until the orange is peeled)
- *cognitive:* judgment (e.g., when is enough membrane removed), memory (procedural, e.g., how to peel an orange), reasoning (e.g., where to discard the peels), planning (e.g., remove all the peels before starting to eat), decision making (e.g., which orange to take), concentration (e.g., to attend until the task is finished)
- *perceptual:* body awareness (e.g., where is the hand in relation to the orange); figure-ground (e.g., selecting one orange from several in a basket); eye-hand coordination (e.g., to pick up an orange section and put it in mouth); color, shape/size discrimination (e.g., how large a section can be eaten)
- *sensory:* vision, hearing, taste
- *social:* communication (e.g., with leader or staff person), sharing (e.g., sharing with other group members)

Value of the Activity

- *sensory stimulation:* senses involved—taste, touch, sight, smell, hearing, movement
- *motor:* range of motion in the fingers and arm, gross coordination, pinch strength, grip strength
- *emotional:* self-esteem (e.g., in being able to do a familiar task), independence (e.g., being able to do an independent activity), choice (which orange to take), enhance reminiscence (e.g., association with getting an orange in a Christmas stocking)

15.0 ASSESSMENT: SELECTING GROUP MEMBERS

Assessment is very complex, and yet it is so crucial. It is complex because the abilities of persons with ADRD vary so much from skill to skill and from hour to hour. For instance, a person may require total assistance with bathing and dressing and yet be able to function as a competent hostess in a group. Someone may have almost no verbal skills and yet be able to respond to and enjoy a specially structured sensory stimulation group. Assessment is crucial because only with an understanding of someone's preserved and continuing skills can the group leader encourage maximal participation in the group. It is also essential for documenting the effects of group involvement.

In addition, the assessment of "activity pursuit patterns" is legally mandated, as part of the 1987 federal nursing home law, OBRA87 (Perschbacher 1991). This assessment, documenting time awake, average time involved in activities, preferred activity settings, general activities preferences, and preferences for more or different activities, is designed to serve as a trigger for individual activities planning.

The most essential overall guideline for assessment is to avoid hard-and-fast rules. Do not decide what someone can or cannot do on the basis of the stage of the disease. While some have developed lists that describe symptoms and deficits at various stages, many others state that the course of ADRD is so variable from skill to skill and person to person that such classifications are not very useful (Baum et al. 1988; Cohen 1988; Cohen & Eisdorfer 1986; Dippel & Hutton 1988; Mace 1990; NIHCD 1987; OTA 1987; Teri et al. 1990; Volicer et al. 1987, 1988). Staging becomes particularly difficult with advanced dementia (Davis et al. 1990). For those who lead activity-based groups, the usefulness of determining the stage of the disease is even more questionable. Well-planned and well-designed groups are meant to call on remaining skills, skills that may not be so easily observed in standard self-care situations; for example, social skills, emotional memory, sensory appreciation.

Mental status questionnaires are commonly used to screen for cognitive impairment. The most commonly used mental status test is the Folstein Mini-Mental State (MMS) (Folstein et al. 1975; Katzman & Jackson 1991; Rubenstein et al. 1989). These scores can give the activity leader a general idea about whether the person is moderately or severely impaired. In practice, in relation to activity groups, this author uses MMS scores of 20 to 26 as indicative of mild impairment, scores of 11 to 19 as indicative of moderate impairment, and scores of 10 and below as indicative of severe impairment. This is supported by the information in the literature (Burns et al. 1991b; Cooper et al. 1990). However, because mental status tests are based primarily on verbal and reasoning skills, the scores are not predictive of performance in a social, nonverbally focused group. Similarly, studies have concluded that mental status tests are not good predictors of performance in the activities of daily living (Reed et al. 1989).

Because of their difficulties with abstract thinking and verbal skills, the best way to assess how persons will function in a group is by observation of actual activity performance and a trial in the group (Mace 1990). Gathering some basic information from the records, other staff, and a brief one-to-one assessment will indicate which groups to try.

An assessment should include four parts:

1. review of information from charts, staff, and family
2. informal discussion/interview with the person
3. group participation
4. ongoing evaluation of group participation and reassessment

Each facility should develop forms and formats that best suit its needs. The following is an outline of information that must be used in an assessment. Documenting activity assessments and progress is now legally required. Of even greater significance is the vital role of documentation in making use of personally significant information during groups and for measuring progress toward goals and objectives. The information contained in these assessments is confidential.

15.1 Background Information

Background information is absolutely essential. It helps in planning activities, in using cues to encourage responses, to fill in the blanks when someone does respond, and above all to build self-esteem by reaffirming the value of previous life experiences. This information allows you to understand something about the person as a whole, and not just as someone with ADRD. It is useful to keep this information on large file cards or in a small portable binder for easy and quick reference, should it be needed during a group. It is recommended that this review be done before an interview, as it will help in deciding what other information you need and how best to gather it. However, be very careful not to let this information influence you to decide in advance about the person's group skills.

15.2 Format for Recording Background Information

1. Full name (including birth name for married women):
2. Preferred form of address (Mr., Mrs., Miss, Ms., first name, or lifelong nickname):
3. Birthplace:
4. Birth date:
5. Parents' names and occupations (for many, these associations are very important):
6. Family members and significant others:
7. Spouse:
8. Children's names and place of residence:
9. Siblings' names and place of residence:
10. Special friends:
11. Other relatives:
12. Places lived as an adult:
13. Most recent place of residence:
14. Occupations:
15. Significant personal accomplishments (related to occupation, recreation, entertainment, hobbies, athletics, politics, etc.):
16. Religious affiliation and involvement (it is very important to be aware of religious backgrounds, in order to orient the person to important celebrations):
17. Hobbies and interests:
18. Favorite foods:
19. Medical and dietary precautions (e.g., diabetic or low-salt diet, unsteady on feet, precaution for choking, allergies):
20. Sensory functioning
    —Vision (e.g., wears glasses, has cataracts):
    —Hearing (hears in one ear better than another):
    —Hand dominance (This is very important. Many persons with ADRD have been thought to be less capable than they really were simply because they were left-handed and were being treated as if they were right-handed):
21. Mobility (chair-dependent, requires assistance to walk, etc.):
22. Self-care (level of independence):

15.3 Pre–Group Assessment

A very brief screening interview, in combination with the information gathered in the first stage of the assessment, will help to place the person in a trial group at the most suitable level. It is best to do the interview in a quiet, private room, but this may not be possible for reasons of time or space. The emphasis during this time is to meet the person; begin to establish some rapport; and get a broad understanding of his or her social, communication, and functional skills. The climate should be one of positive acceptance and nonthreatening. It is essentially a "conversation" and sharing of information. A standard interview format would be too threatening for the person with ADRD. The use of specialized communication skills is essential. Crepeau (1986) provides an excellent outline for an activities assessment that offers other useful suggestions.

The following is a suggested format only. Introduce yourself and extend a hand in greeting. Ask how the person is. Depending on verbal skills, ask other "getting to know you" type questions such as "Where were you born?" and "What did you work at?" If possible, have tea, coffee, or juice together. This begins to establish rapport and allows observation of motor and cognitive skills. Attempt some other simple activity that might be done in a group, such as putting flowers in a vase or looking at an interesting object (e.g., an old camera). Offer a pen and paper and ask the person to write his or her name. During this brief session, make the following observations:

- social skills: Responds to greeting, shakes hands, smiles, verbalizes, introduces self, makes eye contact?
- verbal skills: Uses single words, phrases, logical sentences? Exhibits understanding, normal structure to conversation? Follows directions? Has difficulties such as word finding, perseveration (getting stuck)?
- nonverbal communication: Uses facial expression, gestures, voice tone? Responds to caring personal touch?
- cognitive skills: Shows attention, concentration (easily distracted) (length of time able to attend), memory (immediate and short-term), initiative, ability to make choices? Follows one-, two-, or three-step verbal commands? Able to read? Comprehends simple written phrases?
- mood: Happy, sad, angry, changeable, appropriate to the situation?
- motor skills: Hand grasp, catches ball (one-handed or two), hand dominance, manipulates small and large objects?
- spontaneous movements: Demonstrates spontaneous movements? Any restlessness? Able to write name?

- posture and mobility: Maintains normal posture, slumps, requires support to sit upright, etc.? Walks assisted or unassisted? Immobile?
- self-stimulating behavior: If present, what kind?

15.4 Group Participation

Assessment during groups is an expansion of the observations made during the initial assessment. These may be recorded on a chart, such as that suggested for sensory stimulation or reminiscence groups (see Chapters 6 and 7). Consider the following:

- response to verbal prompting
- response to nonverbal prompting, such as hand-over-hand guidance
- favorite types of activities, especially self-directed ones
- preferred sensory modality (e.g., auditory, visual, touch)
- level of cuing required (e.g., encouragement, verbal prompt, physical prompt, demonstration, hand-over-hand guidance).

15.5 The Activity Plan

Developing the specifics of the activity plan is the responsibility of the activity leader. However, coordinating the plan with the overall goals for the person is the responsibility of activity leaders together with the whole treatment team. Activities are essential. They are most effective when they are a part of the total plan for the person. Activity leaders can gain useful pointers about the person from other team members, such as hand strength and perceptual skills from the occupational therapist, ambulation from the physiotherapist, mental status from the psychiatrist, and self-care from the nursing staff. Other team members can learn useful information from activity leaders, such as social skills and interest and ability in self-directed activity. Successful treatment is a total team effort.

It is very important that persons with intact cognitive function be involved in developing their activity plans and personal objectives. Such involvement is usually beyond the capability of persons with advanced ADRD. However, the activity leader becomes their advocate by developing an activity plan based on an assessment of their previous interests, needs, and expressions of interest in particular activities. Individual participation in developing these plans usually cannot be based on discussion; instead, it can be based on observation of positive responses to activities. Offering manageable personal choice, usually between two alternatives, maintains an element of personal involvement. For example, the person could make a choice between tea and coffee, choose which book to look at, choose which color paper to use, etc. Some persons may also be able to decide whether they would rather be involved in, for example, music group or exercise group.

On the basis of the assessment, the activity group leader must set some concrete, individual objectives for the participant. Some examples are

- assist in plant care activities two times per week
- increase verbalization to at least three times per group
- improve concentration by attending during one-to-one contact for at least five minutes
- participate in music activities at least once a week
- improve motor skill by participating in at least three exchanges of the exercise ball or beanbag
- participate in baking and tea group at least once a week

Having set these goals, measuring progress becomes a simple matter of describing whether or not the objectives have been met.

15.6 Ongoing Assessment

Since ADRD is progressive, continuous assessment is essential. The activity leader should be particularly observant about any unusual or sudden changes in behavior, as this may indicate another illness or problem.

16.0 CHALLENGING BEHAVIORS

A great many challenging behaviors, such as wandering, restlessness, day/night reversal, and repeated questioning, are associated with ADRD. Although these behaviors challenge and stress personal and professional caregivers, and are often cited as a primary cause of admission to long-term care, there has been very little study of either the cause or the most effective approach in dealing with these behaviors (Cooper et al. 1990; Jackson et al.1989; Mace 1990).

The level of cognitive impairment is loosely associated with certain behaviors (Jackson et al.1989; Teri et al. 1988). One study of 3,351 Rhode Island nursing home residents found that 26.4 percent of the residents had exhibited some form of disruptive behavior in a two-week period. Moderate to severe cognitive impairment was associated with the highest rate of disruptive behavior (Jackson et al. 1989).

However, a more recent in-depth study of 680 subjects with probable AD, seen at the California

Alzheimer's Disease Diagnostic and Treatment Centers, found only a small positive correlation between level of cognitive impairment and the presence of five behaviors: agitation/anger, personality change, wandering, hallucinations/delusions, and insomnia and depression (Cooper et al. 1990). Although a study by Teri et al. (1988) found an association between cognitive impairment and wandering and agitation, a subsequent study (Teri et al.1990) found no such association. These authors suggest that since the correlation is weak, other factors such as coexisting diseases, emotional disorders, drug reactions, and environmental and social factors are more important than cognitive function in relation to problem behaviors. Another study of 346 residents of intermediate care facilities found no association between cognitive impairment and behavior problems (Everitt et al. 1991).

Problem behaviors, then, are not an inevitable consequence of cognitive decline. There is much that can be done to prevent or minimize the occurrence of these behaviors. Whether or not these behaviors are a problem depends to a large extent on the setting and on the training caregivers have received to deal with these behaviors. A study of behavior problems and the related staff distress had some interesting findings. While agitation was the most common behavior problem among 42 percent of the 346 residents, it was found to be severely distressful to staff only 6 percent of the time. In contrast, 33 percent of the residents were reported to demonstrate withdrawn behavior, and it was found to be distressful to staff nearly 66 percent of the time (Everitt et al. 1991).

Above all else, it is essential to understand that these difficult behaviors are symptoms of a physical brain disease. They are not under the conscious control of the person, nor are they deliberate attempts to be difficult or aggravating. Persons with ADRD are struggling, as best they can, to cope with deteriorating skills in a world that is becoming increasingly difficult for them to understand. As caregivers, we cannot possibly expect our impaired clients to try any harder than they already are. Instead, we have to try harder to understand why the behavior is occurring and what we can do about it. For caregivers who take a problem-solving approach to these behaviors, they become a challenge rather than a problem.

Unfortunately, in the past, the all-too-common response to these challenging behaviors was the use of chemical and/or physical restraints. These approaches often, in fact, increase agitation and certainly decrease function. Restraints are the approaches of last resort, and are to be used only when the safety of others or of the person is in question. In fact, there is little evidence that drugs (chemical restraints) are effective in the management of problem behaviors associated with ADRD. Improvement is likely to be only moderate, and only those patients with the most severe problems are likely to have a response (Phillipson et al. 1990). Everitt et al. (1991) found a substantial level of behavior problems despite the use of psychoactive medication.

It is becoming increasingly recognized that provision of a supportive and stimulating physical and social environment is preventative and the best approach to dealing with these behaviors (Eimer 1989; Katzman & Jackson 1991; Knopman & Sawyer-DeMaris 1990; Mace 1990; Stone 1990; Strumpf et al. 1990; Taft & Barkin 1990). In addition, there is now legislation in the United States that requires drug audits to be conducted in nursing homes at least once a month, by a licensed pharmacist. There are strict guidelines for use of psychotropic drugs, which include a statement that "antipsychotics are inappropriate if used simply to control such symptoms as anxiety, wandering, restlessness or insomnia" (Taft & Barkin 1990, 8). This legislation will have far-reaching effects, given that studies report that 43 to 87 percent of the residents of nursing homes are given psychotropic medication (Taft & Barkin 1990). Similarly, in October 1990, a United States federal mandate required the reduction of the use of physical restraints in nursing homes, which is estimated to include more than 30 percent of nursing home residents (Strumpf et al. 1990).

Personnel conducting activities programs are challenged to support this mandate, to develop alternatives to physical and chemical restraints in dealing with problem behaviors. This is essential not only for legal reasons, but even more importantly, for the humane and compassionate reason of protecting adult dignity. This challenge must be dealt with not only within the larger context of the residential environment but also within the smaller environment of groups and one-to-one activities.

We are challenged to examine such factors as the milieu of our groups, our approach to the person, the activities presented, and our communication techniques to determine the source and develop a solution for these behaviors. Permanent exclusion of the person from participation in activities is not an acceptable solution. In fact, an environment devoid of meaningful activity and stimulation is one cause of difficult behaviors such as restlessness, and repetitive, self-stimulating behaviors such as loud, repetitive clapping or banging. Other causes of these behaviors require much more study, but also included are other aspects of the physical and social environment, the degree of damage to the brain, other factors that create excess disability (e.g., an acute illness), and the person's lifelong methods of coping.

Responses to the challenge of these difficult behaviors in ways that maintain maximal function and that cause the least stress for the person and the caregiver cover a very large area. They are discussed in more detail in other publications dealing with direct care (Altman 1987; Dippel & Hutton 1988; Jarvik & Winograd 1988; Mace 1990; Volicer et al. 1988). For the purposes of this book, this brief section considers only those behaviors and approaches that may be a concern during activity groups.

First of all, review the principles of group work, especially such important factors as unconditional positive regard and providing success experiences that do not confront persons with their disabilities. Careful attention to these principles and the provision of a reassuring, supportive group milieu will go a long way toward preventing these difficult behaviors.

In dealing with disruptive behaviors, the first step is to take an *organized approach*. Consider the following important questions:

- What is the real consequence of or problem with the behavior? Is this something that is disturbing or dangerous to others? Is the behavior a problem only for you and can you ignore it? For example, is behavior such as watering the plants too often, eating with the wrong utensil, wearing mismatched clothing, or rubbing or patting the chair arms a problem for you or for the participant?

- What are the possible causes of the behavior? Is the behavior caused by the environment, frustration, illness, boredom, misinterpretation, lack of attention, or attention for negative behavior?

- When, and under what circumstances, does the behavior occur? Where, when, and with whom? Keep a chart or use another recording system.

- What change is necessary? Eliminate the behavior, reduce the frequency, increase the frequency, or change caregiver expectations? Pick one solution and try it.

- Did the first solution work? If not, why not?

- Is there something else that can be tried?

16.1 Guidelines for Preventing Problem Behaviors

The following guidelines are based on the literature and my personal experience in dealing with challenging behaviors.

Constantly assess the group milieu, being sure that it is calm, comforting, and reassuring, and neither overstimulating nor understimulating. This is the first line of preventative action and one that is arrived at in your setting, with your participants, by using some of the basics presented in this book and elsewhere, along with trial and error.

Be consistent in general programming, scheduling, and approach. Programs should be given at the same time and in the same place, and follow the same format. Changes should be introduced gradually. However, consistency should not be confused with rigidity. Each person is unique, the disease is progressive, and behavior changes from day to day and even from hour to hour. Particular individual approaches must be reevaluated constantly and adapted if necessary. If something is not working, discontinue it.

Distract rather than confront. Offering alternate attention, such as a walk or a snack, may help the person to forget what was disturbing him or her. In this case, memory loss can be used to advantage. For example, if someone is clapping repetitively (perhaps initiated by some music used in the group), offer another activity that is less disruptive but equally repetitive, such as sanding a cutting board. Physical and motor distractions are more successful than other distractions (see Chapter 7).

Never shout or display anger. The verbal message of shouting will not be understood, but the emotional message will cause further alarm for the person with ADRD as well as for others in the group.

Use gentle humor as part of the nonverbal approach. Remember, however, that humor involves laughing with, and not laughing at, the person. Sense of humor is very much individualized, so be sure that your comments will be amusing to others, not just yourself.

Isolate the person from the group—briefly—for disruptive or disturbing behavior. See the behavioral approaches section of this chapter. This action is very effective with some individuals, but it should be used carefully and consistently.

Analyze the circumstances surrounding the behavior and try to prevent them from happening again. The seating arrangement, overstimulating music, glare from a window, cold room temperature, or an overly demanding activity are all factors that could cause agitation or distress.

Provide a bridge from the group to the usual routine of the day, and vice versa. This is a crucial issue. Change is frightening and upsetting for persons with ADRD. We must provide them with the cues and reassurance they need in order to adapt. If a person is summarily taken to a group, without a gentle introduction and explanation, he or she may be so upset with the change that settling into the group is impossible. Even more commonly, after the pleasure and stimulation of the group, he or she may have difficulty resettling into the regular routine. Say a lengthy goodbye, review the group theme, remind the person when you will return, leave a memento of the group, and connect the person with direct-care staff, as necessary.

Pay particular attention to nonverbal communication such as tone of voice, facial expression, and gestures. Watch for signs of increasing agitation or anxiety and intervene to relieve concerns and prevent further escalation.

If the behavior is unusual for the person, report it to other team members. Investigate possible physical causes such as fever, constipation, illness, or uncomfortable clothing.

Build self-esteem by providing success experiences. Be aware of the individual's capabilities and do not offer activities that are too difficult or too easy. Display completed craft and art projects for everyone to appreciate, and compliment the person.

Offer meaningful activities, walks, and exercise to reduce boredom and frustration.

Use gentle, reassuring personal touch as appropriate, but do not restrain unless absolutely necessary for safety reasons.

Explain all procedures, especially changes of location, to those who are wheelchair-dependent.

Speak slowly, in short simple sentences.

Never lie, make false promises, or give insincere reassurances. It is absolutely a mistake to believe that such reassurances are harmless because of the individual's memory loss. The person may not remember the facts, but he or she will remember the emotion associated with being deceived. This feeling undermines the establishment of a trusting relationship.

Evaluate interventions and responses and try to understand what works best with each person.

Schedule activities at times of the day when the person is most alert, usually in the morning, or most in need of activity, often at the end of the afternoon and after supper.

16.2 Specific Behaviors

Wandering, Pacing, and Restlessness

These behaviors are frequently cited as problem behaviors associated with ADRD (Cohen-Mansfield et al. 1990; Dawson & Reid 1987). In fact, wandering and/or pacing can provide an outlet for physical energy and relieve stress. One study of 402 nursing home residents found that 39 percent of these residents were pacers (Cohen-Mansfield et al. 1991). Of great interest in that study was the finding that residents who paced were not only more cognitively impaired than those who did not, but also healthier (i.e., they had significantly fewer physical diagnoses, less pain, better appetites, and less impaired eating skills and received fewer medications).

These residents were also more likely to have had past stressful life experiences. From this perspective, then, the challenge with wandering and pacing behaviors is to provide a safe environment that allows this activity (see environmental section of this chapter as well as McGrowder-Lin & Bhatt 1988; Rader 1987). It is also important to pay careful attention to nutrition, as persons who pace may require up to 1,600 calories more per day (Rheaume et al. 1988).

In a group setting, these behaviors may be a problem when someone first comes to the group, especially if he or she already has a tendency to pace. As the individual becomes more familiar with the group, reassured by the milieu and rewarded by participation, wandering almost always becomes less and less of a problem (Bryant 1991). The study by Cohen-Mansfield et al. (1991), in fact, reports that pacing is less likely to occur when other people are close at hand. With reassurance and familiarity, most come to join the group at the table. Until this point is reached, allow the person to wander about the group room, bearing the following considerations in mind:

- Check to make sure that no dangerous materials such as poisonous plants, hot water taps, a stove, craft supplies, or sharp objects are accessible.

- Disguise the exit with a curtain or removable cloth strips, paint the handle and frame the same color as the door, and try a two-dimensional grid in front of the door (for further information see Hussian & Brown 1987; Namazi et al. 1989).

- Do not try to integrate more than one wanderer at a time.

- Remember that at least a part of the wandering behavior is related to searching for the familiar. Constant reassurance provides a message that the person is safe and cared for.

- Take the materials from the group to the wanderer.

- Encourage the wanderer to join the others at the table for tea or coffee. This is a particularly good time to draw the group together.

- Check to see whether the person needs to go to the bathroom.

- Provide a safe outlet for the energy used in pacing (e.g., a rocking chair or exercise bicycle). If the person wanders from the group or the facility, walk with him or her, matching pace. Gradually change direction and return to the facility.

Repetitive Questioning

Accept repeated questions! Because of severe memory loss, the person really does not remember having just asked the same question. Be patient and reassuring. If the question has to do with finding a loved one, such as a parent, a spouse, or a child, tell the person that you are there and will care for him or her. Identify with the need to recall this person and assist him or her to reminisce.

- Offer a variety of materials, experiences, and activities.
- If the person perseverates (gets stuck on one phrase) offer some interesting and distracting activity or materials to redirect.
- For some, providing a large-print card with the answers to frequent questions is helpful.
- Provide ample orienting cues in the environment, such as calendars and clocks, and reality reassurance during conversation.
- Look for the emotional need and meaning behind repeated questions.

Disruptive Repetitive Behaviors

Repetitive hand clapping, banging, or shouting can be a problem during group activities. These behaviors are a particular problem for a few participants and often are the result of boredom. Lacking stimulation, these persons provide their own. The behavior may be complicated by the tendency to perseverate (repetitively clapping, or shouting one word) and by the attention it gets—even if it is negative attention. These behaviors may be less of a problem in groups, but may occur when the leader is busy with another participant. The best approach is to distract with self-directed repetitive activity that is not disruptive, for example, looking at a book or magazine, feeling or holding onto a varied-textured cloth book or quilt, sanding, or batting a foam ball attached to a bat with a string. For more suggestions see the self-directed activities in Chapter 7.

Incontinence

Toileting schedules and incontinence are usually managed by direct-care nursing staff. No matter how demented, incontinence is extremely embarrassing for the individual. Always be especially careful to protect dignity and self-esteem at such times. Persons running activity groups should participate in whatever program has been set up and be aware of the following pointers:

- If it is not already part of the routine, suggest that participants be toileted just before a group.
- If someone appears particularly restless or uncomfortable, try to find out, discreetly, whether he or she needs to go to the bathroom.
- If a participant has an accident during the group, quietly assist the person to go, or to be taken, to direct-care staff to be changed.

- Offer a large amount of fluids during the day, as a full bladder is necessary to convey the message of the need to urinate. Cutting back fluids reduces this message.
- Report unusually frequent urination to medical staff, as this may be a sign of a urinary tract infection.

Suspiciousness and Hallucinations

Because of their cognitive losses, especially their inability to remember and to understand what is going on around them, persons with ADRD may become suspicious that family, staff, or peers are taking their things, trying to harm them, etc. Some may also have visual or auditory hallucinations. The following approaches are helpful:

- Provide reassurance and respond to the emotion of the concern. For example, if a person says, "That nurse took my purse," reply, "Mrs. MacDonald, I know you must miss having your purse with you. I will help you find it after the group. For now, would you help me by holding onto this purse [or book] for me?"
- Never lie to or deceive the person.
- Never play into the misperception or hallucination or attempt to argue with or reason the person out of it. These misconceptions are not reasonable to us, but they are firmly fixed and represent the person's best attempt at explaining what is happening to him or her.
- Provide order and consistency in the environment, making it easier for the person to function.
- Provide safe, secure, but accessible places for prized personal possessions. Mount family photos on the wall near the bed; attach pouches or carry bags to personal chairs; attach "fanny packs" for personal possessions. Such pouches or packs can be made in materials of various textures so that they also provide sensory stimulation.
- Be sure that vision and hearing are checked regularly and that glasses or hearing aids are properly cleaned and worn.
- Avoid ambiguous or confusing designs and pictures.
- Explain sounds or events that may cause alarm or confusion. For example, "That noise is the truck picking up the garbage."

Agitation and Aggressive Behavior

All of the preceding suggestions are preventions for the escalation of agitated behavior that may lead the person to strike out. It should be stressed again that a calming, reassuring environment and approach is of utmost importance in preventing these incidents. Agitation or aggressive behavior is much less likely to occur in an activity group than in the more intimate situations involving personal care. In fact, in three years of working with the most severely impaired persons with ADRD, I had a patient strike out at me only once. This was quite understandable, as I was attempting to get him to stop eating from the sugar container, a very rewarding activity! Watch for warning signs, and if a person is becoming agitated or upset, intervene at once; either remove the person to a quieter setting or try some of the procedures already suggested. Other pointers:

- Remain calm.
- Never approach or move the person unexpectedly. Persons with ADRD may have a return of the "startle response," a reflexive reaction to a sudden noise, touch, or change of position.
- Avoid confrontation, except in cases of safety.
- Speak calmly and quietly, responding to the person's emotional concerns.
- Call for help if you are at all concerned for your safety or that of other participants.
- Keep your distance and allow the upset individual personal space.
- Reduce stimulation in the area by, for example, turning off music.
- Remove any potentially harmful objects in the environment.

Catastrophic Reaction

Catastrophic reaction is an extreme, agitated, inappropriate response accompanied by extreme anger, agitation, crying, etc., to what may appear to be a simple or unimportant occurrence. These reactions occur when the person with ADRD feels overwhelmed, perhaps by something as apparently simple as dropping the exercise ball. Again, these reactions are best avoided by following the preventative actions already discussed and watching for signs of increasing agitation and concern. In the event that a catastrophic reaction does occur, follow these pointers:

- Speak calmly and reassuringly.
- Move slowly.
- Do not restrain, but do use reassuring physical touch, as appropriate.
- Remove the person to a calmer environment.
- Call for assistance, as necessary.
- Use gradual distraction.

Important preventative measures are:

- Avoid challenging the person beyond his or her capacity to act and respond.
- Avoid overstimulating environments.
- Analyze the circumstances surrounding the reaction and try to prevent them in the future.
- Evaluate the action taken and determine how effective it really was.

Inappropriate Sexual Behavior

Inappropriate sexual behavior is extremely unusual. Sometimes a person's confused actions, such as undoing buttons or zippers or attempting to remove clothing, may be incorrectly interpreted as sexual behavior. In reality, the person may have to go to the bathroom and be unaware that he or she is in a public place, or cannot find the toilet. Sometimes removing clothing or undoing buttons and zippers is another form of self-stimulation or self-directed activity. Other persons may masturbate, being unaware that they are in a public place.

Still others may misinterpret a caregiver's touch as a sexual gesture. This is an extremely sensitive and difficult subject for all caregivers—especially family members, who will be upset at their relative's seeming loss of social control. Cohen and Eisdorfer (1986) discussed these issues very carefully and in detail. The reader is referred to their excellent book, *The Loss of Self*. The following pointers may be helpful to the activity group leader:

- Be aware that the individual with ADRD has continuing needs for caring and affection, which may be unmet in an institutional setting. Provide caring, personal touch to meet those needs, but be sure that they are appropriate: a touch on the arm, shoulder, or hand, a hug around the shoulders, taking a person's arm or hand as you walk to group, rubbing on hand cream, a shoulder or neck massage. Make sure actions cannot be misunderstood, as would, for example, sitting very close beside someone on the bed.
- Protect individual dignity. Never make a game or a joke of sexual overtures from clients to staff or client to client. A show of affection between clients may be good for both, but if it is distressing to one person he or she should be protected and ensured of personal dignity.
- Provide and respect the need for privacy.
- Provide ample opportunity for bolstering self-esteem and receiving important positive attention.

Bringing these back—work and love, meaning—
"centered" him, gave him back a firm base of
identity and health, and alleviated the violent
physio-logical oscillations he had been having.

Art and play, and drama and rite, had a
therapeutic power as strong as L-dopa, as strong
as any drug; but it was clear these worked in a
different way. They worked, one felt *to evoke a
self,* and not in some partial and mechanical way.

—Oliver Sacks

Therapeutic Activities

1.0 ACTIVITIES OF DAILY LIVING

Bathing, grooming, dressing, eating, and toileting are the most basic, the most essential, and the most frequently overlooked human activities. For independent adults, these activities are so fundamental that we do them as if by rote, scarcely giving the fact that we have brushed our teeth or had a bath today a second thought. We, for instance, would be unlikely to highlight these activities when discussing the day's accomplishments with friends or colleagues.

When, however, an illness or a long-term disability interferes with performing these routine activities of daily life, we come to appreciate their profound importance to our sense of personal competence. Persons who have had to depend on someone else to brush their teeth, comb their hair, or feed them truly appreciate the significance of independence in self-care routines.

Deficits associated with ADRD have a progressive, negative effect on the performance of the activities of daily living (ADL) (Aronson et al. 1992; Birren & Schaie 1990; Doble 1991; Edwards et al. 1991; Myton & Allen 1991; Teri et al. 1989; Venable & Mitchell 1991). In the early stages, the person may forget a hair appointment or how to get home from the shop. As the disease progresses, the person may be unable to initiate hair combing, or apraxia may cause difficulty in co-ordinating the necessary movements. At this stage, the person requires 24-hour care with assistance and supervision for most ADL. Unfortunately, this requirement

often progresses far too quickly to a complete dependence on others for every aspect of ADL. Even if the resident continues to perform most activities of daily living independently, the scheduling and structure are determined by the facility. This often contributes to the resident's feeling of dependence. The findings of a survey of cognitively well residents of two long-term care facilities are of particular interest in this regard (Winger & Schirm 1989). Despite the fact that 97 percent and 95 percent, respectively, of these residents were independent in eating, only 40 percent of each group saw themselves as actually being in control of this activity. The timing, location, and content of this essential activity of daily living were determined by others and negatively affected their sense of being in control.

An institutional setting particularly fosters the dependence of persons with ADRD (Burgener & Barton 1991; Heacock et al. 1991; Reichenbach & Kirchman 1991; Solomon 1990). This can lead to a situation of excess disabilities, discussed in Chapter 2. Regardless of lifelong personal routines, they must fit into the daily institutional routine of, for example, being dressed for breakfast by eight o'clock. It is particularly difficult for the person with ADRD to adjust lifetime habits to this new schedule. Perhaps the person never dressed until noon and was accustomed to puttering about in the morning with frequent cups of tea. Perhaps, as is the case with many older people, he or she was accustomed to sponge baths, rather than showers or tub baths. (A very lovely new facility in our province has private one-piece shower units, which are all being used for storing luggage!) In an effort to have the person with ADRD meet this new routine, care staff often fall into "doing for" rather than enabling and "doing with." In one very interesting controlled study of 63 newly admitted nursing home residents, nursing staff were informed that half of these residents were expected to do much better than most people with their particular disabilities. At a three-month post-test, these residents were found to have significantly fewer depressive symptoms, but they also had significant losses in functional independence (Learman et al. 1990). It seems likely, as the authors suggest, that nursing staff expressed their interest and encouragement for these high-expectation residents by doing more for them, rather than by encouraging independence.

In addition, the institutional environment is frequently missing familiar cues that prompt functional behaviors (see Chapter 4). Perhaps nowhere else is this more obvious than with regard to eating. Persons with ADRD may not try to feed themselves because the institutional dining area does not look like a place to eat, nor does the food or serving method look familiar. In this instance, and others, the lack of initiative, a common symptom of ADRD, is interpreted as a lack of skill or a lack of interest.

Unfortunately, the frequent institutional response to difficulties with self-feeding tends to be to feed the person, rather than to design environments and programs to encourage independent eating (Birren & Schaie 1990; Nolen & Garrard 1988; Rogers & Snow 1982). This is the end result of several factors, in addition to those already mentioned involving the institutional tendency to encourage dependence rather than independence. Staff may be concerned about maintaining proper nutrition. This concern is, indeed, a valid one. Several studies have found that the food intake of seniors in long-term care is below the recommended dietary allowance in several nutrients (Welch et al. 1986). One study found this to be the case, regardless of whether the residents ate in the dining room or in their own rooms (Welch et al. 1986). Others report that persons with AD who pace constantly require as much as 1,600 calories more per day (Rheaume et al. 1988).

Lacking an understanding of how to enable self-feeding, staff will feed persons with ADRD. In one survey, more than half of the 84 residents were fed lying in bed, which neither encourages self-feeding nor promotes safe swallowing (Rogers & Snow 1982). There is also a misperception that more time is required to encourage or enable self-feeding rather than to spoon-feed. In fact, the opposite was found to be true in one survey of 106 nursing home residents. An average of

13.4 minutes was required to spoon-feed a resident and 3.1 minutes to supervise and encourage a resident (Nolen & Garrard 1988). Another study showed that interventions that are not time-consuming can have a great impact on nutrition. The nutrient intake of 21 institutionalized elderly patients (Group A) with a primary diagnosis of chronic organic brain syndrome, who were capable of eating independently, was compared with that of a matched control group (Group B). Both groups were encouraged verbally to eat. In addition to verbal encouragement, persons in Group A were touched lightly on the arm five times during the course of a one-hour meal. Persons in Group A demonstrated a significant increase in food intake, 29 percent more calories and 36 percent more protein (Eaton et al. 1986). Unfortunately, interventions such as these that encourage independence are not widely used. Consequently, persons with ADRD become deprived of participation in self-feeding and other essential ADL, having a further devastating effect on their self-esteem. It must be considered, at least in part, that resistance to care provision is a last desperate effort to assert the need for independence in ADL.

How would the care burden of overworked direct-care staff, the difficulties of activity staff in planning meaningful activities at which the person with ADRD can be successful, and, most of all, the stress on individuals with ADRD living in institutional settings be altered if enabling individual involvement in ADL were to become a primary and integrated part of the activities of the day? This reversal of approaches has been found to have positive effects for all concerned in special care facilities such as Welsley Hall in Michigan, Baycrest in Ontario, and Beechgrove Special Care Unit in Prince Edward Island, as well as being widely recommended in the clinical literature (Coons 1991a, 1991b; Edelson & Lyons 1985; Mace 1990; Zgola 1987).

From this perspective, the day's routine becomes a more natural one. The pressure to finish bathing, grooming, and dressing by 9:00 a.m. is removed. Assistance with self-care can become a time for precious one-to-one interaction. The routine can be individualized according to personal habits, and functional behavior is encouraged through cuing procedural memory. One person may get up at 5 a.m., have coffee, and look at the paper, as he or she has always done. Another may choose to sleep until 10:30 a.m., washing and dressing in time to eat a substantial lunch. After the morning self-care routine, social and activity programs then become the focus. Just as in community living, after preparing for the day the resident moves on to visiting with friends, attending meetings or groups, or participating in hobbies. These essential activities provide a meaningful reason for the morning routine, and involvement in ADL contributes to self-esteem. Restoring a balance to the content of daily activities allows leisure activities and ADL to mutually support each other.

Of course, such a "non-routine" in the morning requires the cooperation of the entire team: dietary, recreation, housekeeping, and direct-care staff. Whether or not such a comprehensive program is possible in your facility, it is important to focus some aspects of an activity program on these essential ADL. What are the advantages of such a focus?

- It provides an obvious and easily identifiable purpose.

- It offers familiar, overlearned activities that provide an opportunity for success.

- It allows targeting the asset of procedural memory.

- It enhances individual self-esteem by supporting competence in daily routines.

- It provides an opportunity for one-to-one interaction.

- It provides an opportunity for individualization of the daily routine.

- It provides an excellent opportunity for the use of caring personal touch.

- It allows for the development of an integrated, interdisciplinary approach to care.

1.1 Premises for Enabling Independence in the Activities of Daily Living

The same general premises apply to ADL as described for other activities. Some of the more essential features are highlighted below.

Break ADL into manageable steps, giving guidance/ instruction for one step at a time. To suggest that the person with moderately advanced ADRD brush his or her teeth is usually too complex. Instead, assist with one step at a time. For example: "It's time to brush your teeth. Come with me to the bathroom and I will help you. Here is the toothpaste. Take the top off. Here is the toothbrush. Squeeze some toothpaste onto the brush. Put down the toothpaste. Take the brush to your mouth. [Demonstrate by gesture and help to initiate with hand-over-hand guidance, as necessary.] Now brush your teeth."

Begin the activity at the step where the person can succeed. In the preceding example of brushing teeth,

the person may be unable to put the toothpaste on the brush. In this case, begin instead with the brush prepared.

Help to initiate, as necessary. The person may, for instance, be able to feed herself or himself if assisted with hand-over-hand guidance to make the first few hand-to-mouth movements. He or she may be able to wash hands and face if the hands are guided to the warm water and the face cloth.

Organize necessary materials and equipment in advance. For example, prepare the bathroom in advance of a bath by having the water drawn and towels, soap, powder, shampoo, and clothes ready. This advance preparation allows you to give full attention to the person.

Provide familiar environmental cues. This was stressed in the sections on the environment. The bathroom and dining room, in particular, should look as homelike as possible.

Use multimodel cues. For example, the person can be cued that it is lunch time by the smell of the food and the sight of a familiar dining room, by being verbally cued that it is lunch time, and by the feel of the cutlery in the hand.

Reduce distractions. To be successful in ADL tasks, a person with ADRD needs to concentrate on the task at hand. Turn off music or radios, attend to the person, and do not be in conversation with others. Locate the activity in an area where disruptions are least likely. Unrelated conversations among staff are especially distracting during mealtime. Facilities with tray service meals should serve one course at a time, to avoid confusion.

Ensure privacy. This is particularly important for personal activities such as toileting, bathing, and dressing. Congregate living can make privacy more difficult, but not impossible, to achieve. After providing any needed physical assistance, a person may be left in private on the toilet, physically supported as necessary by, for example, a toilet safety frame. Cover the person with a large beach towel if he or she is embarrassed about receiving assistance with the bath. Dressing should be done in a bedroom with the doors closed and the drapes pulled.

Provide manageable choice. Offer alternatives of two or three items of clothing. Provide choice in condiments with meals and as much other choice of foods as possible. It is particularly important to provide choice with regard to daily routines. For example, ask, "Would you like your bath now, or after breakfast?"

Ensure consistency in routines and approaches. Staff communication is absolutely essential in this regard. Once a successful approach is arrived at, it should be followed by all staff at all times. Consider, for example, Patrick and his eating patterns:

> For many months Patrick's refusal to swallow had been a problem for his wife. He would load his mouth with food without swallowing. Sometimes repeated cuing would help, but more often than not, he would spit the food into the garbage. Patrick was eventually admitted to our unit for assessment. The introduction of softer and puréed foods had no effect on his reluctance to swallow. Patrick was referred to eating stimulation group. The problem was alleviated somewhat by giving him only small portions, with touch stimulation of the throat muscles to encourage swallowing between portions. One day, to my amazement, Patrick took an orange from the fruit basket on the table, peeled it and ate it, and had no problem whatsoever with swallowing! Inspired by this, during the next session, I offered him not only fruit to peel, but also bread to butter and crackers to spread with peanut butter and cheese spread. He prepared, ate, and swallowed it all! With the assistance of the dietitian, Patrick's meal tray was changed entirely, so that it was made up of these and other finger foods such as sandwiches and vegetable pieces. This new diet required some time for direct-care staff to adjust to. Accustomed to Patrick's usual lack of initiative, they would spread the cheese on the crackers or peel the orange. And Patrick would continue to refuse to swallow. However, eventually they came to understand his capabilities and provided small portions of these foods, which Patrick prepared and swallowed.

There are countless examples of such interventions. One person prefers to bathe in the evening, immediately before bed; another gets dressed willingly if clothes are laid out after breakfast. Consistency of approach from direct-care staff reinforces these independent behaviors.

Accommodate familiar personal routines as much as possible. Family and significant others can be of great assistance in this regard. What was the usual morning routine—bathe, dress, and breakfast? Or did the person have breakfast late, shave, and dress afterward? Finding out the details of these routines, and following them as much as possible, will greatly enable function, as it facilitates procedural memory for familiar activities. This is particularly important in regard to bathing,

which can be a difficult and frightening activity for the person with ADRD. Many persons from the current older generation are not accustomed to daily baths or may be accustomed to sponge baths. Unless they are incontinent, why cannot this routine be continued?

Provide opportunities for reminiscence and sensory stimulation. Self-care routines provide a perfect opportunity for one-to-one reminiscence and sensory stimulation. See Chapters 6 and 7 for specific suggestions.

1.2 Meal Groups

Mealtime activities are particularly important, as eating and self-feeding are profoundly affected by the deficits associated with ADRD (Bucht & Sandman 1990; Helen 1990; Kolassa et al. 1989; OTA 1987; Rheaume et al. 1988; Suski & Nielson 1989). It is widely reported in the clinical literature that persons with ADRD are at risk of becoming dependent in eating (Cohen & Eisdorfer 1986; Davis & Kirkland 1988; Edelson & Lyons 1985; Jarvik & Winograd 1988; Kalicki 1987; Mace & Rabins 1981; OTA 1987; Volicer et al. 1988). However, only a small number of studies have documented the actual incidence of eating difficulties.

A careful survey of 106 elderly residents found that those who were passive and preoccupied and had a diagnosis of dementia (43 percent of the residents) required significantly more assistance with eating. Those with positioning and swallowing problems, symptoms that frequently occur in the end stage of ADRD, also required feeding some or all of the time, and another 25 percent required encouragement and/or supervision (Nolen & Garrard 1988). An Office of Technology Assessment study, based on caregiver reports, found that 32 percent of those with ADRD required some assistance with eating and another 34 percent were completely dependent in eating (OTA 1987). The OTA also reported that 6 percent of those in New York State with severe dementia required assistance with feeding. A study of 88 patients at various stages of ADRD, ranging from the year of symptom onset to 17 years after onset, found that 50 percent were unable to eat independently 8 years after onset (Volicer et al. 1987). In a survey of 90 moderately to severely impaired Alzheimer's patients, 66.6 percent required "coaxing and constant supervision to eat" (Volicer et al. 1988, 96). A survey of 400 institutionalized ADRD patients in 30 wards in Sweden reported that 17.5 percent of these patients had eating difficulties so severe that they had to be fed (Michaelson et al. 1987).

The impaired ability to self-feed raises diverse and complex considerations. Of primary importance is the impact on the individuals themselves. The assistance of, or the complete dependence on, others for eating has a negative effect on individual self-esteem and frequently on the attitudes of significant others and staff toward the individual (Beck 1981; Duncan 1987; Hames-Hahn & Llorens 1989; Helen 1990; Nolen & Garrard 1988; Ott et al. 1990, 1991; Perket 1986). The centrality of food to special celebrations (e.g., birthdays and weddings) and the pleasurable social and sensory aspects of mealtime give eating an importance that goes far beyond nutrition alone. Persons with ADRD who have difficulty eating may also be deprived of these meaningful experiences.

There are also other important considerations, such as health issues (e.g., effect of inadequate nutrition on increasing the severity of the symptoms of ADRD and increasing the vulnerability to other diseases); practical issues (e.g., home care versus institutional care; increased staff time required for feeding); and ethical issues (e.g., use of invasive methods such as tube-feeding when individuals can no longer be spoon-fed). While some of these difficulties are an inevitable consequence of ADRD, the use of mealtime groups can prevent excess disabilities in relation to eating.

Mealtimes are the perfect, natural occasion for people to be gathered together in groups. The social setting of mealtime encourages social behavior, improves appetite, and promotes overlearned functional responses, such as self-feeding (Ott et al. 1991). By specially structuring the setting and the activity, self-feeding, socialization, and self-esteem can be enhanced. For higher-functioning individuals, preparing their own breakfast or lunch as part of a "club" can be very satisfying. William is a good example: For most meals in the unit dining room, William had to be coaxed to leave his bed. After participating in the breakfast club for a couple of months, he appeared at the door almost before I had my coat off, ready for his job of making the toast. Sometimes he was even waiting for me!

For the more severely impaired, a variation of sensory stimulation, eating stimulation, is described in Chapter 7.

Breakfast or Lunch Club Group

Purpose

To provide a normalized, homelike setting for a breakfast or lunch meal that will facilitate functional meal preparation activities, appetite, and independence

Goals

- to improve the appetite of both the participants and other residents by preparing a home-cooked meal

- to facilitate participation in functional meal preparation activities (e.g., setting the table, making toast or sandwiches, washing dishes)
- to promote socialization
- to facilitate independent eating
- to enhance self-esteem through involvement in meaningful activities
- to facilitate reminiscence and thus reaffirm the value of previous life experiences

Meal Group Setting

The group should take place in a cozy, quiet room that can be rearranged to look like a homey dining room (Figure 5-1). If a separate room is not available, private space in a large room can be adapted by using screens or room dividers. Wonders can be done with even the most barren of areas by adding donated items such as plants, vintage furniture, draperies, afghans, pillows, pictures, etc. If the room must be used for other purposes at other times, sturdy folding tables can be used. Socialization is enhanced by using small tables seating four to six persons. Even though food will be prepared, the area does not need to have a stove. Perfectly wonderful, simple meals can be prepared by using a toaster, an electric kettle, and an electric frying pan. If dishes, cutlery, etc. cannot be stored in the room, a sturdy plastic trolley, such as the kind used for busing in restaurants, is very convenient for transporting dishes and other supplies. In the "dining room," it serves as a convenient work and cooking space. The addition of a dishpan and drain rack creates a convenient area for washing dishes. A portable tape recorder with age-appropriate music greatly enhances the atmosphere. Have the daily paper available, since reading the paper while waiting for the meal, or after eating, is a natural activity. Even if the participants are unable to read lengthy articles, it is an excellent normalizing activity. It can

Figure 5-1 Meal group setting

also be used by the group leader for introducing orienting information.

Selecting Participants

Meal club groups are most appropriate for individuals who are able to eat independently and who have persisting functional and verbal skills. This would include moderately impaired individuals, scoring, for example, 11 or above on the Folstein Mini-Mental State examination. As with other groups, it is very helpful to have at least one or two participants who are higher functioning and can serve as a role model. It is best to begin such a group with four or five participants who you are sure will be responsive. As you become more comfortable with the group, one group leader can easily work with eight to ten moderately impaired participants. Eating stimulation groups, a variation of sensory stimulation, is a meal group activity for the more severely impaired. For more details, see Chapter 7.

Meal Group Frequency and Duration

Obviously the more often such a group can be run, the better. However, given the usual busy schedule of an activity program, once per week is realistic. Once the group is established, it may be possible to train interested direct-care staff to lead the group. Duration depends on the number and functional level of the participants. With eight participants who were moderately to severely impaired, the breakfast club run by this author required two hours from initial preparation to the final cleanup.

Participant Evaluation

The eating group evaluation sheet (Exhibit 5-1) was developed for a research project on the eating stimulation group (Rogers et al. 1989). It identifies positive eating behaviors and can be used as a checklist to monitor progress or maintenance. Inter-rater reliability scores ranged from 69 percent to 85 percent with a mean of 78.4 percent, which is well within the acceptable range.

Group Format

The format should mimic, as closely as possible, a regular home mealtime routine. The group leader adapts this, following the guidelines for group work in Chapter 4, and divides the preparation and cleanup activities according to participant skill level. It is important that everyone has a job to do, to feel part of the group. Use activity analysis and break the activities into manageable steps. Any potentially dangerous activities, such as frying bacon, should be done by the group leader. To encourage socialization, bring in vintage kitchen equipment, cookbooks, favorite family recipes, and local and seasonal favorite foods.

1.3 Breakfast Club Group

The following are some suggested activities for a breakfast club meal serving bacon, eggs, toast, and beverage:

- Spread the tablecloth or place mats and set the table.
- Fold the napkins.
- Select the music.
- Put flowers in water or arrange another table centerpiece.
- Lead the blessing for the meal.
- Make and butter toast.
- Make the tea or instant coffee.
- Serve out the plates.
- Clear the plates and dishes.
- Wash the dishes.
- Dry the dishes.
- Sweep the floor.
- Put away the furniture.

1.4 Suggestions for a Lunch Club Group

Ideas for simple lunch club foods can be found in Appendix 5-A. Items that may take longer to prepare or cook can be done in stages in advance of the group meeting. It is important that, as much as possible, the participants be involved in planning the menu. However, simply saying "What do you want to make for lunch next week?" is probably too overwhelming. Listen for cues of favorite foods during conversation. Offer choice among two or three items. The following are some suggestions for satisfying lunch foods that can be broken down into easy steps:

- sandwiches (each person makes own from a selection of favorite fillings and breads)
- fruit and vegetable pieces with crackers and cheese
- grilled cheese or other hot sandwiches
- corned beef hash (made from canned corn beef)
- eggs and toast
- salad and fresh biscuits
- hamburgers
- beans and hot dogs
- sausages and sauerkraut
- chowder
- soup (liven up commercial soup by adding fresh vegetables and other ingredients)
- pancakes

Exhibit 5-1 Eating Group Evaluation Sheet

Activity	Date/time	Never	Occasionally	Often	Always
Chews Food					
Swallows liquids					
Brings food from table to mouth independently					
Brings liquids from table to mouth independently					
Eats with minimum of spillage					
Attempts to clean up spills					
Takes appropriate-sized mouthfuls					
Acknowledges peers/staff appropriately					
Initiates appropriate verbal communication					
Responds appropriately to verbal communication					
Shows interest in food					
Smiles or reflects positive mood					
Shows interest in the environment					
Indicates completion of meal with appropriate comment or action					
Amount of food intake is appropriate					

1.5 Grooming Groups

Personal hygiene activities are private, but some grooming activities have a group context in the community (for example, visiting the barber shop or beauty parlor) and can continue to do so in a long-term care setting. Using the same principles as for other groups, grooming groups can be organized around a particular theme. They provide a good opportunity to improve self-esteem through enhanced personal appearance. Certainly, one of the most therapeutic times for our female patients was their weekly visit to the hairdresser. They not only looked great, but the hairdresser's cheerful and encouraging conversation lifted their spirits. The leader should give appropriate feedback on the "new look" and encourage other group members to do the same. Mirrors may be used, but with caution, as some may be frightened when they do not recognize their own reflections. Small hand mirrors are preferable to large wall mirrors. A grooming group should be scheduled for a time of day when these activities would usually occur. For shaving and hair care, this would most logically be in the morning. Doing manicures, makeup, and jewelry with female participants can be connected to a regular or special event such as an evening entertainment or dance, a special visitor, or getting ready on Friday for the weekend. These activities present an excellent opportunity to involve volunteers and to solicit donations of makeup and jewelry from companies and local stores.

Follow the generic guidelines and design a group that will meet the needs of your residents. Personal grooming supplies should be kept separate by using individual stacking storage bins or some other system. Take precautions with potentially hazardous materials, such as the sharp pins on brooches or manicure equipment, and be aware of the potential for some persons to put objects in their mouths. The following are two suggested groups:

The barber shop—a grooming group in which men do their own shaving and comb their own hair. Add sensory appeal with aftershave lotions and talcum powder.

The beauty parlor—a group in which women do their own hair, nails, and makeup and put on accessories such as jewelry and scarves. This could be presented in a sensory stimulation type of format (see Chapter 7).

2.0 FOOD-RELATED ACTIVITIES

Activities related to food preparation and eating are tremendously motivating and among the most successful with any age group. For individuals with ADRD, food-related activities meet almost all of the requirements of an ideal activity.

- They have an obvious purpose.
- They provide an immediate reward.
- They are highly motivating.
- They provide an opportunity to participate in a familiar, overlearned activity.
- They provide multisensory stimulation.
- They stimulate long-term memory.
- They are designed for adults.
- They can easily be broken down into simple steps.
- Ingredients and equipment are readily available.
- They provide a manageable opportunity for choice and decision making.
- They are an excellent means of involving volunteers and other staff members.

2.1 Goals

- Improve or maintain muscle strength and tolerance (e.g., hand muscles, through prolonged grasp during the stirring of foods).
- Improve or maintain gross hand coordination (e.g., spooning batter into muffin pans).
- Improve or maintain joint range of motion (e.g., reaching for ingredients or materials).
- Improve or maintain concentration/attention (e.g., cutting a cookie and placing it on a baking sheet).
- Increase food intake through the stimuli of preparing the food, tasting the food, and smelling the aromas while the food is cooking.
- Enhance self-esteem (e.g., by serving cookies that participants have helped to make to family members or staff).
- Encourage socialization (discussing associations, opinions during food preparation). There is also a normal stimulus to socialize while sharing the food.
- Provide sensory stimulation (rich sensory stimuli from textures, smells, movements, sights, and tastes).
- Stimulate reminiscence, long-term memory (What is your favorite kind of cookie? Did your mother make them?).
- Stimulate procedural memory (lifelong familiar activities, e.g., stirring, chopping, drying dishes).

2.2 Selecting Food Activities

The most successful food activities are those that

- are simple, failure-free recipes for familiar foods, such as baking powder biscuits
- are quick to prepare, such as no-bake chocolate drop cookies

- include simple, repetitive actions such as peeling and chopping for fruit salad, stirring cookie batter, churning ice cream, mixing pastry
- can be done in stages over several days, such as pies or tarts
- do not require a high level of skill or precision, such as a coffee cake as opposed to an angel food cake
- can be broken down into several steps requiring various skill levels (e.g., for apple crisp, peeling and chopping apples require more skill than mixing the topping, but everyone can put the apples and topping in the pan)
- are associated with the current season (e.g., strawberry shortcake in summer) or a festival (e.g., pumpkin pie for Thanksgiving)
- are favorite local specialties (e.g., in Nova Scotia, green tomato chow-chow)
- have nutritional value (e.g., oatmeal cookies as opposed to very sweet sugar cookies)
- are aromatic and help to stimulate the appetite (e.g., baking bread dough, simmering stew)
- are adaptable for use with mixes and prepared foods in order to save time (e.g., coffee cake made from biscuit mix)
- are an adaptation, as necessary, of a favorite family or personal recipe of a particular resident, client, or patient.

A selection of recipes is found in Appendix 5-A.

2.3 Precautions

- Wash hands thoroughly before beginning.
- Be aware of food allergies among the group.
- Adhere to diabetic, low-salt, and other dietary restrictions. Be sure to provide alternate treats for these individuals.
- Avoid foods that may cause choking (e.g., cookies with nuts).
- Have the staff prepare foods that involve the use of hot pots, the stove, and the oven. Because of problems with judgment, burns can easily happen.
- Do not permit severely impaired individuals to use sharp knives and peelers; permit others to do so only with one-to-one supervision.
- Be aware of those individuals who tend to put everything in their mouths, and take precautions accordingly.

2.4 Basic Procedures

1. If you are unfamiliar with cooking and baking, try the recipes first yourself.

2. Assemble all needed materials and ingredients and lay them out in an orderly fashion before the participants arrive.

3. Premeasure ingredients and partially prepare, as appropriate (e.g., measure all dry ingredients together and all liquid ingredients together, ready for mixing). This will not be necessary for higher-functioning individuals. However, because of difficulties with judgment, decision making, and comprehension, measuring and following a recipe is difficult for those who are moderately to severely impaired. A volunteer who likes to bake could do this step.

4. Initiate desired movement with hand-over-hand guidance as necessary.

5. Encourage spontaneous activity based on procedural memory. For example, place a biscuit cutter in the person's hand and have dough ready to cut and a cookie sheet nearby.

6. Assess skill level and involve participants in various tasks of the activity, providing assistance as necessary. For example, some may be able to break an egg into the cookie batter; others may be able only to stir, with hand-over-hand guidance.

7. Focus attention on the associated sensory cues with verbal suggestions such as the following:

   —"Here is some vanilla to put in the cake. Does it smell familiar to you?"

   —"Here is a sturdy wooden spoon to stir the batter. How does the handle feel to you?"

   —"Here is a biscuit warm from the oven. How does it taste to you?"

8. Use opportunities to facilitate reminiscence. For example, make use of the following kinds of lead-in or information-seeking questions: "Did you bake often? What was your specialty? What favorite food did your mother used to make? What was the best meal you ever had?"

9. Provide choice, as manageable. For example, offer the plate of freshly baked cookies and let the person select one, or ask whether the person would like butter on the toast.

10. Involve participants in repetitious, familiar activities such as drying the dishes or mixing the dry ingredients for pastry.

11. Use equipment and materials that are familiar to the participants, which provide multisensory stimulation and an opportunity for reminiscing. Some suggestions are colorful, textured oven mitts, aprons, and tablecloths; old-fashioned manual timer; old-fashioned baking utensils such as hand-held eggbeaters, ceramic mixing bowls, wooden butter bowls, cookie tins, and storage jars; illustrated cookbooks, especially old ones; vintage recipes that list ingredients such as "butter the size of an egg" and directions such as "bake in a quick oven."

2.5 Adaptations

- Stabilize the mixing bowl with a non-skid material or a damp cloth.

- Use adaptive equipment as necessary, such as a one-handed chopping board, rocker knife, built-up handles, pot stabilizer, or plate guard.

- For those who are moderately and severely impaired, use the parallel presentation format to present the steps. For example, move around the table and have each person take a turn at stirring the batter. Then go around again, with each person taking a turn to drop some batter onto the cookie sheets.

2.6 Cooking Methods

Just because your facility does not have a kitchen or even a stove does not mean you cannot do food activities. First, see "No-Bake/No-Cook Suggestions" in Appendix 5-A for ideas for sandwiches, snacks, and sweets requiring no baking or cooking. Second, consider alternate baking and cooking methods. The staff room may have a microwave oven, or a small one could be purchased by the auxiliary or by monies from a fund raiser. The recipes in Appendix 5-A include suggested microwave cooking times, or use the directions for your particular microwave oven. The microwave oven has the advantage of being faster for baking, but there is some sacrifice in browning and texture. A Crock-Pot may be borrowed or purchased and used to make soup, stews, chowders, puddings, etc. A small toaster-oven is relatively inexpensive and can be used for baking in small batches.

Using the Electric Frying Pan for Food Activities

Probably the most successful and least expensive alternative to a stove is an electric frying pan. Foods such as soups, stews, sauces, puddings, and eggs can be cooked directly in the pan, according to standard methods.

For baking, the frying pan can be turned into a mini-oven. The more expensive models, with crockery liners, become mini-ovens simply by covering the pan tightly. For other types, place a metal baking rack or several Mason-type jar rings in the bottom. Cover with the lid, with the steam vent closed. Set the thermostat approximately 50 degrees higher than for a standard oven (e.g., cookies to be baked in a 325-degree oven would be baked at 375 degrees in the frying pan). Baking requires approximately 20 percent more time. For example, cookies normally requiring 10 minutes will require 12 to 13 minutes. Suggested electric frying pan baking times are given with the recipes. Use pie or cake pans as baking sheets.

The frying pan oven method produces delicious baked goods. However, the items will not be as brown or as light in texture as they are when baked in a regular oven. They are, nonetheless, a delicious treat to the nose and the palate and give enormous pleasure to the participants, who may not have had fresh, home-baked food, especially from their own hands, for some time.

2.7 Recipe Format

For individuals who may not be able to see and/or follow a regular recipe, these adaptations may be helpful. Use large print on oversized recipe cards, a flip chart, a Bristol board, or a blackboard. Use simple step-by-step directions illustrated with a simple drawing or picture. Provide individual recipes in large print. For individuals who are severely impaired, it is best not to confuse them with a recipe. Provide individual verbal and physical direction and cues while proceeding through the steps of the recipe.

2.8 Presentation Format

Activities can be presented as part of ongoing groups, for example, sensory stimulation or reminiscence groups, or as special-occasion activities. A very effective use of food activities is to develop a breakfast or lunch club (see Section 1.2). Participants are encouraged by the normal mealtime milieu to plan and prepare as much as possible of their own meals and then to share the results.

2.9 One-to-One Techniques

Do a baking activity with one participant, adapting assistance to his or her skill level as needed. Do one-to-one baking activities with severely impaired individuals on their unit. In this case, each resident does one simple, final step; for example, he or she might put the muffin or cookie batter in pans to bake, shape the dough for hot cross buns or rolls, or put the filling in tart shells. Bake the prepared foods on the unit and return to serve each participant his or her baking, or have the residents do the serving. The most efficient way of doing this is to prepare a cart in advance, with the dough or batter; baking pans; and wash cloths, towels, and a basin for hand washing.

2.10 Equipment and Supplies

If baking is done other than in a standard kitchen, it is a great timesaver to gather basic supplies and equipment and keep them all in one place or on a mobile cart. Basic equipment should include mixing bowls, spoons, dishpan, soap, dishcloth, tea towels, measuring cups and spoons, rubber spatula, baking pans, and potholders. Measures that provide an exact amount when full (for example, a one-half-cup scoop) are easiest, since they require less judgment and decision-making skill.

Basic supplies should include flour, salt, vanilla, baking powder, baking soda, shortening, oil, brown and white sugar, milk powder, paper plates and cups, napkins, muffin papers, tea, coffee, and powdered coffee creamer.

2.11 Time Required

The food activities in Appendix 5-A were designed to be completed within the course of one-hour group sessions. Those that take longer can be adapted to be completed in several steps spread over several sessions. On special occasions, one long session may be scheduled. These activities may include making pickles, preserves, or special holiday foods. Activities with the moderately impaired will take less time, since they require less guidance. Time will also vary according to the number of participants. Time estimates given are for six to eight severely impaired participants.

The recipes have been categorized according to time requirements: Preparation time indicates the approximate time for preparation *in the group,* and excludes the parts completed by the leader before or after the group session.

- cakes/muffins/quick breads/squares: preparation time 15 to 20 minutes; baking time 30 to 60 minutes
- cookies/candy/biscuits: preparation time 10 to 15 minutes; baking time 10 to 15 minutes
- desserts, cobblers, crisps, puddings: preparation time 15 to 20 minutes; baking time 30 to 45 minutes
- miscellaneous (pancakes, appetizers, ice cream): total time 30 to 60 minutes
- no-bake/no-cook food activities: preparation time 10 to 30 minutes
- yeast breads and rolls (quick method): 2 hours from start to finish

2.12 Number and Skill Level of Participants

Using the adaptations as suggested, food activities can be adjusted for all skill levels. If advanced preparations are made, one experienced staff person can do a food activity with up to ten severely impaired individuals. When beginning, it is wise to have a smaller number of participants. With fewer participants there is also more opportunity for member participation.

2.13 Suggested Activities during Baking/Cooking Time

- Look at and discuss associations with cookbooks, particularly older cookbooks, and old-fashioned kitchen equipment such as apple peelers, butter pats, and cookie tins and cutters.
- Music appreciation: hum, sing, tap, clap along with familiar tunes. This is especially good during seasonal activities, for example, sing Christmas carols while baking Christmas cookies.
- Discuss favorite foods and favorite recipes.
- Locate or generate a recipe for a favorite food that can be made at a future group.
- Moderately impaired individuals enjoy watching a short film, with assistance to focus on cues; or playing a simple but adult-associated game, such as "I am baking cookies and I'm going to put in ...," with each participant adding an ingredient and, if possible, naming those already put in. This game is good for memory and concentration and is enthusiastically greeted by the participants when presented in an adult manner. Precise recall is not emphasized, and humor is encouraged.
- Complete a familiar phrase or saying related to food:

I'm so hungry, I could eat a _____. (horse)

This meat is as tough as_____. (leather, nails)

Feed a cold and starve a _____. (fever)

An apple a day keeps the _____ away. (doctor)

An apple pie without some cheese is like a kiss without a _____. (squeeze)

These phrases may be spoken or presented on individual cards, sheets, or large flip charts, depending on the skill level of the participants. This is a very successful activity with persons with ADRD because it depends on recognition, not recall, and is based on overlearned, familiar phrases.

3.0 HANDICRAFTS

Handicraft activities can be an excellent modality with individuals with ADRD. However, because these activities may require more skill or may be less familiar to some, great care must be taken in planning the activities. See Appendix 5-B for some appropriate handicraft activities.

3.1 Guidelines to Selecting and Planning Handicraft Activities

Activities must be adult in focus and presentation. A restatement of this guideline is particularly important in relation to handicraft activities. It is unfortunately the case that in order to simplify handicraft activities to match the skill level of individuals with ADRD, activities that are intended for children are used. On this point I am very emphatic: *Activities that are obviously intended for and associated with children are an insult to adult dignity and should never be used.* There *may* be a slight gain in having the person's time occupied briefly, but the loss to dignity and self-esteem, no matter how advanced the dementia, is immeasurable. It is my experience, and that of others, that no matter how pervasive the cognitive losses, the individual with ADRD remains acutely aware of his or her status as an adult. Children's coloring books, juvenile large-piece puzzles, infant "busy boxes," babies' cuddle toys, nursery school stringing beads, and other such materials have *ABSOLUTELY* no place in an adult setting. The associations of these with childhood is firmly fixed. Persisting long-term memory and recall of familiar activities make these associations very much available to the individual with ADRD. Being asked to color in a children's coloring book is a flagrant insult to an already fragile self-esteem. When you are 65, 74, or 92, cognitively impaired or not, do you want someone to offer you a coloring book and crayons?

Even if these materials are presented to the individual in the most adult of ways, there are other implications. They present an image to other staff and to visitors that the person is childlike. This image is all too often translated into talking to and treating the person as if he or she were a child, a further insult to adult dignity. I take great exception to the all-too-familiar expression, "They are in their second childhood." NOT TRUE. *The person with ADRD has lost skills and capacities, but he or she is not in any sense a child and is not to be treated as such.*

"Simple activities" do not have to mean activities suitable for children. Adaptation of these activities to an adult format is essential. Artistic pictures and adult line drawings can be completed with pastels or markers, or liquid embroidery pens can color in bold designs on fabric, if this is an interest of the individual. There are now available adult-theme large-piece jigsaw puzzles, large-size dominoes, adult self-directed activities, and age-appropriate stimulation materials (see Chapter 7). Out with coloring books, in with paint by number!

In addition to selecting handicraft activities that are adult in content, activities must be simple and straightforward; directions must be concise and clear; and the language and manner adult.

Handicraft activities must be purposeful and have an obvious or identified use. Handicraft activities have been one of the favorite trinity of activities with the elderly, what some people call the BBC—bingo, bowling, and crafts. For older individuals, with or without cognitive impairment, busywork or craft activities with no obvious use unfortunately have been used all too often. Activities that have no purpose or meaning are not helpful or therapeutic for anyone. For the individual with ADRD, being presented with activities that have no use, as far as he or she can tell, is a further insult to self-esteem. So, first of all, in relation to the previous section, make sure the activities have an *adult* purpose or meaning. Cutting out paper dolls or decorations for bulletin boards may have a purpose, but is it an adult purpose that will be obvious to the individual with ADRD? Although it is essential to enliven the decor of long-term care facilities, we must be sure that they look like an adult residence, not a nursery school.

Second, for the individual with ADRD, a special effort must be made to communicate the purpose of the activity. Many older adults have had little time in their working lives for purely leisure activities. Knitting or woodworking projects were done as a gift for someone else, or because they were needed. Comments such as the following help to clarify the purpose of the activity. "Let's make this place mat for the table. It will look pretty and help with tidying up after mealtime." "This is an unsanded cutting board. I will help you sand and finish it. It will be a good present for your daughter." "Your grandchildren would like this beautiful decoration. I will help you make one for them."

The purpose or the use of the activity must be made clear from the outset. Bear in mind the need for using simple language and concrete examples. For instance, if a project such as painting building blocks for nursery-school children is to be done, at least have some of the children visit first. The visit will make the purpose much clearer than any verbal explanation.

The purpose, and the creator, of the project must also be made clear to other staff. If items are to be sold in a gift shop or used for table centerpieces or wall decorations, the article should clearly identify the artisan by a tag or signature. This will further reinforce the value of the project to other staff and to visitors.

Finally, the handicraft activity must be purposeful for that particular individual. For individuals who are cognitively impaired this is sometimes difficult to determine. As has been so frequently mentioned, it is important to know as much as possible about previous life experiences, values, and interests in order to select the proper handicraft activity—and sometimes even then there are surprises:

Bob was a gruff, rather cantankerous old man who was severely demented as a result of Korsakoff's syndrome. He and his wife had had a stormy 57-year marriage. There were many battles, especially after his drinking bouts. It was almost Valentine's Day, and the sensory stimulation group participants were going to make valentines for friends or relatives. I was in a quandary about Bob's involvement in this activity. I was sure that, in of all their 57 years of marriage, Bob had never given his wife a valentine. I was also pretty sure of his reaction to being involved in what might seem like such a sissy activity.

Oh well, fools rush in where angels fear to tread, and I showed Bob a finished sample card. I suggested, with bated breath, that together we could make one for his wife. What a surprise I got! He smiled and said, "All right, let's get the hell at it."

This project was spread out over several days in the group. As he completed each stage, Bob was obviously more and more pleased with his efforts. When the whole card was finished he was absolutely tickled pink. With help, he addressed the card to his wife and signed his name.

Handicraft activities must be carefully selected so as not to confront an individual with ADRD with his or her losses. In order not to do so, a careful assessment of persisting skills is necessary. Someone may have been a proficient knitter but, because of reduced concentration and initiative, he or she is no longer able to follow a pattern, even though the overlearned basic stitches of knitting are still very familiar. Some may be able to do plain knitting, such as a scarf. Some may not have the initiative necessary to maintain this repetitive activity. For others, depending on the individual personality, doing such a simple activity may be a flagrant reminder of their losses.

For some, a related activity may hold some of the pleasures associated with a previous skill, without confronting them with lost skills. To continue with the knitting example, for someone who was a talented knitter great pleasure may be derived from the smell, feel, and colors of various types of yarn while winding wool from skeins into balls or making an "eye of God" ornament. The feel of the sandpaper and wood and the smell of the sawdust may stimulate pleasurable recollections of previous accomplishments for a woodworking hobbyist.

Assessing in advance whether handicraft projects are within the capabilities of the individual, the "just-right challenge," ensures success experiences and avoids discouraging failures. The fragile self-esteem of an individual with ADRD is greatly affected by failure.

Fine motor skills deteriorate before gross motor skills and are almost always difficult for individuals with advanced dementia. Handicraft activities requiring careful placement of small objects and other such precise details should be avoided or adapted. Mosaic pictures using small stones or seeds in detailed patterns can be replaced with large patterns filled in with larger materials. Large, simple design stencils should be substituted for smaller, finer patterns. Steps of the activity requiring fine motor skills can be done in advance by the group leader or a volunteer. For example, in making valentines, the participants in sensory stimulation were able to trace out a large heart using a cardboard stencil. Before the next group, a volunteer cuts out the hearts, as these individuals were unable to manage scissors.

Handicraft activities should have a few simple, repetitive steps. Once the person learns these steps, procedural memory and the rhythmic nature of the repeated movements enables continuing with the activity. Some examples of this type of handicraft activity are fringing napkins, stuffing pillows, winding yarn for an "eye of God," and making rubbings.

Handicraft activities should be connected to familiar, overlearned activities and movements. Activities that connect with the better-preserved long-term and procedural memory are more likely to be accepted and successful. Frequently, providing hand-over-hand guidance is all that is necessary to initiate overlearned actions such as sanding wood or winding yarn.

Use materials and supplies that have sensory appeal and rich associations with long-term memories. Colorful yarns and fabrics, sweetly scented woods, soft dough, pillow stuffing, textured seeds, mosaic tiles, crackly sandpaper, and other such sensory-rich materials improve the level of alertness, help to focus attention, and motivate involvement (see Chapter 7). Materials such as old-fashioned jars used to do rubbings, which have long-term associations, stimulate interest and reminiscence. The group leader facilitates responses by connecting the materials with the life experiences of the individual.

The end product should be pleasing and a demonstration model available. A pleasing end product is related to some of the earlier guidelines. The end product should be pleasing according to adult standards. The lopsided and endearing craft projects of children are not rewarding or pleasing to adults. In order to accomplish a pleasing and satisfying end product, the project must be within the capabilities of the participant. It is more rewarding and supportive of self-esteem to have a nicely turned out wooden trivet than a poorly completed corner bracket.

Handicraft activities should provide opportunity for self-expression, creativity, and manageable choice. Although too much choice can be overwhelming for individuals with ADRD, offering manageable choice (for instance between two colors of yarn or two pictures for decoupage) is essential to promote self-esteem and a sense of personal control. Similarly, although it is essential to provide structured guidelines, allowance must be made for self-expression and creativity. The designs of the mosaic must be already made, but the individual can select a particular design and fill it in with colors and materials of his or her choosing. The arrangement of cloth pieces for a fabric collage or the distribution of colors in an "eye of God" provide an opportunity for creativity and self-expression.

Avoid materials and equipment that may be dangerous. When doing handicraft activities with individuals with advanced ADRD, one must always be aware that some may tend to put dangerous or inedible objects in their mouths. Avoid materials such as pins, toxic glues, and varnishes, or complete the steps requiring these materials for the participants. Always pay careful attention when these individuals are doing craft activities. Provide hand-over-hand guidance and one-to-one supervision as necessary.

Sharp and dangerous equipment that may be used inappropriately by the cognitively impaired should be used only under one-to-one supervision by the moderately impaired. Those in advanced stages should have any necessary cutting, sawing, and hammering completed for them.

3.2 Goals of Handicraft Activities

- Provide an opportunity for creativity and self-expression, such as creating the color and arrangement for a greeting card.
- Enhance self-esteem through success experiences, such as making place mats for the community dining room.
- Provide an opportunity to give something to others, such as a napkin holder or cutting board for a friend.
- Facilitate reminiscence, for example, through associations with the colors and textures of fabrics.
- Provide sensory stimulation through the many sensations of touch, vision, sound, and movement associated with the activity.
- Improve or maintain muscle strength and tolerance, joint range of motion, and hand coordination, for example, while gripping the sandpaper or tying the macramé.
- Improve level of alertness through the focused stimulation involved in the project.
- Encourage socialization, through sharing materials and working on projects with peers.

4.0 HORTICULTURAL ACTIVITIES

The art, the science, the pleasure of working with plants is a very old one indeed. Keeping house plants and tending an outdoor garden are familiar and accepted pastimes for many older people. For individuals with ADRD, horticultural activities are an excellent medium as they are most often familiar, hence calling up overlearned skills and long-term memories. The use of horticulture as therapy is becoming widely recognized for its benefits with many populations. It is used for vocational and work skills training with the mentally handicapped and chronic psychiatric patients, as a motivating and rewarding modality with the physically disabled, and as a pleasurable and satisfying hobby for nursing home residents. In many settings in Great Britain the use of horticulture for therapeutic purposes is highly developed. In North America, its development and application is proceeding rapidly. There are at least nine American universities that offer degrees in horticultural therapy. In the United States, in 1973, the National Council for Therapy and Rehabilitation through Horticulture was formed. This organization has a yearly conference, a process of registration for becoming a certified horticultural therapist, and publishes a newsletter. In conjunction with this professional framework, there are countless therapeutic programs in schools, hospitals, and seniors' centers across North America.

In Canada, the development of horticulture as therapy is also growing rapidly. The Royal Botanical Gardens, Hamilton, Ontario, operates outreach and training programs in horticulture as well as facilitating the establishment of the Canadian Horticulture Therapy Association. The University of British Columbia Botanical Gardens also operates horticultural therapy programs.

Some of the advantages of horticulture as a therapeutic modality are as follows:

- It is a dynamic and responsive medium.
- It is uniquely motivating in that the need, for example, to water the plant or pick off dead leaves is obvious and, for those with experience, an automatic response.
- It has an obvious, intrinsic purpose.
- Plants are living and responsive, but nonthreatening and nonjudgmental.
- Plants have a positive effect on the environment.
- Horticultural activities can be easily broken down into simple steps.
- Horticulture provides tasks that are adaptable to all skill levels.
- It provides opportunity for year-round activities.
- Materials are inexpensive and readily available.
- Working with plants helps to put people in touch with the natural life cycle of growth, change, development, and death. It can serve as an impetus to talk about their own life cycles.
- Horticulture is a good activity for involving volunteers.

The healing and restoring properties of working with plants and natural materials is widely recognized by gardeners, farmers, therapists, and the patients themselves (Burgess 1990).

Cleome was hospitalized for severe depression and suspected early Alzheimer's disease. While in the hospital, she became very much involved in the occupational therapy department plant club. One day, while she was happily engaged in repotting some begonias, her doctor passed the door and stopped to say hello. She looked up from her work and said, "This, doctor, is medicine for the spirit."

John Angus had worked all of his life with the land and with plants. He had been one of the first commercial blueberry growers in the province and was justifiably proud of his accomplishments. He had also developed commercial greenhouses, growing bedding plants and potted flowers. For John Angus, growing things was more than a way to earn a living, it was his life.

When I met John Angus, he was in the advanced stages of Alzheimer's disease. His language was quite well preserved, but he was particularly troubled by motor coordination and movement difficulties. He had so little command or sense of his body that he required full assistance to get dressed or even to sit in a chair. Independently tending a garden or plants was out of the question.

He had been living in various institutions for several months when I suggested that he come to the occupational therapy department to do some potting. The very suggestion brightened him up immensely. As I guided his hands to the potting soil, tears began to run down his smiling cheeks. With hands immersed in his beloved soil, John Angus said, "This is just heaven, just heaven, and I had no idea that it was so handy to home."

With hand-over-hand guidance, John Angus potted several begonias. On each visit, also with assistance, we watered, fertilized, and pruned the plants. By Christmas time, the begonias were in full bloom. There are hardly words to describe the pleasure and satisfaction it gave John Angus to present them to his family as Christmas gifts—or, indeed, the pleasure his family had in receiving them.

There are literally countless anecdotes such as these to illustrate the powerful therapeutic effect of horticulture. It is most unfortunate that there is almost no empirical research to further support its effectiveness. However, the research that has been done has positive results. One study found that the very simple intervention of having flowers on the table during meals significantly increased the amount of verbalization, the length of time spent in the dining room, and the amount of food consumed among chronic psychiatric patients (Talbot et al. 1976). In another study the introduction of an indoor gardening activity resulted in the active involvement of 90% of the attenders (Powell et al. 1979).

As with many other therapeutic modalities, there is a pressing need for careful research which will further validate the large number of descriptive accounts of the therapeutic effectiveness of horticulture, as well as to better define techniques and projects which are the most effective with individuals with ADRD.

In the meantime, the following goals have been widely identified in the existing literature and are supported by my personal experience.

4.1 Goals of Horticulture As Therapy

- Provide a nonthreatening opportunity to nurture and care for a living thing. Plants are responsive. In return for proper care, they grow and produce new shoots, flowers, and edible parts. Individuals with ADRD so frequently are the recipients of care; working with plants provides a manageable opportunity to be the caregiver.
- Provide an opportunity to give something to others (e.g., a gift plant for a friend, dried herbs for the kitchen).
- Improve self-esteem through success experiences (e.g., picking and displaying the flowers grown).
- Provide an opportunity for involvement with a dynamic medium (e.g., watching the amaryllis bud fatten and open).
- Provide an opportunity for creativity and self-expression (e.g., arranging the flowers or designing a cone wreath).
- Improve or maintain joint range of motion, muscle strength and tolerance, and motor coordination in a uniquely motivating way (e.g., while misting the house plants or digging the garden).
- Provide widely varied sensory stimulation (e.g., the feel of the soil, the smell of the flowers, the sound of the rustling leaves, the sight of the vibrant colors of the garden in bloom, the taste of a fresh-picked tomato).
- Promote reminiscence and stimulate the use of overlearned, familiar actions (e.g., the potted geraniums that mother kept on the windowsill; watering the plants).

- Encourage socialization (e.g., sharing information about the plants, previous gardening experiences, complimenting each other on flower arrangements).

- Improve the general level of alertness and help to maintain cognitive functions such as attention, reasoning, and judgment (e.g., deciding when the plant has had enough water, which leaves need removing).

4.2 Selecting Horticultural Activities

Use plant materials that are easy to manage, hardy, and adaptable. In order to have a plant or product that is satisfying, both in the end stage and during the growing, it must be able to survive less than professional care and the usually poor growing conditions of an institution. It is better to have a healthy spider plant than spindly orchids or sickly African violets. Some easily grown house plants are Swedish ivy, grape ivy, wandering sailors (many types), peperomia. Table 5-1 gives a listing of easy-to-grow house plants and their light requirements.

Start with a small, manageable project, indoors or out. It is easy to become so enthusiastic about an outdoor garden that before you know it there is more garden to weed or produce to use than can be easily managed. Unlike craft projects, horticultural projects are living and require thought to their care every day of the week.

Avoid poisonous plant materials and other products, as participants may put leaves or plant parts in their mouths. Some of the more common poisonous plants are poinsettia, dieffenbachia, rhubarb leaves, and holly. Contact the local poison control center for a complete listing. Avoid the use of toxic and noxious chemicals for pest control. Use organic sprays, such as insecticidal soap.

Select plant materials that have familiar associations for the participants. Using familiar house or garden plants will stimulate long-term and procedural memory. For example, geraniums are a common and relatively easy-to-grow house plant. Tomatoes and lettuce are among the most popular garden plants.

Use plant and other materials that have sensory appeal. Scented geraniums and herbs and textured, brightly colored pots and containers in interesting shapes add greatly to sensory appeal and hence increase the alertness of the participants.

Include plant- and nature-related activities that will expand involvement in horticulture. Appendix 5-C has numerous suggestions for related activities, such as making a terrarium, pressed-flower pictures, or plant motif hasty notes.

Relate indoor activities to the season, to promote reality reassurance. This is usually determined by necessity, such as starting transplants in the spring. However, it is important to remember to bring the outdoors in, to highlight seasonal changes. Some examples are pussy willows and fruit blossoms in spring, fresh-picked strawberries in summer, pumpkins in autumn, evergreen boughs at Christmas.

4.3 Basic Horticultural Considerations and Procedures

The process, and not the end product, is the most important feature of horticultural therapy. The emphasis of the program should not be on the quality or quantity that the participant produces, but on encouraging the person's involvement. Staff and volunteers must not be so concerned about getting things done properly or quickly that they do the job for the person. This would defeat the whole purpose of the program.

On the other hand, every effort should be made by staff and volunteers to ensure that the project will be as successful as possible. The better the plants prosper, the more positive the reward for the participant. It is crucial that anyone wishing to establish a horticultural therapy program understand that he or she is working with a living system that has specific care requirements. A collection of seeded flats cannot have the door shut on it for the long weekend, in the same way that this is possible with craft projects. Arrangements must be made, at the outset, for staff or participants who will regularly care for the plants. Second, the person setting up the program should have knowledge of or learn the basic principles of indoor plant care. There are many excellent references that can be of assistance; several are listed at the end of this section. For the purposes of this book, I mention only a few areas of horticultural practice that, in my observation, are particularly important in setting up a program.

Growing plants indoors is a severe modification of their natural environment. In order to achieve the best plant growth, the indoor environment must be adapted, as far as possible, to suit the plant. The adaptations fall into the general categories of light, media, moisture, and temperature.

4.4 Light

Since available light is such a key factor in determining plant growth, projects must be planned according to the light available. So, before deciding on plant types, the program planner must select the location. This will determine the plants that can be grown. The Vancouver Botanical Gardens has a simple test that is very helpful in determining the amount of available light, and hence which plants will grow there:

1. Place a piece of white paper where you wish to set the plant.
2. Hold your hand a foot above the paper and look at the shadow:
   —bright light: the shadow is dark and clear
   —average light: the shadow is faded but clear
   —low light: the shadow is fuzzy and unclear
3. Nearly all plants can be divided into these light groupings and have common characteristics:
   —bright-light plants: often fast-growing, flowering; brightly colored leaves, variegated leaves, tiny leaves; desert plants
   —average-light plants: average speed of growth; average-sized leaves, green in color, even if variegated
   —low-light plants: slow-growing; large leaves, often straplike, very deep green, and, if variegated, usually very limited color or in greens

Light can be improved by placing plants on reflective white or foil surfaces (such as white plastic or aluminum or white enamel trays). Foil-covered cardboard can be placed behind plants to reflect the light back on to the leaves. Finally, make sure the windows are clean!

If there are no suitable windows, a fluorescent light garden (Figure 5-2) is inexpensive and has the additional advantage of being portable. It is not necessary to spend a lot of money on fluorescent light systems. Demolition and surplus warehouses usually have secondhand fluorescent light fixtures at a very low price. Be sure that the bulbs in the fixture face down, rather than out. Fixtures can be mounted on warehouse shelving or suspended by chains. To maximize the amount of light that reaches the plant, a white reflective surface (white styrofoam is excellent) should be placed above

Figure 5-2 Fluorescent Light Garden

the fixtures. Two or more fixtures placed side by side are more efficient than single fixtures. Eight-foot fixtures are more efficient than two- or four-foot ones. There is absolutely no evidence that the very expensive grow-light bulbs will give any better growth than the ordinary cool-white fluorescent bulbs. It is much more important that the bulbs be kept free of dust and that they be replaced as soon as dark areas appear at the ends.

If plants begin to shed their lower leaves, this could be a sign that they are not getting enough light. Any plant that is moved from a high-light area, such as a greenhouse or outdoors, will respond in this way unless it is gradually acclimatized to the lower-level, indoor light. The presence of long spindly stems with big distances between leaf internodes is a sure sign that plants are not receiving enough light. Plants growing in windowsills should be turned 90 degrees every few days, to prevent the leaning-tower-of-Pisa effect. Frequently pinch off ½"–1" of the growing shoots to encourage the development of leafy plant growth.

4.5 Growing Medium

The growing medium for indoor plants is also crucial. Under no circumstances will pot plants thrive in ordinary garden soil. First of all, it is absolutely essential that soil be pasteurized to kill diseases, insects, and weed seeds. Pasteurized soil may be purchased, or garden soil can be pasteurized by maintaining it under moist conditions at a temperature of 70 degrees C for 30 minutes. This can be done in an oven. However, the smell of the hot soil is pervasive. A local nursery or greenhouse is often willing to do this free of charge for institutions.

Second, the soil must be amended to provide proper aeration, drainage, and moisture-holding capacity for the confined growing area of a pot. Adding materials such as sand, perlite, or Turface improves drainage and aeration. Adding peat or vermiculite will improve moisture-holding capacity. Many references give mixes that are suitable for various types of plants. A good standard pot plant mix is one-third soil, one-third perlite, and one third vermiculite. Mixing these ingredients is a good, repetitive activity. Moisten the ingredients slightly to keep down the dust. Plants should be repotted once a year, usually moving to a pot one or two inches larger in diameter. With very large plants, add one or two inches of rich new soil to the top of the pot. If a plant slows in growth and begins dropping leaves, it may be root-bound. Loosen between the pot and the soil with a knife, tap the bottom of the pot, and remove the plant. If returning the plant to the same size pot, loosen the root ball with fingers or a knife, removing old soil and some of the roots, especially those at the bottom. Add two inches of new soil to the pot bottom. Replace the plant and add water.

4.6 Water

A common problem in many programs is over-watering. Participants often become so interested in caring for the plants that they tend to water more than necessary. This presents a very serious problem for plant growth. Plant roots, like people, need air to breathe. The plant will quite literally drown if water occupies all of the air space around the roots. A plant with soil that is too wet will develop droopy leaves and eventually drop its leaves, just as it will if it is too dry. Countering overwatering with instruction, signs, etc., is one possibility, but it is rather difficult to accomplish. A helpful remedy would be increasing the proportion of perlite, even up to 50 percent, in the soil so that the mix is very porous and water will drain freely.

Another important aspect of drainage is the container. Pot plant containers can be virtually anything as long as they have drainage holes. It is often said that adding a layer of gravel to crocks or jars will provide drainage. This is not really accurate. Gravel merely provides a place for water to drain, so that the plant roots are not standing in it. This method should be avoided, especially for small containers.

Another commonly held fallacy is that a gravel layer in the bottom of the pot will improve drainage. In fact, just the opposite is true. Putting gravel in the bottom of a pot reduces drainage because it reduces the length of the soil column. The shorter the soil column, the poorer the drainage.

This important point can be illustrated by a simple experiment. Saturate a tea towel with water and wring it out lightly. Hold the towel up so that it is draining from the long edges (the shortest column). After it has stopped dripping, turn the towel so that it drains from the short edges (the longest column). The amount of water that now comes from what was thought to be a drained towel is surprising.

Drainage is slowed down by layers of different particle size. The potting medium must be thoroughly mixed to avoid this effect. Plant pots should never sit in water. Drainage saucers or trays should be emptied. To maximize root aeration, it is important that the pot size be suited to the plant size. When a small plant is in a large pot, especially if there is a problem with overwatering, there is not enough root volume to create air spaces and absorb water, which makes the water saturation problem worse.

Participants who like to overwater plants could have their energies directed toward misting the plants instead. The air in virtually every institution is too dry for optimal plant growth. Regular misting will certainly benefit plants and will not harm any plant types, including African violets, as long as the misting water is the same temperature (never colder) as plant leaves. Setting plants on trays of pebbles with a layer of water in the bottom will also help humidify them.

4.7 Temperature

Temperature is the fourth important environmental variable. Little can be done about the room temperature for plants growing in an institution. However, care should be taken to avoid extremes in temperature. Do not put plants near radiators, heat vents, or drafts from doorways. Avoid locations that are close to windows that become very cold in winter or overly hot on sunny days. Most plants appreciate a temperature lower at night than during the day, but they do not appreciate— any more than people do —the frying-freezing syndrome.

4.8 Insect and Pest Control

The most serious maintenance problems for any gardener are insect pests and diseases. An ounce of prevention here is worth more than a pound of cure. Carefully examine plants, including those from commercial greenhouses, that come into the program. Ruthlessly pitch out any that carry insects or show evidence of mildew or fungus diseases. Remove all dead and diseased leaves. Never reuse pots, unless they are scrubbed with a 25 percent bleach solution. Soil that is to be reused must be repasteurized. Do not store uncleaned pots or dead plants near healthy plants. Repot plants every year to maintain optimal growth. Insects go first of all for sickly plants.

Some insects, such as aphids, cannot abide regular encounters with water. Washing plant leaves with plain water or a mild soap solution not only will help control aphids, but will remove dust and dirt, which slows down growth. This is another activity for the person who is likely to kill plants with kindness by overwatering.

To keep an insect invasion under control, plants should be checked regularly for any signs of pests. Washing, as mentioned, is a first control. The use of chemical sprays in enclosed institutional areas, where many are likely to have health problems, should be avoided. Spraying with insecticidal soap provides good control for most house plant pests. This spray is not harmful to people or the environment. It must be kept in mind that not even toxic chemical sprays can totally eliminate all insects. The soil, pots, and all areas around the infected plants should be sprayed. Seriously infected plants can be placed in a plastic bag, sprayed, sealed up, and left for 24 hours, effectively fumigating the pests. Since insects such as aphids have a seven-day life cycle, the plants should be sprayed once a week for three to four weeks. For those with greenhouses, a predator wasp, *encarcia formosa,* successfully controls whiteflies in many commercial greenhouses. Gnats and ladybugs are effective against aphids. Sources are listed at the end of this section. Another useful control for whiteflies is provided by yellow boards or yellow paper coated with a sticky substance such as that used for painting the trunk of trees to trap insects. The insects are attracted to the color yellow and fly toward it.

4.9 Feeding

Feeding is perhaps one of the most neglected areas of house plant care. There is simply not enough nutrient in potting soil to maintain healthy plant growth. Feeding biweekly with a standard dilution of a water-soluble 20-20-20 plant fertilizer is essential. For flowering plants, when blooming, use a fertilizer high in phosphorus, such as 10-30-20. These numbers represent the proportions of the essential plant nutrients in the fertilizer mix. The first number is nitrogen, which supports leaf growth; the second is phosphorus, which encourages flowering and fruiting; and the third is potassium, which supports healthy roots and stems. For those who wish to use only organic products, fish emulsion is good for leaf growth. To support flowering, bone meal should be included in the potting mix. When plant growth is slow (for example, during winter months), cut back on fertilizer to every three to four weeks. Adding finished compost to the potting mix supports healthy plant growth, improves soil aeration, and fights against plant diseases. Sprinkling finished compost on the surface of already potted plants gives them a boost.

4.10 Plant Propagation (Starting New Plants)

Plant materials are unique among the therapeutic modalities, because you can produce more for no cost! However, care must be taken in starting new plants in order to have healthy ones. The common practice of putting a cutting in a glass of water until roots form is a very poor one. The new plant develops a tangled set of roots that are adapted to growing in water, hence water absorption is easy. When these roots are transplanted to soil they are like a fish out of water. These roots are not

adapted to the more difficult task of water absorption from soil. The plant quite literally will sit and sulk for days or weeks until new roots can be grown.

The following is an outline of the proper and most successful method for starting new plants (Figure 5-3).

1. Select propagation containers. Any container 2½ to 3½ inches deep with drainage holes will serve the purpose. For individual propagation boxes, fiber pack grow trays work well, as do plastic food containers with holes punched in the bottom. Plants can be started right in the pot, as long as it is a small pot for one cutting, or several cuttings are put in a large pot. For starting individual plants, paper cups with a hole punched in the bottom work well. Individual two-inch or three-inch pots made of peat are biodegradable and can be put right into the larger pot at transplant time. The root system is thus not disturbed by the transplant process.

2. Loosely fill the container with a dampened rooting medium. A mixture of equal parts of soil, vermiculite, and perlite works well, as does commercially prepared soil-less potting mix.

3. Using a small dowel or pencil as a dibble, make one-inch deep holes in the mix, about a half-inch apart.

4. Using a sharp knife or scissors, take three- to four-inch stem cuttings from succulent, but sturdy, sections of a healthy, insect-free plant. Do not use tough, woody cuttings, because they are difficult to root and do not produce healthy plants.

5. Remove the bottom leaves, ensuring that each cutting has at least one leaf axil node, as this is where the new roots form.

6. Dip the cut ends in rooting hormone powder (auxin), using the appropriate strength for the type of plant to be propagated (see the directions on the package). Tap off excess powder. (*Note:* Remove from the container only as much rooting hormone as will be needed. Extra hormone powder should not be returned to the container because of the possibility of contamination.) Plants that are easy to root do not require rooting hormone. Common easy-to-root house plants are

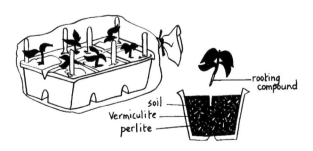

Figure 5-3 Starting New Plants

Table 5-1 Easy-to-Grow House Plants

Low-Light Requirements

Asparagus Fern	Nerve plant
Baby's Tears	Parlor Plant
Cast-Iron Plant	Peperomia
Chinese Evergreen	Spider Plant
Devil's Ivy	Variegated Snake Plant
Dracaena	White Flag
Kentia Palm	

Moderate-Light Requirements

Aluminum Plant	Jade Plant
Arrowhead Vine	Piggyback Plant
Artillery Plant	Prayer Plant
Boston Fern	Rubber Plant
Creeping Fig	Swedish Ivy
Dumb Cane	Wandering Sailor (formerly
Grape Ivy	known as Wandering Jew)
Ivies	

Bright-Light Requirements

Begonia	Flame Violet
Blood Leaf	Geranium
Butterfly Palm	Inch Plant
Coleus	Lipstick Plant
Croton	Medicine Plant

Table 5-2 Easy-to-Propagate House Plants

Aluminum Plant	Lipstick Plant	Rosemary Vine
Arrowhead Vine	Miniature Holly	Shamrock
Artillery Plant	Monkey Plant	Silk Oak
Blood Leaf	Nerve Plant	Spider Plant
Coleus	Peperomia	Star of Bethlehem
Devil's Ivy	Polka Dot Plant	Swedish Ivy
Fibrous Begonia	Purple Passion	Teddy Bear Plant
Geranium	Plant	Umbrella Tree
Grape Ivy	Purple Heart	
Inch Plant	Rosary Vine	

room moisture. When roots have formed, use a large spoon or trowel to lift the new plant and as much surrounding soil as possible to a pot half-filled with soil mix. Sprinkle soil, as needed, around the stem. Gently firm the soil, and water as needed.

4.11 Outdoor Container Gardening

Container gardens outdoors are an excellent choice for individuals with ADRD. They provide an outdoor gardening experience without the difficulty of preparing and maintaining a garden space. Containers can be placed in areas most accessible to the individuals. Each participant can have his or her own container garden. Container gardens are easier to tend for individuals who are physically frail and have coordination problems.

Container gardening outdoors requires specialized horticultural practices, most particularly in connection with container site, variety selection, and growing medium. As for indoor potted plants, the container can be virtually anything as long as it has drainage holes. Some of the least expensive containers are plastic buckets of varying sizes (usually up to five gallons) in which many bulk foodstuffs (e.g., peanut butter, flavored syrups, margarine, etc.) are packed. These are available free or at small cost from cafeterias or restaurants. Drainage holes are easily made with a small electric drill. If a drainage saucer is required, the lid can be used. The variety of inexpensive or free containers is limited only by one's imagination—old bathtubs, wooden cribs from concrete sewer pipes, and gallon paint cans can all serve as containers for a lush garden. Wooden window boxes can be made in all shapes and sizes. Once again, drainage holes are important. The wood should be treated and painted to slow rotting. Pressure-treated wood makes an excellent lifetime container, but it is very expensive. An effective and inexpensive wood preservative can be made by combining one bar of melted paraffin wax with one liter of linseed oil and three liters of mineral spirits.

spider plants, swedish ivy, philodendron, peperomia, and wandering sailor. Others are listed in Table 5-2. Other plants may root without using rooting powder, but the success rate is poor.

7. Place the prepared cutting in the holes in the container and gently firm soil around the stem.

8. Mist the cuttings and soil.

9. Place wire hoops, dowels, or popsicle sticks in the corners of the container so that they come about two inches above the level of the plant leaves.

10. Carefully cover the whole container with a clear plastic bag or plastic wrap.

11. Inflate the bag, to keep the plastic off the leaves, and fasten with a twist tie.

12. Place the container in a moderately lit, moderately heated area until roots are well formed (two to three weeks for most common house plants). Never place in direct sun. Check for root formation by gently tugging on the plant stem. If there is resistance, there are roots. If the plastic becomes laden with moisture, open the bag for a few hours. Watering is rarely necessary, as this mini-greenhouse maintains its own moisture. However, if the soil should become dry, mist the plants and soil and reseal the container.

13. A few days before transplanting, open the plastic covering to provide a gradual adjustment to regular

Wood preservatives such as creosote and Pentox presently are under scrutiny by the Canadian government as potential health hazards, and can be bought only with a license in the United States. They should be used with extreme caution, and never on containers for vegetable production.

Durable, but expensive, raised growing beds, which are accessible from wheelchairs, can be made from railway or landscaping ties. Great care must be taken to securely fasten the ties to contain the weight of the earth safely. There are many attractive design possibilities, which incorporate raised beds with a patio area. When developing a new site for gardening with the disabled, it must be carefully planned for easy-reaching access from wheelchairs. Bed width, height, walkway size, and slope must all be considered. Generally beds should not be more than four feet wide.

The next consideration is site selection. In many cases there will be little choice, but if the facility has large grounds, there are important factors to consider. Of utmost importance is accessibility. For those who have physical disabilities, a difficult or tiring procedure to reach the garden will defeat many of the positive aspects. While some sites at a distance may be more suitable horticulturally, the prime concern must be accessibility. The site can then be designed to improve its growing capability by selecting plant varieties appropriate for that particular microclimate, by adapting the sun-shade patterns, by trimming trees, or adding sun screens or windbreaks.

If indeed there is a choice of accessible locations, then selecting a site with maximal sunlight is of prime importance. Other factors to be considered are soil, interference from surrounding tree roots, susceptibility to damage from pedestrian traffic, and access to water.

Outdoor container gardens will not thrive if grown only in ordinary garden soil. As for potted house plants, this specialized growing area must have soil amendments to provide good aeration, drainage, and moisture-holding capacity. The standard potting mix of $1/3$ rich garden soil or compost (pasteurization is not necessary outdoors), $1/3$ perlite, and $1/3$ peat or vermiculite is also suitable for outdoor container gardens. However, this mix would become very costly for a large number of containers. Once again, it is a good idea to scout around to see what materials are available free or at low cost. Excellent container gardens can be grown by preparing the containers as follows (Figure 5-4):

1. Place a one- or two-inch layer of sphagnum moss (gathered in the woods) in the bottom of the container.

2. Fill the container to a point three inches from the top with alternating layers of two to three inches of rotted sawdust mixed with horticultural lime and half-inch

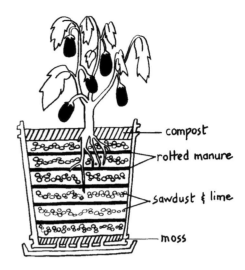

Figure 5-4 Container Garden

to one-inch layers of well-rotted manure. Begin and end with sawdust. Sawdust is available free from sites around lumber yards or sawmills.

3. Add a two-inch layer of finished compost. Other types of free or inexpensive container growing media are spent mushroom compost, ground-rotted bark (try the municipal parks and grounds dumping site), and rotted tree leaves. Sand directly from a sand and gravel company is usually much cheaper than perlite as a drainage component. A trial batch of a few containers using a new growing medium should be attempted before any large-scale planting is done.

Full-scale, raised-bed gardens, which are one to two feet deep, require the same soil amendments as regular garden soil and can be prepared in the same manner. A soil test is a good guide for the required nutrients. In Canada, soil tests are provided free of charge by the provincial departments of agriculture. Since the roots of a container-grown plant are confined to the container soil for nutrient absorption, it is important that this soil be well enriched and routinely fertilized. A standard dilution of liquid 20-20-20 or fish emulsion is good for containers in which only leafy plants are growing. Flower- or fruit-producing plant containers should have a higher phosphorus fertilizer, such as 10-30-10, or compost or manure tea. To make these teas, fill a bucket or barrel one-third full of compost or manure, fill with water and let "steep" for two days. Water containers with the rich liquid. Containers using a soil-less mix will require constant fertilization.

Plant and cultivar (variety) selection should be based on container size and light availability at the site. Cultivars of some vegetables have been specifically selected for container growing and will give much better results than common garden cultivars. In full-sun areas, vegetables such as peppers, eggplants, patio or Sweet-100 tomatoes, bush cucumbers, or zucchini; or flowers such as dahlias, snapdragons, geraniums, or marguerites grow well. In areas receiving less than six hours of sun, try leaf lettuce or Swiss chard; herbs such as parsley, mint, or chives; or flowers such as begonias, impatiens, coleus, fuschia, or lobelia.

4.12 The Outdoor Garden

There are shelves and shelves of books describing techniques and principles for outdoor flower and vegetable gardening. This small section serves merely as an introduction for getting started. As a trained horticulturalist and a lifelong gardener, my absolute and unapologetic bias is toward organic gardening. These methods not only provide healthy produce without damaging the environment, but they are the easiest and most failure-free methods for getting the maximal yield from the least space. As a gardening instructor and consultant, I repeatedly found that peoples' gardening failures and frustrations were due to inadequate preparation of the soil for growing. If these initial preparations are made, the routine yearly maintenance of the garden is easy and the production prolific. No amount of chemical addition can compensate for poor soil. What follows is a thumbnail sketch of how to develop and plant an intensive, bountiful, organic vegetable garden. Further references are found at the end of this section.

Bountiful back yards do not mean back-breaking labor. Did you know that an area the size of a double bed can produce six months or more of daily salads? Or that an area the size of the average living room can supply fresh vegetables for a whole season? This and more can happen when your backyard becomes bountiful.

Bountiful back yards do not mean

- large amounts of time, money, and yard space
- good existing soil and climate
- having a green thumb

Bounty in the back yard does mean

- saving money
- produce of unbuyable flavor, freshness, and variety
- a satisfying and relaxing hobby

This bounty is made possible through

- organic soil preparation
- crop selection
- special planting techniques
- early start/late finish

Organic Soil Preparation

Regardless of what sort of soil (or nonsoil) is in your back yard right now, adding large quantities of organic matter means extremely high production because

- It provides a constant supply of food for plant growth.
- It creates soil that lets roots grow deep and holds moisture and nutrients.
- It attracts worms and microbes, which keep the soil loose and break down nutrients for plant growth and plant food.

Preparing and Maintaining the Garden (Figure 5-5).

The first year

1. Do a soil test to determine soil acidity (a pH of 6.5 is best for most vegetables).
2. Remove and set aside the top 6 to 8 inches of soil (less, of course, if that is all there is). This is most easily accomplished by working in 18- to 24-inch sections. Remove the soil from the first section to a tarpaulin-covered grass area beside the bed. Do steps 3 and 4 below. Finish with the topsoil from the next section. Continue until the whole area is prepared. Move the topsoil from the first section to cover the last section.
3. Loosen but do not turn over the remaining soil for another 16 inches (or as far as possible). Remove rocks, tree roots, and other debris.
4. Chop and add sod removed from the garden site. Add an 8- to 12-inch deep organic sandwich of alternating organic material and soil (see "Rotting Advice").
5. Rake in five pounds of bone meal and three pounds of wood ash per 100 square feet. Add amendments to change soil pH, as necessary. In Canada such tests are free from provincial departments of agriculture.

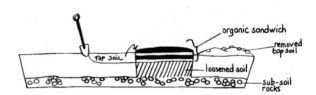

Figure 5-5 Soil Preparation

6. One inch of worked compost or aged manure sifted into the topsoil with a digging fork will boost growth.

7. The work is done: plant the garden.

Every year

1. Loose soil means lively growth, so *never* walk on prepared soil or spade muddy or extremely dry soil.

2. Do not disturb natural soil layers by mixing soil and subsoil when digging.

Preparation

1. Every fall, spade in three to four inches of fresh manure (two inches of rotten manure), lime, and bone meal if required by soil test.

2. Cover with a thick mulch, or plant with fall rye.

3. The following spring remove the mulch or spade in the rye. Rake the mulched ground and plant. Allow the rye to decompose for three to four weeks before planting.

4. If the soil test shows that potassium is needed, rake in one or two pounds of wood ashes per 100 square feet.

5. If available, one inch of finished compost sifted into the topsoil will boost vegetable yields.

6. Dig extra-large transplant holes. Add two inches of manure, one inch of soil, and one tablespoon of bone meal and fill in around the transplants with worked compost.

Spring preparation

Follow steps 1, 4, 5, and 6 above, using only aged manure.

A Plant's Food Guide for Health.

- Manure (an excellent source of humus and plant food, but varies widely in content according to type, amount of bedding material included, and how it was aged; be sure of this information)
  1. fresh manure
     —still smells
     —is high in nitrogen
     —must *never* touch plant roots or leaves
     —must be mixed with dry organic matter and covered or turned into the soil to prevent nitrogen loss
  2. aged manure
     —looks like black, humus-rich soil
     —has no offensive smell

     —will not burn plants, but using too much causes excessive leaf growth
     —should be kept covered
  3. sources
     —pigeon keepers and horse stables (most cities have them)
     —classified ads, gardening section (many will deliver)
     —local farmers
     —other gardeners may share their sources
- High-carbon material
  1. breaks down slowly
  2. generally dry material, such as fall leaves, sawdust, dry plant material, straw, newspapers, dry seaweed, dry eel grass
- High-nitrogen material
  1. breaks down quickly
  2. generally wet material such as fresh grass clippings, fresh vegetable wastes, green plants and weeds, manure, fresh seaweed
- Compost
  1. best all-around, balanced food for plant growth

Rotting Advice. To get a good rot going, there should be four parts of carbon to one part of nitrogen by percentage of composition. For example, one garbage bag of fresh grass clippings or five gallons of fresh vegetable waste, or two to three gallons of fresh manure, will break down one garbage bag of dry leaves. Make sandwich-type layers of these materials in an open pile, a compost bin, or a box with good aeration. Top with a thin layer of soil to add microorganisms and worms and to eliminate any smell. The compost is ready more quickly if it is turned often and if the original material is in small pieces.

Crop Selection

Good Things Come in Small Packages. To get the most from the smallest space, select these crops: beans (pole types), carrots, celery, chard, cress, leeks, leaf lettuce, onions (bunching), radish, tomatoes, turnip greens, spinach, zucchini (bush type).

Good Things Come Expensive at the Store. For the best dollar value for garden space used, select these crops: asparagus, broccoli, Brussels sprouts, cauliflower, cucumbers, eggplant, herbs, lettuce (specialty types such as romaine), melons, parsley, parsnips, peppers, and snow peas. The spacemongers corn, potatoes, and peas are in a category by themselves, since the flavor of these just-picked plants cannot be found elsewhere. Many standard home garden vegetables such as beets, cabbage, cooking onions, squash, and turnips are missing from these lists because they are all relatively inexpensive, readily available, and travel and store well. Generally, it does not make sense to grow them in a small back yard garden.

Varieties of Varieties. Each vegetable has several different varieties. There are 500 varieties of tomatoes alone. Read seed catalogues carefully and select those that seem most suited to your climate and offer the highest production. Keep experimenting, and ask other gardeners about their favorites.

Think before You Plant.

- Plant heat-loving crops in the sunniest places.
- Plant cool-weather crops in the shadier places.
- Arrange plants from tallest to shortest, moving across the garden from north to south.
- Do not grow vegetables that are not suited to the climate or season.

Special Planting Techniques

Bed or Block Planting. Bed or block planting results in more production by 4 to 30 times and requires less weeding, watering, digging, and feeding. Beds can be any length but must be narrow enough to reach across from the sides (four to five feet). Beds are easier to work and grow better, due to warmer soil temperatures, if they are raised. The edges of the beds should be supported by railway ties, planking, or other material. Some pointers for bed planting are:

- Scatter or broadcast seeds, or set out transplants, the same distance apart in all directions as the distance recommended between plants in rows.
- Leaves of plants three-fourths mature should just touch.
- Use the intensive planting scheme below, especially for transplants.

```
┌──────────────────────────────┐
│  X  X  X  X  X  X  X  X       │
│    X  X  X  X  X  X  X  X     │
│  X  X  X  X  X  X  X  X       │
│    X  X  X  X  X  X  X  X     │
└──────────────────────────────┘
```

Intercropping. Plant together crops with

- different growth areas, e.g., climbing cucumbers and beets; carrots and Brussels sprouts, celery, or romaine lettuce; parsley and staked tomatoes; asparagus and snow peas

- different maturity times, e.g., green onions and broccoli; romaine lettuce transplants and cauliflower; tomatoes and head lettuce; radishes and carrots (beets, broccoli, cauliflower); cress and swiss chard

Plant the last vegetable three to four weeks before the first finishes: leaf lettuce and zucchini (bush beans); cauliflower (broccoli) and bush beans; peas (bush or pole) and beans (bush or pole).

Succession Growing. As soon as one crop is harvested, more seeds or plants go in. Keep a plant nursery (especially for lettuce and broccoli seedlings) to provide plants for empty spaces.

Favorite Combinations. Table 5-3 shows vegetables listed in order of planting, from spring through summer and fall.

Vertical Growing (Saving Space). Good climbers for netting: pole beans, peas, cucumbers, melons, pumpkins, squash; for trellises and poles: melons, pumpkins, squash, tomatoes, zucchini.

Early Start, Late Finish

Plant Early. Plant as soon as the ground is thawed (if prepared in the fall) or as soon as it can be worked. These vegetables can withstand frost: cress, green onions (from sets), kale, lettuce, peas, radishes, spinach, Swiss chard, and turnip greens. Plant and cover with plastic to warm the soil. Remove plastic when seedlings appear. When days are consistently above ten degrees C, plant beets, carrots, parsley, and parsnips.

Harvest Late. The first fall frosts do not mean the end of fresh produce if you remember the following:

- Cool-weather crops (see "Plant Early") also thrive in autumn.
- You can determine the planting date for fall crops by adding two weeks (because of the shorter fall days) to the number of days to maturity. Now count backward from the usual date of the final

Table 5-3 Favorite Combinations by Season

Spring	Summer	Fall
Peas	Lettuce	Radishes, Green Onions
Spinach	Bush Beans	Romaine Lettuce
Turnip Greens	Tomatoes (Peppers and Eggplant)	
Leaf Lettuce, Green Onions	Carrots	Cress
Leaf Lettuce	Broccoli (Cauliflower)	
Cauliflower	Bush Beans	Fall "Greens"

fall freeze; this will be the approximate planting date.

- The soil must be enriched before replanting.
- Mulching in the fall helps keep the soil warm.
- Chinese vegetables such as Psai chai, bok choi, and Chinese broccoli do very well in the short days of fall.

Begun Is Half Done. Start transplants inside, about six weeks before they are planted outside. Plant outside when the average daytime temperatures reach 10 degrees C: broccoli, Brussels sprouts, leeks, lettuce, Swiss chard. At 18 degrees C, put out cucumbers, tomatoes, and zucchini. Cucumbers and zucchini have sensitive roots, so start early in peat pots or pellets. At 21 degrees C, put out eggplant, melons, and peppers.

Clever Tricks To Beat the Heat Problem. Presprouting seeds eliminates the need for the warmer soil temperatures required for germination. Try this with beans, cucumbers, melons, peas, and zucchini. Permanent, clear plastic mulch raises soil temperature by 6 degrees C.

4.13 Horticulture Resources

Horticulture As Therapy

Beems, J. 1985. *Adaptive Garden Equipment.* Available from Craig Hospital, 3425 South Clarkson, Englewood, CA 80110 ($2.50). Instructions and drawings on how to adapt gardening equipment for better grip.

Chaplin, M. 1978. *Gardening for the Physically Handicapped and the Elderly.* London: Redwood-Burn Ltd. A small but comprehensive book on adaptations and horticultural projects.

Coson, M. 1978, 1979, 1980. *Gardening As Therapy.* A series of three 32-page booklets outlining ten or more sessions each for horticulture as therapy in spring, summer, and fall. There is also a general booklet, *Horticulture As Therapy.* All are available from

    The Botanical Gardens
    University of British Columbia
    6501 NW Marine Drive
    Vancouver, British Columbia
    Canada V6T 1W5

Moore, D. 1989. *Growing with Gardening: A Twelve Month Guide for Therapy, Recreation and Education.* Chapel Hill, N.C.: University of North Carolina Press.

Olszowy, D. 1978. *Horticulture for the Disabled and Disadvantaged.* Springfield, Ill.: Charles C Thomas Publisher.

Rothbert, E., and J. Danbert. 1981. *Horticultural Therapy for Seniors Centers, Nursing Homes, Retire-*

ment Living. This is a 118-page book that provides practical information and resources for establishing gardening programs with older people. It is available from

    Chicago Horticultural Society
    P.O. Box 400
    Glencoe, IL 60022

General Gardening

Carr, A., et al., eds. 1978. *The Encyclopedia of Organic Gardening.* Emmaus, Pa.: Rodale Press. An excellent encyclopedia guide to garden plants, herbs, perennial flowers, and basic organic gardening tecniques.

Halpin, A. 1980. *Rodale's Encyclopedia of Indoor Gardening.* Emmaus, Pa.: Rodale Press. An excellent and comprehensive guide to basic indoor gardening techniques, special projects, and growing guidelines for many house plants.

Jeavons, J. 1979. *How To Grow More Vegetables Than You Ever Thought Possible on Less Land Than You Can Imagine.* Berkeley, Calif.: Ten Speed Press. A clear and detailed description of how to develop intensive vegetable gardening in raised beds.

Seymour, J. 1980. *The Self-Sufficient Gardener.* Garden City, N.Y.: Doubleday & Co. An excellent guide to intensive organic gardening emphasizing moderate- and cold-climate gardening.

Magazines

Growth Point is a quarterly journal on topics related to horticultural therapy. It is published in England by the Society for Horticultural Therapy and Rural Training (see "Organizations").

Organic Gardening is published ten times per year by Rodale Press. It has excellent practical articles on gardening and thoughtful pieces on the importance of growing things for the health of the individual and the planet.

    Rodale Press
    33 E. Manor St.
    Emmaus, PA 18098

Organizations

    American Horticultural Therapy Association
    9220 Wightman Road, Suite 300
    Gaithersburg, MD 20879

    Canadian Horticultural Therapy Association
    c/o Royal Botanical Gardens
    P.O. Box 399
    Hamilton, Ontario
    Canada, L8N 3H8

The Society for Horticultural Therapy and Rural Training Ltd.

> Goulds Grounds, Vallis Way,
> Frome, Somerset, BAI 3DW,
> United Kingdom

Local gardening clubs or specialist groups such as the Rose Society or the Orchid Growers Organization can be an excellent source of volunteers, information, and perhaps supplies. Perhaps the annual show or exhibit could be hosted in your facility's auditorium.

Supplies and Adaptive Equipment

> Dominion Seedhouse Ltd.
> Georgetown, Ontario
> Canada L7G 4A2
>
> Equipment Consultants and Sales
> 2241 Dunwin Drive
> Erin Mills, Mississauga
> Ontario, Canada L5L 1A3
>
> Green Garden
> P.O. Box 278
> Mount Prospect, IL 60056
>
> Mellingers Inc.,
> 2310 W. South Range
> North Lime, OH 44452

Seeds

There are many mail-order seed houses. Check with local gardeners for their favorite in your area. Local seed houses will be more likely to carry the most successful varieties for your region. The following is a brief list of some seed companies with mail order catalogues.

> W. Atlee Burpee Co.,
> 300 Park Ave.
> Warminester, PA 18974
>
> Dominion Seed House
> Georgetown, Ontario
> Canada L7G 4A2
>
> Joseph Harris Co., Inc.,
> Moreton Farm
> 3670 Buffalo Rd.
> Rochester NY 14624
>
> George W. Park Seed Co.
> South Carolina Highway 254 North
> Greenwood, SC 29647
>
> Stokes Seed Co.
> P.O. Box 548
> Buffalo, NY 14240
> or
> 39 James St., Box 10

> St. Catherines, Ontario
> Canada L2R 6R6

Year-old seeds for community and therapeutic gardens are available for the cost of postage. You will receive 50 packets of seeds of your choice of herbs, flowers, or vegetables. Write to

> America the Beautiful
> 219 Shoreham Bldg.
> Washington, DC 20005

Cuttings, Pots, and Supplies

Have staff, volunteers, and families save pots and other suitable containers as well as donate cuttings. Greenhouses, flower shops, and supermarket plant departments may donate spent plants for cuttings, and the pots may be recycled. Funeral homes may donate flower arrangements, which can be taken apart and used to make smaller arrangements.

5.0 INTERGENERATIONAL ACTIVITIES

There has been great enthusiasm recently for programs that bring young and old together, in senior centers, day-care programs, nursing homes, and schools. When well planned and organized, these programs can be tremendously successful. It is essential, however, that these programs be thought over with care, particularly when involving older individuals with ADRD. Simply putting children and old people together and assuming that good will come of it can lead to disaster. There has been very little research in this area, and the results now available are mixed (Haber & Short-Degraff 1990). The program must be designed to meet the needs of the older and the younger participants while preserving the dignity of both. The children's capacity for enthusiasm and energy and the capacity of older persons to share their wisdom and compassion can then be mutually beneficial, the coming together beautiful to watch.

> The occupational therapist on the pediatric service and I thought that our two client groups would have much to offer each other. After considerable planning and discussion, we decided to introduce them. The children made cookies to bring. During the cookie baking, staff talked with them about grandparents and other older people they knew. They also talked about the older people they would meet. Most of them were grandparents too, probably older than their own grandparents. Some would be hard of hearing and have difficulty seeing, some wouldn't. Like the children, they too were in the hospital, mostly because they were feeling very sad.

Just like growing up was hard sometimes, so was growing old.

The children were firmly reminded that because the people they were visiting were not feeling well, they would find loud noises and obnoxious behavior especially upsetting. Most of the children (ages 8 to 12) had been hospitalized because of severe behavior problems at home and at school. In the hospital they were on strict behavioral programs. So, even though only the children with the highest level of privileges were allowed to participate, their potential for "acting up" during the visit was the biggest concern about the program by the staff.

The older people were also told about the children's visit, about the cookies and the tea party, and about the suggested activity of making terrariums together. Clients who were judged to be well enough were specially invited by the occupational therapist. They were told the ages of the children and that they were in the hospital because of problems in getting along with their families or in school. Many of the older clients were amazed and saddened to learn that such young children would have to be in a psychiatric hospital. They felt very sorry for the children, but most were somewhat reluctant to be involved because they weren't sure they were well enough to cope.

What a surprise awaited all involved! Ten children with problem behaviors and ten depressed older adults came together for a gardening activity and a social time, and all stereotypes melted away. The pediatric staff were absolutely amazed that they didn't have to give a single time out during the one-and-one-half-hour visit. The older people were smiling from ear to ear as they and their young partners worked on their terrariums. By cookie-sharing time the room was abuzz with conversation and laughter. The young visitors also passed cookies to the seniors who didn't come to the group. They were positively beaming with the praise they got for their cookies.

When the time came for the children to leave, one senior participant spontaneously hugged each child. As I was told afterward, it was at this point that the pediatric staff were literally holding their breath. Some of these children had great difficulty accepting and giving affection and would be just as likely to

level you as hug you. But hug they all did, and loved every minute of it!

5.1 Planning Intergenerational Programs

Intergenerational programs involving the cognitively impaired elderly must be undertaken with extra special care and planning. With severely impaired individuals, one must consider that young children, and even college students, will find it too difficult to deal with their impairments. In addition, dealing with such seriously impaired older people may lead to the development of negative stereotypes of all older people.

Before embarking on an intergenerational program, carefully think through what the goals of such a program might be, and if indeed they are reasonable goals for your particular population.

5.2 Goals of Intergenerational Activities

- Provide an opportunity for nurturing and expressing affection.
- Improve self-esteem through affirming the value of the person's role as parent or grandparent.
- Promote a normalized atmosphere, by including different generations and age groups.
- Provide an opportunity for pleasure given by observing the energy and enthusiasm of children.
- Provide a unique motivation for involvement in activities, a concrete reason for projects such as writing cards.
- Encourage socialization.
- Provide an opportunity for caring touch and physical contact.

5.3 Planning Intergenerational Activities

What are the key ingredients to successful intergenerational programs? The following guidelines are based on my experience and the limited literature that is available (Haber & Short-Degraff 1990; McDuffie & Whiteman 1989; Struntz & Reville 1985; Ventura-Merkel 1983).

Select the older participants carefully. Individuals with unpredictable or difficult behavior should not be included. Select the older participants according to the age of the children. For individuals in advanced stages of ADRD, either very young children, or, older college or high school students who can understand something of the disease process, are the most suitable. The youngest children will more likely be able to communicate on a nonverbal, emotional level and not be troubled by the communication problems of persons with ADRD. Babies and toddlers will appreciate touch and cuddles from the seniors. Brief visits will be positive for both.

Select the younger participants carefully. Children visiting with older people with ADRD must be given some background on the disease, presented in a way that they can understand. There are several children's story books, written about grandparents with memory problems. These include: *Grampa Doesn't Know Me Any More* (Guthrie & Arnstee 1986); *My Grammy* (Kibbey 1988), *Always, Gramma* (Nelson 1988) and *Maria's Grandma Gets Mixed Up* (Sanford 1989). Children who are too rambunctious will be upsetting for the older participant.

Remember that coordination between staff working with the older participants and those working with the children is essential. The success of any intergenerational program depends upon a thorough knowledge of the needs, values, and skills of the participants. The respective staff members must work together in selecting participants and planning activities that will be of mutual benefit.

Respect the right of any potential participant not to be involved. There is no absolute affinity between all older people and all children. Some older people will find the children too tiring or demanding. Others may prefer to watch from a distance, rather than be directly involved. Individuals in the middle stages of ADRD may be worried that they will appear "stupid" to the inquisitive child. If the program has been carefully explained and a positive invitation offered, the refusal must be respected. When children from day-care centers or schools are included, the parents must be informed.

Keep the activities simple and the visits brief to avoid overstimulation for individuals with ADRD. Plan visits around simple activities that both groups of participants will enjoy. If the children and the older individuals are strangers to each other, it is especially important to focus the gathering around an activity that both will enjoy. Although it is important to plan carefully for these activities, one must also be careful not to overplan. The program should allow for spontaneity between the seniors and the children.

Some suggested activities are

- churning ice cream
- food preparation (e.g., making lemonade, bread, cookies)
- gardening activities indoors or out (for an outdoor garden, try making a scarecrow together)
- looking at and trying out memorabilia or artifacts of mutual interest (e.g., old-fashioned apple peeler, butter churn, old-time clothing)

- music activities (e.g., dancing, folk songs, teaching each other favorite songs)
- parties (especially birthday parties or for special occasions such as Easter)
- pet visitation
- photograph session (looking at old cameras, taking pictures of each other with a Polaroid camera)
- picnics, preparations for special occasions (e.g., Halloween, Valentine's Day)
- walks and indoor exercises

Since children are also involved, take extra care that the activities and the approach with the adult are adult. Just having children present does not make doing childish activities any more acceptable. Indeed, it may be a further insult to old persons with ADRD to have such a graphic illustration that their skills are on the same level as those of children. However, if an activity is presented so that the child and the adult are helping each other, it can be enjoyed by both.

Develop a "grandfriends" program. This type of program could be very beneficial for individuals who are mildly to moderately impaired. Children and adults gather as a group a few times a year for special occasions or parties. Each older adult is matched with a child, as a "special friend." In between visits, letters, cards, and perhaps phone calls can be exchanged. Such an activity can be coordinated with the language arts program in the children's school. For the older adults, the cards and letters can be part of an activities program, which will help to stimulate cognitive function and give purpose to these activities.

Use opportunities for older adults to observe and enjoy children from a distance. Sitting on a park bench and watching children play can bring much enjoyment to persons with ADRD, without placing any demands on them.

6.0 MOVEMENT AND EXERCISE

Until the end stages of the disease, primary motor function is a persisting ability of persons with ADRD. Movement and exercise are essential to maintenance of these physical abilities as long as possible, in addition to the well-known benefits of exercise, such as improved breathing, heart function, appetite, and general energy level (Larson & Bruce 1986; Leitner & Leitner 1985; National Resource Center on Health Promotion and Aging 1991a; Posner et al. 1992; Rogers et al. 1990; Schilke 1991; Short & Leonardelli 1987). Movement stimulates alertness, provides an acceptable outlet for energies, and is in itself a pleasurable experience. Intense exercise therapy may improve the cognitive function of persons with AD (Lindemuth & Moose 1990). It is not surprising that movement and exercise programs are very popular in ADRD day programs and long-term care settings. Kalicki (1987) noted that 83 percent of the 18 ADRD specialty units surveyed had an exercise program. Movement and exercise programs were the second most popular activity in the ADRD day programs surveyed. With adaptation, movement and exercise programs can provide the individual with ADRD with an activity at which they can succeed, as well as important health benefits. Movement and exercise can also play an important role in reducing night-time pacing (Robb 1985). As the disease progresses to its final stages, movement becomes even more important in order to prevent painful contractures and to help to maintain breathing patterns and digestion. In these latter stages the individual will require one-to-one assistance to maintain movement.

6.1 Goals of Movement Programs

- Improve or maintain range of motion, strength, and general endurance. Maintenance of function is a very important goal for individuals with progressive diseases such as ADRD.

- Improve or maintain cardiorespiratory function. The importance of exercise to a healthy heart is well recognized.

- Improve general alertness through movement stimulation. Support for the importance of movement stimulation is found in Chapters 1 and 7.

- Provide an opportunity for the pleasure of movement and physical contact with others. Until deprived of the opportunity for movement, few realize how essential it is to general well-being. Exercise groups also provide an opportunity for all-important touch from others (e.g., holding hands in a group or pairs to do exercises).

- Provide an outlet for restless energy. Good exercise programs can help to reduce restlessness and wandering.

- Provide an opportunity for self-expression through movement.

6.2 Selecting Participants for Movement Groups

In order to participate in an exercise group an individual should
- have some residual skill in following verbal and nonverbal directions given to the group as a whole
- be able to attend to the group process for at least five minutes

- have a predictable pattern of behavior (i.e., not prone to unpredictable agitation)
- be able to move limbs independently

Group exercises with only one or two leaders are not appropriate for persons in the more advanced stages. Although movement continues to be very important, they will require one-to-one or one-to-two assistance in order to follow the directions. If volunteers are available, exercises could still be carried out in a group; however, this should be monitored carefully, as the group may cause too much stimulation and be too confusing for participants.

6.3 Precautions

- Check with clinical staff on health-related activity restrictions. Before beginning any exercise program, the individual should have medical clearance.

- Avoid overexertion, especially with persons who have been inactive for some time. Be very careful not to overstress fragile joints and bones. Monitor carefully for signs of fatigue, and slow down or stop immediately if present.

- Be aware of limitations in range of motion.

- Avoid exercises and movements that require leaning the head and neck backward. This may cause dizziness due to loss of blood supply to the brain.

- Do not use props that could cause injuries (e.g., wooden dowels).

- Avoid jerky, bouncy movements. Keep the routine smooth and rhythmic.

6.4 Guidelines for Exercise/Movement Groups

Develop a regular routine of types of exercises and follow it consistently. All sessions should begin with 5 to 10 minutes of gentle stretches and warm-up exercises to all body parts, followed by 15 to 20 minutes of more strenuous activity. The session should close with 5 to 10 minutes of cool-down, relaxation-type movements. These times may be shortened, depending on the tolerance of the participants.

Run the group in a comfortable room that is separated from the main living areas, to prevent distractions and interruptions. Participants should wear comfortable, loose-fitting clothes and sturdy, supportive footwear.

Provide supportive straight-back chairs (preferably with arms to make getting up easier), and seat participants in a circle, according to ability. Alternate seating of higher-functioning and lower-functioning individuals allows for one to model the behavior of the other. Those with hearing loss should be seated opposite the leader, those with visual deficits or who need extra assistance should be seated beside the leader. In this group no table is present, in order to allow for foot movements.

Help to initiate the desired movements as necessary, with hand-over-hand guidance.

Use exercises in which the movements mimic familiar, functional activities. It is, however, very important to introduce these activities carefully, with ample reality reassurance, so that they do not increase confusion and disorientation (e.g., so that the person thinks he or she is actually on a boat). The use of safe, related props is a help in overcoming this problem. In verbal introductions, emphasize reality reassurance through frequent use of words such as *pretend*, *imagine*, and *as if.* Encourage humming, which not only adds to the enjoyment of the group, but underlines the fact that these are make-believe activities.

Use rhythmic, instrumental music to stimulate movement. It is best to avoid music with words during exercise groups, as this can be too distracting. Match the rhythm to the speed of the exercises; slower rhythmic music to open the group, more fast-paced in the middle, and calming and melodic music for a relaxing ending. Music helps to keep the movements smooth and rhythmic.

Be aware of primitive reflexes and avoid stimulating them (see Chapter 3). There is one exception to this guideline. The grasp reflex can be used positively in order to get someone to hold onto a prop. Similarly, the common deficit of perseveration can be used to engage the individual in a repetitive movement. Be prepared, however, with a distraction or an appealing stimulus (e.g., a drink or a snack) to break the person out of the movement, when necessary.

Use videotaped and audiotaped exercises only for the mildly impaired. Most persons with ADRD require the presence of a real person to guide them through exercises. The videotape will be too abstract.

Develop an adult story sequence in which many body movements are incorporated into the telling of the story. For example, in a story about getting out of bed in the morning, the leader does each movement as the story is told. Eliminate the more abstract parts for persons who are more impaired.

It's the start of another day. You blink your eyes open. Stretch your arms above your head. Stretch out your legs and wiggle your toes. You reach over to shut off the alarm. But too late, it rings anyhow. Ouch,

that's a noisy way to start the day. *[Hands over ears, shaking head]* Oh well.

You throw back the covers and sit straight up in bed. You swing your legs over the side of the bed and wiggle your feet into your slippers. You rub the sleep out of your eyes and stand up. Reach over and push apart the drapes. It's a great day, but that sun sure is bright in the eyes. *[Shield eyes with hand]*

This sequence provides a concrete way of loosening up and stretching many muscle groups. Use your imagination to develop other such sequences. Similar sequences can be developed for the strenuous portion of the group. For example, going for a boat ride (Figure 5-6):

It's such a great day, I think I will go for a canoe ride. Let's walk to the wharf. *["Walk," raising the feet while remaining seated]* Oh, here we are. Reach over and grab the sides of the boat. Lift one foot at a time. And settle down on the seat. Untie the rope, and take the oar (a sponge baton). It's a calm, beautiful day and we can really make some time. Let's paddle! *[Paddle as vigorously as can be tolerated for two to three minutes on one side.]* That arm is getting tired, let's paddle on the other side. My goodness, the wind is getting

Figure 5-6 Going for a Boat Ride

up. The boat is rocking from side to side *[Hang onto the chair sides and rock from side to side 10 to 12 times, going as far over as possible]* and it's swaying to and fro like a rocking chair. *[Rock back and forth strenuously 10 to 12 times]* We'd better get paddling and head for shore. *[Paddle strenuously, changing sides, according to participant energy level; and continue as tolerance allows]*

Phew, we made it back to shore. Let's just sit here for a minute and rest. Take some deep breaths and relax. Lay that paddle down and shake the stiffness out of our hands. Wipe the sweat off your forehead and roll your head around to get the stiffness out of your neck. Ouch! My legs are stiff. Let's shake those out too. Oh, that's better. Phew that feels good. Take some more deep breaths and relax.

For this cool-down stage, a short session of guided imagery can be used, depending on the capacity of the person to participate in this abstract activity. Guided imagery in a group is not appropriate for persons severely impaired with ADRD, but it can be very effective with some when done individually. Guided imagery encourages people to relax, visualizing in their minds a pleasant and peaceful place. It is an excellent way to wind down from the stimulation of the exercise and to provide a bridge back to the daily routine. Encourage the participants to close their eyes, get comfortable in their chairs, and take long, slow breaths in and out. Quiet, soothing, instrumental music or a related nature-sounds tape helps set the mood. Select a scene or setting that would be familiar and comforting to the participants. Invite them to follow along with you in their imagination, picturing the scene in their minds. Speak slowly and in a calm, gentle voice. Use words such as *imagine*, *as if*, and *pretend* frequently. After the experience, take great care to reorient the participants to the present.

Following the above exercise sequence, a guided imagery such as the following might be used:

Let's just sit here sit here and relax for awhile. Close your eyes and take some long breaths in and out. *[Demonstrate.]* Keep on with the slow breathing and keep your eyes closed. Now follow along with me in your imagination. Let's imagine that you are sitting on the shore, overlooking a beautiful, calm lake. The lake is so still it looks like a sheet of blue glass. As you gaze out, you see a perfect reflection of the puffy white clouds in the lake. Imagine that along the far shore there is a beautiful grove of trees, tall birches with their shimmering white trunks, topped by the golden glow of their leaves, colored by the autumn temperatures. Standing even taller, behind the stately birches, are magnificent maples in glorious autumn colors—fiery reds, brilliant oranges, and dazzling yellows. And imagine that scattered among these glorious colors are stately pines, with their green lacy branches, providing a perfect contrast for the maples and the birches. Now imagine that you look down from these beautiful trees at the lake and see this whole wonderful scene reflected in the perfectly still water of the lake.

Also imagine that the air is as still as the water. Pretend that your skin is touched by a gentle, warm breeze carrying the scents of the pines and the autumn leaves. Imagine that there is no other sound but the gentle lapping of the water on the shore and the rustle of the golden leaves on the birches. All of your senses feel calm and refreshed, as you imagine this beautiful scene and breathe slowly and deeply.

Then, in the distance, imagine that you hear the evening call of an owl—"whoo whoo whoo"—a signal that the day is ending. Imagine now that you look to the western shore of the lake, where the sun, a glowing scarlet ball, is slowly sinking into the clouds, tingeing all of the edges of the clouds with magnificent colors of yellows, oranges, and finally reds and scarlets. The sky is like a wonderful, living picture of colors, all perfectly reflected in the still water of the lake. Imagine that the sun has now disappeared from the sky, leaving the clouds and the lake in a rosy, scarlet glow. You breathe deeply of the woodland pines, the fresh lake air, and think "Pink sky at night, sailor's delight." You feel calm and relaxed thinking that tomorrow will be a good day. Keep your eyes closed and breathe very calmly. Rest for a few minutes before leaving this beautiful imagined scene. *[Silence is appropriate.]*

Now, feeling very relaxed, you open your eyes and come back to the room where we were doing exercises.

At this stage, gently provide important reality reassurance information, calling each person by name. Gently provide information such as where they are, what the date is, where they will be going next, and when you will see them again. This is an essential part of guided imagery.

Use some other suggested functional activities for exercise. With a sponge baton (cut from one-inch regular foam two to three inches wide and two to three feet long):

- beat the eggs or the fudge
- cast the fishing rod
- sweep the floor
- hoe the garden
- rake the leaves
- shovel the snow

Using a fabric prop (e.g., squares of fabric, towels, scarves, or a large handkerchief):

- hang up the clothes
- shake out the dust cloth or mats
- polish the car (or the silver)
- wave the flag

Use a parachute. Parachutes are commercially available or can be purchased from an army surplus store, or stitch one from old sheets or light fabric. The parachute, especially if it is brightly colored, can be a very stimulating exercise prop. It is suitable only for moderately impaired individuals, because of the need to follow directions and coordinate movements with other group members. Each participant takes a firm hold of the edge of the parachute, rolling it up as necessary. Raising arms swiftly up and then slowly down causes it to puff up. When it is pulled tight, balls can be rolled or bounced on it, with participants moving their arms up and down. Hand-over-hand movements rotate it around the circle. Shaking it can simulate shaking the rugs.

Other suggestions for movement/exercise activities using beanbags and balls are found in the kinesthetic stimulation section of Chapter 7. Variations on games of catch are very effective, as the movement response is automatic. Swimming, walking, and dancing provide excellent, adult-appropriate exercise. Remember that it is also important to warm up for these exercises by stretching and walking slowly for the first five minutes.

6.5 Resources

Organizations

The American Alliance for Health, Physical Education, Recreation and Dance
P.O. Box 704
Waldorf, MD 20604
Telephone 1-800-321-0789

This organization has numerous publications on exercises for the older adult, including the following:

Elder-Fit: A Health and Fitness Guide for Older Adults, a 66-page guide written for instructors.

Mature Stuff: Physical Activity for the Older Adult, a 245-page book with information on aging and ideas for standing and chair exercises, dance, and pool exercises.

Other Resources

Step-by-Step: Planning Walking Activities. Photocopies are available free from The National Resource Center on Health Promotion and Aging, American Association of Retired Persons, 601 E Street NW, 5th Floor, Washington, DC 20049. This is a kit on how to plan and develop a walking program.

Resource Guide for Fitness Programs, a 116-page manual on developing fitness programs for the older adult (order number 2019, $5.00 plus $2.00 handling). It is available from

National Council on Aging
Department 5087
Washington, DC 20061-5087.
Telephone 1-202-479-1200

The Healthline Workout for Bone and Muscle Fitness, a series of simple exercises using inexpensive surgical tubing. It is available from

Healthline Inc.
P.O. Box 55231
Madison, WI 53705

7.0 MUSIC

John's melodious tenor voice and his large carpenter's hands on the ivories had led many a church sing. Now, severely demented, he scarcely spoke, and when he did it was a few mumbled phrases that were hard to make sense of. However, whenever there was familiar music, John's strong and true voice chimed in, the words perfectly recalled. He and I developed a ritual of singing some favorite songs while walking to and from groups.

We were all delighted to have a piano donated to the unit. It had sat in open view in the living room for several weeks, but John had never ventured near it. One day, I decided to continue our sing while seated on the piano bench. John appeared to pay no attention to the keyboard in front of him. I gently placed his hands on the keys and began singing one of his favorites, "Let Me Call You Sweetheart." Slowly his fingers began to move. The melody, and then the chords, soon were flowing from his hands. John continued for another ten minutes. With prompting he played one golden oldie after another until his hands and head dropped in fatigue. John wasn't always able to play; sometimes he was too tired or agitated or withdrawn. But when he did play, his hands, his face, and his whole body took on a marvelous, powerful air.

John was not the only person to respond to music. While listening to the jigs and reels during sensory stimulation group, Mr. Boudreau became very animated and joyous. He told me how he and his fiddle had played well into the night at many a dance and community gathering. He said he would love to play again, but didn't have his fiddle any more. The next day I brought my son's fiddle to the group.

Mr. Boudreau picked it up lovingly and eagerly. He set bow to string and scratched out a few notes. He then laid it down sadly. Tears filled his eyes as he told me, "Dat fiddle, it is no good. De fiddles, dey don't make dem de same no more. Not de same no more."

Mr. Boudreau's inability to play the fiddle was a painful reminder of his lost abilities. Mr. Boudreau touched the wood of the instrument, gently and lovingly, many times throughout the group, but the sadness on his face remained. The next time there was fiddle music during the group, Mr. Boudreau tapped his feet, clapped and sang, and named some of his favorite pieces. Neither of us suggested that he play again.

The above anecdotes illustrate two very important points about the therapeutic use of music with individuals who have ADRD: Music can have a pervasive effect that facilitates movement, speech, and the reactivation of old skills. However, both the music medium used and the response are very much dependent on the individual's personality and history.

Music, often described as the universal language, has an amazing capacity to speak, to enliven, and to enhance, regardless of cognitive ability. It is this very characteristic that makes it such a powerful and effective therapeutic modality for individuals with ADRD (Smith 1990). Music can be used as a way to communicate, to express feelings, to enliven rich memories that bypass the communication difficulties caused by the disease. The noted neurologist, Oliver Sacks, speaks of the power of music to enliven patients with severe Parkinson's disease or others with postencephalitic syndromes. He described the experience of one patient as follows:

> Another patient of mine had extensive frontal lobe damage, rendering him completely "flat" emotionally, seemingly incapable of any normal feeling. But he loved music (country music especially), and when he sang, as he sometimes did spontaneously, he would come alive in the most remarkable way, as if the music could give him, transiently, what his cortex had lost. (Sacks 1990, 47)

He describes the effect of music as follows: "One such way of 'centering,' of recalling a self, the active powers of a self, from the abyss of pathology, can be given by music, by art of all kinds" (Sacks 1990, 46).

In neurological terms, the "musical" areas of the brain are usually in the nondominant hemisphere, the side of the brain that does *not* control language. Appreciating, responding to, and becoming involved in music do not require the areas of the brain that are usually damaged by the disease processes of ADRD (Bright 1988; Clair & Bernstein 1990; Kartman 1984; Sacks 1990). In one study, the use of music during a reminiscence group resulted in higher measures of life satisfaction and a greater level of enjoyment, compared to a control group which did not use music (Bennett & Maas 1987).

Now the second important point identified by the anecdotes must be emphasized: Great care must be taken to tailor the use of music to individual interests and competencies. Music is not really a universal language; that is, music of all types does not necessarily speak to every person. Response to music is highly individual, depending on personal taste and background. Some may tap toes and fingers and be moved by the heart-stirring rhythm and lyrics of country and western music; others find it offensive. Sitting and listening to Beethoven's Fifth Symphony may be uplifting to some and have no meaning at all to others. The mistaken assumption that music is a universal language is the basis for elevator music or the background music piped through shopping malls. It is not the basis for the use of music therapeutically. To be therapeutic, particularly for individuals with ADRD, music must be carefully selected according to individual preferences and personal history. Furthermore, it must be introduced with empathy, in order to meet individual therapeutic goals. Music played as a background, the large group sing-along, and entertainment by visiting musicians all have an important recreational value for the older person who lives in an institution. However, in order to be truly therapeutic, in order to promote individual change—especially for the person with ADRD—there must be someone to make the bridge between the music and the person, to engage the individual with the music. The goal-directed nature of this engagement with music changes it from entertainment to therapy. For some, engagement with the music may mean singing along or dancing; for others it may mean an increased level of alertness or a calmer mood. For the person in the final stages of ADRD, visible engagement may not be possible; however, listening to familiar music can be reassuring and therapeutic (Figure 5-7).

7.1 Goals of Music as a Therapeutic Modality

- Provide a unique opportunity for nonverbal expression of emotions through the emotional cues associated with particular songs and the use of movements and rhythms that express sorrow, happiness, anger, etc.

- Stimulate vocalization and communication through the recall of familiar song lyrics and the sharing of music experiences in a group.

- Stimulate movement through responses such as clapping hands and tapping feet to rhythmic music, and dancing or other movement to music.

- Stimulate reminiscence through associations with familiar and favorite songs.

Figure 5-7 Engagement in the Music

- Enhance self-esteem through the recall of familiar, overlearned skills and procedural memory for certain songs or playing a particular instrument.
- Facilitate relaxation and alleviate stress through the calming effect of familiar music.
- Help to set the mood for other activities, such as a lively rhythm for exercises or calming music at bedtime.
- Provide an opportunity for creativity through encouraging unique personal interpretations in movement, rhythm, and lyrics, and perhaps painting or drawing to music.
- Provide an opportunity for a pleasurable activity. For individuals with ADRD, who live so much in the present moment, this is a very important goal.

7.2 Guidelines for the Use of Music Therapeutically

The group leader must have a combination of therapeutic and musical skills. The leader must have enough musical skill to engage the individual with the music and enough therapeutic skill to establish an appropriate goal for the use of music. Certified music therapists have intensive training, which makes them the most suitable personnel to run therapeutic music groups. Unfortunately, their numbers are few, and only a few facilities are fortunate enough to have funding for a certified music therapist. Music is such a powerful medium for individuals with ADRD that it would be a tragedy to deprive persons without access to a certified music therapist of its benefits. If care is taken to establish therapeutic goals and the leader has some musical background, beneficial music programs can be implemented. The group leader can use an easily played instrument such as an autoharp, a guitar, or a ukulele.

Small, portable keyboards are easy to play and are a great boon to music programs. Portable cassette tape players are very useful if the leader engages people with the music. Leaders with a therapeutic background in various fields can transfer these skills to a music program. Music therapy workshops are frequently offered across the continent, and attendance would further enhance the leader's skills. Perhaps the musical talents of a volunteer could be used, with the group leader supplying the therapeutic direction.

The individual must be assisted to become engaged with the music, to facilitate active involvement. Much has already been said about the difficulty persons with ADRD have in showing initiative. Although music is a familiar medium, there is no guarantee of automatic involvement. The individual with ADRD often remains as passive and unengaged during a large group sing-along as they do during an exercise class.

> Every week after lunch two good-hearted volunteers came to play the piano for the residents of the dementia unit. They played and sang old-time and lively songs for about an hour. The piano was positioned against one wall, and the residents were lined up in chairs along the other walls. Occasionally, one of the more mobile residents would stand by the piano and sing a bar or two. Mostly the residents just slept or stared into space.

What is wrong with this picture? What about the pervasive effect of familiar music? In a nutshell, there was no one to provide the bridge, to engage the individual with the music. The musicians were faced away from the residents and were occupied with their music. Some of the staff were at lunch and others were busy with after-lunch duties. If someone had been available to move about the room, taking a hand, touching a shoulder, helping to start the singing of the familiar words, this would have been a very different picture. Another problem was the time of day. Most of the residents were tired after the morning and were ready for a rest.

Some techniques to facilitate engagement in music are suggested as follows:

- Face the person, make eye contact, take a hand, and begin singing the words of the song or gently swaying in time to the music.
- Take hands and initiate clapping in time to the music.
- Provide large-print song books and assist in turning to the proper page. Even if the person has difficulty reading, the familiar activity of holding a song book is a cue to initiating the singing of familiar words.
- Assist the person to stand and do some simple dance steps or movement to the music. A person in a wheelchair can be "danced with" in the chair, moving it in time to the music. Stand facing the person. If he or she is unable to copy your movement, use gentle physical guidance to initiate movement of the feet.
- Encourage associations with particular songs (e.g., Do you recall dancing to this song? Where? With whom?) to enhance and enrich the hearing of the music with personal memories.
- Use connected sensory cues to increase arousal and alertness (e.g., use actual sleigh bells with "Jingle Bells," flags for patriotic songs, a rose for "My Wild Irish Rose").

If the person is in the advanced stages of ADRD and is engaged in self-stimulating rhythmic movements (e.g., rocking back and forth or rubbing the chair arms) or sounds, make a bridge to her or his world by mimicking these sounds and movements. This will often bring the person's attention to you and provide an opportunity to introduce an actual song of a similar rhythm, and thus encourage vocalization.

Select music according to the background and personal preferences of the individuals. This is particularly important with individuals with ADRD, as the familiarity with loved pieces will stimulate response and involvement. Family members and significant others are good sources of information about favorite pieces and the general type of music preferences. Popular songs from the era of their youth and young adulthood are always good choices (see Table 5-4 for some suggestions). Frequently, there are popular and well-known regional folk songs and types of music. For example, in Nova Scotia, fiddle jigs and reels and seafaring songs such as "Farewell to Nova Scotia" and "I'se the Bye" are almost universally known, and call forth a response. Ethnic or religious music that has been important to the individual is also evocative. Observe participant responses to various types of music, and record, mentally or physically, successful pieces. Try as much as pos-

sible to offer individual choice in music selection. Highlight favorites of participants during the group. Announcements such as, "Let's sing 'My Wild Irish Rose'; Paddy will lead us, as it is his favorite song," make the individual feel special and improve self-esteem.

Relate music selections to the season, the weather, and special holidays to facilitate reality reassurance. Sing patriotic songs at the time of a national holiday, for example, or "April Showers" in spring.

Use carefully selected music to set the mood or to stimulate, as appropriate. Quiet waltzes and ballads are calming during meals; more lively march tunes may help to get people going in the morning. Favorite music played on a tape player in a quiet room may help to calm agitation or induce sleep.

Use music to enhance other activities. Play stirring, rhythmic music for exercise groups; emotional, expressive music during a free-style painting group; and music associated with the theme during reminiscence groups.

Select music and musical activities that are appropriate to the participant's skill level. It is very important to try to avoid confronting individuals with their loss of skills, as happened to Mr. Boudreau in the opening account. Related musical activities, such as listen-

Table 5-4 Popular and Seasonal Songs for Music Therapy

Popular Songs

Ain't She Sweet?	Easter Parade	It's a Long Way to	She'll Be Comin' Round the
Ain't We Got Fun?	Faraway Places	Tipperary	Mountain
America	Farewell to Nova Scotia	Let Me Call You Sweet-	Shine on Harvest Moon
Anchors Aweigh	God Bless America	heart	Side by Side
Annie Laurie	God Save the Queen	Mairszy Dotes	Silver Threads among the Gold
Aunt Dinah's Quilting Party	Good Night, Irene	Maple Leaf Forever	So Long, It's Been Good to
Baby Face	Good Night Ladies	Meet Me in St. Louis	Know You
Beautiful Dreamer	Grandfather's Clock	Mocking Bird Hill	Sweet Rosie O'Grady
Believe Me if All Those	Has Anybody Seen My Gal?	Moonlight Bay	Take Me Out to the Ball Game
Endearing Young Charms	Heart of My Heart	My Bonnie Lies Over	Toot, Toot, Tootsie
Bicycle Built for Two	Home on the Range	the Ocean	When Irish Eyes Are Smiling
Billy Boy	Home Sweet Home	My Wild Irish Rose	When You and I Were Young,
Clementine	I Want a Girl	O Canada	Maggie
Cockles and Mussels	I Dream of Jeannie	O Dear, What Can the	White Cliffs of Dover
Coming through the Rye	I'm Looking Over a Four Leaf	Matter Be?	Yankee Doodle
Daisy, Daisy	Clover	On Top of Old Smoky	Yellow Rose of Texas
Danny Boy	I've Been Working on the	Red River Valley	Zippity-Do-Dah
Don't Fence Me In	Railroad	Roll Out the Barrel	
Down by the Old Mill Stream	In the Good Old Summer	Rose of Tralee	
Drink to Me Only with Thine	Time	Row, Row, Row Your Boat	
Eyes			

Christmas Favorites

Deck the Halls	Jingle Bells	Silent Night	Winter Wonderland
Frosty the Snowman	Joy to the World	We Wish You a Merry	
I'm Dreaming of a White	Santa Claus Is Coming to	Christmas	
Christmas	Town		

ing to or commenting on favorite music, are good choices. On the other hand, musical activities must always be adult in content and form. The use of childish songs or formats, although they are simple, is an insult to adult dignity. In this connection, a word must be said about rhythm instruments. Although these instruments are satisfying and simple, they are also associated with children and must be presented very skillfully, in an adult fashion, to avoid damaging fragile self-esteem. In the name of "music therapy," I have seen a man with Huntington's chorea handed a plastic tambourine decorated with pink ballerinas. This should never be. About rhythm bands, the music therapist Ruth Bright (1988) has the following to say:

> So-called "Rhythm Band," the simple hitting of drums, tambourines etc. in time to a record or accompaniment, is not very therapeutic in that it fails to meet any latent creativity (p. 56). But one should not either encourage or permit the endless thumping which in some places passes for music therapy, as a constant background to all singing and all conversation. (p. 34)

Instruments must be of good quality, adult in design, and presented empathetically and with dignity.

Use a variety of types of music and presentation formats. This is the opposite of Musak, which blends into the background and is not a source stimulation because it is always there, independently droning on. Switching tempos and styles, e.g., from instrumental to voice— with appropriate bridging—increases stimulation. To balance this, one must also remember the importance of consistency and structure for individuals with ADRD. Certain favorite songs should be used consistently for ritual opening and closing. The predictability of the structure, not necessarily the content, is reassuring.

Be prepared for, and accepting of, the sadness that can be triggered by associations with particular music. It is much easier and more satisfying when people respond to music with laughter rather than with tears. The expression of sorrow and the release of unhappy emotions, however, are vital to emotional health. In most cases a "good cry" and another's empathetic support are all that are needed, and the person will return to a normal mood. It is not healthy to discourage the natural expression of sadness. There is frequently little opportunity for such expression in a long-term care setting. However, if the person has unusual difficulty in resuming a normal mood, it is essential that a physician be notified and the individual assessed and treated, as necessary, for depression. If particular songs are too upsetting for individuals and distress them unduly, those

songs should be avoided. The distress of these individuals may also spread to other members of the group.

Music groups, like all groups, should be run in an area free from distractions. It will be difficult to assist the individual to respond to or to focus on music while in an area such as the common room, with the frequent coming and going of staff, other residents, and visitors. It has also been my experience that staff or visitors may, with the best of intentions, involve themselves inappropriately in the music selection.

Use music activities on a one-to-one basis, during activities of daily living. Softly singing a favorite tune while assisting with morning dressing or playing a favorite tape during a bath or when settling for bed can be calming and reassuring.

7.3 Resources

Music Books

Dallen, L., ed. 1980. *Heritage Songster.* Dubuque, Iowa: William C. Brown Co.

Freeman, G., ed. 1962. *Mitch Miller Community Songbook.* New York: Remick Music Corp.

Okun, M., ed. 1978. *The New York Times Country Music's Greatest Songs.* New York: New York Times Book Co.

Large-print song books—sources local Canadian National Institute for the Blind (C.N.I.B.)

Local seniors' projects (e.g., New Horizons Projects in Canada)

Other Resources

American Association for Music Therapy, 66 Morris Avenue, Springfield, NJ 07081; Telephone 1-201-379-1100.

National Association for Music Therapy, Silver Spring, MD; Telephone 1-301-589-3300.

Karras, B., ed. 1988. *You Bring Out the Music in Me.* New York: Haworth Press. A monograph also published as *Activities, Adaptation and Aging.* 1987. 10, no. 1/2.

MMB Horizon Music series: MMB Music Inc., 10370 Page Industrial Boulevard, Saint Louis, MO 63132.

- Volume 1: *Accent on Rhythm: Music Activities for the Aged.* rev. 3rd ed. (by Donna Douglas)
- Volume IV: *Music Therapy and the Dementias: Improving the Quality of Life* (by Ruth Bright)
- Volume VI: *Music Therapy for Living: The Principle of Normalization Embodied in Music Therapy*

Recordings for Recovery is a nonprofit organization that lends cassette tapes free of charge. It has a very large collection of music, including tapes of many vintage songs and environmental sounds. The tapes are mailed out, as in a lending library, or they may be purchased. These tapes are intended for persons who are institutionalized or homebound or otherwise limited by handicaps. Contact the nearest regional library for a catalogue:

Michigan (and headquarters)
Michael Hoy
413 Cherry St.
Midland, MI 48640
Telephone 1-517-832-0784

8.0 THE THERAPEUTIC USE OF PETS

The age-old bond between humans and animals translates into certain facts: In North America more money is spent on pets than on all hobbies combined; more people visit zoos than attend all spectator sports; 50 percent of all American families have a pet (Prebis & Whitesell 1990). The popularity of pets has also translated into an enthusiasm for using pets therapeutically with a wide variety of populations, such as disabled children, prisoners, physically handicapped adults, and residents of nursing homes. A large volume of anecdotal and descriptive literature describes the positive effects of pets, particularly with the elderly. However, these effects have not been supported by the few empirical research studies that have been undertaken (Beck 1985; Beck & Katcher 1984; Hendy 1987; Wallace & Naderman 1987; Wilson & Netting 1987; Winkler et al. 1989).

In actual fact, the research literature consists of only a few uncontrolled studies claiming to have significant positive results. These results have been quoted and requoted. One such frequently quoted study is that of

Mugford and M'Comisky (1975). In that study, of only 19 community-dwelling elderly, the authors found that giving a bird, as opposed to a plant or nothing, had some positive effects on social behavior. This study is misquoted by numerous others, implying that the birds effected a significant improvement in health and well-being (Beck 1985). In general, the few attempts to study the therapeutic effects of pets have been limited by poor study design, especially the absence of control conditions and valid, objective outcome measures (Beck 1985; Beck & Katcher 1984; Hendy 1987; Wallace & Naderman 1987; Wilson & Netting 1987; Winkler et al. 1989).

Some controlled studies have found that the effect of people visitors was equivalent to or greater than that of pet visitors (Hendy 1987; Wallace & Naderman 1987). Another recent careful study of the effects of introducing a resident dog on one floor of a nursing home had some very interesting findings (Winkler et al. 1989). Six weeks after the dog came to the unit there was an increase in resident social interactions, but the level had returned to normal by 22 weeks. This is in agreement with results of most of the research on pet visitors, that any observed effect is short-lived. There was, however, a continued increase in interaction among the staff at 22 weeks. Furthermore, the dog spent more time with staff than with residents, and, not surprisingly, staff were more enthusiastic about the positive effects of the dog than were the residents. In addition, about one-third of the residents interviewed felt that the dog did not like them, and several commented that this made them feel sad.

Although the preceding is by no means a comprehensive review of the research literature, it does summarize the findings to date. The intent is to emphasize that the introduction of pets to the elderly living in institutions is not necessarily therapeutic. Although there is ample anecdotal information that pets can provide momentary pleasure for some, and that for a small group it is uniquely motivating, there is no empirical evidence to support these effects.

In this regard, the use of pets is no different from other therapeutic modalities, such as horticulture, music, or handicrafts. The difficulty is that the introduction of pets to the elderly has become a "motherhood and apple pie" type of issue. It has been assumed to be unequivocally good. Pictures of smiling old people holding a cuddly puppy have universal appeal in the popular press and are good public relations for institutions. Most of those involved in implementing pet programs, and indeed researching them, are themselves pet owners, and their enthusiasm has biased their research. There has been, in general, a suspension of critical evaluation of the therapeutic value of introducing pets to the institutionalized elderly. Beck (1985) describes this situation as follows:

> In short, it is hard to resist a therapy that is not expensive, part of everyday life, appears to give immediate results, receives a great deal of public attention, and reinforces the interests and beliefs of many of society's more wealthy and influential citizens. (p. 366)

The preceding is not intended to dismiss the use of pets from useful therapeutic modalities for persons with ADRD or the elderly in general. It is intended to put the introduction of pets into perspective. Pets can be a useful therapeutic and recreational medium, encouraging some people to make temporary positive responses. This can be particularly beneficial for the person with ADRD (Beyersdorfer & Birkenhauer 1990). However, the use of pets is not any more effective or guaranteed to be successful than the introduction of any other unique experiences, such as human visitors, music, children, horticulture, outings, picnics, parties, etc. It is not a magic cure for all that ails frail old people, as one would sometimes conclude when reading the popular literature. The therapeutic benefits of keeping pets can be put into perspective by considering the effects on elderly pet owners. Although there is no doubt that these elderly individuals derive great satisfaction from their pets, there is no evidence that they are healthier or happier than non–pet owners.

In addition, because of health and safety concerns, the introduction of pets into institutions can be very complicated. Pet therapy programs are dependent on the presence of willing and competent volunteers, without whom the programs would be too expensive. All of these issues must be considered before introducing pet therapy, and they must be considered in relation to the use of other therapeutic modalities with fewer potential complications.

8.1 Goals for the Therapeutic Use of Pets

- Encourage movement, as in reaching to pet or play with the animal and walking and caring for them.
- Encourage socialization by providing a familiar and common topic of discussion, as well as speaking to the animal.
- Provide an experience of unconditional positive regard. The affectionate response of a healthy, good-tempered animal can be very meaningful for a person with ADRD, who may be desperate for attention and affection.

- Provide sensory stimulation. The soft textures of fur and warm skin and the movement and sound responses of the animal are all wonderful sources of sensory stimulation.
- Enliven and normalize the environment, particularly for persons who have been pet owners.
- Provide a nonthreatening opportunity for expressions of caring and nurturing for individuals who are primarily recipients of care.
- Encourage reminiscence. For those who were pet owners at one time there are many memories and associations.
- Provide reality reassurance through using the animal to provide orientation information (e.g., "It's time to give the dog his supper").
- Provide an opportunity for nonverbal communication. Physical communication, through petting and holding the animal, can be very rewarding for individuals with difficulties in verbal communication.

8.2 Selecting Participants

- Select persons who have been pet owners and animal lovers. It is very important to be aware of the individuals' history and interests. Some people simply have never been interested in animals or, in fact, are offended by them; the introduction of a pet for these people would not be appropriate.
- Select individuals without open sores or infections. There is a danger not only of communicating diseases from the animal to the person through open sores, but also for the animal to get such things as respiratory infections from the person.
- Select individuals whose behavior is predictable and calm. Do not include individuals who are prone to disruptive, unpredictable, or aggressive behavior. The introduction of the new stimulus may trigger the behavior, and it is possible that the animal may be accidentally harmed.
- Select individuals who are not allergic to the animals involved.

8.3 Selecting the Animals

Animals used in pet visitation programs most often belong to staff members or volunteers or are Humane Society animals brought to the facility by Society staff or volunteers. The success of a pet program depends on selecting appropriate animals that will be able to relate reliably with individuals with ADRD. Before introducing pets, the following selection criteria should be considered:

- Animals must be obedience-trained and house-trained. Community or staff volunteers should present appropriate certificates of obedience training to the coordinator of the program. It is absolutely essential that the behavior of the animals be controllable and predictable, no matter what may arise during the visit. Although young animals such as puppies or kittens are almost irresistible, they may not be good choices because of their unpredictable behavior.

- Animals must be healthy, certified as such by a veterinarian, with up-to-date immunization. Animals must be free of fleas, hookworm, and wounds or sores. Immunization should include

  1. for dogs:
     —distemper
     —hepatitis
     —leptospirosis
     —parvovirus
     —rabies (4 months)
  2. for cats:
     —panleukopenia
     —rhinotracheitis
     —calicivirus
     —rabies (4 months)

- Animals must be clean, well-groomed, and free of loosened hair or flea dander. If the animals come inside on a stormy day, wipe paws and coats before bringing them to the participants.

- Animals must be good-tempered, friendly, and capable of relating to a wide variety of people. Some animals are shy or relate only to particular people, and would not be helpful in a pet program.

- Animals should be spayed or neutered.

- Kittens should have their claws clipped.

- Select animal types that are familiar. Dogs, cats, birds, and perhaps rabbits are good choices for indoor programs. If an outdoor space is available, visits by horses from a riding school, or by other farm animals in a rural area, can be very successful. Small animals such as gerbils, guinea pigs, and hamsters are easy to care for and portable but they may not be suitable for use with the individual with ADRD. These animals usually are not familiar to the older generation and, because of disease-related difficulties in interpreting the environment, may even be frightening. In addition,

the behavior of these animals is unpredictable, and they are not suitable for holding or petting.

8.4 Procedures for Using Animals

Pet programs for individuals with ADRD may involve either pet visitation or a resident pet in a day program or residential center. Pet visitation programs have the advantage of requiring less day-to-day care of the pet and may be simpler to arrange administratively. In addition, visits provide an element of surprise or novelty, which may contribute to increased alertness among the participants. On the other hand, a resident pet has the advantage of contributing to a normal, homelike atmosphere 24 hours a day, providing for the possibility of developing strong relationships with individual residents. The care and feeding of the pet can provide a meaningful activity.

In either case, great care must be taken to ensure that the program has the approval of administrators and health officials and that measures are taken to provide for liability in the case of an injury during the program. Volunteers should be screened and trained by the program coordinator and follow the usual route for facility volunteers. Any bites, scratches, or other injuries must be reported immediately to the appropriate authority.

8.5 Guidelines for an Animal Visitation Program

Choose the location for the visits carefully. An outdoor lawn or patio area is ideal, reducing problems with having an animal in residential areas, which can be a particular difficulty in health care facilities. The disadvantage of an outdoor location is the provision of security for those who may wander, possible complications with transportation of participants outdoors, and lack of availability during poor weather.

An indoor area should have easy access from the outdoors, for the animal and the handler. In health care settings, this access should avoid resident living areas. In all settings, the animal should never be in kitchen and food preparation areas, in active treatment areas, in laundry areas, or near people who are ill. An indoor location for group pet visits should be separate from the rest of the unit, in order to control access for residents who may not wish to, or should not, attend. The room should be large enough to hold the participants, the animal, and the handler and allow for some freedom of movement. However, a room that is too large can be overwhelming for the participants and can lead to problems in managing the animal. The floor and furniture should be of natural material that can be easily cleaned of animal excretions. As with all groups for individuals with ADRD, the room should be as comfortable as possible. If necessary arrangements are made administratively, some individuals may benefit from private visits in their rooms. The animal should be on a lead or under the control of an experienced handler at all times.

Make sure that everyone present has an opportunity to interact with the animal if he or she wishes to do so. Follow the general guidelines for leading groups for individuals with ADRD. Particular attention should be paid to helping to initiate the interaction between the participant and the animal by focusing attention on sensory aspects and making personal associations. Because of their deficits, individuals with ADRD may not respond spontaneously to an animal visitor. Care must also be taken to avoid overstimulation.

Introduce the animal to the participants, using frequent cues, and encourage a functional response such as talking to the animal, petting it, or playing with it. If treats are provided to give to the animal, make sure that they are safe for human consumption in case the participants put them in their mouths.

Give ample warning that the visit is ending. If participants become very involved with the animal, they may have a hard time separating from the group and returning to their daily routine. Provide advance cues that the group is ending, such as "Pat Lassie for one last time today, as she soon has to go back to her kennel."

Limit the time of the visit. Groups should be about an hour long, certainly no more than an hour and a half. Both the animal and participants will become too fatigued by a longer group.

Animal handlers must accept, in advance, the responsibility of cleaning up any excrement. Always have paper towels or rags on hand for such emergencies. The animal should be exercised before a visit.

8.6 Considerations Regarding Resident Pets

Carefully consider the goals of having a resident pet. Is a pet being considered because the residents would benefit or because the staff would like it? If a resident pet improves staff morale this is a worthwhile goal, but it should be recognized as the main intent. Care must be taken to ensure that staff do not become involved with the pet to the extent that the residents are ignored.

Be aware of institutional or government policies that prohibit the presence of an animal in the facility. This area must be investigated very thoroughly with regard to issues of liability and infection control. If there are many barriers to introducing a resident pet, be very sure that the advantages are going to be worth all of the trouble involved. If so, prepare a carefully researched document in support of your application. Use research

literature and examples of other successful local programs. Potential benefits can be demonstrated by introducing a pet visitation program first.

Follow the previous guidelines for animal selection. With a resident pet, one must be particularly careful to ensure that the animal is able to relate to everyone. Bear in mind that small animals such as cats and smaller dogs can be a hazard for older individuals with ADRD, who have difficulty interpreting their environment and may also be unsteady on their feet. Other types of pets require less care than cats or dogs. Fish are sometimes a good option, but it must be remembered that they also require proper care in order to be aesthetically pleasing. Birds such as budgies or canaries can be a good addition and are easy to care for. They should be fed seed containing special antibiotics to prevent the spread of disease from the droppings or the dust.

One or two staff members should be designated as primary caregivers or coordinators of the pet. These staff members should know or learn something about the management of the animal and be sure that the animal is well cared for and neither underfed nor overfed. Residents should be involved in feeding and other pet care duties.

Make arrangements so that the animal can be kept away from individuals who do not wish contact because of allergies, unpredictable behavior, or personal preference. In one facility I visited, the resident cat had free range. Most residents welcomed this fluffy white visitor. However, one gentleman did not care for cats, especially this one, because it liked to lie across his jigsaw puzzles. Unfortunately, the only solution for this gentleman was to close his door to keep the cat out. This also shut him off from fellow residents.

Use opportunities to focus the attention of residents on the pet and encourage appropriate responses. The advantage of a resident pet is that it can make an institution seem more homelike. The disadvantage is that it may fade into the woodwork and be taken for granted. Individuals with ADRD need help to relate to the animal in order to derive therapeutic benefit.

8.7 Suggestions for Other Programs with Animals

- Sponsor a pet show for staff and families on the grounds of the facility. Residents can attend and/ or participate as judges or assistant handlers.

- Invite groups such as dog obedience classes, animal care classes, 4-H clubs, or riding schools to visit and put on a demonstration.

- Plan outings to zoos, demonstration farms, fall fair animal exhibits, horse shows, or pet shops.

- Hang a bird feeder near a window to invite wild birds, which are fascinating to watch. Mixing food or making seed balls for the birds can be an excellent activity. A birdhouse may be placed near a window in nesting season.

8.8 Resources

The Delta Society
P.O. Box 1080
Renton, WA 98057
Telephone 1-206-226-7357

This society has information and resources, including videotapes on pet therapy.

Consider the local Humane Society and pet fancier groups such as kennel clubs, cat fancier groups, or bird watching groups.

9.0 SPIRITUAL ACTIVITIES

Spiritual or religious activities have not necessarily been a part of the life experience of all individuals with ADRD. However, for those for whom it has played an important role in the past, continued involvement can contribute greatly to their self-esteem and general well-being. This is supported by the results of a study of 100 older adults who were asked to describe how they coped with their most stressful life situations (Koenig et al. 1988). Religious behavior was the most frequently reported coping behavior. Forty-five percent of the sample reported religious behavior as a way of coping with one of the three stressful life events described. Seventy-five percent of these religious coping behaviors were related to personal religious attitudes, such as faith, trust in God, and private prayer. This is significant for our purposes, as individuals with ADRD—with related losses in cognition—will likely have difficulty independently maintaining their lifelong personal religious activities. Another significant finding from this study is that the second most common coping behavior in dealing with stress was involvement in pleasurable, meaningful activities.

Although there have been relatively few such studies, the results of other studies were similar (Conway 1985–86; Manfredi & Pickett 1987; Rosen 1982). These studies suggest that religious coping behaviors are common among older adults, regardless of sex, place of residence, race, or socioeconomic status. In further support, a study of 836 older adults found a strong correlation between positive morale and involvement in religious activities (Koenig et al. 1988).

The results of these studies have particular significance for individuals with ADRD. There is no doubt that coping with their disease is an extremely stressful experience. Unfortunately, lifelong ways of coping with stress, including personal religious practices, are negatively affected by the disease itself. Individuals with ADRD require the support and assistance of others to adapt ways of coping, including religious behaviors (Edelson & Lyons 1985; Martin & Fuller 1991).

Supporting the person with ADRD in maintaining lifelong religious practices requires great sensitivity to both the disease process and to personal beliefs. The activity specialist's role is interpreting the disease process and working with a religious leader, volunteer, or family member of the same faith, in order to adapt religious activities to the individual's present abilities. The activity specialist applies the same principles of communication, group leadership, activity selection, etc. to religious activities as applied to other activities. However, the understanding and experience of the particular faith must come from someone within the faith. Inclusion in religious activities must be based on lifelong practices, and care must be taken not to offend family members and significant others.

Residential facilities that are run or designed for members of a particular faith will undoubtedly have activity directors of that faith, who will be able to lead religious activities themselves and utilize support from others in the religious community. Great care must be taken neither to exclude other residents of different backgrounds nor to require participation. If the resident wishes, relevant activities from her or his background should be developed. In some cases, if the individual expresses an interest and the family agrees, she or he may benefit from inclusion in religious activities of other traditions within a faith.

Generations of Alice's family had been strong adherents of the protestant Christian faith. Participation in worship services and other church activities had always been a central part of her life. As Alice's Alzheimer's disease progressed, participation in these activities became even more important. The familiar hymns and prayers provided a reassuring structure in a world that was more and more without an understandable order. As her disease progressed, Alice required 24-hour care and became a resident in a nursing home that was run by the Roman Catholic Church. There was a chapel where daily mass was said. Accompanying her fellow residents, Alice went to mass for the first time in all her 81 years. Although it was not part of her traditional religious practices, Alice was enchanted with the beauty of the mass. It spoke to her and reassured her.

9.1 Why Consider Religious/Spiritual Activities?

- They are a recognized source of support and reassurance during the stress of coping with ADRD.
- They provide an opportunity for spiritual and emotional expression.
- They are familiar and reassuring activities that call upon overlearned, familiar activities and behaviors.
- They are an important part of the life experience of many; thus they are essential to holistic treatment.
- They represent a unique way of communicating, which can be very meaningful when standard communication fails.
- They are meaningful, adult activities.
- They provide an opportunity for reminiscence.

9.2 Guidelines for Planning Religious Activities

Be very familiar with the religious backgrounds of the participants and select activities accordingly.

Work together with a religious leader of the particular faith to plan adapted individual or group activity. Some community members may be hesitant to become involved, but the assistance of the activity leader in interpreting the changes associated with ADRD and the importance of continued involvement should overcome these hurdles.

Plan activities built around religious holidays and festivals that include traditional observances, music, food, and dress.

Use familiar, nonverbal cues to prompt the familiar activity (e.g., setting, special music, special dress, traditional order). One article reported that on-unit church services on a dementia unit were not particularly satisfying to either the staff or the residents. Residents became restless; others not involved interrupted the service, etc. However, when the service was moved to the chapel, clergy were dressed in their traditional garb, residents were helped to dress as they would for church and were offered a role in the service, and the service was adapted (e.g., shortened and included many familiar hymns), the residents participated and responded very well. They looked forward to the weekly service (Harrison & Law 1985).

Adapt the activities to the current abilities of the participants. Familiar hymns and prayers may be recalled if the participant is cued with the first few words. Familiar scripture may be read if it is provided in a large-print format.

Use religious activities and associated materials on a one-to-one basis. This encourages reminiscence and verbalization and provides reality reassurance. Read familiar passages from religious texts, sing religious songs as appropriate, or look at pictures of important religious buildings or personalities.

9.3 Resources

The Ecumenical Council of Health and Ministry of Marin (E.C.H.M.M.), P.O. Box 2447, San Rafael, CA 94712; Telephone 1-415-455-9727. This organization has a number of worship resources for Christian services in nursing homes. Audiotapes, videotapes, and printed liturgies are available for purchase or rental.

10.0 THE VISUAL AND EXPRESSIVE ARTS

There are a number of expressive activity modalities that can be successful on their own or as a part of other activities. These art forms are a potent means of nonverbal communication that can add a great deal to activity programs, if appropriately used. This brief section is by no means an exhaustive listing, but hopefully it will provide some guidelines and suggestions for use.

10.1 Creative Writing

One controlled study of eight-week creative writing groups conducted in six nursing homes found significant improvements in group process measures such as participation, interest, and enjoyment (Supiano et al. 1989). Participants with cognitive impairment made the most significant gains. There were also significant improvements in levels of depression, particularly for persons with higher cognitive functioning.

Providing opportunities for creative writing can serve to enhance self-esteem, provide opportunities for self-expression, and encourage mutual support. Even when physical writing skills have vanished, adapted creative writing provides the individual with ADRD with an opportunity for self-expression. Provide a physical cue, such as a simple thematic picture or a reminiscence-type artifact (e.g., an old-fashioned school slate or a cookie tin). Assist the individual to make personal associations. Using communication guidelines, assist the individual to express her or his feelings about the occasion or article or event. As these thoughts and feelings are expressed, write them down in the person's own words and style, but make complete sentences, as necessary. Read each sentence back to the person for approval, and make corrections as necessary. Write or type out the writing in clear, distinct letters. If a theme picture was used (for example, a Christmas card picture for Christmas, a poppy for Remembrance Day, a cornucopia for Thanksgiving), mount it and the written associations on posterboard or construction paper. Assist the person to put his or her name on the finished product. Display the creation on a personal or public bulletin board or on the individual's door.

These "reflections" may be put together in a three-ring binder, which makes a good focus for visits with family and friends. In this way, your skills in helping the person with ADRD to express thoughts and feelings can also open up communication with staff and significant others. A part of the person that the family may have thought had vanished, or that staff members never knew, is thus enlivened. The individual satisfaction derived from these simple self-expressive activities is fantastic. Given the appropriate cues and encouragement, it is astounding what touching and profound thoughts are expressed. The following are some examples of assisted creative writing by individuals in the advanced stages of dementia.

> Frank on Thanksgiving: It is good to remember how lucky we are. I'm thankful for my health. When I was a boy, we always had a big Thanksgiving dinner, with turkey and all the trimmings. But we remembered other people too. At school there would be a collection of turnips and other vegetables and preserves for the poor.

> Mabel on Christmas: What I remember most is Christmases when the children were small. It was always so busy, never enough time for anything. I liked to bake Christmas cookies with them and their friends. And the concert at church. I always helped with the music. I still love the Christmas music, but it's not so busy now. It makes me sad too.

Some may enjoy hearing familiar or stirring passages read. This may inspire their own writing. Suggested passages are found in an article by Wenzel (1990).

10.2 Films

Showing feature-length movies in the day room or another community room is usually not a successful activity for individuals with ADRD. It provides too much unfocused stir and uninterpretable stimulation. However, for persons who are moderately impaired, short (15- to 20-minute) films that are related to the topic at hand and are presented in a quiet, controlled setting can be very effective.

Selecting Films

- Select short films (15 to 20 minutes long).
- Select films that are related to a current theme, e.g., in reminiscence group or the season.
- Select films related to life experiences familiar to your participants (e.g., a first car, springtime maple sugaring, favorite local attractions or events, well-known people).
- Select films with a clear, simple dialogue or narration that can be appreciated even without understanding the details of the language.
- Select films that are documentary in nature and thus do not require attending during the entire sequence in order to appreciate portions of it.
- Play music that sets the mood and is appropriate to the theme.
- Use comedy shorts of old-time favorites (e.g., Laurel and Hardy, Buster Keaton, the Marx Brothers, Charlie Chaplin).

Presenting Films

- Use a small, comfortable room to prevent unnecessary interruptions.
- Show the films in a semidarkened room (to avoid undue confusion about the time of day, etc.), being sure to avoid glare on the screen. Use good projection equipment that will present a clear picture and good sound. Use a good-quality screen. A projector and screen are preferable to a videocassette recorder, because the picture is larger and easier to see.
- Arrange comfortable chairs at a reasonable distance from the screen. Seat the participants while the lights are on and turn the lights on again as soon as the film is finished.
- While the film is in progress, move from participant to participant, quietly assisting them to focus on the film and providing cues to help them link the film with their personal experiences. This is the most important point in making the experience of the film available to the individual with ADRD.
- Select participants who retain some ability to attend and verbalize. Although the use of cuing does make films available to persons with ADRD, even this is not enough in the advanced stages.
- Keep the group small (8 to 12 participants) so that it is possible to provide individual cuing.

- Freeze the film if you wish to point out a particularly interesting sequence.
- Make a card file of useful films; include source, length, topic, and other comments such as appealing music, local scenes, etc.

10.3 A Note on Audiotapes

Audiotapes of discussion or contemporary comedy would probably be lost on individuals with moderate and advanced ADRD. There are simply not enough cues to make it meaningful. However, if an old-fashioned radio (a large, wooden, floor type) is available it is possible to simulate the pre-television pastime of gathering around the radio to listen to dramatic shows. The radio need not be working. Cassettes of old-time radio comedies and dramas (e.g., "The Jack Benny Show," "The Roy Rogers Show," "Sergeant Preston of the Yukon," "The Shadow") can be played on a good-quality cassette player nearby. These characters will be familiar and will provide a good opportunity to reminisce and share in some laughter. Be sure to provide ample reality reassurance information before, during, and after the show so that the setting does not result in further disorientation.

10.4 A Note On Slides

Slides, selected and presented according to the guidelines for films, can also be beneficial. Keep the presentation short. Use a pointer to highlight particular features of interest. Pre-prepared slide-tape presentations may be more "available" to the participants if the commentary is done instead by a group leader.

10.5 Film Sources

- Community educational centers (e.g., high schools, community colleges, and universities, especially through continuing education, noncredit courses)
- Museums and public libraries. Most now have educational, historical, or short feature films available.
- Provincial/state department of education film boards. Many have a catalogue and a convenient system for mailing films. Excellent promotional films often are available at the provincial/state tourism departments.
- The National Film Board of Canada (NFB) has an excellent collection of short, topical films that are available for a small rental fee. NFB titles related to reminiscence themes are found in Appendix A

of Chapter 6. A catalogue of films costs $5.00 (Canadian). Many titles are also available in video format. These may also be purchased at a relatively small cost. For example, a 15- to 60-minute video costs $26.95 (Canadian). For Canadian customers, these may be purchased from the many regional offices or the head office:

National Film Board of Canada
Customer Services, D-10
P.O. Box 6100, Station A
Montreal, Quebec, Canada, H3C 3H5

In Canada, films may be booked up to 90 days in advance. Canadian customers may call a toll-free reservation number for their region:

Atlantic Canada   1-800-561-7104
Quebec 1-800-363-0328
Ontario 1-800-267-7710
Western & Northern Canada 1-800-661-9867

The NFB will ship films to regional locations; the return cost of shipping is the responsibility of the customer. Many local libraries in Canada also carry NFB titles. For distribution information on NFB films for use in the United States contact:

The National Film Board of Canada
1251 Avenue of the Americas, 16th Floor
New York, NY 10020
Tel. 1-212-586-5131
Fax. 1-212-575-2382

10.6 Pictures

Folk wisdom has it that "a picture is worth a thousand words." For individuals with ADRD, this continues to be true; if the pictures are carefully selected and presented, they can compensate for difficulties in verbal communication.

Selecting Pictures

- Select clear, simple pictures without a lot of confusing detail.
- Select pictures with good contrast between the main focal point and the background.
- Select pictures related to a current theme or season.
- Select pictures that are significant to the life experiences of the participants.
- Select pictures with a matte finish to avoid glare.

Presenting Pictures

- Mount pictures on posterboard or construction paper for ease of handling.

- Organize a picture file or album, according to theme.
- Point out significant features and help the individual to relate them to personal life experiences.
- Use a commercial photo album, personal photos from family or friends, and information about significant life experiences to prepare a personal "biography" with the participant. These albums can be a source of great personal pleasure, provide a focus for visits, improve self-esteem through emphasizing life accomplishments, and introduce other staff members to another side of the person. The biography may also be mounted on a large Bristol board in the resident's room or on the door.

Sources

The following are some suggested sources for good, clear pictures:

Calendars: Calendars are one of the most inexpensive sources of clear pictures, especially discards from the year past. Calendars of beautiful local scenes or of well-known landmarks, animals, flowers, etc., can all be used effectively.

Coffee-table or illustrated books. There are some beautiful productions of these books on local or national areas, animals, flowers, etc. Often they can be purchased relatively inexpensively at yard sales, flea markets, or used book stores. Some individuals may enjoy leafing through the whole book, but for most it will be necessary to help them focus on a particular picture and make associations.

Greeting cards. Some beautiful artwork goes into greeting cards. Have friends and family save the color picture portion. These may be mounted for display interest. They are also useful cues for creative writing. Participants can choose a favorite among a small selection.

Magazines. Magazine illustrations and pictures should have any distracting wording cut off and be mounted for ease of handling. *Ideals* magazines are published eight times per year and contain excellent pictures, stories, and poems of interest to older adults. If they are not available in your area write to:

Ideals Publishing Corporation
P.O. Box 2100
Milwaukee, WI 53201

Promotional posters and pictures. Some excellent color posters are available from tourist offices, departments of agriculture, and promotional groups (such as the Milk Producers Association).

Seed catalogues. Seed catalogues are a free source of some beautiful pictures of flowers and vegetables.

10.7 Poetry

Although poetry is a verbal expression, its emotional and rhythmic qualities add a unique dimension that, like music, makes it more accessible to persons with cognitive losses. The "feeling" communication found in poetry helps to bridge the gap of losses in standard verbal communication. The message of poetry is able to bypass the words themselves. The hearing or reading of well-loved and familiar poems, like the lyrics of familiar songs, can stimulate verbalization and reminiscence. The writing of simple, unrhymed, nonmetrical poems, individually or in groups, can provide a unique opportunity for the expression of feelings and thoughts, for creativity, for socialization, for encouraging mutual support, and for reminiscence as well as providing success experiences. Poetry does not demand the same precision of fact or logical sequence as other forms of writing. Although group poetry-writing sessions are more suitable for persons who are in the early and middle stages, even persons with advanced ADRD will appreciate hearing familiar poems read. Memorizing poems and "elocution" classes were familiar activities for some members of this generation.

10.8 Guidelines for Poetry Writing Sessions

Select individuals who retain some language capacity, who are able to attend to the group process for at least five to ten minutes, and who will be comfortable with each other. The ideal group size is four to eight participants, depending on functional level.

Run the group in a quiet, cozy, and comfortable room.

Begin the group with examples of simple poetry in an unrhymed, nonmetrical form. Poems written by other seniors are a good inspiration for the first poetry-writing groups. Koch (1977) published numerous such poems in his book, *I Never Told Anybody.* Hearing, reading, and seeing poems previously written by the group provide inspiration, promote self-esteem, and remind participants of what they can accomplish. Seek out other examples of poetry, for example, the works of Walt Whitman or Robert Frost.

Select a theme or topic, or offer a choice between two or three topics. Although participants may take another route, providing a topic eliminates many problems with initiative and decision making. Select topics that are related to the current season or events (e.g., "spring," "Christmas," "birthdays," "the fall fair"), including topics used in ongoing reminiscence groups. Topics should be related to the participants' life experiences.

Provide concrete artifacts or cues related to the topic. For example, provide a bouquet of spring flowers, an old-fashioned school bell, a basket of apples, or an old photo.

Use communication techniques to encourage verbalization. Ask open-ended questions such as "What do you remember about your first day at school?" "What is the best Christmas you can remember?" "Who were you with? Where? What did you do?" "Why was it the best?" Use fill-in-the-blank responses: "My favorite season is _____ because _____." "If I could be anything I wanted it would be _____ because _____ ." Assist the person to connect the theme with his or her personal life experiences. Emphasize thoughts and feelings. Encourage imaginative involvement, being sure, at the same time, to provide adequate reality reassurance: "I want you to pretend or imagine that _____."

Move around the group, making sure that everyone has a chance to participate. Some may offer a word or a line, others a whole verse. Some may not speak at all, until encouraged by the contribution of others.

Record the contributions. For most participants, recording what they say relieves concern about writing and spelling and frees them up to become involved in the poetry. Read back the contribution for clarification and correction. When corrected, writing the contributions in large letters on a flip chart allows participants to read them and provides a concrete reinforcement for their efforts.

Praise and highlight individual contributions.

"Publish" the poems by writing them neatly in large letters or typing them in large print. Name the authors prominently. Poems should be posted to be enjoyed by staff and visitors and to encourage feedback to the authors. Individual authors should have their own copies, which can be posted and/or kept in a binder or album. Attractive illustrations or pictures are a good idea. Submit poems for publication in the facility newsletter or the local newspaper or seniors' letter.

Use these same techniques to conduct individual poetry-writing sessions, as appropriate.

Use familiar verses or ditties as a basis for rewriting, adding personal information. For example, "roses are red, violets are blue, sugar is sweet, and so are you," or begin instead with "petunias are pink."

10.9 Resources

Curley J. 1982. Leading poetry writing groups in a nursing home activities program. *Physical and Occupational Therapy in Geriatrics* 1, no. 4: 23–34.

Koch K. 1977. *I Never Told Anybody: Teaching Poetry Writing in a Nursing Home.* New York: Random House.

Sources of Poems

- vintage school textbooks/readers
- poetry anthologies
- *Ideals* magazines

Some Familiar Poems

- "Casey at the Bat"
- "The Wreck of the Hesperus"
- "The Cremation of Sam McGee"
- "In Flanders Fields"
- "The Village Blacksmith"
- "I Wandered Lonely As a Cloud"

11.0 GENERAL ACTIVITY RESOURCES

Activities, Adaptation and Aging, a quarterly journal with some good practical and research articles on activity; many focus on Alzheimer's and related dementias. Available from:

Haworth Press
10 Alice St.
Binghamton, NY 13904-1580

Activity Director's Guide, a monthly newsletter for those who conduct activities with elderly persons, including ideas for working with persons with Alzheimer's disease. Available from:

Eymann Publications, Inc.
1490 Huntington Circle
Box 3577
Reno, NV 89505

Activity Ideas for Older Adults, a mail-order company with a small catalogue of books, booklets, games, and other resources for working with older adults. Available from:

Elderpress
731 Treat Ave.
San Francisco, CA 94110

American Association of Retired Persons, 1909 K Street, NW, Suite 400, Washington, DC 20036; Telephone 1-202-296-5960. Has resources for reminiscence and intergenerational programs as well as other books and the loan of audiovisual materials.

Bifocal: Carries a selection of resources for reminiscence, including slide-tapes, videos, and resource kits on particular themes. Available from:

Bifocal
911 Williamson
Madison, WI 53703
Telephone 1-608-251-2818

Eldergames: Carries a variety of materials for various functional levels—memory games, trivia questions, and fabric books for stimulation. Available from:

Eldergames
11710 Hunters Lane
Rockville, MD 20852

Keep in Touch, a practical guide for groups and activities with disabled older adults. Available ($7.00 Canadian + postage $1.60) from:

M. Judd
1379 Dudley Cr.
Winnipeg, MB, Canada R3M 1P1

Mental Aerobics, a 350-page book of quizzes, holiday theme activities, word games, and memory games designed for older adults ($51.95 Canadian, plus postage and handling). Available from:

Mental Aerobics
4417 Torrington Road
Victoria, BC, Canada, V8N 4N8

Nottingham Rehabilitation Equipment: In addition to standard rehabilitation equipment, Nottingham carries an interesting selection of adapted adult games; large-piece, adult jigsaw puzzles; oversize dice and other large-size games; and adaptive gardening equipment. It also carries an interesting assortment of pic-

tures, slides, and music for reminiscence. Available from:

Nottingham Rehabilitation Equipment
Distributed through Physio E.R.P.
1170 Burnamthorpe Rd. W., #32
Mississauga, ON, L5C 4E6
Telephone 416-566-4092

Potentials Development, a mail-order service with a catalogue of booklets and small publications giving practical plans for activities of many types with older adults. Available from:

Potentials Development
775 Main St.
Buffalo, NY 14203

Sensory Stimulation Products for Alzheimer Patients, a small selection of safe, self-directed activities for persons with advanced ADRD (e.g., adult, cloth books). Available from:

Geriatric Resources Inc.
5450 Barton Dr.
Orlando, FL 32807
Telephone 1-800-359-0390

CAKES, MUFFINS, AND QUICK BREADS

BANANA BREAD

Banana bread is an old favorite and a good way to use up over-ripe bananas.

Ingredients

> $^1/_3$ cup shortening
> $^2/_3$ cup sugar
> 2 eggs, slightly beaten
> $1^1/_3$ cups sifted all-purpose flour
> $2^3/_4$ teaspoons baking powder
> $^1/_2$ teaspoon salt
> 1 cup mashed, ripe bananas

Method

Cream together shortening and sugar until light and fluffy. Add eggs and beat until thick and pale lemon-colored. Sift dry ingredients and add alternately with the mashed bananas. Blend well after each addition. Pour into greased 4" × 4" × 8" loaf pan, and bake at 350 degrees for 60 to 70 minutes (cake tester inserted in the center should come out clean).

Microwave. Microwave on medium high for 9 to 12 minutes (cake tester should come out clean). The top will be glossy but will set after 15 minutes' standing time.

Electric Frying Pan (EFP). Bake directly in the pan. Spray pan with vegetable nonstick product or grease well. Heat to 300 degrees. Bake for 20 to 30 minutes or until done.

LOW-CALORIE BANANA BREAD

Ingredients

> $1^3/_4$ cups sifted flour
> 2 teaspoons baking powder
> $^1/_4$ teaspoon baking soda
> $^1/_2$ teaspoon salt
> $^1/_4$ cup melted shortening or vegetable oil
> 2 well-beaten eggs
> 2 tablespoons liquid sweetener
> 1 teaspoon vanilla
> 2 medium bananas, well-mashed

Method

Sift dry ingredients together. Combine liquid ingredients and add, stirring until flour is moistened. Fold in mashed bananas. Pour into greased 4" × 4" × 8" loaf pan and bake at 350 degrees for 50 to 60 minutes.

Microwave and EFP. Bake same as regular banana bread.

BASIC ONE-EGG CAKE

Ingredients

2 cups sifted flour
1 cup sugar
3 teaspoons baking powder
1/2 teaspoon salt
1/2 cup shortening
1 egg
1 cup milk

Method

Sift together dry ingredients. Add shortening and milk. Beat until well mixed and smooth. Beat in egg. Pour into two greased 8" layer cake pans or a 2" × 8" × 12" rectangular pan. Bake at 350 degrees for 30 to 35 minutes. Frost as desired.

Microwave. Microwave at medium high for 7 to 9 minutes per layer or 11 to 15 minutes in rectangular pan.

EFP. Bake one layer at a time, on rack, at 400 degrees for 35 to 40 minutes.

ADAPTATIONS

Shortcake

Bake in layers. Serve warm with fresh fruit (e.g., strawberries, peaches, cherries). Put whipped cream between the layers and on top. Slice into wedges to serve.

Fruit Cobbler

Reduce shortening to 1/4 cup and make batter as directed. Use 2 1/2 cups of canned pie filling (e.g., blueberry, cherry, apple, rhubarb) or prepare 2 1/2 cups of thickened fruit. Pour fruit into greased 2" × 8" × 12" cake pan. Pour prepared batter on top. Bake at 350 degrees for 45 to 50 minutes, until tester inserted in cake comes out clean or cake springs back when lightly touched. Bake directly in EFP at 325 degrees for 25 to 30 minutes.

Cottage Pudding

Prepare batter as above, but reduce shortening to 1/4 cup. Bake in 2" × 8" × 12" pan, as directed. Cut in squares and serve warm with warm thickened fruit sauce, chocolate sauce, butterscotch sauce, or lemon sauce.

Upside-Down Cake

Heat 1/3 cup butter or margarine and 3/4 cup brown sugar in 2" × 8" × 12" pan until bubbling. Remove from oven or microwave. Arrange canned pineapple slices, pear halves, or peach halves in the sauce. Pour batter, made as directed, over fruit. Bake at 350 degrees for 45 to 50 minutes.

Microwave. Microwave on high for 11 to 13 minutes.

EFP. Heat topping and fruit directly in the pan. Pour batter on top. Bake at 275 degrees for 25 to 30 minutes.

BISHOP'S BREAD

This is delicious and foolproof. It is an excellent substitute for the more expensive and complicated Christmas cake.

Ingredients

3 cups all-purpose flour
2 teaspoons baking powder
1 teaspoon salt
4 eggs, beaten
1 cup sugar
1 cup chopped nuts
2 cups chopped dates
1 cup candied cherries
1 1/2 cups chocolate chips

Method

Combine dry ingredients. Stir in fruit, nuts, and chips. Beat the sugar into the eggs until fluffy. Pour into fruit mixture and stir well. Pour into well-greased tube pan or two large loaf pans. Bake at 325 degrees for 1 to 1 1/2 hours. Add a flat pan of hot water to the oven to preserve moisture. Cool thoroughly. Wrap carefully. (Keeps very well.)

QUICK BLUEBERRY COFFEECAKE, BREAD, OR CUPCAKES

Ingredients

5 cups all-purpose flour
2 cups white sugar
2 tablespoons baking powder
1 teaspoon salt
3/4 cup butter or margarine.
1 cup chopped nuts (optional)
3 cups fresh or frozen blueberries
4 eggs
1 cup milk
1/4 cup brown sugar
1/4 cup wheat germ or oat bran
3 teaspoons cinnamon

Method

Mix flour, white sugar, baking powder, and salt. Add butter and cut in with pastry blender or two forks until mixture resembles coarse meal. Stir in nuts and berries. Beat the eggs with the milk and add to the flour mixture. Stir until thoroughly combined. Pour batter into a greased 2" × 8¹/2" × 14" pan. Mix brown sugar, wheat germ or oat bran, and cinnamon together and sprinkle over cake batter. Bake in 350-degree oven for 40 to 50 minutes.

Microwave. Microwave in ring or bundt pan on high for 14 to 16 minutes or in flat glass pan on medium high for 14 to 16 minutes.

EFP. This cake is not at its best in a frying pan, but small batches can be cooked in layer pans on a rack in a 400-degree EFP for 35 to 40 minutes.

Method for Bread

Pour into two greased 4" × 4" × 12" loaf pans. Bake at 350 degrees for 40 to 50 minutes. Microwave on high heat for 12 to 14 minutes per loaf (bake one loaf at a time).

Method for Cupcakes

Put 1 tablespoon (heaping) of batter in greased or paper-lined muffin pans. Bake at 375 degrees for 15 to 20 minutes. Ice as desired.

Microwave Muffins

Use microwave muffin pans or improvise with 1" high cut-off bottoms of paper drink cups filled with muffin papers. Fill papers half full. Arrange in a circle on a plate. Bake on medium high for 2¹/2 to 4 minutes for 6 muffins.

ADAPTATIONS

Oat Chocolate Chip

Substitute 2 cups of oat bran for 2 cups of flour and add 3 cups of chocolate chips instead of the blueberries.

Cranberry

Substitute 3 cups washed whole cranberries (fresh or frozen) for blueberries. Add grated rind of 2 oranges to batter.

Raisin or Date and Spice

Substitute 1 cup of applesauce for milk, 3 cups of raisins or dates for blueberries; add 3 teaspoons of cinnamon and 1 teaspoon of nutmeg.

BLUEBERRY MUFFINS

Ingredients

1 cup butter or margarine
¹/2 cup sugar
1 beaten egg
1¹/2 cups flour
¹/2 teaspoon salt
2 teaspoons baking powder
¹/2 cup milk
1 cup blueberries

Method

Cream butter and sugar. Beat in egg. Sift together dry ingredients and add alternately with milk. Fold in blueberries. Spoon into greased muffin pans. Bake at 375 degrees for 15 to 20 minutes. Makes 1 dozen.

Microwave. Microwave on medium high for 3 to 4 minutes for 6 muffins.

BRAN MUFFINS

Bran muffins are healthful, familiar, and easy to make. This is my father-in-law's recipe. They were always delicious despite the fact that he seldom followed the usual direction of mixing muffins only gently and lightly!

Ingredients

¹/2 cup vegetable oil
¹/4 cup brown sugar
¹/4 cup molasses
2 eggs
1¹/4 cups milk
2¹/2 cups whole-wheat flour
1¹/2 cups cooking bran
1¹/2 teaspoons baking powder
¹/2 teaspoon each of salt and baking soda
³/4 cup chopped dates or raisins

Method

Mix together liquid ingredients. Add remaining ingredients and stir until combined. Put into greased muffin pans. Bake at 350 degrees for 20 to 25 minutes. Makes 2 dozen.

Microwave. Microwave on medium high for 2¹/2 to 4 minutes for 6 muffins.

LOW-CALORIE BRAN MUFFINS

Ingredients

2 cups all-purpose flour
1½ cups cooking bran (can use ½ to ¾ cup of this amount as wheat germ)
¾ teaspoon salt
1¼ teaspoons baking soda
2 tablespoons brown sugar
2 cups sour milk, yogurt, or buttermilk
1 beaten egg
¼ cup honey or molasses
2 tablespoons soft butter, margarine, or oil
1 cup raisins

Method

Combine dry ingredients with raisins. Beat together liquid ingredients and combine with dry ingredients. Spoon into greased muffin tins (or use papers). Bake at 375 degrees for 20 to 25 minutes. Makes 2 dozen.

Microwave. Microwave on medium high for 2½ to 4 minutes for 6 muffins.

QUICK BROWNIES

Ingredients

¾ cup all-purpose flour
½ teaspoon baking powder
¼ teaspoon salt
½ cup butter or margarine
¼ cup cocoa
¾ cup sugar
2 eggs
1 teaspoon vanilla
1 cup chopped nuts (optional)

Method

Sift dry ingredients together. Place margarine in 8" square pan and melt over low heat in oven or microwave. Pour melted butter into mixing bowl, add cocoa, and mix well. Cool to lukewarm. Beat in the sugar. Add eggs and vanilla and beat until smooth. Mix in dry ingredients until smooth. Add nuts, if desired. Spread evenly in pan, scraping down the sides. Bake at 350 degrees for 25 to 30 minutes. Frost when cool, if desired.

Microwave. Microwave on high for 6 to 7 minutes.

EFP. Pour directly into greased pan. Bake at 275 degrees for 20 to 30 minutes.

CARROT CAKE

Carrot cake is healthful and delicious and a good group activity. Grating carrots is a simple repetitive activity, but be careful of scraped fingers.

Ingredients

1 cup sugar
1 cup vegetable oil
4 eggs
½ teaspoon salt
1½ teaspoons baking powder
1½ teaspoons baking soda
1½ teaspoons cinnamon
½ teaspoon nutmeg
2 teaspoons vanilla
2½ cups all purpose flour
3 cups grated carrots
1 cup raisins
½ cup nuts (optional)

Method

Beat sugar and oil until smooth. Add vanilla. Add eggs one at a time and beat until smooth. Stir together dry ingredients and add. Fold in carrots, raisins, and nuts. Pour into greased 2" × 8½" × 13" pan. Bake at 300 degrees for 45 to 55 minutes. This cake is so moist it does well without a frosting. However, if you wish you can frost with the traditional cream cheese frosting.

Microwave. Microwave on high for 13 to 15 minutes.

EFP. Not a good candidate for skillet cooking.

CORN BREAD OR JOHNNIE CAKE

This is an old-fashioned favorite that should stir up lots of memories, along with the batter. Almost everybody has a favorite recipe. This is my personal favorite.

Ingredients

2 cups yellow cornmeal
½ cup flour (white or whole-wheat)
¼ teaspoon baking powder
1 teaspoon baking soda
¼ cup sugar
½ teaspoon salt
1 beaten egg
2 cups buttermilk, sour milk, or yogurt
¼ cup oil (or melted lard for an indulgence in old fashioned taste!)

Method

Stir together dry ingredients. Stir together liquid ingredients, except the oil or lard. Heat the lard in a 10" cast-iron frying pan until melted. Pour into liquid ingredients, swishing all around the sides of the pan first. If using oil, pour in frying pan and coat sides before adding oil to liquid ingredients. Place greased pan in 400-degree oven and heat. The pan should be smoking hot to make a nice crisp crust. Stir liquid ingredients into dry ingredients and mix until ingredients are just combined. Pour into hot pan. Bake at 400 degrees for 30 to 35 minutes. Turn down to 375 degrees if cake is browning too much.

Microwave. The microwave will not give that nice thick crust, but if an oven is not available, microwave at medium high for 9 to 11 minutes.

EFP. Pour batter directly into the hot greased pan. Bake at 350 degrees for 30 to 40 minutes. Lower heat if the bottom is browning too much. Serve warm, with butter, molasses, or maple syrup.

DATE BREAD

Ingredients

  2 cups chopped dates
  1½ cups boiling water
  1 cup brown sugar
  2 tablespoons butter or margarine
  2 eggs
  2¾ cups all-purpose flour
  1 teaspoon salt
  2 teaspoons baking soda
  1 teaspoon vanilla

Method

Pour boiling water over dates and let cool to room temperature. Add baking soda. Beat together sugar, shortening, and eggs. Add to date mixture. Add remaining ingredients and mix well. Pour into greased 4"× 4" × 12" loaf pan. Bake at 350 degrees for 50 to 60 minutes, until tester inserted in the middle comes out clean.

Microwave. Microwave on high for 9 to 12 minutes.
EFP. Not suitable.

DATE SQUARES

Ingredients

  1 cup flour
  1 teaspoon baking soda
  3 cups oatmeal
  1 cup brown sugar
  1 cup butter or shortening
  ½ teaspoon salt
  2 cups dates
  water to just cover dates
  ½ teaspoon lemon juice

Method

Cook dates in water until soft. Add lemon juice and let cool. Mix dry ingredients. Cut in butter until crumbly. Press half of crumb mixture into 2" × 8" × 12" pan. Add date mixture and sprinkle with remaining crumb mixture. Bake at 350 degrees for 30 to 35 minutes.

Microwave. Microwave on high 7 to 9 minutes.
EFP. Not suitable.

ADAPTATION

Fruit Squares

Substitute one 24-ounce can of fruit pie filling for the date filling; cherry is particularly good.

DEVIL'S-FOOD CAKE

This cake is absolutely moist and wonderful and easy. I have never had a failure.

Ingredients

  1 cup sugar
  ¾ cup cocoa
  1 cup milk
  1 egg
  1 cup sugar
  ¾ cup shortening
  2 eggs
  ½ cup milk
  ⅛ teaspoon salt
  1 teaspoon baking powder
  1 teaspoon vanilla
  2¼ cups flour

Method

Beat first four ingredients together. Heat, stirring frequently, until the consistency of custard. Cool to lukewarm. Sift together flour and other dry ingredients. Add with remaining ingredients and beat well. Pour into greased 8" layer cake pans or a 2" × 8" × 12" rectangular pans. Bake at 350 degrees for 30 to 35 minutes for the layers and 40 to 45 minutes for the rectangular pan.

Microwave. Layers: 7 to 9 minutes per layer on medium high. Rectangular pan: medium high for 11 to 15 minutes.

EFP. In layers on rack at 400 degrees for 35 to 45 minutes.

GINGERBREAD

This is an old Nova Scotian favorite, served with fresh applesauce, lemon sauce, or whipped cream.

Ingredients

1 cup molasses
$1/2$ cup sugar
1 teaspoon cinnamon
1 teaspoon ginger
$1/4$ teaspoon cloves
2 teaspoons baking soda
1 cup boiling water
$2^1/2$ cups of flour
2 beaten eggs

Method

Dissolve baking soda in boiling water. Mix ingredients in the order given, stirring in the eggs last. Pour into a greased 9" × 9" pan and bake at 350 degrees for 30 to 35 minutes.

Microwave. Microwave on medium high for 5 to 6 minutes.

EFP. Bake directly in greased skillet at 275 degrees for 25 to 35 minutes. Check for burning and turn down accordingly.

WACKY CAKE

Wacky cake is an easy, foolproof cake

Ingredients

$1^1/4$ cups all purpose flour
$3/4$ cup sugar
$1/4$ cup cornstarch
1 teaspoon cinnamon
1 teaspoon baking soda
$1/2$ teaspoon salt
3 tablespoons cocoa or carob powder
$1/3$ cup oil
1 tablespoon vinegar
1 cup cold water

Method

Stir together dry ingredients. Mix liquid ingredients and stir into dry. Pour into greased 8" × 8" pan. Bake at 325 degrees for 25 to 35 minutes.

Microwave. Microwave on high for 8 to 10 minutes.

EFP. Bake on rack at 400 degrees for 30 to 35 minutes.

ADAPTATIONS

Layer Cake

Double recipe ingredients to make two layers.

Cupcakes

Bake in greased muffin pans or papers. Makes 1 dozen.

Diabetic

Use carob and use $1/2$ cup of sugar substitute, such as Sugar Twin, instead of sugar.

COOKIES/CANDIES/BISCUITS

BAKING POWDER BISCUITS

Ingredients

2 cups all-purpose flour
4 teaspoons baking powder
2 teaspoons white sugar (optional)
$^1/_4$ cup vegetable shortening
$^1/_8$ teaspoon cream of tartar
$^3/_4$ cup milk

Method

Mix dry ingredients. Cut in shortening with two forks or pastry blender, until mixture resembles fine meal. Stir in enough milk to make a soft but manageable dough. Knead together lightly, 10 to 12 turns, on a floured surface. Pat to $^1/_2$" thickness. Cut with sharp-edged cutter. Place on a greased cookie sheet. Bake in regular oven at 425 degrees for 12 minutes or until lightly browned.

Microwave. Microwave on high for 5 minutes.
EFP. Bake at 475 degrees for 15 minutes.

adaptations to the method

Make a large batch of the dry ingredients with the shortening cut in. Store in a tightly covered jar and use as needed. Mixing these ingredients is a simple, repetitive activity that a participant could do, especially someone who has a need for motor activity and tends to perseverate. To prepare biscuits or adaptations from the dry mix add $^3/_4$ cup of milk to $2^1/_2$ cups of dry mix.

Time Saver

Flour a paper plate and knead dough lightly together on it. Pat out and cut dough on the plate. Cover cookie sheet with foil for baking. A commercial biscuit mix can be used for plain biscuits or for the adaptations that follow.

adaptations to the recipe

For Increased Nutrition

- substitute $^1/_4$ cup of wheat germ, wheat bran, or oat bran for $^1/_4$ cup of flour
- mix $^1/_4$ cup milk powder into the milk
- beat one egg in measuring cup and add milk to usual level

- use 1 cup of whole-wheat flour and 1 cup of white flour
- add 1 cup grated cheese

For Variety Add

- finely minced chives or parsley
- $^1/_3$ cup berries or chopped apples
- $^1/_2$ cup raisins, currants, coconut, candied fruit

Pinwheel Variations

Pat dough into a rectangle and spread with

- grated cheese
- butter, brown sugar, cinnamon, and raisins
- thick jam, preserves, or pie filling
- onions sautéed in butter and mixed with poppy seeds

Roll up like a jelly roll, cut in $^1/_2$" thick slices, and bake at 350 degrees for 15 to 20 minutes.

Fruit Shortcakes

Substitute $^1/_3$ cup butter for shortening and increase sugar to $^1/_4$ cup. Cut in fancy shapes as desired. Sprinkle with sugar and bake as usual. Split in half. Place fresh fruit and whipped cream on bottom half. Add top, and more fruit and whipped cream.

Appetizers (Pigs in a Blanket)

Pat dough into a circle about $^1/_4$" thick. Cut into 8 wedges. Place cooked, small sausage at wide end of the wedge. Roll up. Bake for 15 minutes at 400 degrees. Other savory or ground meat fillings may be used.

Meat Pie

Heat desired meat filling in a casserole or baking pan. Pat biscuit dough $^1/_2$" thick and into a shape that will cover the filling. Place over hot filling. Bake at 400 degrees for 15 to 20 minutes until dough is baked and filling is hot.

Fruit Cobblers

Place stewed, thickened fruit or commercial pie filling in 2" deep casserole or baking pan. Substitute butter or margarine for shortening, increase sugar to $1/2$ cup, and use beaten egg in a 1-cup measure, adding enough milk to equal 1 cup. Drop batter by spoonfuls on the prepared fruit. Sprinkle with sugar and cinnamon, if desired. Bake at 375 degrees for 25 to 30 minutes, until bubbling and golden.

CHOCOLATE DROP COOKIES

These are quick, easy, and very adaptable.

Ingredients

$1/3$ cup butter or margarine
$1/2$ cup milk
2 cups sugar
3 cups oatmeal
6 heaping tablespoons cocoa or carob powder

Method

Combine butter, milk, and sugar and bring to a full boil. Boil for 1 minute, stirring frequently. Remove from heat and stir in dry ingredients. Drop by spoonfuls on waxed paper or cookie sheets. Let cool and store in a container with a tight-fitting lid.

adaptations

Shaping

When the mixture has cooled enough to handle it shapes very easily into whatever the occasion calls for. Some suggestions are: shape into hearts, roll in coconut, and decorate with red candy hearts; shape like mini-pumpkins and roll in orange-tinted coconut.

Diabetic Substitute

- 1 cup Sugar Twin for 1 cup sugar
- increase oatmeal by $1/2$ cup

Additions

Add 1 cup of raisins or 1 cup of desiccated coconut along with the oatmeal.

Reduced Sugar

Use only 1 cup of sugar and increase oatmeal by $1/2$ cup.

EASY CHOCOLATE FUDGE

Ingredients

1 package chocolate pudding and pie filling mix
$1 1/2$ cups icing sugar
$1/4$ cup butter or margarine
$1/4$ cup milk

Method

Combine pudding mix, milk, and butter and boil for 1 minute, stirring constantly. Remove from heat and stir in sugar. Mix well. Pour into greased 8" square pan. Cool and cut in squares.

EASY SHORTBREAD COOKIES

Ingredients

$1/2$ cup cornstarch
$1/2$ cup icing sugar
1 cup flour
$3/4$ cup margarine or butter

Method

Sift dry ingredients together. Blend in margarine or butter to form a smooth dough. Shape into 1" balls and place on an ungreased cookie sheet. (Dough may be chilled for 1 hour for easier handling.) Dough may also be rolled to $1/4$ inch thickness and cut with a cookie cutter. Bake at 300 degrees for 15 to 20 minutes.

NEVER-FAIL CHOCOLATE FUDGE

Ingredients

2 tablespoons butter or margarine
$1 1/3$ cup sugar
$2/3$ cup evaporated milk
$1/2$ teaspoon salt
2 tablespoons cocoa
2 cups miniature marshmallows

Method

Measure butter, sugar, milk, and cocoa into a pan. Place on medium heat, bring to a boil, and cook for 5 minutes, stirring constantly. Remove from heat and stir in marshmallows. Stir until marshmallows are melted. Pour into greased 8" square pan. Cool and cut in squares.

OLD-FASHIONED ROLLED GINGERBREAD

Ingredients

1 cup shortening
1 cup white sugar
1 cup molasses
1 beaten egg
5$\frac{1}{2}$ cups flour
1 tablespoon ginger
1 teaspoon cinnamon
1 teaspoon salt
1 tablespoon baking soda
1 tablespoon vinegar

Method

Boil shortening, sugar, and molasses for 2 minutes. Let cool to room temperature. Dissolve baking soda in the vinegar and add to cooled mixture, along with remaining ingredients. Add enough flour to make a smooth, not sticky, dough for rolling. (It should not be too stiff.) Chill for 1 or 2 hours. Do not overcool, as this makes the dough too stiff and unmanageable. Roll out on lightly floured board or table, using a floured pin. Dip cutters in flour. Place shapes on a greased cookie sheet and bake for 10 to 12 minutes at 325 degrees.

Microwave. Microwave on high, 1 to 3 minutes.

EFP. Bake on a greased pan, on rack, at 400 degrees for 12 to 15 minutes. Store cooled cookies in an airtight container to retain crispness. The rolling of the cookies may be a well-preserved skill for some. For others, their contribution may be to cut shapes from sheets of rolled dough, which can be prepared on foil-covered cardboard for moving from individual to individual for cutting.

OATMEAL CHOCOLATE CHIP COOKIES

Ingredients

$\frac{1}{2}$ cup butter or margarine
$\frac{1}{2}$ cup brown sugar
$\frac{1}{2}$ cup white sugar
1 egg
1 tablespoon water
1 teaspoon vanilla
$\frac{3}{4}$ cup flour
$\frac{1}{2}$ teaspoon baking soda
$\frac{1}{2}$ teaspoon salt
1$\frac{1}{2}$ cups oatmeal or oat bran
1$\frac{1}{4}$ cups chocolate chips

Method

Cream together butter and sugars. Beat in egg, water, and vanilla. Stir in dry ingredients and chocolate chips.

Drop by spoonfuls onto greased cookie sheets. Bake at 350 degrees for 10 to 12 minutes.

Microwave. Microwave on high for 1 to 3 minutes.

EFP. Bake on a greased pan, on a rack, at 400 degrees for 12 to 15 minutes.

OATMEAL DROP COOKIES

Ingredients

1 cup shortening, butter, or margarine
1 cup each of brown and white sugar
2 eggs
2 cups flour
2 cups oatmeal
1 teaspoon baking soda dissolved in 1 tablespoon hot water
$\frac{1}{4}$ teaspoon ground nutmeg

Method

Cream together butter and sugar until light and fluffy. Beat in eggs and baking soda water. Add flour, oatmeal, and nutmeg and mix well. Drop by teaspoons on greased cookie sheets. The cookies spread, so keep them well apart on the cookie sheets. Bake at 350 degrees for 8 to 10 minutes. They should be golden brown on the bottom. Don't let them overbake, as this makes them too hard.

Microwave. Microwave on high for 1 to 3 minutes.

EFP. Bake on a greased pan, on a rack, at 400 degrees for 12 to 15 minutes.

PEANUT BUTTER COOKIES

Ingredients

1 cup white sugar
1 cup brown sugar
1 cup butter or margarine
1 cup peanut butter (crunchy or smooth)
2 eggs
3 cups flour
2 teaspoons baking powder
$\frac{1}{2}$ teaspoon salt

Method

Cream sugars and butter. Beat in egg and peanut butter until mixture is light and fluffy. Add flour and mix well. Drop by spoonfuls onto greased cookie sheet. Flatten with a fork dipped in water. Bake at 350 degrees for 10 to 12 minutes.

Microwave. Microwave on high for 2$\frac{1}{2}$ to 3 minutes.

EFP. Bake on greased pan on rack at 400 degrees for 12 to 15 minutes.

SCONES

This is a delicious and rich variation of tea biscuits.

Ingredients

2 cups flour
2 tablespoons sugar
3 1/2 teaspoons baking powder
1/2 cup shortening
1/2 cup milk
1 egg

Method

Mix flour, baking powder, and sugar. Cut in shortening until the mixture resembles coarse meal. Beat together the egg and the milk. Reserve 2 tablespoons. Add remainder to the dry ingredients and mix gently. Knead on lightly floured board 10 to 12 times. Shape into 8 to 10 round flattened balls or one large one pressed to 1/2" thickness. Place on greased sheet. Score large "scone" into 8 pie-shaped wedges. Brush with reserved egg mixture. Sprinkle with sugar. Bake at 400 degrees for 12 to 15 minutes.

Microwave and EFP. As for baking powder biscuits.

adaptation

Add raisins or other dried fruit, as for baking powder biscuits.

SUGAR COOKIES

Ingredients

2 1/2 cups flour
1/2 teaspoon baking soda
1 cup butter, margarine, or vegetable shortening, or a combination
1 cup white sugar
1 teaspoon almond or vanilla extract
1 egg
2 tablespoons milk

Method

Cream sugar and butter together until fluffy. Beat egg and extract. Add dry ingredients and mix well. Add milk and mix well. Drop by teaspoons on a greased cookie sheet. Flatten with a glass dipped in sugar (colored sugar may be used, according to the season). Bake at 350 degrees for 10 to 12 minutes.

Microwave. Microwave at high for 2 1/2 to 3 minutes.

EFP. Bake on greased pan on rack at 400 degrees for 12 to 15 minutes.

SUGARLESS FRUIT COOKIES

Ingredients

1/2 cup chopped dates
1 cup raisins
1 cup water
2 eggs
1/2 cup margarine or butter
3 tablespoons liquid sweetener
1 teaspoon vanilla
1 cup flour
1 teaspoon cinnamon
1 teaspoon baking soda

Method

Combine dates, raisins, and water. Boil for 3 minutes and let cool. Cream together eggs, margarine, sweetener, and vanilla. Add sifted dry ingredients alternately with fruit mixture. Chill for several hours. Drop by spoonfuls on greased baking sheets. Bake at 350 degrees for 10 to 12 minutes. For cake, pour mixture into greased 8" square pan. Bake at 325 degrees for 20 to 25 minutes.

DESSERTS

BATTER-STEAMED PUDDING

This is an old family recipe, easy to make, and completely adaptable to what is in season or favorite fruits.

Ingredients

2 cups all-purpose flour
2 tablespoons shortening
$1/2$ cup white sugar
1 egg
2 teaspoons baking powder
$3/4$ cup milk

Method

Cream shortening and sugar. Beat in egg. Add flour and baking powder. Stir in milk. Layer in pan of a steamer with fruit slices (e.g., apples, pears, peaches, pineapple) or fresh or frozen berries (e.g., blackberries, raspberries, blueberries, cherries, cranberries). Steam over boiling water for about 1 hour, until the dough is cooked through. Serve warm with sugar and milk or favorite sauce.

ADAPTATIONS

Steaming

Most people will have to improvise a steamer. The pudding can go in any flat dish (e.g., a pie plate), and should be tightly covered with foil. Select a large kettle with a tight-fitting cover that will hold the pudding with height to spare. Place a lid or jar rings on the bottom of the kettle so that the pudding will not sit directly on the bottom. Put about 2" of water in the kettle (do not let it come up to the pudding), cover tightly, and bring to a boil. Puddings can be steamed in the same fashion in an electric frying pan.

Combinations

- *Oat and date:* Substitute 1 cup of oat bran for 1 cup of flour. Use chopped dates instead of fresh fruit.
- *Cranberry orange:* Use undiluted concentrated orange juice instead of milk; add 1 tablespoon grated orange peel and use fresh or frozen cranberries for the fruit.
- *Spicy with fruit:* For apples, add 2 teaspoons of cinnamon with the flour; for blueberries, $1/2$ teaspoon nutmeg; for pears, $1/2$ teaspoon ground ginger; for pineapple, 2 teaspoons lemon zest.

- *Diabetic substitute:* Use $1/3$ cup Nutrasweet for the sugar.

CUSTARD

Custard is a healthful and versatile dish that is easy to swallow and digest.

Ingredients

2 cups milk
3 whole eggs
$1/2$ cup sugar
$1/8$ teaspoon salt
1 teaspoon vanilla

Method

Heat milk until steaming, being careful not to boil. Beat eggs thoroughly. Add $1/4$ cup hot milk to beaten eggs, beating while slowly pouring in the milk. Repeat. Slowly pour the egg mixture into the hot milk, beating constantly. Cook and stir constantly over low-medium heat until the custard coats the back of the spoon. Do not boil. Stir in vanilla. Pour into serving dish(es) and cool at room temperature. Cover with waxed paper and chill. Sprinkle top with grated nutmeg, or sugar and cinnamon, if desired.

Baked. Beat together above ingredients. Pour into baking dish or custard cups. Sprinkle with nutmeg, if desired. Bake at 300 degrees for 40 minutes or until set. A knife inserted in the center should come out clean. Do not overcook, as it spoils the texture.

Microwave. Reduce milk to $1/2$ cup. Scald milk on high for 3 to 4 minutes. Add to egg as above. Cover dish and microwave on low for 10 to 12 minutes. Place paper towel between lid and dish to absorb moisture while cooling. Sprinkle with nutmeg before serving, if desired.

EFP. Pour combined ingredients into greased custard cups or bowls. Place the cups on racks in the pan. Add boiling water to come half way up the sides of the cups. Cover and simmer until custard is set (10 to 12 minutes). The custard can be made, according to the stirred method, directly in the EFP.

adaptations

Butterscotch

Use brown sugar instead of white sugar.

Chocolate

Increase sugar to ¹/₃ cup and mix it with 3 tablespoons of cocoa. Stir hot milk into the cocoa sugar mixture to make a thick paste. Return to hot milk, stirring well. Proceed as above.

Coconut, Date, or Raisin

Stir in ¹/₂ cup of coconut, dates, or raisins into cooked stove-top custard, or add to the bottom of the baking dish for baked custard.

Cheese

Omit sugar and add ¹/₂ cup grated cheese to the bottom of the baking dish for baked custard. Sprinkle the top with paprika. Bake as usual.

FRUIT CRISP

Ingredients

enough peeled, chopped fruit to fill 8¹/₂" × 2" × 13" pan to within 1" of the top (apples, rhubarb, peaches, blueberries, or plums are all good)
¹/₂ cup butter or margarine
1 cup oatmeal
1 cup brown sugar
1 cup flour

Method

Cut butter into dry ingredients until crumbly. Place fruit in pan. Sprinkle over fruit and bake at 375 degrees for 35 to 40 minutes, until fruit is soft and top is golden brown. For apples, add 3 teaspoons of cinnamon; for peaches, sprinkle ¹/₂ teaspoon of nutmeg over the fruit; for rhubarb, add extra sugar according to taste. Serve warm with ice cream or whipped cream.

adaptations

This is a wonderfully adaptive dish with jobs for every skill level—preparing fruit, mixing the topping (a good repetitive activity), or spooning over the topping. Try a combination of apple, blueberry, and cranberry. Delicious!

GRAHAM CRACKER CRUMB CRUST

Ingredients

1¹/₂ cups graham cracker crumbs
¹/₄ cup melted butter or margarine
¹/₄ cup sugar
2 teaspoons cinnamon

Method

Combine ingredients and press into 9" pie pan. Bake at 325 degrees for 5 to 7 minutes.
Microwave. Microwave on high for 3 to 4 minutes.
EFP. Bake on a rack at 400 degrees for 8 to 10 minutes. The shell may be filled unbaked, but it does not hold together as well.

ICE CREAM

This is guaranteed to be a successful project—calling forth so many memories, giving exercise, and tasting so good.

Ingredients

5 cups milk
¹/₂ teaspoon salt
³/₄ cup sugar
4 beaten eggs
2 cups light cream
1 cup whipping cream
2 teaspoons vanilla

Method

Rinse a large pan with water, to prevent sticking. Heat milk and creams until steaming. Add sugar and stir until dissolved. Add small amount of hot milk to the eggs, beating while adding. Slowly add another cup of hot milk, beating eggs constantly. Slowly pour this mixture back into the hot milk, whisking or beating constantly. This process is very important in preventing the custard from curdling. Heat over medium low, stirring constantly, until the mixture is thick and coats a metal spoon. Stir in vanilla, cover, and chill. Pour into ice-cream churn container. Churn according to freezer directions.

adaptations

Chocolate

Increase sugar to 1¹/₂ cups. Stir ¹/₂ cup cocoa into the sugar. Add hot milk and stir until cocoa is dissolved. Return to hot milk and proceed as above.

Fruit Flavor

During the last 10 minutes of churning add 2 cups chopped peaches, strawberries, cherries, bananas, whole blueberries, or other fruit or 2 cups thickened fruit or fruit purée.

NEVER-FAIL PIE CRUST

Ingredients

5 cups all purpose flour
1 pound good-quality shortening
1 teaspoon baking powder
1 teaspoon salt
1 tablespoon brown sugar
1 beaten egg
1 tablespoon vinegar

Method

Mix dry ingredients together. Cut in shortening until mixture resembles coarse meal. Beat egg in a 1 cup measure and add vinegar. Add water to equal 1 cup. Add to dry ingredients and mix gently into a smooth ball. This dough keeps in the refrigerator for at least 2 weeks. It may be divided into 6 portions (enough for six 9" pie shells), wrapped, and individually frozen. The portions may be rolled into pie shells and frozen before baking. This makes enough for 2 double crust pies and 2 single crusts. It may be cut in half.

This recipe is very forgiving and can be rerolled several times and still give good results. However, it is best to handle it as gently as possible. Roll out only enough for one shell at a time ($^1/_6$ of the dough). Lightly flour the board and the pin. Roll gently from the center out. It rolls best if *slightly* chilled.

adaptations

This is an excellent activity for a special occasion, such as pumpkin pies for Thanksgiving. Individuals who are familiar with baking and can do repetitive activity would be very good at mixing the dough. You may wish to roll out the pastry yourself. However, it is amazing how these familiar skills come back if someone is given some dough and a rolling pin. Everyone can assist in preparing the filling, cutting and sieving the pumpkin, etc. And everyone can put filling in the shells independently or with assistance. The aroma and the associations are matchless.

MISCELLANEOUS (PANCAKES AND CONDIMENTS)

Pancakes are an old-fashioned favorite for breakfast or a winter supper. Among your participants there is certainly a favorite family heirloom recipie.

WHOLE WHEAT PANCAKES

Ingredients

2 cups whole-wheat flour
$^1/_2$ cup wheat germ
4 teaspoons baking powder
3 tablespoons oil
2 beaten eggs
milk to make good pouring batter (1$^1/_2$ to 2 cups)

Method

Stir together dry ingredients. Beat eggs and stir in oil and 1 cup of milk. Stir into dry ingredients and add milk to reach desired consistency. Bake on hot, greased griddle or electric frying pan at 375 degrees. Pancakes are ready to turn when small bubbles form on the top.

Note: With one-to-one guidance each participant can pour the batter and flip own pancake. This brings great satisfaction! Smaller pancakes are easier to manage.

OATMEAL-BLUEBERRY PANCAKES

Ingredients

1$^1/_2$ cups oatmeal
$^1/_2$ cup flour
1 tablespoon baking powder
$^1/_2$ teaspoon salt
1 beaten egg
3 tablespoons oil
1$^1/_2$ cups milk
1 cup fresh or frozen blueberries

Method

Mix together dry ingredients. Beat together liquid ingredients and add, stirring just enough to mix. Bake as above. Sprinkle blueberries over pancake while first side is cooking. Flip and cook on second side. Grease the pan very well for these, as the blueberries tend to stick.

DILL PICKLES

Ingredients

4 quarts dill-size cucumbers
8–10 heads of fresh dill
2 tablespoons mixed pickling spice
4 cloves of garlic, peeled
3 cups water
2 tablespoons sugar
1/4 cup coarse salt
1 cup white vinegar

Method

Scrub cucumbers to remove spines. Place 1 head of dill, 1 clove of garlic and 1/2 tablespoon pickling spice in the bottom of a 1-quart jar. Pack with clean cucumbers. Add a head of dill for the top. Combine water, sugar, salt, and vinegar and bring to a boil. Pour brine over cucumbers and fasten lids securely. It is not necessary that these pickles be sealed. For best flavor, leave in a cool place for 3 months.

GREEN TOMATO CHOW-CHOW

Ingredients

15 pounds green tomatoes
5 pounds onions
1/2 cup coarse pickling salt
3–4 cups cider vinegar (to taste)
2–3 cups brown sugar (to taste)
1/2 cup mixed pickling spice, tied in a cheesecloth bag
1 tablespoon ground cinnamon
1 teaspoon dry mustard

Method

Chop vegetables in large chunks and sprinkle with salt. Let stand overnight in a stainless steel, glass, or plastic container. Drain well in the morning and place in a large, heavy-bottomed kettle. Bury the bag of spices in the middle. Add the vinegar and bring slowly to a boil. Uncover and let cook gently for 1 1/2 hours, stirring to avoid sticking. Mix cinnamon and mustard with the sugar and stir in. Cook and stir for 10 minutes until seasonings are well blended. Taste, and add sugar and vinegar as desired (this is fun with a group, as everyone can offer an opinion). Bottle in sterilized jars.

GREEN TOMATO PICKLE (UNCOOKED)

Ingredients

2 quarts green tomatoes
2 quarts cabbage
8 large onions
6 red sweet peppers
1 hot red pepper

Method

Wash and prepare vegetables, cutting into chunks that will fit into a hand grinder (this portion should be done by staff, a volunteer, or a high-functioning participant). Grind with a medium blade, using a manual grinder (a good repetitive activity). Mix ground vegetables with 1/2 cup coarse salt. Let stand overnight. Drain well. Mix with 6 cups of white sugar, 2 teaspoons of dry mustard, 1 quart of vinegar, 2 teaspoons of celery seed, and 2 teaspoons of turmeric powder. Bottle in clean jars or store in a large crock. This relish does not require sealing.

CRANBERRY-ORANGE RELISH

Ingredients

4 cups whole cranberries
1 whole orange, cut in pieces
2 cups sugar

Method

Grind cranberries and oranges on medium blade of food grinder. Stir in sugar. Store in a cool place.

NO-BAKE/NO-COOK SUGGESTIONS

APPLESAUCE SQUARES

Ingredients

1 can condensed milk
1 cup thick applesauce
$1/3$ cup lemon juice
3 egg whites, beaten stiff
3 egg yolks, beaten
whole graham wafers

Method

Line bottom of a 2"× 8" × 12" pan with whole graham wafers. Combine milk, applesauce, lemon juice, and egg yolks. Fold in egg whites. Pour over wafers and chill. Cut in squares.

CRISPY PEANUTS

Ingredients

1 cup crisp rice cereal
1 cup peanut butter
1 cup powdered sugar

Method

Combine above ingredients. Shape and roll in plain or tinted desiccated coconut.

DREAM BARS

Ingredients

2 cups miniature marshmallows
1 cup chopped dates
$1/2$ cup desiccated coconut
1 cup chopped maraschino cherries
$1/2$ cup chopped nuts
24 graham crackers, rolled into fine crumbs ($1^1/_2$ cups crumbs)
1 10-ounce can condensed milk

Method

Mix all ingredients, adding the milk last. Sprinkle 9" x 9" pan with powdered sugar. Press in mixture and chill. Sprinkle top with powdered sugar. Cut into squares.

EASY CHERRY FROZEN TREAT

Ingredients

19-ounce can cherry pie filling
14-ounce can crushed pineapple
10-ounce can condensed milk
3 tablespoons lemon juice
$1/2$ teaspoon almond flavoring
2 cups whipping cream, 2 envelopes topping mix, or 4 cups prewhipped dairy topping

Method

Combine all ingredients except the cream. Whip cream or topping and fold into other ingredients. Spoon into muffin tins lined with papers. Freeze.

PEANUT BUTTER FUDGE

Combine 1 cup smooth peanut butter, 1 cup honey, and 1 cup instant skim milk powder. Shape in balls and roll in toasted coconut or powdered sugar. Chill.

PINEAPPLE-STRAWBERRY PARFAIT

Ingredients

1 can evaporated milk
2 packages strawberry jelly powder
1 14-ounce can crushed pineapple

Method

Pour milk into shallow pan and put in the freezer compartment until ice crystals begin to form. Dissolve jelly in 1 cup of boiling water. Drain pineapple, reserving juice. Add 1 cup of reserved juice to the jelly. Chill jelly until the thickness of corn syrup. Whip chilled evaporated milk until it stands in soft peaks. Fold into jelly. Fold in pineapple. Pour into serving glasses or dish or prebaked graham cracker pie shell. Chill and serve.

"STRAWBERRIES"

Ingredients

1 package strawberry jelly powder
1 can condensed milk
2 cups desiccated coconut

Method

Mix together and shape like strawberries, rolling in icing sugar. A green icing "stem" may also be made. Chill well.

OTHER NO-BAKE SUGGESTIONS

- Fruit shortcake (see "Biscuits" for method, substituting commercially baked shortcakes for biscuits)

- Fruit or vegetable trays with dips
- Instant pudding mixes
- Punch
- Salads
- Sandwiches
- Sundaes

YEAST BREADS AND ROLLS

BASIC NO-KNEAD BREAD DOUGH

This is an easy recipe, requiring approximately 2 hours from start to finished rolls.

Ingredients

3 cups lukewarm water
$1/2$ cup sugar
6 tablespoons oil
1 teaspoon salt
2 eggs
4–5 cups flour
2 tablespoons instant yeast

Method

Beat liquid ingredients together. Mix yeast and flour. Add liquid ingredients to flour and yeast and beat well. Add 3 to 4 cups more flour; mix well to make firm dough. Let rise for 15 minutes and then stir down. Let rise again for 15 minutes and shape as desired. Bake loaves at 350 degrees for 30 to 40 minutes. Bake rolls at 400 degrees for 10 minutes.

ROLLED-OAT BREAD

This is an old fashioned Nova Scotian favorite that does not require kneading. It is also known as porridge bread.

Ingredients

2 cups boiling water
1 cup rolled oats
$1/2$ cup molasses
$1/2$ tablespoon salt
1 tablespoon butter
1 package (1 tablespoon) granulated yeast
$1/2$ cup warm water
5 cups flour (all-purpose)

Method

Pour boiling water over rolled oats and let stand 1 hour. Sprinkle yeast in the lukewarm water and let stand 10 minutes. Add, along with the salt, molasses and butter to the oats mixture. Add flour 1 cup at a time and mix well after each addition. Let rise and stir down three times. On the third time, beat well. Pour into two greased 4" × 4" × 12" loaf pans. Let rise until double. Bake at 425 degrees for 10 minutes. Reduce heat to 350 degrees and bake 30 to 35 minutes more.

SWEET ROLLS

These are yeast rolls that require kneading. However, they are light, easy, and so delicious. The dough can be made a day in advance and left to rise in the refrigerator.

Ingredients

1 cup lukewarm water
1 cup boiling water
1 tablespoon yeast
1 teaspoon sugar
1 teaspoon salt
1 egg
$1/3$ cup shortening
$1/2$ cup sugar
5 cups flour

Method

Dissolve the teaspoon of sugar in the lukewarm water. Sprinkle the yeast over the top. Cream together sugar and butter. Beat in the egg. Add the boiling water. Cool to lukewarm. Add the dissolved yeast. Beat in 2 cups of flour. Beat for 3 to 5 minutes. Mix in remaining flour 1 cup at a time. Knead on a floured board until smooth and elastic and no longer taking up flour (5 to 10 minutes). To make the lightest rolls, the dough should be slightly sticky. Replace in the mixing bowl and let rise in a warm place (80 to 85 degrees) while covered with a damp tea towel. Let rise until double in bulk. When ready, the dough should retain the mark of a lightly touched finger. This takes about 1 hour. Punch down and let rise again until double in bulk. Shape into rolls or loaves. Let rise until double. Bake rolls at 425 degrees for 10 minutes and bread at 350 degrees for 35 to 40 minutes. When done, the bread should sound hollow when tapped on the bottom.

ADAPTATIONS TO THE METHOD

Set the batter the night before and leave to rise overnight in the refrigerator or in a cool, but not freezing, place. Shape as desired and let rise in a warm place. The rising will take two or three times longer than usual. Bake as usual.

Baking

Personally, I do not find the results of microwave or EFP baking of yeast foods satisfying.

Freezing the Dough

Immediately after kneading, the dough may be divided into portions according to need and frozen in plastic bags. Allow plenty of room in the bags, as dough will continue to rise for some time. Allow to thaw for several hours. Shape and let rise (two or three times as long as normal). Bake as usual. Purchased frozen commercial bread dough is easy and provides a wonderful aroma while baking.

ADAPTATIONS TO THE RECIPE

Raisin Bread (Loaf)

After second rising, divide dough in half. Shape each half into a smooth ball; let rest, covered with a damp towel, for 10 minutes. Roll one half out into a rectangle

$1/2$" thick. Sprinkle evenly with 1 cup raisins, pressing raisins into the dough. Roll up jelly roll fashion, pressing the overlapping pieces of dough firmly together with each full roll. Seal the edges by pinching firmly. Place seam side down in a greased 4"x 4"x 12" loaf pan. Let rise until double and bake at 350 degrees for 35 to 40 minutes.

The second piece of dough can be shaped into rolls or whatever is desired. If the whole batch is going to be raisin bread, add the raisins to the dough with the flour and shape as for basic loaves.

Cinnamon Buns

After the second rising, divide the dough in half. Roll one half into a $1/2$" thick rectangle. Spread generously with soft butter or margarine. Sprinkle on brown sugar and cinnamon to taste. Sprinkle with raisins. Roll into a long roll. Slice in 1" thick slices, place wide side down in a greased $8^1/_2$" x 13" x 2" pan. Bake at 325 degrees for 40 to 45 minutes.

Coffee Ring

Form a "jelly roll" of raisins, sugar, and cinnamon as for cinnamon buns. Place roll on a greased cookie sheet. Join open ends to form a circle. Make cuts $3/4$" apart along the outside edge, leaving 1" to 2" of the inner edge of roll intact. Arrange cut portions so that they fan out from the inner ring. Let rise until double. Bake at 300 degrees for 35 to 40 minutes.

Hot Cross Buns

Add with the flour to the original recipe 2 cups raisins, 1 cup cut, mixed peel, 3 teaspoons cinnamon, $1/2$ teaspoon nutmeg, $1/2$ teaspoon ground cloves.

Mix and let rise as for original recipe. Shape into 2" to 3" rolls and place well apart on greased cookie sheet. Let rise until double. Cut a cross in the top of each roll with a sharp knife. Bake at 325 degrees for 10 to 15 minutes. When cool, outline cross with icing, if desired.

SUITABLE DIABETIC RECIPES

- Baking powder biscuits
- Chocolate drop cookies (made with sugar substitute)
- Custard
- Low-calorie banana bread
- Low-calorie bran muffins
- Pancakes
- Sugarless fruit cookies or cake
- Wacky cake (diabetic version)

Suggested Handicraft Activities

DÉCOUPAGE

This is a very simple, satisfying activity.

Materials

- colorful, good quality pictures
- $\frac{1}{2}$" thick pieces of wood for mounting
- sandpaper
- a clear, quick-drying découpage finish such as "Podgy"
- glue
- paintbrush
- hanger

Method

1. Select a colorful, pleasant picture from a magazine, seed catalogue, calendar, or greeting card.
2. Select a $\frac{1}{2}$" thick piece of wood that is at least 1" larger in dimension than the picture. Sand and prepare wood. For more "rustic" projects a cedar shingle or a piece of rough-hewn barn board may be used.
3. Glue the picture in place and let dry.
4. Cover with 2 to 3 coats of "podgy" or other découpage sealer. The more coats, the more depth to the finished product.
5. Insert commercial hanger on the back.

variations

- Make brooches, key chains, or refrigerator magnets, using diagonally sawed pieces of 2" branches or attractive pieces of scrap wood. Glue on brooch pin findings or magnets (available at most hobby stores), as appropriate.
- Add glued or screwed on rubber legs and use as a trivet.

DOUGH ART

The dough is easily and cheaply made from available ingredients, and many attractive items can be created. Working with the dough provides good hand exercise as well as an outlet for creativity. The material is less fragile than ceramics for painting. The dough is made of all edible ingredients, in case any should be accidentally eaten. There are two dough recipes, one of which is suitable for rolling and air drying or oven baking. The other may be shaped as desired and then baked. A few drops of vegetable food coloring may be added with the liquid ingredients. The color will change with baking, so this works best with recipe #1.

Materials

- dough art recipe #1 or #2
- craft glue
- plastic bags
- rolling pins (recipe #1)
- foil covered cookie sheets
- whole or ground aromatic spices (e.g., cinnamon, cloves, nutmeg)
- essential oils (e.g., rose or other flower scents)
- dried flowers, ribbon, lace scraps and other attractive decorations
- tempera paints and brushes
- wide-tip felt markers
- food coloring

Dough Recipe #1

Ingredients

2 cups baking soda
1 cup cornstarch
1 1/4 cups cold water

Method

Mix baking soda and cornstarch in a saucepan. Stir in water. Cook over medium heat, stirring constantly, until mixture is the consistency of mashed potatoes. Cool on a plate covered with a damp cloth. When dough is cool enough to handle, it may be rolled or shaped as desired. Air dry objects at room temperature for 2 days. Smaller objects can be dried in a preheated 350-degree oven for 10 to 15 minutes. Once dry, objects can be painted or decorated, as desired. After decorating, the finish may be preserved by spraying, brushing, or dipping with varnish or shellac or liquid plastic. To color the dough, add a few drops of liquid food coloring to the water before mixing. Lightly kneading in a small amount of dye powder to the finished dough gives a marbleized effect.

The dough keeps well in a tightly sealed plastic bag in the refrigerator. Bring to room temperature before using.

Dough Recipe #2 (to be hand-shaped and baked)

Ingredients

1 cup flour
1/2 cup table salt
1/2 cup cornstarch
1/2 cup water
1 teaspoon glycerin (available in drugstores)

Method

Sift dry ingredients together. Mix glycerin and water very thoroughly. Slowly stir into sifted dry ingredients and mix thoroughly. Add water as necessary to get a dough that will hold together but not be sticky. Knead for approximately 10 minutes, until smooth and elastic. Dough will keep, well covered in plastic bags, for 1 to 2 months in the refrigerator. Bring to room temperature before shaping. When working with the dough, use only small amounts at a time, as it dries very quickly. Shape dough as desired, using glue diluted with equal parts of water, to fasten ends and pieces together. Bake on foil-covered cookie sheet for 30 minutes to 1 hour, depending on the size of the item. It should be firm and dry but not overly brown. Cool. Brush with glue diluted with equal parts of water and decorate or sprinkle with spices as desired.

Suggested Dough Art Projects

- Roll dough 1/4" thick and cut with cookie cutters or other shapes to make Christmas ornaments, mobiles, name plaques, or signs.
- Ornaments: Punch a hole with a skewer or toothpick when dough is still soft. A paper clip can be inserted as a hanger. Allow to air dry on a flat surface for 1 or 2 days, depending on room humidity. Paint with tempera paint and decorate with glitter, dried flowers, bric-a-brac, or beads. For a mobile,

cut out several bird shapes and let dry; paint as desired (e.g., all red for cardinals). Glue on a black bead for an eye and some craft feathers. Hang individually or in groups as a mobile.

- Nameplates (for residents' doors or community rooms such as the kitchen): Cut letters from rolled dough using a stencil and a very sharp knife. This should be done by a leader or a volunteer. Alternately, roll out ³/₈" to ¹/₂" thick ropes from recipe #2 dough. Shape into letters on baking sheet and bake. Letters can be painted. Glue with epoxy onto a shingle or piece of scrap wood. Decorate with mementos of personal significance (e.g., a small fiddle for a violin player or dried flowers for a gardener. Such items can often be found in craft stores). Spray (outdoors or in a well-ventilated room) with varnish. Insert fastener for hanging.

- Wreaths: Roll dough from recipe #2 into ropes. Make 3 pieces equal in length, fasten end, and braid. Fasten ends with diluted glue to form a circle. Bake. Brush with diluted glue and decorate as desired. Two pieces of dough may be used and the length twisted instead of braided. These wreaths may be any size desired—6" lengths for individual mini-wreaths to 18" lengths for large door wreaths. Twisting shorter lengths is easier to manage. For scented wreaths, add essential oils with the liquid ingredients or powdered spices with the dry. The scent can be renewed by adding a drop of oil to the finished wreath.

- Napkin Rings: Roll dough from recipe #1 ¹/₄" to ³/₈" thick. Cut in 1¹/₂" wide strips, using a sharp knife. Cut in lengths that will fit around a cardboard roll (plus ¹/₂" overlap) from wrapping paper, waxed paper, etc. Cover the roll with foil. Place strips around roll, sealing overlap with diluted glue. Leave a 1" space between rings. Arrange joins all on one side of the roll. Thread a sturdy string through the roll and tie ends to form a long loop. Hang by the loop so that the joins are on the top of the roll and no dough touches walls or other surfaces. Leave until firm and dry. Slide off foil. Paint or decorate as desired.

- Pencil holders or desk dishes: Shape dough around cans or boxes. Smooth with moistened hands. Let dry, decorate, and paint as desired. Shapes cut from dough recipe #1 may also be stuck on with diluted glue.

These are just a few suggestions for this inexpensive and versatile material. Use your imagination.

EYE OF GOD

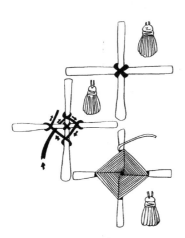

Eye of God is a simple, but colorful handicraft using a repetitive motion.

Materials

- yarn of various colors and textures (scraps are fine, but they should be several yards long)
- 8" lengths of ¹/₄" dowel; sturdy, straight, tree branches; or ¹/₂" wide smooth wood strips

Method

1. Mark the midpoint of each wood piece and lash the pieces together at midpoint to form a cross.
2. Fasten the center color of yarn and begin winding, as illustrated.
3. Change colors, as desired, fastening securely on the back, and continue winding until ¹/₂" to ³/₄" of wood remains.
4. Fasten the yarn end securely.
5. Add tassels to 3 of the wooden ends, if desired.
6. Tie sturdy cord or decorative ribbon or braid for hanging.

variations

- Use longer pieces of wood to make a very large wall hanging.
- Make as a group project, with individuals each winding a section.
- Make smaller "eyes," using, for example, popsicle sticks as a frame, and hang as a mobile. *Note:* these will be too small for many to maneuver.

FABRIC PROJECTS

Many participants will have spent a great deal of time in previous years sewing—making new clothes, "making over" clothing, and mending. Although these more complex skills are probably beyond individuals with moderate and advanced ADRD, there is still great pleasure to be found in the colors and textures of fabric. These are some simple projects that provide an opportunity to re-experience these pleasures. Remnants are easily collected from staff and family members or donated from textile and drapery stores.

Butterflies

Materials

- remnants of colorful fabric, cut with pinking shears into 3", 4", 5", or 6" squares.
- 10" pipe cleaners in various colors
- magnets (refrigerator magnet size)
- glue

Method

1. Crinkle fabric square in the middle to form two wings.
2. Select a smaller square of the same material or a complimentary fabric and crinkle in the middle to form the lower wings.
3. Select pipe cleaner and bend one end around the two wings to form the butterfly body.
4. Shape upper part of the same pipe cleaner to form the butterfly antennae.
5. Repeat steps 3 and 4 with a second pipe cleaner.
6. For use as a magnet, glue magnet onto the back of the butterfly body. Use to decorate walls, windows, doorways.

Fringed Napkins or Place Mats

This is a safe, repetitive, self-directed activity.

Materials

- fabric—washable, open-weave fabric that can be frayed easily (drapery remnants are excellent)
- for napkins, square pieces of fabric at least 8" or 10"
- for place mats, rectangular pieces of fabric approximately 12" x 16"
- matching thread
- sewing machine

Method

1. Zigzag around the fabric piece, 3/4" from all outer edges. Repeat at least twice more, stitching over previous stitching, to form a sturdy mat of stitches to prevent fraying beyond this point.
2. Pull the lengthwise strands of the fabric out as far as the stitching, forming a fringe border.
3. Press the completed project.

Pillows

The completed project can provide reassuring, adult-appropriate, tactile stimulation for those with ADRD, as well as being useful in supporting a good seating position.

Materials

- colorful, soft-textured fabric remnants (many sizes are useful; even a small pillow can tuck in beside a hip or bring pleasure when laid underneath frail hands.)
- material for stuffing (cut up, discarded panty hose, commercial cotton, or fiberfill stuffing) *Note:* Foam chips are frequently used in stuffing small pillows, but they are not suitable for this project because they are difficult to handle and hard to clean up, as static electricity causes them to cling to everything.
- matching thread
- sewing machine

Method

1. Cut two fabric pieces of the same size. Use of contrasting textures and colors for the front and the back will increase stimulation. Providing the participant with manageable choice in the selection of the fabric will increase his or her interest and involvement. Depending on the volunteer assistance available for sewing, even greater

stimulation is provided by a patchwork design of various colors and textures.

2. Pin right sides together and machine-stitch along the one narrow side and the two long edges of the pillow.

3. Turn right side out. *Note:* these steps must be completed by staff or a volunteer. This is a good project for involving local community groups (e.g., 4-H clubs, scouts, or church groups).

4. Assist the participant to stuff the pillow.

5. Fold in $1/2$" on open end of pillow. Pin and stitch closed.

Quilt Collage

Materials

- colorful fabric remnants, cut in 2" squares
- pieces of ticketboard, Bristol board, or construction paper ($8^1/2$" × 11")

- wide tipped black felt pen
- glue
- 6" × 6" firm cardboard or plastic square

Method

1. Center 6" square on mounting paper and trace around it with the marker (using hand-over-hand guidance as necessary).

2. Assist participant to select 9 squares of fabric, arranging them in rows of 3 x 3 on the large square. Encourage associations with favorite colors, textures, quilts, etc.

3. Glue pieces in place.

4. Assist to sign the person's name and possibly write down associated reflections.

5. This project may be turned into a greeting card, a picture, or a place mat. For place mats, mount on ticket board and cover with clear self-adhesive shelf paper or have plasticized.

GREETING CARDS

Making greeting cards provides an opportunity not only for creativity and self expression, but for orientation, reminiscence, and facilitation of the expression of thoughts and feelings. Every effort must be made, however, to ensure that the activity is adult and that the end product is pleasing. A wide variety of materials may be used. These are but a few suggestions.

Materials

- good-quality bond or art paper
- glue

- good-quality pictures from calendars, magazines, used greeting cards
- colored paper (construction paper, colored bond, ticketboard) (Scraps of good-quality colored paper are often available free or for little charge from printing companies.)
- cardboard, Bristol board, or thin plastic for making stencils
- attractive materials for decorating (e.g., paper doilies, scraps of ribbon and lace, sequins, glitter, colored foil paper)
- tempera paints
- black and colored felt-tip markers

Method

1. Introduce the theme of the card (e.g., Valentine's Day, birthday, Christmas).

2. Help the person to select whom he or she wishes to make the card for. Throughout the activity, keep reconnecting the participant with the person and the theme.

3. Fold the bond or art paper to the appropriate size for a card.

4. Make the outside cover. Some suggestions:

   —Make a simple stencil of an appropriate design (e.g., a heart for Valentine's Day or a bell for Christmas) that is at least $1^1/2$" smaller than the card. Fold the paper in half, then in quarters. One folded edge is the top, the other the spine. Trace the stencil design onto the card cover. Cut out. Glue an appropriate picture, a colorful piece of fabric, attractive wrapping paper, or colored foil or paper doily on the inside of the cover.

—Outline a related design (e.g., a star for Christmas) or make an abstract design with glue on a heavy paper card cover. Sprinkle with salt that has been tinted with food coloring; shake off excess salt. If essential oils are mixed with the salt (e.g., rose scent for the outline of a flower), the card will also be scented. To tint the salt, mix in a drop of food coloring and let stand to air dry, or quickly dry in the oven or microwave.

—Decorate card cover with sponges dipped in various colors of tempera paint to make an abstract design, or fill in a stencil design.

—Potato prints: Draw a simple design into the cut side of a potato. Carve around the design with a sharp knife to leave a design that stands out from the surface by $1/4$" to $1/2$". Dip the potato stamp into tempera paint and press firmly onto the card cover.

5. Assist to write a thought or sentiment of the person's choosing or copy a familiar verse in black felt pen.

6. Assist the person to write the receiver's name and sign their own name, using a regular pen.

"LEATHER" VASES OR JUGS

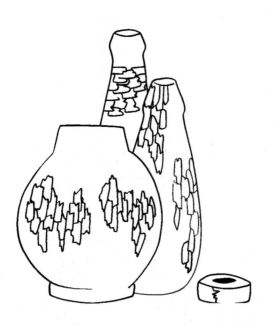

This is a simple, repetitive activity with a pleasing end product.

Materials

- clean jars or bottles with an interesting shape (e.g., salad dressing jars, wine bottles)
- $1/2$" masking tape
- wood stain or shoe polish
- shellac

Method

1. Stick 1" to 2" pieces of masking tape in overlapping layers in a random design on the outside of the bottle until the bottle is completely covered. Tear off pieces of tape and use hand-over-hand guidance, as necessary, to get the activity going. The bottle should be completely covered and 2 or 3 layers deep overall.

2. Stain the tape with wood stain applied with a brush, or rub with a shade of brown shoe polish. Allow to dry thoroughly.

3. Finish with 3 or 4 coats of shellac, allowing to dry between coats.

LIQUID EMBROIDERY

Embroidery is a handicraft familiar to many in the older generation. Those with ADRD who are unable to perform the intricate steps of stitched embroidery can still turn out beautiful products with liquid embroidery. It is also an age-appropriate form of coloring.

Materials:

- liquid embroidery paints
- hoops for liquid embroidery (substitute: cookie tin lid covered with blotting paper and wide, large elastic to secure the fabric over the work surface)
- good-quality polyester/cotton fabric
- simple bold stencils or embroidery transfers in familiar designs

Suggested Projects

- pillowcases
- place mats
- dresser scarves
- fabric nameplates for residents' doors
- tablecloths or runners

Method

1. Iron on embroidery transfer, or trace stencil design onto fabric. Make a special stencil with plastic (from ice cream bucket lids) as necessary.
2. Stretch fabric tightly and smoothly over working surface. Secure with hoop or elastic.
3. Use liquid embroidery paints to fill in any small details that participants might find difficult.
4. Assist, as necessary, to fill in remaining design with liquid embroidery pens.
5. Press fabric and mount as appropriate.

MACRAMÉ PLANT HANGER

Complicated macramé patterns are beyond most persons, even those in the middle stages of ADRD. However, a simple plant hanger involving only one type of knot is a good repetitive activity. Working with jute to tie knots may be more appealing to male participants than some other handicraft activities.

Materials

- jute or cord
- 1" or 1¹/₂" metal ring (from craft stores)
- packing or masking tape
- attractive wooden beads with large holes (optional)
- heavy rubber bands

Method

1. Cut 4 cords 2¹/₂ yards long to use as "filler cords."
2. Fold in half and fasten to ring, using lark's-head knot.

3. Cut 4 cords 6 yards long.
4. Fold in half and fasten to ring with lark's head knot on the outside of the already attached filler cords, making 4 groups of 4 cords each.
5. Roll the outside cords into a ball, leaving about 1 foot of unwound cord, and fasten it with elastic.
6. If the person will work standing, fasten the ring to a secure wall hook that is about waist height. Fasten all but 1 group of 4 out of the way.
7. If the person will work seated, securely tape the ring to a sturdy table. Fasten all but 1 group of 4 cords out of the way.
8. Use the two outside cords to work half-knots over the filler cords until only 10" to 12" of unworked cord remains. Unwind cords from the elastic, as needed. Large decorative beads may be slid onto the filler cords at various intervals, if desired.
9. Work 3 remaining groups of cords as directed in steps 6, 7, and 8.
10. Tie loose ends into a large overhand knot, making sure that the 4 worked cords are of even length.
11. Place potted plant on the ring and hang as desired.

NAPKIN RINGS

These are a simple, functional item that can be made as gifts for family members, for a craft sale, or for use in the dining room. Vary the decorations and colors according to the season.

Materials

- cardboard rolls from waxed paper, foil, wrapping paper, etc.
- strips of felt of various colors
- material for decorating according to the season (e.g., red ribbon, sequins, or small Christmas figures at Christmas time) and availability (e.g., pieces of lace, ribbons, rick-rack, attractive buttons, designs cut out of contrasting colored felt)
- glue

Method

1. Cut cardboard rolls into 1¹/₂" or 2" wide rings. A saw-type bread knife or an electric knife works well without crushing the ring.
2. Cut strips of felt the same width and long enough to cover the rings with a ¹/₂" overlap.
3. Select favorite color of felt and apply glue.
4. Place felt on the cardboard ring and let dry overnight.
5. Decorate with ribbon, ornaments, etc., as desired. These can be personalized by forming initials with ribbon or rick-rack.

PICTURE FRAMES (LASHED)

These can be made in any size and the type of wood adapted to suit the picture. They are an excellent way to display some of the collages, picture associations, and pressed-flower pictures suggested.

Materials

- picture for framing
- 4 wood pieces, 2 for the lengthwise strip and 2 for the width strip (Each should be 1 to 1¹/₂" longer than the dimensions of the picture. Some suggested wood types are doweling, moulding, smooth-finished strapping, narrow strips of pine, or (for a rustic look) small tree branches. New wood may be sanded and stained, if desired. Branches make a particularly attractive frame for a pressed-flower or leaf-print picture.
- lashing material such as jute, heavy yarn, butcher cord, or leather laces
- glue
- carpet tacks
- picture wire

Method

Steps 1 through 5 should be done in advance, for most participants.

1. Place picture to be framed on a flat surface.
2. Put lengthwise frame pieces in place, measuring for an even excess at each end.
3. Place width frame pieces evenly over length pieces.
4. Carefully mark position of width pieces on length pieces with pencil, marker, or knife.
5. Carefully position two corner pieces and fasten with lashing material, as illustrated.
6. Lash corner pieces together securely, as illustrated.

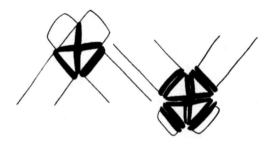

7. Repeat steps 5 and 6 with remaining three corners.
8. Glue or tack picture in place along lengthwise pieces.
9. Mount picture wire on carpet tacks, or use other metal hanging pieces.

PLACE MATS OR DOOR SIGNS

Individualized place mats help to personalize the dining room and can provide important orienting information.

Materials

- ticketboard, Bristol board, or heavy wallpaper pieces cut to place mat size (roughly 12" × 16") (Wallpaper sample books are often available free of charge from decorating stores.)
- attractive greeting card covers, calendar illustrations, or other pictures, varied according to the season
- black or colored wide-tip markers
- colorful fabric strips, cut with pinking shears

- clear self-adhesive shelf paper or access to a plasticizing machine

Method

1. Assist participants, as necessary, to select favorite pictures and arrange on background material.
2. Glue in place and leave to dry overnight.
3. Assist participants, as necessary, to write in name, birth date, month, year, etc. Other personal information such as favorite color, favorite song, etc., can be added as appropriate.
4. Cover both sides with clear self-adhesive shelf paper or have the finished mat plasticized.

RUBBINGS

Designs copied by rubbings can make interesting pictures, greeting cards, or note paper. Use vintage items, which have special meaning for older participants.

Materials

- sturdy parchment-type paper or good-quality bond paper in white and other colors
- soft lead pencils, or pencil crayons (Oil pastels or charcoal may be used but they are more difficult to work with)
- small vintage items with raised designs, such as coins, badges, medals, preserving jars, cast items
- lacquer or fixative spray (for use with charcoal or pastels)
- masking tape

Method

1. Securely fasten paper over design to be copied. Masking tape along the edges works well.
2. Hold pencil or crayons sideways and gently rub back and forth until the design is as clear as desired. Vary colors as desired.
3. Spray pastels or charcoal rubbing with fixative spray.

STENCILING

Fine and complex stencil designs are not suitable. However, large, simple shapes (such as a star, a flower, a heart, a boat, etc.) can help the impaired person produce a lovely design for a card, picture, fabric, or wood project.

Materials

- simple stencils, as described above (Homemade stencils can be made from plastic, e.g., from ice cream bucket lids. Trace design and cut out with sharp scissors.)
- wood, fabric, or paper, as desired
- wide-tipped markers, oil pastels, or tempera paint, as desired (If tempera paints are used, it is best to mix them very thickly or use very little water on block tempera paints, to avoid having the paint run under the stencil. Spray paints can be used but they are expensive, have strong fumes, and are difficult for the participants to manage. They also require less active involvement.)
- masking tape
- pencil

Suggested Projects

- greeting cards
- door nameplate (make from a shingle)
- wooden strawberry boxes with seasonal designs; use as decorative plant pot holders or fill with dried flowers or evergreens for a table centerpiece
- pictures or wooden plaques (add natural materials such as shells, cones, or stones and glue on a rope frame, as desired)

Method

1. Secure stencil onto background material with masking tape. Make sure it is flat to the surface.
2. Paint or color in design as desired.
3. Alternately, the stencil may be used simply as a pattern to trace the design, which is then colored in. If the design is cut out of a piece of paper, a contrasting color or a picture may be mounted behind to make an attractive greeting card.

WOODWORKING

Although moderately and severely impaired persons would not be able to use tools, they can derive great satisfaction from sanding and finishing simple wooden projects that are already cut out. These are good, repetitive, failure-free activities.

Materials

- pieces for small wooden projects such as building blocks (suggest as a gift for grandchildren or the local nursery school), candleholder, cribbage board, cutting boards of various shapes, napkin holder, trivet, or wooden puzzle pieces (Pine is easy to sand and finish.)
- medium and coarse sandpaper
- vegetable oil or commercial finishing wax
- rags
- varnish or shellac and brushes, if this finish is desired

- glue, as necessary to assemble projects, such as the trivet

Method

1. Sand wood with medium sandpaper, if it is rough. Otherwise sand until smooth with fine sandpaper. Sanding is an excellent repetitive activity because it rarely goes wrong. It is also sensory-rich and will facilitate reminiscence for those who have worked with wood. A clamp can be used to hold the wood in place.
2. Wipe sawdust off with a damp rag and let dry.
3. Rub in vegetable oil (nontoxic) or finishing oil or wax (may be toxic) with rags. Several coats and much rubbing are necessary for a good finish. This is also an excellent simple, satisfying, repetitive activity.

CONE WREATHS

Elaborate cone wreaths, with many layers of wired-on cones, are magnificent but beyond the skill of persons with ADRD. However, lovely wreaths can be made without such detailed methods. Depending on the size, the wreaths may be hung on the wall or used as a table decoration.

Materials
- dry, open pine cones
- dried nuts, rose hip berries, small cones, and other items, such as ribbon, to be used as decoration
- bondfast glue
- wire wreath frame (available from florists or hobby supply stores) or a ring of heavy cardboard or plywood

Method
1. If using wire frames, insert cones into the frame, facing alternate directions (stem and tip alternating).

2. For a cardboard or plywood base, glue on cones, facing in alternate directions and placed close together. Allow to dry thoroughly before gluing on other layers or decorations. For many participants the use of glue is too complicated. The whole form may be spread with glue and the cones placed, with guidance as needed. If this is too difficult, have them place the cones, which can be glued on later.

3. Glue on a second and third layer of cones, placing them close together.

4. Decorate by gluing on nuts, dried flowers, or small cones.

5. Spray with varnish.

6. Tie on a bright bow, if desired.

7. If using plywood circles, decorate edges by gluing on ribbon. Small wooden circles with a hole for a candle can be decorated as candleholders.

199

DISH GARDENS

Dish gardens make very attractive table centerpieces and provide an excellent opportunity for creativity. They also make good gifts. They are easier to make than a terrarium, since the container is a flat, open dish.

Materials:

- potting soil mix (two parts pasteurized soil, one part peat moss, one part perlite, and one part sand)
- small, rooted, slow-growing plants such as angel's tears, baby's tears, dwarf creeping fig, dwarf or miniature ivies or peperomia, nerve plant, shamrock, strawberry begonia
- decorative dish, bowl, or clay plant saucer 2" to 4" deep and 8" or more in diameter

- decorative ceramic figures, interesting stones or shells, small pieces of driftwood, or weathered tree branches
- small stones or aquarium gravel
- pieces of charcoal (from an aquarium supply store or the fireplace)
- fiberglass screening
- scissors, trowel, water

Method

1. Place $1/2$" to $3/4$" of gravel in the bottom of the container.
2. Sprinkle with 2 tablespoons of charcoal bits. The charcoal keeps any accumulated water from smelling musty.
3. Cover gravel and charcoal with a piece of fiberglass screening, cut to fit.
4. Add dampened potting mix to come to within $1/2$" of the top of the dish.
5. Arrange plants and other decorative materials to make a miniature landscape. Firm in plants once a pleasing arrangement has been discovered. A flat, open shell can be used as an attractive "pond." It looks lovely with a small fresh flower floating in it.
6. Place in bright, indirect light and check frequently for moisture, as these gardens dry out easily.

DRIED FLOWERS

Many types of flowers and weeds can be dried very simply and make lovely year-round bouquets. The simplest method is air drying. Pick flowers when they are dry, in order to avoid mold. Blooms should be just opening for best results. Remove the leaves from the stems. Fasten the flowers with an elastic band or a piece of nylon stocking and hang upside down in a warm, dark place with good air circulation. Flowers will be dry in two to three weeks.

Some flowers that dry well this way are annuals grown for drying (such as statice and strawflowers), Chinese lantern (seed pods), delphinium, hydrangea, larkspur, ornamental grasses, roses (tight buds), and silver dollars (seed pods). Many weeds found by the roadside are also attractive when dried in this way. Some suggestions are curly dock (collect the seed heads in the green stage), fern fronds, goldenrod (pick before fully mature), Queen Anne's lace, and yarrow.

Other wild plant materials simply require cutting and standing in a box or some other method of storage. Some suggestions are alder branches with cones, bittersweet vine, cattails (collect when firm, about two months before fall freeze), milkweed pods, pussy willows, rose hips on branches, sea heather, and teasel.

Suggested Uses

Bottled Flower Gardens

Select an attractive bottle (juice, salad dressing, or other type) that has an opening wide enough to permit insertion of individual strawflowers, bits of sea heather, or other dried flowers. Add a tablespoon of potpourri mix to the bottom of the jar. Add dried flowers in a random fashion, poking with a chopstick or skewer to place as desired. Cover the top with a circle of floral fabric or lace. Tie in place with a piece of ribbon, lace, or yarn. These make attractive table decorations and can also serve as an air freshener.

Bouquets

Select an attractive or unusual container (e.g., a basket, a crock, a mug with missing handles, a can with a dough art creation around it, an attractive shell). Add a piece of styrofoam or florists' oasis, cut to fit the container. Arrange flowers according to height. Spray with hair spray to make dust removal easier.

Driftwood Planter

Select an interesting piece of driftwood that will sit flat. Arrange flowers in small blocks of oasis or styrofoam, covering the block completely with flowers. Glue or wire the minibouquets in place on the driftwood. Sea urchins or other shells fastened onto the driftwood also make attractive containers.

Tussie Mussies

Gather together a nosegay, a small bouquet of flowers. Fastern together with elastic. Make a background frill of a paper doily or real lace. Wind the stems with ribbon or lace. Use to decorate a bed, a side table, or a bureau.

Wreaths

Select flowers and other plant materials with approximately 2" long stems. Push into place on a premade grapevine, straw, or other type of wreath.

FORCING BULBS

Fall bulbs such as crocus, daffodil, tulip, and hyacinth can all be forced for winter blooms. After indoor blooming, keep the plants watered until the leaves die. Plant outside when the ground thaws. These bulbs will take two or three years to recover from being forced, but if properly fertilized, will yield beautiful blooms outdoors for many years.

Materials

- firm, fleshy, crocus, daffodil, tulip, or hyacinth bulbs
- standard potting mix
- pots

Method

1. Select appropriate pot size. For example, one hyacinth will require a 4" pot, a collection of three hyacinths or five daffodils or tulips will require a 6" pot.
2. Fill pot two-thirds full with dampened potting soil.
3. Push bulbs into the soil.
4. Cover bulbs with soil to 1" below the pot rim.
5. Put pots in a pan or sink and add water to come to the rim of the pot. Leave for one hour.
6. Remove pots and let drain a few minutes.
7. Store pots in a cool, dark place, where the temperature is just above freezing (40 to 45 degrees F). Some suggestions for storage are a basement root cellar; an attic crawl space; outdoors, well banked with leaves; and a refrigerator.
8. Leave the bulbs in this cool location until the roots protrude from the pot hole and the shoots are 1" to 1 1/2" long. Crocus requires about 4 weeks, tulips about 6 weeks, hyacinths about 8 weeks, and daffodils and narcissus about 12 weeks.
9. Bring the pots indoors to a cool place (50 to 60 degrees F) with indirect light. Gradually increase the amount of light over the course of a week.
10. Move to a cool location, with bright indirect light and temperatures of approximately 70 degrees F. Fertilize weekly. Flowers will appear in 4 to 6 weeks.
11. Bulbs such as hyacinth or paperwhite narcissus that have been pretreated can be forced more quickly and do not require soil. Select a glass container twice as deep as the bulb. Fill one-half to three-quarters full with clean gravel. Place the bulbs on top and add more stones, as necessary, to keep the bulbs in position. Store in cool, dark place (50 to 60 degrees F) until the roots are well developed (usually 2 to 4 weeks) and shoots are 2" to 4" high. Adapt to the light, as in the previous method.

LEAF PRINTS

The many attractive patterns of leaves can be used to design writing paper, wrapping paper, or cards. Leaf prints on the sides of wooden strawberry boxes can turn them into attractive containers for dried flowers or Christmas evergreens.

Materials

- fresh leaves with an interesting shape or pattern of veins (for example, maple leaves, ferns, raspberry leaves, ivy leaves, oak leaves, tomato leaves, carrot leaves).
- tempera or poster paint
- wide paintbrushes
- fiberglass screening, elastic, large jar rings, an old picture frame, or a large hoop
- sponges
- colored ink pads, if available
- plain paper folded for cards or hasty notes, or large sheets for wrapping paper

Method

Two types of prints can be made, by using the spatter method or the print method.

Splatter Method.

1. Stretch fiberglass screening over jar ring, picture frame, or other hoop or ring. Faster in place with rubber bands or tacks.
2. Place a leaf or leaves in desired arrangement on the paper.
3. Generously load brushes with tempera paint.
4. Rub brushes over the screen. As the paint falls through the screen it makes a delicate pattern of dots, leaving the outline of the leaves blank. More than one color of paint can be used for a design.
5. Let dry.

Print Method.

1. Dampen a sponge with tempera paint.
2. Press the vein side of a leaf into the sponge, coating it thoroughly with the paint. Alternately, the back of the leaf may be painted with brushes. A stamp pad may also be used, but this ink stains fingers.
3. Carefully place the leaf on the paper, paint side down.
4. Press the top part of the leaf with fingers or a small sponge to transfer the design to the paper.

PRESSED FLOWER CARDS, PICTURES, BOOKMARKS, OR PLACE MATS

The usual method of pressing flowers between pages of a book and then arranging them requires more fine motor coordination than most persons with moderate and severe ADRD could manage. However, this simple method produces very lovely designs.

Materials

- small, flat, flower blooms (such as impatiens, violets, pansies, fibrous begonias, lobelia, salvia florets, sweet peas) and small, attractive leaves (such as small ferns, ivy, daisy leaves, carrot tops)
- good-quality bond or linen paper
- bondfast glue
- heavy books

Method

1. Pick the blooms and leaves when the plants are dry.
2. Provide each participant with a paper, sized according to the project (e.g., bookmark or picture).
3. Offer a selection of fresh flower blooms and leaves and encourage participants to arrange the blooms on the paper as they wish.
4. Set the paper carefully aside and label with the person's name. A volunteer or staff member then secures each bloom or leaf with a drop of glue. Let dry completely.

5. Make sure the flower petals are lying flat, and place the paper under a heavy book for three to five days, until the blooms have dried.
6. Inscribe the picture or card as desired.

7. For place mats, arrange the blooms on ticketboard. After drying and pressing the blooms, cover the ticketboard with clear self-adhesive shelf paper or have it plasticized.

MIMOSA (SENSITIVE PLANT)

The mimosa is listed as a separate project plant because of its unusual properties. The feathery, fernlike leaves fold up gently when lightly touched. After a few minutes, they return to normal. This immediate response from a plant creates great interest and sensory stimulation. If not available in plant form, they can be grown from seed. Seed in moist potting soil, covering seeds with soil. Cover with a newspaper, or place in a dark closet for a few days, to increase germination. Seeds are available from most mail-order seed houses.

ORANGE POMANDER BALLS

Orange pomander balls are an easily made, old-fashioned air freshener. The activity provides wonderful sensory stimulation.

Materials

- fresh oranges
- whole cloves
- sharp skewer or ice pick
- lacy, open-weave fabric
- ribbon or rickrack

Method

1. Cut a 10" square of fabric.
2. Poke holes in the orange at ½" to 1" intervals, using the skewer or ice pick. This should be done by a volunteer or a staff member.
3. Push a whole clove into each hole in the orange.
4. Place the orange in the center of the fabric square.
5. Gather up the edges around the orange and tie securely with ribbon or rickrack.
6. Hang to dry in a warm, airy place for 1 to 2 weeks .
7. Hang in a closet or bathroom.

POTPOURRI

Potpourri is a mixture of dried flowers, herbs, and spices. It is used to provide a natural air freshener. Preparation of the ingredients is an excellent, simple activity that provides wonderful sensory stimulation. Orrisroot is available in drugstores and health food stores. It is a fixative to retain the aroma. Already prepared commercial potpourri mix, available in bulk at health food stores, can be used to make the suggested projects.

Basic Potpourri Mix

- 4 cups of dried flowers and/or herbs
- 1 tablespoon of orrisroot powder
- 2 tablespoons of whole spices
- (optional) a few drops of an essential oil mixed in with the orrisroot powder.

Method

Mix ingredients thoroughly and store in an airtight container for six to eight weeks before use. Suggested herbs: mint, lavender, rosemary, thyme, scented geranium, lemon balm, bayberry. Suggested spices: cinnamon (bark), whole cloves, whole allspice, whole coriander seeds. Make combinations of the above according to individual preferences.

Potpourri Mix # 2

- 4 cups of leaves from a scented geranium (dry in a cheesecloth bag or a mesh onion sack hung in a warm, dark, airy space)
- 2 tablespoons of orrisroot powder
- 2 tablespoons of whole coriander seeds
- 2 tablespoon of whole cloves

Method

Mix ingredients thoroughly. Store in an airtight container for 6 to 8 weeks before using.

To make potpourri, place the mix in a commercial potpourri jar or an attractive jar, dish, or glass container. Cover with lace or netted fabric, if desired. Sachets are little sacks of potpourri mix that can be placed in drawers, hung in closets, etc. Potpourri mix can be placed in pressed fabric sacks and the top fastened with a ribbon. For a quick, no-sewing sachet, cut circles of attractive, loosely woven fabric. Place a spoonful of potpourri mix in the center. Gather edges together and tie with a ribbon, lace, or colored yarn. Alternately, place a circle of fabric over a small hoop (available from craft stores). Place a spoonful of potpourri mix in the middle, place another circle of fabric on top, and fasten together with another hoop.

SPROUTS

Growing fresh sprouts for salads or sandwiches is a quick and easy activity. Alfalfa sprouts are the easiest to grow. A sprouted potato planter is a fun intergenerational project.

Materials

- 2 tablespoons of alfalfa seeds (available in health food stores)
- wide-mouthed glass jar (1-quart size)
- fiberglass screening
- rubber band

Method

1. Place seeds in jar and half-fill jar with lukewarm water. Let stand overnight.
2. Cut a square of fiberglass screening and fasten over the top of the jar with elastic.
3. In the morning drain off the liquid. (This can be used to water plants, as it is rich in nutrients.)
4. Fill jar with lukewarm water and slosh around, tipping sideways and draining out the liquid. Repeat two more times.
5. Lay the jar on its side, near the sink, and rinse at least twice a day until the sprouts are edible size, usually four to seven days, depending on room temperature.
6. Place the sprouts in bright, indirect light for a few hours to turn the leaves green.
7. Drain thoroughly and store in the refrigerator.

Sprouted Potato Planter

Select a large, oblong potato. Slice a ½" layer off the top. Use a knife or serrated spoon to hollow out a ½" deep cavity on the cut side, leaving a ¼" rim. Sprinkle the cavity full of cress seeds. Cover lightly with a plastic bag and leave in bright indirect light. Uncover and let grow as the seeds sprout. This can be made into a potato person—with the sprouted cress as hair—by sticking on eyes, nose, and mouth of buttons, bits of felt, or pipe cleaners.

TERRARIUM

A terrarium is a miniature enclosed garden. It requires very little care, once planted, as the moisture keeps recirculating. I once had a terrarium of wandering sailor that grew, untouched, for five years. They are fascinating to watch grow, and always make an interesting conversation piece.

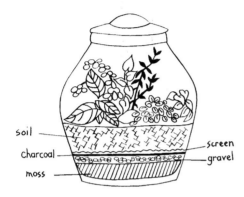

Materials

- potting soil mix: two parts pasteurized soil; one part peat moss; one part perlite; one part sand
- cuttings of plants such as angel's tears, artillery plant, baby's tears, blood leaf, dwarf creeping fig, nerve plant, miniature peperomia, piggyback plant, small spider runners, shamrock, strawberry begonia, swedish ivy, or wandering sailor (Small plants can also be used, but they are much more difficult to manage. Woodland plants such as small ferns; vines such as wintergreen or foxberry; and wildflowers such as violets, spring beauty, or wild orchids also make a lovely terrarium.)
- decorative miniature ceramic figures, stones, or shells
- small stones or aquarium gravel
- bits of charcoal (from an aquarium supply store or the fireplace)
- fiberglass screening
- scissors, trowel, paper plate, long sticks to use as a tool (e.g., pieces of dowel, chopsticks, or the handles of wooden spoons), bottle corks, plant mister, plastic food wrap, sphagnum moss or woodland sheet moss
- wide-mouth glass jars or goldfish bowls (Terrariums can also be made with narrow-mouth glass jars, but this is a much more complicated activity. Gallon jars for pickles, mustard, etc., make excellent, easy-to-work-with terrariums. Restaurants or cafeterias will usually provide them free of charge. For smaller terrariums, use mayonnaise jars or other wide-top jars. If funds are available, decorator storage jars can be purchased for use.)

Method

1. Line the outside of the bottom one-fifth to one-third of the container with sphagnum or sheet moss, green side out. This provides an attractive exterior for the soil area. This step is optional.

2. Place $1/2"$ to $3/4"$ of gravel in the bottom of the container.

3. Sprinkle 1 or 2 tablespoons of charcoal bits over the gravel. The charcoal keeps any accumulated water from smelling musty.

4. Using the bottom of the jar for a pattern, cut a piece of fiberglass screening to fit the jar. With long sticks, poke screening into place on top of the stones and charcoal. This is to keep the soil from filtering into the gravel.

5. Roll the paper plate to make a funnel, or use a regular funnel with a long neck. Place the funnel in the top of the jar. Using the trowel, add soil to the top of the moss container or to fill one-fifth to one-third of the container. Remove funnel and add water, as necessary, to dampen the soil.

6. Use the end of the stick (depending on size) or a cork placed on the end of a small dowel or chopstick to make holes in the potting soil mix for the cuttings. Do not put the cuttings too close together, as they will grow quickly in this environment. Drop cuttings into the hole and firm soil around them with fingers or the cork, as appropriate.

7. Wipe the sides of the jar with damp tissue on a stick.

8. Mist plants gently.

9. Add decorative shells, stones, or figures as desired.

10. Cover tightly with plastic wrap and set in a bright, warm place, but never in direct sun.

11. If the jar fills up with moisture and condensation, it may be necessary to remove the top for a few minutes every day, until the natural cycle is well established. After a couple of weeks the terrarium should not require any maintenance, except for trimming dead leaves and perhaps an occasional watering.

VEGETABLE PRINTS

Designs cut into potatoes or other root vegetables make inexpensive stamps for designer wrapping paper, greeting cards, stationery, or pictures, which do not require artistic skill to make.

Materials

- fresh potatoes
- sharp knife
- tempera paint
- brushes
- paper

Method

1. Cut potato in half lengthwise or sideways, depending on the size of the design.
2. Draw or trace the outline of an abstract shape or a simple seasonal design (e.g., a shamrock for Saint Patrick's Day, a heart, a Christmas star or bell) onto the cut surface of the potato. Cookie cutters are a good source of simple designs.
3. Cut the design 1/2" deep into the potato.
4. Carve away a 1/2" deep section of the potato, surrounding the area of the design.
5. Dip the design in tempera paint and stamp onto paper. For more involved creations use several colors of paint and several stamps.

You need only claim the events of your life to make yourself yours. When you truly possess all that you have been and done, which may take some time, you are fierce with reality.

—Florida Scott-Maxwell

Day-to-day living for Mr. Comeau had become a never-ending trial. Where was his lifelong companion of 60 years? Where were his teeth? What day was it? When was dinner? Where is the bathroom? Where is *he*? Tormented by his inability to determine the answers to these questions, he spent his days wandering the corridors inquiring hopelessly, again and again, from each passer-by.

One day, Mr. Comeau came to a reminiscence group on cars. At first he sat quietly, listening to the others describe their first car ride or about walking in to get their first driving license. Mr. Comeau, too, responded with some brief comments. He had owned a Chevrolet. He said he still drove a blue Ford. However, when he looked at the picture in his booklet of a British Touring Car, he really found some answers. After studying a rather indistinct photocopy of the car, he told us all, in animated detail, why it had never been a success. The door, he said, opened out from the center post and it simply had never been accepted in North America. From there, he went on to describe driving vacations he had taken and how he had done his own car repairs. Calmed by the group's affirmation of the value of his previous life experiences, Mr. Comeau sat smiling happily, sharing in the refreshments at the end of the group.

1.0 INTRODUCTION: WHAT IS REMINISCENCE?

What is reminiscence? This deceptively simple question is really a very complex one. The answer depends on the type of reminiscence and the perspective taken by the respondent. Let me begin, then, by stating what I mean by reminiscence, in the context of working with individuals with ADRD. This chapter focuses on what has been called simple or recreational or informative or story-telling reminiscence. It is, quite simply, the recollection of previous life experiences. These previous life experiences are remembered for the pure pleasure of re-experiencing happy or satisfying occasions or to pass information on to others.

By contrast, what is called life-review reminiscence is focused primarily on analyzing, evaluating, and coming to terms with unpleasant or unhappy previous life experiences. Undoubtedly, simple reminiscence frequently has some evaluative characteristics, but the crucial difference is one of emphasis. For example, life-review reminiscence centered on the depression years would focus on an unresolved issue, such as having to drop out of school because of finances. Guided life-review sessions are conducted by a trained therapist, who assists the person to work through his or her lifelong resentments about having dropped out of school, and, with successful life review, come to terms with this disappointment.

Simple reminiscence about the depression would focus on recalling the experiences and circumstances of the time. The individual may have left school to help support the family, but the emphasis in the reminiscence session would be directed toward how people helped each other out and found ways to economize; the session would thereby provide support for the person by affirming the value of the sacrifice he or she made in leaving school.

Further discussion of the types of reminiscence are found in Section 1.4 of this chapter.

1.1 What Is a Reminiscence Group?

A reminiscence group is a structured group activity in which the group leader assists and guides the group members to recall previous life experiences and facilitates the group's affirmation of the value of these experiences. These groups may be strictly verbal, but the addition of multisensory artifacts and props enriches the experience and further facilitates reminiscence.

1.2 Why Groups Focusing on Reminiscence?

People of all ages reminisce about past experiences. However, for the elderly, reminiscence is particularly important. Reminiscence provides an opportunity, as they come to the end of their lives, to look back on their life experiences; to recall, recollect, and to rethink all that they have seen, done, accomplished, and left undone. It provides an opportunity to accomplish what Erikson et al. (1986) described as the final life task of summing up, of coming to terms with life accomplishments.

Butler (1963) was the first clinician to identify reminiscence as a positive, purposeful activity for the elderly. He stated:

> This paper postulates the universal occurrence in older people of an inner experience or mental process of reviewing one's life. I propose that this process helps account for the increased reminiscence in the aged, that it contributes to the occurrence of certain late-life disorders, particularly depression, and that it participates in the evolution of such characteristics as candor, serenity, and wisdom among certain of the aged. (p. 65)

Butler's thoughts on reminiscence among the aged and his recommendations for developing life-review groups revolutionized earlier thinking. Previously, the tendency of older people to reminisce was viewed as negative—an unhealthy dwelling on the past. Despite the fact that it remains unclear whether life-review reminiscence is in fact a universal human process, the valuable contribution to healthy aging made by reminiscence is now widely acknowledged by clinicians and researchers (see Sections 2.0 to 2.5 below).

In the clinical literature one finds recommendations such as the following: "The personal identity of an older person is enhanced when the person is encouraged to discuss the past and describe the experiences that created the unique self." (Maguire 1985, 47). From an elderly woman, there is the affirmation by octogenarian Florida Scott-Maxwell quoted at the beginning of this chapter (cited in Kiernat 1983, 47).

For the frail elderly requiring institutional care, coming together with others in a group to share memories and offer mutual support and affirmation provides an opportunity that may not be otherwise available to them, because of their reduced contact with family and friends. The facilitation of a group leader enables individuals, who most often are strangers to each other, to develop a supportive atmosphere for sharing personal memories and discussing common life experiences. Sharing their life experiences as a group provides an opportunity to develop new friendships. It also provides a rich opportunity for direct-care staff to come to know, and appreciate, the whole life experience of the older resident.

1.3 Why Reminiscence Groups with Individuals with ADRD?

Like all aging persons, individuals with ADRD have a need to sum up, to look back over their life experiences. Those whose disease has progressed to the stage where they are in need of full- or part-time institutional care require the direct assistance of others not only to meet their physical needs, but also to meet emotional needs, such as the need to sum up. Although long-term memory is less affected than short-term memory, these individuals almost always require the assistance of others to elicit these memories. Multisensory cues and artifacts (for example, churning ice cream), organized and presented by a group leader, target the better-preserved function of recognition, as opposed to recall. The sensory associations with particular reminiscence themes (e.g., the smell, feel, and sight of evergreen boughs in association with Christmas) help to trigger long-term memories. Familiarity with individual experiences and accomplishments allows the group leader to use this information to elicit and guide reminiscing. The leader affirms the value of previous life experiences and encourages other group members to do the same.

The individual with ADRD is thus enabled to re-experience not only the event but the emotions associated with a time when he or she was capable and in control.

Lo Gerfo (1980) reminds us that "stimulating informative reminiscence may arouse the younger competent person who slumbers inside the seriously impaired elder" (p. 41). This act alone enhances self-esteem. Devastated as they are by the losses associated with their disease, opportunities for enhancing self-esteem are vital for persons with ADRD. Recalling previous experiences also recalls the associated pleasant feelings and brings further pleasure. Recalling unhappy experiences provides an important opportunity, which may not be readily available, to give expression to sorrow in a supportive environment. The group leader helps the individual identify the positive aspects of these experiences.

To return to the introductory anecdote, Mr. Comeau's recollection of a particular car was triggered by the picture prop. This recollection was encouraged and praised by other members. Mr. Comeau felt better about himself and was encouraged to discuss related experiences. These experiences reminded him of his previous competencies and further enhanced his self-esteem.

1.4 What Is the Theory behind Reminiscence Groups?

As previously stated, Butler (1963) was the first to identify the tendency to reminiscence as a positive—indeed necessary—attribute of the aged. Butler's theory was built on the developmental theories of Erikson (1953). What Butler called life-review reminiscence was necessary to accomplish the primary life task of the aged, to sum up, to resolve the crisis of ego integrity versus despair. In life review, older individuals re-examine and re-evaluate their life experiences. This process enables the elderly person to put successes, failures, and experiences in perspective. Successful life-review reminiscence allows the older person to feel that his or her life has been worthwhile, to resolve feelings about old conflicts and failures, and to attain ego integrity. Butler suggested that some elderly people, depending on their personality, require the assistance of a skilled therapist and/or group support in order to achieve ego integrity. He stated:

> I conceive of the life review as a naturally occurring, universal mental process characterized by the progressive return to consciousness of past experiences, and, particularly, the resurgence of unresolved conflicts; simultaneously, and normally, these revived experiences and conflicts can be surveyed and reintegrated. (Butler 1963, 66)

In life-review reminiscence, the older person actively struggles with the past in order to come to terms with negative and difficult experiences. This process may be associated with negative affect until the crisis has been resolved.

As others began to explore reminiscence and aging, other types of reminiscence were identified. On the basis of the spontaneous reminiscing tape-recorded over the course of two years of 48 men and women living in sheltered housing in London, Coleman (1974) described three categories of reminiscing:

1. simple reminiscing, recalling past experiences
2. informative reminiscing, recalling the past in order to give others important information
3. life-review reminiscing, recalling personal past experiences in order to resolve conflicts and come to terms with negative experiences

McMahon and Rhudick (1967) studied 150 elderly outpatient veterans and also described three types of reminiscence:

1. story-telling reminiscence, for personal pleasure and for history
2. life-review reminiscence
3. defensive reminiscence, which is characterized by a glorification of the past and indicates an unhealthy adjustment to the present

Lo Gerfo (1980) described three categories, which are similar to those of McMahon and Rhudick (1967):

1. informative reminiscence, which focuses on factual recall to provide pleasure
2. evaluative reminiscence (life review)
3. obsessive reminiscence, preoccupation with past events that is not adaptive (this is similar to Butler's unsuccessful life review)

Clements (1982) added the term *recreational reminiscing*, which is reminiscing primarily for fun and pleasure, as opposed to a more specific therapeutic purpose. It appears akin to, if not identical with, simple or informative or story-telling reminiscence.

In summary, various investigators have identified at least three types of reminiscence: story-telling/informative, life-review, and obsessive. Some differentiate between informative and story-telling reminiscence. For the purposes of this book, it seems useful to combine them, following Merriam (1980, 1989), and call the two dimensions together "simple reminiscence."

Unfortunately, clarification of the types of reminiscences being studied has scarcely been attempted in the research literature (Haight 1991; Kovach 1990; Merriam 1980, 1989; Molinari & Reichlin 1984–85; Thornton & Brotchie 1987). Most empirical research has been based on a global, undefined type of reminiscence. This has presented great difficulties in drawing conclusions based on the research, as is discussed in the next section. However, more to the point here, it has also meant a very limited development of the essential theoretical knowledge base of reminiscence.

A study by Merriam (1989) is one of the few attempts to develop this knowledge base further. The transcripts of tape-recorded simple reminiscence sessions, which focused on particular topics, were analyzed according to content and structure. From these 170 pages of notes, Merriam derived consistent categories that describe the structure of simple reminiscence. These categories are:

- *selection:* The person searches his or her "mental files" in order to select a particular experience.
- *immersion:* The person becomes fully involved in recalling a particular experience. Merriam describes this phase as conveying a sense of immediacy and being rich in sensory detail.
- *withdrawal:* The person begins to distance self from the experience, frequently by making comparisons to the present.
- *closure:* The person relinquishes involvement in the memory by summing up the experience, and frequently by describing the wisdom gained from it.

Merriam was struck by the consistency of this pattern. Individuals would follow this structure with one memory, and often begin it all over again as they switched to another. Although much more investigation must be done, Merriam has made an important start at broadening the theoretical knowledge base of simple reminiscence.

Butler's early work (1963) on life-review reminiscence describes it as being particular to the old and as being primarily an intrapersonal experience. It is now widely accepted that people of all ages reminisce and that the quantity of reminiscence may not actually increase with age, but more likely the quality or the focus will change (Greene 1982; Kiernat 1983; Molinari & Reichlin 1984–85). Furthermore, interpersonal aspects of reminiscence, such as the present social context, have been identified as having an important influence on the function and nature of reminiscence (David 1990; Merriam 1980; Molinari & Reichlin 1984–85; Rattenbury & Stones 1989).

1.5 Summary

Although advances have been made in developing the theoretical foundation of reminiscence since the early work of Butler (1963), much remains to be clarified. In addition to life-review reminiscence as described by Butler (1963), for purposes of evaluation, it is now clear that simple reminiscence, for purposes of pleasure and information sharing, is also a viable and important process with the elderly.

There is an impressive array of anecdotal and descriptive literature supporting the effectiveness of reminiscence interventions (e.g., Buechel 1986; Burnside 1988; Coleman 1974; Dietsche 1979; Ellison 1981; Harwood 1989; Havighurst & Glasser 1972; Jones & Clark 1984; Kiernat 1979; Lazarus 1976; Lesser et al. 1981; Lewis 1971; Sable 1984; Sullivan 1982; Weiss 1989). Views such as the following typify this literature:

> In summary, the validating, integrating, guiding and connecting functions of reminiscence combine to facilitate a re-patterning of the older person's life. Through reminiscence, one develops a firm sense of identity and a balanced concept of time. He fulfils his responsibility to guide the younger generation and gains knowledge about the type of relationship he has with his environment. (Sullivan 1982, 43)

Review of descriptive and anecdotal literature is the first step in accumulating evidence for the effectiveness of any intervention. This preliminary literature enthusiastically and emphatically endorses the therapeutic benefits of reminiscence for the elderly. Correlational studies also support the importance of reminiscence for the elderly.

2.0 EMPIRICAL RESEARCH ON REMINISCENCE

The limited, empirical study of reminiscence that has been undertaken presents inconclusive, and sometimes contradictory, findings. This should not be taken to mean that therapeutic reminiscence has been tried and found wanting. In fact, the vast majority of the results indicate the positive effects of reminiscence. In a comprehensive review of 97 published articles on reminiscence, Haight (1991) reported that only 7 did not have positive outcomes. Five of these seven were individual interventions of one hour or less. However, because of the many inconsistencies in the research itself, no definitive conclusion can be reached. Because of a vague definition of the type of reminiscence being measured, widely varying subject populations, and many other differences in study design, reminiscence research does not present a cohesive body of literature. In general, empirical research has not been built on the findings of previous studies. Furthermore, the existing studies have numerous flaws (David 1990; Haight 1991; Kovach 1990; Lo Gerfo 1980; Merriam 1980, 1989; Molinari & Reichlin 1984–5; Rattenbury & Stones 1989). Some of these flaws are as follows:

- absence of objective outcome measures (e.g., Buechel 1986; Dietsche 1979; Jones & Clark 1984; Lazarus 1976; Lesser et al. 1981; Sable 1984)
- lack of control conditions (e.g., Harwood 1989; Kiernat 1979; Parsons 1986);
- outcome measures lacking in sensitivity or reliability or validity (e.g., Goldwasser et al. 1987; Scates et al. 1985–86)

Given the overwhelmingly positive reports from staff and families about reminiscence interventions and the sometimes slight significance of empirical measures with the same subjects, it is suggested that the outcome measures have not been directed at the proper characteristics (Kane & Kane 1987; Kiernat 1979; Kovach 1990). For example, with a physically frail elderly population, changes in socialization would be reasonable outcome measures, but the often-used changes in self-care ability would not. Many studies have relied on interview and/or subject-completed scales of life satisfaction or self-esteem; but objective, behavioral measures are likely to be more sensitive and accurate. Some additional flaws are

- small sample size (e.g., Baines et al. 1987; Perotta & Meacham 1981–82; Rattenbury & Stones 1989)
- short intervention times (This includes virtually all of the studies, as the majority were not more than eight weeks long and some were much shorter. For example, the subjects in the study by Froehlich and Nelson [1986] met for only one session.)
- a lack of attention to defining or identifying the type of reminiscence (e.g., life-review or simple social reminiscence) and a wide variation in characteristics such as age, residency (community or institution), health, cognitive function, and the social setting (e.g., individual or group)

Recent literature reviews and articles on reminiscence (e.g., David 1990; Haight 1991; Kovach 1990; Merriam 1989; Rattenbury & Stones 1989) echo the conclusion of research from a decade earlier that called for more rigorous investigation into the therapeutic effects of reminiscence, specification of the types of reminiscence intervention, characteristics of subjects,

and the circumstances under which reminiscence is most effective (Lo Gerfo 1980; Merriam 1980). There are now, however, a number of well-controlled studies of simple reminiscence interventions with positive results. There is a great need for replication of these studies (Baines et al. 1987; Goldwasser et al 1987; Lappe 1987; Rattenbury & Stones 1989) in order to strengthen the positive findings.

The absence of a conclusive body of empirical literature should not be interpreted as a signal to abandon the therapeutic use of reminiscence. It is a signal that here, as in most other areas of intervention with the elderly, there is a great need for much more research *and* much more careful research. Indeed, it must be emphasized that throughout the existing literature the findings are overwhelmingly positive. Within this positive context, it is the obligation of clinicians to advocate further research and to apply and further develop reminiscence techniques, which indicate so much promise of therapeutic benefit for the elderly.

The existing research on reminiscence is examined, first of all, with reference to the investigation of life-review reminiscence. Next, the whole body of research has been divided according to residence—community or institution—of the subjects. Since the primary focus of this book is on individuals who are resident in an institution, the research from this population is described in some detail in the final section. However, important considerations have emerged from research on reminiscence among the community-dwelling elderly. These are highlighted in the middle section.

2.1 Life-Review Reminiscence

Life-review reminiscence, as described by Butler (1963), has been tested by various research studies. In general, these studies have numerous methodological weaknesses and have not been carefully designed to either match or test Butler's theory. The existing research, which is primarily correlational, provides rather weak evidence that some elderly do engage in life-review reminiscence (Boylin et al. 1976; Coleman 1974; Havighurst & Glasser 1972; Kovach 1990; Molinari & Reichlin 1984–85; Taft & Nehrke 1990). Except for the study by Coleman (1974), these studies are all based on correlations using self-completed surveys of frequency and type of reminiscence and are therefore subject to bias. There is, in addition, the usual uncertainty of relating cause and effect in correlational studies. These correlational studies provide tentative evidence that life-review reminiscence is associated with healthy aging. High frequency of reminiscence, as reported in the self-completed surveys, was associated with high ego integrity (Boylin et al. 1976), support for ego integrity in times of stress (Lewis 1971; Lieberman & Falk 1971), absence of depression (McMahon & Rhudick 1967), and increased life satisfaction (Havighurst & Glasser 1972). Coleman (1974) found that reminiscence was adaptive for those who are dissatisfied with their past.

The results of the few studies of applied life-review reminiscence are also inconclusive. The strongest support comes from the study by Fry (1983). This researcher implemented structured and unstructured life-review reminiscence with 162 depressed, community-dwelling, elderly individuals in eight major North American cities. Subjects were directed to reminisce about negative life events. Both treatment groups improved in ego-strength measures and decreased in depression measures, compared with the no-treatment control. Those trained in structured reminiscence improved more than those trained in unstructured reminiscence. Two other studies, using group life-review interventions with small groups of community-dwelling elderly, found no significant treatment effect as measured by improved self-esteem, decreased depression (Perrotta & Meacham 1981–82), or life satisfaction and anxiety (Scates et al. 1985–86). However, these studies were of short duration (five sessions and six sessions, respectively), had small sample sizes, were conducted by personnel who were unfamiliar with their subjects' histories, and (perhaps most important of all) were conducted with community-dwelling elderly individuals whose scores on the measured scales were already well within the normal range. There was, in fact, little room for improvement.

In contrast, a one-session intervention study comparing the effective meaning of a discussion and activity-based life-review intervention, but without a control group, found that participants saw life review as good, powerful, and active (Froehlich & Nelson 1986). This would support the suggestion that previous studies of life-review reminiscence have not selected appropriate outcome measures for the community-dwelling elderly.

Applied studies of life-review reminiscence with the institutionalized elderly were not located. A correlational study reported that those who engaged in frequent life-review type reminiscence had the strongest ego integrity (Taft & Nehrke 1990).

In summary, there is little empirical support for the effectiveness of life review reminiscence with the community-dwelling elderly, and none for the institutionalized elderly, but this is primarily attributable to the methodological and design errors of the research. The theory itself has scarcely been tested, nor the theoretical base developed. Butler's contention (1963) that life-review reminiscence is a naturally occurring, universal mental process has been neither proven nor disproven.

There has been no study of life-review reminiscence with the institutionalized elderly. This *may* be coincidental; however, it is more likely that, as Molinari and Reichlin (1984–85) suggest, life-review reminiscence is not an appropriate therapeutic tool with the institutionalized elderly, who have much more limited options for resolving old conflicts. Furthermore, for individuals with ADRD, the focus on verbalization, reasoning, and problem solving makes life-review reminiscence difficult. This, combined with the necessity for group leaders of life-review reminiscence sessions to be highly skilled professionals, makes simple reminiscence a much more appropriate intervention for persons with ADRD. Discussion of the empirical evidence of its effectiveness is found in a later section.

2.2   Simple Reminiscence Research with the Community-Dwelling Elderly

On reviewing the reminiscence research with the community-dwelling elderly as subjects, several considerations that have a bearing on reminiscence work with the institutionalized elderly emerge.

1. Mood can be improved and positive moods maintained through recalling and reminiscing about pleasant previous experiences (Brennan & Steinberg 1983–84; Coleman 1974; Fallot 1980; Fry 1983; Haight 1988; Havighurst & Glasser 1972; Ingersoll & Silverman 1978; McMahon & Rhudick 1967). These findings with the community-dwelling elderly are particularly interesting, since they were less likely than the institutionalized elderly to have a depressed mood, and hence there is less room for measurable change. A small study of 21 community-dwelling elderly by Perrotta and Meacham (1981–82), did not find a significant reminiscence treatment effect, as measured by the Zung depression scale. However, a much larger study of 162 community-dwelling elderly, who were identified as depressed by the Beck depression inventory, did show significant improvement with structured one-to-one reminiscence therapy (Fry 1983). The intervention in both studies consisted of five one-to-one structured reminiscence treatment sessions. However, the interventions used by Fry (1983) focused on reviewing negative life events and lasted 90 minutes, as opposed to 45 minutes in the study by Perrotta and Meacham (1981–82).

This brief comparison of two reminiscence studies with conflicting results illustrates the difficulty in drawing conclusions from empirical work that is so widely varied in basics such as subjects and intervention methodology. However, the bulk of the research on reminiscence and depression indicates that structured reminiscence can have a positive effect on mood. Perrotta and Meacham (1981) themselves pointed out the limitations of their study in relation to the small sample size, the relatively "normal" pretest scores of the subjects, the global nature of the reminiscence intervention, and the absence of a social aspect to the reminiscence intervention.

2. Self-esteem and life satisfaction can be supported and improved by reminiscence interventions (Fallot 1980; Haight 1988; Havighurst & Glaser 1972; Hughston & Merriam 1982; Ingersoll & Silverman 1978; Lappe 1987; Lewis 1971; Merriam & Cross 1982; Olivera 1977). These studies suggest that recollecting previous life experiences improves satisfaction with the past and that present self-esteem is enhanced.

3. Reminiscing about previous positive experiences is a pleasant activity that is associated with a positive mood (Brennan & Steinberg 1983–84; Deitsche 1979; Havighurst & Glasser 1972; Hyland & Ackerman 1988; Kovach 1990; Olivera 1977).

4. Providing a structure or framework for reminiscence enhances the outcome (Fry 1983; Jones & Clark 1984; Merriam 1989; Weiss 1989). Fry (1983) directly studied the effects of structure with 162 depressed, community-dwelling elderly. Both structured and unstructured reminiscence session subjects demonstrated significant gains in ego strength and decreased depression compared with a no-treatment control group. Those subjects trained in structured reminiscence made significantly greater improvements than did subjects trained in unstructured reminiscence. These effects persisted during a 15-week follow-up period.

5. Reminiscence experiences are vivid and rich with sensory detail, and have the effect of making the previous experience seem immediate once again (Hyland & Ackerman 1988; Kovach 1990; Merriam 1989; Molinari & Reichlin 1984–85; Revere & Tobin 1980–81). Merriam (1989) describes this as follows: "The memory is recalled in such detail that the reader or listener feels transported to the scene" (p. 763).

6. The social context of reminiscence is an important variable in terms of both the particular social circumstances of the individual and the social setting of the reminiscence intervention. Stressful or uncertain social circumstances tend to increase the amount of time spent reminiscing. For example, Lieberman and Falk (1971) found that older persons on a waiting list for a nursing home reminisced more than did those living in a stable community situation or those already in a nursing home. Lewis (1971) found that, when individuals who were classified as "high reminiscers" were presented

with an experimental social threat, there was a significant increase in the similarities between present and past self-concept, as compared with "low reminiscers."

Others report differences in the amount and nature of reminiscence, depending on place of residence or sex. Molinari and Reichlin (1984–85), in their review of the life-review reminiscence literature, suggest that life review may be positive for the community-dwelling elderly. However, it may be associated with a negative effect for the elderly living in institutions, as they have less opportunity to resolve old conflicts. Hughston and Merriam (1982) found that men had a less positive attitude toward reminiscence than did women. In contrast, David (1990) found that the evaluation of memories and high peer contact was associated with positive life adjustment for widowed men, but the opposite was true for widowed women. For widowed women, connecting to the present and self-focus were associated with high self-esteem. The sample size of both these studies is rather small, but the findings do indicate the importance of social factors and the pressing need for more study of how they influence reminiscence.

The social situation surrounding the particular reminiscence experience is also important. Habegger and Blieszner (1990), in a study of 50 community-dwelling elderly, found that having opportunities to reminisce was significantly associated with oral and silent reminiscence. In addition, they found that those who reminisced during earlier life stages engaged in more reminiscence as they aged.

The majority of the studies of the community-dwelling elderly are based on one-to-one interviews. The outcome may be very different for reminiscence that takes place in a group setting. Indeed, the literature strongly suggests that a group setting greatly enhances the positive effects of reminiscence, as the group provides mutual support and decreases the feelings of isolation (Buechel 1986; Burnside 1988; Butler 1963; Dietsche 1979; Ellison 1981; Froehlich & Nelson 1986; Kibbee & Lackey 1982; Kiernat 1979; Lazarus 1976; Perrotta & Meacham 1981–82; Sable 1984; Scates et al. 1985–86; Schafer et al. 1986; Zgola & Coulter 1988). It is certainly highly likely that the relative paucity of group reminiscence interventions with the community-dwelling elderly accounts, at least in part, for the inconclusive results of some of this research.

In summary, although the results of the empirical studies of reminiscence with the community-dwelling elderly are inconclusive, the literature does provide much evidence of positive effects and indications of how to proceed with empirical study and clinical application.

2.3 Empirical Reminiscence Research with the Institutionalized Elderly

As with reminiscence research with the community-dwelling elderly, there is very little empirical research. A brief outline of the existing research is given in Table 6-1.

2.4 Discussion

Although variations in methods and measures and flaws in research design prevent drawing absolute conclusions, the 11 studies in Table 6-1 all report positive findings about the effectiveness of reminiscence interventions with the institutionalized elderly. This research endorses the need both for more research and for developing clinical expertise in reminiscence interventions. Examination of the research in more detail provides some useful information for designing reminiscence interventions.

Given the focus of this book, studies with the cognitively impaired elderly are of particular interest. The studies by Baines et al. (1987), Goldwasser et al. (1987), Holland (1987), Kiernat (1979), and Weiss and Thurn (1987) were conducted with subjects who were described as confused, disoriented, or cognitively impaired. These five studies lend very encouraging support to the effectiveness of reminiscence with this population. The studies by Baines et al. (1987) and Goldwasser et al. (1987) are particularly significant, as these were careful research projects employing control groups and validated outcome measures.

Goldwasser et al. (1987) reported that mildly to moderately demented individuals were significantly less depressed after involvement in ten structured reminiscence sessions than were those who were involved in support-type discussion groups or the no-treatment control group. Although there was no measured change in functional behavior (e.g., self-care) or cognition, this may have been due to the limited sensitivity to small changes in the assessment measures, the Katz activities of daily living scale and the Folstein Mini-Mental State. In addition, measures of social responsiveness would be more likely to demonstrate change as the result of a reminiscence intervention. These effects were not maintained at 5 weeks postintervention, a finding that supports the need for ongoing intervention to maintain maximal functioning of individuals with degenerative cognitive diseases. Reminiscence group leaders in this study used an intensive system of verbal cuing to stimulate recall.

The study by Baines et al. (1987) found that moderately to severely cognitively impaired institutionalized elderly individuals who participated in reminiscence

sessions that were preceded by reality orientation sessions improved on measures of cognitive and behavioral function. These gains were maintained at one-month follow-up assessments. The treatment control groups, and those who participated in reminiscence groups previous to reality orientation groups, did not show these improvements. Although this study was conducted with a small number of subjects (15), the results are extremely interesting. To interpret the results and determine salient variables for further research and clinical work, the interventions themselves must be considered in more depth. The reality orientation intervention was based on the format of Holden and Woods (1982). These groups are *not* the standard classroom reality orientation sessions using only reality orientation information and repetition. This reality orientation group made use of multisensory materials and many other elements common to sensory stimulation groups. Reminiscence materials, such as old photographs and newspapers, were also used. References to the past were always connected, by comparison, to the present day. The intervention was purposely social, and group interaction was encouraged. This laid an important foundation for group cohesiveness and sociability for the reminiscence group sessions that followed. In contrast, the reminiscence group sessions used preprogrammed audiotape slide presentations supplemented by personal photographs, memorabilia, and artifacts. The emphasis was on personal reminiscence, and no specific comparisons were made to the present. The members of this group did not develop cohesiveness and sociability. Even subsequent reality orientation sessions apparently did not overcome the lack of sociability established in the preceding reminiscence sessions

The work of Schafer et al. (1986) with 185 institutionalized, cognitively alert elderly further supports the important contribution of socialization to the effectiveness of reminiscence interventions. This study also used prepackaged reminiscence materials, in this case an audiotape presentation from the National Council on Aging. Those who participated in guided group discussion, in addition to listening to the tapes, demonstrated enhanced interaction with other residents, compared with the participants who only listened to the audiotapes. Furthermore, those who did not use the tapes at all but who participated in structured discussion groups on the same topics as on the tape made even greater gains in socialization. Those residents who made the greatest gains in socialization and life satisfaction from reminiscence discussion groups were those who were least adaptable to the changed living circumstances found in the nursing home environment (Berghorn &

Table 6-1 Empirical Reminiscence Research with Institutionalized Elderly

Study	Subjects	Intervention	Results
"Reality Orientation and Reminiscence Therapy: A Controlled Cross-over Study of Elderly Confused People" (Baines et al. 1987)	$N = 15$ with moderate to severe cognitive impairment; residents of a large British nursing home who rarely participated in social activities.	Random assignment to groups, crossover design; (A) 4 weeks' RO (according to Holden & Woods 1982) and 4 weeks' reminiscence with auto-slide programs, artifacts, personal photographs, books, etc.; (B) 4 weeks' RO & 4 weeks' reminiscence; (C) no treatment control. 2 leaders per 5 subjects.	Mental ability declined for all, but less for Groups A and B. Group A improved significantly more than B in communication and behavior. Gains were maintained at a 1-month follow-up; significant gains in staff knowledge of residents.
"The Effects of Reminiscing on the Perceived Control and Social Reactions of the Institutionalized Elderly" (Schafer et al. 1986)	A stratified random sample from 32 nursing homes in eastern Kansas; 10–12 residents of each who were mentally alert, ambulatory, and capable of listening and speaking to others.	(A) Audiotape of program of self-discovery for seniors, plus discussions with trained leader; (B) unstructured group discussions with a trained leader using the same themes as A; (C) Audiotapes, as in A, broadcast by closed-circuit radio with call-in opportunity; all groups, 1-hour sessions each week for 12 weeks; (D) no treatment control. One leader to 10–12 subjects in Groups A, B, C. All groups were focused on reminiscence.	Pre- and post-test measures of life satisfaction, social interaction, activity, and memory. Both discussion groups enhanced interactions with other residents. The nontape discussion group resulted in significantly higher interaction with other residents and in knowing more residents. Group C participants demonstrated a significant decrease in perceived personal control. Limited support for reminiscence discussion-type groups.
"Reminiscence Intervention in Nursing Homes: What and Who Changes?" (Berghorn & Schaffer 1987). A further analysis of the data from the preceding study by Schafer et al. (1986)	See Schafer et al. (1986).	See Schafer et al. (1986).	Portions of the pre- and post-tests, as they related to mental adaptability and degree of change with reminiscence, were analyzed. Those who were least adaptable (mentally) to the change to a nursing home environment demonstrated the most significant change in life satisfaction and interaction after involvement in reminiscence groups.
"Reminiscing and Ego Integrity in Institutionalized Elderly Males" (Boylin et al. 1976)	$N = 41$; male residents of a DVA unit in New York. Mean age 64.4 years.	Correlational study comparing frequency of reminiscing with scores of ego adjustment, using a modification of Havighurst and Glasser's reminiscence scale (1972) and an author-developed ego adjustment scale.	Those who reminisced most frequently had higher ego integrity scores. Negative affect was moderately correlated with reminiscing.
"Cognitive, Affective and Behavioral Effects of Reminiscence Group Therapy on Demented Elderly" (Goldwasser et al. 1987)	$N = 27$; nursing home residents with moderate to severe dementia.	(A) Reminiscence group, emphasizing cuing and nonverbal communication; organized around themes. (B) Support group, emphasizing present/future events and problems. (C) No-treatment control group. A and B met for 30 minutes, twice weekly for 5 weeks. Two leaders per 10 subjects.	Reminiscence group was significantly less depressed (measured by pre- and post-test Beck depression scale) after intervention compared to the support group and the control group. Effects were not maintained at 5-week follow-up testing.

Table 6-1 continued

Study	Subjects	Intervention	Results
"The Use of Life Review Activity with Confused Nursing Home Residents" (Kiernat 1979)	N = 23; residents from 3 Wisconsin nursing homes who had been charted as confused for at least 3 months.	Reminiscence sessions organized around themes, progressing in chronological order from childhood to the present. Positive associations were emphasized. Multisensory materials were used. Two sessions of 45 minutes to 1 hour each, per week, for 10 weeks. Two leaders for 6–10 subjects. No control group.	Measurement scales were poorly designed and use was discontinued. Anecdotal records show that 48% of participants improved in behavior over the course of the intervention (e.g., reduced restlessness, improved cooperation, increased socialization and attention).
"Reminiscing: The Life Review Therapy" (Lappe 1987)	N = 83; cognitively alert residents of 4 urban nursing homes.	(A) Reminiscence groups for 10 weeks meeting (a) once a week (b) twice a week, using focus themes and memorabilia. (B) Current events groups for 10 weeks meeting (a) once a week and (b) twice a week, discussing current news items. Interpersonal approach and structure were identical in all groups. No control group. One leader to 8–14 subjects.	Reminiscence group subjects demonstrated a significantly greater increase in standardized self-esteem scores, compared to current event groups. There was no significant difference in improvement between groups that met once a week and groups that met twice a week.
"A Controlled Evaluation of Reminiscence and Current Topics Discussion Groups in a Nursing Home Context" (Rattenbury & Stones 1989)	N = 24; cognitively alert residents of an urban nursing home.	(A) Reminiscence group. Structured discussion around themes progressing from childhood to the present. (B) Current topics structured discussion group. (C) No-treatment control group. Two half-hour sessions, per week, for 4 weeks. 2 leaders for 4 subjects.	Both treatment groups made a significant gain on a standardized measure of happiness. Individuals who participated the most made the greatest gains. Gains raised participants to the norm for community-dwelling elderly.
"Reminiscence, Life Review, and Ego Integrity in Nursing Home Residents." (Taft & Nehrke 1990)	N = 30; cognitively alert residents from 4 nursing homes in rural Wisconsin.	Correlational study of amount and type of reminiscing with the degree of ego integrity using a 13-item reminiscence scale and the ego integrity scale developed by Boylin et al. (1976).	Life-review reminiscence was positively correlated with ego integrity; 67% of the subjects reported using reminiscence for life review.
"A Mapping Project to Facilitate Reminiscence in a Long-Term Care Facility" (Weiss & Thurn 1987)	N = 15; nursing home residents who were identified by nursing staff as having mild to moderate levels of disorientation.	One-to-one sessions with student volunteers who had preliminary training sessions on working with the elderly and dementia patients. Developed personally meaningful maps of home, lifetime travels, and a creative mapping project (e.g., dance steps, garden, scrapbooks illustrated by maps), and a "heritage map." Met 4 hours per week for 4 weeks.	Evaluated by content analysis of student volunteer anecdotal record. Positive responses to projects increased substantially over time; 77% of the visits elicited reminiscing.

Table 6-1 continued

Study	Subjects	Intervention	Results
"Perceived Effects of a Training Program to Enhance Family Members' Ability to Facilitate Reminiscing with Older Disoriented Residents." (Weiss & Thurn 1990)	*N* = 12; volunteer relatives of mildly to moderately confused nursing home residents.	Training sessions for relatives focusing on confusion, memory, and reminiscence; 1 group meeting followed by 2 individual sessions. A no-intervention control group of relatives was able to receive the training after the study.	Intervention group of relatives showed a significant, positive improvement on needs assessment scales measuring skill and satisfaction in relating to and reminiscing with disoriented relatives.

Schafer 1987). Although the evidence is indirect, it lends support to the potential effectiveness of reminiscence groups with persons with ADRD, since, because of disease-associated deficits, they too have great difficulty adapting to changed environments.

A recent study by Rattenbury and Stones (1989) with 24 cognitively alert nursing home residents further supports the importance of socialization/discussion-type interventions. All groups were randomly selected. Compared with the control group, subjects in reminiscence and current events discussion groups made significant gains on a standardized, validated measure of happiness. Those who participated most in the discussion made the greatest gains.

Because the present focus is on reminiscence groups, the fact that this study reports no difference in effectiveness between reminiscence and current events discussion groups bears further consideration. This could be accounted for by at least three factors: First, reminiscence discussions, as opposed to current events, are likely to be particularly effective with the cognitively impaired elderly because long-term memory and previous experiences are better preserved than recent experiences and information requiring new learning. The subjects in this study, however, were not cognitively impaired. Second, group leaders were not on the staff of the nursing home and hence were not familiar with the history and background of the subjects. Their ability to elicit and encourage reminiscence would have been limited by their unfamiliarity. Indeed, unfamiliarity with the subject's history is an important consideration that might have limited the positive outcome of other reminiscence research, such as that of Fry (1983), or played a significant role in the absence of positive treatment effects in the other studies (e.g., Perrotta & Meacham 1981–82; Scates et al. 1985–86). Finally, the reminiscence group intervention was strictly discussion-based. It is possible that the use of artifacts and memorabilia, as was done in the study by Baines et al. (1987), would have enhanced the outcome of the reminiscence group.

A larger (*N* = 83) study by Lappe (1987) also compared reminiscence and current events groups with cognitively alert nursing home residents. In that study, the reminiscence groups were somewhat different from those of Rattenbury and Stones (1989). Those groups incorporated memorabilia, after the initial groups the participants helped to generate the topics, and the intervention was longer in duration (ten weeks rather than four weeks). These differences account, at least in part, for the more positive findings of this study in favor of the reminiscence groups.

The study by Lappe (1987) found that those involved in reminiscence groups made significantly greater gains in self-esteem, as measured by a standardized scale, than those involved in current events discussion groups. The researcher made every effort to ensure that the structure and the interpersonal approaches in the two group types were the same. It is unfortunate that the researcher did not also use a control group, as it would have further strengthened the validity of these positive findings. There was no significant difference between the gains made by groups that met twice a week and groups that met once a week.

Lappe's study (1987) is a good illustration of the continuing confusion about the type of reminiscence studied. The title, "Reminiscing: The Life Review Therapy," and the introductory sections about Butler and life review seem to indicate that this research focuses on life-review reminiscence. However, both the description of the reminiscence intervention and the reference by the author to simple reminiscing indicate that this, in fact, was a study of simple reminiscence. Despite these shortcomings, the positive findings of this study support the continuing development of simple reminiscence group interventions.

In an attempt to facilitate reminiscence during family visits, Weiss and Thurn (1990) carried out an interesting study. Senior therapeutic recreation students were given intensive training in understanding and responding to individuals who were confused and disoriented. In turn, they were involved in three training sessions with 12 volunteer family members. Family members in the training sessions, as compared with those in the control group, made significant gains in understanding and skill in relating to and reminiscing with their confused relatives. It would be interesting to have a follow-up study of actual communication between the trained relatives and the resident. Nonetheless, this study again underlines the importance of communication and, further, the importance of adapting communication to suit the individual.

Another positive outcome of reminiscence groups is the opportunity for staff to become more familiar with the life history of the resident with ADRD. The study by Pietrukowicz and Johnson (1991) demonstrated that this knowledge can have a positive effect on attitudes of nursing staff toward residents. Nursing staff who read a chart that contained a one-page personal history viewed the resident as more acceptable and autonomous than did those who read a chart that did not contain this history.

Kiernat (1979) conducted a study of a group reminiscence intervention with 23 confused, disoriented nursing home residents. The intervention was 20 sessions long. Over the course of the ten weeks, the sessions worked through the entire life span. Multisensory materials were used, as appropriate to the session theme. Unfortunately, this study employed neither a control group nor a valid outcome measure. However, analysis of the anecdotal records found that the behavior of 48 percent of the participants improved (e.g., reduced restlessness, improved cooperation, increased socialization and attention). Those who were the most regular attenders made the greatest gains. Although this study is descriptive, it does contribute supportive evidence for the potential therapeutic benefits of structured reminiscence groups.

A correlational study of the institutionalized elderly reported that individuals who reminisced the most had the highest ego integrity scores (Boylin et al. 1976). In contrast, the study by Taft and Nehrke (1990) found that it was not the quantity but the type of reminiscing that was associated with ego integrity. Those who were involved with life-review type reminiscence had high ego integrity scores. This more recent study had a relatively small sample size ($N = 30$); was rather unique in that it attempted to determine the type of reminiscence; and employed subjects from a nursing home, as opposed to all-male residents of a Veterans Administration facility, who were the subjects of the earlier study. The subjects in both studies were cognitively alert. In a multistrategy, daily program of one hour, which included the use of reminiscence, improvements were noted in morale, activities of daily living, and mental functioning (Reichenbach & Kirchman 1991). The 72 subjects in this study, conducted in two 100-bed nursing homes, had identified organic brain syndrome; there were equal numbers of persons who were mildly, moderately, and severely impaired. The project lasted for four months. One-half of the subjects, who were not significantly different in age or mental ability, were assigned to the control group, which used standard nursing home care. This care included some activities that were conducted by the staff, who also ran the multistrategy group. Together with the findings from studies with the community-dwelling elderly, these results suggest that reminiscence supports self-esteem.

2.5 What Is the Empirical Evidence for the Therapeutic Effectiveness of Reminiscence?

A review of the literature makes it clear that the empirical evidence to date is inconclusive. This is not because of negative outcomes. In fact, the vast majority of the studies reported positive findings (for example, a review of 97 published articles on reminiscence found only 7 that did not report positive outcomes [Haight 1991]). Rather, the inconclusiveness can be attributed to the relatively small number of studies, the poor design of many of the earlier studies, limited theoretical knowledge about reminiscence, and failure to replicate studies with successful outcomes. The empirical literature on reminiscence lacks cohesiveness. Having said this, one must also reiterate that, although the flaws in the research prevent a definitive conclusion, there is virtually universal agreement that the positive outcomes of the majority of the work that has been done endorse the importance of forging ahead with more research and clinical application. The research to date on the therapeutic use of reminiscence gives strong indication that it is an intervention with tremendous potential. Furthermore, the more recent, carefully controlled, studies of group interventions of simple reminiscence all report significant positive outcomes with regard to decreased depression (Goldwasser et al. 1987), improved cognitive and behavioral function (Baines et al. 1987), measures of happiness (Rattenbury & Stones 1989), and increased self-esteem (Lappe 1987). This potential seems to be particularly promising with the cognitively impaired who live in institutions.

The lack of thorough empirical study with regard to reminiscence is, sadly, perfectly consistent with research into other therapeutic interventions for the institutionalized elderly. As Kane and Kane (1987) point out, "much has been written on this subject, but relatively little has been studied" (p. 228). In their comprehensive survey of interventions and programs with nursing home residents they also conclude that the limited amount of research was flawed by small sample sizes, lack of replication, poor generalization, and poor subject selection criteria. They, too, go on to emphasize that the existing evidence gives strong support for the importance of forging ahead with interventions. They raise an interesting question of values and quality of life, which are particularly pertinent to persons with ADRD: "Is it necessary to prove the benefit of every single intervention in a nursing home setting? Can we not assume some services are worthwhile simply as decent, humane things to do?" (Kane & Kane 1987, 236). Reminiscence group interventions with the cognitively impaired elderly have shown sufficient preliminary evidence of improving self-esteem and increasing socialization. Giving these disabled individuals even a temporary sense of control by calling up memories of past competencies is a "human and decent" necessity; furthermore, it sustains health and well-being.

2.6 Implications of the Research for Reminiscence Group Sessions

Structure is important, most particularly with the cognitively impaired.

Recreational or story-telling reminiscence is associated with the most positive outcomes. This is true particularly for persons who live in institutions and are cognitively impaired, as they may be unable to resolve old conflicts. Life-review type reminiscence has rather uncertain outcomes and should be undertaken only by highly trained professionals (Kovach 1990; Merriam 1989; Molinari & Reichlin 1984–85). It is, however, very important to listen to and acknowledge the negative experiences and the expressions of unhappiness that may arise during reminiscence sessions. There may be little other opportunity for individuals to give vent to these feelings. It is equally important to move on from validating these feelings to helping the individuals identify positive aspects or virtues in the way in which they handled the negative experience.

Reminiscing is influenced by the social setting. Particular attention must be given to establishing a supportive group atmosphere. The personal involvement of the group leader in discussion and facilitation of the group is very important for persons with ADRD, who may need specific cuing to facilitate recall. Familiarity with the individual's history and life experiences is essential.

The most successful outcomes with reminiscence groups use an integrated approach. Such an approach involves multisensory cues (Baines et al. 1987; Kiernat 1979; Lappe 1987; Weiss 1989; Weiss & Thurn 1987; Zgola & Coulter 1988), provides verbal and nonverbal cues to facilitate reminiscence (Baines et al. 1987; Goldwasser et al. 1987), makes use of nonverbal communication such as touch (Kovach 1990), and encourages connecting reminiscence with the present.

3.0 THE REMINISCENCE GROUP

The general goal of a reminiscence group is to provide a social setting for the thematic, multisensory presentation of memorabilia, which will stimulate reminiscing, in order to reaffirm the value of previous life experiences.

3.1 Specific Goals

- Provide pleasurable experiences through recalling and re-experiencing positive events of the past.
- Enhance self-esteem through recalling previous accomplishments and competencies.
- Enable the expression of emotions associated with previous life experiences.
- Assist individuals to identify positive aspects of negative or difficult experiences.
- Decrease the sense of isolation by enabling and encouraging mutually supportive behavior among peers.
- Assist to maintain cognitive functioning through stimulating long-term memories.
- Provide reassuring orienting information through connecting memories and themes to present-day events.
- Develop empathy between the group leader and the participants through the leader's enriched understanding of the participants' life histories.
- Provide opportunities for the involvement of significant others (e.g., in providing memorabilia and information and in doing one-to-one projects).
- Encourage socialization.
- Provide opportunities for direct-care staff to learn about the life stories and accomplishments of residents.

3.2 Selecting Participants

Select persons who are mildly to moderately cognitively impaired. These persons score in middle ranges on mental status tests (for example, 10 or above on the Folstein Mini-Mental State; Reisberg stages 3, 4, 5, and possibly 6 [Reisberg 1983]). These scores are only general guidelines. Someone with Mini-Mental State scores well below 10 may respond very well to the group, because of the previously discussed unevenness in function and the supportive nature of the group.

Select persons with persisting structural verbal skills. This characteristic is very difficult to quantify. Individuals whose verbalizations are limited to a few words or familiar phrases and who have little spontaneous speech would *probably* not do well in a reminiscence group because of the focus on verbalization. They would be better suited to appreciating the props and memorabilia in the context of a sensory stimulation group. In order to participate in a reminiscence group, individuals should have some capacity for following conversational structure, responding to questions with sentences, and taking initiative in making alternate responses. However, this skill should not be confused with verbal skills with regard to content or comprehension. The guidance of the leader and the facilitation of the reminiscence materials are designed to overcome difficulties, such as in naming, that are common at this stage of ADRD.

Select persons with persisting attention skills. This characteristic also cannot be easily quantified. In general, individuals who require direct one-to-one contact in order to maintain brief attention are not suitable. On the other hand, it is not necessary that the person be able to attend to a standard group process, as the group structure is adapted to accommodate reduced attention. The individual should be able to attend independently to a conversation or other stimulus for at least four to five minutes.

Select persons who respond well to a group setting. As was discussed in Chapter 4, the best evaluation is a trial in the group. It is very difficult, if not impossible, to judge how a person will respond to the specialized structure and stimulation of a reminiscence group on the basis of performance in other areas such as self-care or large group activities. The individual may be lost in a crowd and overwhelmed by the stimulation of an institutionwide Christmas party, but the intimate setting and focused presentation of cues in a reminiscence group may call forth not only memories of Christmas past, but familiar social behavior.

It is good practice to select participants with varied functional levels. A group of all lower-functioning individuals would be very difficult. Having at least one participant who is verbal, spontaneously responsive, and enjoys reminiscing and storytelling provides an excellent role model and stimulus for the other participants.

3.3 Setting

The reminiscence group should take place in a quiet, comfortable room that is as homelike as possible. This room or area should be free of distractions. A corner of the day room or living room or a portion of the activities room, where other activities are also taking place, is *not suitable*. The coming and going of other residents and staff are too distracting and disruptive. A room with a door to separate the group from distractions is very important. If the only choice is a large room, it should somehow be partitioned off with furniture or room dividers, so that the large open space does not interfere with the feeling of group togetherness.

A table around which all participants can be seated is essential. Gathering participants around the table is an effective and concrete cue for promoting a normalized atmosphere. The aim is to have participants feel as if this is a gathering of friends sharing information and activities over a cup of coffee or tea. Unlike other types of therapeutic groups, where a table may be a barrier to communication, for persons with ADRD the table at center enhances communication. The addition of a brightly colored, textured cloth and a seasonal centerpiece further enhances this concrete, focal center for the group.

3.4 Time

- Meet at the same time and day of the week. Structure and predictability are reassuring.
- Meet at frequent intervals; twice a week is preferable, but if only once a week is possible it is still worthwhile.
- Meet for 30 to 60 minutes.

The length of time is variable, depending on the numbers in the group, the amount of material presented, and the responsiveness of the participants. It must be remembered that the individual need not be able to attend to the group process for the whole time. Since participants receive periodic individual attention and cuing, they are not as likely to become fatigued or restless, as they would during a regular group.

3.5 Group Size

Once familiar with the group format and the participants, it is possible for one staff member to lead a group of up to eight people. Even for a highly skilled leader, a group containing more than eight participants can be difficult, as it does not allow for the individual attention and facilitation necessary to promote reminiscence. Until the leader becomes comfortable with reminiscence groups, starting with a smaller group of three or four participants is recommended.

3.6 Participant Evaluation

Evaluation of the participants and of the particular activities and programs must be ongoing. The most important evaluation is observation of how the participants respond to materials and activities presented in the group. Communicate with direct-care staff about any carry-over effects to other settings. Group leaders with clinical training may do more formal evaluations, such as mental status tests or self-care, self-esteem, or socialization scales. During the evaluation process, it is very important to keep in mind that, for persons with a progressive disease such as ADRD, maintaining existing levels of functioning is a crucial and valuable goal. It is also essential to recall that persons with ADRD live most fully in the present moment. Therefore, the most important evaluation is how the group activity affected their personal happiness or pleasure and encouraged responsiveness at that particular moment. An evaluation form (Exhibit 6-1) was developed for use in evaluating participants' responses over time. It may be adapted to suit the needs of different programs and facilities.

3.7 Group Format

For individuals with ADRD, even those with persisting verbal and attention skills, an adaptation of standard group methods is necessary. Detailed guidelines are found in Chapter 4. For reminiscence groups an adaptation of the parallel presentation format is effective. In this format, the particular prop or artifact is presented to each participant in turn and personal associations, remembrances, or opinions are facilitated. In this way, the group leader is able to use verbal cues that are meaningful to the individual and that will stimulate long-term memory. Depending on the functional level of the participants, there may be times when the process will proceed naturally. The associations of one participant may trigger spontaneous responses from others. The group leader may simply need to ensure that everyone has an opportunity or is encouraged to participate. This, however, is a rather rare occurrence. More often the group leader will need to structure the group and facilitate responses in order to compensate for the deficits of individuals with ADRD.

3.8 Group Order

1. Introduction. Individually welcome each participant and informally introduce the topic while walking to the group or when each person enters the room. When everyone is gathered, briefly introduce the topic.

If the group membership changes frequently, members should introduce themselves or be introduced each time. If the group has a stable composition, this is necessary only when new members join. The emphasis here is on encouraging sociability and identifying personal similarities (e.g., one person is from the town where the other's mother was born), not on factual recall of each other's names. Emphasize individual names by calling each person by name when addressing him or her during the group. As leader, include yourself in these introductions (e.g., also say where you were born). When the leader shares information and remembrances, it helps the participants to feel less self-conscious about doing the same.

2. Begin, if possible, by providing an associated item, the "initial cue," to each participant (e.g., a Valentine's Day card, an apple for a group on apples, a small paper flag, a Christmas decoration, an Easter egg, or photocopied pictures or illustrations). Setting these items at each place at the table will begin the process of focusing on the topic and stimulating personal reminiscences before the group even begins. If the budget allows, the participants can take these items with them as a souvenir and reminder of the group. Further reminiscence can then be stimulated as the item is discussed with staff and visitors. For example, in Nova Scotia, with its thousands of miles of coastline, reminiscence sessions on boats are very popular. For one such session, every participant received a photocopied, illustrated map of the province. The map was copied from a restaurant place mat and was illustrated with important local attractions, including a lighthouse and a famous sailing ship. As they came to sit at a place at the table, almost all the participants spontaneously picked up the map and began to look at it. Going from person to person, the leader encouraged each participant to locate and mark his or her birthplace, talk about how close it was to the water and boats, and identify the famous sailing ship by name. After the group, the participants' maps, with important personal places identified, were placed in their rooms. Staff and family members frequently remarked on the maps and the places marked, and thus further reminiscence was encouraged.

3. The next prop(s) or cue(s) should be multisensory, concrete, and commonly associated with the theme. These will trigger long-term memories and associations (e.g., a model wooden boat, a school bell for the school days group, or a horseshoe or other gear for a group on horses). Several are suggested in the resource guides (Appendix 6-A). Present these cues one at a time and use verbal and nonverbal cues to facilitate individual reminiscence.

Exhibit 6-1 Reminiscence Group—Individual Evaluation

Response	Date/Time	Never	Occasionally	Often	Always
Identifies materials present	Week 1				
	Week 2				
	Week 3				
	Week 4				
Connects presented material with personal experience	Week 1				
	Week 2				
	Week 3				
	Week 4				
Discusses personal life experiences	Week 1				
	Week 2				
	Week 3				
	Week 4				
Demonstrates insight about personal life experiences	Week 1				
	Week 2				
	Week 3				
	Week 4				
Makes appropriate social responses to group leader	Week 1				
	Week 2				
	Week 3				
	Week 4				
Makes appropriate social responses to peers	Week 1				
	Week 2				
	Week 3				
	Week 4				
Attends to the general group process	Week 1				
	Week 2				
	Week 3				
	Week 4				
Makes appropriate voluntary contributions to the group	Week 1				
	Week 2				
	Week 3				
	Week 4				
Attends entire session	Week 1				
	Week 2				
	Week 3				
	Week 4				

4. At this stage a short film or slides are appropriate, if they are to be used. The preceding cues will have provided a focus and stimulated memories as well as alertness, so that a brief presentation of this sort will be appreciated. During the presentation, guide participants in relating the presentation to their lives and to the theme. Quiet, one-to-one comments, such as "Do you remember riding in a horse and buggy like that?" help to focus attention. For further suggestions see "The Visual and Expressive Arts," Chapter 5.

5. A related activity, if a film is not used, is appropriate at this stage (e.g., making Christmas decorations or Christmas baking, taking a photograph for a group on cameras, or planting some seeds for an indoor gardening group).

6. Artifacts or modern-day props that help to refocus attention on the present day should be presented at the end of the group (e.g., illustrations or examples of modern watches and clocks for a group on watches/time; contemporary train schedule, tickets, or brochures for a group on trains).

7. Close the group with a social time. Serve tea/coffee/juice with any refreshments that may have been made. Continue conversation about the topic at hand, always returning to the present moment to provide reality reassurance.

3.9 Closing/Bridging

Return participants to their rooms or the communal living room, as appropriate. Give them a warm and personal goodbye. Remind them of what they have done and discussed in group that day. Clasp their hands and give praise, highlighting their particular contributions. Remind them of the time and topic of the next group. It is very important that each participant be assisted to settle back into the regular routine. Some may need reassurance from their direct caregiver.

The group leader is responsible for making sure that this bridge from the group to the daily routine is in place. Not to do so defeats the purpose of the group intervention. If a participant returns from a group and is too stimulated or disoriented to be able to participate in the unit routine, direct-care staff will be rightly skeptical about the overall value of the group. Leaving each participant with a concrete memento of the group, such as the initial cue, is reassuring.

3.10 Presentation of Artifacts or Props

Reminiscence groups, of necessity, have a verbal focus. However, because of their disease-associated deficits, persons with ADRD require special techniques to enable verbalization. The use of props, artifacts, or memorabilia is very important in assisting the verbal recall of previous experiences. These items trigger memories in ways that abstract verbal questions or comments are unable to do. Gathering together these materials does take some time. The leader, however, should not feel too overwhelmed. Even one or two items related to a theme are very helpful. Once the group is under way, other staff and family often appear with interesting items from their closets or basements.

Review Chapter 3, on "Communication," for suggestions on stimulating verbalization.

Emphasize recognition, not recall. Do not ask, "What is this called?" Questions with a "right" answer are threatening to persons with ADRD, as it confronts them with their disabilities. Use information/opinion-seeking questions, sometimes called lead-in questions. For example:

- Does this look familiar to you?
- What do you like best about_____?
- What do you recall about_____?
- Where do you recall seeing this before?
- How would you use this?
- Have you ever_____?
- What do you think of_____?
- What is your favorite_____?

Encourage touching and handling the artifacts, as the sensory stimulation will help to prompt associations (Byrd 1990). Memories are usually rich with sensory details. Help to focus on these sensory aspects by verbal cues, such as "Does this feel rough (or smooth or soft, etc.)?" See Chapter 7 for more detailed suggestions.

Emphasize associations based on long-term memory. Begin the group with the earliest associated memories and progress, through the group, to more recent memories. Although there are losses to long-term memory, it remains more intact than recent memory. Targeting a persisting skill improves self-esteem and confidence and encourages further participation.

Link artifacts with the individual participant's background and experiences. Because of disease-associated deficits, individual recollections probably will not be spontaneous. However, if verbal cues based on familiarity with the participant's history are provided, rich associations are often opened up. For example, one participant with advanced Alzheimer's disease had been a farmer and did not seem to have much to contribute to a reminiscence group on boats. However, when he was reminded that he had visited his brother who was stationed on a World War II corvette, he began to describe his visit in detail. He was also proud to tell us all that, although he was a landlubber, all the sailors were amazed that he never got seasick, even in the roughest weather.

Target associations that are "mountaintop" lifetime experiences. Memorable events such as the first day of school, first car, first boyfriend or girlfriend, bar mitzvah, wedding day, first day on the first job, going off to or coming home from war, and the assassination of President Kennedy are usually imprinted in memory in vivid detail. Call up personal associations with these experiences—what the person was wearing, who they were with, where they were living, how they felt—and thus re-enliven the experience. Individual accomplishments or experiences that were significant have equally rich associations. Learn what these are from significant others, and encourage reliving winning the championship, being elected mayor, bringing in the first crop, delivering the baby, etc. As a reminiscence group leader, it soon became obvious to me that the retelling and reliving of these significant personal events, sometimes every week, had a powerful positive effect on mood, self-esteem, and sociability.

Continually reinforce reality through then-and-now comparisons. Reminiscence groups are meant to reaffirm and enliven the past, but not to encourage living in the past. This is particularly important as the group comes to a close and participants must return to their daily routine.

Assist participants to make connections with others with common experiences and provide mutual support and affirmation.

During a session on boats Beth recounted how she had fallen overboard during an evening row in the harbor. She was a terrified teenager, flailing about in the frigid North Atlantic. She couldn't swim. One of the young men on the wharf jumped in and pulled her from the icy water. Understandably, she hasn't enjoyed being in boats ever since that time! The leader commented on how frightened she must have been, but what a fortunate thing it was that someone was standing by. A fellow participant chimed in, "Sure was, otherwise we wouldn't have her here with us now."

Beth was still feeling shaken, recalling this frightening experience at the start of what turned out to be, on the whole, a rather unhappy life. She commented that she didn't know who would save her now. Without any direction from the leader, her fellow participants spontaneously said they sure would.

Some who could swim said they would jump in for sure. Others had ideas about buoy lines and boats. Some said they would warm her up afterward with blankets, hot chocolate, maybe even a rum toddy!

As her peers poured forth their concern and obvious affection, Beth's expression changed from fright to pleasure, and she quipped that, with all of this help, it might not be so bad falling out of the boat again!

Present only one cue at a time. For individuals with ADRD, too much stimulation is overwhelming and increases difficulties with concentration and decision making.

Select cues of personal and local significance.

Multisensory cues help to stimulate long-term memory.

Artifacts that have an action component encourage involvement and stimulate procedural memory (e.g., butter churn, ice cream churn, musical instruments, vintage camera). One of the most popular artifacts in my groups was an old-fashioned crank telephone donated by a family member. When participants cranked the handle—often doing the ring at their childhood home—and picked up the receiver, the memories came pouring forth in vivid and animated detail. One recalled using the emergency ring to summon distant neighbors when her mother was having a baby. Another recalled five- or six-way conversations among boyhood chums on the same line, and how they had worked out code messages. Another remembered the neighborhood gossip who always listened in, and how disappointed she was with the advent of the dial telephone.

It is important to put this animated discussion in perspective. Previous to the group, these same individuals were sitting in the day room, staring into space or restlessly pacing the halls. The old telephone gave them a focus, as individuals, to recall previous life experiences and, as a group, to share experiences and stories. They concluded, as a group, that the old crank telephone had lots of faults but that it was probably better for community togetherness than the modern system.

Incorporate music related to the theme. Music is such a potent cue for stimulating memories. It is a language—beyond words—that can transport, without the interference of memory loss, to another place and another time. Songs associated with important life events can unlock a kaleidoscope of thoughts, associations, and reflections. One study involving 26 cognitively well women living in a nursing home compared life-review reminiscence sessions with and without music (Bennett & Maas 1987). Groups met for the same length of time, covered the same themes, and were matched in personal characteristics. However, in the music groups, discussion was preceded by listening to a related piece of music. Those in the music group showed a significant gain in life satisfaction compared with the verbal group, which actually showed a decline. Those in the music-based group also reported enjoying the group more than did the verbal group. The use of music is discussed in Chapter 5.

Music in reminiscence groups is very important. The music should be related to the theme and should be the focus cue, not used as background. Background music can be too distracting when presenting other cues or trying to stimulate conversation. Encourage singing along with tape-recorded familiar songs. In fact, in most cases little encouragement is needed. Even persons who are primarily nonverbal usually recall the words of familiar and favorite songs, such as the national anthem. This recall stimulates others and encourages verbalization. In a group on the national holiday, participants were given a small Canadian flag. One hummed the opening bars of "Oh Canada," and everyone joined in. Posture improved, faces beamed, and they spontaneously applauded their efforts. After this opener, the stories of Dominion Day parades and picnics, the first raising of the new Canadian flag, and fond remembrances of the old Union Jack poured forth.

Music is also a good way to close a group, leaving participants with a positive and tuneful memory of the group.

Share a related personal reminiscence. Telling brief, associated anecdotes encourages the participants to do the same. Care must be taken to do this only to stimulate, not to dominate, the discussion.

Use humor. Amusing personal incidents are often told and retold, becoming part of the family folklore. These memories therefore may be more easily recalled. Group leaders can set the tone by telling a funny story, related to the theme, about themselves or someone they know. Collect such stories from participants' families and significant others.

3.11 Unhappy Memories

The focus of simple reminiscence groups is not, as it is with life review, to encourage discussion and struggle with negative past experiences. It is inevitable, however, that in the context of a reminiscence group these experiences will surface. It is very important that the group leader listen attentively and empathize with the sad feelings, as he or she does with the happy ones. Do not be afraid of tears; they are an expression of a healthy human emotion, just as a smile is. Reassure the person that you appreciate how unhappy a time that

must have been. It has always been my experience that simply being able to talk about the experience and receive expressions of support and empathy is in itself helpful in dealing with the unhappiness. The group leader then assists the person to identify the positive aspects of how he or she dealt with the situation or what was learned from it. If the group leader is concerned that the experience continues to disable the participant, the person should be referred for professional, one-to-one counseling.

A New Year's reminiscence group provided time for looking back and looking ahead. William said, without hesitation, that the best year of his life was the year of his marriage. He told again, with obvious satisfaction, how he had driven all the way to New York City from Sydney, Nova Scotia, on his honeymoon. He and his bride had seen all of the sights at the New York World's Fair. He reflected on the harmony of their years together, sharing in the joys and sorrows of day-to-day life. Then, suddenly, the peaceful expression on his face turned to one of fear. He began to speak quickly, in staccato sentences. The hospital called. The nurse said his wife was worse. He drove to the hospital. Quickly. He ran to his wife's room. She was dead.

William sat sobbing, mourning the death of his wife seven years earlier. The tears flowed freely, for the first time in those seven years. The leader put an arm around his shoulder. Other group members touched his hand and expressed their sympathy. Gradually the tears subsided. The leader thanked William for sharing with the group the wonderful story of his loving devotion to his wife. He was reminded again of their many years and adventures together. When the time came to propose the New Year's toasts, the serenity had returned to William's face, and he raised his glass high to Enid, his life companion.

4.0 THE REMINISCENCE GROUP: PUTTING IT INTO PRACTICE

The content and specific order of a reminiscence group must, by definition, be unique to each setting and group of participants. The incorporation of local folklore, customs, stories, and experiences makes the experience meaningful. In addition, it is very important that the group leader be familiar with the individual participant's history in order to stimulate the recall of personal experiences.

The group resource guides in Appendix 6-A are intended only as suggestions—to be elaborated on, embellished, and personalized with colorful and significant local experiences. The guides were written from the cultural perspective that was most familiar and significant to the participants in my groups. They are presented not as recipes or formulas, but as examples that hopefully will inspire the development of reminiscences significant to the participants in your groups. Each resource guide contains several suggested props or artifacts, but it is by no means necessary to have all of these materials for a group. Similarly, numerous verbal cues are suggested. However, it is not intended that all of the questions be asked; they are merely suggestions. The group leader can select the ones appropriate

to his or her participants. Each resource guide provides enough materials and suggestions for at least two groups on the same theme.

The thematic calendar (Exhibit 6-2) provides a suggested yearlong thematic program guide. The sensory stimulation theme charts in Chapter 7 follow this same calendar. There is considerable overlap in suggested materials for the two groups, thus reducing preparation time. Directions for suggested activities or projects are found in Chapter 5.

The films listed in Appendix 6-A are available from the National Film Board of Canada (NFB). Call numbers and length are included. For ordering information see Chapter 5, Section 10.5, "Film Sources." Also see other resources, particularly "General Activity Resources," Chapter 5, Section 11.0.

Exhibit 6-2 Thematic Calendar

January	*February*	*March*	*April*
1. New Year's/New Beginnings 2. Winter Fun 3. Party Time (Grooming) 4. Winter Evenings at Home 5. Animals in Winter	1. Groundhog Day/Hoping for Spring 2. Valentine's Day 3. Lent: Mardi Gras/Shrove Tuesday (as appropriate) 4. Indoor Planting	1. Cameras/Pictures 2. Trains 3. Easter or Passover (as appropriate) 4. Pets	1. Birthdays (party) 2. Spring 3. Planting a Garden 4. Spring/Summer Games 5. Fishing
May	*June*	*July*	*August*
1. Gardens/Boats 2. Mother's Day 3. Music Appreciation 4. Victoria Day (Canada) or Spring (see April) 5. Farming	1. Flowers/Gardening 2. Weddings 3. Father's Day 4. Carpentry/Woodworking	1. National Holiday 2. Beaches/Oceans/Lakes 3. Vacations 4. Garden Harvest or Cars	1. Fishing (see April) 2. Boats (see May) 3. Indoor Planting (see February) 4. Garden Harvest or Pets (see March)
September	*October*	*November*	*December*
1. School Days 2. Watches/Clocks 3. Autumn 4. Trains (see March)	1. Getting Ready for Winter 2. Thanksgiving (Canadian) or Music Appreciation (see May) 3. Horses 4. Halloween	1. Cameras/Pictures (see March) 2. Veteran's Day/Remembrance Day 3. Thanksgiving (American) or Music Appreciation (see May) 4. Birthdays (see April)	1. Telephone 2. Quilts 3. & 4. Christmas or Hanukkah (as appropriate)

NEW YEAR'S/NEW BEGINNINGS

Initial Cue	Individual punch glasses, ingredients for punch, punch bowl
Verbal Cue	Who would you like to make a New Year's toast to? Why?
Nonverbal Cue	Mix the punch; serve, make toasts, and taste.
Prop/Artifact	Party streamers, hats and horns, top hats, candles, evening bag, gloves, New Year's "crackers"
Verbal Cue	Special New Year's traditions? Foods? Parties? With whom? Where? Go dancing? With whom? What sort of music? What dances? Any New Year's babies (or close)?
Nonverbal Cue	Try on hats; blow the noisemakers; light candles and make wishes; do some dances.
Prop/Artifact	Hourglass (e.g., egg timer with sand)
Verbal Cue	Ever see one? Own one? Use one? For what? Does time fly?
Nonverbal Cue	Tip the hour glass.
Prop/Artifact	Calendar for the New Year (get free donations from local businesses)
Verbal Cue	Where did you hang the calendar at home? Where did it come from? Local store? Picture on it? Keep track of anything special on it? What do you think is going to be special about this new year?
Nonverbal Cue	Look through the calendar. Pick out special occasions in various months and mark them, especially birthdays; hang the calendar in the participant's room.
Audiovisual	Videotape of Guy Lombardo in Times Square
Music	"Auld Lang Syne"
Activities	Make and serve punch and propose toasts; make New Year's sheets (photocopied, decorated with cutouts from newspaper); be sure to post these sheets for sharing with other staff. Include the following:

For 199? my New Year's resolution is_____.

Best remembrances_____ Year_____ Day_____ Fun _____Person_____

WINTER FUN

Initial Cue   Winter clothing (hats, mittens, scarves, fur muff), a bowl of snow

Verbal Cue   Remember getting dressed for the cold as a child? Favorite hat or mittens? Color? Homemade? By whom? Did you like playing in the snow? Special games? Fox and goose? Make snow angels? Snow forts? Sledding? Where? With whom?

Nonverbal Cue   Try on hats, scarves, etc. (use a mirror as appropriate); make a snowball (with mittens on).

Prop/Artifact   Ice skates (vintage if possible), hockey stick, hockey sweater, sports page with current hockey standings.

Verbal Cue   Ever go skating? Where? With whom? Outdoor rink or indoor? Make a rink in your backyard? Children skate? Grandchildren? Play hockey? Figure skate? Remember skating parties? Special outfit? Sledding parties? Follow professional hockey? Have a favorite team? Favorite players? Old-time? Now?

Nonverbal Cue   Play "Skaters' Waltz"; look at the skates and try them on; take a shot with the hockey stick; check the hockey standings.

Audiovisual   *The Sweater*, NFB 1 0180 079, 10 minutes (the story of a boy and a hockey sweater); *The Joy of Winter*, NFB. 1 0162 023, 15 minutes (humorous look at making the best out of winter). Brief video of hockey game or professional figure skating, such as *Blades and Brass*, NFB 1 0167 061, 10 minutes (highlights of the 1967 National Hockey League season set to the lively music of the Tijuana Brass).

Music   "Skaters' Waltz," "Winter Wonderland," "Frosty the Snowman"

Activities   Make hot chocolate, mulled cider to "warm up."

PARTY TIME

Initial Cue	Perfume, talc, after shave lotion
Verbal Cue	Associate with getting "decked out." Favorite scent? Favorite place to go? Favorite party?
Nonverbal Cue	Put on perfume or after shave lotion, as appropriate.
Prop/Artifact	A selection of vintage clothing (party accessories), e.g., ties, dress gloves, top hat, "minks," cummerbund, cuff links, jewelry
Verbal Cue	Ever own a similar item? What was it like? Where did you get it? Where did you wear it? What was your favorite "dress outfit"? Where did you go? With whom? What sorts of things did you do to celebrate special occasions? What occasions?
Nonverbal Cue	Try on the items; view in mirror.
Prop/Artifact	Various types of "party music" (e.g., Big Band, square dance); a dance card program
Verbal Cue	Favorite dance music? Favorite dance? Like to dance, or just watch? Most memorable dance? Why? With whom? Where?
Nonverbal Cue	Dance steps, or keep time to the music while seated; fill in the dance card.
Prop/Artifact	Various decks of cards ("vintage" if possible); cribbage board; bridge tally cards
Verbal Cue	Play cards? What game? With whom? Where? Any good stories about memorable card games?
Nonverbal Cue	Play cards.
Music	Favorite party or dance music
Activities	Make party foods (e.g., cookies, sandwiches, relish tray). Have everyone dress in "Sunday best" for an actual party with the theme decided by the group.

WINTER EVENINGS AT HOME

Initial Cue	Kerosene lamp, with pieces of lamp wick for each person
Verbal Cue	Ever use one? What was it like? Whose job to clean and prepare? How best to do it?
Nonverbal Cue	Light the lamp; polish the brass; trim the wick; clean the chimney.
Prop/Artifacts	Old-fashioned crank telephone
Verbal Cue	Have one? Which house? Where was it? Who else lived there? What was your ring? Listening in on conversations-recollections? Most important phone call? From whom? About what? First dial phone? Prefer new or old phones? Why?
Nonverbal Cue	Crank the phone.
Prop/Artifact	Vintage radio/contemporary radio
Verbal Cue	First radio? Who owned it? Favorite show? Where listened to? With whom? Who were the stars? Favorite station? Listen to radio now? What station? Comparisons to TV.
Nonverbal Cue	Tune the dial of vintage and/or a new-style radio.
Prop/Artifact	Home games—crokinole, checkers, dominoes, jigsaw puzzles
Verbal Cue	Personal associations as appropriate (favorites? playing partners? best game?, etc.)
Nonverbal Cue	Move the pieces; play a game.
Prop/Artifact	Vintage book/magazines and contemporary issues of the same magazines
Verbal Cue	Personal associations as appropriate (like to read? favorite book/magazine? why? prefer old or modern version?)
Nonverbal Cue	Examine and pick out familiar/favorite items.
Audiovisual	*For You, Mr. Bell* NFB 1 0171 106, 16 minutes (lively story of Bell and the invention of the telephone). Audio of vintage radio shows (e.g., "The Shadow," "The Jack Benny Show," "The Lone Ranger," "Sergeant Preston of the Yukon")
Music	Dance music (Big Band sounds)
Activities	If I could call up anyone I wished right now it would be _____ and I would tell them _____. Play crokinole, checkers, dominoes, cards; crack walnuts; play charades (if appropriate); do dramatic readings of favorite stories/poems, make tea biscuits, candy; have a taffy pull.

ANIMALS IN WINTER

Initial Cue   Playing cards, note paper, or napkin with colorful bird/animal illustration

Verbal Cue   Ever see this animal/bird? Where? With whom? Where do they spend the winter? Where would you like to spend the winter?

Nonverbal Cue   Deal out cards; write a note on paper.

Prop/Artifact   Stuffed (real) small animals (e.g., rabbits, squirrels, etc.) and birds (available from local museums, collectors, or taxidermists)

Verbal Cue   Personal associations with animals/birds presented; Seen one? With whom? Where? Personal anecdotes/experiences? Ever go hunting? Get anything? Know anyone who did?

Nonverbal Cue   Pet and touch the animals.

Prop/Artifact   Pieces of fur, fur hats, muffs, collar pieces

Verbal Cue   Ever own one? Ever own a fur coat? Know anyone who did? What was it like? Where did you/they get it?

Nonverbal Cue   Try on the garments.

Prop/Artifact   Posters, photographs, calendars, books with animal pictures; bird feeder; bird whistle, bird caller

Verbal Cue   Did you ever feed the birds? What sort of feeder? What kind of bird feed? What birds came? Where did the feeder hang? Favorite bird? Why? Least favorite? Why?

Nonverbal Cue   Try the bird whistle; select favorite birds from pictures/books.

Audiovisual   *The Winds of Fogo*, NFB 1 0169 059, 20 minutes (two fisherman visit Fogo Island, off the coast of Newfoundland, and discover the many birds found there). *The Flight of the Snows*, NFB 1 0174 538, 27 minutes (the story of the snow goose migration). *Fly Away North*, NFB 1 0164 171, 10 minutes (bird migration). *Wild in the City*, NFB 1 0185 039, 16 minutes (animals such as raccoons that have adapted to city life). *Images of the Wild*, NFB 1 0178 834, 22 minutes (the story of Robert Bateman and his wildlife paintings).

Music   Tapes of environmental, animal, or bird sounds

Activities   Make a simple bird feeder; make suet and seed balls for the birds.

GROUNDHOG DAY/HOPING FOR SPRING

Initial Cue	Clear, simple picture of a groundhog; article from a local paper with a groundhog's picture (photocopy for each participant)
Verbal Cue	Discuss the saying "If the groundhog sees his shadow there's six more weeks of winter." Ever hear this? From whom? Believe it? Ever see a groundhog? Know any other sayings about the coming of spring?
Nonverbal Cue	Read the story.
Prop/Artifact	Other signs of spring: budding branches, spring bird songs, "spring tonic" medicine bottles (dose of sulfur and molasses), long johns to put away for summer
Verbal Cue	Recognize these? Remind you of anything? What do you think of when you think of the coming of spring? The end of winter? Ever have to take a "spring tonic?" What was it? Who gave it to you? Did you like it? Did it work? What do you like best about spring? About winter?
Nonverbal Cue	Put the branches in water to force the leaves; taste some fresh spring greens (e.g., watercress, spinach); try to imitate bird songs; do ones they know or name the bird songs they recognize.
Music	"Zippity Do-Dah"
Activities	Plant some wheat kernels, to watch the sprouts grow; force a heat-treated hyacinth bulb or narcissus; make chocolate mud-pie cookies and roll them in green coconut (connect with things turning green in spring).

VALENTINE'S DAY

Initial Cue	Valentine's Day cards (vintage or reproduction if possible)
Verbal Cue	Remember getting a special valentine card? What was it like? Who was it from? Recall Valentine's parties at school? As an adult?
Nonverbal Cue	Look at the cards and read the verses.
Prop/Artifact	Paper doilies, red roses (silk with scent or other artificial if real is impossible), cinnamon hearts, red heart (e.g., a satin one from a candy gift box or other fancy hearts)
Verbal Cue	The person whom I cared about the most in my life was _____ because _____. How did you meet? Where did they live? What did they look like? What did you do together?
Nonverbal Cue	Taste cinnamon hearts; arrange cookies or other treats in Valentine's box.
Prop/Artifact	Contemporary Valentine's Day card
Verbal Cue	Ever send a Valentine card? Ever get one? From whom? What was it like? Who would you like to send a card to now? (emphasize reality reassurance) What would you like to say on the card?
Nonverbal Cue	Pick one they like the best; address it and sign name.
Audiovisual	Read or have read the story of Saint Valentine.
Music	"Let Me Call You Sweetheart," "Heart of My Heart"
Activities	Make heart-shaped cookies from sugar cookie recipe; make valentines (per sensory stimulation suggestions); have a Valentine's Day tea party; make up rhymes from "Roses are Red"; complete the sayings with "love" in them ("Love makes the _____ [world go round]).

MARDI GRAS/SHROVE TUESDAY

Initial Cue   Paper eye masks (made from construction paper if not otherwise available)

Verbal Cue   Connect with Mardi gras theme (celebration before Lent begins). Ever go to a Mardi gras parade? Party? Where?

Nonverbal Cue   Try on the mask or design one (decorate with sequins, spray glitter, etc.).

Prop/Artifact   Old-fashioned pancake griddle or spider or cast-iron frying pan

Verbal Cue   Ever see one? Where? What was made on it? Ever use one? Own one? Did you make pancakes on Shrove Tuesday? What kind? Pancake suppers at church? Pancake flipping contest?

Nonverbal Cue   Examine griddles; flip pancakes.

Prop/Artifact   Costumes appropriate for Mardi gras parade (e.g., fancy capes or hats that can be tried on)

Verbal Cue   Ever in a Mardi gras parade? What did you wear? Where was it? Who with? Ever dress up for another type of party?

Nonverbal Cue   Try on costumes; decide which they like the best.

Music   Lively Mardi gras type music

Activities   Mix up pancake batter, cook and enjoy; have a pancake supper party; have a costume parade (with music) with all staff participating.

INDOOR PLANTING

Initial Cue   Branch with swelling buds or seed packet (large seeds such as nasturtiums or beans) or seed catalogue

Verbal Cue   Focus on signs of spring associated with the props; personal associations, e.g., Ever bring in branches to force flowers? What branches? Where did you pick them? Anybody with you? How did you do it? Start your own seeds in spring? Which ones? How? Know anyone else who did? What are signs of spring for you? (assist with local examples as appropriate, e.g., pussy willows, bird songs, etc.)

Nonverbal Cue   Feel the swelling buds (put the branches in warm water for forcing); open the seed packets and plant some seeds; look through seed catalogues and find favorites; identify associations.

Prop/Artifact   Vintage garden tools (e.g., seeder, trowel, spade); clear color pictures of the signs of spring in nature; spigot and bucket for tapping maple syrup; finished maple syrup or sugar or cream; pictures of maple syrup making

Verbal Cue   Have a garden? Where? What did you grow? Ever use these tools? Where? With whom? Ever start plants indoors for the garden? What plants? Where did you put them? Ever tap trees? Where? How? Who with? Make maple syrup? Go to a sugaring-off party? Been to a maple bush? A sugar shack? Know anyone who used to make maple syrup? What did you like maple syrup on best? Share favorite recipes?

Nonverbal Cue   Examine artifacts; taste maple syrup.

Audiovisual   *Nonoonse Anishinabe Ishichekewin Ka Kanawentank*, NFB 1 0680 054, 10 minutes (the Indians near Lake Manitoba making maple syrup).

Music   Environmental sounds tape with spring sounds, bird songs

Activities   Plant seeds for spring garden (easy-to-grow favorites like tomatoes, onions, marigolds); start indoor house plants (associate with being too early to garden outside but can do inside); visit a greenhouse or a maple bush; make a terrarium, dish garden.

CAMERAS/PICTURES

Initial Cue	Photocopy of vintage photo of well-known local scene or streetscape of years gone by
Verbal Cue	Photographs capture things as they were; identify personal associations; discuss changes
Nonverbal Cue	Find familiar details in the pictures.
Prop/Artifact	Vintage camera, vintage photos or albums, photographs of favorite local scenes
Verbal Cue	Ever own a camera like this one? Or another camera? What was it like? Where did you get it? What/who do you like to take pictures of? Ever develop your own pictures? Does this photo remind you of anyone? Do you have a favorite picture of yourself? Of someone else? What is it like? Where? What were you doing?
Nonverbal Cue	Look at camera, focus, and try to use it; examine vintage photos; make personal associations with people or objects.
Prop/Artifact	Contemporary camera (preferably Polaroid type)
Verbal Cue	Ever see a camera like this? Use one? Which type of camera do you prefer (vintage or modern)?
Nonverbal Cue	Take a Polaroid photo of each other (or have picture taken by staff).
Audiovisual	*Great Days in the Rockies*, NFB 1 0183 029, 11 minutes (photographs and techniques of photographer Byron Harman, who photographed the Rockies in the early 1900s). *Fixed in Time: A Victorian Album*, NFB 1 0180 039, 20 minutes (a picture of Victorian Halifax, Nova Scotia, based on the photographs of Oliver Massey Hill).
Activities	Mount photographs (on Bristol board mat); label and hang in room or send to person of participants' choice; make "picture biography" of favorite personal photographs (seek help from family/significant others); make picture collage (from magazines) of favorite pictures or focus on a theme (e.g., favorite foods).

TRAINS

Initial Cue	Photocopy of steam engine or other vintage train
Verbal Cue	Ever ride on a train like this? See one? Discuss the details of the train and make personal associations
Nonverbal Cue	Examine pictures and locate various features.
Prop/Artifact	Engineer's striped denim hat, conductor's cap, model train (ideally from a model train club), book/ photos of vintage trains/engines
Verbal Cue	Train near your childhood home? What time did it go through? Heading to where? Ever ride on it? With whom? Going where? Did you eat on the train? What? Ever work on the trains? Doing what? Know anyone who worked on the trains? Do you think you would like the job of conductor/porter/engineer? Ever hitch a ride? Ride the rails?
Nonverbal Cue	Try on caps; run the model train or move individual cars; examine and discuss details (e.g., cowcatcher, steam engine).
Prop/Artifact	Train sound effects (recorded—engine, whistle, "all aboard," railway crossing signals)
Verbal Cue	What do these sounds remind you of? A trip? Travel? Adventure? Someone going away? Who?
Nonverbal cue	Blow a trainlike whistle; call "all aboard."
Prop/Artifact	Modern-day train schedule; tactile or regular map of the region, state, province, or country
Verbal Cue	Been on a modern train? With whom? Going where? What do you like about modern trains? About the old trains? What's your favorite way of travel (train, plane, car, boat)? Where would you travel to if you could go anywhere you wanted? How would you get there?
Nonverbal Cue	Find familiar places on the schedule, map.
Audiovisual	*Railroaders* NFB 1 0158 008, 21 minutes (a film about the crews that maintain the rail lines in British Columbia, Canada). *The Railrodder*, NFB 1 0165 062, 25 minutes (a humorous silent film starring Buster Keaton, showing a trip across Canada on a railway jigger).
Music	"I've Been Working on the Railroad," "Far Away Places"
Activities	Visit train station/restored steam train/model train club; prepare a box lunch for a train trip; plan a train trip to desired destination, using maps.

EASTER

Initial Cue	Easter lilies
Verbal Cue	Recognize this? Ever have one? Get it as a gift? From whom? Have any special memories for you? Ever grow one?
Nonverbal Cue	Smell and touch the flowers.
Prop/Artifact	Easter basket, Easter bonnets (vintage if possible), spring flowers, Easter rabbit or chicks (live if possible, otherwise good-quality stuffed ones), special decorative Easter eggs (e.g., Ukrainian painted eggs)
Verbal Cue	Did you go hunting for Easter eggs when you were young (or older)? Where? With whom? Do you remember having a special Easter basket? What was it like? Ever get a rabbit or a chick for Easter? Or have one for a pet? Have to take care of them on the farm? Did you (or your wife/ girlfriend, mother/sister) get a new Easter bonnet? Remember a favorite one? What was it like? Did you do anything special for Easter? Special memories of Easter dinner? What did you eat? With whom?
Nonverbal Cue	Examine the Easter basket; rearrange the eggs; pet and/or feed the rabbits/chicks; try on the Easter bonnet(s).
Prop/Artifact	Pussy willows, branches with swelling buds
Verbal Cue	It is Easter now (associate with spring/new life). Ever go to pick pussy willows? Have a favorite place/memory of this? Ever "force" branches to flower? Which ones? Where did you get them?
Nonverbal Cue	Touch the willows/branches; arrange a bouquet.
Music	Easter hymns (as appropriate), "Hallelujah Chorus," "The Easter Parade," "Here Comes Peter Cottontail"
Activities	Make hot cross buns or chocolate mud pies rolled in colored coconut to look like Easter eggs; decorate and fill Easter baskets for a nursery school or visiting grandchildren. Have an Easter party with everyone in special finery, perhaps even an Easter parade involving the staff (make sure that it's age appropriate); force bulbs for early bloom (e.g., hyacinths, crocus, daffodils). Paint Easter eggs (with tempera paint or dampened, colored tissue paper designs) (make sure that this is presented in an age-appropriate way)— a good intergenerational activity.

PETS

Initial Cue	Writing paper or cards with picture/illustration of dogs/cats/birds
Verbal Cue	Ever have a cat/dog/bird as a pet? What was its name? What color? Where did you get it? What did you like best about this pet? Have any unusual pets (e.g., skunk, raccoon, ferret, etc.)
Nonverbal Cue	Select favorite, sign name.
Prop/Artifact	If possible, live pets (see "The Therapeutic Use of Pets," Chapter 5). Otherwise use high-quality realistic stuffed animals as well as posters, pictures of family pets, glass collection of animals and china figurines, pictures of famous pets (e.g., Lassie, Rin Tin Tin)
Verbal Cue	Continue with personal associations as outlined above. Special tricks your pet could do? Amusing stories about you (or someone else) and a pet?
Nonverbal Cue	Interact with animals (see "Therapeutic Use of Pets," Chapter 5).
Prop/Artifact	Pet paraphernalia (e.g., leashes, brushes, rawhide bones, catnip mice, bird cage)
Verbal Cue	Discuss favorite type of dog/cat. What would you have for a pet if you could get anything you want? What would you call it?
Nonverbal Cue	Examine items, focusing on sensory aspects and stimulating associated personal memories.
Music	"How Much Is That Doggie in the Window?," "Yellow Bird," "Kookaburra Sits in the Old Gum Tree"
Activities	Visit a pet store or the Humane Society, or have them bring animals in, if possible. Make homemade treats for the pets (e.g., homemade doggie biscuits, stuffed catnip mice, suet balls to feed the wild birds). Groom, walk, feed, pet the live animals. Prepare a goldfish bowl with gravel, etc., to make an easy and cheap aquarium. Make a group project collage of pictures of animals from magazines; decoupage picture/plaque of pet.

BIRTHDAYS

Initial Cue Birthday card (can be front cover of an already used one) or birthday napkin

Verbal Cue Introduce topic with personal associations. When is your birthday? Remember any birthday as very special? Or a special birthday party for someone else you know?

Nonverbal Cue Put birthdays on large yearlong calendar (single sheet).

Prop/Artifact Vintage clothing items for special occasions; different types, scents, colors, and sizes of birthday candles

Verbal Cue Continue personal associations. Ever wear items like these for a birthday or other special occasion? What was the occasion? What did you wear? How did you get there? Who else was there? What sort of food was served?

Nonverbal Cue Try on the clothing; place the candles on the cake and light them; sing "Happy Birthday" to each person. (Emphasize reality reassurance.)

Prop/Artifact Birthday party invitations; material to make birthday cards and/or cakes

Verbal Cue Reality reassurance, reviewing birth date and the present date. Know anyone whose birthday is this month? Who would you like to send a card to? Explore information about this person. Favorite type of birthday cakes that you've had before? Who made it? Who else was there? If you could have any type of cake you wanted now, what would it be? Why? Who would you share it with?

Nonverbal Cue Plan birthday party for second session; make birthday cards.

Music "Happy Birthday" (and variations)

Activities Grooming (manicure, after shave talc, hand cream, etc.) in preparation for party. Try on fancy vintage clothing (e.g., top hats, women's hats, long gloves, ties). Make goodies (cakes, cookies, etc.) and other preparations for a birthday party. Have a birthday party. Make birthday cards for each other, special friends, relatives, staff. Have a poetry writing session to write verses for the cards. Pass the present: Wrap a package of treats with one for everyone (e.g., cookies, flowers, candies) with birthday wrapping paper. Wrap with plain newsprint, inserting directions for whom to pass the present to (e.g., someone who wears glasses). Include a layer and a cue for every person in the group. The first person unwraps one layer and passes it to another person who fits the enclosed cue. Continue until the actual present is unwrapped. Share the goodies. This is a good warm-up activity to start a group. Some suggested cues are: someone who likes to sing; someone who has a nice smile; someone who likes to laugh; someone who has curly hair; someone with blue eyes.

SPRING

Initial Cue	Clippings or pot of fresh green grass
Verbal Cue	Memories of spring from childhood, e.g., walking barefoot in the new grass, playing in the mud puddles, getting the first dandelion, walking in the spring rain. What do you like best about spring? What do you like least about spring? What is your favorite season?
Nonverbal Cue	Smell and feel the grass.
Prop/Artifact	Fragrant spring flowers (e.g., mayflowers, hyacinths, narcissus), pussy willows, forsythia, dandelions, pot of chives or other herbs; watercress, color photos of local spring scenes
Verbal Cue	Have special memories of walks to pick spring flowers? Where? With whom? What kind of flowers? Herbs? Grow these flowers in your garden? Other spring flowers? Favorite memories of spring? Favorite place in spring? What do you like best about spring? What is your favorite season? Why?
Nonverbal Cue	Smell and touch the flowers and arrange in water; taste the herbs.
Prop/Artifact	Maple syrup/cream/butter and maple syrup equipment as available (e.g., spigot, bucket, brace and bit); maple branch with swelling buds
Verbal Cue	Ever have maple syrup/sugar/butter before? Make it? With whom? How's it made? Discuss maple syrup–making techniques now. Been to a sugaring-off party? Heard of it? What do you do?
Nonverbal Cue	Taste the maple syrup or other treats.
Audiovisual	*Nonoonse Anishinabe Ishichekewin Ka Kanawentank*, NFB 1 0680 054, 10 minutes (the Indians near Lake Manitoba making maple syrup)
Music	Tapes of nature sounds (woodlands in spring with running water, bird songs, etc.); "April Showers," "Zippity Do-Dah"
Activities	Make a woodland spring terrarium (one each using a large jar, or a group one in a small fish tank); visit a sugar bush; boil down maple syrup to make sugar; make "grandpères" (dumplings cooked in maple syrup); have a "sugaring-off" party; make theme pictures with associated "reflections" using favorite flower pictures from seed catalogues or magazine pictures or spring bulb company leaflets.

PLANTING A GARDEN

Initial Cue	Seed catalogue or seed packet with color picture
Verbal Cue	Getting ready to plant a garden. Ever have a garden? Where? What did you grow? Remember a special garden from childhood?
Nonverbal Cue	Pick out favorites from catalogue; open seed packet and plant the seeds.
Prop/Artifact	Vintage (or contemporary) small garden tools (trowel, clippers, watering can); small seeder; pictures of well-known local or other famous gardens
Verbal Cue	Continue with personal associations with gardening. Keep a garden at your home as an adult? What did you grow? What did you like best from the garden? Favorite job? Least favorite job? Know anyone with a good garden?
Nonverbal Cue	Do activities suggested below.
Prop/Artifact	Fresh produce (tomato, tropical fruits, fresh greens)
Verbal Cue	Favorite produce fresh from the garden? Ever grow it? Pick it? Tropical gardens—ever see one? Favorite tropical fruit? Why?
Nonverbal Cue	Prepare and sample foods.
Audiovisual	*My Urban Garden*, NFB 1 0184 012, 26 minutes (high production in a small backyard garden, with Carol Bowlby as commentator). *The Vacant Lot*, NFB 1 0177 147, 16 minutes (the lively story of how a vacant lot in Montreal is turned into a garden by a group of seniors).
Music	Nature sounds tape (spring); tropical /jungle sounds tape
Activities	(All of these activities are good for intergenerational programs.) Begin to prepare and plant accessible outdoor garden space; start seedlings for outdoor garden; prepare and plant indoor potted garden (e.g., cress, parsley, or other herbs in pots, tomato planter, potato barrel); sprout seeds from oranges, lemons, grapefruit, avocado, or grow pineapple tops; visit a greenhouse/ garden shop. See Chapter 5 and the horticulture section for details.

SPRING/SUMMER GAMES

Initial Cue	Pictures of famous baseball players from participants' era (e.g., Shoeless Joe, Babe Ruth, Yogi Berra, Jackie Robinson)
Verbal Cue	Associate with springtime and baseball season starting. Did you follow baseball? Have a favorite player? Recognize the players?
Nonverbal Cue	Examine the pictures.
Prop/Artifact	Baseball, glove, cap, bat
Verbal Cue	Play baseball as a child? As an adult? What team? Place? Position? Who else was in the league? How did your team do? Know anyone else who played? Famous "play" stories?
Nonverbal Cue	Try on the glove, cap; toss the ball.
Prop/Artifact	Skipping rope (old-fashioned type with wooden handles)
Verbal Cue	Skip as a child? Where? With whom? Remember skipping rhymes? Special types of skipping (double Dutch, etc)?
Nonverbal Cue	Try turning the rope.
Prop/Artifact	Colored kite(s), string, and fabric scraps
Verbal Cue	Ever own one? Fly one? Make one? What was it like? How did it fly? Where did you fly it? With whom? Secrets for flying? Making? Other favorite spring games/pastimes?
Nonverbal Cue	Make a tail for the kite by tying the fabric scraps onto the string.
Prop/Artifact	Contemporary baseballs cards, team pennants, hats, "new-fashioned" aluminum bat; video clip of a current favorite local team
Verbal Cue	Follow baseball now? Favorite team? Favorite player? Opinion of teams now compared to the old days? What do you think of the aluminum bat?
Nonverbal Cue	Examine cards and other props.
Audiovisual	*King of the Hill*, NFB 1 0174 106, 57 minutes (rather long; may want to show in portions: the story of Fergie Jenkins, Hall of Fame pitcher, who played for the Chicago Cubs in the early 1970s)
Music	"Take Me Out to the Ball Game," skipping chants (favorite local ones, e.g., "Cinderella dressed in yella," etc.)
Activities	Dramatic reading of "Casey at the Bat"; make ball game snacks (e.g., hot dogs, popcorn) while watching clips of famous players or World Series or contemporary game (good intergenerational activity).

FISHING

Initial Cue	Variety of fishing lures (without hooks) or brochure from a government department of fisheries
Verbal Cue	Ever go fishing? As a child? As an adult? Favorite fishing places?
Nonverbal Cue	Look at and feel the various lures.
Prop/Artifact	Fishing gear (vintage as available): reel, kreel, various floaters and lures, fishing hat, fish net (hand-held or piece of large seine nets)
Verbal Cue	Continue to explore personal associations/stories about fishing. Who did you fish with? As a child? As an adult? Places? What were they like? Ever do a long fishing trip? Fish for a living? Biggest fish? Best "fish story?"
Nonverbal Cue	Examine materials and try, as appropriate.
Prop/Artifact	Mounted specimens of prize fish; pictures of people with prize fish; books/pictures of local fish species, favorite fishing spots
Verbal Cue	Recognize these places? Others you know of?
Nonverbal Cue	Examine items; point out familiar locations.
Prop/Artifact	Samples of favorite local fish treats (e.g., fish cakes, fish chowder, solomon gundy, pickled herring, smoked oysters)
Verbal Cue	Like to eat fish? Favorite kind? Special way of serving? Any special dish you made? What ingredients did you use? Who did you serve it to? Friends or relatives who were good fish cooks? What did they make? (If this discussion is begun during the first session it will provide ideas for foods to make/serve during the second session.)
Nonverbal Cue	Make, serve, taste, and enjoy.
Audiovisual	*Change by Degrees*, NFB 1 0175 008, 9 minutes (story of a small Nova Scotia fishing village). *The White Ship*, NFB 1 0166 039, 15 minutes (a Portuguese schooner doing traditional fishing off the coast of Newfoundland). *Fisherman's Fall*, NFB 1 0167 010, 14 minutes (about salmon fishing in British Columbia).
Music	"Squid Jigging Ground," "I'se the Bye"
Activities	Make favorite fish dishes, according to local custom. Turn it into a party, e.g., an oyster supper, a fish fry, a clambake; visit an aquarium or a local pet store with a good collection of tropical fish; organize a fishing trip; prepare a simple aquarium or goldfish bowl; record and illustrate favorite heirloom fish recipes.

BOATS

Initial Cue	Photocopied booklet of different types of ships and boats
Verbal Cue	Ever been on a boat? What type? Where? With whom? (focus on earliest memories)
Nonverbal Cue	Look at the different types of boats and comment on ones recognized.
Prop/Artifact	Map of province/state/region
Verbal Cue	Identify place of birth and other places lived. How far from the water?
Nonverbal Cue	Write name on map near birthplace or on a large textured map.
Prop/Artifact	Model boats/ships of various types, as available (e.g., ships in bottles, decorative model ships, vintage toy boats, modern models); sou'wester, ship's bell, compass, barometer, sail or sail-cloth, oiled rope, and other boat/ship-related items
Verbal Cue	Continue associations with boats (toy, model, real) beginning with childhood and working to the present. Ever see a boat like this? Own one? Make one? Anyone you know make model boats? Ships in bottles? What sorts of boats have you been in? With whom? For how long? Have any adventures? Favorite type of boat? Favorite place to be in a boat?
Nonverbal Cue	Examine the various models.
Audiovisual	*The Sea Got in Your Blood*, NFB 1 0165 118, 28 minutes (stories of the sea and sailors from Atlantic Canada). *The Last Corvette*, NFB 1 0179 230, 28 minutes (former crew members reminisce about serving on the corvettes, accompanied by songs and news clips from the World War II era) *Steady as She Goes*, NFB 1 0181 049, 27 minutes (humorous and fascinating story of a retired man whose hobby is making ships in bottles).
Music	"Row, Row, Row Your Boat," "Sailor's Hornpipe," "What Do You Do with a Drunken Sailor," "Anchors Aweigh," "Shores of Tripoli"
Activities	Make a collage of boat pictures or a decoupage picture of a boat; plan a "boat trip" using maps; visit a marine museum (if available) or a hobbyist who makes model boats.

MOTHER'S DAY

Initial Cue	Fresh flowers
Verbal Cue	Associate having/wearing flowers with special occasion. What was your mother's favorite flower? Did she grow it? Did you grow it? What is your favorite flower?
Nonverbal Cue	Make individual boutonnieres and wear for the day or arrange a bouquet.
Prop/Artifact	Vintage photo of woman dressed up (participant's mother's picture if available), vintage hats, jewelry, hair ornaments, combs, hairpins, perfume atomizer or perfume bottles, old-fashioned aprons
Verbal Cue	Does this photograph remind you of your mother? How so? How different? Assist in personal associations with the mother. What did she look like (hair color, height, etc.)? What was her full name? Where was she born? What did she like to do best? What do remember best about your mother? About special times/events with your mother (e.g., learning to cook, taking care of you when sick, sewing a special outfit)? Special foods or treats mother made? Discuss associations with items with memories of mothers. Are there people who have been like a mother to you?
Nonverbal Cue	Try on items (as appropriate); look at and feel individual items.
Prop/Artifact	Contemporary Mother's Day cards (store-bought or made in the group)
Verbal Cue	Mother's Day coming up. Use information about personal history to talk with those who are mothers (parents) about their children's names. Where do they live? Are you a grandparent? Special remembrances of Mother's Day for you (surprises? special presents?). If some participants have not had children, approach this topic with sensitivity. Focus on their mothers or perhaps people who have been like children to them.
Nonverbal Cue	Make Mother's Day cards; sign and send to someone whom they would like to remember on Mother's Day.
Audiovisual	*Great Grandmother*, NFB 1 0175 108, 28 minutes (a Victorian "photo album" of mother during pioneer days on the prairie; a rather slow-moving film).
Music	"M-O-T-H-E-R," "The Little Old Shawl That Mother Wore," "Billy Boy," "I Want a Girl Just Like the Girl"
Activities	Make Mother's Day cards for someone special. Organize a Mother's Day tea for participants, with significant others, if possible; dress in special-occasion clothes; make corsages or boutonnieres; generate and make mother's favorite recipes; do creative writing focused on memories of mother (individually or as a group). Create a group poem or other form using the letters from *mother*, e.g., *M* is for _____?

MUSIC APPRECIATION*

Initial Cue   Songbook/song sheet vintage or selection of old favorites

Verbal Cue   First memories of music as a child? With whom? What songs? What instrument? Favorite song from childhood?

Nonverbal Cue   Look at song sheets and pick out or hum and sing favorites.

Prop/Artifact   A selection of small instruments, particularly local favorites (e.g., the fiddle in the Maritimes), including mouth organ, recorders, "spoons," ukulele

Verbal Cue   Play an instrument? Which one? Who did you play with? Favorite songs? Type of music you liked best? Know anyone who plays an instrument? For pleasure or for their job? Most memorable occasion with music (e.g., dance, concert, family gathering, religious service)? If you could hear any music you wanted to, what would it be? Who would you like best to sing or play it?

Nonverbal Cue   Examine and try out the instruments.

Prop/Artifact   Selections of favorite musical pieces

Verbal Cue   Which is your favorite singer, band, type of music?

Nonverbal Cue   Listen to the selections and comment after each one.

Prop/Artifact   Brief selections of contemporary music of various types

Verbal Cue   What do you think of the contemporary music? Why? What do you like about it? Dislike about it?

Nonverbal Cue   Listen to music selections and comment after each one.

Audiovisual   *Good Bye Sousa*, NFB 1 0173 032, 17 minutes (an old-fashioned brass band plays toe-tapping music in a small Ontario town). *Boy Meets Band*, 1 0161 022 -11 minutes (excellent snapshot of a West Vancouver boys' band that plays lively music). *Don Messer: His Land and His Music*, NFB 1 0171 015, 64 minutes (popular Maritime fiddler and his music; very well received, can be played in two or more sessions). *Celtic Spirits*, NFB 1 0178 911, 28 minutes (familiar folk and fiddle music performed in Cape Breton, Nova Scotia, and the Scottish Highlands). *The Fiddlers of James Bay*, NFB 1 0180 001, 29 minutes (two cree fiddlers play their traditional music and travel to the Orkney Islands, the original home of the music).

Music Activities   Use information from the discussions and play a favorite for each session.

Begin making a songbook of group favorites; have a dance with favorite local music or visiting musicians, or go out to a concert; listen to a memorable piece of music and use it as a stimulus for creative writing, or look at a free-flowing piece of art to stimulate memories and associations.

*For more detailed suggestions see music section, Chapter 5.

VICTORIA DAY

Initial Cue   Small Union Jack flag or napkin with flag or royal family picture

Verbal Cue   Victoria Day coming up. Do you recall celebrating Queen Victoria's birthday as a child? Who was queen/king when you were a child? Ever see them during a royal visit? Were you or your family a fan of the royal family? Why? Why not? (There are bound to be strong feelings here, so be prepared to give everyone a chance to give an opinion.)

Nonverbal Cue   Sing "God Save the Queen" (many will be more familiar with "King") together.

Prop/Artifact   Picture books, posters, photo albums, or scrapbook pictures of the royal family. (Focus on particular pictures; work through the pictures in chronological order). The "Queen Mum' is familiar and particularly popular with the older generation; commemorative plates, spoons, cups, and memorabilia

Verbal Cue   Who was queen/king during the time you were a young adult? What do remember about them? Ever see them when on tour? Where? When? Do you have a favorite member of the royal family? Least favorite? Why? Recall any amusing stories or anything else about the members of the royal family?

Nonverbal Cue   Look at the pictures and make personal associations.

Prop/Artifact   Focus on current Queen Elizabeth II (using pictures)

Verbal Cue   Do you remember the coronation? Watch it on TV? Where? With whom? What do you think of the current monarch, Queen Elizabeth? What's good about her? Not so good? Do you think that she should step down and have Charles become King? Why? Why not? What else do you recall about the current royal family (e.g., surname, Windsor; husband, Prince Philip; the Queen's father was King George VI)?

Nonverbal Cue   Examine pictures; select favorite/least favorite.

Audiovisual   *The Queen, the Chef, and the President*, NFB 1 0174 113, 22 minutes (the 1973 visit of Queen Elizabeth to a tiny Acadian village on Prince Edward Island, Canada).

Music   "God Save the Queen," "Rule Britannia," "The Maple Leaf Forever"

Activities   English tea party.

FARMING

Initial Cue	Fresh clover (e.g., from roadside or vacant lots) or a handful of hay
Verbal Cue	Smell remind you of anything? Ever live on a farm? Visit a farm? Work on a farm? Where? When?
Nonverbal Cue	Smell and feel the clover or the hay; tie with a ribbon to make a wall decoration.
Prop/Artifact	Focus portions of the session on various farm animals, in turn, using associated materials: cow—cowbell, milking stool, butter churn, and other equipment; sheep—sheepskin, spinning wheel, wool carders, colored skeins of yarn; chickens—egg basket, feathers, grain (for feeding the hens)
Verbal Cue	What do you remember most about your time on the farm? What did you like best about the farm? Least? Continue with personal associations with particular animals and farm activities (e.g., milking the cows, shearing the sheep, gathering the eggs, bringing in the hay, slopping the hogs, driving the tractor, hitching the horses). As materials are examined use sensory associations (e.g., does the feel of the sheepskin remind you of anything) to help call forth memories.
Nonverbal Cue	Examine materials and use as appropriate (e.g., ring the bell, turn the butter churn, wind the yarn into a ball).
Prop/Artifact	Tastes of farm fresh foods (e.g., homemade bread with freshly made butter, home-cured bacon or sausage, freshly made buttermilk biscuits)
Verbal Cue	Do you recall having these foods? Making them? Where? When? With whom? Focus discussion on farming now and how it has changed (e.g., mechanization, large farms). Would you rather live on the farm or in the city now? Why? Advantages of each? What animals would you raise if you lived on a farm? What would you grow?
Nonverbal Cue	Make and taste the foods.
Audiovisual	*Prairie Album*, NFB 1 0179 226, 14 minutes (farm life on the prairies during the depression). *Potatoes*, NFB 1 0176 164, 27 minutes, illustrated by watercolor paintings (the story of the modern shifts in potato farming). *Cattle Ranch*, NFB 1 0161 068, 20 minutes (a vivid picture of the life, and music, of a cowboy on the open range). *How Things Have Changed*, NFB 1 0171 025, 10 minutes (comparison between the modern and traditional cattle drives). *New Denmark*, NFB 1 0180 007, 28 minutes (the story of how the Danish immigrants to New Brunswick established potato farming).
Music	"We're Poor Little Lambs Who Have Lost Our Way," "Red River Valley," "Oklahoma!"
Activities	Visit a farm or a museum farm operation; have a hog-calling contest; make butter from fresh cream (use a real churn if available, otherwise a hand rotary beater); complete the expressions: You can wait until the _____ (cows come home); He is a _____ (wolf) in _____ (sheep's) clothing; They eat like a _____ (pig/hog); You can't make a silk purse out of a _____ (sow's) ear; He's as stubborn as a _____ (mule); I'm so hungry, I could eat a _____ (horse).

FLOWERS/GARDENING

Initial Cue	Selection of fresh, fragrant flowers attractively placed in vintage flower basket
Verbal Cue	Do you recall a particular flower/flower garden during your childhood? Where was it? Who grew it? What kinds of flowers? Which was your favorite?
Nonverbal Cue	Pick favorite flower(s) and make into a boutonniere or arrange in vase; encourage appreciation of the smell, feel, and visual beauty.
Prop/Artifact	Various representations and uses of flowers (vintage if possible), pictures of Victorian gardens, famous flower gardens (local and international), embroidered items, wallpaper, floor coverings, famous paintings, sachets, dried flowers
Verbal Cue	Grow flowers at your home as an adult? Inside? What kind? What colors? Favorites? Friends or family members have special flower gardens? Get flowers or flower greeting card as a special present? What were they? From whom? What was the occasion? Have any of these items (i.e., wallpaper, embroidery, etc.) in your home? What was it like (color, design, location)? Special memories of anything similar? Use items to continue personal associations. What is your favorite flower? Why? What color? What flowers?
Nonverbal Cue	Examine items and focus on sensory aspects to encourage personal reminiscences.
Prop/Artifact	Seed catalogues with color pictures of flower; greeting cards or stationery with flower illustrations
Verbal Cue	What is your favorite flower? Why? What color? Who would you like to send a "flower" greeting to (using cards or stationery)? What flowers (focus attention on current friends/family)? What greeting or wish?
Nonverbal Cue	Select favorites from catalogue; write greetings on card.
Audiovisual	*What Price Beauty*, NFB 1 0173 108, 15 minutes (magnificent shots of wide variety of flowers and discussion of how they were developed).
Music	"When You Wore a Tulip," "The Yellow Rose of Texas," "My Wild Irish Rose," "Sweet Violets," "Moonlight and Roses," "Lonely Little Petunia in an Onion Patch"
Activities	Make pressed flower pictures or cards; visit a florist's shop or greenhouse with flowering plants, or a popular local park or garden with a flower garden; make a collage or decoupage of favorite flower pictures; dry flowers for arrangements or sachets; create new verses for "Roses are red, violets are blue." (See horticulture section, Chapter 5 for more details.)

WEDDINGS

Initial Cue	Vintage wedding photographs (or photocopies)
Verbal Cue	Do you remember going to a wedding as a child? Whose wedding? Where was it? What was the bride's dress like? What sort of food was served? What did you wear?
Nonverbal Cue	Look at details of pictures and make personal associations.
Prop/Artifact	Clothing items for weddings (vintage if possible): lace, veil, gloves, top hat, cummerbund, dress tie, silk pocket scarf, the bride's garter; pictures of famous weddings (e.g., Queen Elizabeth, Grace Kelly)
Verbal Cue	Have you ever seen a picture from your parents' wedding? Where was it? When? Did they celebrate any special anniversaries? What were the clothes like? Continue with associations with other weddings. (If there are members of the group who have never married or married unhappily, approach this topic with sensitivity to their feelings.) Their own wedding? Weddings of their children? Friends? Silver and golden wedding anniversary celebrations? Ever been to a chivaree? Know any good stories about chivarees? What was the most beautiful marriage? Where? Were you there?
Nonverbal Cue	Try on items.
Audiovisual	Films, clips of famous weddings (e.g., the British royal family)
Music	"Wedding March," "Daisy, Daisy," "Me and My Gal," "Wedding Bells are Breaking Up That Old Gang of Mine"
Activities	Arrange an outing to watch the wedding photo sessions at a local park; make the punch and other goodies for a "celebration."

FATHER'S DAY

Initial Cue	Assortment of vintage ties (available at rummage sales, garage sales, etc.)
Verbal Cue	Did your father wear a tie? Often, or just on special occasions? Which one of these would he have liked the best?
Nonverbal Cue	Examine and try on ties.
Prop/Artifact	Vintage photo of man dressed up (participant's father if available); vintage men's hats (e.g., fedora, straw hat, top hat, worker's cap); vintage items such as ties, cane or walking stick, cuff links, tiepins, dress "collars," shaving cup
Verbal Cue	Does the photograph remind you of your father? How so? How different? Assist in making personal associations with the father. What did he look like (hair color, height, etc.)? What was his full name? Where was he born? What did he work at? What did he like to do for fun? What do you remember about your father? About special times/events with your father (e.g., fishing trip, camping trip, special trips or presents, working together in his workshop)? Discuss associations with items with memories of father. Are there people who have been like a father to you?
Nonverbal Cue	Try on items (as appropriate); look at and feel individual items.
Prop/Artifact	Contemporary Father's Day card (store-bought or made in the group)
Verbal Cue	Father's Day coming up. Use information about personal history to talk with those who are fathers (parents) about their children: Names? Where do they live? Are you a grandparent? Special remembrances of Father's Day for you (surprises, special presents)? If some participants have not had children, approach this topic with sensitivity. Focus on their fathers or perhaps people who have been like children to them.
Nonverbal Cue	Make Father's Day cards; sign and send to someone special whom they would like to remember on Father's Day (emphasis on reality reassurance).
Audiovisual	*David and Bert*, 1 0175 036, 27 minutes (story of a 40-year friendship between a prospector and a native Indian and the passing on of their stories to grandchildren).
Music	"My Grandfather's Clock," "When Father Papered the Parlor"
Activities	Picture collage of individuals' fathers (use background information you know to preselect a limited choice of materials (favorite sports, occupation, hobbies, birthplace, etc.); Make Father's Day cards for someone special; do creative writing focused on memories of father (individually or in group); create a group poem or other form for creative writing, using the letters from *Father*: F is for _____, etc.

CARPENTRY/WOODWORKING

Initial Cue   Wood "curls" from planing or pieces of 1" × 1" cut for making a trivet
Verbal Cue   Does the smell and feel of the wood remind you of anything or anyone from childhood? Know anyone who worked with wood? As a carpenter? As a handyman? Who? Where was their shop? What did they make? Did you like to help?
Nonverbal Cue   Focus on the sensory aspects of the wood; arrange curls into a picture design

Prop/Artifact   Vintage hand tools (e.g., plane, hand drill, hammer, level, square); carpenter's apron; small hand-crafted wooden items, vintage if possible (e.g., sewing boxes, bookends, corner brackets, napkin holders, candlesticks, wooden toys)
Nonverbal Cue   Examine the items and explore the sensory aspects.

Prop/Artifact   Pieces of wood of various types, sandpaper
Verbal Cue   Favorite type of wood? What would you like to have made out of it? Do you prefer wooden chairs to the modern metal chairs?
Nonverbal Cue   Examine the wood and do some sanding.

Audiovisual   *John Hooper's Way with Wood*, NFB 1 0177 281, 18 minutes (a woodworking craftsman at work).
Activities   Make a small wooden item (see "Woodworking Activities" in Chapter 5).

NATIONAL HOLIDAY

Canada: July 1—Canada Day (Dominion Day)   United States: July 4—Independence Day

Initial Cue	Small national flag (often sold as party favors)
Verbal Cue	Recall celebrations of Dominion Day/Independence Day as a child? Parade? Picnic? Fireworks? Where? Who were you with?
Nonverbal Cue	National Anthem
Prop/Artifact	Full-sized flag; national items, mottoes, crests, as appropriate, e.g., Canada (maple leaf, maple products, beaver pictures, national game—hockey), U.S.A. (the eagle, apple pie, national game—baseball); coffee table books showing good pictures of various parts of the country
Verbal Cue	Which national holiday celebration as an adult do you remember the most? Why was it special? Where? Who with? What did you do? Ever been in the parade? What did you do? Ever help organize the parade? The picnic? Was there a community picnic? Where? What did you eat? Horse races? Remember one in particular? (For those who have a particular ethnic background, focus on national holiday customs of this country.)
Nonverbal Cue	Look at items and make personal associations.
Prop/Artifact	Full-sized map of the country; sparklers, small firecrackers, pictures of firework display
Verbal Cue	Reality reassurance focusing on present date, age of the country, and present location. Favorite place(s) in the country? Why? If you could live anywhere you wanted to, where would it be? Why? Ever set off firecrackers? Go to a display? Where? With whom?
Nonverbal Cue	Locate places on map as discussed.
Audiovisual	*Here is Canada*, NFB 1 0172 568, 28 minutes (beautiful film portrait of Canada from coast to coast).
Music	Parade music (marching bands); "This Land Is Your Land"; national songs: Canada—"Oh Canada," "God Save the Queen," "Maple Leaf Forever"; United States—"America," "God Bless America," "My Country Tis of Thee"
Activities	Have a picnic with homemade ice cream; arrange outings to the local parade, fireworks, other events.

BEACHES/OCEANS/LAKES

Initial Cue	Seashells (small) in small plastic containers of sand (e.g., yogurt containers)
Verbal Cue	Remember going to the beach as a child? Which beach? What was it like? (small, big, crowded, sandy, rocky, color of sand, water temperature)? Whom did you go with? What did you like best about it? Least? Did you have a picnic there? What did you eat? How did you get there? Did you collect seashells? Make anything out of them?
Nonverbal Cue	Find the seashells in the sand, focusing on the sensory aspects of feel, color, variety.
Prop/Artifact	Pictures of popular local beaches, "swimming holes" (including vintage pictures of a swimming party); pictures of famous ocean or lake beaches; swimming gear (e.g., goggles, bathing cap, bathing suit); beachcombing treasures (e.g., driftwood, shells, beach glass, beach pebbles, dried seaweed)
Verbal Cue	Continue with associations with times at the beach/swimming as an adult. Where? When? With whom? Favorite beach? Why? Like to swim—outdoors or in a pool? Like to walk on the beach? Collect treasures? Ever find anything special? Ever put a note in a bottle? Ever find one? Special memory of a happy day at the beach or swimming? Ever take a trip to a far away or famous beach?
Nonverbal Cue	Write a note and put it in a bottle.
Prop/Artifact	Large conch type seashell; seafood taste treats, as appropriate to local favorites (e.g., smoked oysters, pickled herring, sardines, fish and chips)
Verbal Cue	If you could go to any beach you wanted to now, where would it be? With whom? What would you do there (e.g., walk, swim, watch the sunset)? What is your favorite type of seafood? (give examples as necessary) Ever caught it? Cooked it?
Nonverbal Cue	Listen to the sound of the ocean; taste the foods.
Music	"In the Good Old Summertime," "Swimming, Swimming"
Activities	Have a picnic/outing to the beach or swimming spot, indoor pool party; write note/messages to send in bottles; make a decorative item with polished driftwood and other beachcombing treasures.

VACATIONS

Initial Cue	Local, provincial, or state map
Verbal Cue	Do you remember going on any trips as a child? How far? How did you travel? Who with? What did you do there? Did you visit anyone special? Did you do anything special (assist with cues appropriate to the place, as necessary)
Nonverbal Cue	Examine the map and find birthplace, present location, favorite local attractions.
Prop/Artifact	Small vintage suitcase packed with some items for travel (e.g., vintage clothing, hat, towel and face cloth, comb, brush, camera); clear pictures or post cards of favorite local or world famous travel spots (e.g., Niagara Falls, Statue of Liberty, Eiffel Tower, etc.)
Verbal Cue	Did you take any trips as an adult? Where to? (Niagara Falls, Statue of Liberty, Eiffel Tower, etc.) Do you like to travel? Why? Why not? Did you have to travel for work? (What for? etc.) Know anyone who was a traveling salesperson or had to travel for work? Or made exciting trips for adventure? Any good stories of travel adventures (getting lost, etc.)?
Nonverbal Cue	Sample food items appropriate to travel locations.
Prop/Artifact	Family crest, emblem, family tree
Verbal Cue	Ever go to a family reunion? Family name? Have a crest? How far did you go? Did anyone travel farther? What did you do? Did it happen every year?
Nonverbal Cue	Examine items.
Prop/Artifact	Travel brochures, train schedules, plane/train tickets
Verbal Cue	If you could travel anywhere you wanted to right now, where would it be? What would you do there? How would you like to travel (train, plane, car). Ever traveled by plane? What did you like about it? What didn't you like about it?
Nonverbal Cue	Look at brochures and pick favorite places.
Audiovisual	Travelogue films of interesting places. *The Mighty Steam Calliope*, NFB 1 0178 094, 10 minutes (a fun summer afternoon with a working calliope).
Music	"Faraway Places," "Slow Boat to China"
Activities	Make a collage of travel spots; make a scrapbook of actual trip participants have made; make a short "trip" to a favorite local destination; design a family crest using an outline.

CARS*

Initial Cue Old and/or modern "dinky" cars
Verbal Cue Ever have a toy car? Favorite? Other favorite toys of childhood? Children or grandchildren play with these? What are their favorite toys?
Nonverbal Cue Look at the cars; in an adult appropriate way encourage "racing" the car along the table.

Prop/Artifact Antique toy car or model, old license plate, manual car horn, old hubcap; illustrated books, posters, and calendars of vintage cars; vintage photographs of people or families beside their cars
Verbal Cue First car ride? First car driven? First car owned? Where did you go? With whom? For what occasion? What kind of car? What color? How much did you pay for the car? How much was gas? Did you ever have your picture taken beside a car? What car? Who did it belong to? Anything special about the car? What was the occasion for the picture?
Nonverbal Cue Touch, feel, and try out the props (e.g., honk the horn); look at the photos and books and relate to personal life experiences.

Prop/Artifact Photocopied "booklets," one for each participant, of popular cars from their era, including advertisements
Verbal Cue Ever ride in a car like that? Own one? Anybody you know have one? Favorite model? Why? Least favorite? Why? Recall the advertising slogans?
Nonverbal Cue Encourage/assist participants to write their names on the booklets as well as other comments about favorite cars, recollections, etc.

Prop/Artifact Road map or outline map of province, state, or county
Verbal Cue Longest, favorite, most memorable car trip. To where? With whom? In what car? What did you do there?
Nonverbal Cue Locate home, birthplace, another place visited by car; trace route of a remembered long-distance trip or favorite "Sunday drive" route.

Prop/Artifact *Motor Trend* or other modern-day car magazine; colored, contemporary car advertisements mounted on construction paper or Bristol board
Verbal Cue Favorite modern car? Make? Model? Color? Prefer old model or new model cars? Why? Cost of new cars now compared to your first car? Cost of gasoline now? Then?
Nonverbal Cue Examine pictures and select a favorite.

Audiovisual *The Bates Car*, NFB 1 0174 017, 15 minutes (a humorous true story of an older English inventor who develops a methane-powered car). *Just One of the Boys*, NFB 1 0175 212, 16 minutes (an excellent film about a blind mechanic who specializes in repairing and restoring vintage cars). *The Oshawa Kid,* NFB 1 016 029, 24 minutes (the story of the car industry at Oshawa, Ontario, from the early days). Bi-Focal Productions has a kit, "Remembering Automobiles," that includes a slide carousel or videotape on vintage cars.
Music "Daisy, Daisy," "There Was a Little Ford," "The Low Backed Car," "In My Merry Oldsmobile," "Meet Me in St. Louis"
Activities Plan outings to a car museum, antique car show, new car show, car salesroom; a Sunday drive for ice cream. A popular destination for a drive was for ice cream or a picnic; the drive may not be possible, but the picnic or the ice cream bar can partially be recreated indoors. Fill in the blanks: "imagine" games are a good way to close the group, returning to the present while encouraging creativity and imagination. Keep the preamble adult: If I could have any car at all, it would be a _____. If I could get in a car now and go anywhere, I would want it to be _____.

*For other summer themes, see Fishing, Boats, Indoor Planting, and Garden Harvest.

SCHOOL DAYS

Initial Cue Piece of chalk, shiny red apple (an "apple for the teacher")

Verbal Cue *Note: Reality reassurance is especially important throughout this session.* What do you remember about your first day of school? Where? Name of school? Teacher? How did you get there? Who else was in your class? What did you wear? Were you nervous? Did you bring your lunch to school?

Nonverbal Cue Write name with chalk on slate or chalkboard; do opening exercises in age-appropriate fashion (e.g., national anthem, pledge of allegiance to the flag).

Prop/Artifact Vintage schoolbooks (readers, spellers, etc.); book bag; lunch pail (lard pail); book strap; slate and chalk; school bell; old wall maps of region, state, or province; straight pen and bottled ink; abacus; vintage pictures of school classes/schools, as appropriate to the locality (in Canada a picture of Queen Victoria was hung in almost every school attended by this age group).

Verbal Cue Continue with associations (as above) with schools attended at various ages. Favorite subjects/teachers? Least favorite? Why? Ever play hooky? To do what? Favorite recess games? Last year of school? Where? Best friend? Special memories? Study as an adult? Teach? Anyone in your family a teacher? What do you remember about school and your children/grandchildren/nieces/nephews/neighborhood children? Help with homework? Report card time? Did you (or they) get special presents for "grading"?

Nonverbal Cue Look at books and pick out familiar ones or familiar content; try writing name with a straight pen (with assistance as appropriate); find familiar places on maps.

Prop/Artifact Contemporary schoolbooks; regional, provincial, state, or country map; modern globe

Verbal Cue What do you think about these books compared to the ones you used? What do you like better about school in your day? Now? How has the map of the country/globe of the world changed? What would you like to study/learn about now?

Nonverbal Cue Compare contemporary and vintage books and maps.

Audiovisual *We're Gonna Have Recess*, NFB 1 0167 090, 9 minutes (lively film of children playing at recess).

Music "School Days, School Days"

Activities Intergenerational gathering comparing then and now with school-age children (could include the children doing an oral history project). Make cookies or other favorite after-school snack (e.g., bread and molasses). Depending on cognitive function of participants, have a spelling bee or geography match.

WATCHES/CLOCKS

Initial Cue	Photocopied page of watches from vintage catalogue
Verbal Cue	Did you ever own a watch that looked like any of these? Which one? Where did you get it? How much did it cost?
Nonverbal Cue	Find familiar watches and prices.
Prop/Artifact	Vintage pocket watches, shelf clocks, alarm clocks, etc., as available; pictures of grandfather's clock, other types of large clocks; well-known local or international clocks (e.g., Big Ben), sundial (or pictures); hourglass (available as modern minute timers)
Verbal Cue	What was your first watch like? Where did you get it? How much did it cost? Was it a gift? From whom? For what occasion? Did you ever own a watch/clock like this? Did you buy it? Was it a gift? How long did you have it? Did it keep good time? Ever own a clock that chimed? A cuckoo clock? A grandfather's clock? Know anyone who did? Ever have a sundial in your yard? Did it work? Discuss other ways of keeping track of time (e.g., the noon whistle, angle of the sun).
Nonverbal Cue	Wind the watches/clocks as appropriate.
Prop/Artifact	Contemporary watches, clocks, etc.; contemporary catalogue with watches.
Verbal Cue	What do you think of modern watches/clocks? Advantages? Disadvantages? Which type do you like best? Why?
Nonverbal Cue	Compare prices/features of vintage and contemporary watches.
Music	"My Grandfather's Clock," recordings of well-known clock chimes
Activities	Outings to see any well-known local clock (e.g., town clock); complete the sayings: Tomorrow never _____ (comes). Don't put off until tomorrow what _____ (you can do today). Time and tide waits for _____ (no man). A watched pot _____ (never boils). Time flies when you're _____ (having fun).

AUTUMN

Initial Cue   Brightly colored fall leaves of various shapes, sizes, and colors

Verbal Cue   Do you remember playing in the fall leaves as a child? Burying yourself in piles of leaves? Making leaf "houses"? Pressing colorful leaves in books? Making a collection for school? Having a fall bonfire of leaves?

Nonverbal Cue   Arrange the leaves for pressing to make a collage picture or card.

Prop/Artifact   Harvest basket (vintage wicker basket or hamper if possible) with fall produce, Indian corn, gourds; nuts in the shell (and in the outer shuck if possible); vintage preserving jars, crocks, jugs, etc.

Verbal Cue   What do you remember about fall as an adult? Getting food ready for winter? Harvest excursions (in the 1920s to help with the prairie grain harvest)? Storing food in the root cellar? Canning and preserving? Special relish/preserve favorites? Who made them? Did you have extra work in the fall? Ever shuck walnuts? Other nuts? Go to fall work bees?

Nonverbal Cue   Examine items, focusing on sensory aspects.

Prop/Artifact   Local or regional map; pictures of local or other spots with the fall foliage; vintage clothing for fall (sweaters, caps, mittens)

Verbal Cue   Go on any trips or drives to see the fall colors? Where? Have a favorite spot to see the colors? Where? What was it like? Remember getting out fall clothing like these? What were they like (color)? Where from?

Nonverbal Cue   Find favorite autumn spot on the map; try on clothing.

Prop/Artifact   Picture of the autumn countryside (local if possible); freshly harvested apples, dried apples, cider, old-fashioned apple peeler (perhaps available at a local museum)

Verbal Cue   What do you like best about autumn? Least? What's your favorite season? Why? Favorite apple? Favorite way of eating apples? Who made it? Ever see an apple peeler like this? Used one?

Nonverbal Cue   Taste different types of apples; make apple foods (applesauce, apple jelly, apple pie, hot mulled cider); try apple peeler.

Audiovisual   *Morning on the Lievre*, NFB 1 0161 024, 13 minutes (autumn scenes in the Quebec countryside). *An Apple for All Seasons*, NFB 1 0164 536, 7 minutes (the growing and harvesting of luscious apples).

Music   Autumn nature sounds tape, "Harvest Moon"

Activities   Make apple crisp. While waiting for it to bake, play "apple peel game." Peel several apples, keeping the peel in one long piece. Twirl the piece three times overhead and let it land on the floor. Decide what letter the peel makes. Originally this was done during apple peeling bees, to make dried apples, and the letter represented the initial of the person you would marry. Some may have played this in the past. Now this can be adapted to cue memory, naming appropriate categories such as a type of flower, tree, food, a place name, a person's name, etc. Iron colorful leaves between sheets of waxed paper to make cards or pictures. Make autumn decorations of gourds, Indian corn, squashes, dried leaves, and grasses. Drive to see the fall colors. Rake the leaves to mulch the garden. Make an excursion to apple orchard or cider mill. Plant fall bulbs (e.g., tulips, daffodils, crocus). Make simple, local specialty fall relish or preserves. Participants can help prepare the fruits and vegetables. Actual canning should be done by the group leader or a volunteer because of the danger of burns and spills. Making preserves can be a good party occasion. Play festive, lively music while working to encourage conversation and reminiscing. While preserves are cooking, show a popular video or film. Involve participants in tasting the preserves as they cook, and making recommendations on anything that needs to be added.

THANKSGIVING*

November (U.S.A)		October (Canada)

Initial Cue Small pumpkin(s), gourds, Indian corn, or other

Verbal Cue What do you remember about Thanksgiving as a child? Was it a big celebration in your home? Where was it? Which town? Whose home? Who came? What kinds of foods did you eat? Any special family traditions at Thanksgiving?

Nonverbal Cue Examine the item.

Prop/Artifact Harvest basket*; cornucopia; autumn-colored leaves; dried flowers, weeds, and grasses; Indian corn

Verbal Cue Continue associations with Thanksgiving as an adult. Where was Thanksgiving held? If family home, focus on associations, descriptions of family home. Where? What sort of house? Who came? Did you travel far to be home for Thanksgiving? How did you travel? Who came the farthest? How did they travel?

Nonverbal Cue Arrange cornucopia and other items for dining table or other centerpieces or decorations.

Prop/Artifact Pictures of the harvest, the countryside in autumn, Thanksgiving dinner, meals and gatherings

Verbal Cue Did you ever have the family Thanksgiving in your own home? What did you have for the meal? What kind of stuffing was the favorite at your home? Who made it? What was the happiest Thanksgiving you can remember? Why?

Nonverbal Cue Examine pictures.

Prop/Artifact Cornucopia or other picture

Verbal Cue If you could have anything you wanted for Thanksgiving dinner, what would it be? Whom would you invite? Where would you have it?

Nonverbal Cue Use picture as a cue to trigger associations/things to be thankful for and record as for creative writing.

Music "Harvest Moon"; If appropriate to participants' background, Thanksgiving hymns such as "Bringing in the Sheaves," "Come Ye Thankful People Come," "We Plough the Fields and Scatter"

Activities Make pumpkin pies from scratch (see "Sensory Stimulation," Chapter 7). Decorate with produce, leaves etc. Depending on the functional level of participants, assist them to prepare a group Thanksgiving dinner. Make a collage of favorite things, things to be thankful for, using magazine and other pictures; make a decoupage picture of a favorite autumn scene.

*See "Autumn" (September). Adapt content and discussion to current season. The harvest basket should contain winter storage vegetables such as carrots, potatoes, squash, onions (done in braids if possible), turnips, and pumpkin. Make a fall relish such as green tomato pickle or uncooked chili sauce.

HORSES

Initial Cue	Playing cards, stationery, or napkins with a horse picture
Verbal Cue	Do you remember riding a horse/going for a buggy ride/sleigh ride as a child? What was the horse like (color/size/name)? Where did you go? Who was with you? Did you like the ride? Why/Why not?
Nonverbal Cue	Examine items.
Prop/Artifact	Horseshoe, horse blanket and pin, pieces of horse harness or saddle, riding crop, curry comb, sleigh bells or similar items
Verbal Cue	Continue adult associations with horses. Ever use horses for your work (e.g., farmer, milk delivery, rancher, bread wagon, or other)? Anyone you know use a horse for their work? Ride for pleasure? Ever fall off a horse? Have any adventures (e.g., lines breaking, runaway horse)? Ever go to a rodeo? Take a long trip on horseback? A horse-pulled sleigh ride?
Nonverbal Cue	Examine items.
Prop/Artifact	Calendar or illustrated book of different types of horses
Verbal Cue	Which type of horse is your favorite? Why? What color? If you had a horse of your own, what would you call it? Where would you go? Horseback or buggy? What was best about getting around with horsepower? With cars?
Nonverbal Cue	Select favorite.
Audiovisual	*Heavy Horses*, NFB 1 0181 091, 14 minutes (a good, visual film about raising Clydesdale heavy horses; not much commentary or music). *Heavy Horse Pull*, NFB 1 0177 116, 15 minutes (a humorous look at a heavy horse pull in Ontario). *Chuckwagon*, NFB 1 0164 162, 9 minutes (fast-moving film about the chuckwagon races in Calgary). *Precision*, NFB 1 0169 033,10 minutes (shows the musical ride of the Royal Canadian Mounted Police).
Music	"Camptown Races," "The Old Grey Mare," "She'll be Comin' Round the Mountain"
Activities	Visit a horse farm or riding stable, or if nearby have the riding stable visit you. Watch a videotape of a famous horse race (e.g., the Kentucky Derby, the Queen's Plate). Make oatmeal muffins or cookies or oatcakes; associate with the fact that horses eat oats, but oats are also a healthful food for people.

HALLOWEEN

Initial Cue	Large pumpkin to make a jack-o'-lantern, as a group project
Verbal Cue	Do you remember carving a jack-o'-lantern as a child? Who helped you? Did you make scary ones or friendly ones? Did you grow the pumpkin? Where did you get it? Did you go out trick or treating? With whom? What costume did you wear?
Nonverbal Cue	Remove seeds (with long-handled spoon) and prepare pumpkin; work out design; group leader cuts design and adds candle or flashlight, depending on safety regulations.
Prop/Artifact	Various masks, hats, jackets, scarves, wigs, etc., to make do-it-yourself costumes (vintage if possible)
Verbal Cue	Continue adult associations with Halloween. Ever go to a costume party? What was your costume? Where was the party? Who else was there? Did you give out Halloween treats for the children? Homemade? What? Ever have a "trick" played on you? Ever play any tricks? Any good stories about Halloween tricks? Best costume you ever saw? Ever help a child with their costume? Who? What costume? Remember bobbing for apples?
Nonverbal Cue	Try on various articles; this can be an excellent and laughter-filled group, but the presentation must be done in an age-appropriate fashion. Have a mirror handy for people to look at the effect (a small hand mirror is best; anything larger may be frightening).
Prop/Artifact	Contemporary masks and costumes
Verbal Cue	Who would you dress up as now for Halloween? Where would you go trick or treating? What treats would you hope for? What amusing "tricks" would you do?
Nonverbal Cue	Try costumes on; select favorite.
Music	Favorite music as appropriate
Activities	Have a costume parade with visiting children, costume parade by staff. Have a Halloween party with bobbing for apples, making caramel corn, and other such activities. Make chocolate drop cookies and roll them in orange tinted coconut to look like pumpkins. Have a pumpkin-carving contest (using small pie-type pumpkins).

VETERANS DAY/REMEMBRANCE DAY*

This will be a highly emotional topic for many, with the intimate connections of the older generation to having served in either World War I or World War II or having lost loved ones in war. Be prepared to offer support for the expression of sadness.

Initial Cue	Lapel pin poppy
Verbal Cue	Assist to recall associations with the poppy.
Nonverbal Cue	Put on the poppy.
Prop/Artifact	National flag, military beret, tam or cap (as appropriate), medals or other military decorations
Verbal Cue	Did you serve in World War I or II? Did anyone you know? Where? How long? What rank? What regiment? Did you go to Remembrance Day ceremonies? Participate? How? Where were the ceremonies? Parade? Help to sell poppies?
Nonverbal Cue	Examine the artifacts.
Prop/Artifact	Stencil of large poppy; white paper, red construction paper, pencil, pen, scissors; trace poppy on red paper with stencil; assist to cut out as necessary; place on white paper
Verbal Cue	Use poppy picture to do assisted creative writing with thoughts and reflections on Remembrance Day. Name people they would like to remember. End on a positive note with words of appreciation for these people. Introduce happy wartime memories with favorite wartime music (e.g., "White Cliffs of Dover," "Waltzing Matilda")
Nonverbal Cue	As appropriate, taps, moment of silence, and reveille
Audiovisual	*Fields of Sacrifice*, NFB 1 0164 199, 20 minutes (moving film of the battlefields of World War I and World War II). Canadian National Film Board has numerous films about Canada during the war.
Music	Favorite wartime music (e.g., Vera Lynn songs, "Waltzing Matilda," "It's a Long Way to Tipperary").
Activities	Plan a simple Remembrance Day service involving participants in selecting the hymns, doing readings, and sharing memories; share in refreshments after the service.

*Other programs for this time of year: Thanksgiving (American), Music Appreciation (see May), Birthdays (see April).

TELEPHONE

Initial Cue	Photocopies (one per person) of vintage telephones or, if appropriate to participants, tin can and string "telephone" system (associate with childhood toy)
Verbal Cue	Did you always have a telephone in your home as a child? When did you get a telephone? Where was it? What was it like (e.g., old-fashioned crank telephone)? Do you remember your number? Ring (on a party line)?
Nonverbal Cue	Identify the features of the telephones.
Prop/Artifact	Vintage telephone(s), particularly a crank-type, may be available from a museum; an artifact from the local telephone company; vintage telephone book from the locality
Verbal Cue	Continue associations with the telephone in their own homes as adults. What type? Where was it? What was the number/ring? Any amusing stories with party lines? Listening in? Stories about wrong numbers? Telephone helped you out in the case of an emergency? Use the telephone for your work? Do you like "visiting" on the telephone? What is the farthest distance you ever called or talked on the phone?
Nonverbal Cue	Try out the phone(s); crank or dial your ring or that of others you know; find the telephone number of friends or others in the vintage directory.
Prop/Artifact	Contemporary phones, adaptive telephone equipment (local telephone company may have an adaptive equipment display)
Verbal Cue	Compare differences between modern telephones and early telephones, advantages/disadvantages of each; include modern devices such as answering machines and cellular phones. Who would you like to call on the telephone right now? What would you say? (Reality reassurance is important.)
Nonverbal Cue	Look at and try out equipment.
Audiovisual	*For You Mr. Bell*, NFB 1 0171 106, 6 minutes (photographs and memories of Alexander Graham Bell at his home in Baddeck, Nova Scotia, where he worked on many of his inventions).
Activities	Visit telephone company display center with contemporary telephones and adaptive equipment and/or a display of vintage telephones. Play a telephone game (presented in an adult manner); whisper a message from one person to the next and compare the differences between the beginning and the ending messages; one-to-one time, as appropriate, to call someone special. Write out telephone messages they would like to give to favorite persons.

QUILTS

Initial Cue	Full-size quilt spread on the table or, if unavailable, quilt patches
Verbal Cue	Did you sleep under a quilt as a child? Remember homemade quilts in your home? Who made it? What was the design like? What colors? Do you remember a favorite or special quilt?
Nonverbal Cue	Feel the quilt; look at different shapes, size, colors
Prop/Artifact	Quilt patches of various colors and textures, quilt batting, thimble(s); books or magazines with pictures of vintage quilts
Verbal Cue	Continue with associations with quilts, as an adult. Have quilts in your home? Who made them? What colors? What design? Ever make a quilt? Know anyone who did? What design? What colors? How long did it take? Where did it get used? Ever go to a quilting bee? Where? Who else was there? Any good stories?
Nonverbal Cue	Look at patches/quilt designs and select favorite; trace out design of favorite remembered quilt.
Prop/Artifact	Various quilted items (e.g., potholders, pillows, place mats, tea cozy, clothing)
Verbal Cue	(Show contemporary quilt design.) Ever do anything like this? Own anything like this? What? What do you think of "modern" quilt designs? Do you prefer blankets or quilts as covers? Why?
Nonverbal Cue	Examine items and select favorite.
Audiovisual	Bi-Focal kit on quilts
Music	"Aunt Dinah's Quilting Party"
Activities	Make quilt collage with fabric scraps glued on paper. Organize a quilt show among staff, family, interested community members. Invite members of a local quilting guild in for a demonstration or display.

CHRISTMAS

Initial Cue	Evergreen boughs with red velvet ribbon or holly branch or Christmas decoration. Note: Because of fire hazards, evergreen boughs should not be left about in communal living situations.
Verbal Cue	Did you decorate your house with evergreens at Christmas when you were a child? Where did you get them? Who with? Where did you put them? Have a Christmas tree? Where from? What kind? How big? Where did you put it? What sorts of decorations? Have any special favorites? Is there a Christmas tree that you remember especially well, or a favorite? What was it like? What house? Who decorated it?
Nonverbal Cue	Tie bow onto the bough; arrange pieces and ribbon in a wide-mouth glass jar to make a table centerpiece.
Prop/Artifact	Selection of Christmas decorations, ornaments (vintage if possible), red candles, and candleholders; Christmas tablecloth, napkins, or place mats; Christmas stockings; cone wreaths (or other dried wreaths); selection of Christmas cards (or the cover page of used cards)
Verbal Cue	Continue with associations with Christmas through adulthood. Where was Christmas held? Whose house? Who was there? What kind of tree? Other decorations? How did you get there? Ever get snowed in at Christmas? Other favorite stories or adventures at Christmas time? Favorite family stories always told at Christmas? (May help to start off by telling something from your own Christmas memories.)
Nonverbal Cue	Look at the ornaments and select favorites (put on a tree if possible); put candles in the holders and light; decorate table; select favorite Christmas card and write poem or reflections to go with it.
Prop/Artifact	Peppermint candy cane, Christmas hard candies, chocolates, favorite homemade or commercial Christmas treats (e.g., fruitcake, shortbread, mince tarts, cranberry sauce)
Verbal Cue	What was your favorite food at Christmas time? Who made it or where did it come from? What did you usually have for Christmas dinner? Who cooked which things? What did you make? What was your specialty? What ingredients did you use? Which Christmas dinner do you remember especially well? Who was there? What did you have for dinner? Who cooked it? If you could have anything you wanted for Christmas dinner, what would it be? Who would you like to cook it? Who else would you invite? What would you wear? Where would it be?
Nonverbal Cue	Try out the treats; make some as suggested in the activities section.
Audiovisual	*Christmas Lights*, NFB 1 0169 024, 9 minutes (beautiful film of Christmas lights, with music and no words). *I've Never Walked the Steppes*, NFB 1 0175 018, 28 minutes (the story of Christmas festivities with a Ukrainian family). *A Figgy Duff Christmas*, NFB 1 0178 233, 10 minutes (the traditional Christmas music of Newfoundland, Canada).
Music	A selection of favorites such as "Jingle Bells," "White Christmas," "Silent Night," "Rudolph," "I Saw Mommy Kissing Santa Claus." Recordings of Christmas favorites by popular singers for this generation, such as Bing Crosby, Vera Lynn, Frank Sinatra.
Activities	Christmas has such rich and wide-ranging associations and so many special activities that the list of possible activities is endless. Here are a few suggestions: Plan a group Christmas dinner, including as many favorite foods as possible, and having participants do as much of the preparations as possible (spread out over several days as suggested by activity analysis). Make special Christmas foods such as easy shortbreads, fudge, bishop's bread, gingerbread cookies, sugar cookies (cut in Christmas shapes), chocolate drop cookies shaped into wreaths and decorated with green coconut and maraschino cherries. Making these together is a good intergenerational activity. Decorate a Christmas tree. Include old fashioned decorations such as strings of popcorn and cranberries. This can be quite a difficult activity, so be sure your participants have the motor and visual skills necessary. Use large needles and stale popcorn. Family members may bring in favorite personal decorations. Make a personalized Christmas place mat. Mount a favorite Christmas card scene on ticketboard. Assist, as necessary, to write in favorite Christmas food, name, and December 199?. Plasticize the end product.

That's a life, James, I'll tell you, not as if you didn't know—standin out there in the maple grove countin up your buckets like a banker, and lookin out over the hills as the whole world outside and inside unlocks. First the pussy willows come, and the rivers run emerald green. . . .
Then the robins arrive, sometimes flocks of two or three hundred, brightening the bare brown southern cants. About the same time, spring peepers stot up. Then fields begin to green. Some reason, the green always appears first where the snow's melted last.

—John Gardner

Sensory Stimulation

1.0 INTRODUCTION: MR. D. AND THE PUMPKIN

Meet Mr. D., a distinguished, balding, elderly man with an engaging smile. Trouble is, neither his wife of more than 50 years, nor his children, nor the staff in the institution where he lived saw it much any more. What they saw was a severely disabled man who apparently recognized none of his loved ones or caregivers and, out of the gray confusion that made up his world, forcefully resisted the full care he so much needed. He no longer fed himself, and spent most of his day sleeping or staring off into space. On rare occasions he might utter a solitary, unconnected word. Mr. D. was severely impaired due to Alzheimer's disease.

It was almost Halloween the first time Mr. D. came to sensory stimulation group. When his gerichair was wheeled to a place at the table, he didn't even open his eyes during this change of scenes. Our department garden had produced a fine, brilliant orange pumpkin, which I had brought to group that day. I placed the pumpkin in front of Mr. D. No response. While verbally introducing myself, the day, the season, I gently guided Mr. D.'s hands to the cool, ridged surface of the pumpkin. Contact! His eyes were open, spar-

kling with life. This man, who hadn't spoken a sentence in weeks, hefted the pumpkin, eyed it approvingly, and said, "Well, now, isn't that a dandy. Wherever did you get that?" That day, after the other sensory experiences of the group and almost every day thereafter, Mr. D. put in the milk and sugar and stirred his own tea.

This account may leave you shrugging and thinking to yourself, "Well, I guess you had to be there!" Truer words were never spoken! Unless you have stepped into the world and hearts of people severely disabled by ADRD you cannot begin to imagine the significance of being able to perceive, appreciate, and respond to an ordinary item in the environment, such as the lowly pumpkin, or the immense satisfaction of being able to prepare your own tea. These simple acts of daily life have become rare gifts—gifts that enable individuals with ADRD to be competent once again and feel affirmed in their humanness. Caregivers who are able to appreciate these occasions as gifts also share in them. Mrs. D. once said to me, "If only I could see him smile once again, it would do my heart such good." In fact, she saw this and much more.

A few months later Mr. D. became one of the participants in a special variation of sensory stimulation, which I call eating stimulation. Prompted by the physical and verbal cues, the homelike environment, and the enhanced sensory cues of the tastes and smells of premeal activities in this group, Mr. D. began to feed himself for the first time in seven months.

Such progress is not possible for every individual severely disabled by ADRD. However, with enhanced and guided sensory stimulation, it is possible for everyone to appreciate and respond to the rich sensory world of smells, movement, feels, sights, sounds, and tastes, from which they are often isolated by their disease.

1.1 What Is Sensory Stimulation?

Sensory stimulation is an individual or group activity for the cognitively impaired elderly who have difficulty in relating and responding to their surroundings. Meaningful and familiar smells, movements, feels, sights, sounds, and tastes from their immediate and larger surroundings are presented systematically and in a format that can be understood by the individual.

1.2 What Is the Purpose of Sensory Stimulation?

Through focusing attention on specific, concrete, sensory cues, individuals are assisted to explore these materials, relate them to familiar life experiences, and are thus enabled to make appropriate responses to their world. Sensory stimulation is designed to compensate for the sensory deprivation that these individuals may experience as a result of ADRD.

1.3 For the Individual with ADRD, What Is the Meaning of Being Enabled To Make Appropriate Responses?

No one can say for certain what being enabled to make appropriate responses means. However, the experimental evidence and the clinical observations outlined in the next section, and old-fashioned common sense, strongly suggest that persons who are able to participate in the social and self-care aspects of their lives feel better about themselves and are more calm and more alert. The best way to try to understand this is to stand, imaginatively, in the shoes of the person with ADRD. How would you feel if you were completely dependent on other persons and totally unable to relate to the world and people around you?

For example, try this brief experiment: Go to an area far removed from the kitchen for dinner, preferably not even in your house. A friend blindfolds you. Without speaking or being spoken to, you are fed a tepid, bland meal, which you had no hand in preparing and no say in its content. As a final gesture, your friend wipes the spilled food from your face. Write down all of the feelings and thoughts you have during this brief experiment in reduced sensory stimulation, dependency, and disassociation from the normal mealtime environment. Mul-

tiply this times 24 hours a day, times seven days a week and try, if you can, to overlay your reactions with the frustration of your incomprehension as to why it is not possible any longer to feed yourself. I have participated in this experiential exercise many times, with many people, and it has always been an overwhelming experience. On one occasion, a physician told me that, despite every conscious effort he made to participate fully, he was so repulsed by being fed that he found himself absolutely incapable of opening his mouth when the spoon was on his lips!

1.4 What Purpose Does Sensory Stimulation Serve for Caregivers?

Individuals who are more able to relate to and participate in their surroundings feel better about themselves and are more calm, more alert, and more functional; hence, care is less demanding.

2.0 THE THEORY BEHIND SENSORY STIMULATION

2.1 Sensory Deprivation

Numerous experiments have shown that when normal, healthy adults are deprived of sensory stimulation they exhibit negative effects such as decreased motivation, poor concentration, impaired motor coordination, difficulty with abstract reasoning, and an increase in disorientation and somatic complaints (Ernst et al. 1978; Parent 1978; Zubek 1969). These effects were increased by perceptual deprivation (that is, being in a meaningless environment) and further increased by immobilization. This decreased functioning persisted for some time—longer with extended deprivation—after return to a normal environment. Sensory deprivation has also been observed to produce these negative effects in cases of acute illness and/or long-term hospitalization (Downey 1972; Jackson et al. 1962).

Persons with ADRD are especially at risk of sensory deprivation. The sources of this risk are as follows.

Age-associated changes in the sensory systems: Older individuals may not see, hear, feel, taste, smell, or move about as well as they once did (see Chapter 1).

Deficits that accompany ADRD: Individuals with ADRD frequently are unable to interpret and act on what their senses tell them. Disease-related impairments in reasoning, judgment, memory, perception, language, and motor skills render their environment effectively meaningless. They are essentially living in a perceptually deprived environment.

Potential for under- or overstimulation of the senses due to institutionalized living: Sources of understimulation are such things as the decrease in caring personal touch, the sameness of each institutional day, the presence of bland colors and textures, and the absence of familiar objects and people. One study compared perceived body images of nursing home residents with those of community-dwelling elderly. The nursing home residents were found to have significantly impaired body images (Bruneau et al. 1981). Overstimulation can also cause sensory deprivation, since the information cannot be understood or processed. Sources of excess stimulation are the coming and going of staff and supplies, blaring radios or television, and public address systems (Cleary et al. 1988). In addition, there is the real possibility of apathy and decreased motivation, leading to decreased interaction, due to institution-induced learned helplessness (see Chapter 4).

Multiple effects: For persons with ADRD, the above three factors magnify each other and increase the risk of sensory deprivation and of the associated negative effects. Because of cognitive deficits in reasoning and memory, adapting or learning new behavior is difficult. The usual institutional environment does not reinforce or support their remaining abilities. Thus the behaviors they have learned over a lifetime are not necessarily useful in this relatively new environment. It is difficult to appreciate new sensory experiences or to make use of overlearned patterns such as finding the bathroom. Consequently, the individual acts and responds less frequently, and the level of sensory input is decreased yet again; thus a vicious, self-perpetuating cycle begins. In addition, many of the observed symptoms of sensory deprivation are similar to those associated with ADRD (e.g., disorientation and decreased motor coordination). The result can be a magnification of symptoms beyond that caused by the disease itself.

2.2 Sensoristasis

Sensoristasis is the level of sensory stimulation necessary for alertness and normal brain functioning. Brain function in turn regulates behavior. When the level of stimulation is too little, too much, or too difficult to understand, behavior becomes disorganized (Parent 1978). The "just right" level of stimulation encompasses not only quantity, but quality. In qualitative terms, effective stimulation includes elements of surprise, change, and diversity. For individuals with ADRD this issue is especially complex. On the one hand, a certain predictability to the environment is essential in order to compensate for deficits in such skills as decision making, memory, judgment, attention, and initiative. On the other hand, this must be balanced by an adequate level of stimulation to prevent sensory deprivation. This issue is discussed in more detail in the environmental section of Chapter 4.

2.3 Circular Effects

Sensory and perceptual deprivation lead to disorganized behavior and/or a decreased level of activity. This reduced level of activity may be voluntary, due to apathy, or involuntary, due to chemical or physical restraints to control disruptive or unsafe behavior. A reduced level of activity further reduces sensory stimulation, which leads to still more disorganized behavior, etc. In this way a downward spiral of decreasing function is set in motion. This is often observed, for instance, when someone with or without ADRD moves from the community to institutional care (Kane & Kane 1987).

2.4 Planned, Controlled Sensory Stimulation: Breaking the Cycle

By introducing carefully planned, meaningful sensory stimulation, some of the conditions of sensory and perceptual deprivation can be reversed (Figure 7-1). The individual is enabled to make a response, to reach out to his or her world in an appropriate way, for example, by giving a smile and a thank you to the staff member who brings breakfast. The person in the environment responds in return, and more sensory input is received; for example, smiling and gently touching his shoulder the staff person replies, "You're welcome, Mr. C. Enjoy your meal." And so an *upward spiral* can be initiated.

Just such a simple interaction as the one above can have amazing effects. One study demonstrated a significant increase in the intake of food: 29 percent more calories and 36 percent more protein. Twenty-one patients with chronic organic brain syndrome who were capable of eating independently were lightly touched on the arm five times, while they were verbally encouraged to eat, during the course of a one-hour meal (Eaton et al. 1986). These gains were maintained at other meals, and in the week following the intervention. Twenty-one other patients, matched for diagnosis and level of function, who were only verbally encouraged showed no increase in food consumption. Sensory stimulation—so simple (a touch), so effective (improved nutrition)!

Of course, for persons with ADRD the upward limit of this spiral is determined by their neurological deficits. However, all too often the level of function, their behavior in response to their surroundings, is determined not by neurological deficits but by the limitations imposed by an impoverished and inappropriate environment. Their level of disability is in excess of that caused by their disease alone (Brody et al. 1971). Persons with ADRD require an organized environment

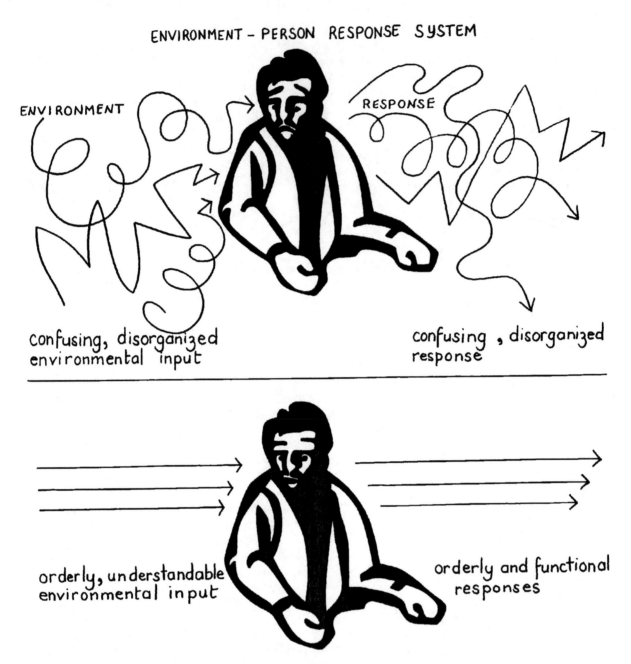

ENVIRONMENT - PERSON RESPONSE SYSTEM

ENVIRONMENT

RESPONSE

confusing, disorganized environmental input

confusing, disorganized response

orderly, understandable environmental input

orderly and functional responses

Figure 7-1 Environment-Person Response System

and planned, enhanced, sensory input to support their optimal functioning. Sensory stimulation helps to eliminate excess disability through building on an asset, since the primary sensory areas of the brain remain relatively untouched by ADRD.

Many elderly individuals have dementia-like symptoms, which cannot be explained by organic causes alone but can be attributed to sensory deprivation. For these individuals, appropriate sensory stimulation treatment can open the door to a truly phenomenal transfor-

mation. One such case is documented by Rogers et al. (1987):

Maude's status from the time of admission to the nursing facility until the initiation of the sensory training program 2 years later remained essentially unchanged. She was disoriented to persons, time, and place, totally dependent in self-care, and hostile when being cared for. Over the 5½ weeks, during which she participated in about twenty, 30- to

45-minute sessions of intensive sensory stimulation, she exhibited impressive gains in orientation, attention, concentration, self-feeding, mobility, communication, and ability to cooperate with caregiving. Having made these personal gains, Maude became a person to staff. Staff members were able to interact with her through general conversation and in physical care in more productive and meaningful ways. This, in turn, provided additional stimulation, although not as focused as the modalities used in the sensory training program, and contributed to the maintenance of program gains. (p. 675)

These gains were maintained throughout the one year of follow-up.

2.5 Why Will Attending Regular Activities Programs Not Have the Same Effect?

Certainly, there are many sensory elements in regular activity programs—the allure of music, the taste of special foods, etc. However, the individual severely impaired because of ADRD has great difficulty making sense out of it. Frequently, large group gatherings are overstimulating and lead to extremely disorganized behavior (e.g., catastrophic reactions). On the other hand, understimulation can cause the individual with ADRD to become, in effect, lost in a crowd—unable to follow the conversation or to decide which cookie to take; he or she withdraws in *apparent* apathy. Perhaps you have had an experience similar to the one below:

> On numerous occasions, a wonderful film on traditional Cape Breton fiddle music, *Celtic Spirits* (National Film Board of Canada) had been well received by both cognitively well and moderately impaired older adults. So, one afternoon I decided to turn the day room into a movie theater and show this film to a group of persons severely impaired because of ADRD. They had always responded well to rhythmic fiddle music in small groups. But what a disaster followed. Some slept in their chairs or continued to stare into space. One began to bang the wall and demand to go to supper. Another grabbed the hair of the lady beside him. Before the film could be stopped, the panic and chaos had spread to many others, and those who had been enjoying the film retreated to the calm of their rooms.

For persons severely impaired because of ADRD, the crucial point is not merely the presence of sensory stimulation, but *how* and *what* is presented. Otherwise it is inaccessible. Because of their deficits, stimulation must be presented in manageable and understandable ways. They must be assisted to focus on a particular sense and enabled to interpret and respond to the stimulation. Sensory stimulation groups, to be effective, must be carefully planned and conducted. They must be designed so that the sensory materials are presented in an order and a manner that is based on an understanding of neurological functioning. It is, above all, an interactive process that is tailored to the needs and abilities of the individual. Effective sensory stimulation is not a passive group activity. Because of disease-related deficits in the ability to initiate activity and to interpret the stimulation, the sensory elements of regular group activities are usually inaccessible to persons with ADRD.

2.6 Why Is Not the Normal "Sensory" Milieu of the Environment and Daily Activities Enough?

If persons with ADRD lived in an ideal world, i.e., a specially designed unit with large numbers of exceptionally well-trained staff, it might be. Unfortunately, the world in which most individuals with ADRD live is far from ideal. They require the extra support and facilitation of specialized sensory stimulation programs to meet their needs and enable function; and, even in specialty units, separate sensory stimulation groups continue to play an important role. For instance, in one survey of 18 specialty units, 44 percent also had sensory stimulation programs (Kalicki 1987).

Some critics of sensory stimulation groups have suggested that it is more logical to conduct sensory stimulation as an integrated part of care, e.g., during sensory-rich times such as eating and bathing (Davis & Kirkland 1988; Folsom et al. 1978; Peer 1976). This, of course, is essential and very effective. However, a good sensory stimulation group program is also designed to be an integrated, meaningful part of the individual's daily life (i.e., the use of meaningful materials, thematically organized, conducted in a normalized "social club" milieu). In the ideal world mentioned earlier, it is not a replacement for, but an important supplement to, a holistic, sensory-rich environment. In the more usual, less than ideal, world sensory stimulation serves the general goal of overcoming the effects of sensory deprivation and enabling function, of beginning an upward spiral of success. It also serves as a demonstration to other staff of the real capabilities of their withdrawn, sensory-deprived residents. Furthermore, it can serve as a demonstration of some sensory stimulation techniques that can be used effectively during daily activities.

The relative physical isolation of the group provides an environment in which the individual's attention and response can be more easily focused, free of the hubbub of the comings and goings on the unit. Here, there is an opportunity to introduce sensory-rich materials from the larger environment—important sights, sounds, smells, and tastes of the community and the home. Many of these materials (e.g., evergreen boughs at Christmas), often cannot be safely left about a facility occupied by confused residents. Returning to the theory of sensoristasis, the introduction of these materials is essential, providing an element of novelty, surprise, and extra stimulation. The sensory stimuli of the daily environment quickly become habituated, and although this is comforting and to a certain degree necessary, it is not stimulating. Furthermore, the social milieu of this group setting enhances function (see Chapter 4). Finally, to conclude on a practical note, the group represents an efficient use of staff time. It provides an opportunity to develop an expertise in one area and allows involvement with several individuals at once.

2.7 What Is the Difference between Sensory Stimulation and Sensory Integration?

Sensory integration is an occupational therapy intervention that was originally developed for use with learning-disabled children (Hames-Hahn & Llorens 1989; Yack 1989). It is based on neurological developmental principles. The details of these principles and the subsequent assessment and intervention are complex. The basic foundation is, in deceptively simple terms, the use of sensorimotor activities to strengthen neural connections and form an essential foundation for more complex cognitive and neural functioning (Corcoran & Barrett 1987). These techniques have been adapted for use with other populations, including regressed geriatric patients. Although this approach has not been well developed in geriatrics, the two studies in the literature report some remarkable improvements in functioning (Corcoran & Barrett 1987; Hames-Hahn & Llorens 1989).

Since both interventions are based on multisensory therapy, there is frequent confusion among therapists, and others, about their similarities and differences. Unfortunately, the important distinctions between these two approaches have not been clearly defined in the literature to date. Table 7-1 provides an analysis of these distinctions based on study of the available literature and my clinical experience with the two interventions. It must be emphasized that sensory integration is a highly complex and skilled treatment modality that requires the assessment and intervention skills of a qualified therapist. There has been very limited application of sensory integration with regressed elderly, and although it is widely used with children, it remains controversial even with that population (Yack 1989).

2.8 Similarities between Sensory Stimulation and Sensory Integration

- There is an underlying premise that the "excess disability" (Brody et al. 1971) of the institutionalized elderly can be, at least partially, accounted for by sensory deprivation.
- Both are based on neurological principles.
- Studies have demonstrated remarkable improvements in, for example, social interaction and self-care.
- There is a limited number of controlled research studies.

2.9 Concluding Summary

Sensory stimulation is a more appropriate modality for persons with ADRD. Since it does not focus on cognitive skills, as such, it is more suitable for individuals with generally lower functioning as a result of neurological deficits. In addition, it can be implemented by staff without an extensive background in neurodevelopmental theory and treatment. However, in some cases, the actual sensory integration intervention itself is remarkably similar to that of sensory stimulation groups (Hames-Hahn & Llorens 1989). Based on these similarities, the effectiveness of these sensory integration interventions can be interpreted as a measure of support for sensory stimulation itself.

3.0 RESEARCH EVIDENCE: SOUNDS GOOD, BUT DOES IT REALLY WORK?

Sensory stimulation is a group intervention that makes sense according to neurological, psychological, and environmental principles. It is a logical and valid treatment based on sound clinical judgment. Unfortunately, there is not extensive empirical research evidence to support its effectiveness. This is not because it has been tested and found lacking, but because its effectiveness has scarcely been tested experimentally. In fact, the existing studies have very positive results (see Table 7-2). This same situation exists in virtually every area of psychosocial intervention with persons with ADRD. Although the amount of research in the field

Table 7-1 Differences between Sensory Stimulation and Sensory Integration

Topic	*Sensory Stimulation*	*Sensory Integration*
Target Population	The "regressed" elderly and, minimally, the profoundly mentally handicapped	Learning-disabled children, adult schizophrenics, and (minimally) the "regressed" elderly
Prevalence	Commonly used by occupational therapists in work with the sensory-deprived elderly; variations widely used by many doing "activities" with the elderly	Only a few accounts of use with the elderly
Theoretical Frame of Reference	A compensatory/rehabilitative approach within a neurodevelopmental/environmental framework (making use of already acquired skills)	An acquisitional/developmental approach within a neurodevelopmental/environmental framework (acquiring new skills)
Goals	To compensate for sensory deprivation; to stimulate environmental awareness; to prompt performance of overlearned behaviors	To improve central nervous system organization; to strengthen neural interconnections as a foundation for more complex mentally and socially adaptive responses (Corcoran & Barrett 1987)
Client Characteristics	Ability to perform higher-level cognitive functions usually impaired	Capable of integrating sensory information and learning or relearning higher-level cognitive functions
Focus of Stimuli	Enjoyment; to stimulate previously learned responses and increase general level of alertness	A foundation for more cognitively complex activities in the group (e.g., puzzles, word games, object identification) and elsewhere (e.g., self-care)
Sensory Cues	Focus on one sense at a time, presented in an orderly progression (e.g., olfactory, kinesthetic, touch, visual, auditory, gustatory) and emphasized throughout the session	Multisensory stimuli presented in the context of activities; initial emphasis on tactile, vestibular, and proprioceptive input; olfactory and gustatory introduced later; emphasis on stimuli providing vestibular input
Motor Activities	Vestibular input may occur incidentally, but is not a focus (and is sometimes contraindicated due to client deficits)	Planned, vestibular stimulation is a fundamental component
Cognitive Responses	Generally de-emphasized in favor of automatic, overlearned responses; verbal responses as such are facilitated but not targeted	Higher cognitive activities are central focus of the progression of therapy; verbal responses are targeted

has increased phenomenally in recent years, the vast majority has been directed toward the search for a cure for ADRD. The primary focus of the clinical literature has been on support for caregivers.

These are undoubtedly vital areas of research and investigation. It is, however, well past time that more research was dedicated to investigating the effectiveness of therapeutic interventions that can minimize the suffering and dependence and maximize the quality of life of individuals already affected by ADRD (Estes & Binney 1989). Clinicians and activities personnel can scarcely keep their heads above the demanding waters of their regular duties, and may not have the necessary research skills. They can, however, lobby the faculty and students of nearby universities and colleges to make use of their programs as a site for research and/or clinical experience. In the end, such research makes all of our jobs easier. For instance, groups and interven-

Table 7-2 Sensory Stimulation Studies

Study	Subjects	Intervention	Results
"Sensory Stimulation of Elderly Patients: Preliminary Report on the Treatment of Patients with Chronic Brain Syndrome in an Old Age Home" (Ernst et al. 1978b)	Subjects N=6; elderly nursing home residents diagnosed with chronic organic brain syndrome	Group sessions twice weekly for 3 months, which included sensory stimulation, simple exercises, and social activities; no control group; 3 leaders to 6 subjects	Improved scores on tests for chronic organic syndrome and improved socialization; maintained for 1 year after therapy
"The Effectiveness of Sensory Stimulation for Geropsychiatric Inpatients" (Paire & Karney 1984)	Subjects N=30; psychiatric inpatients from a 300-bed geriatric/psychiatric unit of a large mental hospital; 81% with a primary diagnosis of schizophrenia, 19% with a primary diagnosis of organic brain syndrome (all selected as the most regressed patients by their treatment teams)	(A) Sensory stimulation (SS), individual within a group; (B) staff attention using music, reading newspapers, sharing snacks; (C) control group receiving standard hospital care; A and B met for 12 weeks, 4 times per week; 2 leaders for 5 patients	Significant improvement in doing own personal hygiene of both treatment groups, but maintained at 6 weeks post-treatment only by the SS group; increased interest and participation in group activities by SS group; effect maintained at follow-up
"Re-establishing Independent Eating through Sensory Stimulation" (Rogers et al. 1989)	Subjects N=5; elderly psychiatric inpatients (acute) with a primary diagnosis of senile dementia (3 Alzheimer's type and 1 multi-infarct); 1 with a primary diagnosis of Huntington's chorea; all partially or fully dependent in eating	Group intervention using premeal sensory stimulation, a familiar mealtime environment, and cuing to encourage independent eating; single-subject research design with each subject serving as own control; 1 leader to 5 subjects	Significant increase in positive mealtime behaviors (e.g., independent eating, intake, socialization) for all 5; carryover of behaviors to the other meals in the regular dining room
"An Eclectic Group Program for Nursing Home Residents with Dementia" (Maloney & Daily 1986)	Subjects N=16; elderly nursing home residents; 8 disoriented with major physical limitations; 8 partially oriented with motor and sensory impairment; all were previously unable to participate in group activities	Sensory-based activities presented in the following order: smell, touch, movement, breath (e.g., singing), motor planning, and taste; socialization was emphasized. (A) Maintenance group (less impaired) 1 hour; (B) intervention group (more impaired) 30–45 minutes; 2 or 3 leaders per 6 residents; a 3-year pilot project, not a controlled study; members had a comprehensive assessment every 6 months; weekly observation notes were kept	10 of 16 (63%) maintained or improved cognitive and social function; 45% showed actual improvement (smiling, eye contact, initiation and responsiveness in conversation, and increased participation in other group activities)
"Effects of a Multi-Strategy Program upon Elderly with Organic Brain Syndrome" (Reichenbach & Kirchman 1991)	Subjects N=72, from two 100-bed urban nursing homes; subjects were identified as having organic brain syndrome, 12 with mild, 12 with moderate, and 12 with severe impairment	An eclectic social/activity group that included sensory stimulation, reminiscence, reality orientation (as in reality reassurance), music, movement, touch, and socialization; 1 hour per day, 5 days a week for 4 months; leaders were home activity workers with 4 hours of special training by an occupational therapist.	Intervention multistrategy group showed significant improvements compared with control group on scores of morale, mental functioning, and activities of daily living

Table 7-2 continued

Study	Subjects	Intervention	Results
		Control group: regular nursing home program with intermittently scheduled reality orientation, remotivation, exercises, outings, and numerous passive activities	
"Maude: A Case of Sensory Deprivation" (Rogers et al. 1987)	Case study of a self-care-dependent, nonmobile, nonverbal, disoriented 90-year-old woman who had been living in a 58-bed skilled nursing home facility for 5 years	Sensory stimulation focusing on visual, auditory, olfactory, gustatory, tactile, and proprioceptive senses; 30-minute sessions 4 days a week for 5 weeks; individual treatment in a group with 5 other regressed elderly residents; 1 leader for 6 participants	Pre- and postevaluation by an occupational therapist not involved in the treatment; marked improvement in orientation, verbalization, alertness, and attempts at independence in eating and propelling a wheelchair; gains maintained for the entire year of follow-up; % of responses to stimuli made, without assistance, increased from 29% in week 2 to 69% in week 5

tions that are validated by research are much more readily supported in terms of staff and material resources.

As a consequence of the limited amount of applied clinical research, closely related areas of research are also included in this section.

3.1 Sensory Deprivation Studies

As has already been mentioned, short-term sensory deprivation experiments with healthy adults have shown significant negative changes in electroencephalographic patterns, cognitive and motor function, and motivation after periods of sensory and/or perceptual and/or motor deprivation (Ernst et al. 1978; Zubec 1969). These negative effects are reduced by the inclusion of a simple exercise routine in the deprived environment. There is also an extensive literature from animal studies, which identify distinct, destructive brain cell changes as the result of sensory deprivation (Ernst et al. 1978).

3.2 Neurological Plasticity

In the not-very-distant past, it was widely believed that the human neurological system (principally the brain) and its functioning developed during a certain critical period of childhood and was thereafter fixed. However, in recent years much evidence from human clinical studies and laboratory animal studies has re-

futed this earlier belief. In fact, the mammalian brain remains to some extent plastic, that is, capable of change and growth throughout adulthood and into old age. There are many examples in the literature. Just a few of the more relevant ones are mentioned here.

The brain has an extensive "map" of the external sensory body. When this sensory system is damaged (e.g., nerve damage) the brain cells reorganize the map to enable continued sensory messages (Merzenich 1984). Damage to sensory systems increases the acuity and sensitivity of the remaining sensory systems, exemplified by the increased touch and auditory acuity of a blind person (Greenough 1984). Finally, the extensive experiments of Diamond (1984) in providing enriched environments (specifically, provision of a succession of toys for manipulation) for laboratory rats demonstrated substantial brain growth in both young and old rats in this environment, including both nuclear growth and change in the number and size of dendrites (Birren & Schaie 1990; Cohen 1988; Diamond 1984; Schaie 1989; Timiras 1988). The evidence is speculative, but hopeful, that despite damage to brain cells caused by ADRD, the remaining cells are capable of growth (e.g., creating new connections) or reorganization (strengthening existing but previously underused pathways) to compensate for this damage.

Sensory stimulation is vital to the development (e.g., shown by work with premature infants [Gottfried & Gaiter 1984]) and maintenance of the neural system. It is important to recall again in this context that the sensory areas of the Alzheimer's diseased brain remain relatively unaffected by the disease (Birren & Schaie 1990; Ernst et al. 1978). Thus, the case for the provision of enhanced sensory stimulation for persons with ADRD is supported by the work on neural plasticity.

3.3 Environmental Effects

As has been previously discussed (see Chapter 4), persons with ADRD are exquisitely sensitive to their environment. Sensory stimulation groups are, in effect, carefully controlled environmental interventions. Indeed, a premise of sensory stimulation is that the relative sensory deprivation of the environment can contribute to decreased functioning. The effectiveness of other environmental inventions implies support for sensory stimulation itself (Birren & Schaie 1990; Calkins 1988; Cleary et al. 1988; Coons 1991a, 1991b; Davis & Kirkland 1988; Edelson & Lyons 1985; Heacock et al. 1991; Hiatt 1987b; Hyde 1989; Johnson 1989; Karlinsky & Sutherland 1990; Mace 1990; McCracken & Fitzwater 1990; Namazi et al. 1989; Negley & Manley 1990; OTA 1987; Volicer et al. 1988; Zgola 1987).

3.4 Sensory Integration Studies with Geriatric Subjects

As outlined previously, there are many commonalities between the techniques and materials used in sensory stimulation and those used in sensory integration. The studies in Table 7-3 provide collateral support for the effectiveness of sensory stimulation.

3.5 Summary: Research Findings

Unfortunately, a body of well-controlled research evidence supporting the effectiveness of sensory stimulation does not exist. However, the results of the one controlled study (Paire & Karney 1984) were very positive, showing significant improvements in participants' ability to carry out their own personal hygiene, and increased interest and participation in group activities. The study by Reichenbach and Kirchman (1991) was also a controlled study with positive and supportive findings. Although the multistrategy program they describe is not specifically sensory stimulation, these techniques are central. In practice the group is remarkably similar to the sensory stimulation groups that I have led. Although sensory stimulation is the focus, other techniques such as reality reassurance, reminiscence, movement, and music are always incorporated in the group plan. This study is particularly significant

because it demonstrates the potential for improvement in activities of daily living and general morale, even by the severely impaired. It is important to note that these groups used regular activity staff, who were given special training, and that the program took place daily over a longer period than most research studies (four months).

Related studies, uncontrolled case studies, and descriptive accounts report encouraging improvements in positive mealtime behaviors (Rogers et al. 1989), improved communication, mood, and behavior (Bryant 1991); improvements in self-feeding (Hames-Hahn & Llorens 1989); an increased level of alertness and interest in activities with specific smell stimulation (Brouillette & White 1991); improved scores on tests for chronic organic brain syndrome (Ernst et al. 1978b); improved cognitive and social function (Maloney & Dailey 1986); and improved self-care and socialization (Rogers et al. 1987). The existing evidence for the effectiveness of sensory stimulation and sensory-based activities is encouraging, although it indicates a tremendous need for more research. There is, however, already sufficient evidence that sensory stimulation interventions are essential, and caregivers must forge ahead to put them in place. The conclusion of Kane and Kane (1987), in a comprehensive literature review of long-term care, is particularly pertinent here: "The efforts to improve the milieu of nursing home residents by adding pleasant routines or thoughtful opportunities for interesting activities are likely to pay off in increased well-being" (p. 236).

4.0 THE SENSORY STIMULATION GROUP

The overall goal of the group is to provide organized, understandable, sensory stimulation to enable environmental awareness and responsiveness. An improved understanding of the environment is the foundation for a happier mood and an improved ability to participate in self-care and to relate to other people.

4.1 Specific Goals

- Improve environmental awareness through enhanced sensory cues.
- Prompt familiar, functional behaviors.
- Improve general level of alertness.
- Enable appropriate social and environmental responses.
- Provide reassuring, orienting information.
- Provide pleasurable, sensory experiences.
- Provide opportunities for emotional expression

Table 7-3 Sensory Integration Studies

Study	Subjects	Intervention	Results
"Using Sensory Integration Principles with Regressed Elderly Patients" (Corcoran & Barrett 1987)	Subjects *N*=11; nursing home residents identified by nursing staff as their most regressed; diagnosis not stated	(A) Sensory integration therapy following the outline of Ross & Burdick (1981); (B) control group received biomechanical treatment (as assessed by an occupational therapist) in a group setting; each group met for 40 minutes twice weekly for 16 weeks; 1 leader for 5 subjects	Tester blind to group assignment; based on clinical observations by an occupational therapist; control group, no change; sensory integration group, marked improvements in attention span, postural and motor control, communication, orientation, and social interaction; no statistical analysis undertaken
"Impact of a Multisensory Occupational Therapy Program on Components of Self-Feeding Behavior in the Elderly" (Hames-Hahn & Llorens 1989)	Subjects *N*=12; nursing home residents with moderate to severe regressive behavior, sensory loss; required assistance in feeding and had a history of receptiveness to group intervention; no diagnosis given	(A) Sensory integration therapy following the 5 stages of Ross & Burdick (1981), progressing to more and more complex activities; 45-minute sessions 5 days per week for 8 weeks; 2 leaders for 5 subjects. (B) Involvement in regularly scheduled group activities 5 or more days per week (precise time not given); 3 or 4 leaders for 15–25 participants; blind pre- and postintervention administration of an author-developed feeding scale	5 out of the 6 improved in raw scores on feeding scale compared with controls; statistical analysis not undertaken; feeding scale items included independence in feeding, psychosocial behavior during feeding, and appropriate lip, tongue, and jaw movements

and communication.

- Enhance self-esteem.

4.2 Selecting Participants

If possible, it is helpful to include participants of differing functional levels. Managing an entire group of individuals who are low functioning would be difficult. An individual who is in need of sensory stimulation, and responds to it particularly well, serves both as a role model for other participants and as a source of encouragement for the group leader.

Individuals with the characteristics to respond well to the group

- are moderately to severely cognitively impaired (score, for example, in the lowest range of scores of a mental status questionnaire, such as 0 to 10 on the Folstein Mini-Mental Status questionnaire [Folstein et al. 1975] or Reisburg [1983] Stages 6 and 7)
- demonstrate a need for sensory stimulation by repetitive, self-stimulating actions, such as rubbing table trays or chairs

- have limited or absent verbal skills
- are able to remain in an upright position for 30 to 45 minutes
- are capable of deriving pleasure from sensory experiences (includes everyone, no matter how impaired)
- are capable of participating in a group setting

The last criterion is difficult to define. Performance in other areas, such as in the day room or in self-care, are not necessarily indicative of how the individual will respond in a sensory stimulation group. The stimulation, structure, and personal affirmation of the group often has a transforming effect (Bryant 1991; Rogers et al. 1987). In addition, self-care activities emphasize cognitive and motor skills, whereas sensory stimulation groups emphasize sociability and emotional and sensory experiences. In self-care activities individuals with ADRD are confronted with their disease-related losses. In contrast, sensory stimulation groups seek to build on remaining abilities.

The best way to determine an individual's group capacity is to try him or her in the group, preferably several times. Remember also to make use of the gradual group integration techniques discussed in Chapter 4.

Even individuals with extremely disruptive behavior may eventually be able to be included in the group through the use of behavior modification time outs. Only those individuals whose behavior is a danger to themselves or others, or whose behavior is totally disruptive to the group, should be excluded. Even in such cases, repeated trials are always worthwhile.

4.3 Setting

The room should be quiet and comfortable and as homelike as possible. See group milieu section, Chapter 4, for more details.

A table around which all participants can be seated is essential. Gathering participants around the table is an effective and concrete cue that promotes a normalized atmosphere. The aim is to have participants feel as if this is a gathering of friends, sharing information and activities over a cup of coffee. Unlike other types of therapeutic groups, in which a table may be a barrier to communication, for persons with ADRD the table at the center enhances communication. The addition of a brightly colored, textured cloth and a seasonal centerpiece provides a concrete, focal center for the group. Although the table is essential as a group focal point, it is not essential that everyone be seated all the time. Provided there are no safety hazards, those who are restless may get up and wander about the room. Eventually, they will return to the group. It has been my experience that allowing those who are restless to wander at the start gives them the ease to eventually settle into the group and remain at the table with their peers. However, having more than one person at a time who is restless and wandering would be too disruptive. Some settle in more comfortably to the group if they observe from a distance, at another chair or table, and are encouraged gradually to join the others.

The setting is especially enriched by familiar music. A portable cassette tape player is convenient. Begin with stimulating music (for example, fiddle jigs and reels) to increase arousal, and then use more soothing music (ballads and waltzes) as the group progresses. Further information on music is found in Chapter 5.

4.4 Time

- Meet at the same time, every day, or as often as possible.
- Meet in the morning, as individuals with ADRD are usually more alert then.
- Meet for 30 to 60 minutes.

The time is variable, depending on the numbers in the group and the amount of time spent with each participant on each cue. It is commonly recommended that groups for persons severely impaired by ADRD be no longer than 30 minutes. This recommendation applies to a more traditional group structure in which participants are expected to attend to a general group process. Since participants in this special type of parallel group receive periodic individual attention, they are not as likely to become fatigued or restless during a longer group time. Some may rest, or even sleep, except during one-to-one time. Others may watch and listen.

4.5 Group Size

Once familiar with the group format and the participants, it is possible for one staff member to lead a group with eight to ten severely impaired participants. However, until the leader becomes comfortable with the group process, a smaller number (four to six) is recommended.

4.6 Participant Evaluation

Evaluation of the participants and the particular activities and programs must be ongoing. The most important evaluation is observation of how the participants respond to the materials and activities presented in the group. Communicate with direct-care staff about any carry-over effects to other settings. Group leaders with clinical training may do more formal evaluations, such as mental status tests or self-care or socialization scales. During the evaluation process, it is very important to keep in mind that, for persons with progressive diseases such as ADRD, maintenance of existing levels of functioning is a crucial and valuable goal. It is also essential to recall that persons with ADRD live most fully in the present moment. Therefore, the most important evaluation is how the group or activity affected their personal happiness or pleasure, and encouraged responsiveness, at that particular moment. An evaluation form (Exhibit 7-1) was developed for use in evaluating participant responses in a group, over time. It may be adapted to suit the needs of different programs and facilities. To score, draw a line to the appropriate response level.

4.7 Group Format: Parallel Presentation

Because of the severity of the deficits of persons in need of sensory stimulation, an adapted form of a parallel group format is the most effective. Each participant is individually presented with the particular sensory cue or activity in turn. For example, the group leader moves around the table, individually focusing attention on the smell of a fresh orange section and encouraging

Exhibit 7-1 Sensory Stimulation Group—Individual Evaluation

Response	*Date/Time*	*Never*	*Occasionally*	*Often*	*Always*
Makes eye contact	Week 1				
	Week 2				
	Week 3				
	Week 4				
Connects presented material with personal experience	Week 1				
	Week 2				
	Week 3				
	Week 4				
Responds to verbal prompting	Week 1				
	Week 2				
	Week 3				
	Week 4				
Responds to nonverbal prompting	Week 1				
	Week 2				
	Week 3				
	Week 4				
Makes appropriate nonverbal response to stimulus	Week 1				
	Week 2				
	Week 3				
	Week 4				
Makes appropriate verbal response to stimulus	Week 1				
	Week 2				
	Week 3				
	Week 4				
Attends when being individually addressed	Week 1				
	Week 2				
	Week 3				
	Week 4				
Attends to group process	Week 1				
	Week 2				
	Week 3				
	Week 4				
Makes appropriate voluntary response	Week 1				
	Week 2				
	Week 3				
	Week 4				
Attends entire session	Week 1				
	Week 2				
	Week 3				
	Week 4				

participants to pick it up and eat it. The group leader then moves around the table, focusing each individual's attention on a beanbag, and encouraging participants to catch and toss it. The group proceeds in this manner until every individual has been presented with every cue. Group interaction should be encouraged, and may take place, but should not be expected because of the disease-related deficits of the participants. This format has several advantages:

- Repetition with each participant reinforces the information.
- By beginning with a higher-functioning individual, his or her response can serve as a model or cue for others.
- The format compensates for memory loss and reduced attention span.
- The format allows adapting the presentation and cuing to individual interests, needs, and capabilities. For example, the soft fur of a mink pelt collar was used to stimulate one gentleman to reminisce about his previous occupation as a hunter and trapper, and for another lady about getting dressed for church in the winter.
- The format provides individual attention and feedback within a group setting.

Immediately after presenting a particular cue, the leader should focus on enabling a related functional response. The targeting of functional responses may take some practice. The verbal responses (i.e., question and answer) we are so used to focusing on are not suitable, because of the negative effects of ADRD on verbal communication. The focus, instead, should be on automatic, overlearned responses (e.g., clapping in time to music) and nonverbal communication (e.g., smiling). Verbal responses should be facilitated, but not emphasized. Verbal responses are stimulated by using lead-in, or opinion-seeking, questions as opposed to questions that have a right or wrong answer. For example, do *not* ask what color an object is. Rather, ask, "What does this color remind you of?" or "What else can you recall that is this color?" or "Do you like this color?" Everyone can offer an opinion.

Because of the cognitive deficits, the most successful cues are subcortical (i.e., do not require cognitive processing) and make use of nonverbal, multisensory stimuli to elicit a familiar or overlearned response. For example, the participant has just smelled the aroma of a freshly cut orange. The functional response is to pick up the orange section and eat it. This may be cued spontaneously by the smell itself or, failing that, by placing the orange within the line of vision and near the

person's hand. Finally, it may be necessary to gently guide the person's hand to the orange section or to place the section in the hand and guide the hand to the person's mouth. During this process, verbal cues such as "Doesn't that smell delicious?" or "Have a taste of the orange" are helpful. However, verbal cues alone are frequently inadequate. It is important to link the verbal suggestion with personal associations and to facilitate reminiscence. Participant responses must be constantly reinforced and encouraged by verbal praise and caring personal touch.

4.8 Sequencing of Sensory Cues

It is absolutely essential that the presentation of sensory materials be done in a planned, organized manner. Bringing a collection of materials and passing them around is *not* sensory stimulation. Persons with moderate to severe impairment due to ADRD do not have the independent ability to interpret what is presented to them, nor to respond appropriately to it. However, when sensory-rich materials are presented in an organized and understandable manner, a functional response is made possible. The presentation of sensory cues must adhere to the following principles:

- Organize the cues around a particular theme or focus.
- Direct the cues toward enabling an associated functional response.
- Present the cues in a sequential manner, gradually increasing the complexity of the sense targeted.

Sensory cues should be presented in the following order: smell, movement, touch, vision, hearing, and taste. This order of presentation was developed according to the current literature and my personal experience. Many of the suggested sensory cues are in fact multisensory. However, only one of these senses is targeted. Thus, while a pine bough may stimulate smell, touch, and sight, emphasis must be given to only one sense at a time, such as the feel of the needles and the pine bark. Adaptations for age-related sensory losses are important to keep in mind (see Chapter 1).

4.9 Characteristics of Useful Sensory Cues

- Use familiar objects with a particular sensory aspect that can be targeted. For example, knitted red mittens are better than a ball of wool or a red fabric square. In addition to color, attention can be focused on the texture. Suggested functional responses are to put on the mittens, identify the color, name the mittens, or recollect wearing mittens as a child, to play in the snow.

- Use natural materials that are related to the current season (e.g., pine boughs at Christmas; fresh, green grass in spring).
- Use everyday sensory-rich materials. Institutional life deprives individuals with ADRD of contact with the rich array of sensory experiences that others take for granted. Bring in materials that are part of your normal everyday life (e.g., freshly brewed coffee) or part of seasonal activities (e.g., a pumpkin at Halloween).
- Use materials with an obvious associated functional response (e.g., a beanbag to catch, an apple slice to eat).
- Do not use materials or activities that are primarily associated with children (e.g., coloring books, baby toys).
- Avoid materials that may cause allergic reactions.
- Avoid potentially dangerous materials (e.g., ammonia, because of cardiovascular effects; poisonous plant materials). Be aware that many severely cognitively impaired individuals tend to put things in their mouths.

5.0 SPECIFIC CUES FOR EACH SENSE

5.1 Olfactory Sense (Smell)

Smell is the first cue presented, because of its pervasive capacity to arouse and stimulate. The sensation of smell is "wired" to the reticular activating system of the brain, the system responsible for general arousal and alertness. The sense of smell is one of the first to develop in the human infant, before acute vision and hearing, for instance. The "sense of smell" occupies a larger area of the brain than any other sensory system (Rosenbloom & Morgan 1986). The deterioration of olfactory capacity is thought to be a symptom of Alzheimer's disease that takes place out of developmental sequence, that is, before losses in vision and hearing (Jarvik & Winograd 1988; Serby 1986). However, familiar and pleasant aromas still have a general stimulating or arousing effect (King & Parachek 1986; Maloney & Daily 1986; Paire & Karney 1984; personal observations). This effect is particularly important at the beginning of a group. King and Parachek (1986) described some smells as alerting or arousing (e.g., vinegar, vanilla, almond extract) and others as calming or soothing (e.g., banana oil, nutmeg, heavy flower scents). However, no evidence could be located in the literature to support this contention.

Since one gets used to a particular smell very quickly (habituation), several shorter exposures are preferable to one lengthy one. Essential oils or extracts are best presented by perfuming a cotton ball or tissue (one per participant to avoid the spread of respiratory diseases) or by soaking absorbent cotton and placing it in a small spice jar, with the plastic shaker piece in place. With severely cognitively impaired individuals, stimulating the sense of smell has a tendency to trigger an automatic response—to put the object in the mouth. When using inedible materials such as cotton balls, keep a firm grip! Persons with a previous history of alcohol abuse frequently will attempt to "bottoms up" the spice jar. In both cases, be prepared with a distraction, such as a peppermint candy after the peppermint extract cue. When collecting materials, use extracts or essential oils, rather than flavorings used in baking. Strawberry flavoring, for instance, may taste like strawberries in baking but it does not smell much like them. Of course, whenever possible, the real thing is best of all.

When encouraging a functional response that involves tasting, be sure to be aware of dietary restrictions, allergies, and difficulties with swallowing. Be particularly alert to choking or aspiration of sample foods. Always check with the clinical staff about precautions. Do not give sample foods to individuals at risk.

A list of suggested olfactory materials is presented in Table 7-4. These have been found to be effective by the author and others (King & Parachek 1986; Maloney & Daily 1986; Paire & Karney 1984).

5.2 Kinesthetic Sense

The kinesthetic sense is the sensation of the movement of body parts through space. This sense frequently is not included among the basic senses, and yet it is crucial. The excitement and invigoration that many derive from the strenuous movement of athletic activities are obvious. The pleasurable sensations and stimulating effect of less strenuous exercise, or even the body movements of ordinary daily activities, may not be so obvious until such movements are no longer possible. Persons with ADRD are subject to the normal physical effects of aging (see Chapter 1) as well as to those associated with their disease. Because of cognitive impairment and/or apraxia, the purposeful movements involved in daily activities (e.g., getting dressed) may be curtailed as they become more and more dependent. Because of balance problems and gait disturbance, independent walking may no longer be safe. To further complicate the picture, the individual may also have an extraordinary need to move as a result of the restless-

Table 7-4 Olfactory Sensory Cues and Responses

Sensory Cue	Suggested Functional Response
Fresh fruits (orange sections, apple slices, banana, grapes, strawberries, melon, and other familiar and seasonal fruits)	Pick up and eat the portion or peel and eat; recall associations, such as apple picking in the autumn; name favorite fruit
Peppermint extract	Pick up and eat a peppermint candy; what does this remind you of?
Pickles (favorite local specialties, e.g., green tomato chow-chow or pickled herring in Nova Scotia)	Pick up and eat the pickles or chow-chow; recall associations
Scented fresh flowers	Arrange the flowers in a container of water or on paper to make a pressed-flower card or picture; recall favorite flowers and places for them in the garden; wear as boutonnieres (do not attach with pins)
Fresh green grass	Recall associations with the spring, cutting the grass, etc.
Cinnamon sticks	Taste cinnamon heart candies, recall associations; add to mulled cider
Freshly made, fragrant herbal tea	Taste the tea, make verbal associations, such as chamomile tea, with something mother gave when ill
Aftershave or hand lotion or perfume (be particularly aware of allergies)	Rub onto hands or face, recall associations (e.g., dressing up for a party, favorite perfumes)
Familiar live herbs or scented plants such as chives, spearmint, lemon geraniums, watercress	Pick a piece and taste it; verbal associations, such as finding the first watercress in spring
Pine cones, evergreen boughs	Place for table arrangement or wreath; identify associations, perhaps with Christmas
Lavender sachet or potpourri mix (in jar to make air freshener)	Tie drawstring top of sachet (if possible); identify associations
Coffee (make a fresh, fragrant pot in the group room)	Taste the coffee; associations with making coffee, e.g., flavor preferences, coffee breaks with friends, a bridge club
Scented candle	Assist individuals to light the candle; blow out the candle; insert in a candleholder; identify associations
Freshly baked bread or biscuits (see food activities section in Chapter 5 for shortcut suggestions)	Butter and taste the bread; identify associations
Maple extract	Taste maple syrup or maple sugar; identify associations with making maple syrup, pancakes, and pancake suppers
Fir bark chips or sawdust	Arrange, as mulch, around potted plant or terrarium; identify associations
Chocolate (candies, chips, hot chocolate)	Unwrap and eat candy; stir and taste hot chocolate
Cut lemon	Squeeze out juice using hand juicer; mix and stir lemonade; recall associations

ness sometimes associated with ADRD or the side effects of medications such as haloperidol (Everitt et al. 1991). This particular situation is discussed in more detail in Chapter 4, with regard to challenging behaviors.

The end effect of reduced body movement is not only the reduction of still another stimulating sensation; it also can be the beginning of a vicious cycle. For the elderly, in particular, reduced movement very quickly leads to muscle wasting. For example, the large thigh muscles that are essential for standing up begin to decline after two days of bed rest. Reduced movement means reduced oxygen intake, which in turn decreases the level of cognitive alertness and promotes the appearance of primitive reflexes, which interfere with normal function. Consequently, the brain receives less feedback of body part location, and apraxic symptoms are magnified. This, in turn, can lead to less food intake and a compromised nutritional status, as well as to reduced cardiac output. The end result is a further decline in overall function and a further cycle of reduced movement and sensory stimulation. Or, if the individual persists in "restlessness" or " agitated movement," the worst scenario may be further chemical and/or physical restraint.

Kinesthetic stimulation is introduced early in the group to increase alertness and arousal, as well as to provide an appropriate outlet for the need to move. As an individual becomes more impaired with ADRD, standard exercises become more and more difficult to follow. One-to-one assistance is necessary, and frequently even this may be ineffective or resisted (see "Movement/Exercise" in Chapter 5).

In sensory stimulation group, effective movement activities are those that

- have a concrete, logical stimulus for movement (e.g., playing catch)
- are one-step repetitive movements (e.g., clapping to music)
- do not require complex motor planning (e.g., shaking a tambourine or maraca)
- are overlearned movement patterns (e.g., shaking hands)

Precautions

- Supervise the use of materials that may be thrown and potentially injure another participant.
- Be prepared with a diversion if a participant perseverates on a disruptive movement (e.g., loud, repetitive clapping).
- Avoid sudden or rapid movements or changes in position, as this may provoke a startle response or a catastrophic reaction.
- Avoid movements that cause hyperextension of the neck (leaning the head too far back), as this may cause a transient ischemic attack (temporary loss of blood to the brain).
- For individuals with a positive grasp reflex (see Chapter 3), avoid stimulating the palm of the hand.

The way in which kinesthetic activities are presented is particularly important. The tone and purpose must be adult, so that they are not seen as games meant for children and cause some to withdraw. The activities are best introduced as exercises, "something to help you get moving," "wake you up." Participants are almost always receptive to this approach. John Angus is a good example. He had severe proprioceptive and movement impairments. However, he retained some insight into the nature of his disease and was delighted when he was asked to exercise. He saw this as a sign that there was some help for his disabilities. He asked for a beanbag for his room. He frequently used it to "exercise," by playing catch with staff and his family. It is interesting to note that, although John Angus had such severe proprioceptive problems that he could not seat himself in a chair unaided and such severe apraxic problems that he could not dress himself, his ability to catch and throw was excellent.

Grading kinesthetic activities according to ability is important. For example, many severely impaired individuals do not respond at all when a beanbag is gently tossed at their hands. In this case, begin with hand-over-hand guidance, accompanied by verbal cuing. Place the beanbag in the person's dominant hand and assist him or her to pass it to your hand. Gradually increase the distance the beanbag must be passed, and reduce the amount of hand-over-hand guidance. It is amazing that even the most severely impaired individuals are able to progress from the passive movement of the beanbag from their hands to yours, to moving farther distances without assistance, to a short toss, finally to catching and tossing it independently. Reinforce the progress with verbal praise and reassuring personal touch.

Kinesthetic activities provide a good opportunity for encouraging group interaction. For example, with leader guidance as needed, the beanbag can be passed or tossed around the table from one participant to the next. This can sometimes continue spontaneously, even with the most severely impaired participants.

With kinesthetic activities, the functional response is inherent in the activity itself. The stimulation of the activity can be capitalized on by cuing for more complex verbal responses (e.g., while playing catch, "Did you ever play baseball?" "What position?" "What's your favorite baseball team?").

Kinesthetic Activities

Beanbag Catch. This is a particularly excellent and stimulating activity. Beanbags can be made cheaply and easily by using bright scraps of textured fabric. Sizes and weights can be graded according to individual hand strength. Participants can exercise choice by selecting one of a favorite color. Move your position to increase the distance thrown, and incorporate crossing the midline and using both hands. Adaptations:

- toss at a large bull's-eye target on the table or floor
- toss into a basket
- toss through a hoop
- toss through a hole in a vertical target

Other Types of Catch

- nerf balls (good if concerned about some participants throwing so hard or inaccurately that others might be injured)
- inflatable beach balls (with some higher-functioning participants this may be adapted to a game of kickball; also good for simulated volleyball)
- balloons (bat or push from one to another) (These are bright, light, and easy to manage; however, balloons should be used with caution because the noise of a bursting balloon may cause a startle response or even a catastrophic reaction. Light beach balls or the more sturdy type balloons are preferable.)

Movement to Music

- Pattern or initiate the movement with hand-over-hand guidance as needed.
- Incorporate other body movements, following the rhythm patterns of the music; e.g., swinging arms to a march, swaying to a waltz, tapping toes to a jig, nodding head in time with jazz.
- Encourage individuals to do some familiar dance steps if they are able.
- Use rhythm instruments (e.g., tambourine, maracas, spoons) to keep time to the music. Introduce these in an adult fashion (see Chapter 5).
- Encourage singing or whistling along, as this is good exercise for the lungs and increases oxygen intake.
- Encourage individuals to use kazoos, slide or tin whistles, or harmonicas if they are able.

Adaptive Games

- lightweight "horseshoes"
- lightweight Velcro darts and dart board
- paper airplanes (for most, the leader will need to fold the plane; some may be able to follow through or copy the leader)
- plastic bowling pins and balls (too complex for the severely impaired)
- dice (oversized fabric or foam)

5.3 Touch

The skin is the body's largest "sense" organ, and the sensation of touch has a powerful and pervasive effect. Even before use of sight and sound, the infant first begins to explore and interpret the world through touch. Touch is a very effective means of nonverbal communication. Many different messages can be conveyed with touch, depending on the type of touch and the context. The elderly living in institutions are frequently starved for caring personal touch. For further discussion of the use of personal touch, see Chapter 3.

Some general principles to recall here are as follows:

- Never touch a person without alerting in other ways (e.g., by vision, voice).
- Be aware of individual differences and customs in the use of personal touch (e.g., for some, anything beyond a handshake is an invasion of personal space).
- Be especially careful not to use personal touch in a way that could be interpreted sexually by a confused elderly individual (e.g., arm around the waist).
- Be aware that light touch (e.g., touching the hand or shoulder briefly, brushing a soft fabric over the hands) is stimulating or alerting.
- Be aware that pressure touch (e.g., a firm handshake or clasp or a hug) is calming and reassuring.
- Be aware that light touch around the lips can stimulate a rooting or sucking reflex, and should be used only by a clinician trained to direct these reflexes toward functional responses (for example, improved fluid intake).

Touching other objects and materials is usually very satisfying, and the individual may continue this independently (see self-directed activities). There is an enormous variety of effective materials, most particularly the tactile-rich materials of everyday life. Only a small sampling is listed in Table 7-5, by way of an introduction to selecting materials and related functional responses for your particular population. Presenting two related but contrasting textures is effective (e.g., warm and cold, wet and dry, smooth and rough, soft and hard). This is also a way to build on the increased arousal level following the previous stimulus. It may be necessary to guide the participants' hands gently to the materials or to encourage them to run their hands over them. When presenting two contrasting textures, present one at a time. In most cases, the functional response is the feeling or use of the materials themselves. Connect the materials with the individual's previous

Table 7-5 Tactile Cues and Responses

Tactile Cue	*Functional Response*
Nonpoisonous plants, leaves, branches, bark, cones, selected as seasonally appropriate (e.g., a branch of apple blossoms in spring, a basket of colored leaves in the fall); other horticulture materials (pots, soil, trowel, plant mister bottle)	Several ideas for functional responses to these materials are found in the horticulture section (Chapter 5). The activities can be broken down into parts and spread out over several days. If each participant has his or her own plant, a good (weekly) tactile exercise is to feel the leaves, then the soil for moisture and water, as necessary. The functional response is to water the plant or mist the leaves. Associations with plant materials can be particularly rich.
Different sizes, shapes, and textures of wood (contrast can be between rough and smooth wood or between wood and sandpaper)	Sand the wood.
Nails and screws of different sizes, fastened securely onto a board (use with caution around fragile, aging skin)	Turn the nut onto a bolt.
Familiar kitchen utensils	Use as appropriate to the utensils (e.g., whip cream with a hand rotary beater, mix dough with a pastry blender). See the food section of Chapter 5 for more detail.
Various textures of fabric and materials (fabric beanbags can be used again here); an actual fabric object is best (e.g., scarf, collar, mittens, potholders, hat, gloves, pillowcase, cloth bags or purses with zippers or other fasteners, a textured pillow, picture or quilt made of squares of various fabrics)	Enjoy the pleasurable feel of the fabric and the use associated with the object (e.g., put on the mittens, collar, or scarf; put a pillow in the pillowcase, etc.).
Vintage camera, crank telephone, pocket watch, old-fashioned alarm clock, perfume atomizer	Assist to focus and click shutter of camera; crank telephone and pick up receiver; wind clock and assist to set at correct time.
Grooming materials (e.g., comb, brush, talc, hand cream, bracelets, necklaces, earrings for women)	Encourage use as appropriate.
Bucket of soft sand	Find shells buried in the sand; make sand pictures, sand candles.
Rocks of various textures	Lift and compare the surface feel.
Whole, fresh fruits and vegetables (related to the season and special occasions)	Encourage response as appropriate (e.g., peel vegetables, section the orange, prepare a jack-o'-lantern at Halloween; see "Horticulture Activities," Chapter 5, for additional ideas).
Horseshoe, saddle, leather, rope	Facilitate the rich associations these materials will have for some.
Pens, papers, envelopes, and other writing and office supplies	Hold the pen, write the person's name (hand-over-hand guidance for some); sign a card; put paper or cards in envelopes.
Leather- and clothbound books (old copies of familiar classics are excellent), magazines	Feel the textures and contrasts; turn the pages; some may spontaneously read a portion or comment on a picture (facilitate this response).
Snow, ice cubes (as seasonably appropriate)	Make a snowball (this is very popular; some may want to use mittens); remove ice cubes and put in a glass or pitcher of water.

continues

Table 7-5 continued

Tactile Cue	Functional Response
Damp sponge or dishcloth, dry tea towel or bath towel	Wipe table or tray; make a "sponge painting"; wash and dry dishes.
Various textures of dry foods (e.g., rice, grains, seeds, beans, whole spices)	Do related cooking activities; make a seed and grain mosaic picture; plant some seeds.
Vintage toys (e.g., old cars, train pieces, dolls, teddy bears, tops, etc. (age-appropriate presentation is essential)	Feel, enjoy, experience, and relive the memories.
Sports equipment (e.g., fishing reel, baseball glove, ball, skipping rope)	Touch, explore, try out, and relive the memories.
Musical instruments (e.g., mouth organ, violin, recorder, banjo)	Touch, explore, try out, and relive the memories.
Feathers	Tickle to elicit laughter.

life activities. For example, for a cue such as a piece of wood, the handyman might be given verbal prompts related to carpentry projects. For someone who likes to cook, the cue of a wooden spoon could be associated with favorite recipes. At this stage, the goal is to build on the stimulation from previous cues, and it is usually possible to facilitate more complex functional activities (e.g., steps of a horticulture, baking, or handicraft project). Directions for suggested projects are found in Appendixes to Chapter 5.

5.4. Visual

Taking in and interpreting visual cues is a very complex activity. For persons with ADRD, the interpretation is complicated by their disease, and the taking in can be complicated by age-related changes in vision (see Chapter 1). It is essential to bear these losses in mind when introducing visual cues. Visual cues are used at this stage in order to build on the stimulation provided by earlier cues and to direct it toward appreciating and responding to these more complex cues.

Some factors to bear in mind when selecting visual cues are as follows:

- Use clear, uncomplicated pictures with bright colors, high contrast, and an unambiguous focus (e.g., a white clapboard church set against a bright blue sky; a brown horse in a green pasture).
- Remember that matte finishes are best, as glossy finishes or some plastic coatings cause glare.
- Use real objects of a single, solid color to provide extrasensory and associated-use cues, which help interpret visual stimuli (e.g., a red rose, a skein of green yarn).

- Focus on the visual aspects of the activity materials begun with tactile cues (e.g., potting a plant: tactile cues are the feel of the leaves, pot, soil, trowel, etc.; visual cues are the color of leaves, the pot, the ink in the marker used to write a label).
- Use accompanying verbal prompts that are non-threatening:
  1. What color would you say this is?
  2. What is your favorite color?
  3. Does this color remind you of anything?
  4. What do you think of this color?
  5. Did you ever have a _____ this color?
  6. Where did you get it?
  7. Use it? With whom?
  8. These gloves are a beautiful brown (blue). Just like your eyes.

The cues given in the preceding sections also have visual aspects, which can be focused on at this stage of the group, making use of the suggested functional responses and verbal prompts. Calendars are an excellent, low-cost source of pictures. Thematic vintage or regional calendars (e.g., antique cars, flowers, the mountains) are especially good. If the picture is not sturdy, it can be mounted on Bristol board, making a contrasting matte border. These pictures can also be put on the walls, creating a rotating art gallery that adds visual stimulation to the room and improves the general milieu.

A simple, clear, outline map of the region, state, or province is an excellent visual cue. Frequently such a map is available in the form of place mats used in local restaurants. Participants can be assisted to locate their home towns and familiar geographical features (e.g., the capital, the main river, favorite recreation area). It is amazing what even the most severely impaired can recall, with some prompting. This recollection is very satisfying and reassuring. Participants can take copies of the map with them, with the names of their home towns or other associations printed in place.

This activity proved so successful that, to facilitate place finding, I designed a tactile map of our province. The coast was outlined with green yarn, beaches with sand, rivers with blue yarn, and mountains with small stones; there was a replica of the famous Nova Scotia Bluenose sailing in the coastal waters. This map was very well received by participants of all functional levels, and is highly recommended as a group resource. It would make a good project for higher-functioning residents or volunteers.

Mirrors are sometimes suggested as a visual cue. These should be used with caution, and only when you know your participants very well. The more severely impaired may not recognize themselves and thus become very frightened by their own images. This can cause agitation or even a catastrophic reaction.

5.5 Auditory Sense

Like vision, auditory cues are complex and require a high level of interpretive skills. Hearing deficits associated with aging are common. This, combined with the generalized difficulty of persons with ADRD in interpreting their environment, makes the use of auditory cues particularly difficult. For minimally to moderately impaired individuals, tapes with several repetitions of familiar sounds may be useful and stimulating (e.g., nature sounds; kitchen sounds; laughter of children playing; cash register ring; car horns; traffic sounds; siren; musical instruments; workshop sounds such as a drill, hammer, or saw). If the tapes are homemade, the sounds should be very clear and include numerous repetitions. There is a commercially available tape of such sounds that is designed for children (see resources). It is well done, but requires careful editing and selection for use with adults with ADRD. Nature and environmental sound tapes are also available in most record stores. These can be used to focus on a particular auditory cue but may also provide milieu or background music when tied in with the group theme (e.g., bird sounds for a group on spring, ocean sounds for a group on boats). Taped auditory cues are most usefully presented in the following manner: "I have brought a sound for you to listen to." Play several repetitions of the sound, well within the participants' hearing range, with the tape recorder in their line of vision. Use verbal prompts such as the following:

- What does that sound like to you?
- Do you recognize that sound?
- Does that sound familiar to you?
- Does that sound remind you of anything? Let's play it again.

If the sound has not been identified the first time, try some more verbal prompts and then identify the sound. Play the sound a third time, for reinforcement.

In my experience, the use of taped auditory cues is too confusing for the more severely impaired participants. Without the associated sensory cues, they are unable to identify the sound and become perplexed or possibly agitated trying to locate it. With auditory tapes, the targeted functional response is verbal, which, especially without other sensory cues, is too difficult for more severely impaired individuals.

Music and environmental sounds tapes, however, are an essential part of the milieu of sensory stimulation groups. They provide auditory stimulation throughout the group. It is best to use rhythmic and stimulating music (e.g., folk, marching, ethnic) to begin the group and more calming music (e.g., environmental sounds, waltzes, classics) for the last half of the group. Participants can be cued to this music by clapping hands or tapping toes, humming or singing, or whistling along. With other auditory cues, the participants' functional response is to make the sound themselves, such as ringing the bell, blowing the whistle, or responding to the music as suggested above. The most meaningful auditory cues are those associated with activities. The group leader presents the cue by prompting the participant to focus on it (e.g., crumpling the newspaper used while potting plants; striking the match to light a candle; clinking ice cubes while stirring punch).

Some other auditory cues are

- musical instruments (maracas, tambourine, banjo, mouth organ, whistles, small drum)
- bells (cowbell, school bell, sleigh bells, "chow" bell triangle)
- alarm clock, minute timer
- cassette tape recorders and/or Walkman type players with headphones
- bird or other whistles, duck call
- party noisemaker, bicycle horn

5.6 Gustatory Sense (Taste)

Like auditory cues, taste experiences are used throughout the group and are an important functional response to earlier cues (for example, picking up and eating the banana piece, after identifying the smell). Taste is important at the end of the group because of its rewarding and reinforcing effect. The serving of refreshments is a standard closing for many social gatherings and encourages socialization. Some pointers for the use of gustatory cues are as follows:

- Be aware of dietary restrictions and precautions for persons with swallowing difficulties.
- Use seasonal foods or items prepared in the group.
- Avoid excessive use of empty-calorie food.
- Use food related to the group theme, when possible.
- Focus cuing on whether an item tastes salty (e.g., crackers) or sweet (e.g., digestive cookies).
- Do not disrupt participant enjoyment of refreshments by seeking complex verbal responses. This is a time to wind down and relax, after the more demanding responses that were encouraged earlier in the group.
- Encourage maximal independence in feeding themselves and adding their own milk and sugar to tea or coffee (hand-over-hand guidance may be needed by some to cue into this overlearned behavior).
- Offer a choice of hot beverages, juice, or milk.
- Use this relaxed and "normalized" portion of the group to encourage socialization.

Some suggested taste treats are digestive cookies, social teas, and other "light" cookies; crackers and cheese; toast (participants should butter their own); fresh fruits; fresh biscuits, muffins, or cookies made in the group (see Chapter 5).

5.7 Self-Directed Activities

While the group leader focuses on one individual, the other participants may appreciate some simple, self-directed activities. These may be particularly helpful for participants who become restless or disruptive. These should be selected according to the participants' interests and capabilities, as well as being certain that they will not cause harm to themselves or others when not directly supervised. Bringing these activities back to the unit may also help some to settle more happily into the daily routine. These activities make use of the tendency to perseverate, once the leader helps to initiate the movement. Some activities that I have found useful are the following:

- looking at magazines and books (with colorful and familiar pictures) or illustrated seed catalogues

- looking at the local newspaper (even if participants are unable to read it, they often enjoy holding or folding it and turning the pages)
- writing on a sheet of paper and/or folding it and putting it in an envelope
- writing or drawing on newsprint taped over wheelchair or geri-chair trays
- holding or moving a beanbag from hand to hand
- mixing the dry ingredients for pie dough or biscuits
- mixing soil for plants (be certain the person will not put soil in mouth)
- wiping the table or tray with a damp sponge or cloth
- sanding or polishing a cutting board or other wooden item (clamp item in place as necessary)
- winding yarn into a ball (from a skein, or unraveling a no longer useful hand-knit item)
- rearranging items (e.g., tissues, papers, photos) in a purse or wallet
- manipulating large-piece, adult-appropriate jigsaw puzzles (requires moderate-level functioning or assistance)
- shuffling, dealing, arranging playing cards
- feeling, folding, or repeated turning of the pages of fabric books (pages of different-colored, textured fabrics, *not* children's cloth books) or quilts
- manipulating the beads on a small abacus
- turning the parts of a Rubik's cube
- polishing shoes, silver, apples, brass
- rolling or tossing oversized foam or fabric dice
- playing tick-tack-toe, using oversized sheets (with an X and an O in place to help initiate)
- removing dead leaves from plants (If someone has previously kept house plants it is amazing how long this skill will persist; take precautions against putting things in mouth.)
- manipulating a foam bolo ball and bat (ball attached by a string to a small paddle).

6.0 SENSORY STIMULATION GROUP FORMAT

The following is a detailed outline of a sample sensory stimulation group. By employing this outline as a guide, group leaders can then develop a large variety of sessions. Select a theme from the thematic calendar (see Exhibit 6-2). Suggested accompanying cues are listed on the weekly theme charts (Appendix 7-A) and detailed in the preceding sections on sensory cues and associated functional responses. If the cues are related to a particular activity (for example baking or a craft), details are found in Chapter 5. It must be emphasized that these are suggestions and guidelines only. There is no recipe for groups with persons with ADRD. It is essential that the cues and responses be adapted to the interests and capabilities of individual participants.

The sample group which follows is focused on the activity of potting a house plant. Specific horticultural directions are found in Chapter 5. The olfactory and kinesthetic cues (the peppermint plant and the green color of the beanbag) are related to this theme, but only indirectly, to ease preparation and presentation. Each section has several suggested questions for the leader. The intention is that the leader use only one or two of these, as appropriate, and allow ample time for the participant to respond, as suggested in Chapter 3, "Communication."

If there are several participants, it may not be possible for everyone to complete potting a plant in one session, but the activity is easily spread out over two or more sessions.

6.1 Sensory Stimulation Group

Table Arrangement

White or pale yellow table cover (a sheet is practical); large spider plant and several plantlets placed in the middle.

Invitation to the Group

Leader: "Good morning, Mrs. MacDonald," shaking her hand, "How are you this sunny, cold Tuesday in February? It is too cold for plants to grow outside, but they can grow inside. I would like you to help put some plants into pots. You can have one to enjoy for yourself." Continue to support, reassure and connect the activity with Mrs. MacDonald's past life experiences and interests while walking toward the group.

Olfactory Stimulation

Sensory Cue: Peppermint (fresh leaves or extract, as available; a potted peppermint plant or a scented peppermint geranium is ideal)

Approach from the individual's line of vision. Put an arm reassuringly around the person's shoulder or touch her hand, as appropriate. "Good morning, Mrs. MacDonald, how are you this cold Tuesday morning in February? I have brought something nice for you to smell. This will wake up your nose this morning." Pass the mint scent near her nose and make an audible sniffing noise as you inhale. After she has smelled it, remove it briefly.

"How does that smell?" (Offer the scent again.) "Do you recognize that smell? What does it remind you of?" (Offer the scent again.) "This is peppermint. Did you ever grow mint like this in a garden or a pot? Did you ever drink peppermint tea? Did you ever use peppermint in baking? Did you ever have fresh mint with a roast of lamb?" (Offer the scent again.) "Isn't that a nice, fresh smell? Do you like peppermint candies? Here is one for you to taste." (Use sugar-free candies for diabetics.)

Repeat with each participant.

Kinesthetic Stimulation

Sensory Cue: Beanbag catch, using various textures and shades of green beanbags, if available.

Adapt the activity to each individual's capacity, as described in the kinesthetic section. A more directly related kinesthetic activity is mixing potting soil in a large bucket. With higher-functioning participants, this may be successful, although messy, and the dust may be bothersome for some individuals. For lower-functioning participants, this may be too difficult, especially if they tend to put things into their mouths.

"Good morning, Mrs. MacDonald. Did you enjoy that peppermint candy? Now I have some exercises for your hands, to help get them moving this morning, before we do the planting." Engage Mrs. Macdonald in one to three minutes of beanbag toss, encouraging and assisting as appropriate. Be sure to give positive feedback. "That was an excellent throw!" or "Very good, your hands are getting stronger every day." "Did you ever play baseball? What position did you play? Who did you play with, etc.?"

Repeat with each participant. After every participant has had an individual game of catch, encourage the members of the group to pass or toss the beanbag around the table, saying each participant's name in turn.

Tactile Stimulation

Sensory Cue: Soft potting soil, hard trowel handle

"Hello, Mrs. MacDonald. It is too cold out this morning for plants to grow outside, but we can grow some inside. I would like you to help me get the pot ready to plant. Here is the soil. Doesn't it feel nice and soft?" Guide the participant's hand or finger to feel the soil. Keep a close eye on those who might try to taste it. Some may want to really feel it, if plants and gardening have been a previous activity. Others, for whom soil is dirt, may just poke one finger in and that is enough. Guide as necessary to use the small trowel or a spoon to three-quarters fill a four-inch pot. Choose contrasting-color pots if possible, such as red or white. Do this activity on newspaper to speed cleanup.

Encourage recollections while doing this activity. "Do you keep house plants? Which ones? What were your favorites? Did you ever get a plant as a gift? Who gave it to you? What was the occasion?"

Repeat with each participant.

Visual Stimulation

Sensory Cue: Spider plantlets

"Mrs. MacDonald, you have prepared the pot. Now let's put this little spider plant in the pot." Gently guide her hands, as necessary, to do this activity. "What color would you say this plant is? What else does the color green remind you of?" (Supply hints as necessary, e.g., green grass, tree leaves, etc.). "This is a very healthy little plant. You have done a good job of helping me plant it. Do you think it will grow to be as big as this spider plant? Did you ever have a plant like this before? I will keep this here for you and we will check it often to see how it grows." Label quickly with tape. "Thank you for your help, Mrs. MacDonald." (After the group, add more soil as necessary.)

Repeat with each participant.

Auditory Stimulation

Sensory Cue: The newspaper from each participant's "potting area"; audiotape of birds singing

"Hello again, Mrs. MacDonald. Now that the plants are all potted, it is time to clean up for tea (or coffee). Would you rumple up this paper for me? Thank you. That made a lot of noise didn't it? It sure is good to have the cleaning up done. Now you can hear the music of the birds singing. Does that sound familiar? We have just potted a plant for an indoor winter garden. Now you can imagine that the birds are singing in our indoor garden."

This latter activity may be too abstract for the more disabled, and should be used with discretion. For some severely impaired participants who might eat or throw the soil, the cleanup of the potting area may need to be done immediately. Assist the participants to wipe their hands clean.

Repeat with each participant.

Gustatory Stimulation

Sensory Cue: Digestive cookies and tea or coffee

"Hello, Mrs. MacDonald. Now that you have potted the plant, I have a snack for you. Here, have a taste of this. How does it taste to you, salty or sweet?" (Many will say neither, or observe that it is just about right, due to confabulation or the actual inability to distinguish.) "Enjoy the cookie. The group is almost over for today.

It is time to get finished up. Would you like tea or coffee? I will be back with it soon."

Repeat with each participant.

"How was the cookie, Mrs. MacDonald? Here is your tea, Mrs. MacDonald. Do you take milk in your tea?" Assist, as necessary, to add milk. "Enjoy your tea. It is almost time to go back to the day room now."

Repeat with each participant.

Closing

Return all participants to their rooms or the day room. Give them a warm and personal goodbye. Clasp their hands and give praise for their accomplishments in the group. Remind them of what they have done in group that day. Wish them goodbye and tell them that you will see them tomorrow (or as appropriate). It is very important to be sure that each participant is helped to resettle into the daily routine after the stimulation of the group. Some need reassurance from their nurse or caregiver. Leaving them with a safe, and appropriate, memento of the group also reassures them. You might give them a seed catalogue or a flower after a gardening group, a fresh cookie after a baking group.

7.0 EATING STIMULATION: A VARIATION OF SENSORY STIMULATION

Purpose

The general goal of this group is to promote independent eating through the use of a normalized milieu and specific sensory stimulation. The targeted functional response for the sensory cues is independent eating. Other goals are identical with those for regular sensory stimulation groups. Related research is described in Table 7-2 (Rogers et al. 1989).

A five-week research project found that participants in an eating stimulation group significantly improved in positive meal time behaviors and that these behaviors were carried over to other meals eaten in the community dining room (Rogers et al. 1989). The study of Hames-Hahn and Llorens (1989) demonstrated improved self-feeding after involvement in sensory integration activities. Eating stimulation groups tend to be well received and supported by staff of all disciplines because of the obvious purpose and directly observable effects. The participants themselves perceive the group as a special occasion, like being invited out for lunch, and are usually eager to come and to remain.

Murray, who almost never spoke, was always the last one to leave and usually needed extra encouragement to do so. One day, at the end of the group, he looked around to the others at the table and said with a broad smile on his face, "I like this, one, two, three, four,—and you."

Dierdre worried when she came to the group for her fourth time that she didn't have on the proper shoes or dress to be eating out in such a lovely place.

Setting

See Breakfast and Lunch Club groups, under "Activities of Daily Living" in Chapter 5. A setting which, as much as possible, resembles a home dining room or family meal in the kitchen is particularly important for this group. The familiar setting helps to prompt the over-learned behavior of self-feeding. Since these participants are more likely to be physically disabled and to have difficulty in maintaining an upright posture, special attention must be given to seating and positioning. Be sure that chairs maintain knees and hips at 90 degrees, feet are flat, and the back is supported, with the neck slightly flexed, for good swallowing. Special seating needs should be assessed and prescribed by a registered occupational therapist. Tables should be the appropriate height for eating and allow access for individuals in wheelchairs and gerichairs.

Selecting Participants

This group is intended for severely impaired individuals who have difficulty feeding themselves, despite the persisting physical capacity to do so. Swallow and gag reflexes should be intact. As with other groups, it is wise to begin with a smaller number until you become comfortable with the group methods. With experience, it is possible for one experienced staff member to run an eating stimulation group for up to five participants.

Duration and Frequency

Total preparation, group, and cleanup time require one and a half to two hours for five participants. With this group, it is best to serve the regular food service meals. In regard to frequency, once a week is the minimum, twice a week is preferable. Interested direct-care staff can be trained to take over the actual running of the group.

Participant Evaluation

See Lunch/Breakfast Club in Chapter 5.

Suggested Sensory Materials

The following are some materials that I have found to be successful. As in sensory stimulation, many materials stimulate more than one sense, but only one sense is targeted.

Smell. Commercial dry onion soup mix, prepared in a concentrated form, heated and placed on the window sill; fresh fruits and vegetables (in season) in a basket as a table centerpiece; flowers, herbs, plants, and natural materials in season (e.g., evergreen boughs at Christmas) arranged as a table centerpiece; aromatic traditional foods (e.g., green tomato chow-chow, pickled herring, cheese)

Touch. Frequent, reassuring personal touch; comfortably hot water for personal grooming; soft terry cloths and towels; an old-fashioned enamel basin; baking utensils and ingredients for biscuit making

Vision. In addition to the visual aspects of the above materials, the following items are suggested: posters of food; colorfully illustrated cookbooks (particularly vintage ones); regional pictorial magazines and books; the local newspaper; colorful aprons; tablecloths, napkins, dishcloths and potholders

Auditory Sense. Frequent verbal cuing and orienting information used for reassurance, not for prompting recall (e.g., time of day and year, weather, foods being served, connectors with personal biographical information); an old-fashioned brass bell or dinner bell; familiar and favorite background music (generally stimulating music, e.g., traditional fiddle music, to begin the group; more soothing music during the meal, e.g., Bing Crosby favorites) played on a cassette tape recorder

Taste. As allowed by dietary restrictions, appetizers of stimulating premeal foods: fresh fruits and vegetables; crackers and cheese; freshly made baking powder biscuits; relishes (e.g., pickles); hot tea, coffee, or juice, as preferred

Kinesthetic Sense. Ambulation to the group and being seated at the table (if physically capable); washing own hands and face; preparing biscuits (pouring, mixing, cutting, placing on baking sheet); adding milk and sugar to tea or coffee; ringing the bell

Format

1. The participant is invited to come to a special luncheon and is seated at the table. When appropriate prescribed seating cannot be obtained, proper positioning should be supported by the use of rolled towels or blankets.

2. The activities that follow are introduced to each group member in turn. Optimal verbal and nonverbal responses are encouraged by focusing on the sensory cues and facilitating personal reminiscences. All members are presented with a particular cue or activity before the next cue is introduced.

- Facilitate independent washing of hands and face, using terry cloths and an old-fashioned enamel basin filled with hot water.

- Encourage/enable participation in pouring the milk, stirring the ingredients, and cutting the baking powder biscuits (once per week). Use the shortcut method described in Chapter 5.

- Provide olfactory stimulation, encouraging association with the coming mealtime and reminiscing about favorite foods. Provide taste stimulation with appetizers, as described above, immediately after individual olfactory stimulation.

- Provide further taste stimulation with hot tea, coffee, or juice as preferred. Encourage participants to add and stir in their own milk and sugar.

- Provide visual stimulation, focusing on pictorial cookbooks, magazines, the local newspaper, plants, flowers, and seasonal table decorations.

3. Serve the regularly provided meal service. Since persons with ADRD can be confused by being presented with an entire meal tray at once, each course should be served separately.

4. The following cues and/or environmental supports should be provided, as needed, based on assessment by an occupational therapist or an appropriately qualified professional:

- proper positioning and postural support for eating
- adaptive eating equipment (e.g., plate guard, spouted cup, weighted cutlery, built-up handles)
- hand-over-hand guidance, with the utensil in the participant's hand, to initiate hand-to-mouth movements
- backward chaining of self-feeding behaviors (e.g., the first step being hand-to-mouth movement)
- reminders to swallow and/or stimulation of throat muscles to facilitate swallowing
- frequent verbal orienting cues to the meal (what is being served, etc.)
- encouragement and positive reinforcement for independent eating, provided verbally and through reassuring personal touch on the hand, arm, or shoulder
- active encouragement of socialization and verbalization

5. After completion of the meal, assist the participants, as necessary, to wash their hands and faces and return to the daily routine. Provide bridging as for other groups.

6. Communicate information to other team members, as appropriate (e.g., food intake, helpful cues, supports and assistive equipment to nursing staff; food preferences or dislikes to dietary staff; equipment needs to the social worker).

7.1 Sensory Stimulation during Activities of Daily Living

The sensory appreciation and inherent stimulation of these activities can be targeted, just as they are in sensory stimulation groups, and the related functional response can thus be encouraged. For example, during dressing, the individual's attention can be focused on the soft texture of a sweater or socks and the beautiful color of a shirt. The same techniques and principles used in groups can be applied to the activities of daily living. These principles, in brief, are as follows:

- Introduce the activity, using the person's proper or preferred name. As you speak to the individual, provide reassuring orienting information, such as, "Good morning, Mrs. MacDonald. I have brought you some toast for breakfast on this sunny Wednesday in June."

- Use a verbal approach that encourages a positive response, and nonverbal cues that communicate warmth and reassurance.

- Target one particular sense at a time, such as the delicious smell of the morning toast.

- Reduce confusion and competing stimuli. Place only the toast in front of the person, not the whole breakfast tray.

- Provide verbal and nonverbal prompts to encourage a related functional response. For example, provide hand-over-hand guidance to bring the toast to the mouth.

- Make connections with personal interests or habits. "Here is some delicious strawberry jam to put on your toast. What is your favorite kind of jam? Did you ever make strawberry jam?"

- Give ample—but not excessive—positive feedback, using caring personal touch. Squeeze the person's hand or put your arm around his or her shoulder. Give verbal praise: "Great! You have eaten that whole piece of toast. That will give you energy for the day."

Enhance Functional Responses

- Use appropriate hand-over-hand guidance (e.g., hair brush in hand guided to the hair).

- Begin the first steps of the activity (e.g., put toothpaste on the brush and place the brush in the person's hand).

- Prompt familiar, overlearned behaviors through the use of equipment, and a setting that is as homelike and familiar as possible.

- Use the opportunity for caring personal touch (e.g., rubbing in hand cream).
- Connect with previous life activities (e.g., "How did you wear your hair when you were a girl?") and current events (e.g., "It will be good to get your hair done now, because your son Bill will soon be coming to visit").
- Provide manageable choice (e.g., between two shirts).

Bathing

As previously discussed, bathing is often a frightening experience for persons with ADRD and frequently may be resisted. Enhancement of the pleasant sensory experiences of bathing helps to overcome this problem. Enhance the milieu through

- a homelike, comforting bathroom decor (The white ceramic tile, shiny fixtures, and glare from fluorescent lights of many institutional bathrooms are cold and unwelcoming and may be frightening. This can be toned down by adding warmly colored curtains, wallpaper, incandescent lamps, and nonskid bathmats.)
- calming music or environmental sounds audiotape
- pleasantly scented air (Counteract antiseptic institutional cleaners with sachets; potpourri; scented candles; pleasantly scented soaps [such soaps can be used to perfume the air, even if they cannot be used on sensitive skin]; and aromatic plants, such as a lemon geranium or a flowering hoya.)
- a comfortably warm temperature (Because of age-related changes in heat sensitivity, this may seem too warm to others.)

Enhance sensory cues by

- using soft, brightly colored bathrobes, towels, and washcloths
- rubbing on moisturizing creams or dusting on talc, as appropriate, after the bath

Dressing

- Enhance the milieu by ensuring privacy and comfortably warm temperatures.
- Enhance sensory cues by selecting clothing in a variety of appealing textures and colors and in favorite personal colors and styles (consult with family and significant others).
- Enhance functional responses by
  1. having a limited (no more than two) selection of a particular type of clothing from which to choose

2. offering one item at a time
3. arranging clothes in the order in which they are to be put on
4. targeting associated reminiscences
5. providing reality reassurance as a cue for dressing (e.g., "You have just had your breakfast here at Sunshine Manor. It is Sunday morning. Now it is time to get dressed, because your daughter will be here to take you to church.")

Grooming

- Enhance the milieu through a homelike bathroom (as described previously) or dressing table setting. Mirrors must be used with caution, as many persons with severe cognitive impairment are unable to recognize themselves and become frightened by their reflections in the mirror. Cover mirrors as appropriate, with fabric or a blind. Small hand mirrors may be less frightening than large wall mirrors.
- Enhance sensory cues by providing grooming materials that have a variety of *textures* (e.g., smooth handles on hairbrushes, a soft powder puff); *scents* (as skin and allergy sensitivity allow, talc, hand cream, perfume, aftershave lotion); *colors* (incorporate personal color favorites in items such as combs and toothbrushes); *contrast* (e.g., in color to distinguish the brush from the dresser; see "Environmental Theories" in Chapter 4).

7.2 Sensory Stimulation during Visits

Families and significant others are in a better position than anyone to enhance function through sensory stimulation. Since they are well acquainted with their relative's or friend's personal preferences, lifelong habits, and previous life experiences, they can not only pass this information on to staff members but use it during visits. They can greatly enrich the individual's sensory stimulation and give a focus to what are sometimes awkward visits by bringing in favorite personal mementos and other items, which the person may not safely or conveniently keep at the facility. If the individual is able, and the weather allows, a short walk or wheelchair ride outside is very stimulating and something staffing routines often do not allow. However, be sure to check with direct-care staff first, as this may be overstimulating or make settling back into the daily routine too difficult. The outdoors provides ample sensory materials to which the individual can be cued.

A visitor can bring special stimulation and individual attention to the person with ADRD. It is important, however, to adapt the visits to make them as rewarding and nonthreatening as possible for both parties. The following are some guidelines for visits.

Introduce yourself. This is first and foremost. Expecting the individual with ADRD to recall your name—sadly enough, whether you are a wife of 50 years or a volunteer—is too stressful. Given time and reassurance, your relative or friend will almost always show other signs of recognition. However, the loss of memory for names is a deficit that usually appears quite early. It is essential to begin the visit with a tone of reassurance ("Hello, mum, this is your daughter-in-law, Carol. I have come to visit you on this beautiful Sunday afternoon in July") rather than a contest ("What's my name? Don't you remember me?"). Although visitors have a need to be recognized and recalled, this must be sought in ways which do not confront the individual with his or her disability (e.g., connect with especially memorable times you have shared; use favorite photos, songs, shared expressions).

Make use of special communication tips. See the suggestions in Chapter 3 emphasizing nonverbal communication and unconditional positive regard.

Visit in a pleasant but quiet area free from the distraction of the comings and goings of the unit.

Have a concrete focus for the visit (e.g., a family photo album, music, flowers to arrange, or the other suggestions that follow). Visiting is usually centered around conversation. Since conversation as such (i.e., the exchange of information and ideas) is a deficit area, the focus should be on a concrete activity, sociability (e.g., having tea together), sensory appreciation, and nonverbal communication. Although it is not the usual image of "visiting," for persons with ADRD just sitting and holding hands with a loved one while listening to favorite music is enriching and comforting.

Use reminiscence techniques. Focus on significant personal experiences or accomplishments, shared personal experiences, or important generational experiences (e.g., life during the depression). Bring physical cues or artifacts and use information-seeking questions as described in Chapter 6.

Provide a bridge to help the individual resettle into the daily routine when you leave. It is helpful to leave him or her with a memento of your visit (e.g., a magazine, card, or book; a bouquet to admire). Return the person to the unit area and make a connection with direct-care staff, such as, "This is your nurse, Joan. She will help you get ready for supper now." Give a warm, personal farewell, using ample reassuring touch. Provide reassuring orienting information, adding in your name and the time of your next visit, and thank the person for today's visit. If the person is still able to read,

leaving a card with your name, the time of your visit, and what you did together is reassuring.

The following are some activity suggestions for use during visits:

- Put cut flowers in a vase.
- Bring cones and evergreen boughs or other materials with which to make a table centerpiece.
- Bring a skein or a ball of wool to wind.
- Bring strawberries to stem for a strawberry shortcake (can be passed and shared with other residents).
- Clap, hum, sing, dance, tap toes, or whistle along with favorite music.
- Look at clippings of stories and pictures of personal interest from newspapers, magazines, or family photo albums.
- Write postcards or cards to friends or family (see Chapter 5 for facilitating techniques).
- Help with simple, repetitive tasks that the person may have done previously (e.g., stuffing envelopes, folding flyers, shelling peas, folding napkins). This not only gives a focus to the visit but adds to the individual's self-esteem, as he or she feels useful being able to help you.
- Help with personal grooming, such as doing hair and nails (or makeup with women).
- Share tea or coffee and a favorite treat. If the facility does not have a kitchen or space for preparation, bring it, already prepared in a thermos. The occasion can be made extra special by bringing cups and saucers, or a favorite mug, and having a proper "tea."

8.0 CONCLUSION

After covering many topics and techniques varying from behavior modification to the therapeutic use of plants and pets, it is fitting to close the final therapeutic activities chapter with some suggestions for visiting, spending time with another person, because it is such a commonplace and essential activity of daily life. As ADRD progresses, even this simple act becomes difficult. However, by adapting the visit so that the focus is on nonverbal activities, anyone—a friend, family member, or paid caregiver—can once again make a visit a meaningful and therapeutic time for the person with ADRD. It is a time when the visitor and the person with ADRD can share experiences of the heart and the senses, bypassing the deteriorating capacity of the mind. When we "speak" from the heart, we are understood and appreciated.

9.0 RESOURCES

Auditory sound tapes are available from:
KALS Inc.
P.O. Box 126
Kitchener, Ontario
Canada N26 3W9

Back to the Table. An excellent guide to developing dining programs in residential facilities. Available from the author:
Suzanne Perkett, O.T.R.
9518 West St. Martins Rd.
Franklin, WI 53132

Parachek Geriatric Rating Scale and Treatment Manual. This is a booklet with good suggestions for sensory stimulation activities. It is available from:
Center for Neurodevelopmental Studies, Inc.
8834 North 39th Ave.
Phoenix, AZ 85051

Sensory Stimulation Fragrance Projects. Pauletta B. Gwinnup. This is a booklet of suggested sensory activities, suitable for the mildly and moderately impaired. It is available from:
Potentials Development
775 Main St.
Buffalo, NY 14203

Sensory Stimulation Products for Alzheimers. This is a small catalogue of safe, self-directed activity materials for persons with advanced ADRD. It is available from:
Geriatric Resources Inc.
Orlando, FL 32807
Telephone 1-800-359-0390

Recordings for Recovery. This is a catalogue of tapes of music and environmental sounds that are available for free loan. For regional addresses see "Music Resources" in Chapter 5.

Thematic Calendar and Sensory Stimulation Theme Charts

Key for Sensory Cues

Smell	S
Kinesthetic Sense	K
Touch	TO
Vision	V
Auditory Sense	A
Taste	TA
Functional Response	>

THEMATIC CALENDAR

January	*February*	*March*	*April*
1. New Year's 2. Winter Fun 3. Party Time (Grooming) 4. Winter Evenings at Home 5. Animals in Winter	1. Ground Hog Day, Hoping for Spring 2. Valentine's Day 3. Lent, Shrove Tuesday, Mardi Gras (as appropriate) 4. Indoor Planting	1. Cameras/Pictures 2. Trains 3. Easter or Passover (as appropriate) 4. Pets	1. Birthdays (party) 2. Spring 3. Planting a Garden 4. Spring or Summer Games 5. Fishing
May	*June*	*July*	*August*
1. Gardens/Boats 2. Mother's Day 3. Music Appreciation 4. Victoria Day (Canada) or Spring (see April) 5. The Farm	1. Flowers, Plants, Gardens 2. Weddings 3. Father's Day 4. Carpentry/Woodworking	1. National Holiday 2. Beaches, Oceans, Lakes 3. Vacations 4. Garden Harvest or Cars	1. Fishing (see April) 2. Boats (see May) 3. Indoor Planting (see February) 4. Garden Harvest or Pets (see March)
September	*October*	*November*	*December*
1. School Days 2. Watches/Clocks 3. Autumn 4. Trains (see March)	1. Getting Ready for Winter 2. Thanksgiving (Canadian) or Music Appreciation (see May) 3. Horses 4. Halloween	1. Cameras/Pictures (see March) 2. Veteran's Day, Remembrance Day 3. Thanksgiving (American) or Music Appreciation (see May) 4. Birthdays (see April)	1. Telephone 2. Quilts 3. /4. Christmas or Hanukkah (as appropriate)

NEW YEAR'S

Sensory Cue	*Sensory Stimulation Activities*
Day 1	
S	Scented candle > light it
K	Beanbags
TO	Velvet cummerbund or vest
V	Calendar (for the New Year) with a clear, simple picture
A	Party horn
TA	Leftover Christmas sweets
Day 2	
S	Perfume/aftershave lotion > rub some on
K	Shake maracas in time to appropriate music
TO	Candle
V	Velvet cummerbund or vest
A	"Auld Lang Syne"
TA	Crackers and cheese
Day 3	
S	Oranges > squeeze orange juice for punch
K	Beanbags
TO	Fancy evening bag
V	Party horn
A	Strike a match, light candle, blow out match
TA	Apple or orange pieces or digestive cookies
Day 4	
S	Lemons > squeeze juice for punch
K	Pour in ingredients and ice, and stir the punch
TO	Fancy punch glass
V	Fancy evening bag
A	Ice rattling in the punch cup > toast to the New Year
TA	Punch and party goodies, as available

WINTER FUN

Sensory Cue	*Sensory Stimulation Activities*
Day 1	
S	Skein of real wool or unspun wool
K	Make snowballs from a bucket of snow (wear mittens)
TO	Fur muff (or other fur), associate with animals keeping warm
V	Simple picture of a snow-covered landscape
A	"Winter Wonderland"
TA	Hot chocolate
Day 2	
S	Spices for mulled cider (stick cinnamon, whole cloves) > put in cider
K	Measure and stir the cider and spices for "mulled cider" (use Crock-Pot or electric frying pan if stove not available)
TO	Skates (vintage if possible)
V	Colorful woolen scarf, mittens, or hat
A	Sounds of children playing in the snow
TA	Hot mulled cider and digestive cookies
Day 3	
S	Peppermint extract > taste peppermint candy
K	Slide a hockey puck (rubber one) along a table or tray or shoot the puck with a stick (if appropriate)
TO	Warm sweater (preferably heavy, homemade, one with different textures in the pattern)
V	Newspaper with picture of a hockey game or the hockey scores
A	Short audio portion of a hockey game (e.g., "He shoots, he scores!" and cheering)
TA	Cheese and crackers
Day 4	
S	Banana
K	Beanbags or appropriate "make it snow" winter scene paperweight > shake the paperweight
TO	Real snow
V	Paper snowflakes mounted on colored background
A	Auditory sounds (if appropriate): howling winds, snowstorm, or crackling fire
TA	Social teas or popcorn

PARTY TIME/GROOMING

Sensory Cue	*Sensory Stimulation Activities*

Day 1—Dance Party

S	Perfume/talc/aftershave lotion > put some on
K	Dancing/movement to age-appropriate music
TO	Collection of vintage hats, ties, scarves, jewelry, as appropriate > emphasize contrasting texture
V	Comb/brush (focus on color) > do hair (use mirror with discretion)
A	Square dance or other type of appropriate party music
TA	Party snacks (e.g., fancy crackers, cookies, chips) served in a party atmosphere

Day 2—Apple Party

S	Stick cinnamon > sprinkle ground cinnamon on cooked apples
K	Push cut, cooked apple quarters through sieve to make applesauce
TO	Old-fashioned apple peeler (if available) or dried apples > contrast feel with fresh apples
V	Different colors of apples, arranged in a basket
A	"Johnnie Appleseed"
TA	Applesauce

Day 3—Card Party

S	Peppermint > taste peppermint candies
K	Shuffle and deal out cards
TO	Cribbage board
V	Face cards in one suit (e.g., king, queen, jack of hearts); use oversized cards, as necessary
A	Rattle of dice
TA	Pretzels or other

Day 4

S	Perfume/talc/aftershave lotion
K	Mix and prepare applesauce squares
TO	Comb/brush (focus on feel)
V	Colorful party accessories (as on day 1); select only one or two per participant
A	Party music (as appropriate)
TA	Applesauce squares > serve on a party plate; use real cups

WINTER EVENINGS AT HOME

Sensory Cue	*Sensory Stimulation Activities*
Day 1	
S	Kerosene lamp or candle > light it
K	Vintage radio > turn the knobs and dials
TO	Checkers game, crokinole, or dominoes > move the pieces
V	Vintage magazines or books (or photocopies of appropriate sections) > turn the pages
A	Taped introduction to a popular radio show (e.g., "The Shadow," "The Jack Benny Show," "The Lone Ranger")
TA	Dried apples (or in Maritime Provinces, roast dulse over candle flame)
Day 2	
S	Whole black walnuts (or other whole nuts) > crack open and smell (take precautions with regard to choking or putting shells in the mouth)
K	Move pieces of checkers, crokinole, or dominoes
TO	Vintage radio
V	Quilt or quilt pieces, hooked rug, or other vintage handicraft
A	Cracking open the nuts
TA	Nuts (if appropriate), popcorn, or applesauce squares
Day 3	
S	Cheese > taste
K	Grate the cheese and mix dough for cheese tea biscuits
TO	Cut out biscuit dough and place on cookie sheet
V	Focus on visual aspects while cutting biscuits
A	Minute timer (timing the biscuits)
TA	Cheese tea biscuits
Day 4	
S	Peppermint > taste peppermint candies
K	Winding yarn from a skein into a ball or bean bags
TO	Vintage magazine, book, or vintage handicraft
V	Checkers game (emphasize red and black contrast)
A	Shaking dice
TA	Cheese tea biscuits or social teas

ANIMALS IN WINTER

Sensory Cue	*Sensory Stimulation Activities*

Day 1

S	Peppermint
K & TO	Petting or grooming real animal, stuffed mounted animal, or good-quality synthetic animal
V	Simple poster or photo of animal in winter
A	Animal sounds tape (as appropriate) > identify particular animals
TA	Crackers and cheese

Day 2

S	Banana
K	Beanbags
TO	Vintage fur collar or pelt or fur scraps (available from furriers)
V	Stuffed animals as on day 1
A	As on day 1
TA	Digestive cookies

Day 3

S	Apple pieces
K	Fill bird feeder or make suet-seed balls for the birds (hang near a window)
TO	Bird feathers or stuffed real bird
V	Real bird or photo or picture of a common bird
A	Bird whistle or tape of bird sounds
TA	Applesauce

Day 4

S	Cut orange sections
K	Beanbag, or peel and prepare fruit for TA
TO	Animal as on day 1
V	Fur collar or fur pieces
A	Animals sounds tape as on day 1
TA	Fruit pieces

GROUNDHOG DAY/HOPING FOR SPRING

Sensory Cue	*Sensory Stimulation Activities*
Day 1	
S	Soil/wheat kernels (associate with planting for spring)
K	Plant wheat kernels (cover with plastic and put in a warm, bright place)
TO	Branches with swelling buds > put in water for forcing
V	Clear, simple picture or poster of a groundhog
A	Spring bird songs
TA	Fresh vegetables (e.g., lettuce, parsley, watercress, other greens)
Day 2	
S	Peppermint (associate with the fresh smell of spring)
K	Put on and take off wool sweater (associate with warmer weather coming)
TO	Hyacinth bulb (heat-treated) > place in special jar for sprouting
V	Branches with swelling buds
A	Spring bird songs
TA	Digestive cookies
Day 3	
S	Fresh, scented flower (e.g., freesia, narcissus, hyacinth; if unavailable try essence with flower scent)
K	Beanbags (various textures and shades of green)
TO	Contrast between heavy winter jacket or sweater and spring jacket
V	Local newspaper with the story of the groundhog highlighted
A	Rattling newspaper
TA	Crackers and cheese
Day 4	
S	Fresh sprouted wheat blades > pick a piece and taste
K	Shape prepared chocolate drop cookie dough and roll in coconut tinted green
TO	Emphasize contrast in texture between dough and coconut
V	Flower as on day 3
A	Favorite background music
TA	Chocolate drop cookies

VALENTINE'S DAY

Sensory Cue	*Sensory Stimulation Activities*
Day 1	
S	Fresh flower, essential oil scent on good-quality silk flowers, potpourri mix
K	Using cardboard or pastic stencil trace heart outline on red paper (for Valentine card, staff or volunteer to cut out, before next group)
TO	Paper doily
V	Fancy red heart (e.g., satin heart from a candy box)
A	"Heart of My Heart," "Let Me Call You Sweetheart"
TA	Crackers with strawberry jam > spread own jam
Day 2	
S	Vanilla > shake a drop in sugar cookie dough
K	Mix dough for cookies (chill dough)
TO	Cutout of red heart (from day 1) > place paper doily behind the heart
V	Valentine cookie cutter (red plastic is good) or commercial Valentine card
A	"Roses are Red" etc. (recite and encourage participants to join in)
TA	Red apple slices
Day 3	
S	Cinnamon > taste cinnamon hearts
K	Roll and cut out Valentine cookies (assisted as needed); decorate with cinnamon heart candies
TO	Fancy heart as on day 1
V	Sign card made on day 2 (assist as appropriate)
A	Music as on day 1
TA	Valentine cookies
Day 4	
S	Hot chocolate (association of chocolate with Valentine's Day) > drink
K	Fold Valentine party napkin
TO	Red fabrics of different textures (velvet, corduroy, satin, etc.)
V	Flowers (fresh if possible) > put in vases to decorate tables
A	Music as above
TA	Valentine cookie/tea party

LENT/SHROVE TUESDAY/MARDI GRAS

Sensory Cue	*Sensory Stimulation Activities*
Day 1—Shrove Tuesday	
S	Maple extract > taste maple sugar or maple candy
K	Mix premeasured ingredients for pancakes
TO	Focus on the many touch sensations while pouring batter and cooking own pancake
V	Rich brown syrup, as it is poured on
A	Focus on sounds of pancake cooking
TA	Pancakes (begin to eat as each is cooked); serve tea and coffee after
Day 2	
S	Aftershave lotion/hand cream or perfume > put some on (associate with preparing for a party)
K	Tambourine/maracas > shake in time to lively Mardi gras music
TO	Mask (as worn for Mardi gras costume)
V	Single-color costume or garment (as worn for Mardi gras parade)
A	Lively parade music
TA	Crackers and cheese
Day 3	
S	Peppermint > taste peppermint candies
K	Beach ball catch
TO	Colored costume as on day 2
V	Mask
A	Light a sparkler
TA	Digestive cookies
Day 4	
S	Orange sections
K	Beanbags
TO	Tambourine or maraca
V	Local newspaper with a picture of Mardi gras or Shrove Tuesday celebrations
A	Lively parade music
TA	Fresh fruit pieces

INDOOR PLANTING

Sensory Cue	*Sensory Stimulation Activities*

Day 1

S	Peppermint (preferably fresh plant or extract)
K	Stir potting soil and put in pot
TO	"Wheat" planted in January (check for moisture and water as necessary)
V	Large, green house plant (e.g., spider plant)
A	Rumpling up newspaper during cleanup
TA	Crackers and cheese

Day 2

S	Potpourri mix
K	Write name on tongue depressor (use as plant label)
TO	Pot, plantlet, soil > put plantlet in pot and add extra soil as needed > push in name marker
V	Wheat planted in January
A	Rumpling newspaper
TA	Digestives

Day 3

S	Apple slices
K	Beanbags in shades of green
TO	Tree branch (focus on contrast between the feel of the buds and bark)
V	Clear picture of apple tree in bloom (use reality reassurance to actual season)
A	Bird songs/nature sounds tape
TA	Apple jelly and crackers > spread own jelly

Day 4

S	Scented geranium or other herb
K	Beanbags in shades of green
TO	Feel potted plant soil > water as necessary
V	Tree branch as on day 3
A	Bird songs/nature sounds tape
TA	Fresh fruit pieces

CAMERAS/PICTURES

Sensory Cue	*Sensory Stimulation Activities*
Day 1	
S	Aftershave lotion/talc/hand cream > rub on (associate with getting ready for photo)
K	Brushing hair
TO	Vintage camera > look through lens and take picture
V	Vintage photo (e.g., family portrait type in vintage frame)
A	Click of the shutter on the camera
TA	Crackers and cheese
Day 2	
S	Aftershave lotion, etc. (as on day 1)
K	Brushing hair
TO	New camera (preferably Polaroid type)
V	Flash of the camera (take picture of person if Polaroid; show when done)
A	Winding the film forward
TA	Digestive cookies
Day 3	
S	Flower (e.g., hyacinth, forced in group)
K	Mount the photo on paper mat, sign name and other message
TO	Vintage photo (contrast with new)
V	Photo of favorite local scene (e.g., from a calendar or coffee table book or album)
A	Favorite music
TA	Fresh fruit
Day 4	
S	Vanilla > add drop to premeasured cookie dough
K	Stir premeasured cookie dough and drop spoonfuls onto greased cookie sheet
TO	Terry cloth and water to wash hands
V	Vintage cookie tins or cutters
A	Minute timer (for cookies)
TA	Fresh cookies

TRAINS

Sensory Cue	Sensory Stimulation Activities
Day 1	
S	Coal (associate with coal-fired steam engines)
K	Beanbags
TO	Railway engineer's type hat (striped denim) or conductor's hat
V	Pieces of realistic model train (ideally a model train club might come with some items)
A	Train whistle (recording) or a whistle to blow that sounds like a train whistle
TA	Social teas
Day 2	
S	Banana (associate with exotic places to travel to)
K	In an adult manner, push or shove railway car or model train
TO	Trace the route of a train journey on a tactile map of your local area
V	Railway hat
A	Train chugging (recording), "Faraway Places"
TA	Soda crackers
Day 3	
S	Apple (associate with favorite local fruit)
K	Beanbag toss at a local map target (where would you travel?)
TO	Model train pieces as on day 1
V	Photo or book of vintage steam trains (looking at such things as the cowcatcher)
A	"All Aboard," clanging the bell
TA	Apple
Day 4	
S	Cheese (associate with traveling food)
K	Mix biscuits, cut, and put on cookie sheet (food for travel)
TO	Tactile map or piece of railway tie
V	Modern-day train schedule
A	"I've Been Working on the Railroad"
TA	Fresh biscuits and cheese

EASTER

Sensory Cue	*Sensory Stimulation Activities*
Day 1	
S	Spring flowers (fresh if possible, Easter lily or other)
K	Easter-color balloons for balloon volleyball (or if not suitable, beanbags)
TO	Easter basket
V	Easter bonnet (vintage if possible) with lace and flowers
A	"The Easter Parade," "Peter Cottontail"
TA	Easter eggs
Day 2	
S	Orange
K	Pet Easter rabbit or chicks (live if possible; otherwise good-quality stuffed ones)
TO	Spring flowers
V	Easter basket
A	Sounds of baby chicks
TA	Fresh fruit pieces
Day 3	
S	Chocolate or cut, mixed peel
K	Mix premeasured dough for chocolate drop cookies or hot cross buns (chill dough)
TO	Easter bonnet
V	Easter rabbit or chicks as on day 2
A	Nature sounds, "Woodlands in Spring"
TA	Chocolate drop cookies or digestive cookies
Day 4	
S	Flowers (fresh)
K	Shape chocolate drop cookies like Easter eggs (roll in tinted coconut) or shape hot cross buns
TO	Focus on touch sensations of the dough
V	Easter basket with Easter "goodies"
A	"The Easter Parade," "Peter Cottontail"
TA	Chocolate drop cookies or hot cross buns

ANIMALS

Sensory Cue	Sensory Stimulation Activities
Day 1	
S	Catnip (dried form available from health food stores)
K	Pet and groom live cat or kitten (if not possible use realistic, good-quality stuffed animals)
TO	Focus on touch sensations of cats
V	Calendar or picture book of cats with clear pictures > select favorite
A	Animals sounds tape of cats (if appropriate)
TA	Cheese and crackers
Day 2	
S	Fresh grass (associate with dogs rolling in the fresh grass or eating it in the spring)
K	As on day 1 but with dogs
TO	As on day 1 but with dogs
V	As on day 1 but with dogs
A	As on day 1, but with dogs barking or song "How Much Is That Doggie in the Window?"
TA	Fruit pieces
Day 3	
S	Banana
K	Beanbags
TO	Live bird or stuffed bird from a collection
V	As on day 1 but with birds
A	Bird calls or bird whistle; songs, "Yellow Bird," "Kookaburra"
TA	Social teas
Day 4	
S	Peppermint
K	Nerf ball catch
TO	Check soil from plant from earlier session > add water as needed
V	Review favorites from previous three sessions
A	Review favorites from previous three sessions
TA	Digestive cookies

BIRTHDAYS

Note: Emphasize reality reassurance throughout—this is about birthdays, not a participant's birthday now.

Sensory Cue	*Sensory Stimulation Activities*
Day 1	
S	Hand cream/aftershave lotion (associate with "getting ready for something special")
K	Heavy-duty "Happy Birthday" balloon for catch or balloon volleyball (alternate beanbags)
TO	Colored marker and paper > write name, birth date (keep for the week, then post in room)
V	Colorful pictures or decals > select and place on paper from above
A	Light candle and blow out
TA	Graham crackers
Day 2	
S	Scented candle > place in holder for table centerpiece
K	As on day 1
TO	Scoop and flour > measure flour for cake (e.g., six people, 3 cups flour, $\frac{1}{2}$-cup scoop each)
V	Birthday wrapping paper (clear, simple design) or small wrapped gift (e.g., cookie or candy bar) > unwrap gift
A	Party horn > blow the horn (wipe clean with alcohol swabs between users)
TA	Crackers and cheese
Day 3	
S	Vanilla extract > shake a drop in premeasured ingredients for cake batter
K	Add liquid ingredients to dry; stir cake batter
TO	Spoon cake batter > put spoonful of batter into muffin papers
V	Party invitation > invitation to next day's party or simple colorful birthday card > identify colors/associations
A	Minute timer ticking
TA	"Cakelets" (1 tbsp. batter in muffin paper; bake at 350 degrees for 10 minutes; when cakelets are done, bake remaining batter in standard cupcake size)
Day 4	
S	Chocolate icing >spread on cupcake with a popsicle stick (or table knife); lick the popsicle stick
K	As on day 1, variation while singing "Happy Birthday"
TO	Colored sugar sprinkles > sprinkle on cupcake
V	Birthday candle (colored) > place in cupcake and light
A	Sing "Happy Birthday," party music
TA	Cupcakes (make the sharing a "party" atmosphere)

SPRING

Some seasonal updates of materials are suggested below. These materials are multisensory, but focus on one sense per session. New materials for May sessions: branches in bloom or full leaf; fresh greens (e.g., dandelion, sorrel, lettuce); rhubarb > prepare and cook stewed rhubarb.

Sensory Cue	*Sensory Stimulation Activities*
Day 1	
S	Sweetly scented spring flower (e.g., in Nova Scotia the mayflower)
K	Arrange flowers in water
TO	Pussy willows
V	Green grass (dug from outside and put in a pot)
A	"April Showers"
TA	Fresh fruit
Day 2	
S	Peppermint (fresh or extract)
K	Beanbags (in various shades and textures of green)
TO	Spring flowers
V	Clear, simple picture of a local scene in spring > identify colors/objects
A	"Zippity-Do-Dah"
TA	Fresh fruit
Day 3	
S	Garden chives (in a pot)
K	Beanbags
TO	Green grass (as on day 1)
V	Dandelions or other early flowers (emphasize personal associations)
A	Spring nature sounds tape (e.g., running brook, bird songs)
TA	Digestive cookies
Day 4	
S	Maple extract > taste maple syrup or maple sugar
K	Check previously planted plants, water and prune, as necessary
TO	Maple syrup spigot
V	Branch with swelling buds (maple if possible)
A	Selections from previous days
TA	Maple syrup with ice cream or toast

PLANTING A GARDEN

Note: Outdoor (O) and indoor (I) activities are listed for those without outdoor garden space.

Sensory Cue	Sensory Stimulation Activities
Day 1	
S	Potted chives or other herb plant > taste
K	Mix soil for potting
TO	Trowel, pot, soil > put soil into pot
V	Already-grown cress pot or other lush green plant (preferably outdoor type)
A	Rattle of cress seeds in packet > plant seeds in pot (use salt shaker or candy mint dispenser as necessary)
TA	Fresh "greens" (e.g., parsley, mint, spinach, watercress) with cheese or other sandwich spread > put on crackers
Day 2	
S	(O) Focus on the smell of fresh air; (I) fresh air at the window or fresh green grass in a pot
K	(O) Walk to outdoor garden plot or planter boxes; (I) beanbags (green shades)
TO	(O) Spade or dig soil as appropriate; (I) potato with "eyes" sprouting > cut for planting and air dry 1 day
V	(O) Focus on green grass, blue sky, etc.; (I) seed catalogue (focus on one bright, clear picture)
A	(O) Focus on bird songs, wind, etc.; (I) nature sounds tape
TA	Digestive cookies
Day 3	
S	Cut tomato > taste
K	Fill 3-gallon bucket with soil for planting
TO	Bucket, potato eyes, trowel > plant potatoes in bucket (indoors or out)
V	Red, ripe tomato/picture of full-grown tomato plant with ripe tomatoes
A	Pour warm water on "Jiffy pellets" (associate with preparing to plant tomatoes)
TA	Green tomato chow-chow or other tomato relish > spread on crackers
Day 4—Tropical Gardens	
S	Orange pieces (associate with tropical gardens) > taste
K	Prepare (as possible) and mix the fruit for a fruit salad
TO	Tomato seeds and soaked "Jiffy pellets" > plant (associate, as appropriate, with tomato as a fruit)
V	Unusual tropical fruit such as a pineapple or a tropical house plant (can plant the pineapple top)
A	Tropical bird songs
TA	Fruit salad

SPRING/SUMMER GAMES

Sensory Cue	*Sensory Stimulation Activities*

Day 1

S	Green grass
K	Participant to hold one handle of skipping rope and turn while leader holds other end (if not possible, Nerf ball)
TO	Vintage type skipping rope with wooden handles
V	Clear picture of child skipping
A	Familiar skipping chants (e.g., "Cinderella Dressed in Yella") > encourage joining, in an adult-appropriate manner
TA	Digestive cookies

Day 2

S	Peppermint
K	Wind up kite string
TO	Fabric strips > tie to make a kite tail
V	Brightly colored kite(s)
A	Sounds of children playing outdoors (as appropriate)
TA	Crackers and cheese

Day 3

S	Freshly popped popcorn (pop in room, if possible, to increase aroma); associate with snacks at a baseball game
K	Nerf or other soft baseball > play catch
TO	Baseball glove
V	Baseball team shirt or hat from favorite local team
A	"Take Me Out to the Ball Game"
TA	Popcorn (crackers or other for those who do not like popcorn)

Day 4 (*Note:* **Good outdoor theme for a barbeque, if possible.**)

S	Mustard (associate with hot dogs at a ball game)
K	Baseball catch as on day 3
TO	Baseball team shirt or hat
V	Pictures of famous baseball players from participants' era (e.g., Babe Ruth, Shoeless Joe, Yogi Berra, Jackie Robinson)
A	Recorded sound of a baseball game or umpire calls
TA	Hot dog (if appropriate—take precautions for choking); prepare own (with assistance), putting dog in bun, adding relish, etc.

FISHING

Sensory Cue	*Sensory Stimulation Activities*
Day 1	
S	Solomon gundy (pickled herring) or other local favorite, aromatic seafood treat
K	Cast out and wind in reel of shortened fishing rod (no hooks, of course)
TO	Fishing lures or floats of various textures
V	Colorful poster or picture of different types of fish > identify favorites or one recognized
A	Woodland sounds (water, streams, bird calls)
TA	Solomon gundy and crackers (alternate crackers and cheese)
Day 2	
S	As on day 1
K	As on day 1
TO	Tackle box or kreel > open, examine contents
V	Live goldfish or lures as on day 1
A	As on day 1
TA	Digestive cookies
Day 3	
S	Cooked fish (according to favorites, e.g., canned tuna or salmon or poached white fish)
K	Mix premeasured ingredients and shape for fish cakes
TO	Fishing rod and reel
V	Colorful fishing hat
A	Sound of fish cakes frying (using electric frying pan)
TA	Fish cakes (provide an alternate as necessary)
Day 4	
S	Fish cakes (leftover)
K	As on day 1
TO	Fish net (piece of net in coastal fishing areas or sports fishing net with handle)
V	Fishing lures as on day 1
A	Ocean sounds (if appropriate)
TA	Cheese and crackers or fresh fruit

GARDENS

Note: These groups should be outdoors as much as possible. Emphasize sensory aspects while doing simple gardening activities, as suggested. Focus attention on particular sensory aspects and take precautions not to overstimulate. Alternate indoor activities are indicated by (I).

Sensory Cue	*Sensory Stimulation Activities*
Day 1	
S	Fresh herbs, as available (e.g., chives, mint, oregano, thyme) > pick and eat on the spot. (I) Potted herbs
K	Walk to the garden and plant, with assistance as appropriate (suggested activities: raised planter box or barrel of peas; toss dahlia tubers or potatoes into predug holes; scatter seeds of radish, lettuce, nasturtium, beans, spinach, beets; set out hardy, easy-to-grow flower transplants such as marigolds, snapdragons, or pansies. (I) Beanbags
TO	Tomato seedlings > feel to see if dry and water as appropriate
V	Emphasize visual aspects. (I) Green plant (e.g., cress pot or sprouting potato barrel)
A	Emphasize auditory aspects, e.g., bird songs, wind. (I) "In the Merry, Merry Month of May"
TA	Fresh vegetables, as available
Day 2	
S	Scented flowers (e.g., narcissus, daffodil, tulip, pansy, lily of the valley)
K	See day 1
TO	Trowel/hoe (contrast feel of wooden and metal parts)
V	See day 1. (I) Fresh flowers, as available (e.g., dandelions)
A	See day 1. (I) Nature sounds tape
TA	Cheese and crackers
Day 3	
S	See day 1
K	See day 1
TO	Potato barrel > water as needed
V	See day 1. (I) Clear picture of a garden
A	See day 1
TA	Digestive cookies
Day 4	
S	See day 2
K	See day 1. (I) Prepare and mix vegetables for a salad
TO	Fresh produce (e.g., rhubarb)
V	See day 1. (I) Red, ripe tomato
A	See day 2
TA	Fresh salad

BOATS

Note: Adapt according to types of boats used locally.

Sensory Cue	Sensory Stimulation Activities
Day 1	
S	Coiled rope (as used on boats) > tie a simple knot
K	"Row, Row, Row, Your Boat" (or other song) as appropriate to level of functioning; do simulated movements associated with boating, such as rowing, hoisting sails, bailing out, leaning fore and aft, starting the engine, rough waters (emphasize reality reassurance)
TO	Boat model or replica as available (preferably vintage)
V	Picture of well-known ship or local type of boat (e.g., in Nova Scotia, the Bluenose)
A	Clanging of the ship's bell
TA	Ship's biscuits (or other type of biscuit)
Day 2	
S	Favorite local canned, dried, or smoked fish snack
K	See day 1
TO	Yellow sou'wester and hat > try it on
V	Boat model as on day 1
A	Foghorn
TA	Snack, as in S (provide alternate)
Day 3	
S	Seaweed (dried seaweed in inland areas)
K	See day 1
TO	Sailcloth or canvas
V	Sailor's hat or tunic > try it on
A	Selection of seafaring songs: "Row, Row, Row Your Boat," "What Do You Do with a Drunken Sailor?" "A Capital Ship," "Anchors Aweigh"
TA	Social teas
Day 4	
S	Vanilla > add to premeasured cookie dough
K	Mix and drop cookies on greased cookie sheet
TO	Sailor's hat
V	Sou'wester
A	"Shores of Tripoli," "Bluenose Is Sailing Once Again," "I'se the Bye"
TA	Fresh cookies

MOTHER'S DAY

Sensory Cue	Sensory Stimulation Activities

Day 1

S	Perfume/talc/hand lotion, as appropriate (associate with scent that mother wore)
K	Rub hand cream thoroughly onto hands, arms, or face
TO	Vintage hat (associate with the type that mother wore)
V	Vintage photo of woman dressed up (make associations with mother)
A	Poem or song, "M Is for the Many Things You Gave Me"
TA	Social teas

Day 2

S	Dried sachet mix
K	Make sachet bag or jar (see Appendix 5-C)
TO	Emphasize touch aspects of sachet
V	Vintage jewelry, hair ornaments, combs > select favorite
A	"Billy Boy," "The Little Old Red Shawl That Mother Wore"
TA	Digestive cookies

Day 3

S	Vanilla or other extract used in cookies > shake a drop in premeasured cookie dough
K	Mix cookie dough (select old-fashioned favorites like mother made, e.g., molasses, sugar, oatmeal); drop on greased cookie sheets
TO	Vintage jewelry as on day 1
V	Colorful, old-fashioned apron
A	Music as on day 2 or other favorite vintage songs
TA	Just-made cookies

Day 4—Mother's Day Tea

S	Fresh flowers > arrange in water
K	Grooming hair in preparation for the tea
TO	Icing tube and cookies > decorate cookies (e.g., write mother's first name or initials)
V	Colorful tablecloth, real cups and saucers, napkins > lay the table for tea
A	See day 2
TA	Special Mother's Day tea

MUSIC APPRECIATION

Note: Select one musical instrument per day, according to what is available (e.g., guitar, recorder, fiddle, slide whistle, ukulele, banjo, harmonica, spoons, autoharp).

Sensory Cue	*Sensory Stimulation Activities*
Day 1	
S	Fresh flowers as available
K	Movement in time to music. Vary movements through the week, according to the type of music used (e.g., toe tapping, clapping, swaying, dancing). See Music, Chapter 5.
TO	One instrument as suggested above > hold and attempt to make a sound on the instrument
V	Vintage song book or sheet music
A	Recording of instrument selected—use favorite local songs > encourage singing along
TA	Social teas or cookies from previous week
Day 2	
S	Peppermint
K	As on day 1
TO	As on day 1
V	Pitch pipe or tuning fork > play and hum note (as appropriate)
A	As on day 1
TA	Crackers and cheese
Day 3	
S	Orange pieces
K	As on day 1
TO	As on day 1
V	Music stand
A	As on day 1
TA	Digestive cookies
Day 4	
S	Cheese
K	As on day 1
TO	As on day 1
V	Musical instrument
A	As on day 1
TA	Fruit pieces

VICTORIA DAY (CANADA)

Sensory Cue	Sensory Stimulation Activities
Day 1	
S	Cheddar cheese
K	Cricket bat (if possible) > bat the ball (on the floor); or use croquet mallet, sponge ball
TO	Plate, cup, spoon, or other memorabilia of the royal family
V	Colorful, clear poster of the Queen (e.g., coronation picture); associate with memories of the coronation
A	"God Save the Queen" (very familiar—encourage to sing along) (may know "God Save the King" better)
TA	Shortbreads
Day 2	
S	Peppermint
K	Beanbags
TO	Union Jack
V	Memorabilia as on day 1
A	Bagpipe music (associate with being the Queen's favorite)
TA	Digestive cookies
Day 3	
S	English Leather aftershave lotion
K	"British Grenadiers"; march while seated, if necessary, or clap in time to the music
TO	See day 1
V	Union Jack
A	"God Save the Queen"
TA	Cheddar cheese and crackers (English variety, e.g., Carr's water biscuits)
Day 4	
S	Dried currants
K	Mix premeasured ingredients for scones; cut out and place on greased cookie sheet
TO	See day 1
V	Photo album, scrapbook, or coffee table book of Prince Charles or other members of the royal family
A	Favorite music related to theme
TA	Scones and jam

FARMING

Sensory Cue	*Sensory Stimulation Activities*

Day 1—Cows

S	Hay or straw (often available at urban garden centers)
K	Beat cream into butter using small hand churn or rotary egg beater (save buttermilk)
TO	Butter bowls, paddles, prints, or churn as available
V	Picture or poster of cattle grazing in the pasture or in the barn
A	Cowbell > ring it
TA	Toast (preferably from homemade-style bread) with fresh butter

Day 2—Sheep

S	Fresh sweet butter > spread on a cracker
K	Wind yarn from a skein to a ball
TO	Sheepskin or lamb's wool
V	Spinning wheel or wool carders or shuttle or colored skeins of yarn or knitted item
A	Sounds tape of sheep (if appropriate), "We're Poor Little Lambs," "Baa, Baa, Black Sheep"
TA	Cheese and crackers

Day 3—Pigs

S	Smoked sausage or cooked bacon
K	Beanbag toss at bull's-eye target
TO	Rough wood barn board (genuine article painted red on one side is good)
V	Photographs/calendar or other reproductions of pigs (e.g., pig-shaped cutting board, piggy bank)
A	Hog calling (from premade tapes); some participants may know how
TA	Bacon/sausage/salami with bread or crackers

Day 4

S	Fresh clover (available along roadsides or in vacant lots, even in the city) > taste the blooms of red clover
K	Mix premeasured ingredients for buttermilk biscuits (use buttermilk from churning); cut and place on greased cookie sheet
TO	Hay or straw
V	Barn board
A	Farm animal sounds tape or children singing "Old MacDonald," "Little Boy Blue"
TA	Buttermilk biscuits

FLOWERS/PLANTS/GARDENS

Carry on with gardening tasks appropriate to the season (see "Horticultural Activities" in Chapter 5). Indoors, use a flowered tablecoth on the table (a sheet works well).

Sensory Cue	*Sensory Stimulation Activities*
Day 1	
S	Fragrant fresh flowers as available > arrange in water > wear one as a boutonniere
K	Beanbags with flowered print
TO	Check soil for dryness > water potted plants as necessary
V	Beautiful specimen of flowering plant (e.g., bring in outdoor planter) or huge bouquet of fresh flowers
A	"You Wore a Tulip," "My Wild Irish Rose," "Sweet Violets," "Moonlight and Roses"
TA	Edible flowers (chive blossoms, clover, nasturtium) or alternate
Day 2	
S	Flower-scented cologne, hand cream, soap
K	Arrange single blooms of small flat flowers (see "Horticultural Activities" in Chapter 5) on card or blotter paper for picture or card
TO	Emphasize touch sensations of above activity
V	Seed catalogue, calendar, poster, or coffee table book; focus on one type of flower or flowers of a particular color
A	"Rose of Tralee," "A Lonely Little Petunia in an Onion Patch," "Yellow Rose of Texas"
TA	Fresh fruit
Day 3	
S	Sachet
K	Sign card or picture made on day 2
TO	Crewel work or embroidered flowers on pillowcases or picture
V	See day 1
A	"Roses are red/violets are blue," etc. > encourage reciting together; make up new verses, as appropriate
TA	Digestive cookies
Day 4	
S	Fresh strawberries
K	Beanbags
TO	Fresh flowers/petals (focus on different textures)
V	Greeting cards with flower pictures
A	Sayings: "A rose by any other name would smell as sweet," "A rose between two thorns"
TA	Fresh vegetable tray (could include radish roses or tomato flowers)

WEDDINGS

This is a thoughtful topic that will stir up many memories, both happy and sad. Be sure to allow for the expression of sadness, but end with reinforcing, positive aspects.

Sensory Cue	*Sensory Stimulation Activities*
Day 1	
S	Aftershave lotion/talc/perfume/hand cream; associate with dressing for a special occasion
K	Rub on hand cream
TO	Lace (antique if possible)
V	Vintage photo (bride and groom) > associate with parents' wedding (or own wedding, being sensitive to singles)
A	"The Wedding March"
TA	Social teas
Day 2	
S	Fresh orange or lemon > squeeze the juice for punch
K	Mix ingredients for punch
TO	Satin cummerbund, black bow tie or special tie, silk pocket scarf or top hat
V	Contemporary wedding photo (of famous wedding, e.g., Diana and Charles, Queen Elizabeth II, Grace Kelly)
A	Toast to the bride and groom (clink glasses, encourage everyone to say, "To the bride and groom," and to name a favorite bride and groom)
TA	Cheese and crackers
Day 3	
S	Vanilla > shake a drop into premeasured liquid ingredients for cake
K	Mix premeasured ingredients for white cake (or use cake mix); make cake and "cakelets" as in April "Birthdays" session
TO	Decorative bride and groom top for wedding cake
V	See TO, day 1
A	"Wedding Bells Are Breaking Up That Old Gang of Mine," "Me and My Gal," "Daisy, Daisy"
TA	Cakelets
Day 4	
S	Flowers > wear as boutonniere or corsage
K	Spread prepared icing on cake; decorate with sprinkles or icing flowers
TO	Wedding garter
V	Wedding cake photo
A	See day 3
TA	Cake, served in a party setting

FATHER'S DAY

Sensory Cue	Sensory Stimulation Activities

Day 1

S	Aftershave lotion/shaving soap (associate with what father used to wear)
K	Bowling (if able, otherwise bean bags)
TO	Old-fashioned wooden cane or walking stick
V	Vintage photo of man dressed for special occasion (associate with own father)
A	"My Grandfather's Clock"
TA	Crackers and cheese

Day 2

S	Peppermint
K	Casting out with fishing rod and reel
TO	Vintage tie(s) of interesting textures and colors
V	Contemporary Father's Day card
A	Favorite music, as appropriate
TA	Fresh fruit

Day 3

S	Fresh wood pieces (associate with father's workshop)
K	Sanding
TO	Vintage men's hats as available—fedora, straw hat, top hat, working cap > try on, associate with what their fathers wore
V	Plain colored background paper to begin picture collage; "MY FATHER" in large letters on the top > write father's name at top, participant's name at bottom.
A	As on day 1 and day 2
TA	Digestive cookies

Day 4

S	Aftershave lotion/shaving soap
K	Picture/collage of individual's father; use background information you know to preselect a limited choice of materials (favorite sports, occupation, hobbies, birthplace)
TO	As in K above, emphasizing touch sensations
V	As in K above, emphasizing visual sensations
A	As on day 1 and day 2
TA	Toast > spread on butter

CARPENTRY/WOODWORKING

Sensory Cue	*Sensory Stimulation Activities*
Day 1	
S	Fresh cedar wood or shingle
K	Sand or oil wood to make cutting board or other simple item (see "Handicraft Activities" in Chapter 5)
TO	Contrast smooth piece of finished lumber with log or branch
V	Small wooden item (planter, trivet, candleholders, tray)
A	Sawing
TA	Crackers and cheese (serve on wooden bowl or tray)
Day 2	
S	Pine bough
K	As on day 1
TO	Sandpaper
V	Hammer
A	Hammering
TA	Digestive cookies (serve as on day 1)
Day 3	
S	Spruce gum (associate with chewing it as a child)
K	As on day 1
TO	Nails/screws (be very careful with those who might put them in their mouths)
V	Hand drill
A	Power drill
TA	Social teas (serve as on day 1)
Day 4	
S	Freshly cut branch of maple or other deciduous tree
K	As on day 1
TO	Small wooden item, as on day 1
V	Plane
A	Planing
TA	Fresh fruit (serve as on day 1)

NATIONAL HOLIDAY—CANADA DAY

Note: Canada Day is best known as Dominion Day to most older participants today.

Sensory Cue	*Sensory Stimulation Activities*
Day 1	
S	Maple extract (associate with the national emblem, the maple leaf) > taste maple syrup or maple sugar
K	Variations on hockey, the national game (e.g., floor hockey—pass the rubber ball or shoot into nets; canes make good hockey sticks—slide rubber puck along table)
TO	Canadian flag
V	Real maple leaves
A	"Oh Canada"
TA	Seasonal fresh fruit
Day 2	
S	Seasonal fresh fruit, as available (e.g., strawberries)
K	Clap or stomp feet in time to parade music (associate with First of July parade)
TO	Small firecrackers or sparklers
V	Clear color photo of fireworks (make personal associations with going to fireworks display)
A	"Oh Canada," "The Maple Leaf Forever"
TA	Seasonal fresh fruit
Day 3	
S	Vanilla > shake a drop into premeasured liquid ingredients for cake
K	Cake and "cakelets" as on April Birthdays
TO	Union Jack (associate with the old flag)
V	Picture of a beaver or a mounted stuffed beaver (e.g., from a local museum; associate with being the national animal)
A	"God Save the Queen"
TA	Cakelets

Day 4—Have First of July picnic outdoors, if possible

S	Mustard or onions (associate with hamburgers/hot dogs and First of July picnic)
K	Prepare hot dog (put meat in bun and add condiments > eat)
TO	Spread icing on cake; decorate with small flags or with squeeze-on tubes of red icing to make Canadian flags; focus on touch and visual cues, as appropriate
V	As in TO above
A	"Oh Canada" or other patriotic songs and parade music as appropriate
TA	Hot dogs, hamburgers, Canada Day cake

NATIONAL HOLIDAY—FOURTH OF JULY

Sensory Cue	*Sensory Stimulation Activities*

Day 1

S	Fresh apple (associate with "as American as apple pie")
K	Catch with a Nerf or a soft plastic type baseball (associate with baseball as the national game)
TO	American flag
V	Clear picture of an eagle (or mounted stuffed eagle, if available; associate with the national symbol)
A	Patriotic songs: "Stars and Stripes," "America," "This Land Is Your Land," "The Shores of Tripoli"
TA	Apple pie (commercial or make in group, as appropriate; use shortcut with prepared filling and premade crust)

Day 2

S	Seasonal fresh fruit (e.g., strawberries)
K	Clap or stamp in time to parade music (associate with Fourth of July parade)
TO	Small firecrackers or sparklers
V	Clear photo of fireworks (make personal associations with going to fireworks displays)
A	See day 1
TA	Seasonal fresh fruit

Day 3

S	Vanilla > shake a drop into premeasured liquid ingredients for cake
K	Cake and cakelets as on April Birthdays
TO	Eagle as on day 1
V	American flag, Stars and Stripes
A	See day 1
TA	Cakelets

Day 4—Have Fourth of July picnic, if possible

S	Mustard or onions (associate with hamburgers, hot dogs, and Fourth of July picnic)
K	Prepare hot dog or hamburger (put meat in bun and add condiments > eat)
TO	Spread icing on cake; decorate with small flags or sprinkles or squeeze tubes of icing to make the American flag; focus on touch and visual cues, as appropriate
V	As in TO above
A	"Happy Birthday, America," parade music and others as on day 1
TA	Hot dogs, hamburgers, Fourth of July cake

BEACHES/OCEANS/LAKES

Sensory Cue	*Sensory Stimulation Activities*
Day 1	
S	Seaweed (fresh or, if not available, dried)
K	Catch with a beach ball
TO	Sea shells of various types and textures
V	Clear picture of a famous ocean beach or a popular local one, as appropriate
A	Nature sounds tape with ocean waves, sea birds, etc.
TA	Seafood treats as appropriate to local favorites (e.g., smoked oysters, pickled herring, sardines)
Day 2	
S	Seafood treat (as on day 1 under TA)
K	Find the seashells buried in a tray of sand; focus on movement and touch sensations
TO	Find the seashells buried in a tray of sand; focus on movement and touch sensations
V	Focus on colors of the seashells
A	As on day 1
TA	As on day 1
Day 3	
S	Freshly cut lemon (associate lemons or juicer with making lemonade > squeeze juice for lemonade)
K	Stir lemon juice, sugar, water, ice to make lemonade
TO	Bathing cap, swim goggles, bathing suit, as appropriate
V	Vintage picture of swimming party at the beach or "swimming hole"
A	"In the Good Old Summer Time"
TA	Lemonade and digestive cookies or social teas
Day 4	
S	Peppermint (associate with fresh outdoor smell)
K	Driftwood pieces, shells, dried seaweed, and other beachcombing treasures; rub and polish driftwood and combine with shells, etc., to make a decorative centerpiece; focus on kinesthetic, touch, and visual cues, as appropriate
TO	As in K above
V	As in K above
A	Favorite music
TA	Ice cream

VACATIONS

Sensory Cue	*Sensory Stimulation Activities*

Day 1

S	Aftershave lotion/perfume/talc (associate with preparing for a special occasion)
K	Small vintage suitcase packed with some items for travel (e.g., vintage clothing, hat, towel and face cloth, comb, brush, camera); unpack and repack the suitcase, focusing on specific sensory cues in turn (e.g., the feel of the suitcase, the color of the hat, etc.); emphasize reality reassurance throughout
TO	As in K above
V	As in K above
A	"Faraway Places"
TA	Cheese (associate with being a good travel food)

Day 2

S	Cheese
K	Trace the route to a favorite destination on tactile local map, globe, or road map, as appropriate
TO	Globe
V	Clear pictures or post cards of favorite local or world famous travel spots, especially those with personal significance (e.g., Niagara Falls, Statue of Liberty, Eiffel Tower)
A	Music appropriate to picture (e.g., "The Last Time I Saw Paris" for the Eiffel Tower)
TA	Food item as appropriate to travel spot (e.g., French bread for Paris)

Day 3

S	Smell of leather (associate with leather suitcases, car or train upholstery)
K	Write local postcard (with assistance as necessary) to friend or relative
TO	Souvenir items from popular local travel spots (e.g., spoons, plates, mugs, hats)
V	Globe
A	Travel sounds, from a tape, as appropriate (e.g., train sounds, ship's bell, car horn)
TA	Foods from exotic places, as appropriate to the ethnic background of participants

Day 4—Summer Cottage

S	Evergreen boughs
K	Windup fishing reel (associate with fishing at the cottage)
TO	Moss, bark, or other "woodsy" items
V	Kerosene lantern > light it (with assistance, as needed)
A	Nature sounds tape (e.g., loon calls, waterfalls, bird calls)
TA	Camp food (e.g., baked beans)

GARDEN HARVEST

Note: This may involve more than four sessions.

Sensory Cue	Sensory Stimulation Activities
Day 1	
S	Fresh flowers > put in water
K	Basket of fresh produce, according to local availability (or picked from the therapeutic garden), e.g., tomatoes, peppers, cucumbers, beans; take items out of basket and focus on touch and visual aspects, as appropriate
TO	As in K above
V	As in K above
A	Favorite music
TA	Favorite produce from the basket (assist to prepare as necessary)
Day 2	
S	Tomato leaves and freshly cut tomato
K	Outdoor walk focusing on the feel and visual aspects, as appropriate. Visit the therapeutic garden, if one is available
TO	As in K above
V	As in K above
A	Favorite music as appropriate
TA	Fresh vegetable pieces; cheese and crackers
Day 3	
S	Vanilla > shake a drop into the custard mix for homemade ice cream
K	Beat together liquid ingredients for custard for ice cream (staff to cook and cool)
TO	Ice cream scoop
V	Picture of favorite local ice cream shop
A	Favorite music
TA	Fresh fruit, according to local season
Day 4	
S	Fresh fruit according to local season > crush to add to ice cream
K	Churn ice cream, with everyone taking a turn at the crank; focus on touch and visual aspects as appropriate; associate with personal memories of churning ice cream, favorite kinds, etc.
TO	As in K above
V	As in K above
A	Favorite music
TA	Home made ice cream

Other August themes may include fishing (see April); boats (see May), indoor planting (see February).

GARDEN HARVEST

Note: This may involve more than four sessions.

Sensory Cue	*Sensory Stimulation Activities*
Day 1	
S	Fresh flowers > put in water
K	Basket of fresh produce, according to local availability (or picked from the therapeutic garden), e.g., tomatoes, peppers, squash, cucumbers, melons; take items out of the basket and focus on touch and visual aspects, as appropriate
TO	As in K above
V	As in K above
A	Favorite music
TA	Fresh Fruit
Day 2	
S	Tomato leaves and freshly cut tomato
K	Wash vegetables for making simple uncooked relish (e.g., green tomato relish)
TO	As in K above, focusing on touch sensations
V	Vintage preserving jars
A	"Harvest Moon"
TA	Fresh fruit pieces
Day 3	
S	Vinegar or spices for the relish
K	Turn the handle to grind prepared vegetables for the relish; focus on touch and visual properties, as appropriate
TO	As in K above
V	As in K above
A	Favorite music
TA	Crackers and cheese
Day 4	
S	Finished relish
K	Selection of dried flowers, attractive weeds, bulrushes, and branches suitable for a dried flower arrangement; make individual bouquets, selecting favorites with assistance as appropriate; focus on touch and visual aspects in turn
TO	As in K above
V	As in K above
A	Favorite music
TA	Fresh fruit

SCHOOL DAYS

Sensory Cue	Sensory Stimulation Activities

Day 1

S	Cheese (associate with good food for school lunch)
K	Slate and chalk (or scribbler) > write name
TO	Vintage schoolbooks (readers, spellers, etc.)
V	Vintage school group photo or picture of a school building
A	School bell > ring it
TA	Crackers and cheese

Day 2

S	An apple (cut pieces to increase aroma); associate with an apple for the teacher
K	Beanbag or sponge ball catch (associate with games played at school); use schoolyard rhymes, in age-appropriate fashion (e.g., "Anti anti over, the cows are in the clover")
TO	School bell
V	Slate and chalk
A	"School Days, School Days"
TA	Apple pieces

Day 3

S	Peppermint (or, in the Maritime Provinces, molasses; associate with a favorite after-school treat, bread and molasses)
K	See day 2
TO	Slate and chalk
V	Vintage schoolbooks
A	Sounds tape, with children laughing and playing
TA	Digestive cookies

Day 4

S	Vanilla > shake a drop into premeasured ingredients for chocolate drop cookies (or other cookies)
K	Stir together and shape chocolate drop cookies (associate with after-school snack)
TO	Straight pen and ink > dip in pen and write name (with assistance, as needed)
V	Vintage schoolbooks > find familiar passages
A	"School Days" or schoolyard chants
TA	Chocolate drop cookies

WATCHES/CLOCKS

Sensory Cue	*Sensory Stimulation Activities*
Day 1	
S	Fresh flowers > put in water
K	Beanbag catch
TO	Vintage pocket watch > wind the watch or set it
V	Vintage catalogue page of watches (associate with first watch)
A	"Tick, tick" from Big Ben-type alarm clock (the real thing)
TA	Digestive cookies
Day 2	
S	Apple
K	Beanbag toss at bull's-eye target
TO	Big Ben type alarm clock > wind the clock or set it
V	Clear picture of well-known public clock, e.g., in Nova Scotia, the Citadel clock or in London, Big Ben
A	Clock chimes (ringing the half hour, etc.)
TA	Apple
Day 3	
S	Cheese
K	Beanbag catch
TO	Watch fob, watch chain, or small vintage shelf clock
V	Clear picture of grandfather clock or other large floor clock
A	"My Grandfather's Clock"
TA	Crackers and cheese
Day 4	
S	Fresh pear (if available)
K	Beanbag toss at bull's-eye target
TO	Modern wristwatch
V	Vintage pocket watch (contrast with modern watch)
A	"Tick, tick" of a pocket watch
TA	Fresh pears or other fruit

AUTUMN

Sensory Cue	*Sensory Stimulation Activities*
Day 1	
S	Relish (local, homemade favorite)
K	Take out and rearrange harvest basket of gourds, squash, apples, and other fall produce
TO	Branches of brightly colored fall leaves
V	Clear picture of local or other autumn scenes
A	The rustling of the leaves
TA	Relish and crackers
Day 2	
S	Apple
K	Beanbag catch (autumn colors, if possible)
TO	Indian corn
V	Harvest basket of fall produce (see day 1)
A	Favorite music, "Harvest Moon"
TA	Apples and other fall fruits
Day 3	
S	Cinnamon > sprinkle into cooked apples to make applesauce
K	Turn handle on purée mill (or push cooked apples through sieve) to make applesauce
TO	Harvest basket (see day 1)
V	Branches of brightly colored fall leaves
A	Nature sounds in autumn (e.g., the wind, crickets)
TA	Applesauce
Day 4	
S	Hot mulled cider
K	Basket as on day 1
TO	Old-fashioned preserving jar
V	Indian corn
A	Corn popping
TA	Popcorn, cider (cold or hot mulled cider)

GETTING READY FOR WINTER

Sensory Cue	*Sensory Stimulation Activities*

Day 1

S	Onion from basket
K	Harvest basket (as in August harvest theme) with winter/fall produce for storage (e.g., carrots, potatoes, turnip, squash, apples, winter pears, grapes); take out items from basket and focus on the feel and the visual aspects in turn
TO	As in K above
V	As in K above
A	"Harvest Moon," fall nature sounds tape
TA	Produce from basket (with help to prepare as needed)

Day 2

S	Vinegar > taste a finished pickle
K	Wash and prepare vegetables for making a simple relish that is a local favorite, focusing on the feel and the visual aspects as appropriate (e.g., cranberry orange relish, green tomato chow-chow)
TO	As in K above
V	As in K above
A	Favorite music (lively), played while working
TA	Crackers and cheese

Day 3

S	Apple
K	Turn handle of food grinder to prepare vegetables for relish
TO	Vintage preserving jars
V	Brightly colored wool cap, mittens, or scarf > try it on
A	As on day 1 and day 2
TA	Apple, dried apple, or apple jelly and crackers

Day 4

S	Relish
K	Beanbag catch (or nerf football, as appropriate)
TO	Wool cap or mittens (see day 3)
V	Vintage preserving jars
A	As on day 1 and day 2
TA	Finished relish, cheese and crackers

THANKSGIVING (CANADIAN)

Sensory Cue	Sensory Stimulation Activities
Day 1	
S	Homemade relish (local specialty or favorite)
K	Scrape seeds out of a pie pumpkin to make pumpkin pies (after group, leader or volunteer prepares and cooks pumpkin)
TO	As in K above
V	Selection of a variety of colors, sizes, and shapes of autumn leaves
A	Thanksgiving hymns, appropriate to participants' backgrounds: "Come Ye Thankful People," "We Plough the Fields and Scatter," "Bringing in the Sheaves"
TA	Relish, cheese and crackers
Day 2	
S	Cranberry sauce
K	Turn handle of purée mill or push through sieve to prepare pumpkin for pies
TO	Harvest basket or cornucopia
V	Picture of prepared, cooked turkey or turkey dinner > name Thanksgiving dinner favorites
A	See day 1
TA	Thanksgiving taste treats (cooked turkey, cranberry sauce, rolls)
Day 3	
S	Cinnamon stick (rub hands over it to get the full scent)
K	Help to mix dry mix for pastry for pumpkin pies, or mix graham cracker crust
TO	Press pastry or graham crumbs into tart tins > place pastry scraps on greased sheet, sprinkle with sugar and cinnamon, and bake
V	Indian corn
A	See day 1
TA	Baked pastry scraps
Day 4	
S	Nutmeg > grate or grind whole nutmeg for pumpkin pie filling
K	Mix pumpkin pie filling (premeasured ingredients)
TO	Spoon filling into tart shells made on day 3, or use commercially prepared pastry shells
V	Harvest basket or cornucopia
A	Favorite party music
TA	Pumpkin pie/tarts

HORSES

Sensory Cue	*Sensory Stimulation Activities*

Day 1

S	Leather from horse harness
K	Toss rubber horsehoe in simulated game of horseshoes; if not appropriate, beanbags
TO	Horseshoe (real)
V	Clear color picture of a horse
A	Recorded horse race commentary
TA	Cheese and crackers

Day 2

S	Apple (associate with a treat that horses like)
K	As on day 1
TO	Horse blanket with pin
V	Ceramic or other reproductions of a horse (e.g., a hobby horse)
A	"The Old Gray Mare," "Camptown Races," "She'll Be Comin' Round the Mountain"
TA	Apple and other fresh fruit, as available

Day 3

S	Mulled, spiced cider
K	As on day 1
TO	Piece of horse harness or saddle, as available
V	Horse blanket with pin
A	Sleigh bells or other types of bells used on horses
TA	Mulled cider and graham crackers

Day 4

S	Vanilla > shake a drop into premeasured baking ingredients
K	Mix premeasured ingredients for oatmeal muffins (or oatmeal cookies or oatcakes); shape for baking
TO	Oats (associate with food for us, but also a good food for horses)
V	Harness or saddle
A	Selections from day 1, 2, or 3
TA	Baked goods

HALLOWEEN

A good intergenerational activity.

Sensory Cue	*Sensory Stimulation Activities*
Day 1	
S	Peppermint
K	Remove seeds from a large pumpkin (use large metal spoon)
TO	As in K above, focusing on touch sensations
V	Picture of finished jack-o'-lantern
A	Favorite music
TA	Digestive or other cookie
Day 2	
S	Apples (associate with bobbing for apples or candied apples at Halloween)
K	Beanbags (fall colors, if possible)
TO	Finished jack-o'-lantern (done by leader or volunteer)
V	Witch's hat and broom (or similar)
A	Favorite music
TA	Apples or other fruit
Day 3	
S	Hot mulled cider
K	Beanbags
TO	Various hats, which could be part of a Halloween costume > try on
V	Put candle in jack-o'-lantern > light (with assistance, as appropriate; use long matches)
A	Popcorn popping (do in air popper)
TA	Popcorn, or crackers and cheese for those who do not like popcorn
Day 4	
S	Vanilla > shake a drop into premeasured ingredients for chocolate drop cookies
K	Mix chocolate drop cookie dough; roll in orange-tinted desiccated coconut to shape like pumpkins
TO	As in K above, focusing on touch sensations
V	Halloween masks
A	Favorite music
TA	Chocolate "pumpkin" cookies

VETERANS DAY/REMEMBRANCE DAY

This will be a very emotional topic for many. It is important, however, to provide an opportunity for expression of the feelings associated with these memories. The last session includes preparing food, as a time for reassurance and coming together, as happens at a wake.

Sensory Cue	*Sensory Stimulation Activities*
Day 1	
S	Relish/pickle
K	Use a stencil to trace an outline of a large poppy on red paper (volunteer or staff to cut out after group)
TO	Lapel pin poppy > put it on (use safety pins)
V	Military beret, tam, or cap
A	Taps, followed by a moment of silence (as appropriate)
TA	Digestive cookies
Day 2	
S	Apples
K	Marching in place to military music
TO	Military hat; see V on day 1
V	Red paper poppy from day 1 > mount on white paper
A	Military marching band tunes, e.g., "Shores of Tripoli"
TA	Apples and other fruit
Day 3	
S	Peppermint
K	As on day 2
TO	Paper poppy from day 2 > write names of people to remember (with assistance as needed)
V	Medal or medallions as available
A	Favorite wartime songs (e.g., Vera Lynn, "White Cliffs of Dover")
TA	Crackers and cheese
Day 4	
S	Vanilla > shake a drop into premeasured cookie dough
K	Mix and shape no-bake cookies
TO	National flag
V	Lapel pin poppy
A	National anthem
TA	Cookies

TELEPHONE

Sensory Cue	Sensory Stimulation Activities

Day 1

S	Apple
K	Vintage telephone > turn the crank or dial the number (recall own ring or number, as appropriate)
TO	Telephone book (vintage if possible); emphasize contrast between the feel of the pages and the cover
V	Modern telephone > dial own number
A	Telephone ring
TA	Apple and other fresh fruit

Day 2

S	Peppermint
K	Beanbag catch
TO	Vintage telephone; see day 1
V	Telephone book (focus on the contrast in color between white pages and yellow pages)
A	Telephone busy signal (unless too disorienting for your participants)
TA	Fresh fruit or digestive cookies

Day 3

S	Relish
K	Beanbag catch
TO	Modern telephone
V	Vintage telephone; see day 1
A	Favorite music
TA	Social tea or other cookies

Day 4

S	Cheese
K	Mix tea biscuits from prepared dry mix; cut and place on greased sheet
TO	Vintage telephone
V	Modern telephone
A	Favorite music
TA	Cheese and fresh tea biscuits

QUILTS

Sensory Cue	*Sensory Stimulation Activities*
Day 1	
S	Hot mulled cider
K	Beanbags
TO	Brightly colored quilted item (e.g., quilt, pillow, potholder; connect with personal associations with making or having quilts)
V	Quilt patches fabric scraps > select favorite (connect with personal associations with making quilts)
A	"Aunt Dinah's Quilting Party"
TA	Digestive cookies
Day 2	
S	Apple, banana, or other fresh fruit
K	Arrange quilt patches (precut two-inch squares) on ticketboard to make fabric collage (leader glues in place). See Handicraft Activities, Appendix 5-B.
TO	Quilt batting
V	Magazine or book with pictures of quilts
A	Favorite music (begin to introduce Christmas music)
TA	Dried fruits (e.g., apples, apricots)
Day 3	
S	Peppermint
K	Beanbags
TO	Thimble(s) of various types > try on
V	Collage from day 2 > write down associations
A	See days 1 and 2
TA	Crackers and cheese
Day 4	
S	Vanilla > add a drop to premeasured cookie ingredients
K	Mix and shape premeasured ingredients for old-fashioned cookies (e.g., molasses or oatmeal)
TO	Quilt patches or quilted items of various textures
V	Thimble(s) of various types
A	As on day 1 and day 2
TA	Homemade cookies

CHRISTMAS #1

Sensory Cue	*Sensory Stimulation Activities*

Day 1

S	Evergreen boughs (*Note:* Because of fire hazard, evergreen boughs must not be left about in communal living situations.)
K	Beanbag catch (use red and green fabric bags, if possible)
TO	Red velvet ribbon > tie in a bow
V	Select favorite from a small number of cover sheets of (used) greeting cards
A	Christmas music favorites recorded by familiar singers (e.g., Vera Lynn, Bing Crosby, Frank Sinatra)
TA	Crackers and cheese

Day 2

S	Peppermint candy cane
K	As on day 1
TO	Evergreen boughs
V	Favorite card from previous day mounted on place mat–sized ticketboard > write name, favorite Christmas song, favorite Christmas food, December (year); have place mat plasticized
A	As on day 1
TA	Fresh fruit

Day 3

S	Mincemeat
K	Arrange evergreen branches, cones, ribbon, fabric, holly, etc., inside wide-mouth jar for table centerpiece
TO	As in K above, focusing on touch sensations
V	Christmas decorations of various types, especially vintage
A	As on day 1
TA	Mincemeat on graham crackers

Day 4

S	Almong extract > shake a drop into premeasured dough for easy shortbread cookies
K	Mix, shape, and bake shortbread cookies
TO	Holly
V	As on day 3
A	As on day 1
TA	Shortbread cookies

CHRISTMAS #2

Sensory Cue	*Sensory Stimulation Activities*
Day 1	
S	Peppermint candy cane
K	Movement—dance, clap in time to Christmas music
TO	Basket or bowl of Christmas nuts > crack open (if appropriate)
V	Evergreen boughs
A	Christmas music as in previous week
TA	Shortbread cookies (from previous week)
Day 2	
S	Evergreen boughs
K	As on day 1
TO	Christmas tree decoration (vintage if possible)
V	Holly
A	As on day 1
TA	Christmas fruit bowl
Day 3	
S	Chocolate > add chocolate chips to premeasured dry ingredients for bishop's bread
K	Mix premeasured ingredients for bishop's bread; bake one spoonful in muffin papers for "mini-cake." Bake remainder as in directions.
TO	Evergreen boughs
V	Pine cones
A	As on day 1
TA	Bishop's bread, "mini-cakes"
Day 4	
S	Hot mulled cider
K	Put decorations on tree
TO	As on day 2
V	Red velvet ribbon
A	As on day 1
TA	Bishop's bread and other treats

Chapter 8

Administrative and Fiscal Issues

Judith S. Bloomer

1.0 PURPOSE FOR INCLUSION IN A PRACTICE MANUAL

Most clinicians wish to leave administrative and fiscal issues up to administrators. However, there are several reasons why these issues should be considered by practitioners who plan to implement the activities presented in the preceding chapters of this book. These reasons fall into two main (but not mutually exclusive) categories: (1) those issues affecting clinicians who are employees of a health care or social services agency and (2) those issues affecting clinicians who are independent practitioners and consultants.

For clinicians employed within an agency, the implementation of new procedures often must be approved by superiors. A change in treatment interventions often would be a concern of the referring physician who has overall responsibility for the patient. The procedures would be reviewed to determine whether they are in keeping with the overall goals of the agency and service delivery model. Additionally, the costs of implementing the procedures, from a staffing standpoint, and the likelihood of reimbursement for these services would be of utmost concern to the administrator in all times of budgetary constraint. The clinician might be asked to justify the need for a change in programming, particularly when increased cost to the agency is a factor. The efficacy and efficiency of the new programming might be questioned. The clinician should be prepared to document services in such a way as to provide data for program evaluation purposes.

For the private practitioner, who contracts with agencies or independently seeks reimbursement for services directly from funding sources, there are factors to consider in addition to the reasons that are most relevant to nonadministrative clinicians or to line staff employed within a larger organization. Whether certain clinical services are mandated by legislation, whether a physician's referral is required for service provision, and whether specific services are reimbursable are all crucial pieces of information for the independent practitioner proposing to offer services to an outside agency or the public at large.

This chapter addresses the issues discussed above with two general objectives. The first objective is to alert the clinician or private practitioner to the need for adequate planning in proposing new programs. The second objective is to provide an overview of pertinent documents or reference material that enables the clinician to keep abreast of the ever-changing and complex developments in legislation, managed health care, and social policy, all of which affect the delivery of services to the elderly and those with Alzheimer's disease and related disorders (ADRD).

2.0 ETHICAL AND PHILOSOPHICAL BASIS FOR OFFERING SERVICES TO PERSONS WITH ADRD

An initial problem many clinicians face in proposing new services for persons with ADRD is that there is often a lack of knowledge about the need for these new services, based both on numbers of individuals and on why such new services should be offered. To answer the questions of how many and why the clinician often must complete a needs assessment for the particular locale.

2.1 Establishment of Need

Those working with the elderly already know that the over-65 age group is the most rapidly growing segment of the North American population. It is important to understand that ADRD is the primary cause of admission to institutional care, and that these disorders affect 50 to 75 percent of the institutionalized elderly (Alzheimer's Association 1990; Aronson 1988; Carnes 1984; Davis & Kirkland 1988; Dippel & Hutton 1988; Jazwiecki 1988; OTA 1987). In financial terms, one carefully considered estimate suggests that unless innovations are made by the year 2000, the total American health care budget for the elderly will be consumed by the cost of institutional care for those with ADRD (Pfeffer 1989). Nursing homes are the most frequently used residential setting for persons with dementia, and Maslow (1990) reported recent studies that indicate that 40 to 60 percent of nursing home residents have dementia. One study showed that those with dementia were, on average, more impaired in activities of daily living than were other residents and more likely to have the behavioral problems of wandering, verbal abuse, physical aggression, and regressive or socially inappropriate behaviors. This study and another study cited by Mace (1990), which showed that residents with dementia required about 6 percent more staff time than other residents, confirm the belief that dementia patients are more difficult to care for and require more staff time than do other patients. The extent and the severity of the need for intervention with this population is clear. What has not been clear is what needs to be done and why commit scarce resources to a population with a progressive disease that has no cure. The author of this book, Carol Bowlby, has presented an excellent resource manual of what can be done and how it can be provided by staff. How it can be financed is covered later in this chapter by examining reimbursement issues. The question of why commit resources needs to be addressed by examining the philosophical basis of offering such services.

2.2 Goals: Moral versus Medical Treatment Model

Many of the treatment interventions described in the previous chapters are based on therapeutic activities and have their roots in occupational therapy practice in mental health at the end of the last century. Occupational therapy was born of the moral treatment movement of the mid- to late 1800s. Moral treatment was based on the premise that adaptation and engagement in the environment were strong components of health. Productive occupation and productive use of time were used as a remedy for the deterioration of habit and function, in the broadest sense. Function was seen as the ability to do, to be active, and to be appropriately engaged in the environment. Activities were chosen to re-engage the person and to promote health, both mental and physical. Later, at the turn of the century, as the scientific method was embraced and applied to medicine and psychiatry, the moral-emotional model of moral treatment was replaced by a technical-pathological approach (Brochoven 1971). Occupational therapy, as a profession, organizationally aligned itself with the medical profession in the 1930s, by having the American Medical Association establish standards and take over accreditation for occupational therapy schools in the United States. As allied health professionals, occupational therapy adopted a medical model of practice based on assessing pathology and remediating dysfunction. The emphasis on remedial techniques was based on the belief that one could provide a remedy to put an end to disease and restore health—in effect, a corrective intervention or cure.

At present, there is no cure for Alzheimer's disease, although the scientific search for the etiology and cure of the disorder continues. Despite the fact that we now have no intervention to halt or reverse the process of this progressive disease, there are effective approaches and interventions, based on different goals, for persons with ADRD. These goals include maintaining and maximizing residual function and keeping the affected person in the community for the longest period of time possible, as well as minimizing the person's suffering. These goals transcend the physical realm of function to include mental well-being and the maintenance of self-esteem and dignity in the presence of a devastating disorder. At present these goals are not in keeping with the medical model of remediating or curing a disease, and thus there has been little provision—from a policy, procedural, or funding standpoint—to attain these goals in medically oriented facilities such as acute care hospitals, rehabilitation centers, or nursing homes. Those working in medically oriented facilities must propagate an expanded model of service delivery that embraces a more unifying or holistic philosophy of treatment, one that focuses on the whole person and that person's effect on the immediate environment, including family members and other caregivers. The goals must include not only maximizing physical and cognitive maintenance, but also maintaining the quality of the person's emotional self. Cohen and Eisdorfer (1986) report an example of an individual in the early stages of Alzheimer's disease who grieves for the life that is being taken away from him but asks that what is left of his life be meaningful to him:

> I am hungry for the life that is being taken away from me. I am a human being. I still exist. I have a family. I hunger for friendship, happiness, and the touch of a loved hand. What I ask for is that what is left of my life shall have some meaning. Give me something to die for! Help me to be strong and free until my self no longer exists. (p. 21)

It has been pointed out by these same authors that there is loss of memory," as the disease progresses, but people do not exist of memory alone. People have feelings, imagination, desires, drives, will and moral being. It is in these realms that there are ways" to intervene (p. 22). It is time to go back in history, to retrieve that which was valuable in the concept of the moral treatment movement of the late 1800s. A unifying and holistic philosophy that values meaningful intervention is needed, one that helps enable the person with ADRD to be active and engaged in the environment. It is really an issue of values. Policy is based on values, and only when medical and social policies change in regard to the philosophical treatment of those with ADRD will clinical procedures follow.

3.0 DIFFERENCES IN CANADIAN AND AMERICAN HEALTH CARE SYSTEMS: PROVISION OF SERVICES FOR THE ELDERLY

The following section reflecting differences in providing for the needs of those with ADRD via the Canadian and United States health care systems is included in this chapter for two reasons. First, this book was written for staff and caregivers working with persons with ADRD in both countries, thus making it necessary to clarify important differences in the health care delivery and financing systems for each audience. Second, the political climate in the United States is ripe for making changes in the present health care system, particularly in response to underserved populations. In both the current federal legislative body and the recent campaign platforms of those running for presidential and congressional offices, various health care plans have been proposed, some of which are similar to the Canadian system. Given this heightened sensitivity to the

two different systems, it is wise, as well as informative, to review both systems of care for the elderly.

Health care in the United States follows a free-enterprise, fee-for-service model; initially, only those who could afford to purchase health services would receive them. Health insurance was established and based in local and private systems. Payment for health insurance was installed, through the results of organized labor, as an employee benefit controlled by private industry. Although a national health insurance system was proposed as early as 1912 by President Theodore Roosevelt, the American Medical Association successfully campaigned against it. National health insurance was again opposed in 1934 (and defeated) when it was planned to be included as a part of the new Social Security system established after the Great Depression.

In 1965, Congress passed two programs—Medicaid and Medicare—that established certain health benefits to individuals who meet eligibility requirements. Although these two programs are instrumental in financing health care for many elderly and disabled persons, there continue to be many service needs that are not supported—particularly in the area of long-term care, which is essential for persons with ADRD.

Canada's national health care system is based on the concept of universality; that is, the nation's citizens believe that health care is a universal right, just as in the United States the right to bear arms, freedom of religion, freedom of speech, and the provision of basic education are considered universal rights. Consequently, Canada adopted and implemented a national health care insurance program through two major pieces of legislation: the Hospital Insurance and Diagnostic Services Act of 1957 and the Medical Care Act of 1966. This health insurance is supported by taxes and cost sharing between the federal and provincial governments, as agreed upon in the Federal–Provincial Fiscal Arrangements and Established Programs Financing Act of 1977. Although much of the funding for health care comes from the federal level, the individual provinces retain primary control over how and for what health care services the money is spent.

A crucial difference between Canada and the United States is in the financing of long-term care (Kane & Kane 1985). Long-term care is important to review in considering persons with ADRD, because of the progressive nature of the disorder and the need for extended provision of health and social support services.

Long-term care (LTC) is defined as a coordinated continuum of preventative, diagnostic, therapeutic, rehabilitative, supportive, and maintenance services that address the health, social, and personal care needs of individuals who have restricted self-care capabilities.

These capabilities may have been lost or, in other cases, never developed. The services may be continuous or intermittent, but it is generally assumed that they will be delivered for a long time. Long-term programs should promote physical, social, and psychological independence in the least restrictive environment possible (Meltzer et al. 1981; Kane & Kane 1985).

In the United States, LTC generally refers to sustained personal care and health-related services, usually delivered in nursing homes or nursing home alternatives. Such alternatives include home health and homemaker services, day care, congregate housing, seniors' multipurpose centers, telephone reassurance programs, and home-delivered and congregate meal programs. Financial support for these services in the United States has varied from state to state and often is dependent on the individual person's health care insurance (or lack thereof).

All of the above programs are also found in Canada; however, there is great variability in services and programs among provinces and in comparing urban areas with rural areas. A common factor among provinces is the universal health insurance for hospital and medical care, to which many provinces have added a non–means-tested LTC benefit (Kane & Kane 1985, 230). In other provinces, LTC facilities are funded under "social and community services" and therefore are not eligible for health insurance funding for per diem costs, except for physician visits and medication. For those individuals unable to pay for LTC, the municipality pays the difference between their monthly income and the cost of LTC. Despite provincial differences, however, Canada has generally been able to utilize more extensive community-based care, including case management services for those needing LTC, than the United States. Canada also has a longer history of utilizing new technologies, comprehensive assessment systems, and hospital-based geriatric services (Kane & Kane 1985).

Canada has been able to accomplish this expanded range of LTC services in some provinces because of a number of factors. On a basic level, there is the difference in national ethos, or moral character, related to respect for peace, order, good government, and universality among Canadian peoples versus the life, liberty, and the pursuit of happiness as individual rights among those living in the United States. Other differences include the fact that LTC in Canada is built on a foundation of universal health care insurance, and that many Canadians do not have some of the other expenditures that are assumed by citizens of the United States. For instance, it has been proposed that many middle-aged Canadians are more able to assist aged parents needing LTC because they are less burdened by tuition for their college-aged children. The educational burden is shared between individual families and the government, since most Canadian universities are land-grant colleges with subsidized tuition (Kane & Kane 1985). To counter this proposition, many Canadians would be quick to point out that they pay much higher taxes, which support health and social services, than do their counterparts in the United States. The tax rate for many middle-income Canadians, when all levels of taxes are included, can amount to approximately 50 percent of their income. The resultant tax structure contributes to the generally higher cost of living in Canada as compared with the United States.

Another example of different government support services is the fact that Canada's defense expenditures are not as burdensome as the defense budget in the United States, which may again be attributed to a difference in national ethos. Additionally, because of rigid gun-control laws and a less violence-prone society, most Canadian cities are safer than those in the United States. This is thought to influence the likelihood of the utilization of home-based services for the frail elderly in Canada, based on the assumption that they would less likely be victimized in their homes or neighborhoods (Kane & Kane 1985).

Although there is a higher utilization of home-based services in Canada (perhaps due to the greater availability of such services), it is important to note that there is also a slightly higher rate of institutionalization of the elderly in Canada than in the United States. It may be that admission to LTC facilities is more feasible for a greater proportion of Canadians as a result of better government financing of LTC (including institutional) services in general.

Another factor affecting the financing of LTC is that litigation over health and welfare programs is rare in Canada, and thus there is the flexibility to offer more creative community-based programs without the fear of being sued (Kane & Kane 1985).

The structure of the Canadian universal entitlement systems also affects the financing of LTC. Three differences between the United States and Canada are important to note here. The first difference is in the area of income maintenance, which is crucial in determining the feasibility of paying for LTC. The Canadian Old Age Security plan is an entitlement available to all elderly Canadians, and the Guaranteed Income Supplement provides recipients with a minimum guaranteed income. These differ from the Social Security (pension) system in the United States, which is allocated based on duration and income generated from past employment. The Social Security (pension) system in the United States is more analogous to the Canada Pension Plan.

Both countries have need-based federal, provincial, and state supplemental income and welfare programs.

A second difference is the elimination of multiple payment sources for health care in Canada, making the payment system not only simpler but also more efficient on a cost basis than that of the United States. The universal health insurance program of Canada is controlled and dispersed provincially, based on federal funds. In contrast, the funding of health care in the United States is based on a number of sources: third-party reimbursement through private insurance; prospective payment systems such as the federal Medicare program and state Medicaid programs; direct payment on a fee-for-service basis; prepayment in health maintenance and preferred provider organizations; and other managed care systems, which focus on cost containment.

A third and major difference is that LTC in Canada is considered, in some provinces, to be a social program, financed through social and community services funds. In other provinces, it is financed under universal health insurance, or a combination of health and social services. An example of this is seen in the financing of nursing home care. In the United States, nursing home rates often are determined on the basis of a for-profit model in a proprietary enterprise. The expansion of corporate medicine into nursing home chains, home health care agencies, and private rehabilitation services may be the forerunner of the capitalization of LTC. In Canada, where there is a mix of proprietary and nonprofit nursing home providers, the client copayments for nursing homes are set at a low rate in some provinces, and these copayments are covered by a person's Old Age Supplement (OAS), which can be as little as $500.00 per month. The copayments are usually a fraction of the cost of nursing home care, which often range between $2,400 and $3,000 per month. The set rate of copayment, which serves as a regulatory control mechanism, becomes, in effect, a type of subsidized housing not unlike the housing programs offered through social services (Kane & Kane 1985).

In other provinces, the mix of medical and social services supported by the government is similar to the Medicare and Medicaid programs in the United States. Here, per diem rates for nursing homes are set by provincial regulatory bodies, and the difference between the incoming resident's income and the cost of care is covered by the municipality. Therefore, everyone is guaranteed coverage, but only after their personal resources are exhausted and they then qualify for social services. This is similar to the "spend down" phenomenon one sees for individuals in the United States, who may or may not qualify for the national Medicare program, but because of their depleted financial status, would qualify for state-dispersed welfare funds for medical services (Medicaid).

Structural and policy differences, like the example of nursing homes above, also prevail in a variety of organizational settings that offer services to persons with ADRD. A review of differences between Canadian and American service settings is incorporated in the following section on systems analysis.

4.0 SYSTEMS ANALYSIS: A FRAMEWORK FOR PLANNING, DIRECTING, AND IMPLEMENTING SERVICES

Persons with ADRD may be encountered in a variety of settings. The clinician who wishes to work with this population needs to be cognizant of the differences in philosophy and policy by service setting and how these differences potentially affect clinical procedures. On the whole, service settings in Canada and the United States are more similar than they are different. Differences lie more in the name of an agency or organization and the payment for services within that setting. Payment and reimbursement issues, by service setting, are discussed more thoroughly in the section following this one. The focus of this section is on helping the clinician to determine the system-specific factors that influence the planning, directing, and implementation of clinical services.

Services to the ADRD population are generally community-based or institution-based, although some agencies offer a continuum of services. Common service settings are listed below, with the notation of national differences in nomenclature.

4.1 Community-Based Service Settings

Home health care (in the patient's home)—Home-based treatment, personal care, and social support services such as Meals-on-Wheels.

Outpatient geriatric assessment center—Diagnosis and initial treatment recommendations.

Adult day programs—Outpatient treatment, social, and recreational services offered on a per diem basis, at a center away from home. Adult day programs include adult day care and adult day treatment or partial hospitalization, depending on the extent of services offered. The distinction between these types of adult programs is important, as it affects the funding for services. Day care tends to offer more social and recreational activities in addition to basic custodial care, in which the elderly person is supervised and may be fed, if too frail to feed himself or herself. Day treatment or day hospital provides active medical and rehabilitative services and may include social and recreational activities. Day treatment follows a medical model that emulates the daytime program of a hospital (thus called partial hospitalization) in which patients are scheduled for different therapies throughout the day, based on their diagnosis and need. If the therapy is ordered by a physician and provided by qualified rehabilitation or allied health professionals, the service is eligible for health funding or reimbursement, both in the United States and in Canada. Partial hospitalization implies an active treatment mode, and those persons with ADRD who show little rehabilitation potential and who need LTC are generally not eligible for funding for active treatment because of the progressive nature of their disorder. (Reimbursement issues regarding different types of services are discussed in a later section of this chapter.)

Outpatient treatment—Usually provided on an hourly basis at a medical clinic or rehabilitation center.

Case management—Services coordinated by a specified case manager, advocate, or care coordinator to promote the best interest of the patient, to reduce service setting redundancy, and to contain costs. Although the case manager often is community-based, services to the patient can be provided either in the community or in an institution.

Hospice care—Includes community-based programs that provide care for the terminally ill, either at a special community center or through the provision of hospice care in home-based situations. Hospices customarily are considered to be places where hospice care is provided, many of which are institution-based (see more detailed description of hospices in the following section).

4.2 Institution-Based Service Settings

Adult/geriatric congregate living facilities (ACLFs)—Although ACLFs theoretically are considered community-based housing, they can be very large with the number of residents varying from as few as a dozen to more than a hundred, depending on local regulations and licensing standards. ACLFs generally have structured programs, schedules, and staff coverage that are similar to those of a traditional institution.

Domiciliaries—Similar to adult congregate living, but generally restricted to elderly veterans and sponsored by the Veterans Administration (sometimes referred to as "old soldiers' homes").

Veterans' hospitals—VA, or Veterans Administration hospitals in the United States; DVA, or Department of Veterans' Affairs, in Canada. The Veterans Administration also provides LTC for veterans in VA nursing homes and domiciliaries, and (under contract) in community nursing homes and board and care facilities. Some VA medical centers sponsor home care services, adult day care, and respite care (Maslow 1990, 300).

Acute care or general hospitals—Provide acute or general care in a private or public institution.

Geriatric assessment units—Hospital-based diagnostic services for patients admitted on a short-term basis, includes treatment recommendations and referral to appropriate resources for follow-up.

State hospitals—In the United States, exist for publicly funded psychiatric treatment or for the care of persons with severe developmental disabilities.

Provincial hospitals—Canada's counterpart of state hospitals described above. Persons with ADRD who exhibit difficult to manage behaviors are also short- or long-term residents of provincial hospitals.

Skilled facilities—Nursing homes or LTC facilities that are licensed to provide a more intense skilled level of nursing care, generally to patients who have just been discharged from an acute care hospital and who need daily nursing care and rehabilitative treatment. Nursing homes or LTC facilities providing skilled services usually designate certain areas or beds of the facility to care for patients needing skilled care. Skilled care bed patients in the United States are funded by Medicare Part A for discrete periods of time and must be recertified periodically as needing skilled level of care. Other patients who also reside in such facilities are those needing long-term recuperation or palliative care. In Canada, these facilities are sometimes referred to as "extended care" or "chronic care," and are not subject to the Medicare benefit limitation mentioned above.

Nursing homes—Often referred to as rest homes ("homes for the aged" or "hostels" in Canada), nursing homes are extended care facilities providing nursing and personal care services to those unable to care for themselves. Nursing homes in the United States may also be skilled facilities (previously referred to as "skilled nursing facilities"), but not always, as some rest homes are not licensed for skilled care.

Long-term care facilities—Basically nursing homes that provide health care, personal care, and social services on a long-term basis. These facilities are often the last place of residence for persons who are permanently and functionally impaired. Many LTC facilities are also licensed as skilled facilities and provide a more intensive skilled level of care to usually a smaller subset of residents, who are often transferred to special care areas of the facility.

Hospices—Usually are facilities, or units (or programs) of a larger facility, that are specifically designed for the needs of the terminally ill. Pain and symptom control, quality of (the remaining) life, diagnostic honesty, death with dignity, and family follow-up for bereavement purposes are all basic elements of the around-the-clock care that is provided in hospices. Some hospice programs are not in facilities at all but are provided as a home-based service in the community, as noted in the foregoing section on community-based service settings.

4.3 Planning for Program Development

To develop a new service or to expand or enhance an existing program for persons with ADRD, it is recommended that the planner approach the task by using a "goodness-of-fit" model. By this I mean that the planner must conceptualize how the new program will fit into the existing organizational structure. Will the goals of the proposed program be compatible with the mission of the organization? Is the program aligned with the long-range plans of the agency in preparing for future trends? How can the planner propose the program in such a way as to "sell" the concept to the funding source or sponsoring organization?

In order to begin to answer these questions in a well-informed manner, the planner can use a systems approach to analyzing the potential interactions among the proposed program or service; the environment in which it would be placed; and the political, philosophical, financial, and organizational factors that are likely to impinge on the proposed service.

The strategy of using a systems analysis to evaluate the "bigger picture" originated in the field of computer technology, where microlevel input can eventually produce outputs that have macrolevel effects on the integrated system. The schematic diagram in Figure 8-1 helps illustrate the chain of factors that interact and influence the nature or the outcome of other factors that follow in the chain. Figure 8-1 shows the interplay of systems factors, starting with the environmental press at point 1 on the left-hand side of the figure. The political environment, health care trends, or the social and moral state of the time can create forces that are favorable to the development of a new program or service. These forces may result in the passage of new legislation or may create a specific market, often influenced by consumer demand. This legislation, market, or consumer demand usually always helps identify the target population (point 2). What is important for the program planner to note is that he or she can influence the environment or help develop the market by clearly identifying the needs of a target population. Section 5.7 of this

chapter discusses further how a program planner or provider can function as a change agent in influencing policy through the political process and organized effort.

Once the need for a new program or service has been addressed, it is time to develop the program plan (point 3). The planner must give careful thought about the agency, service area of a larger organization, or financial support system to which the plan should be submitted (point 4). The decision (point 5) as to whether to approve and support the new program or service will be moderated by a number of factors (points 6, 7, and 8). The mission or function of the agency (point 6) will influence the decision maker's receptiveness (point 8) to the treatment or service model. For instance, in a hospital or outpatient clinic whose purpose is to treat acutely ill patients by following a medical model of practice, the proposal of a maintenance program to foster optimal functioning and quality of life would stand little chance of gaining support. However, if the planner was able to identify supplemental resources, such as additional external funding and physical space, the same hospital or clinic might be more willing to expand its services. Such was the case of at least one experimental program (the Medicare Alzheimer's Project, which is described more fully in Section 5.6) in which the federal government, regional agencies affiliated with the Council on Aging, a university, and a local hospital collaborated in offering a home-based program utilizing hospital employees to train caregivers of Alzheimer's patients. In other instances, even if the program service model is compatible with the function of the agency, there may be funding limitations or a shortage of space (point 7) for implementing a new service. This might result in a rejection of the proposal or a request for significant revisions. However, if the program plan is accepted and the program is to be implemented (point 9), there are also ongoing factors that may have an impact on how well the program operates. The referral process, the fee-for-service or reimbursement system, and the working relationships of staff are all examples of factors which can make or break a program. These and other influences would be important to assess on an ongoing basis.

It would be wise for the program planner to have included a program evaluation component to the program plan, to help determine the efficiency and effectiveness of the program services. This type of accountability is becoming more standard in today's health care system. Many funding sources and accreditation bodies require a quality assurance or quality improvement plan, either of which can be part of program evaluation. As program needs or deficiencies are identified through pro-

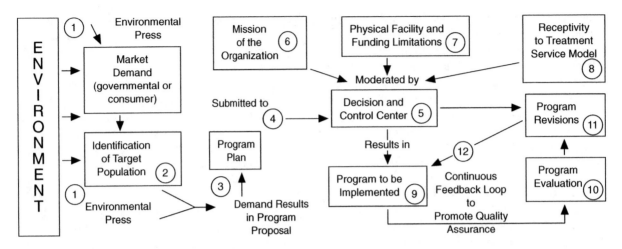

Figure 8-1 Interplay of System Factors

gram evaluation (point 10), program revisions should follow (point 11). The interplay among program implementation, program evaluation, and program revisions ideally should become part of a continuous feedback loop (points 9, 10, 11, and 12), as program revisions will need to be implemented and re-evaluated as to outcome and/or process.

To increase the likelihood of having a new program accepted, the planner should take a proactive stance in assessing the environment in which the program is planned and in analyzing the influence of system factors on how the total system will operate. The planner should address these elements in the program planning stage, prior to completing the formal proposal. The following section proposes questions a planner might consider in making a systems analysis less formidable.

4.4 Crucial Questions for Analyzing the System

- What is the mission, function, or purpose of the sponsoring organization? For instance, if the function of a general hospital is to provide acute care, would a proposal for serving the needs of patients with ADRD be best met in an LTC facility?

- What is the population that the agency serves? Will demographic, diagnostic, or socioeconomic characteristics of the population determine, for instance, eligibility for services?

- What is the philosophy or frame of reference that is predominant in the agency? Does the agency follow a medical model of treatment, a rehabilitation model of functional skills training, a social service model of provision of basic needs? Is this basic philosophy translated into practice or service delivery?

- Does the philosophy or frame of reference of the program developer complement the philosophy of the sponsoring agency? If not, what will be the support for the proposed program?

- What goals are to be met in developing or expanding the proposed program? Do these goals help attain the objectives or mission of the sponsoring organization?

- What resources are available to the program developer in terms of budget and facilities? Are there grant monies available, funding for demonstration projects, and unutilized space or equipment that might be reallocated for the proposal?

- What are the human resources available in terms of staff experience, staff-to-patient ratios, and interest of existing staff in supporting a new program? What is the ratio of professionals to paraprofessionals in implementing the program? How does this division of labor affect workload, reimbursement, or training needs of staff?

- What obstacles or resistances to the program are anticipated? How can they be overcome or redirected into program support?

- What strategies might be helpful in working toward the implementation of the program? Such strategies might include grass-roots organizing, using political strategies of aligning with certain advocacy or policy- and decision-making groups, completing and publicizing a needs assessment, or responding to an already identified need or gap in the service delivery system.

- What interaction with community resources will be required? Looking at the community as a system, what are the inputs and outputs? How are clients referred to the program? What are the criteria for admission or inclusion in the proposed program? What are the criteria for program completion or discharge? Where are clients referred after involvement in the program? What will be the continuum of service delivery in terms of continuity of care?

- Will any components of program evaluation be built into the design of the program? What are the advantages or disadvantages of doing so? Would process or outcome evaluation data be helpful in justifying the need for or continuation of the program?

4.5 Data-Based Decision Making

The answers to the foregoing questions will provide a data base that will enable the program planner to make the informed decisions necessary for program success. Data from the systems assessment should be analyzed as either supporting or not supporting the program as it was originally conceptualized. The planner must then weigh the amount of likely support, and decide whether revisions to the program are needed, to gain a wider base of acceptance.

The necessary revisions should be evident from the analysis. For instance, if the planner has proposed to start a program for persons with ADRD in a general hospital that provides primarily acute care, the concept of providing a program for persons with a long-term illness, such as Alzheimer's disease, may conflict with the mission of the organization (the hospital). To gain support for such a service, the planner may need to revise the program to include only the initial assessment and treatment recommendation process, thereby leaving the longer-term treatment for another community agency to implement. If no such agency in the community exists, the planner may decide to complete a needs assessment and present these data to the hospital, along with a proposal including the potential benefits of providing a new hospital-based outpatient service.

Decisions about staffing may need to be made from a cost basis. Data regarding the requirements for reimbursement of specialized services should be considered prior to hiring staff and in determining the division of labor among staff. Decisions such as these are important, not only for making revisions in the program proposal, but also for determining how to implement the program on a day-to-day basis.

4.6 Implementing the Program: Direction, Division of Labor, Supervision, and Consultation

The program planner may be in an administrative position, but more often than not the planner is a clinician who is interested in expanding his or her services to a targeted population. Whether administrator or clinician, the planner needs to consider what level of staff will be required to implement the program. As mentioned in the previous section, staffing decisions are often made on a cost basis, but the planner must be aware of regulations governing what level of training the staff must have in order to evaluate and treat patients, and for documentation of service delivery. On the basis of cost, it is important to note standard reimbursement guidelines for Medicare, the most-used medical insurance plan for the elderly in the United States.

Medicare guidelines specify reimbursement only if a treatment is prescribed by a physician, delivered by a qualified and skilled professional, and is deemed "reasonable and necessary." This is discussed in more depth in a later part of this chapter, but an examination of the "qualified, skilled, and necessary" stipulation is crucial to the following discussion of staffing issues. Although this book stresses holistic approaches and activities in working with persons disabled by ADRD, the most widely used funding sources of support for these patients are based on a medical model. This distinction is not just a disparity in philosophy; it is also the primary force that drastically reduces the extent of therapeutic activities for those with ADRD because of funding limitations.

Indeed, the crisis in health care financing has affected the nature of service delivery throughout the health care system. In cost containment measures, government regulators and insurance companies have severely restricted the range of therapeutic services that may be reimbursed. Generally, only the most medically necessary procedures for conditions offering the best prognosis are covered. The issue of "how high do we jump" for reimbursement is eloquently discussed by Howard (1991) in questioning the morality of whether therapists should buy into a system in which reimbursement seems to dictate practice.

Recognized experts in the area of long-term care decry this "medicalization" of care and advocate a more balanced sociomedical approach that is not only more holistic but also supported financially by general social program revenues. Given the current funding sources, however, reimbursement regulations often dictate the type and level of therapeutic activities provided for those with ADRD. Therapeutic and psychosocial activities are generally offered through an "activity therapy" department and often are directed by recreational therapists or certified activity directors. Often activities are carried out by these individuals, plus nonprofessional activities personnel, rehabilitation aides, recreationists, and volunteers. Although the program activities are funded via a per diem or facility program charge, there is usually no line item billing for activity therapy because it is not reimbursable as a discrete service under most medical insurance programs. Because of this state of affairs, and the reality of economic considerations for the facility, this chapter primarily focuses on the "skilled" therapies qualified under Medicare for reimbursement: namely, speech, occupational, and physical therapy, all of which have traditionally offered therapeutic activities. This is not to say that other activity therapies are not important in offering a holistic approach.

In medical settings, specific types of treatment are often required if a hospital or nursing home is to meet standards for offering comprehensive services to patients with certain diagnoses. Therefore, for example, if occupational or physical therapy is specified, the agency will not be able to be reimbursed for services delivered if treatment is rendered by a rehabilitation aide. Federal, provincial, and state program standards, as well as requirements posed by third-party payers (see Section 5.0, "Financial and Reimbursement Issues"), must be considered before the planner decides whether to implement the program with the more costly certified therapist, a therapy assistant, or a nonprofessional direct-care staff member.

A model of programming often found in nursing homes in the United States uses state-licensed occupational, physical, or speech and language therapists (trained at the bachelor's or master's degree level) to evaluate patients and develop treatment plans for qualified therapy assistants (such as licensed certified occupational therapy assistants, usually trained at an associate's degree level) to implement, with supervision on a daily basis. Direct-care staff are also used as "treatment extenders" to carry out activities of daily living (ADL) programs in dressing or eating skills. These extended ADL activities would not be billed, of course, as occupational therapy, but the patient would benefit from the therapist-directed programming.

Medicare regulations delineate Medicare coverage for using noncertified occupational and physical therapy aides or rehabilitation aides as skilled therapy extenders. It is important to understand that a certified occupational or physical therapist must be on the premises of a rehabilitation agency or clinic if the person performing the activity does not meet assistant-level qualifications. Other settings, such as private practice, require the actual presence, at all times, of a qualified therapist when services are rendered in a therapist's office or patient's place of residence. The use of certified physical or occupational therapy assistants mandates very specific supervision requirements built into most state licensure laws, and these generally require on-site supervision. Agencies hire the licensed therapist to be at the program site on a frequent basis, although the number of hours of face-to-face contact between supervisor and supervisee generally are not specified. What this allows, in broader interpretation, is the hiring of licensed therapists as consultants on an hourly basis rather than a salaried basis. Therapists working as consultants need to be fully aware of statutes legislating their profession to make sure they are not inadvertently allowing an agency to claim that specific therapies are being provided to the patient population when in reality there is only token professional representation for supervision or training purposes.

In skilled nursing facilities, rehabilitation hospitals, and hospices, Medicare defers to state law or regulation in instances where services are provided by individuals who do not meet assistant-level qualifications. In other words, Medicare will cover therapy services supplied by persons meeting the qualification requirements of state law and standards of practice. Most of the therapeutic activities suggested by Bowlby in Chapters 4, 5, 6, and 7 of this book could be Medicare-covered therapy services, but mainly if billed as part of a per diem rate. In this type of arrangement, the non-certified activity therapist, aide, or direct-care staff member provides program services. The Omnibus Reconciliation Act of 1987 requirement for provision of therapeutic activities can be met, in many states, by the agency's hiring a state-certified activity therapist who has completed a 36-hour training course. The distinction between the activity or recreation therapist and the occupational, physical, or speech therapist again follows a rigid medical model. While all five specialties provide therapeutic activities, "skilled" therapy services refer only to the latter three under Medicare guidelines.

4.7 Program Evaluation

In Chapter 2 of this book Bowlby asks, "Why treat persons with ADRD?" This question in its various forms may well be asked of the program planner, particularly in the proposal stage of program development, when sponsoring agencies may weigh the costs versus the benefits of such an enterprise. Therefore, it behooves the planner to execute the strategy of "the best defense is a good offense" by proactively anticipating concerns and meeting these concerns head-on through ongoing evaluation.

Evaluation of clinical programs generally focuses on quality assurance or quality improvement measures and determination of program effectiveness. Although most agencies continue to use the terminology "quality assurance," new Medicare guidelines are now referring to "quality improvement" as part of a total quality management plan; basically, however, the terms are synonymous as they both refer to evaluation procedures used to monitor and improve the quality of services. Quality assurance is an ongoing problem-solving approach used to improve health care delivery. Whereas quality assurance is often focused on identifying and resolving problems, starting with retrospective records review, the determination of program effectiveness generally requires a planned system of data collection that may or may not be part of the clinical record. The evaluation of program effectiveness may include either outcome data (such as outcome of treatment) or process information (for example, data on the process and/or efficiency of how the treatment is carried out).

The following discussion primarily refers to the type of program evaluation that focuses on program effectiveness in meeting program objectives if one is to answer the question "why treat persons with ADRD?" This is accomplished by operationally defining the program goals in such a way that outcome data can be collected and process evaluation can be completed. In Chapter 2 of this book Bowlby offers three major and functional reasons why treatment for persons with ADRD is important:

1. Without treatment, the progressive disabilities associated with ADRD will result in precipitous downward spiral in function.

2. Treatment reduces the burden of care for family, friends, and paid caregivers.

3. Treatment promotes maximal function and hence reduces the financial burden of care.

The above reasons can be easily restated as goals:

1. to prevent a decrease in function or to maintain the person's optimal functional level

2. to reduce the burden of care for family and caregivers

3. to reduce the financial burden of care

Likewise, each goal can be operationally defined in such a way as to make measurement of goal attainment possible. For example, with the first goal, it is easy to assess a patient's level of function over time and to compare data from the functional assessment with data on similar patients not receiving treatment. The second goal, to reduce the burden of care for family members and caregivers, would require a pre- and postevaluation of the caregiver's responsibilities and other factors such as stress, quality of life, financial and emotional obligations, lost time and income from work, and freedom to pursue personal goals. The third goal, which I take to mean the reduction of public (versus private) financial burden as supported by government funds, can be assessed only on a wider-scale basis. Such an evaluation might attempt to measure the differential cost of treatment in various publicly supported programs, including those in the patient's home, in community-based support programs, and through institutional care. For the individual program planner or clinician, the first two goals would offer a more realistic opportunity in which to initiate a formal program evaluation component to address functional objectives.

Psychosocial objectives are inherent in Bowlby's central goal of all group treatment: that of enhancing self-esteem. Providing success experiences, improving level of alertness, sense of mastery, and maintaining a sense of self-worth are all important in realizing this goal. Program evaluation efforts using consumer (patient and caregiver) evaluation surveys to indicate their satisfaction with services offered, as well as more standardized pre- and postmeasures of self-esteem (if the person with ADRD is able to participate), would be appropriate in measuring these objectives. Consumer evaluation data also would be especially relevant to process evaluation. Process questions might ask for the patient's and caregiver's perspective of how they are engaged in treatment and the quality of the "caring" aspect of professional services or LTC in how treatment is carried out.

5.0 FINANCIAL AND REIMBURSEMENT ISSUES

The first objective of this section of the chapter is to alert the clinician to the need for adequate planning to be sure the program or services have the necessary financial support for survival, particularly during these times of cost containment. A major element of the financial support, in most agencies, is reimbursement for services, but there are also other financial support systems to consider. The second objective of this section is to provide an overview of pertinent documents or reference material that will enable the clinician to keep abreast of the ever-changing and complex developments in legislation and managed health care.

For the provider, it is important to know which specific services are reimbursable in planning a treatment program for persons with ADRD. This knowledge and the decisions that follow from it not only will affect the program budget, but may also justify the program's continued existence in times of meager resources.

Many of the activities described within this practice manual will not be paid by the reimbursement-based service model prevalent in the United States today unless there is documentation that clearly substantiates that the activities increase or maintain the functional status of the person with ADRD. The majority of the therapeutic activities described earlier can be redefined or delivered differently so as to meet the standards of third-party payers. The following sections of the chapter serve as a guide to the program planner in understanding the most common financial support systems in place for those with ADRD, and which therapeutic activities and treatments each system will finance.

5.1 Overview of Financial Support for Those with ADRD

The financing of dementia care is a rising problem throughout the world. The cost of caring for those with ADRD is borne by family, private insurance, and various public (government) support programs at the federal, state or provincial, and municipal levels. Medicaid, in the United States, pays only about 46 percent of the cost for nursing home care; Medicare pays approximately 2 percent; private, long-term care insurance, a little over 1 percent; and the rest is primarily out-of-pocket expense borne by individuals with ADRD and their families (Bonfield 1991, 6; Meltzer et al. 1981, 5). Estimates of what families pay privately vary from 48 percent to 80 percent, depending on whether an individual is eligible for Medicare or Medicaid and whether the services of the "silent providers" on nonreimbursed care are calculated. These latter services include the lost wages of family members needing to stay home to take care of a person with ADRD or the cost of such care had it been paid directly to an out-of-family caregiver (Meltzer et al. 1981, 86).

Despite this multiplicity of support sources, a statistic from the Congressional Budget Office indicated that "only an estimated one-third of the 5 to 10 million adults who may have needed long-term care services in 1975 were receiving them" (Meltzer et al. 1981). There are many reasons why there is such a large underserved population. In addition to a growing number of people at risk for ADRD (due to the growing elderly population), perhaps the most pressing issue is the sharp increase in expenditures for institutional LTC due to spiraling health care costs. Another reason is underutilization of available services by different segments of the population. There are certain socioeconomic and cultural factors that influence health care utilization. However, it is postulated that the complexity of guidelines for funding and reimbursement for health care expenditures has dissuaded many consumers or providers

from seeking or providing the services to begin with. The following section highlights some of the differences in the various financial support programs.

5.2 Government-Financed and Private-Pay Programs

Medicare

Medicare is a national health insurance program for Social Security beneficiaries in the United States. It was developed as Title 18, a part of the Social Security amendments of 1965. To qualify, the beneficiary or his or her dependent spouse must be aged 65 years or older, or have an approved disability for a minimum of two years. Medicare has two major parts, A and B.

Medicare Part A. Medicare Part A (the hospital insurance plan) will pay for inpatient hospital care and skilled nursing home health and hospice care in specified circumstances. To be eligible to receive funds for admission to a skilled nursing facility, the beneficiary must first have spent three days within an acute care facility and must be admitted to the skilled nursing facility within 30 days of discharge. The beneficiary's days of coverage are then limited, and the person must continue to stay on a skilled level of care.

The amount of hospital coverage is determined by the patient's diagnosis via a prospective payment system. There are standard lengths of hospital stays based on diagnostic-related groups (DRGs), although some flexibility is allowed for complicating factors in some illnesses or injuries.

Medicare Part B. Medicare Part B, also known as the supplementary medical insurance plan, pays for services not financed by the basic Medicare plan, Part A. While Part A was financed through Social Security payroll deductions, Part B is voluntarily purchased by the individual already eligible for Part A. It pays for such things as outpatient hospital services and rehabilitation, outpatient health care services, and part of physicians' fees not covered by the basic plan. Most persons have Part B, as it "trails" Part A. By this I mean that Medicare Part A recipients must sign to say they do not want Part B. Otherwise, it is automatically deducted from their Social Security benefit. It is important for both the provider and the beneficiary to realize that, when Part A ends, there is often a copayment because the payment structure for Part B is different. For the service provider to be reimbursed under Part B when there is a copayment, the patient's or his or her family's authorization is first required.

Payment for Therapeutic Services under Medicare. Patients generally have up to 100 days of benefits per disability or illness under Medicare Part A, and qualified therapies (speech, physical, and occupational therapy) and nursing care must be provided daily in order to continue to qualify a patient for Part A services. Currently, it is possible to offer a combination of these three therapies for each period of five days, as long as a therapy is provided daily. The need for physical therapy can qualify patients for home health care, but in nursing homes, occupational therapy can also make the patient eligible for needed skilled services. The therapies listed above must be prescribed by a physician and the therapy must address acute rehabilitative needs, not LTC (Rogers & Hanft 1988). Because they are addressing rehabilitative need, therapy goals must be functional in nature, and progress toward these written goals must be clearly documented. In a hospice situation with a terminally ill patient, therapy can be prescribed to control symptoms and/or to maintain functional level.

The Medicare-approved facility submits the bills for service to Medicare. Private therapy vendors such as consulting speech, physical, or occupational therapists cannot bill Medicare directly for Part A services. It is important to note that the Medicare-approved facility will be reimbursed only for qualified therapies; i.e., the services must be rendered by a certified speech, physical, or occupational therapist directly, or if offered by a physical or occupational therapy assistant, the services must be supervised by a certified therapist. Activity therapies are not reimbursed under this model, except under a per diem facility charge or as part of nursing care, if delivered by qualified nursing personnel.

Payment for therapy services under Medicare Part B allows more flexibility as to where the services are delivered and by whom. Again, the therapeutic services must be offered by qualified therapists or nursing staff, but services may be offered in outpatient hospital clinics, rehabilitation agencies, physician's offices, in approved private vendor office settings, or the patient's home. In all situations except for the services offered by an approved private vendor, the facility bills Medicare directly. When approved for providing therapy services, the therapist receives a Medicare provider number that must be used for all future billing. Certain services have limited coverage. A beneficiary may receive only $500.00 worth of occupational therapy, for instance, per year.

Medicare, whether Part A or Part B, is very limited in paying for services that are needed by those with ADRD. For instance, it will pay for skilled level of care up to 100 days only in a facility licensed for providing skilled services. Also, Medicare Part B pays only 80 percent of reasonable and customary charges, leaving 20 percent for the beneficiary to pay for most outpatient services. Since most patients with ADRD eventually need LTC, it is important to recognize that for 90 percent of the United States population, the cost of LTC will deplete their entire life savings in less than one year. The average cost of nursing home care in the United States now approaches $30,000 a year. Although many Americans think that Medicare will cover those costs, it actually pays only about 2 percent (Bonfield 1991, 7). Individuals and families must pay the rest, until their financial resources—including life insurance benefits and home equity—are depleted to the point that they qualify for medical assistance, which in most cases is provided as part of the Medicaid program.

Medicaid

Medicaid is basically a welfare program that is jointly funded by federal and state government in the United States. It was developed as Title 19 of the Social Security Act and provides grants from the federal government to the states for medical assistance programs. Medicaid is just that: medical assistance given to those whose incomes fall below a designated (poverty) level. The Medicaid program serves not only the impoverished, but also those people who have been forced to deplete most of their financial assets due to the enormous costs of nursing home care and LTC. As it is, the Medicaid program bears the brunt of LTC expenses, paying almost 42 percent of these costs (Bonfield 1991, 7). Many states, if not most, have difficulty managing their Medicaid budgets. On top of very legitimate health care financing, the system is additionally strained by those who fraudulently divert funds and personal assets to meet eligibility requirements.

Eligibility for Medicaid includes residency in the state, not being eligible for Medicare Part A, and the financial limitations referred to above. States must provide coverage to those receiving support from the Supplementary Security Income (SSI) Program, as well as those receiving Aid to Families with Dependent Children (AFDC). Recipients of Medicaid fall into two groups: the "categorically needy," based on cash assistance categories, and the "medically needy," for those who are aged, blind, or disabled. The states are mandated to pay for basic services for the categorically needy, but can offer fewer services to the medically needy. Many of the medically needy also qualify as categorically needy because of large medical bills (Lewis 1989).

Benefits vary from state to state, but generally pay for health care for children, rural health clinics, outpatient hospital services, skilled nursing facilities, physician services, and inpatient hospital services, excluding certain mental disabilities. Payment for therapeutic services under Medicaid is generally more limited than that in the Medicare program in that speech, physical, and occupational therapy services are considered optional. Although states must provide certain mandatory services for Medicaid recipients in hospital settings, outpatient clinics, and skilled nursing facilities, they have the option to provide Medicaid coverage for the therapies listed above. Benefits differ between states, and beneficiaries may choose not to participate in prescribed therapies because of the amount of copayment (usually a minimal charge) that some states may charge.

There are limitations on Medicaid coverage for specific therapeutic services, especially in states that use a flat fee or prospective payment system. However, skilled nursing care; regular nursing care; and rehabilitative, social, and personal care services offered within the context of an LTC program are generally supported by the Medicaid program. National expenditures for nursing home care in the United States were $15.75 billion in 1978, with Medicaid paying approximately 46 percent of the costs of care (Meltzer et al. 1981, 5).

Title 20

Title 20 is a section of the Social Security Act of 1965 and provides for grants from the United States federal government to the individual states for the provision of social services. Generally the federal government will match the state's contribution by a certain percentage of funds. Title 18 (the Medicare program) and Title 19 (the Medicaid program) deals with the provision of medical services; Title 20 is often used in conjunction with either or both of these programs to provide more comprehensive care than health services alone. Title 20 funds are used to fund children's and family support programs, as well as for providing selected services to the elderly. Adult Protective Services is one program that is often supported by Title 20 funds, and this program addresses the needs of the exploited or abused elderly. Homemaker Services is another program that benefits the elderly and is often funded by Title 20.

Title 20 was specifically designated for the provision of economic self-support programs to prevent or reduce dependency; the prevention or remedying of neglect, abuse, or exploitation of children and adults unable to protect their own interests; the preservation of family units; the prevention or reduction of inappropriate institutional care by providing community-based care, home-based care, or other forms of less intensive care; the securing of admission for institutional care when other forms of care are not appropriate; and the provision of services to persons who are in institutions.

Title 20 social services are made available free of charge to those financially needy who are also aged 60 years and older; recipients of AFDC; recipients of general assistance, the Medicare Part B program; and, in most states, recipients of Medicaid. This part of the Social Security Act is used to fund home-delivered meals, congregate meals, homemaker and home health aide services, transportation, chore services, certain health-related services, and community-based care. Geriatric day care is but one example of community-based care that would benefit persons with ADRD. Therapeutic activities offered through a day care or day treatment program that promote independence and maintain functional ability could be paid for through general program funds. Therapeutic activities offered by speech, physical, or occupational therapists and/or nurses would also be covered if the need for such services were medically justified and prescribed by a physician.

Older Americans Act

The Older Americans Act is part of the provisions specified under Title 3 of the Social Security Act. This act set up a nationwide network of area agencies on aging to provide supportive services, senior centers, congregate meals, and home-delivered meals for the elderly. Where Title 20 can include some health care services, Title 3 provides for support services that are nonmedical in nature. Supportive social services include many of the broadly defined social and personal care services described above under Title 20. These services are available to persons aged 60 years or older, regardless of income, although there is an emphasis on targeting low-income, minority, or isolated older persons (Kane & Kane 1987, 75).

The National Administration on Aging provides funds to state and regional councils on aging or municipal senior services agencies. There are national and local chapters of the Alzheimer's Association (United States) and the Alzheimer Society (Canada) that advocate for persons with ADRD and their caregivers. These advocacy groups, councils, and senior service agencies often form a consortium to achieve a common goal or program to benefit the elderly by utilizing the federal and state-dispersed funds described previously. Therapeutic activity programs often receive financial backing from many of these agencies, depending on the program to be provided and the origin of the funds used to support it.

VA Systems

The Veterans Administration in the United States and the Department of Veterans' Affairs in Canada have traditionally hired therapeutic activity staff, including occupational, physical, recreational, educational, and manual arts and kinesio-therapists, as well as vocational rehabilitation staff. These VA staff provide services as part of the daily program for veterans or their dependents in hospitals or domiciliaries.

The elderly are a large part of the VA system's population; although only 14 percent of veterans who use VA hospitals are aged 65 years or older, these 14 percent utilize services three to four times more often than do younger veterans (Kane & Kane 1987, 78). The Veterans Administration provides LTC for eligible veterans in more than 100 VA nursing homes, in 16 large domiciliary care facilities, in state veterans homes, and under contract with many nursing homes and board and care facilities in the community. Maslow (1990) reports that as of 1985, home care services were also provided at 49 of the 172 VA Medical Centers across the United States; adult day care at 9 medical centers; and respite care at 12 centers (p. 300).

Private Insurance and Health Maintenance Organizations

Health maintenance organizations (HMOs) and insurance companies in the United States such as Blue Cross/Blue Shield, Aetna, Prudential, GEICO, and Community Mutual are purchased by an individual, often in a shared arrangement with his or her employer, although private individuals may purchase insurance policies solely for self and family. With costs escalating, this latter option is becoming more and more prohibitive in the United States, and millions of individuals and families therefore are uninsured for health care.

Benefits vary widely among the various companies and are very fluid, i.e., ever changing through the addition of new options and levels. One must examine individual policies to determine what type of therapeutic services are covered under a specific plan. Although preauthorization for therapy is necessary, most insurance companies will pay for therapeutic services by qualified speech, physical, or occupational therapists in an inpatient setting and often in outpatient acute rehabilitation facilities. Standard medical insurance policies generally do not cover the LTC needed by persons with ADRD; however, in recent years, there has been a sharp increase in the number of insurance companies that offer special LTC policies. Unfortunately, these policies have very high premiums, which the average policyholder cannot afford.

Many insurance companies today and most HMOs operate under a "managed care" system in order to control costs and ensure the appropriate utilization of services based on need and—generally—diagnosis. Managed care usually includes mandatory preauthorization for certain services and often sets arbitrary limits on the number of sessions of treatment it will pay full coverage for in a time limited period. For instance, outpatient mental health benefits in some HMOs are limited to 10 therapy sessions per year paid at full coverage and 20 sessions per year with a 50 percent copayment. After 20 sessions, the beneficiary must pay 75 percent of the bill for outpatient services. Inpatient psychiatric services may be limited to 30 days per year by some insurance companies; others have no mental health benefits at all. Since dementia is a psychiatric diagnosis listed in the *Diagnostic and Statistical Manual of Mental Disorders*, those with ADRD are often excluded from medical insurance coverage unless they become eligible for a coexisting physical medical disorder, such as dysphagia or decubitus ulcers.

Canadian Medical Insurance Programs

In Canada, citizens have universal health insurance, which is funded through federal and provincial tax dollars and controlled largely by each province. Each provincial plan varies somewhat with each province, and usually has a unique name. For instance, in Ontario, the government plan is called "OHIP," Ontario Hospital Insurance Plan. Home care in this province is supported by municipal as well as provincial and federal taxes. In Nova Scotia, residents get "MSI," Medical Services Insurance. The government controls overutilization of medical services by requiring the individual's primary care physician, often a general or family practitioner, to make (and thereby approve) referrals to other medical specialties and allied health care providers such as occupational and physiotherapists.

As in the Medicare program in the United States, therapeutic services are most often financed within the context of staffing a program within a facility. When private vendors are hired as consultants or on a part-time contractual basis, however, the funding for this would be paid directly by the agency. Many therapists work under such an arrangement by billing agencies for their services through a private invoice. The agency pays for the contractual services out of general program or staffing funds. Therapists cannot bill the government insurance program directly. A physician's referral is required for authorizing the utilization of allied health therapies in treating specific patients.

As in the United States, Canadians may also purchase private insurance such as Blue Cross/Blue Shield or Maritime Medical Insurance to allow greater coverage and options in health care. For instance, in Nova Scotia, a resident may use his or her basic MSI coverage to pay for an ophthalmology examination; but to cover the price of the corrective lenses and frames, he or she might use a private insurance plan that would pay 80 percent of the other optometric costs.

Private (Individual or Family) Payment

According to the Health Care Financing Administration of the United States, people spent $43.1 billion for nursing home care in 1988. Of that, 48.4 percent was out-of-pocket; 44 percent was from Medicaid, and private long-term care insurance paid only 1.1 percent (Bonfield 1991). What does not have a dollar or a percentage sign attached is the nonreimbursed care given to the elderly by "silent providers" in the home: the family members and friends who serve as caregivers. The cost to the family frequently is not realistically assessed. In addition to money going out to pay for medical care and related services, caregivers usually lose money coming in: the loss in wages from taking off from work or having to leave one's job to shoulder caregiving responsibilities at home.

Early and regionally specific data from an Alzheimer's demonstration project indicate that nearly half of the people with Alzheimer's disease now in nursing homes could live at home if they and their families received financial aid to pay for a variety of alternative services (Bonfield 1991). Unfortunately, note Kane and Kane (1981), there is more incentive (on a government funding level) for nursing home care than for home care because of the view that it is somehow wrong to reimburse persons for fulfilling family duties despite the fact that family members lose income opportunities while delivering extensive LTC (p. 93). This widely held view is a costly one on a national level, given the $43 billion spent on nursing home care. The early data referred to above come from a nationally funded demonstration project, carried out in different regions of the country and specifically designed to determine whether it might be more cost-effective to support alternate sources of care. This Medicare Alzheimer's project is described in more detail later in this chapter, in the section "Experimental and Creative Alternatives to Traditional Health Care Financing."

5.3 General Reimbursement Standards: Documentation, More Documentation, and Billing

Most funding sources require careful documentation of clinical data to justify the provision of adjunctive medical or therapeutic services, particularly in chronic and/or progressive conditions such as ADRD. First and foremost, there must be a physician-approved certification (or recertification) that therapeutic services are required by the patient. The Medicare criterion for whether a service is required is that it must be "reasonable and necessary." *Reasonable* means that there must be a reasonable expectation of improvement within a reasonable period of time, which is specified by the frequency and duration of therapy. *Necessary* means that the service must be skilled (i.e., it must require the skills of a qualified professional or technical person) and that the service must be either provided or supervised by the qualified person.

Additionally, depending on the level of services required, Medicare has minimal requirements for the frequency of service delivery. For patients requiring rehabilitation services only, for instance, therapy must be provided a minimum of two times per week. For those requiring skilled nursing services, therapy must be provided on a daily basis. This therapy can be any combination of speech, occupational, or physical therapy, as long as at least some therapy is offered five days of the week. The patient with ADRD loses out under this model, since active treatment of such frequency often is not necessary. Those with ADRD may be best served by a therapeutic maintenance program, which focuses on strengthening or stimulating residual abilities and maintaining an optimal level of functioning. Such a functional maintenance system is further described later in this chapter.

Generally, the need for therapy is expressed in a broad manner by the physician and can also only indicate that a thorough evaluation by a therapist is requested. Before initiating any therapeutic procedures, the therapist completes an evaluation that provides any information necessary to establish and support any subsequent treatment, as well as a baseline measure of the patient's clinical status and function. The baseline measure is especially important for establishing progress, as it is needed for comparison to subsequent gains in function or goal attainment (Youngers 1988).

Once the need for treatment is established through standard evaluation measures, it is then addressed in a written treatment plan that describes the target problems, the goals of treatment, the type and amount of treatment, and the frequency and duration of services. Goals should be functional in nature, measurable, and achievable. If the therapist is working toward long-term goals, it will be important to designate shorter-term goals that can be used as indicators of progress in meeting more long-term objectives.

Specific interventions are reimbursed by Medicare, as well as payment for very limited durable medical equipment required to improve functional performance. Medicare generally will pay for (or pay for the rental of) wheelchairs, roll-over bedside commodes, walkers, four-pronged canes, and hospital beds in the home. Less durable, or smaller and less expensive equipment such as shower chairs, and adaptive equipment for improvement in self-care function (such as adapted dining room utensils or dressing aids) are not paid for by Medicare, but some are covered under private insurance plans.

In addition to interventions focused on improving performance in self-care, activities to restore physical, cognitive, and psychosocial function are also reimbursed. Reimbursement for the latter activities can be difficult to obtain, however, unless the service provider is very specific as to how cognitive and psychosocial function, for instance, is directly related to practical improvement in adaptive functioning or self-care. For example, it may be necessary to stimulate patients' (cognitive) orientation and alertness in order to attend to environmental stimuli, which can help them locate the bathroom and return to their rooms. Psychosocial problems can often be addressed by their impact on the patient's day-to-day functioning. Depression, for instance, may be the root cause of a patient's refusal to eat; and anxiety caused by a fear of falling may prevent another from participating in rehabilitative activities.

Documentation of progress is essential for continued justification of the service. Part of the initial justification process is to determine what level of staff is required to provide the service. Therapeutic activities that could be offered by an aide, direct-care staff, or a recreation or activity therapist would not be covered if an occupational therapist performed them, because the specialized skills of the occupational therapist would not be required. If it is determined that a qualified therapist's skills are needed, then the treatment plan and progress notes should so indicate (the difference between skilled and unskilled services). This is akin to the distinction between skilled nursing facilities and regular nursing homes, which is based on the type of nursing care needed and provided.

There are quite specific guidelines about what constitutes skilled versus nonskilled services. Youngers (1988, 428) gives an example of this distinction by indicating two different ways of documenting services: "patient seen for dressing and bathing" versus "patient was seen for dressing and bathing training with instruction in use of a sock aid and long-handled sponge." In the former, she points out that the service was seen as nonskilled because anyone can dress or bathe a patient; the latter, an example of skilled service requiring knowledge of compensatory techniques.

Progress notes should relate specifically to the goals stated in the treatment plan. Many agencies require some variation on the content of the treatment plan and progress note, such as that provided below:

- Problems/needs. These are often expressed as behaviors or symptoms. It is important to document when the problem was identified (and treatment initiated).
- Goals of treatment (specification of short-term goals to reach longer-term objectives). Again, the goals must be measurable or observable to determine accurately whether they are attained (for example, "Patient will be able to locate her bedroom on unit, four out of five opportunities").
- Target date. When is it expected that goals will be accomplished?
- Treatment interventions. Specify duration and frequency (for example, "Provide daily 15-minute instruction to train patient to look for and recognize environmental cues for orientation to place").
- Indication of responsible provider. Indicate, for example, "occupational therapist to develop individualized environmental prompts for patient, assistant to train patient in cue recognition."

Documentation of treatment or intervention should be made after every contact and should indicate, at the minimum, what was done, for how long, and who provided it. Any significant response (no response is also noteworthy) from the patient should also be identified. Progress notes and discharge summaries should summarize progress made toward attaining each problem, degree of attainment, and date resolved or modified. Agencies and insurance companies generally have required guidelines as to how often progress notes should be made. Weekly progress notes may be necessary for a patient receiving acute rehabilitation services, whereas in an LTC facility, monthly notes may suffice.

Therapists in the United States should be alerted to the current Medicare guidelines for attainment of acceptable progress. These guidelines vary, depending on whether treatment is to be reimbursed by Medicare Plan A or Medicare Plan B. In the former, increments of progress are generally expected to be greater because of the nature of a more acute illness and/or inpatient hospital stay versus longer-term rehabilitation. The guidelines can be as specific as to expect an increase of at least 20 degrees in range of motion, an increase in attention span of at least five minutes in cognition, and an increase of at least one grade level (of assistance) in activities of daily living.

Medicare will reimburse treatment for certain diagnoses, but not for others. Significant to this book are the reimbursement limitations for those with ADRD. As a primary diagnosis, the following diagnostic categories are generally excluded: organic brain syndrome, Alzheimer's disease, and any chronic condition in which there is no evidence of a recent change in function. However, most acute care physical disabilities or acute exacerbation of chronic physical conditions such as arthritis, multiple sclerosis, or Parkinson's disease are covered, as well as sensory impairment or any psychiatric conditions (other than organic brain syndrome) that are substantiated by a physician.

Billing for therapy services is determined by agency or funding source requirements. Therapists are expected to adhere to a uniform terminology in describing services, not only for billing but for all documentation, including evaluations, treatment plans, and progress notes. For billing purposes in the United States, most medical facilities use physicians' Current Procedural Terminology (CPT) codes. This is a listing of descriptive terms and identifying codes for medical services. Also used are the diagnostic codes found in the ninth edition of An International Classification of Diagnoses (ICD-9).

The Health Care Financing Administration (HCFA), the federal agency that administers Medicare, has modified CPT-4 codes to be used more widely for both Medicare Plans A and B, and the resultant HCFA Common Procedures Coding System (HCPCS) is fast becoming a national system. Blue Cross/Blue Shield is requiring almost all of its participating plans to use the system, and the Health Insurance Association of America has endorsed the use of HCPCS by commercial insurance companies (Scott 1988a, 17).

5.4 Legislative Changes Affecting Reimbursement of Services for the Elderly

Prospective Payment

Federal, state, and provincial legislation is amended frequently, and revisions relating to the cost of health care have been striking in recent years. One major change was the legislated transition from retrospective cost reimbursement for inpatient hospitalization by Medicare to the prospective payment system. These Social Security amendments were signed into law in the United States in 1983, and changed the traditional fee-for-service model into a predetermined (prospective) cost system based on diagnosis. As previously discussed, payment standards have been established for DRGs. Currently rehabilitative and psychiatric hospitals, as well as LTC hospitals, are excluded from the prospective payment system, but HCFA is considering expanding the prospective payment system to post-hospital care. Since 1986, skilled nursing facilities meeting eligibility standards have had the option to shift to prospective payment, and most experts agree that the prospective payment system is on the way for skilled nurs-

ing facilities in general (Glickstein & Neustadt 1992, 10–16).

In 1984, the concept of HMOs was expanded to include a social component especially designed for the elderly. Demonstration sites to study the cost-effectiveness of these social/HMOs were funded as a joint venture of public and private funds. In addition to the core Medicare Part A and Part B components, long-term care and other supplementary benefits were included (Hanft 1988).

Other legislation affecting the elderly included the Medicare amendments enacted in July 1987, which extended coverage of occupational therapy to Medicare Part B beneficiaries. Not only was occupational therapy included as a skilled rehabilitation service (along with physical and speech therapy), but for the first time independent occupational therapy practice (outside of skilled nursing or rehabilitation facilities) could be reimbursed if the therapist became certified as a Medicare provider. There is a $500.00 per year limit of paid occupational therapy services, however, per beneficiary. This type of limit is often referred to in billing practices as "flat rate," versus the fee-for-service reimbursement model. Some states that use the fee-for-service system are months behind in paying providers for Medicaid. Because Medicare contracts with different insurance company intermediaries (such as Blue Cross/Blue Shield) for managing regional accounts, there is often a lot of variance between state Medicare (as well as Medicaid) practices due to the impact of state laws on private insurance carriers or intermediaries. Ohio, for instance, has recently gone to a flat-rate billing model for a two-year trial basis, whereas the neighboring state of Kentucky has just switched from a flat rate to fee for service as a cost-saving measure.

Omnibus Reconciliation Act

Another major change came with the passing of the Omnibus Reconciliation Act of 1987 (OBRA 1987). This legislation was enacted by the United States Congress in response to concerns about improving LTC. The act mandates that any facility receiving federal funds must meet certain guidelines for providing comprehensive assessment and programming for the residents of LTC facilities or nursing homes. In response to this legislation, a standardized resident assessment system is required that meets the criteria of HCFA. HCFA's own standardized instrument, the Resident Assessment System, which was developed and tested over a three-year period, includes a Minimum Data Set (MDS) and 18 Resident Assessment Protocols (RAPS). Recently the MDS has been revised and the expanded version is now referred to as MDS Plus. It is to be used in all LTC facilities by January of 1993. The MDS (both the original and the MDS Plus) provides both screening and assessment components. The RAPS provide the framework from which rehabilitative, psychosocial, and health care plans can be formulated.

The HCFA publication, *State Operations Manual: Provider Certification* (U.S. Department of Health and Human Services 1990), which provides the standardized MDS and RAPS, also provides a review of the statutory requirements for Resident Assessment instruments and other useful information, including definitions of terms, detailed examples of components to be assessed, and guidelines on how to use the system in general. The RAPS identify different types of syndromes or problem areas, which MDS items serve as triggers to indicate the need for further evaluation in the problem areas, common incidence rates for the particular problem in nursing home residents, and utilization guidelines as to how to proceed with the more in-depth evaluation. The Resident Assessment instrument itself which uses the MDS and RAPS standard assessment format is included as an appendix in the HCFA publication.

The 18 RAPS include the following areas to be assessed:

1. cognitive loss/dementia
2. visual function
3. communication
4. ADL/functional potential
5. rehabilitation potential
6. urinary incontinence and presence of/need for indwelling catheter
7–9. psychosocial well being, including separate RAPS on
   7. mood
   8. behavior
   9. delirium
10. activities (activity pursuit patterns)
11. falls and general health conditions
12. nutritional status, oral skills, swallowing problems
13. feeding tubes
14. dehydration/fluid maintenance
15. dental care
16. pressure ulcers, skin care
17. psychotropic drug use and presence of potential psychotropic drug-related side effects
18. physical restraints: alternatives to restraints, conditions associated with, and guidelines for use of restraints

Additional sections include special treatment requirements and procedures, disease diagnoses, the patient's customary routines and preferences at admission, and general demographic and legal information. The specific HCFA assessment system (MDS and RAPS) described above is optional; however, states that choose to develop their own systems must adhere to the same mandated areas of assessment and include the same elements of data and corresponding coding categories as the HCFA system. Any alternate instrument proposed by a state to be used in LTC facilities participating in the Medicare or Medicaid programs must be approved by HCFA.

Since OBRA 1987 is a federal law, OBRA requirements mandate that nursing home and LTC facilities assess patients in the above categories, using the MDS, within 14 days of admission to the facility; promptly after a significant change in any resident's physical or mental status; and now, with the implementation of MDS Plus, quarterly. A care plan of intervention is to be completed within 21 days of admission.

The MDS Plus has several expanded sections which include information on:

- Rehabilitation/restorative care. A new section that lists rehabilitative techniques and training that nurses and direct-care staff (under the direction of nursing staff) carry out. These practices include range of motion exercises, reality orientation, remotivation, splint/brace assistance, dressing/grooming, eating/swallowing, transfer, locomotion, and mobility training or skill practice. Many of these responsibilities have traditionally been carried out by therapy staff. This underscores the importance of documenting why skilled therapy services are needed in addition to what the nursing staff can provide.

- Medication use. Includes a log for recording the name of each medication, the dosage, and the frequency of administration.

- Participation in assessment. Indicates not only which staff have contributed to the assessment, but also whether the resident, family member and/or significant other has participated.

- Use of sign language or braille under communication/hearing patterns.

- Activity pursuit patterns. Expanded to include interests in gardening, volunteer work, and talking or conversing with others.

- Skin problems/care and contractures. Sections have been expanded.

- Special treatments and procedures. Now includes recreation therapy.

- ADL, functional rehabilitation potential. Expanded to include performance which has been restricted due to absence of assistive devices. Compensatory methods or assistive devices have been added to the bathing section and mobility appliances/devices section.

- Personal preferences. Reflected in several sections, includes use of tobacco, preference for bathing in the evening, difficulty in adjusting to changes in routine.

- Miscellaneous additions. Includes clarity of speech and several new indicators of mood and behavior patterns and problems in relationships with others.

Casemix Reimbursement using the RUGS III Classification System

In the United States, the implementation of the RUGS III Classification System (mandated by July, 1993) will drastically change the reimbursement system used in LTC facilities. The intent of the federal mandate is to use the resident assessment information data base (MDS Plus) to delineate needed resources and the eventual payment for such resources. In the latter part of 1992 Ohio was one of six states to pilot the use of the MDS Plus data base to categorize resource utilization by residents in nursing homes and other long-term care facilities. RUGS is an acronym for Resource Utilization Groups and is a system by which residents are classified by the type and frequency of services and rehabilitative care that they require. The data collected using the MDS Plus (i.e., information about the resident's functioning, ADL status, and categories listed previously) are analyzed by computer, using a "grouper" software system. The analysis results in what is referred to as a computer-driven classification system; in other words, the computer classifies residents according to a predesigned and programmed plan. For agencies without computers, residents can also be classified by hand, using the RUGS III Classification System.

The assignment of a resident to a RUG-III group is based on three dimensions: (1) a hierarchy of major resident types, (2) resident functionality as measured by activities of daily living, and (3) presence of additional problems or required services. The hierarchy of resident types includes seven categories of residents who need special rehabilitation, extensive services, or special care; or have clinically complex symptoms, impaired cognition, behavior problems, or specific reduced physical functions. Resident functionality is measured through the resident's ADL status in bed mobility, eating, transfer, and toilet use. The special reha-

bilitation category is further reduced into four subtypes of intensity based on (1) the number of minutes per week of rehabilitation services, (2) the number of rehabilitation therapies involved, and (3) the frequency of therapy. Resident functionality is assessed through ADL status and residents are given an ADL index score. Based on the index and the other two dimensions, the 7 categories of resident types are further divided into a total of 44 classifications.

The RUGS III system is complex and it is reasonable to predict that there will be many revisions as it is implemented across the United States. Most states are using the casemix reimbursement system to guide state Medicaid disbursement, but some areas are also using it to address Medicare reimbursement issues. Data from the MDS Plus is to be submitted by states starting in mid-January, 1993, but the implementation of a reimbursement system based on the casemix classification system is not expected before July, 1993. The new Democratic federal administration is sure to examine the health care delivery system in the United States. Revisions, and perhaps delays, in national implementation of the casemix reimbursement system may result. It is certain, however, that there will be a new system of identification of health and long-term care needs, as well as a way of monitoring the funding of services to meet such needs.

Although the only professional mandated to participate in the Resident Assessment is the registered nurse responsible for coordinating the assessment and certifying its completion, the process is expected to reflect a multidisciplinary effort. The coordinating nurse is responsible for delegating sections of the assessment to those staff members who have the most direct knowledge of the resident in the designated areas. Therefore, it is advisable to have input from social workers; nurses; activity specialists; attending physicians; occupational, physical, and/or speech therapists; dietitians; and pharmacists. Staff who provide therapeutic activities for those with ADRD and other residents of LTC facilities should note their expanded role under OBRA:

> On December 22, 1987, Congress passed a federal law which represented the most dramatic legislative change in federal nursing home regulation since the mid-70's. For the first time in federal nursing home law, "quality of life" was recognized as a key component of nursing home care. Previous regulations and laws had not specified this as a necessary requirement or expectation. (Perschbacher 1991, 22)

Activity professionals should complete the sections of the Resident Assessment system that include assessment of residents' activity pursuit patterns, activity preferences, and customary routines. Those residents having diminished ability to engage meaningfully in any activity, or having functional limitations in participating in preferred activities, will be identified and will need further activity care planning. Many of the therapeutic activities proposed in this book would be recommended as specific interventions to be included in the care plan. This inclusion is likely to be a direct result of having "quality of life" problem areas identified in the Resident Assessment system process.

OBRA 1987 not only required that the Resident Assessment system be implemented by 1990 but also mandated that federally funded facilities comply with federal regulations to facilitate a higher standard of functional ability and quality of life for residents. To do this, agencies were asked to bring up to standard their care planning process, activity department development, restorative programming, restraint reduction, staff training, and documentation development. While most advocates for quality LTC applaud the implementation of higher standards, many providers continue to grapple with the increased costs of quality improvement in expanded activity programs and for financing the additional time spent in staff training and documentation requirements. Despite these providers' concerns about how to implement OBRA, most are pressed into action by warnings on deficiencies and large fines for noncompliance.

It is significant to realize that even by the early part of 1992, there has been no distribution of federal guidelines to address the issue of reimbursement for expanded and improved LTC services under OBRA. Indeed, the topic of reimbursable geriatric service delivery is so important and timely that a new book has just been published that addresses this very issue (Glickstein & Neustadt 1992). These authors take a functional maintenance approach to the delivery of therapeutic services for the geriatric population. This approach not only addresses the mandate of focus required by OBRA, but it also provides guidelines for functional maintenance programs as designed by physical, occupational, and speech therapists. In addition, for therapists in the United States, this book provides valuable reference materials regarding the Medicare insurance system, with numerous appendixes giving actual excerpts from legislation relevant to the care of the elderly and their families.

5.5 System Consolidation

In the United States, one sees the development of strong advocacy groups and coalitions that combine efforts and funding to provide services that would be unattainable for any one group or agency acting alone. Advocacy groups such as the American Association for Retired Persons and the Alzheimer's Association have joined forces to acquire funding for special projects such as Long Term Care 88, a public interest group dedicated to focusing attention on LTC issues. Another such example is the four-year funding support of a program of day care and respite care at 19 centers throughout the United States. This program was made possible by a grant from the Robert Wood Johnson Foundation obtained through the cooperation of the Alzheimer's Association and the Administration on Aging (Mulligan & Cook-Deegan 1990).

Because of the complexity of financial support systems, some communities have taken to reallocating or pooling funds from the various sources described in the preceding sections. One strategy at the state level is to pool the various sources of federal funding and reallocate funds to pay for needed services for the elderly. This also applies to regional and municipal levels. One example of this is the pooling of funds by Santa Cruz County in California. This county took funds from more than 35 federal, state, and county sources to be able to deliver a full spectrum of social services, including day and home care for dementia. County governments in the suburbs of Minneapolis arranged a full array of services by blending the funds available to them through federal sources and redistributing them based on services coordination at the individual county government level (Mulligan & Cook-Deegan 1990, 388).

The above two models begin to approximate the reallocation of federal funds that provincial governments in Canada use to deliver services on a local level. Canadians centralize resources through their concept of "monopsony—the consolidation of payment authority in a single entity" (Kane & Kane 1985, 231). It appears that a monopsony is different from a monopoly in that in the former there is centralized control of the dispersion of funds, but control of the policy making continues to exist in the contributing communities. In a monopoly, there is total control of both policies affecting services provided and the payment of these services. The elimination of multiple payment sources reduces administrative costs and the complexity of the benefit structure for both consumers and providers, and permits a greater amount of control in avoiding gaps in service and overpayment for duplication of services between different service providers. Thus, in effect, the consolidation of funding sources permits greater control of the health care system as well as more deliberate planning for LTC.

Kane and Kane, internationally known experts in the areas of geriatric assessment, services, and LTC, believe the United States can learn a lot about the delivery of health care based on the Canadian model. Service delivery models are suggested in both their 1985 and 1987 publications. They assert that "long-term care is a test of national character. The way we provide for our disabled elderly reveals a great deal about our social values. What is required is an expression of national will. The Canadian experience has shown the way" (1985, 270). Although there are some Canadians who disagree with this statement and even look to the United States as a model for provision of health services, there are increasing numbers of citizens in the United States who support a universal type of health care entitlement. The fact that the provision of health care insurance for the underinsured and uninsured became a hot political issue for candidates for the 1992 United States presidential election only underscores the reality of a system that is not currently effective in meeting the needs of its population.

5.6 Experimental and Creative Alternatives to Traditional Health Care Financing

Medicare Alzheimer's Project

The Medicare Alzheimer's project is a multimillion dollar program financed by the United States Department of Health and Human Services to fund demonstration project research in eight communities in the United States. The objectives of the research are to determine whether family education and training, care coordination, and limited Medicare reimbursement for home and adult day care is cost-effective; and whether the rate of nursing home placement is reduced or delayed for families receiving services not currently covered by Medicare.

Demonstration programs began in 1989 in Cincinnati; Minneapolis; Miami; Memphis; Rochester, New York; Portland, Oregon; Urbana, Illinois; and Parkersburg, West Virginia. Data continue to be collected through April 1993. The study is unique in that it is the first research directed primarily to the caregiver by assessing the effects of providing caregiver support and assistance to keep the patient at home (Bonfield 1991, 20). This project is also a good example of the combined efforts of a consortium of local services for the elderly: four agencies and one university in the greater Cincinnati area submitted a proposal to the federal government that resulted in grant funding for the demonstration project.

Ohio PASSPORT Program

PASSPORT, an acronym for preadmission screening systems providing options and resources today, is an Ohio state program that funds day care services for Medicaid-eligible persons who would otherwise need nursing home coverage. This program was established as a pilot program only in selected Ohio counties in 1987, and it continues to provide funds for day care through the Medicaid waiver program. Medicaid normally pays for nursing home beds and services but, via the waiver, will fund day care as an alternative (Medicaid does not normally pay for day care). The PASSPORT program, in addition to paying for adult day care in preventing nursing home placement, will also pay for homemaker services, transportation, certain medical supplies, and other alternative services (Bonfield 1991, 8–9).

Outcome-Based Reimbursement

More and more third-party payers are examining the extent of progress made as an indication of outcome, and often limit or extend services based on the outcome to date. In the past, the retrospective reimbursement process often led to excessive and sometimes redundant (i.e., in multiple providers) service provision not always justified by patient need. Through managed care (as well as prospective payment), services often need to be preauthorized and there are stricter guidelines for reimbursement.

One creative reimbursement plan was piloted as part of a Health Services Research Project in the early 1980s and funded by the United States Department of Health and Human Services. The project was developed to improve nursing home services and placement by rewarding the achievement of projected outcomes of nursing care. The research was intended for an audience of public officials, policy makers, scholars, and practitioners interested in LTC. It was hoped that the procedures developed in the project might be adopted as an approach to the problem of financing LTC.

This research, conducted by Kane et al. (1983), was important in that it addressed the feasibility of linking payment to outcomes of care in patient functioning, value preferences, and satisfaction. The latter two factors are especially noteworthy in that they represent quality-of-life issues, which so often are neglected in financing care. The specific domains measured as indicators of nursing home resident outcome included physiologic function, pain and symptoms, cognition, affect (or mood), social contact, social activities, ADL (a measure of self-care), and overall satisfaction with many aspects of life in a particular nursing home. In addition to these eight resident outcome categories, the researchers also looked at three broad outcome categories: discharged better, discharged worse (usually to a hospital), and discharged dead. Outcome domains were weighted by value, as assigned by a conference of experts. This project has important implications for those with ADRD in that it was especially progressive in addressing such nursing home outcomes as resident satisfaction, social activities, and self-care—outcomes that would later be mandated by the OBRA 1987.

Residents in the project nursing homes, the patient's family, professionals providing LTC, and government officials were all included as respondents to a survey of the importance of the 11 different domains of outcome, as well as a survey of respondents' judgment of which domains of outcome were likely to be influenced by good nursing home care. Of the nursing home resident respondents, approximately 60 percent of the sample comprised patients with cognitive impairment due to brain injury, cerebrovascular accident, or dementia. Respondents were asked to rate the importance and susceptibility of influence of domains for four different resident categories:

1. those with a high level of cognition and a high level of skills in ADL
2. those with high cognition and low ADL
3. those with low cognition and high ADL
4. those with low cognition and low ADL

It was found that residents' cognition levels had a greater effect on respondent ratings of both importance (of domains) and influence (of nursing care) than the residents' ability to perform ADL. This finding appears to support the idea that cognition and perception of quality of life and the quality of care are of crucial significance to respondents, despite the residents' degree of physical incapacitation. All domains except for discomfort (pain and symptoms) were considered more important for the highly functional cognitive group than for the two (high and low ADL) low-cognitive functioning groups. Ratings for those with low cognition identified as most important the degree of discomfort they might experience. Those with both good cognition and high ADL rated satisfaction, affect, and the social domains as most important. For those with good cognition but poor ADL, physical functioning, ADL, satisfaction, and discomfort were rated most highly. Ratings for residents with high cognition appeared, then, to follow a hierarchy of need, with physical needs a priority over psychosocial factors. For those patients in the low-cognitive category, the respondents consistently placed greater value on all domain improvements for those low-cognitive patients with high ADL, versus the low/low group. Residents assigned the lowest value ratings to low-ADL residents who were cognitively impaired. This discrepancy in value assignment may be

due to the issue of resident bias or discrimination against those patients who are low functioning, and these values may reflect a masked fear of dependency and fear of the loss of functioning as one ages.

Since residents are sensitive to the loss of functioning, which is particularly observable in ADL and self-care, it is important to stress the importance of increasing or maintaining ADL skills for all residents. The importance of activities, interestingly enough, was rated lowest of all domains except for discharged worse or death. The highest ratings for both high and low ADL groups were given to satisfaction. Respondents, in rating the influence of good nursing home care, believed that discomfort is most amenable to treatment, whereas cognition is the least. This research is significant in that it identifies value preferences in LTC and subsequently, this writer believes, sheds light on some of the resistances one encounters to financing services for those with ADRD.

Outcome-based reimbursement gives nursing homes the incentive to produce better resident outcomes by rewarding facilities whose resident care results in better than expected resident outcomes. Correspondingly, it penalizes homes whose residents do worse than expected. In addition to combining quality of care with payment, this approach addresses the questions of what providers, consumers of service, and the public at large expect to achieve and the importance of the various outcomes.

The potential for implementation of outcome-based reimbursement lies in each state because of the fact that states influence nursing homes by the way in which they reimburse homes for Medicaid residents, as well as through quality and capacity regulation and inspection. The outcome-based reimbursement model is seen as preferable to the present mechanism of reimbursement, which provides "perverse incentives to select certain types of residents [only] and to invest minimal effort in maintaining functioning" (Kane et al. 1983, 57). The maintenance of functioning is a crucial issue in expecting reimbursement of services for those with ADRD and is addressed more thoroughly in the following section.

Functional Maintenance As Reimbursable Service

Medicare (and through OBRA 1987, Medicaid also) will fund therapy services that develop programs and methods by which one can maintain an LTC patient's functioning. This, of course, is especially relevant to those with ADRD, as one of the foremost goals of treating a person with ADRD is to stimulate residual skills to maintain the person's optimal functional level as long as possible. Also, as Bowlby emphasizes in Chapter 4, the central goal of group activities is to enhance self-esteem, since the effects of ADRD are so devastating to the individual's sense of competence, independence, and self-worth. The research study on outcome-based reimbursement discussed above clearly illustrates the value preference and importance of residents' maintaining an optimal level of cognition and level of ADL functioning for as long as possible.

Clinical methods of providing therapeutic activities to stimulate and maintain self-esteem and function are presented in Chapters 3 through 7 of this book. In this chapter, various methods of financing therapy and LTC have been discussed; however, the specific challenge of obtaining reimbursement for progressive debilitating dementias has not been addressed. Many service providers assume that reimbursement under Medicare is not possible because of strict requirements related to level of care and/or diagnosis. Although reimbursement is limited, it is possible under certain conditions. Glickstein and Neustadt (1992) provide an excellent resource handbook that presents a functional maintenance therapy system that is a reimbursable geriatric service, when used following recommended guidelines. While this book does not specifically address the ADRD population, it does provide some examples of reimbursable services for those with Alzheimer's disease or progressive dementias.

One frequent misunderstanding that limits application for reimbursement is the confusion over skilled level of care versus skilled service provider. A "skilled" facility is a nursing home or LTC facility that is licensed for skilled beds, those that require the skilled level of care provided by professional nurses. It is important to note that not all beds in a nursing home or LTC facility are skilled. Generally, the facility will have a special unit or units requiring this more intense, or acute, level of care. Although Medicare Part A will pay for therapy for eligible patients requiring such skilled nursing services, it is commonly assumed that when patients are no longer in "skilled" beds of a nursing home, they no longer are eligible for therapy. This is incorrect, as they may still require therapy and the services of a skilled qualified professional, which can be reimbursed as rehabilitation service under Medicare Part B. For those requiring active rehabilitative treatment, the services of a qualified speech, physical, or occupational therapist will be paid. Often, however, the therapist will design an intervention program and train less-qualified staff to carry it out. In these instances, evaluation of the patient, the program development, and training are reimbursable; however, the implementation of the program is not, since it does not require the

expertise of a skilled therapist to carry out. This distinction gets back to the "reasonable and necessary" requirement of the Medicare regulations, discussed previously in this chapter.

Another misunderstanding in regard to potential reimbursement is due to the common knowledge of "red flag" diagnoses that trigger Medicare audits and often bring denials of coverage because the service may be seen as excessive or "unnecessary" for those with chronic, progressive, or old injuries in which maximal rehabilitation potential is assumed to have been already achieved. Such red flag diagnoses include old cerebral vascular accidents, Parkinson's disease, multiple sclerosis, amyotrophic lateral sclerosis, Huntington's chorea, old head trauma, and dementia of any type (Glickstein & Neustadt 1992, 6–14). The misunderstanding comes about when service providers assume that services to individuals with such diagnoses can never be reimbursed. As Glickstein and Neustadt illustrate in their book, their tri-model (functional maintenance therapy) system "is a sensible approach for delivery to individuals with red-flag diagnoses. It offers rehabilitation professionals a model for providing reimbursable consultation services to those individuals who are either not considered to be treatment candidates or for whom expensive and inappropriate active treatment is likely to meet with coverage denials by third party payers" (p. 1:2).

Functional maintenance programs are not appropriate for a patient if no residual functional abilities are identified or if the severity of a psychological disturbance precludes the use of functional maintenance therapy. For instance, Glickstein and Neustadt give the example of an 85-year-old woman with a longstanding history of multi-infarct dementia. A speech therapist evaluated her and found her limitations so great that she was unable to participate in standardized testing. Nonstandardized probes were then used, and this testing indicated that the patient had no residual abilities that could be tapped to establish a functional communication system. Although this patient was not appropriate for functional maintenance therapy, the authors stressed that patients who do have some existing functional abilities, but who are at risk for decreased function if not stimulated or trained, and those who have latent abilities that can be stimulated are candidates for functional maintenance programs (p. 6:23).

For those with ADRD, Medicare has been quite specific about what services are reimbursable. The *Medicare Carriers Manual*, claims process section (U.S. Department of Health and Human Services 1987), mandates that medical management of an Alzheimer's patient's condition would be covered, but not psychiatric treatment. For instance, if an Alzheimer's victim has anorexia and dysphagia due to difficulty in managing soft food, a facility might choose to qualify the patient for skilled level of care by inserting a nasogastric tube to prevent malnutrition. However, such a procedure is invasive and potentially destructive to the patient's level of autonomy and quality of life. This same patient is not eligible for rehabilitation services, since she is able to feed herself but refuses food. Instead, a therapist designs a feeding program, using puréed food and behavior modification at mealtime and is successful in getting the development and dissemination of this program covered as functional maintenance implemented by caregivers (Glickstein & Neustadt 1992, 6:35). For further discussion of the functional maintenance system, please review the Glickstein and Neustadt reference in the annotated bibliography.

5.7 What's a Provider To Do?

Anticipating and Planning for Change

As a provider, it is frustrating to observe inequities in the health and social services system and the resultant impact on those with ADRD. Fortunately, it is not necessary to stand by helplessly in frustrated silence for the next set of government regulations to be implemented. Instead of reacting to policies and procedural regulations, a proactive stance is recommended to anticipate trends and needs and then to act accordingly: to act prospectively as an advocate for the elderly and those with ADRD.

Anticipating needs requires not only sensitivity to the ADRD population, but also sensitivity to the political process of promoting change. As advocates for the elderly and ADRD population, therapists and caregivers can become change agents at the personal, clinical, local, state, and national levels.

Providers As Change Agents

At the most basic level, therapists and caregivers can promote change through their attitude and outlook in working in LTC, through the therapeutic use of self with their patients, through demonstration in the clinic, and by acting as an advocate for persons with ADRD in promoting services. As advocates, therapists could become more active in community organization to develop additional community-based service programs. Expanded program development is possible by engaging the support of such community service clubs or organizations as the Rotary, the Lion's Club, and the Shriners. Since many senior citizens groups, such as the American Association of Retired Persons, the Gray

Panthers, and local government agencies such as branches of the Council on Aging, are quite active in advocating for the elderly, one might wish to combine efforts if objectives are similar. As members of such community planning groups and consumer advisory boards, therapists and caregivers can be effective in mobilizing political interest and action in an advocacy project. Therapists assuming the role of community organizer can use the strategies of locality development, social action, and social planning to promote ventures in the interests of their clients in the community.

Grass-Roots Effect on Political Process

In locality development the therapist, in consulting with groups of interested caregivers and representatives of various community agencies, might coordinate the efforts of active members of the groups toward the accomplishment of various tasks. These tasks might include writing and submitting a program proposal and involving members of power structures (local government and influential agencies or associations) as collaborators in a common venture.

By using the strategy of social action in community organizations, the advocate assumes an activist approach in applying pressure to political groups such as state or county governments to provide more programs or easier access and affordability for those with ADRD. In this role, the advocate might organize the collection of signatures for a grass-roots-initiated petition, or even speak out in favor of certain bills at legislative hearings.

Influencing Policy through Organized Effort

The social planning approach is used in emphasizing the planning process and applying this to community organization. On a community level, the advocate might gather data about the perceived problem, analyze the data, and propose a solution. Within a community agency, the same planning process applies: the therapist employed within an agency would begin by documenting unmet needs of the population, then systematically exploring available resources, suggesting a plan to supplement them with additional services, and developing a procedure to implement the desired service program. The reader is redirected to the earlier sections on systems analysis as a framework for planning, and planning for program development (Sections 4.0 to 4.5) for a review of elements that would be crucial in considering a social planning approach.

Again, it is important to note that much can be done on an individual and more personal level. A therapist or caregiver who comes in contact with people in the community can take the opportunity to educate others about relevant issues. This education can be done on an informal, one-to-one basis, or as part of a more formal dissemination of information by speaking to community groups or participating in training programs for students, new therapists, or caregivers.

Becoming Familiar with Recommendations Made by Experts in the Field

To be effective in influencing others, the therapist or caregiver should be well informed. If he or she is advocating change at a macrolevel of intervention, this would include becoming familiar with existing and proposed policies related to LTC, research, and testimony by experts in the field of gerontology. This can be done by forming study groups through professional associations, formal course work and continuing education, or independent study. Several of the authors mentioned in this chapter are internationally renowned for their expertise in gerontology. Kane and Kane have published prolifically in areas related to LTC and the elderly. Meltzer et al., in their 1981 book, *"Policy Options in Long-Term Care,"* raise issues that are still unresolved and very pertinent today.

Much of this chapter has focused on reimbursement issues, and in discussing current Medicare provisions, it is convenient to forget or abandon a holistic approach to care of those with ADRD. The current reimbursement system is, by far, based largely on the provision of medical services and its resulting overemphasis on institutional and acute care. It is important to understand that quality, or even adequate, LTC involves sustained physical and emotional care. As Meltzer et al. (1981) point out, there is

> much debate about whether LTC is a social or medical service—this is an artificial distinction. Physical care is usually a necessary but insufficient component of the service. In fact, physical needs are so responsive to psychological and social factors that it is almost impossible to separate the two. . . . Dependency can be created or exacerbated because of psychological factors such as fear, depression, or anxiety, and these in turn, are influenced by social factors such as family relationships or the safety of the neighborhood. (p. 84)

For those of us who visualize more holistic services for those with ADRD, there is hope in knowing that the problem of supporting LTC is fast becoming a major social issue and domestic priority not only in the United States, but all over the world. In addition to economics, our value systems are being tested: in an LTC system that has become medicalized, is it preferable to maximize physical safety of the infirm at the expense of

haviing a sterile, hospital-like environment with no privacy and little choice? Meltzer et al. (1981) also question what should be the amount, scope, and direction of public support of LTC compared with the responsibilities and preferences of individuals and families. One thing is certain, political pressures will mount to fund LTC as the elderly population and expense of caring for those with ADRD increase as we approach the turn of the century. It will be important for the "ground troops" of providers to be well prepared to meet the crest of this political-epidemiological wave, if not, in fact, part of the catalyst in shaping a changing system.

6.0 ANNOTATED BIBLIOGRAPHY

Administrative and Fiscal issues

The following seven references are clearly not meant to be an inclusive or even comprehensive listing of resource materials related to administrative and fiscal issues in offering therapeutic activities and services to those with ADRD. It is, however, a concise list of books and resource manuals that have been particularly helpful to me and that I recommend to providers who wish to pursue in more depth selected topics reviewed in this chapter.

Beck, D. 1984. *Principles of reimbursement in health care.* Gaithersburg, Md.: Aspen Publishers, Inc. This is a book about managing reimbursement, written by a business administrator for an audience of hospital administrators and financial services staff. Although it was written at the time the prospective payment system was being introduced to hospitals, Beck gives an analysis of cost reimbursement as well as prospective payment. The book describes the Medicare and Medicaid programs, gives an overview of principles related to cost increases, cost reimbursement strategies, and reports. The appeals process in challenging Medicare denials or overly restrictive regulation is discussed, with suggestions for avoiding the appeals process in the first place. The latter is primarily accomplished through good documentation and accounting techniques, to which Beck commits a whole chapter. Other chapters include a review of the cost allocation process, revenue and pricing strategies, the apportionment process, reimbursement determination, settlements and limits, and corporate reorganization to allow financial flexibility.

Six appendixes are included that review Medicare regulations related to the foregoing chapter topics on cost reports, hospital accounting techniques, cost allocation, revenue and pricing strategies, cost apportionment process, and hospital reimbursement. As anyone knows who has dealt with Medicare and Medicaid, regulations are constantly changing. Therefore, the appendixes included in this book, published in 1984, are clearly out of date. However, the chapter contents include much useful information related to pricing theories and formulas, accounting principles, allocation methods, and accounting and apportionment techniques. The theory, principles, and techniques are general enough to be applied to a variety of health system settings, and therefore the book continues to be a useful resource.

Davis, L., and M. Kirkland, eds. 1988. *The role of occupational therapy with the elderly (ROTE)*. Rockville, Md.: American Occupational Therapy Association, Inc. This training manual is clearly intended for occupational therapists, as it is published by the American Occupational Therapy Association for the purpose of providing a competency-based curriculum, and was initially provided as part of a series of workshops offered throughout the United States. In addition to the manual referenced above, there is also an accompanying trainer's manual (*ROTE II: 1987 Faculty guide*, by Brooks and Davis).

The objectives of the curriculum are (1) to educate occupational therapy personnel in core gerontological knowledge; (2) to train occupational therapy personnel in skills related to the direct care of and program planning for the sick, disabled, frail, and well elderly; and (3) to strengthen the aging services network through the participation of occupational therapy personnel in the continuum of health care for maintenance of independent living. The 442-page manual is divided into four modular sections. All modules lead the trainee through a series of readings (most of which are included), activities and audiovisual training materials, the latter, of course, which were provided in the workshops. Module I presents an explanation of the physical and psychosocial processes of aging and includes material on gerontological theories on aging; specific information related to the anatomical, psychological, and cognitive changes of advancing age; and the physical and psychological pathology of aging.

Module II presents the range of occupational therapy assessment, treatment processes, and settings for practice in gerontology. Module III focuses on a description of major treatment approaches, including activity programming, prevention, care of the terminally ill, activities of daily living, therapeutic adaptations, and cognitive and psychosocial treatment. Module IV presents an overview of important service management issues.

It is for Module IV that I have included this publication for annotated comment. Occupational therapists will find particularly useful the following readings in this section: "Consultation in Gerontic Occupational Therapy," by Lewis; "Federal Legislation Affecting the Elderly: Implications for Occupational Therapy," by Hanft; "Payment for Geriatric Health Care," by Rogers and Hanft; "Reimbursement and Documentation in Geriatric Occupational Therapy," by Youngers; and "Update: Occupational Therapy Medicare Amendments," by Scott.

Glickstein, J., and G. Neustadt. 1992. *Reimbursable geriatric service delivery: A functional maintenance therapy system*. Gaithersburg, Md.: Aspen Publishers, Inc. This publication is best described as a resource manual most useful to speech, occupational, or physical therapists. Another audience would be health facility administrators who wish to expand therapeutic services to meet OBRA regulations. Administrators who would utilize these therapies more if they could justify the cost of employment through increased revenues would also be well advised to review this publication. Glickstein and Neustadt wrote this book based on their experience in obtaining reimbursement for functional maintenance programs through four different (insurance) intermediaries (without a single denial!) for over 450 residents in LTC facilities.

The authors, one of whom is a speech therapist, wrote the manual with the purpose of educating the health care professional "about those parts of the Medicare law that pertain to functional maintenance and to show the professional how to develop a viable continuum of care with reimbursable services" (p. 1:1). Functional maintenance is presented within the philosophical framework of rehabilitation, and the authors present a tri-model system of rehabilitation, one that provides a foundation of a true continuum of care. The tri-model system presents three phases of recovery: restorative I, physiological; restorative II, compensatory; and restorative III, functional maintenance. The last stage, functional maintenance (FM), is particularly relevant to those with ADRD. The two major objectives of FM therapy are to maximize resident functioning and to demonstrate the skilled nature of the service being provided. This latter objective is often the only way it is possible for some patients to be able to continue a rehabilitative process. The authors differentiate between "maintenance," which aims to keep the patient "alive and comfortable" and is basically seen as static and nontherapeutic, and FM, which is the "provision of services intended to enhance those residual functional abilities identified during an evaluation performed by rehabilitation professionals" (p. 4:1). FM is especially important for those patients who have longstanding conditions identified as "red flag diagnoses" by third-party payers and are in need of intervention by rehabilitation professionals. The authors instruct therapists on how to demonstrate the skilled nature of FM so that it is reimbursable and how to provide service to the individuals who need it the most.

The manual includes chapters on the tri-model system itself, describes in greater depth the third phase of rehabilitation, FM, and further identifies three different programs of FM to be used in different situations, based on patient need. Throughout the manual are sample forms the authors have used for evaluation, re-evaluation and adjustment, discharge programs, progress note format, record of treatment, and quality assurance. Also included are samples of resident, staff, and family/friend caregiver questionnaires; training contract forms; and individual and group tracking monitor forms. One of several extremely practical chapters is on service delivery, including training of staff, how to document for reimbursement, different formats for charting entries into the medical record, and some suggestions for billing. Another very practical chapter tells how to apply FM therapy, including how to select candidates for FM programs, how to differentiate them from candidates for ongoing active treatment, and how to design FM programs. Also included are a chapter on orientation to the concept of a working interdisciplinary team, a full chapter explaining and giving excerpts from the OBRA, and chapters describing the American health insurance system, Medicare insurance system, and national and state health insurance programs originating from the Social Security Act. There is a useful appendix explaining health and insurance industry acronyms and standard abbreviations and symbols for documentation, an appendix of definitions, and several appendixes including excerpts from several Medicare documents and the OBRA.

In summary, Glickstein and Neustadt have carefully and competently researched Medicare regulations and OBRA requirements, and their manual has exceptionally good face validity in presenting a reimbursable service specifically aimed toward LTC patients. I recommend this publication highly to therapists who wish to focus on the reimbursable aspects of providing functionally based programming to those with ADRD.

Hertfelder, S., and C. Crispen, eds. 1990. *Private practice: Strategies for success—a comprehensive guide to starting, promoting & building your own private practice.* Rockville, Md.: American Occupational Therapy Association, Inc. Although this manual is published by the American Occupational Therapy Association, the material is generic to any professional setting up a small business. It includes chapters on self-assessment, marketing assessment, and guidelines on how to develop a business plan and loan proposal, and lists resources for additional advice and support. Sample forms used in a business organization are included.

There are chapters on payment for services, Medicare/Medicaid fraud and abuse (how to avoid problems), contracting to provide services, developing a time line and planning calendar, locating space, and ordering equipment. How to set up the books used in bookkeeping, setting up and collecting fees, budgeting, employment issues, patient services, risk management, marketing and public relations, and anticipating practice changes are other very practical topics that are essential for therapists contemplating private practice to consider.

Kane, R., and R. Kane. 1987. *Long-term care: Principles, programs, and policies.* New York: Springer Publishing Co. This is an excellent book for an audience of those generally interested in the future of geriatric services and of LTC in particular. It provides a very good orientation to the LTC field and has a particular emphasis on promoting optimal functioning as the key to good LTC. Kane and Kane have collected useful data describing existing policies and practices regarding LTC in the United States and have assembled, reviewed, evaluated, and synthesized these data with the goal of using them as an aid in decision making about future financing of LTC. The statistics and facts included in the book are sure to be cited as useful references for program planners who would like to strengthen their proposals by using a nationwide data base. The authors also introduce the reader to the complexities of the political, social, and economic factors influencing the delivery of LTC services. They raise thought-provoking issues that question not only how to finance LTC but also whether the current LTC model is a system we would wish to subsidize.

Lewis, S. 1989. *Elder care in occupational therapy.* Thorofare, N.J.: Slack, Inc. This is a general text on working with the elderly. It includes a section on Alzheimer's disease, giving a description of the seven progressive states of the disease as assessed by the Global Deterioration Scale of Reisberg et al. Lewis also describes occupational therapy's role in working with hospice and terminally ill patients, and includes a section on documentation for third-party payers. Medicaid and the Medicare system and amendments are reviewed in a section on health care delivery. The prospective payment system, HMOs, private health insurance, and other sources of third-party payments are discussed. For occupational therapists, this book is helpful in that it addresses many of the reimbursement issues presented in this chapter, but details information that is specific to occupational therapists.

Scott, S., ed. 1988. *Payment for occupational therapy services.* Rockville, Md.: American Occupational Therapy Association, Inc. This is a 465-page manual specific to an audience of occupational therapists. The first three sections of the manual deal with much of the information presented in this chapter, reviewing federal and state sources of payment for therapy services and private insurance systems' reimbursement plans. Another section, on documentation, includes guidelines from the American Occupational Therapy Association giving fundamental elements and types of documentation. Home health care is reviewed, raising many of the administrative and professional issues that apply to therapists working in the home. There is a separate section on billing, including ethical considerations related to improper billing, a discussion of strategies for expanding payment for occupational therapy services, and guidelines for increasing coverage by third-party payers. A useful supplemental table of billing codes is presented, listing occupational therapy intervention by CPT codes. A summary of a grant-funded project in Iowa is described, reviewing that state's success in improving reimbursement for occupational therapy services, including the establishment and operation of a "reimbursement hotline." Also discussed is how the state occupational therapy association obtained state legislation mandating the payment of occupational therapy services in Connecticut; a successful occupational therapy marketing plan in Wisconsin is also reviewed. Finally, the manual includes a glossary of terms used in the insurance industry, and some reprints on reimbursement in geriatric health care and private practice.

Abramson, L. (1978). Learned helplessness in humans: Critique and reformulation. *Journal of Abnormal Psychology, 87,* 49–74.

Advisory Panel on Alzheimer's Disease. (1989). *Report of the advisory panel on Alzheimer's disease.* (DHHS Publication No. ADM 89–1644). Washington, DC: U.S. Government Printing Office.

Age Wave, Inc. (1990). *Face to face with older adults: What's it like to be old?* Emeryville, CA: Author.

Aitken, M. (1982). Self-concept and functional independence in the hospitalized elderly. *American Journal of Occupational Therapy, 36,* 243–250.

Akerlund, B., & Norberg, A. (1986 March/April). Group psychotherapy with demented patients. *Geriatric Nursing,* 83–84.

Alderson, S. (1977). *Hurry up, Bonnie.* Admonton, Alberta, Canada: Three Frog Press.

Allison, N., & Bowlby, C. (in press). The denial of dementia: A critique of Feil's "Validation Therapy."

Altman, H. (Ed.). (1987). *Alzheimer's disease: Problems, prospects and perspectives.* New York: Plenum Press.

Alzheimer's Disease and Related Disorders Association. (1988). *Communicating with the Alzheimer patient.* Chicago: Author.

Alzheimer's Disease and Related Disorders Association. (1990). *Alzheimer's disease statistics fact sheet.* Chicago: Author.

American Psychiatric Association. (1987). *Diagnostic and statistical manual of mental disorders* (3rd ed. rev.). Washington, DC: Author.

Arbuckle, T., Gold, D., & Andres, D. (1986). Cognitive functioning of older people in relation to social and personality variables. *Psychology and Aging 1,* 55–62.

Arkin, S. (1991). Memory training in early Alzheimer's disease: An optimistic look at the field. *American Journal of Alzheimer's Care and Related Disorders & Research, 7*(4), 17–25.

Arnetz, B. (1982). Gerontic occupational therapy–psychological and social predictors of participation and therapeutic benefits. *American Journal of Occupational Therapy, 39,* 461–465.

Aronson, M. (Ed.). (1988). *Understanding Alzheimer's disease.* New York: Charles Scribner's Sons.

Aronson, M., Cox, D., Guastadisegni, P., Frazier, C., Sherlock, L., Grower, R., Barbera, A., Sternberg, M., Breed, J., & Koren, M. (1992). Dementia and the nursing home: Association with care needs. *Journal of the American Geriatrics Society, 40,* 27–33.

Atchley, R. (1980). *The social forces in later life* (3rd ed.). Belmont, CA: Wadsworth.

Atchley, R. (1989). A continuity theory of normal aging. *The Gerontologist, 29,* 183–190.

Avorn, J., & Langer, E. (1982). Induced disability in nursing home patients: A controlled trial. *Journal of American Geriatrics Society, 30,* 397–400.

Backman, L., & Herlitz, A. (1990). The relationship between prior knowledge and face recognition memory in normal aging and Alzheimer's disease. *Journal of Gerontology, 45*(3), 94–100.

Backman, L., Herlitz, A., & Karlsson, T. (1987). Pre-experimental knowledge facilitates episodic recall in young, young-old, and old-old adults. *Experimental Aging Research, 13*, 89–91.

Bakshi, R., Bhambhani, Y., & Madill, H. (1991). The effects of task preference on performance during purposeful and non-purposeful activities. *American Journal of Occupational Therapy, 45*, 912–916.

Baines, S., Saxby, P., & Ehlert, K. (1987). Reality orientation and reminiscence therapy. *British Journal of Psychiatry, 151*, 222–231.

Baltes, M. (1988). The etiology and maintenance of dependency in the elderly: Three phases of operant research. *Behavior Therapy, 14*, 301–319.

Baltes, M., & Baltes, P. (Eds.). (1986). *The psychology of control and aging.* Hillsdale, NJ: Erlbaum.

Barrett, T., & Wright, M. (1981). Age related facilitation in recall following semantic processing. *Journal of Gerontology, 36*, 194–199.

Baum, C., Edwards, D., Leavitt, K., Grant, E., & Deuel, R. (1988). Performance components in senile dementia of the Alzheimer type: Motor planning, language, and memory. *Occupational Therapy Journal of Research, 8*, 357–368.

Bayles, K., & Kaszniak, A. (1987). *Communication and cognition in normal aging and dementia.* San Diego: College Hill Press.

Bayles, K., & Tomoeda, C. (1991). Caregiver report of prevalence and appearance order of linguistic symptoms in Alzheimer's patients. *The Gerontologist, 31*, 210–216.

Beck, A. (1985). The therapeutic use of animals. *Veterinary clinics of North America: Small animal practice, 15*(2), 365–375.

Beck, A., & Katcher, A. (1984). A new look at pet facilitated therapy. *Journal of the American Veterinary Medicine Association, 184*(4), 414–421.

Beck, C. (1981). Dining experiences of the institutionalized aged. *Journal of Gerontological Nursing, 7*, 104–107.

Beck, D. (1984). *Principles of reimbursement in health care.* Gaithersburg, MD: Aspen Publishers, Inc.

Becker, G., & Kaufman, S. (1988). Old age, rehabilitation, and research: A review of the issues. *The Gerontologist, 28*, 459–468.

Begley, S., Hagar, M., & Muir, A. (1990, March 5). The search for the fountain of youth. *Newsweek.*

Beisgen, B. (1989). *Life-enhancing activities for mentally impaired elders.* New York: Springer Publishing Company.

Bennett, S., & Maas, F. (1987). The effect of music-based life review on the life satisfaction and ego integrity of elderly people. *British Journal of Occupational Therapy, 50*, 432–436.

Berdes, C. (1988). The modest proposal nursing home: Dehumanizing characteristics of nursing homes in memoirs of nursing home residents. *Journal of Applied Gerontology, 6*, 372–388.

Berghorn, F., & Schafer, D. (1987). Reminiscence intervention in nursing homes: What and who changes? *International Journal of Aging and Human Development, 24*, 113–127.

Berkman, B., Foster, L., & Campion, E. (1989). Failure to thrive: Paradigm for the frail elderly. *The Gerontologist, 29*, 654–659.

Beyersdorfer, P., & Birkenhauer, D. (1990). The therapeutic use of pets on an Alzheimer's unit. *American Journal of Alzheimer's Care and Related Disorders & Research, 5*(1), 13–17.

Birren, J., & Renner, V. (1980). Concepts and issues of mental health and aging. In J. Birren, & R. Sloane (Eds.), *Handbook of mental health and aging.* Englewood Cliffs, NJ: Prentice-Hall.

Birren, J., & Schaie, K.W. (Eds.). (1990). *Handbook of the psychology of aging.* (3rd ed.). San Diego: Academic Press.

Bonfield, T. (1991, February 25). Elder care: Dealing with a dilemma. *Cincinnati Business Courier.*

Boylin, W., Gordon, S., & Nehrke, M. (1976). Reminiscing and ego integrity in institutionalized elderly males. *The Gerontologist, 16*, 118–124.

Braun, J., Wykle, M., & Cowling, W. (1988). Failure to thrive in older persons: A concept derived. *The Gerontologist, 28*, 809–812.

Brennan, P., & Steinberg, L. (1983–84). Is reminiscence adaptive? Relations among social activity level, reminiscence and morale. *International Journal of Aging and Human Development, 18*, 99–109.

Bright, R. (1988). *Music therapy and the dementias.* Saint Louis, MO: MMB Music, Inc.

Brochoven, J. (1971). The legacy of moral treatment—1800's to 1910. *American Journal of Occupational Therapy, 25*, 223–225.

Brody, E., Kleven, M., Lawton, M., & Silverman, H. (1971). Excess disabilities of mentally impaired aged. *The Gerontologist, 11*, 124–132.

Brody, E., Kleven, M., Lawton, M., & Moss, M. (1974). A longitudinal look at excess disabilities in the mentally impaired aged. *Journal of Gerontology, 29,* 79–84.

Brouillette, M., & White, L. (1991). The effects of olfactory stimulation on the appetites of nursing home residents. *Physical and Occupational Therapy in Geriatrics, 10*(1), 1–13.

Brown, C. (Ed.). (1984). *The many facets of touch.* Skillman, NJ: Johnson & Johnson.

Bruneau, M., Rosseau, M., & Forget, A. (1981). Le Schéma corporel de la personne âgée séjounant en centre d'accueil. *Canadian Journal of Occupational Therapy, 48,* 157–161.

Bryant, W. (1991). Creative group work with confused elderly people: A development of sensory integration therapy. *British Journal of Occupational Therapy, 54,* 187–192.

Bucht, G., & Sandman, P. (1990). Nutritional aspects of dementia, especially Alzheimer's disease. *Age and Ageing, 19,* 32–36.

Buechel, H. (1986). Reminiscence: A review and prospectus. *Physical and Occupational Therapy in Geriatrics, 5*(2), 25–37.

Burgener, S., & Barton, D. (1991). Nursing care of cognitively impaired, institutionalized elderly. *Journal of Gerontological Nursing, 17*(4), 37–43.

Burns, A., Jacoby, R., & Levy, R. (1991a). Neurological signs in Alzheimer's disease. *Age and Ageing, 20,* 45–51.

Burns, A., Jacoby, R., & Levy R. (1991b). Progression of cognitive impairment in Alzheimer's disease. *Journal of the American Geriatrics Society, 39,* 39–45.

Burnside, I. (1988). *Nursing and the aged, a self-care approach.* Toronto: McGraw-Hill.

Burton, M. (1982). Reality orientation for the elderly: A critique. *Journal of Advanced Nursing, 7,* 427–433.

Butler, R. (1963). The life review: An interpretation of reminiscence in the aged. *Psychiatry, 26,* 65–76.

Butler, R. (1975). *Why survive? Being old in America.* New York: Harper & Row.

Butler, R., & Gleason, H. (Eds.). (1985). *Productive aging: Enhancing vitality in later life.* New York: Springer Publishing Co.

Byrd, M. (1990, March/April). The use of visual imagery as a mnemonic device for healthy elderly and Alzheimer's disease patients. *American Journal of Alzheimer's Care and Related Disorders & Research,* 10–15.

Calkins, M. (1988). *Design for dementia: Planning environments for the elderly and the confused.* Owings Mills, MD: National Health Publishing.

Campos, R. (1984). Does reality orientation work? *Journal of Gerontological Nursing, 10*(2), 53–64.

Canadian Medical Association. (1987). *Health care for the elderly: Today's challenges, to-morrow's options.* Ottawa, Ontario, Canada: Canadian Medical Association Committee on Health Care of the Elderly.

Carnes, M. (1984). Diagnosis and management of dementia in the elderly. *Physical and Occupational Therapy in Geriatrics, 3,* 11–24.

Carey, B. (1991, March/April). Architecture for Alzheimer's. *In Health,* 18–19.

Carroll, K., & Gray, K. (1981). Memory development: An approach to the mentally impaired elderly in the long-term care setting. *International Journal of Aging and Human Development, 13,* 15–35.

Christenson, M. (1990). Chair design and selection for older adults. *Physical and Occupational Therapy in Geriatrics, 8*(3/4), 67–85.

Christenson, M. (Ed.). (1990). Adaptations of the physical environment to compensate for sensory changes. *Physical and Occupational Therapy in Geriatrics 8*(3/4), 3–30.

Clair, A., & Bernstein, B. (1990). *Music therapy for severely regressed persons with dementia of the Alzheimer's type.* Paper presented at the American Society on Aging Conference, San Francisco.

Clark, P. (1989). The philosophical foundation of empowerment. *Journal of Aging and Health, 1,* 267–285.

Clarkson-Smith, L., & Hartley, A. (1990). The game of bridge as an exercise in working memory and reasoning. *Journal of Gerontology, 45,* 233–238.

Cleary, T., Clamon, C., Price, M., & Shullaw, G. (1988). A reduced stimulation unit: Effects on patients with Alzheimer's disease and related disorders. *The Gerontologist, 28,* 511–514.

Clements, W. (1982). Therapeutic functions of recreation in reminiscence with aging persons. In M. Teague, R. MacWeil, G. Hutzhuser (Eds.), *Perspectives on Leisure and Aging.* Columbia, MO: University of Missouri.

Cockburn, J., & Smith, P. (1991). The relative influence of intelligence and age on everyday memory. *Journal of Gerontology, 46*(1), 31–36.

Cohen, D., & Eisdorfer, C. (1986). *The loss of self.* New York: W.W. Norton.

Cohen, G. (1988). *The brain in human aging.* New York: Springer Publishing Co.

Cohen-Mansfield, J., & Marx, M. (1990). The relationship between sleep disturbances and agitation in a nursing home. *Journal of Aging and Health, 2,* 42–56.

Cohen-Mansfield, J., Marx, M., & Rosenthal, A. (1990). Dementia and agitation in nursing home residents: How are they related? *Psychology and Aging, 5,* 3–8.

Cohen-Mansfield, J., Werner, P., Marx, M., & Freedman, L. (1991). Two studies of pacing in the nursing home. *Journal of Gerontology, 46*(3), 77–83.

Cole, G., & Scheibel, A. (1989). Lectures in normal and abnormal aging of the nervous system: Alzheimer's disease. Course at the University of California, Berkeley.

Coleman, P. (1974). Measuring reminiscence characteristics from conversation as adaptive features of old age. *International Journal of Aging and Human Development, 5,* 281–294.

Conway, K. (1985–86). Coping with stress of medical problems among black and white elderly. *International Journal of Aging and Human Development, 21,* 39–48.

Coons, D. (Ed.). (1991a). *Specialized dementia care units.* Baltimore: Johns Hopkins University Press.

Coons, D. (1991b). Alzheimer's and the environment. Proceedings of a workshop sponsored by the Alzheimer's Society of Nova Scotia, Halifax, Nova Scotia, Canada.

Cooper, B. (1985). A model for implementing color contrast in the environment of the elderly. *American Journal of Occupational Therapy, 39,* 253–258.

Cooper, J., Mungas, D., & Weiler, P. (1990). Relation of cognitive status and abnormal behaviors in Alzheimer's disease. *Journal of the American Geriatrics Society, 38,* 867–870.

Copstead, J. (1980). Effects of touch on self-appraisal and interaction appraisal for permanently institutionalised older adults. *Journal of Gerontological Nursing, 6,* 747–752.

Corcoran, M., & Barrett, D. (1987). Using sensory integration principles with regressed elderly patients. *Occupational Therapy in Health Care, 4,* 119–128.

Corcoran, M., & Gitlin, L. (1991). Environmental influences on behavior of the elderly with dementia: Principles for intervention in the home. *Physical and Occupational Therapy in Geriatrics, 9,* 5–22.

Cousins, N. (1979). *Anatomy of an illness as perceived by the patient.* New York: W.W. Norton.

Crabtree, D., Antrim, L., & Klenke, R. (1990). The effect of activity levels on controlled information processing in older adults. *Activities, Adaptation and Aging, 14*(3), 77–88.

Craik, F., Byrd, M., & Swanson, J. (1987). Patterns of memory loss in three elderly samples. *Psychology and Aging, 2,* 79–86.

Crepeau, E. (1986). *Activity programming for the elderly.* Boston: Little, Brown & Co.

Cristarella, M. (1977). Visual functions of the elderly. *American Journal of Occupational Therapy, 31,* 432–440.

Cumming, E., & Henry, W. (1961). *Growing old: The process of disengagement.* New York: Basic Books.

Dannefer, D. (1989). Human action and its place in theories of aging. *Journal of Aging Studies, 3,* 1–20.

David, D. (1990). Reminiscence, adaptation and social context in old age. *International Journal of Aging and Human Development, 30,* 175–188.

David, P. (1991). Effectiveness of group work with the cognitively impaired older adult. *American Journal of Alzheimer's Care and Related Disorders and Research, 6*(4), 10–16.

Davis, C. (1986). The role of the physical and occupational therapist in caring for the victim with Alzheimer's disease. In *Therapeutic interventions for the person with dementia,* pp. 15–28. New York: Haworth Press.

Davis, L., & Kirkland, M. (Eds.). (1988). *The role of occupational therapy with the elderly.* Rockville, MD: American Occupational Therapy Association, Inc.

Dawson, P., & Reid, D. (1987). Behavioral dimensions of patients at risk of wandering. *The Gerontologist, 27,* 104–107.

Diamond, M. (1984). Cortical change in response to environmental enrichment and impoverishment. In C. Brown (Ed.), *The many facets of touch.* Skillman, NJ: Johnson & Johnson.

Dietsche, L. (1979). Know your community resources: Facilitating the life review through group reminiscence. *Journal of Gerontological Nursing, 5*(4), 43–46.

Dippel, R., & Hutton, J. (Eds.). (1988). *Caring for the Alzheimer patient.* Buffalo, NY: Prometheus Books.

Doble, S. (1991). A home-based model of rehabilitation for individuals with SDAT and their caregivers. *Topics in Geriatric Rehabilitation, 7*(2), 33–44.

Downey, G. (1972). I.C.U. patients and staffs are subject to emotional stress. *Modern Hospital, 118,* 88–91.

Duellman, M., Barris, R., & Kielhofner, G. (1986). Organized activity and the adaptive status of nursing home residents. *American Journal of Occupational Therapy, 40*, 618–622.

Duncan, L. (1987). Beyond eating skills: Lifestyle considerations for adult treatment planning. *Occupational Therapy in Health Care, 4*, 139–147.

Eaton, M., Mitchell-Bonair, I., & Friedman, E. (1986). The effect of touch on nutritional intake of chronic organic brain syndrome patients. *Journal of Gerontology, 41*, 611–616.

Edelson, J., & Lyons, W. (1985). *Institutional care of the mentally impaired elderly.* New York: Van Nostrand.

Edwards, D., Baun, C., & Deuel, R. (1991). Constructional apraxia in Alzheimer's disease: Contributions to functional loss. *Physical Therapy and Occupational Therapy in Geriatrics, 9*, 53–68.

Eimer, M. (1989). Management of the behavioral symptoms associated with dementia. *Primary Care, 16*, 431–450.

Ellison, K. (1981). Working with the elderly in a life review group. *Journal of Gerontological Nursing, 7*, 537–541.

Emery, O., & Breslau, L. (1988). The problem of naming in SDAT: A relative deficit. *Experimental Aging Research, 14*(4), 181–193.

Erber, J. (1989). Young and old adult's appraisal of memory failures in young and old adult target persons. *Journal of Gerontology, 44*, 170–175.

Erber, J., Galt, D., & Botwinick, J. (1985). Age differences in the effects of contextual framework and word familiarity on episodic memory. *Experimental Aging Research, 11*, 101–103.

Erikson, E. (1953). *Childhood and society* (2nd ed.). New York: W.W. Norton & Co.

Erikson, E., Erikson, J., & Kivnick, H. (1986). *Vital involvement in old age.* New York: W.W. Norton & Co.

Ernst, P., Beran, B., Safford, F., & Kleinhauz, M. (1978). Isolation and the symptoms of chronic brain syndrome. *The Gerontologist, 18*, 468–474.

Ernst, P., Badash, D., Beran, B., Kosovsky, R., Lerner, K., & Kleinhauz, M. (1978). Sensory stimulation of elderly patients: Preliminary report on the treatment of patients with chronic brain syndrome in an old age home. *Israel Annals of Psychiatry and Related Disciplines, 16*, 315–326.

Estes, C., & Binney, E. (1989). The biomedicalization of aging: Dangers and dilemmas. *The Gerontologist, 39*, 587–596.

Evans, D., Funkenstein, H., Albert, M., Scherr, P., Cook, N., Chown, M., Herbert, L., Hennekens, C., & Taylor, J. (1989). Prevalence of Alzheimer's disease in a community population of older persons. *Journal of American Medical Association, 262*, 2551–2556.

Everitt, D., Fields, D., Soumerai, S., & Avorn, J. (1991). Resident behavior and staff distress in the nursing home. *Journal of the American Geriatrics Society, 39*, 792–798.

Fabiano, L. (1984). *Working with the frail elderly: Beyond physical disability.* Seagrave, Ontario, Canada: Education and Consulting Service for Health Care.

Falk-Kessler, J., Momich, C., & Perel, S. (1991). Therapeutic factors in occupational therapy groups. *American Journal of Occupational Therapy, 45*, 59–66.

Fallot, R. (1980). The impact on mood of verbal reminiscing in later adulthood. *International Journal of Aging and Human Development, 10*, 385–399.

Feil, N. (1988). *Validation: The Feil method.* Cleveland, OH: Edward Feil Productions.

Fernie, B., Brown, J., & Fernie, G. (1990). A survey of attitudes toward group programs for Alzheimer's disease patients. *American Journal of Alzheimer's Care and Related Disorders and Research, 5*(6), 27–31.

Finch, C., & Schneider, E. (Eds.). (1985). *Handbook of the biology of aging* (2nd ed.). New York: Van Nostrand Reinhold.

Finlay, O., Bayles, T., Rosen, C., & Milling, J. (1983). Effects of chair design, age and cognitive status on mobility. *Age and Ageing,12*, 329–335.

Folsom, J. (1968). Reality orientation for the elderly mental patient. *Journal of Geriatric Psychiatry, 1*, 291–307.

Folsom, J., Boies, B., & Pommerenck, K. (1978). Life adjustment techniques for use with the dysfunctional elderly. *Aged Care and Services Review, 1*(4), 1–12.

Folstein, M., Folstein, S., & McHugh, P. (1975). Mini-mental state: A practical method for grading the cognitive state of patients for the clinician. *Journal of Psychiatric Research, 12*, 189–198.

Fox, P. (1989). From senility to Alzheimer's disease: The rise of the Alzheimer's disease movement. *The Millbank Quarterly, 67*(1), 58–102.

Foy, S., & Mitchell, M. (1990). Factors contributing to learned helplessness in the institutionalized aged: A literature review. *Physical & Occupational Therapy in Geriatrics, 9*(2), 1–2.

Freeman, S. (1987). *Activities and approaches for Alzheimer's.* Knoxville, TN: The Whitfield Agency.

Froehlich, J., & Nelson, D. (1986). Affective meanings of life review through activities and discussion. *American Journal of Occupational Therapy, 40,* 27–33.

Fromholt, P., & Larsen, S. (1991). Autobiographical memory in normal aging and primary degenerative dementia (dementia of Alzheimer's type). *Journal of Gerontology, 46*(3), 85–91.

Fry, P. (1983). Structured and unstructured reminiscence training and depression among the elderly. *Clinical Gerontologist, 1*(3), 15–37.

Garber, J., & Seligman, M. (1980). *Human helplessness: Theory and applications.* New York: Academic Press.

Gekoski, W., & Knox, V.J. (1990). Ageism or healthism? *Journal of Aging and Health, 2,* 15–27.

Gifford, B. (1990). Report of the Ford Foundation's national commission on testing and public policy. Washington, DC: U.S. Government Printing Office.

Glass, F. (1990). Auditory changes and aging. Lecture. Course on Motor and Sensory Changes in Aging. University of California at Berkeley.

Glickstein, J. (1988). *Therapeutic interventions in Alzheimer's disease: A program of functional communication skills for ADL.* Gaithersburg, MD: Aspen Publishers, Inc.

Glickstein, J., & Neustadt, G. (1992). *Reimbursable geriatric service delivery: A functional maintenance therapy system.* Gaithersburg, MD: Aspen Publishers, Inc.

Goldwasser, N., Auerbach, S., & Harkins, S. (1987). Cognitive, affective and behavioral effects of reminiscence group therapy on demented elderly. *International Journal of Aging and Human Development, 25,* 209–222.

Goodwin, J. (1989). Knowledge about aging among physicians. *Journal of Aging and Health, 1,* 234–243.

Gottfreid, A., & Gaiter, J. (Eds.). (1984). *Infant stress under intensive care: Environmental neonatalogy.* Baltimore: University Park Press.

Green, L. (1991). Humor and light-hearted activities. In D. Coons (Ed.), *Specialized dementia care units.* Baltimore: Johns Hopkins University Press.

Greenblatt, F. (1988). *Therapeutic recreation for long-term care facilities.* New York: Human Sciences Press.

Greene, R. (1982). Life review: A technique for clarifying family roles in adulthood. *Clinical Gerontologist, 1*(2), 59–67.

Greenough, W. (1984). Brain storage of sensory information in development and adulthood. In C. Brown (Ed.), *The many facets of touch.* Skillman, NJ: Johnson & Johnson.

Gregory, I., & Smeltzer, D. (Eds.). (1983). *Psychiatry.* Toronto: Little, Brown & Co.

Gropper-Katz, E. (1987). Reality orientation research. *Journal of Gerontological Nursing, 13*(8), 13–18.

Gross, D. (1990). Communication and the elderly. *Physical and Occupational Therapy in Geriatrics, 9,* 49–64.

Guthrie, D., & Arnsteen, K. (1986). *Grampa doesn't know me.* New York: Human Sciences Press.

Gwyther, L. (1985). *Care of Alzheimer's patients: A manual for nursing home staff.* Chicago: Alzheimer's Association and the American Health Care Association.

Haber, E., & Short-Degraff, M. (1990). Intergenerational programming for an increasingly age-segregated society. *Activities, Adaptation and Aging, 14*(3), 35–50.

Habegger, C., & Blieszner, R. (1990). Personal and social aspects of reminiscence: An exploratory study of neglected dimensions. *Activities, Adaptation and Aging, 14*(4), 21–38.

Hachinski, V. (1983). Differential diagnosis of Alzheimer's disease: Multi-infarct dementia. In B. Reisburg (Ed.), *Alzheimer's disease.* New York: The Free Press.

Haight, B. (1988). The therapeutic role of a structured life review process in homebound elderly subjects. *Journal of Gerontology, 43,* 40–44.

Haight, B. (1991). Reminiscing: The state of the art as a basis for practice. *International Journal of Aging and Human Development, 33,* 1–32.

Hames-Hahn, C., & Llorens, L. (1989). Impact of a multisensory occupational therapy program on components of self-feeding behavior in the elderly. In E. Taira (Ed.), *Promoting Quality Long Term Care for Older Persons,* New York: Haworth Press.

Hancock, B. (1987). *Social work with older people.* Englewood Cliffs, NJ: Prentice Hall.

Hanley-Dunn, P., & McIntosh, J. (1984). Meaningfulness and recall of names by young and old adults. *Journal of Gerontology, 39,* 583–585.

Harrison, D., & Law, M. (1985) 'Services' for the elderly. *British Journal of Occupational Therapy, 48,* 181–183.

Harwood, K. (1989). The effects of an occupational therapy reminiscence group: A single case study.

Physical and Occupational Therapy in Geriatrics, 7(4), 43–57.

Hastings, R. (1986). Let's get together: Group activities in long term care. *Activities, Adaptation and Aging, 9*, 71–76.

Hatter, J., & Nelson, D. (1987). Altruism and task participation in the elderly. *American Journal of Occupational Therapy, 41*, 379–381.

Havighurst, R., & Glasser, R. (1972). An exploratory study of reminiscence. *Journal of Gerontology, 27*, 245–253.

Heacock, P., Walton, C., Beck, C., & Mercer, S. (1991). Caring for the cognitively impaired: Reconceptualizing disability and rehabilitation. *Journal of Gerontological Nursing, 17*(3), 22–26.

Hegeman, C., & Tobin, S. (1988). Enhancing the autonomy of mentally impaired nursing home residents. *The Gerontologist, 28* (Suppl.), 71–75.

Heinemann, A., Colorez, A., Frank, S., & Taylor, D. (1988). Leisure activity participation of elderly individuals with low vision. *The Gerontologist, 28*, 181–184.

Helen, C. (1990). Eating: An Alzheimer's activity. *American Journal of Alzheimer's Care and Related Disorders and Research, 5*(2), 5–9.

Hendy, H. (1987). Effects of pet and/or people visits on nursing home residents. *International Journal of Aging and Human Development, 25*, 279–291.

Henig, R. (1988). *The myth of senility.* Glenview, IL: American Association of Retired Persons.

Hertfelder, S., & Crispen, C. (Eds.). (1990). *Private practice: Strategies for success—a comprehensive guide to starting, promoting & building your own private practice.* Rockville, MD: American Occupational Therapy Association, Inc.

Hiatt, L. (1987a). Environmental design and mentally impaired older people. In H. Altman (Ed.), *Alzheimer's disease: Problems, prospects and perspectives.* New York: Plenum Press.

Hiatt, L. (1987b). Supportive design for people with memory impairments. In A. Kalicki (Ed.), *Confronting Alzheimer's disease.* Owings Mills, MD: National Health Publishing.

Hiatt, L., Brieff, R., Horwitz, J., & McQueen, C. (1982). *What are friends for? Self-help groups for older persons with sensory loss: The USE program.* New York: American Foundation for the Blind.

Hill, R., Sheikh, J., & Yesavage, J. (1989). Pretraining enhances mnemonic training in elderly adults. *Experimental Aging Research, 14*(4), 207–211.

Hoffman, S., Platt, C., Barry, K., & Hamill, L. (1985). When language fails: Nonverbal communication abilities of the demented. In J. Hutton, & A. Kenny (Eds.), *Senile dementia of the Alzheimer type.* New York: Alan R. Liss, Inc.

Hoffman, S., Platt, C., & Barry, K. (1988). Comforting the confused. *American Journal of Alzheimer's Care and Related Disorders and Research, 3*(1), 25–27.

Holden, U., & Woods, R. (1982). *Reality orientation.* Edinburgh, Scotland: Churchill Livingstone.

Holland, L. (1987). Life review and communication therapy for dementia patients. *Clinical Gerontologist, 6*, 62–65.

Howe, C. (1988). Selected social gerontology theories and older adult leisure involvement: A review of the literature. *Journal of Applied Gerontology, 6*, 448–463.

Huang, L., Cartwright, W., & Hu, T. (1988). The economic cost of senile dementia in the United States, 1985. *Public Health Reports, 103*, 3–7.

Hughston, G., & Merriam, S. (1982). Reiminiscence: A non-formal technique for improving cognitive functioning in the aged. *International Journal of Aging and Human Development, 15*, 139–149.

Hultsch, D., & Dixon, R. (1983). The role of pre-experimental knowledge in text processing in adulthood. *Experimental Aging Research, 9*, 17–22.

Hunt, L. (1988). Continuity of care maximizes autonomy of the elderly. *American Journal of Occupational Therapy, 42*, 391–393.

Huss, J. (1976). Touch with care or a caring touch? *American Journal of Occupational Therapy, 31*, 11–18.

Hussian, R. (1984). Behavioral geriatrics. *Progress in Behavior Modification, 16*, 159–183.

Hussian, R. (1988). Modification of behaviors in dementia via stimulus manipulation. *Clinical Gerontologist, 8*, 37–43.

Hussian, R., & Brown, D. (1987). Use of two-dimensional grid patterns to limit hazardous ambulation in demented patients. *Journal of Gerontology, 42*, 558–560.

Hutton, J., & Kenny, A. (Eds.). (1985). *Senile dementia of the Alzheimer type.* New York: Alan R. Liss, Inc.

Hyde, J. (1989). The physical environment and the care of Alzheimer's patients: An experimental survey of Massachusetts' Alzheimer's units. *American Journal of Alzheimer's Care and Related Disorders and Research, 4*(3), 36–4.

Hyland, D., & Ackerman, A. (1988). Reminiscence and autobiographical memory in the study of the personal past. *Journal of Gerontology, 43* (2), 35–39.

Ingersoll, G., & Silverman, A. (1978). Comparative group psychotherapy for the aged. *The Gerontologist, 19,* 201–206.

Jackson, C., Pollard, J., & Kansky, E. (1962). The application of findings from experimental sensory deprivation to cases of clinical sensory deprivation. *American Journal of Medical Science, 243,* 558–563.

Jackson, M., Drugovich, M., Fretwell, M., Spector, W., Sternberg, J., & Rosenstein, R. (1989). Prevalence and correlates of disruptive behavior in the nursing home. *Journal of Aging and Health, 1,* 349–369.

Jagust, W., Pfeffer, R., Scheibel, A., & Terry, R. (1989). Lectures in normal and abnormal aging of the human nervous system: Alzheimer's disease. Berkeley, CA: University of California.

Jarvik, L. (1988). Aging of the brain: How can we prevent it? *The Gerontologist, 28,* 739–747.

Jarvik, L., & Winograd, C., (Eds.). (1988). *Treatments for the Alzheimer patient.* New York: Springer Publishing Co.

Jazwiecki, I. (1988). Long-term care for the elderly in the United States. In T. Schwab (Ed.), *Caring for an aging world: International models for long-term care, financing and delivery.* New York: McGraw-Hill.

Johnson, C. (1989). Sociological intervention through developing low stimulus Alzheimer's wings in nursing homes. *American Journal of Alzheimer's Care and Related Disorders and Research, 4*(4), 33–41.

Jones, G., & Clark, P. (1984). The use of memory 'recall' on a psychogeriatric ward. *British Journal of Occupational Therapy,47,* 315–316.

Judd, M. (1983). *Keep in touch.* Winnipeg, Manitoba, Canada: Author.

Kalicki, A. (Ed.). (1987). *Confronting Alzheimer's disease.* Owings Mills, MD: National Health Publishing; and Washington, DC: American Association of Homes for the Aging.

Kane, R., & Kane, R. (1981). The extent and nature of public responsibility for long term care. In J. Meltzer, F. Farrow, & H. Richman (Eds.), *Policy options in long term care.* Chicago: University of Chicago Press.

Kane, R., & Kane, R. (1985). *A will and a way: What the United States can learn from Canada about caring for the elderly.* New York: Columbia House Press.

Kane, R., & Kane, R. (1987). *Long-term care: Principles, programs and policies.* New York: Springer Publishing Co.

Kane, R., Bell, R., Hosek, S., Riegler, S., & Kane, R. (1983). *Outcome-based reimbursement for nursing home care.* Santa Monica, CA: The Rand Corporation (National Center for Health Services Research).

Kaplan, K. (1988). *Directive group therapy: Innovative mental health treatment.* Thorofare, NJ: Slack Inc.

Karlinksy, H., & Sutherland, A. (Eds.). (1990). Alzheimer's disease and environmental design. *American Journal of Alzheimer's Care and Related Disorders and Research, 5*(3), 3–40.

Kart, C., & Manard, B. (Eds.). (1981). *Aging in America: Readings in social gerontology* (3rd ed.). Palo Alto, CA: Mayfield.

Kartman, L. (1984). Music hath charms. *Journal of Gerontological Nursing, 10*(6), 20–24.

Katzman, R., & Jackson, J. (1991). Alzheimer disease: Basic and clinical advances. *Journal of the American Geriatrics Society, 39,* 516–525.

Keller, M., Leventhal, E., & Larson, B. (1989). Aging: The lived experience. *International Journal of Aging and Human Development, 29,* 67–82.

Kibbee, P., & Lackey, D. (1982, October 29–31). The past as therapy: An experience in an acute setting. *Journal of Practical Nursing.*

Kibbey, M. (1988). *My grammy.* Minneapolis, MN: Carolrhoda Books.

Kielhofner, G. (1983). *Health through occupation: Theory and practice in occupational therapy.* Philadelphia: F.A. Davis.

Kiernat, J. (1979). The use of life review activity with confused nursing home residents. *American Journal of Occupational Therapy, 33*(5), 306–310.

Kiernat, J. (1983a). Environment: The hidden modality. *Physical and Occupational Therapy in Geriatrics, 2*(1), 3–12.

Kiernat, J. (1983b). Retrospection as a life span concept. *Physical and Occupational Therapy in Geriatrics, 3*(2), 35–48.

King, L., & Parachek, J. (1986). *Parachek geriatric rating scale and treatment manual.* Phoenix, AZ: Center for Neurodevelopmental Studies.

Kirasic, K. (1989). The effects of age and environmental familiarity on adults' spatial problem-solving performance: Evidence of a hometown advantage. *Experimental Aging Research, 15,* 181–187.

Kirchman, M., Reichenbach, V., & Giambalvo, B. (1982). Preventive activities and services for the well elderly. *American Journal of Occupational Therapy, 36,* 236–242.

Kite, M., & Johnson, B. (1988). Attitudes toward older and younger adults: A meta-analysis. *Psychology and Aging, 3,* 233–244.

Knopman, D., & Sawyer-DeMaris, S. (1990). Practical approach to managing behavioral problems in dementia patients. *Geriatrics, 45*(4), 27–35.

Knowlton, R., Katzenstein, P., Moskowitz, R., Weaver, E., Malemud, C., Pathria, M., Jimenez, S., & Prockop, D. (1990). Genetic linkage of polymorphism in the type II procollagen gene to primary osteoarthritis associated with mild chondrodysplasia. *New England Journal of Medicine, 322*, 526–530.

Koch, K. (1977). *I never told anybody: Teaching poetry writing in a nursing home.* New York: Random House.

Koenig, H., George, L., & Siegler, I. (1988). The use of religion and other emotion-regulating coping strategies among older adults. *The Gerontologist, 28*, 303–310.

Koenig, H., Kale, J., & Ferrel, C. (1988). Religion and well-being in later life. *The Gerontologist, 28*, 18–28.

Kolasa, K., Schmidt, C., & Bartlett, J. (1989). Feeding Alzheimer's patients. *American Journal of Alzheimer's Care and Related Disorders and Research, 4*(3), 17–20.

Kovach, C. (1990). Promise and problems in reminiscence research. *Journal of Gerontological Nursing, 16*(4), 10–14.

Kral, V. (1978). Benign senescent forgetfulness. In R. Katzman, R. Terry, & K. Bick (Eds.), *Alzheimer's disease: Senile dementia and related disorders.* New York, Raven Press.

Langer, E., & Benevento, A. (1978). Self-induced dependence. *Journal of Personality and Social Psychology, 36*, 886–893.

Lappe, J. (1987). Reminiscing: The life review therapy. *Journal of Gerontological Nursing, 13*(4), 12–16.

Larson, E., & Bruce, R. (1986). Exercise and aging. *Annals of Internal Medicine, 105*, 783–785.

Lawton, M. (1980). *Environment and aging.* Los Angeles: Brooks/Cole.

Lawton, M. (1981). Sensory deprivation and the effect of the environment on the patient with senile dementia. In N. Miller, & G. Cohen (Eds.), *Clinical aspects of Alzheimer's disease and senile dementia.* New York: Raven Press.

Lawton, M. (1983). Environment and other determinants of well-being in older people. *The Gerontologist, 23*, 349–357.

Lawton, M. (1985). Activities and leisure. In *Annual Review of Gerontology and Geriatrics* (Vol. 5). New York: Springer Publishing Co.

Lawton, M., Windley, P., & Byerts, T. (Eds.). (1982). *Aging and the environment: Theoretical approaches.* New York: Springer Publishing Co.

Lazarus, L. (1976). A program for the elderly at a private psychiatric hospital. *The Gerontologist, 16*, 125–131.

Learman, L., Avorn, J., Everitt, D., & Rosenthal, R. (1990). Pygmalion in the nursing home: The effects of caregiver expectations on patient outcomes. *Journal of the American Geriatrics Society, 38*, 797–803.

Leitner, M., & Leitner, S. (1985). *Leisure in later life: A sourcebook for the provision of recreational services for elders.* New York: Haworth Press.

Leng, N. (1982). Behavioral treatment of the elderly. *Age and Aging, 4*, 235–243.

LeSage, J., Slimmer, L., Lopez, M., & Ellor, J. (1990). Learned helplessness. *Journal of Gerontological Nursing, 15*(5), 8–15.

Lesser, J., Lazarus, L., Frankl, R., & Havasg, S. (1981). Reminiscence group therapy with psychotic geriatric inpatients. *The Gerontologist, 21*, 291–296.

Leverett, M. (1991). Approaches to problem behaviors in dementia. *Physical and Occupational Therapy in Geriatrics, 9*, 93–106.

Levy, L. (1990). Activity, social role retention, and the multiply disabled aged: Strategies for intervention. *Physical and Occupational Therapy in Geriatrics, 8*(1/2), 1–30.

Lewis, C. (1971). Reminiscing and self-concept in old age. *Journal of Gerontology, 26*, 240–243.

Lewis, S. (1989). *Eldercare in occupational therapy.* Thorofare, NJ: Slack Inc.

Lewis, T. (1990, May 2). Alzheimer's and architecture: A search for order. *The New York Times.*

Libow, L. (1978). Senile dementia and pseudodementias. In C. Eisdorfer, & R. Freidel (Eds.), *Cognitive and emotional disturbance in the elderly.* Chicago: Year Book Medical Publishers.

Lieberman, M., & Falk, G. (1971). The remembered past as a source of data for research on the life cycle. *International Journal of Aging and Human Development, 14*, 132–141.

Lindeman, R., Tobin, J., & Shock, N. (1985). Longitudinal studies on the rate of decline of renal function with age. *Journal of the American Geriatrics Society, 33*, 278.

Lindenmuth, G., & Moose, B. (1990). Improving cognitive abilities of elderly Alzheimer's patients with intense exercise therapy. *American Journal of Alzheimer's Care and Related Disorders and Research, 56*(1), 31–33.

Lipowski, Z. (1987). Delirium (acute confusional states). *Journal of the American Medical Association, 258*, 1789–1792.

Liu, L., Gauthier, L., & Gauthier, S. (1991). Spatial disorientation in persons with early senile dementia of the Alzheimer type. *American Journal of Occupational Therapy, 45*, 67–74.

Lo Gerfo, M. (1980). Three ways of reminiscence in theory and practice. *International Journal of Aging and Development, 12*, 39–48.

Lonergrin, E. (1990). The aging nervous system: A perspective. Paper presented at Neurological Grand Rounds, University of California at San Francisco.

Lowy, L. (1989). Independence and dependence in aging: A new balance. *Journal of Gerontological Social Work, 13*(3/4), 133–146.

Lyman, K. (1989). Bringing the social back in: A critique of the biomedicalization of aging. *The Gerontologist, 29*, 597–605.

MacDonald, M., & Settin, J. (1978). Reality orientation vs. sheltered workshops as treatment for the institutionalized aged. *Journal of Gerontology, 33*, 416–421.

MacDonald, M., Davidowitz, J., Gimbel, B., & Foley, L. (1982). Physical and social environmental reprogramming as treatment for psychogeriatric patients. *International Journal of Behavioral Geriatrics, 1*, 15–32.

Mace, N. (Ed.). (1990). *Dementia care: Patient, family and community.* Baltimore: Johns Hopkins University Press.

Mace, N., & Rabins, P. (1981). *The 36-hour day.* Baltimore: Johns Hopkins University Press.

Maddox, G., & Busse, E. (Eds.). (1987). *Aging: the universal human experience.* New York: Springer Publishing Co.

Maguire, G. (1985). *Care of the elderly: A health approach.* Boston: Little, Brown & Co.

Maloney, C., & Daily, T. (1986). An eclectic group program for nursing home residents with dementia. *Physical and Occupational Therapy in Geriatrics, 5*, 55–80.

Manfredi, C., & Pickett, M. (1987). Perceived stressful situations and coping strategies used by the elderly. *Journal of Community Health Nursing, 4*, 99–110.

Marino-Schorn, J. (1985/1986). Morale, work and leisure in retirement. *Physical and Occupational Therapy in Geriatrics, 4*(2), 49–59.

Martin, D., & Fuller, W. (1991). Spirituality and aging: Activity key to "holiest" health care. *Activities, Adaptation and Aging, 13*, 37–50.

Marx, M., Cohen-Mansfield, J., & Werner, P. (1990). Agitation and falls in institutionalized elderly persons. *Journal of Applied Gerontology, 9*, 106–117.

Maslow, A. (1970). *Motivation and personality.* New York: Harper & Row.

Maslow, K. (1990). Formal long-term care services and settings. In N. Mace (Ed.), *Dementia care: Patient, family & community.* Baltimore: Johns Hopkins University Press.

Mayers, K., & Griffin, M. (1990). The play project: Use of stimulus objects with demented patients. *Journal of Gerontological Nursing, 16*(1) 32–37.

Mayeux, R., Stern, Y., & Spanton, S. (1985). Heterogeneity in dementia of the Alzheimer type: Evidence of subgroups. *Neurology, 35*, 453–461.

McCracken, A., & Fitzwater, E. (1990). Assessment to guide placement, plan care, and track change in individuals with Alzheimer's disease. *American Journal of Alzheimer's Care and Related Disorders and Research, 5*(1), 24–30.

McDuffie, W., & Whiteman, J. (1989). *Intergenerational activities program handbook* (3rd ed.). Binghamton, NY: Broome County Child Development Council.

McEvoy, C., & Patterson, R. (1986). Behavioral treatment of deficit skills in dementia patients. *The Gerontologist, 26*, 475–478.

McGrowder-Lin, R., & Bhatt, A. (1988). A wanderer's lounge program for nursing home residents with Alzheimer's disease. *The Gerontologist, 28*, 607–609.

McKhann, G., Drachman, D., Folstein, M., Katzman, R., Price, D., & Stadlan, E. (1984). Clinical diagnosis of Alzheimer's disease: Report of the NINCDS-ADRDA work group under the auspices of Department of Health and Human Services Task Force on Alzheimer's disease. *Neurology, 34*, 939–944.

McMahon, A., & Rhudick, P. (1967). Reminiscing: Adaptational significance in the aged. *Archives of General Psychiatry, 10*, 292–299.

McPherson, B. (1983). *Aging as a social process.* Toronto: Butterworth.

Meltzer, J., Farrow, F., & Richman, H. (Eds.). (1981). *Policy options in long-term care.* Chicago: University of Chicago Press.

Merriam, S. (1980). The concept and function of reminiscence: A review of the research. *The Gerontologist, 20*, 604–609.

Merriam, S. (1989). The structure of simple reminiscence. *The Gerontologist, 29*, 761–767.

Merriam, S., & Cross, L. (1982). Adulthood and reminiscence: A descriptive study. *Educational Gerontology, 8*, 275–290.

Merzenich, M. (1984). Functional "maps" of skin sensations. In C. Brown (Ed.), *The many facets of touch.* Skillman, NJ: Johnson & Johnson.

Michaelson, E., Norberg, A., & Norberg, B. (1987, March/April). A quality of life issue: Feeding methods for demented patients in end stage of life. *Geriatric Nursing*, 69–73.

Mitchell, D. (1988). Memory and language deficits in Alzheimer's disease. In R. Dippel, & J. Hutton (Eds.), *Caring for the Alzheimer's patient.* Buffalo, NY: Prometheus Books.

Mitchell, J. (1990). Attitudes and the disabled elderly. *Geriatric Rehabilitation Preview, 2*(2), 1, 7.

Molinari, V., & Reichlin, R. (1984–85). Life review reminiscence in the elderly: A review of the literature. *International Journal of Aging and Human Development, 20*, 81–92.

Moore, J. (1991). *Neurosciences applied to practice: Psychogeriatrics.* Manual from a course presented in January 1991. University of Western Ontario, London, Ontario, Canada.

Morganti, J., Nehrke, M., & Hulicka, I. (1990). Latitude of choice and well-being in institutionalized and noninstitutionalized elderly. *Experimental Aging Research, 16*(1), 25–33.

Mosher-Ashley, P. (1987). Procedural and methodological parameters in behavioral-gerontological research: A review. *International Journal of Aging and Human Development, 24*, 189–229.

Moss, R., & Miles, S. (1987). AIDS and the geriatrician. *Journal of the American Geriatrics Society, 35*, 460–464.

Mugford, R., & M'Comisky, J. (1975). Some recent work on the psychotherapeutic value of cage birds with old people. In R. Anderson (Ed.), *Pet animals and society.* New York: Macmillan.

Mullan, R., & Cook-Deegan, M. (1990). Changing public policy for dementia care. In N. Mace (Ed.), *Dementia care: patient, family & community.* Baltimore: Johns Hopkins University Press.

Munroe, H. (1988, September). Scaling the pyramid: A framework for interventions in nursing homes. Paper presented at the Atlantic Region conference of Occupational Therapists, St. John's, Newfoundland, Canada.

Munson, P. (Ed.). (1991). *Designing facilities for people with dementia.* (Catalog No. H39-200/1991E). Ottawa, Ontario, Canada: Department of National Health and Welfare.

Murden, R., McRae, T., Kaner, S., & Bucknam, M. (1991). Mini-mental state exam scores vary with education in blacks and whites. *Journal of the American Geriatrics Society, 39*, 149–155.

Myton, C., & Allen, J. (1991). Organic mental disorder, self-care deficit and perceived severity: Implications for care and family support. *American Journal of Alzheimer's Care and Related Disorders and Research, 6*(2), 19–23.

Namazi, K., Rosner, T., & Calkins, M. (1989). Visual barriers to prevent ambulatory Alzheimer's patients from exiting through an emergency door. *The Gerontologist, 29*, 699–702.

National Institutes of Health Consensus Development Conference Statement (NIHCD). (1987). *Differential diagnosis of dementing diseases* (1987-181-296: 61128). Washington, DC: U.S. Government Printing Office.

National Resource Centre on Health Promotion and Aging. (1991a). Exercise can benefit everyone. *Perspectives in Health Promotion and Aging, 6*(2), 1, 3, 6.

National Resource Centre on Health Promotion and Aging. (1991b). Fall prevention through health promotion. *Perspectives in Health Promotion and Aging, 6*(3), 1–3.

Negley, E., & Manley, J. (1990). Environmental interventions in assaultive behavior. *Journal of Gerontological Nursing, 16*(3), 29–33.

Nelson, V. (1988). *Always, gramma.* New York: G.P. Putnam's Sons.

Nolen, N., & Garrard, J. (1988). Predicting dependent feeding behaviors in the institutionalized elderly. *Journal of Nutrition for the Elderly, 7*(3), 17–25.

Office of Technology Assessment (OTA), U.S. Congress. (1987). *Losing a million minds: Confronting the tragedy of Alzheimer's disease and other dementias* (OTA—BA-323). Washington, DC: U.S. Government Printing Office.

Oliveria, B. (1977). *Understanding old people: Patterns of reminiscing in elderly people and their relationship to life satisfaction.* Knoxville, TN: University of Tennessee Dissertation.

O'Quin, J., O'Dell, & Burnett, R. (1982). Effects of brief behavioral intervention on verbal interactions of socially inactive nursing home residents. *International Journal of Behavioral Geriatrics, 1*, 3–10.

Ott, F., Readman, T., & Backman, C. (1990). Meal times of the institutionalized elderly: A literature review. *Canadian Journal of Occupational Therapy, 57*, 261–267.

Ott, F., Readman, T., & Backman, C. (1991). Mealtimes of the institutionalized elderly: A quality of life issue. *Canadian Journal of Occupational Therapy, 58,* 7–16.

Ottenbacher, K. (1984). *Evaluating clinical change: Strategies for occupational and physical therapists.* Baltimore: Williams & Wilkins.

Paire, J., & Karney, R. (1984). The effectiveness of sensory stimulation for geropsychiatric inpatients. *American Journal of Occupational Therapy, 38,* 505–509.

Palmer, R. (1990). 'Failure to thrive' in the elderly: Diagnosis and management. *Geriatrics, 45*(9), 47–55.

Parent, L. (1978). Effects of a low-stimulus environment on behavior. *American Journal of Occupational Therapy, 32,* 19–25.

Parsons, C. (1986). Group reminiscence therapy and levels of depression in the elderly. *Nurse Practitioner, 11,* 68–76.

Patterson, R., & Jackson, G. (1980). Behavior modification with the elderly. In M. Hersen, R. Eisler, & P. Miller (Eds.), *Progress in behavior modification* (Vol. 9). New York: Academic Press.

Peer, S. (1976). Therapeutic programs for the long-term care geriatric patient. *Journal of Gerontological Nursing, 2,* 24–26.

Perket, S. (1986). The role of occupational therapy in planning dining programs in institutions for the frail elderly. *Occupational Therapy in Health Care,* 39–48.

Perkins, K., Rapp, S., Carlson, C., & Wallace, C. (1986). A behavioral intervention to increase exercise among nursing home residents. *The Gerontologist, 26,* 479–481.

Perrotta, P., & Meacham, J. (1981–1982). Can a reminiscing intervention alter depression and self-esteem? *International Journal of Aging and Human Development, 14,* 23–30.

Perschbacher, R. (1984). An application of reminiscence in an activity setting. *The Gerontologist, 24,* 343–345.

Perschbacher, R. (1991). Federally mandated nursing home resident assessment: Implications for activity professionals. *Activities, Adaptation and Aging, 13*(1), 21–29.

Peter, L., & Dana, B. (1982). *The laughter prescription.* New York: Ballantine Books.

Pfeffer, R. (1989). Population studies of Alzheimer's disease. Lecture course entitled "Normal and abnormal aging of the human nervous system: Alzheimer's disease." University of California, Berkeley.

Pfeffer, R., Afifi, A., & Chance, J. (1987). Prevalence of Alzheimer's disease in a retirement community. *American Journal of Epidemiology, 125,* 420–436.

Phillipson, M., Moranville, J., Jeste, D., & Harris, M. (1990). Antipsychotics. *Clinics in Geriatric Medicine, 6*(2), 411–422.

Pietrukowicz, M., & Johnson, M. (1991). Using life histories to individualize nursing home staff attitudes toward residents. *The Gerontologist, 31,* 102–106.

Posthuma, B. (1989). *Small groups in therapy settings: Process and leadership.* Boston: Little, Brown & Co.

Powell, L., Felce, D., Jenkins, J., & Lunt, B. (1979). Increasing engagement in a home for the elderly by providing an indoor gardening activity. *Behavior Research and Therapy, 17,* 127–135.

Powell-Proctor, L., & Miller, E. (1982). Reality orientation: A critical appraisal. *British Journal of Psychiatry, 140,* 457–463.

Prebis, J., & Whitesell, R. (1990, April). Consider companion animals: The pet as panacea. Paper presented at the American Society on Aging Conference, San Francisco, CA.

Rader, J. (1987). A comprehensive staff approach to problem wandering. *The Gerontologist, 27,* 756–770.

Rapoport, S. (1983). *Brain in aging and dementia* (NIH Publication No. 83-2625). Bethesda, MD: Clinical Center Office of Clinical Reports and Inquiries.

Rapp, S., & Davis, K. (1989). Geriatric depression: Physicians knowledge, perceptions and diagnostic practices. *The Gerontologist, 29,* 252–257.

Rattenbury, C., & Stones, M. (1989). A controlled evaluation of reminiscence and current topics discussion groups in a nursing home context. *The Gerontologist, 29,* 768–771.

Ray, R., & Heppe, G. (1986). Older adult happiness: The contributions of activity breadth and intensity. *Physical and Occupational Therapy in Geriatrics, 4,* 31–41.

Reed, B., Jagust, W., & Seab, J. (1989). Mental status as a predictor of daily function in progressive dementia. *The Gerontologist, 29,* 804–807.

Reichenback, V., & Kirchman, M. (1991). Effects of a multi-strategy program upon elderly with organic brain syndrome. *Physical and Occupational Therapy in Geriatrics, 9,* 131–151.

Reifler, B., Larson, E., Teri, L., & Poulson, M. (1986). Dementia of the Alzheimer's type and depression. *Journal of the American Geriatrics Society, 34,* 855–859.

Reisburg, B. (Ed.). (1983). *Alzheimer's disease: The standard reference.* New York: The Free Press.

Revere, V., & Tobin, S. (1980–1981). Myth and reality: The older person's relationship to his past. *International Journal of Aging and Human Development, 12,* 15–26.

Rheaume, Y., Riley, M., & Volicer, L. (1988). Meeting nutritional needs of Alzheimer patients who pace constantly. *Journal of Nutrition for the Elderly, 7*(1), 43–52.

Rinzler, C. (1990, June 5). Can your diet prevent wrinkles? Foods that fight aging. *Family Circle,* 40–43.

Robb, S. (1985). Exercise treatment for wandering behavior. *Gerontologist, 25* (abstract special issue), 136.

Robertson, D., Rockwood, K., & Stolee, R. (1989). The prevalence of cognitive impairment in an elderly Canadian population. *Acta Psychiatrica Scandinavica, 80,* 303–309.

Robertson, L. (1987). Memory functioning in those who age normally and abnormally: A literature review. *British Journal of Occupational Therapy, 50*(2), 53–58.

Robins, L., & Wolf, F. (1989). The effect of training on medical students' responses to geriatric patient concerns: Results of linguistic analyses. *The Gerontologist, 29,* 341–344.

Rodeheffer, R. (1984). Exercise cardiac output is maintained with advancing age in healthy human subjects: Cardiac dilatation and increased stroke volume compensate for a diminished heart rate. *Circulation, 69,* 204–210.

Rodin, J. (1986). Aging and health: Effect of the sense of self-control. *Science, 233,* 1271–1276.

Rodin, J., & Langer, E. (1977). Long-term effects of a control-relevant intervention with the institutionalized aged. *Journal of Personality and Social Psychology, 35,* 897–902.

Rogers, C. (1977). *Carl Rogers on personal power.* New York: Delacorte Press.

Rogers, J., Marcus, C., & Snow, T. (1987). Maude: A case of sensory deprivation. *The American Journal of Occupational Therapy, 41,* 673–676.

Rogers, L., Bowlby, C., Grainger, J., & Munroe, H. (1989). Re-establishing independent eating through sensory stimulation. Undergraduate Research, Dalhousie University, School of Occupational Therapy, Halifax, Nova Scotia, Canada.

Rogers, S., & Hanft, B. (1988). Payment for geriatric health care. In L. Davis, & M. Kirkland (Eds.). (1988).

The role of occupational therapy with the elderly. Rockville, MD: American Occupational Therapy Association, Inc.

Rogers, R., Meyer, J., & Mortel, C. (1990). After reaching retirement age physical activity sustains cerebral perfusion and cognition. *Journal of American Geriatrics Society, 38,* 123–128.

Rogers, J., & Snow, T. (1982). An assessment of the feeding behaviors of the institutionalized elderly. *The American Journal of Occupational Therapy, 36,* 375–380.

Rosberger, Z., & MacLean, J. (1983). Behavioral assessment and treatment of "organic" behaviors in an institutionalized geriatric patient. *International Journal of Behavioral Geriatrics, 1,* 33–46.

Rosen, C. (1982). Ethnic differences among impoverished rural elderly in the use of religion as a coping mechanism. *Journal of Rural Community Psychology, 3,* 27–34.

Rosenbloom, A., & Morgan, M. (Eds.). (1986). *Vision and aging: General and clinical perspectives.* New York: Professional Press Books.

Ross, M., & Burdick, D. (1981). Sensory integration. Trenton, NJ: Slack Inc.

Rubenstein, L. (1987). Geriatric assessment: An overview of its impacts. *Clinics in Geriatric Medicine, 3,* 14–28.

Rubenstein, L. (1988). Falls and instability in the elderly. *Journal of the American Geriatrics Society, 36,* 266–278.

Rubenstein, L., Calkins, D., Greenfield, S., Jette, A., Meenan, R., Nevins, M., Rubenstein, L., Wasson, J., & Williams, M. (1989). Health status assessment for elderly patients. *Journal of the American Geriatrics Society, 37,* 562–569.

Ruskin, P. (1983). Aging and caring. *Journal of American Medical Association, 250,* 2550.

Sable, L. (1984). Life review therapy: An occupational therapy treatment technique with geriatric clients. *Physical and Occupational Therapy in Geriatrics, 2*(1), 49–54.

Sacks, O. (1989). *Seeing voices.* Berkeley, CA: University of California Press.

Sacks, O. (1990). Neurology and the soul. *New York Review of Books, 37*(18), 44–50.

Salber, E. (1989). *The mind is not the heart.* Durham, NC: Duke University Press.

Samuel, W., Henderson, V., & Miller, C. (1991). Severity of dementia in Alzheimer disease and neurofibrillary tangles in multiple brain regions. *Alzheimer Disease and Associated Disorders, 5,* 1–11.

Sandford, D. (1989). *Maria's grandma gets mixed up.* Portland, OR: Multnomah.

Scates, H., Randolph, D., Gutsch, K., & Knight, H. (1985–1986). Effects of cognitive-behavioral, reminiscence, and activity treatments on life satisfaction and anxiety in the elderly. *International Journal of Aging and Human Development, 22,* 141–146.

Schafer, D., Berghorn, F., Holmes, D., & Quadagno, J. (1986). The effects of reminiscing on the perceived control and social relations of the institutionalized elderly. In P. Foster (Ed.), *Therapeutic activities with the impaired elderly.* Binghamton, NY: Haworth Press.

Schaie, K., & Schooler, C. (Eds.). (1989). *Social structure of aging: Psychological processes.* Hillsdale, NJ: Lawrence Erlbaum Associates.

Schaie, K. (1989). The hazards of cognitive aging. *The Gerontologist, 29,* 484–493.

Schilke, J. (1991). Slowing the process of aging with physical activity. *Journal of Gerontological Nursing, 17*(6), 4–8.

Schmitz, A. (1991). Food news blues. *In Health, 5*(6), 40–44.

Schnelle, J., Traughber, D., Morgan, D., Embry, A., Binion, A., & Coleman, A. (1983). Management of geriatric incontinence in nursing homes. *Journal of Applied Behavior Analysis, 16,* 235–241.

Schulz, R., & Fritz, S. (1987). Origins of stereotypes of the elderly: An experimental study of the self-other discrepancy. *Experimental Aging Research, 13*(4), 189–195.

Scogin, F., Storandt, M., & Lott, L. (1985). Memory skills training, memory complaints and depression in older adults. *Journal of Gerontology, 40,* 562–568.

Scott, R., Bramble, K., & Goodyear, N. (1991). How knowledge and labelling of dementia affect nurses' expectation. *Journal of Gerontological Nursing, 17*(1), 21–24.

Scott, S. (Ed.). (1988a). *Payment for occupational therapy services.* Rockville. MD: American Occupational Therapy Association, Inc.

Scott, S. (1988b). Update: Occupational therapy Medicare amendments. In L. Davis, & M. Kirkland (Eds.), *The role of occupational therapy with the elderly.* Rockville, MD: American Occupational Therapy Association, Inc.

Sebastion, M. (1992). Investigations into the relationship between diet and osteoporosis. Ongoing research at the University of California at San Francisco Medical Center.

Seligman, M. (1975). *Helplessness.* San Francisco: W.H. Freeman and Co.

Selkoe, D. (1991). Amyloid protein and Alzheimer's disease. *Scientific American, 265*(5), 68–78.

Serby, M. (1986). Olfaction and Alzheimer's disease. *Progress in Neuro-Psychopharmacology and Biological Psychiatry, 10,* 579–586.

Shephard, R. (1987). *Physical activity and aging.* Rockville, MD: Aspen Publishers, Inc.

Shore, H. (1976). Designing a training program for understanding sensory losses in aging. *The Gerontologist, 16,* 157–165.

Short, L., & Leonardelli, C. (1987). The effects of exercise on the elderly and implications for therapy. *Physical and Occupational Therapy in Geriatrics, 5*(3), 65–73.

Skolaski-Pellitteri, T. (1984). Environmental intervention for the demented person. *Physical and Occupational Therapy in Geriatrics, 3,* 55–59.

Sloane, P., & Mathew, L. (1991). An assessment and care planning strategy for nursing home residents with dementia. *The Gerontologist, 31,* 128–131.

Smith, N., Kielhofner, G., & Watts, J. (1986). The relationships between volition, activity pattern, and life satisfaction in the elderly. *American Journal of Occupational Therapy, 40,* 278–283.

Smith, S. (1990). The unique power of music therapy benefits Alzheimer's patients. *Activities, Adaptation and Aging, 14*(4), 59–63.

Soloman, K. (1982). Social antecedents of learned helplessness in the health care setting. *The Gerontologist, 22,* 282–287.

Solomon, K. (1990). Learned helplessness in the elderly: Theoretical and clinical considerations. *Physical and Occupational Therapy in Geriatrics, 8*(1/2), 31–51.

Spangler, P., Risley, T., & Bilyeu, D. (1984). The management of dehydration and incontinence in non-ambulatory geriatric patients. *Journal of Applied Behavioral Analysis, 17,* 397–401.

Stankov, L. (1988). Aging, attention and intelligence. *Psychology and Aging, 3,* 59–74.

Steinkamp, M., & Kelly, J. (1987). Social integration, leisure activity, and life satisfaction in older adults: Activity theory revisited. *International Journal of Aging and Human Development, 25,* 293–307.

Stone, J. (1990). Managing behavior problems in the older adult with cognitive impairment. Presentation at Conference of the American Society of Aging. San Francisco.

Stone, J. (1992). Laugh. *In Health, 5*(7), 52–55.

Stowe, H.B. (1852). *Uncle Tom's cabin.* London: J. Cassell.

Strumpf, N., Evans, L., & Schwartz, D. (1990, May/June). Restraint free care: From dream to reality. *Geriatric Nursing*, 122–124.

Struntz, K., & Reville, S. (1985). *Growing together: An intergenerational sourcebook*. Washington, DC: American Association of Retired Persons.

Sullivan, C. (1982). Life review: A functional view of reminiscence. *Physical and Occupational Therapy in Geriatrics, 2*, 39–52.

Supiano, K., Ozminkowski, R., Campbell, R., & Lapidos, C. (1989). Effectiveness of writing groups in nursing homes. *The Journal of Applied Gerontology, 8*, 382–400.

Suski, N., & Nielson, C. (1989). Factors affecting food intake of women with Alzheimer's type dementia in long-term care. *Journal of the American Dietetic Association, 89*, 1770–1773.

Szekias, B. (1986). Therapeutic activities with the impaired elderly: An overview. *Activities, Adaptation and Aging, 8*(3/4), 1–28.

Taft, L., & Barkin, R. (1990). Drug abuse? Use and misuse of psychotropic drugs in Alzheimer's care. *Journal of Gerontological Nursing, 16*(8), 4–10.

Taft, L., & Nehrke, M. (1990). Reminiscence, life review, and ego integrity in nursing home residents. *International Journal of Aging and Human Development, 30*, 189–196.

Tager, I. (1990). Aging and pulmonary function. Lecture course on Motor and Sensory Changes in Aging, University of California at Berkeley.

Talbot, J., Stern, D., Ross, J., & Gillen, C. (1976). Flowering plants as a therapeutic environmental agent in a psychiatric hospital. *Hortscience, 11*, 365–366.

Tarbox, A. (1983). The elderly in nursing homes: Psychological aspects of neglect. *Clinical Gerontologist, 1*, 39–52.

Teitelman, J. (1982). Eliminating learned helplessness in older rehabilitation patients. *Physical and Occupational Therapy in Geriatrics, 1*(4), 3–10.

Tennant, K. (1990). Laugh it off: The effect of humor on the well-being of the older adult. *Journal of Gerontological Nursing, 16*(12), 11–17.

Teri, L., Borson, S., Kiyak, A., & Yamagishi, M. (1989). Behavioral disturbance, cognitive dysfunction and functional skill. *Journal of the American Geriatrics Society, 37*, 109–116.

Teri, L., Hughes, J., & Larson, E. (1990). Cognitive deterioration in Alzheimer's disease: Behavioral and health factors. *Journal of Gerontology, 45*(2), 58–65.

Teri, L., & Logsdon, R. (1991). Identifying pleasant activities for Alzheimer's patients: The pleasant events schedule-Ad. *The Gerontologist, 31*, 124–127.

Teri, L., Larson, E., & Reifler, B. (1988). Behavioral disturbance in dementia of the Alzheimer's type. *Journal of the American Geriatric Society, 36*, 1–6.

Thomas, C. (Ed.). (1981). *Taber's cyclopedic medical dictionary*. Philadelphia: F.A. Davis Co.

Thomas, D. (1983). *The collected poems of Dylan Thomas*. New York: James Laughlin.

Thornton, S., & Brotchie, J. (1987). Reminiscence: A critical review of the empirical literature. *British Journal of Clinical Psychology, 26*, 93–111.

Timiras, P. (Ed.). (1988). *Physiological basis of geriatrics*. New York: Macmillan.

Trace, S., & Howell, T. (1991). Occupational therapy in geriatric mental health. *American Journal of Occupational Therapy, 45*, 833–838.

Tweedy, J., Reding, M., Garcia, C., Schulman, P., Deutsch, G., & Antin, S. (1982). Significance of cortical disinhibition signs. *Neurology, 32*, 169–173.

U.S. Department of Health and Human Services, Health Care Financing Administration. (1987). *Medicare carriers manual. Part 3—Claims process*. Transmittal No. 1209.

U.S. Department of Health and Human Services, Health Care Financing Administration. (1990). State Operations Manual: Provider certification (Publication No. 7). Transmittal No. 241.

Vaccaro, F. (1988a). Application of operant procedures in a group of institutionalized aggressive geriatric patients. *Psychology and Aging, 3*, 22–28.

Vaccaro, F. (1988b). Successful operant conditioning procedures with an institutionalized aggressive geriatric patient. *International Journal of Aging and Human Development, 26*, 71–79.

Van Horn, G. (1987). Dementia. *American Journal of Medicine, 83*, 101–110.

Venable, S., & Mitchell, M. (1991). Temporal adaptation and performance of daily living activities in persons with Alzheimer's disease. *Physical and Occupational Therapy in Geriatrics, 9*, 31–51.

Ventura-Merkel, C., & Lidoff, L. (1983). *Community planning for intergenerational programming*. Washington, DC: National Council on Aging.

Viney, L., Benjamin, Y., & Preston, C. (1989). Promoting independence in the elderly: The role of psychological, social and physical constraints. *Clinical Gerontologist, 8*(2), 3–17.

Voeks, S., & Drinka, P. (1990). Participants' perception of a work therapy program in a nursing home. *Activities, Adaptations and Aging, 14*(3), 27–34.

Voeks, S., Gallagher, C., Langer, E., & Drinka, P. (1990). Hearing loss in the nursing home: An institutional issue. *Journal of the American Geriatrics Society, 38*, 141–145.

Volicer, L., Seltzer, B., Rheume, Y., Fabiszewski, K., Herz, L., Shapiro, R., & Innis, P. (1987). Progression of Alzheimer-type dementia in institutionalized patients: A cross-sectional study. *The Journal of Applied Gerontology, 6*, 83–94.

Volicer, L., Fabiszewski, K., Rheaume, Y., & Lasch, K. (1988). *Clinical management of Alzheimer's disease.* Gaithersburg, MD: Aspen Publishers, Inc.

Vortherms, R. (1991). Clinically improving communication through touch. *Journal of Gerontological Nursing, 17*(5), 6–10.

Wallace, J., & Naderman, S. (1987). Effects of pet visitations on semi-ambulatory nursing home residents: Problems in assessment. *The Journal of Applied Gerontology, 6*(2), 183–188.

Watts, D., Cassel, C., & Howell, T. (1989). Dangerous behavior in a demented patient: Preserving autonomy in a patient with diminished competence. *Journal of the American Geriatrics Society, 37*, 658–662.

Welch, P., Enres, J., & Rifkin, D. (1986). A comparison of dietary intake of institutionalized elderly fed in two different settings. *Journal of Nutrition for the Elderly, 6*(1), 17–30.

Weiss, C. (1989, Third Quarter). TR and reminiscing: The pursuit of elusive memory and the art of remembering. *Therapeutic Recreation Journal,* 7–18.

Weiss, C., & Thurn, J. (1987, Second Quarter). A mapping project to facilitate reminiscence in a long-term care facility. *Therapeutic Recreation Journal,* 46–53.

Weiss, C., & Thurn, J. (1990, First Quarter). Perceived effects of a training program to enhance family members' ability to facilitate reminiscing with older disoriented residents. *Therapeutic Recreation Journal,* 18–31.

Wenzel, E. (1990). It sure beats looking out the window: Literature for the elderly. *Activities, Adaptation and Aging, 14*(3), 1–16.

West, R. (1988). Prospective memory and aging. In P. Morris, & R. Sykes (Eds.), *Practical aspects of memory: Current research and issues* (Vol. 2: Clinical and educational implications). Chichester: John Wiley.

Williams, H. (1986). Humor and healing: Therapeutic effects in geriatrics. *Gerontion, 1*(3), 14–17.

Williams, R., Reeve, W., Ivison, D., & Kavanagh, D. (1987). Use of environmental manipulation and modified informal reality orientation with institutionalized, confused elderly subjects: A replication. *Age and Aging, 16*, 315–318.

Williamson, P., & Ascione, F. (1983). Behavioral treatment of the elderly. *Behavior Modification, 7*, 583–610.

Wilson, C., & Netting, F. (1987). New directions: Challenges for human animal bond research and the elderly. *Journal of Applied Gerontology, 6*(2), 189–200.

Winger, J., & Schirm, V. (1989). Managing aggressive elderly in long-term care. *Journal of Gerontological Nursing, 15*(2), 28–33.

Winkler, A., Fairnie, H., Gericevich, F., & Long, M. (1989). The impact of a resident dog on an institution for the elderly: Effects on perceptions and social interactions. *The Gerontologist, 29*, 216–223.

Winnett, R. (1989). Long-term care reconsidered: The role of the psychologist in the geriatric rehabilitation milieu. *Journal of Applied Gerontology, 8*, 53–68.

Winocur, G., Moscovitch, M., & Freedman, J. (1987). An investigation of cognitive function in relation to psychosocial variables in institutionalized old people. *Canadian Journal of Psychology, 42*, 257–269.

Wisocki, P. (1984). Behavioral approaches to gerontology. *Progress in Behavior Modification, 16*, 121–157.

Wister, A. (1989). Environmental adaptation by persons in their later life. *Research on Aging, 11*, 267–290.

Woodruff-Pak, D. (1989). Aging and intelligence: Changing perspectives in the twentieth century. *Journal of Aging Studies, 3*, 91–118.

Worden, P., & Sherman-Brown, S. (1983). A word frequency cohort effect in young versus elderly adults. memory for words. *Developmental Psychology, 19*, 521–530.

Wright, L. (1988). A reconceptionalization of the "Negative staff attitudes and poor care in nursing homes" assumption. *The Gerontologist, 28*, 813–820.

Yack, E. (1989). Sensory integration: A survey of its use in the clinical setting. *Canadian Journal of Occupational Therapy, 56*, 229–235.

Yesavage, J., Westphal, J., & Rush, L. (1981). Senile dementia: Combined pharmacologic and psychologic treatment. *Journal of the American Geriatrics Society, 29*, 164–171.

Youngers, K. (1988). Reimbursement and documentation in geriatric occupational therapy. In L. Davis, & M. Kirkland (Eds.), *The role of occupational therapy with the elderly.* Rockville, MD: American Occupational Therapy Association, Inc.

Zarit, S., Zarit, J., & Reever, K. (1982). Memory training for severe memory loss: Effects on senile dementia patients and their families. *The Gerontologist, 11,* 373–377.

Zepelin, H., Wolfe, C., & Kleinplatz, F. (1981). Evaluation of a year long reality orientation program. *Journal of Gerontology, 36,* 70–77.

Zgola, J., & Coulter, L. (1988). I can tell you about that: A therapeutic group program for cognitively impaired persons. *American Journal of Alzheimer's Care and Related Disorders and Research, 3*(4), 17–22.

Zgola, J. (1987). *Doing things: A guide to programming activities for persons with Alzheimer's disease and related disorders.* Baltimore: Johns Hopkins University Press.

Zubek, J. (Ed.). (1969). *Sensory deprivation: Fifteen years of research.* New York: Appleton-Century-Crofts.

Adams, C., Labouvie-Vief, G., Hobart, C., & Dorosz, M. (1990). Adult age group differences in story recall style. *Journal of Gerontology, 45*, 17–27.

Aire, T. (Ed.). (1985). *Recent advances in psychogeriatrics.* London: Churchill Livingston.

Allen, P., & Coyne, A. (1989). Are there age differences in chunking? *Journal of Gerontology, 44*, 181–183.

Backman, L. (1989). Effects of pre-experimental knowledge on recognition memory in adulthood. In A. Bennett, K. McConkey (Eds.), *Cognition in individual and social contexts.* Amsterdam: Elsevier.

Bailey, E. (1989). Red on our head: Communicating in the here and now with Alzheimer's patients. *American Journal of Alzheimer's Care and Related Disorders & Research, 4*(2), 24–27.

Baldwin, L. (1986). Therapeutic use of touch with the elderly. *Physical and Occupational Therapy in Geriatrics, 4*(4), 45–51.

Baltes, M., & Zerbe, M. (1976). Independence training in nursing home residents. *The Gerontologist, 16*, 428–432.

Barnathan, J., & Fox, E. (1990). The new skilled nursing facilities and intermediate care facilities regulations and their impact on activities. Unpublished handout from conference, American Society on Aging, San Francisco.

Barnes, J. (1974). Effects of reality orientation classroom on memory loss, confusion and disorientation in geriatric patients. *The Gerontologist, 14*, 138–142.

Barris, R. (1986). Activity: The interface between person and environment. *Physical and Occupational Therapy in Geriatrics, 5*(2), 39–49.

Beck, C., Heacock, P., Mercer, S., Thatcher, R., & Sparkman, C. (1988). The impact of cognitive skills remediation training on persons with Alzheimer's disease or mixed dementia. *Geriatric Psychiatry, 21*(1) 73–88.

Blocker, W. (1992). Increasing physical activity in the aged. *Geriatrics, 47*(1), 42–56.

Bowlby, C. (1991). Reality orientation thirty years later: Are we still confused? *Canadian Journal of Occupational Therapy, 58*, 114–122.

Brayne, C., & Calloway, P. (1990). The association of education and socioeconomic status with the mini mental state examination and the clinical diagnosis of dementia in elderly people. *Age and Ageing, 19*, 91–96.

Brickel, C. (1986). Pet-facilitated therapies: A review of the literature and clinical implementation considerations. *Clinical Gerontologist, 5*, 309–332.

Bright, R. (1987). The use of music therapy and activities with demented patients who are deemed "difficult to manage." *Clinical Gerontologist, 6*, 131–154.

Brook, P., Degun, G., & Mather, M. (1975). Reality orientation, a therapy for psychogeriatric patients: A controlled study. *British Journal of Psychiatry, 127,* 42–45.

Burgess, C. (1990). Horticulture and its application to the institutionalized elderly. *Activities, Adaptation and Aging, 14*(3), 51–62.

Burton, J. (1989). The model of human occupation and occupational therapy practice with elderly patients, Part 1: Characteristics of aging and Part 2: Application. *British Journal of Occupational Therapy, 52,* 215–221.

Campbell, L., & Cole, K. (1987). Geriatric assessment teams. *Clinics in Geriatric Medicine, 3,* 156–167.

Capuano, E. (1986). The design and implementation of memory improvement classes in the adult day care setting. In E. Taira (Ed.), *Therapeutic activities with the impaired elderly.* Binghamton, NY: Haworth Press.

Carroll, K., & Gray, K. (1983). How to integrate the cognitively impaired in group activities. *Clinical Gerontologist, 14,* 19–30.

Citrin, R., & Dixon, D. (1977). Reality orientation: A milieu therapy used in an institution for the aged. *The Gerontologist, 17,* 39–43.

Clark, B., Wade, M., Massey, B., & Van Dyke, R. (1975). Response of institutionalized geriatric mental patients to a twelve week program of regular physical activity. *Journal of Gerontology, 30,* 565–573.

Coons, D. (1987). Overcoming problems in modifying the environment. In H. Altman (Ed.), *Alzheimer's disease: Problems, prospects and perspectives.* New York: Plenum Press.

Coons, D. (1988). Wandering. *American Journal of Alzheimer's Care and Related Disorders & Research, 3*(1), 31–36.

Cunliffe, P. (1984). Reality orientation with psychogeriatric patients: An initial two month programme. *British Journal of Occupational Therapy, 47,* 341–344.

Curley, J. (1982). Leading poetry writing groups in a nursing home activities program. *Physical and Occupational Therapy in Geriatrics, 1,* 23–34.

Cusack, O., & Smith, E. (1984). *Pets and the elderly: The therapeutic bond.* New York: Haworth Press.

Davis, P., Morris, J., & Grant, E. (1990). Brief screening tests versus clinical staging in senile dementia of the Alzheimer type. *Journal of the American Geriatrics Society, 38,* 129–135.

Dougherty, D. (1985). The effect of the environment on the self-esteem of older persons. *Physical & Occupational Therapy in Geriatrics, 4*(1), 21–31.

Drummond, L., Kirchoff, L., & Scarborough, D. (1978). A practical guide to reality orientation: A treatment approach for confusion and disorientation. *The Gerontologist, 18,* 568–573.

Fabiano, L. (1987). *Supportive therapy for the mentally impaired elderly.* Seagrave, Ontario, Canada: Education and Consulting Service for Health Care.

Fischer, L., Visintainer, P., & Schulz, R. (1989). Reliable assessment of cognitive impairment in dementia patients by family caregivers. *The Gerontologist, 29,* 333–335.

Folmar, S., & Wilson, H. (1989). Social behavior and physical restraints. *The Gerontologist, 29,* 650–653.

Folsom, G. (1985). Reality orientation: full circle. *Bulletin of New York Academy of Medicine, 61,* 343–350.

Foos, P. (1989). Age differences in memory for two common objects. *Journal of Gerontology, 44,* 178–180.

Foster, P. (Ed.). (1986). *Therapeutic activities with the impaired elderly.* Binghamton, New York: Haworth Press.

Gaffney, J. (1986, March/April). Toward a less restrictive environment. *Geriatric Nursing,* 94–95.

Gardner, J. (1976). *October light.* New York: Alfred A. Knopf.

Goldman, L., & Lazarus, L. (1988). Assessment and management of dementia in the nursing home. *Clinics in Geriatric Medicine, 4,* 589–600.

Government & Legal Affairs Division. (1987). *Occupational therapy Medicare handbook.* Rockville, MD: American Occupational Therapy Association, Inc.

Hanft, B. (1988). Federal legislation affecting the elderly: Implications for occupational therapy. In L. Davis, & M. Kirkland (Eds.), *The role of occupational therapy with the elderly.* Rockville, MD: American Occupational Therapy Association, Inc.

Hanley, I., McGuire, R., & Boyd, W. (1981). Reality orientation and dementia: A controlled study of two approaches. *British Journal of Psychiatry, 138,* 10–14.

Harris, C., & Ivory, P. (1976). An outcome evaluation of reality orientation therapy with geriatric patients in a state mental hospital. *The Gerontologist, 16,* 496–503.

Health and Welfare Canada. (1988). *Guidelines for comprehensive services to elderly persons with psychiatric disorders.* Ottawa, Ontario, Canada: Minister of National Health and Welfare.

Heim, K. (1986). Wandering behavior. *Journal of Gerontological Nursing, 12*(11), 4–7.

Helgeson, E., & Willis, S. (1986). *Handbook of group activities for impaired older adults.* Binghamton, NY: Haworth Press.

Hepburn, K., Severance, J., Gates, B., & Christensen, M. (1989). Institutional care of dementia patients: A state-wide survey of long-term care facilities and special care units. *American Journal of Alzheimer's Care and Related Disorders and Research, 4*(2), 19–23.

Hochberg, M., Russo, J., Vitaliano, P., Prinz, P., Vitiello, M., & Yi, S. (1989). Initiation and perseveration as a subscale of the dementia rating scale. *Clinical Gerontologist, 8*(3), 27–41.

Hoffman, S., Platt, C., & Barry, K. (1987). Managing the difficult dementia patient: The impact on untrained nursing staff. *American Journal of Alzheimer's Care and Related Disorders and Research, 2*(4), 26–31.

Hogstel, M. (1979). Use of reality orientation with aging confused patients. *Nursing Research, 28*, 161–165.

Holden, U., & Sinebruchow, A. (1977). Reality orientation therapy: A study investigating the value of this therapy in rehabilitation of elderly people. *Age and Ageing, 7*, 83–90.

Howard, B. (1991). How high do we jump? The effect of reimbursement on occupational therapy. *American Journal of Occupational Therapy, 45*, 875–881.

Johnson, C., McLaren, S., & McPherson, F. (1981). The comparative effectiveness of three versions of classroom reality orientation. *Age and Ageing, 10*, 33–35.

Judd, M. (1971). *Why bother he's old and confused?* Winnipeg, Manitoba, Canada: Author.

Judd, M. (1982). Muriel Driver memorial lecture, 1982. *Canadian Journal of Occupational Therapy, 49*, 117–124.

Kapust, L., & Weintraub, S. (1988). The home visit: Field assessment of mental status impairment in the elderly. *The Gerontologist, 28*, 112–115.

Kremer, E., Nelson, D., & Duncombe, L. (1984). Effects of selected activities on affective meaning in psychiatric patients. *American Journal of Occupational Therapy, 38*, 522–528.

Lamport, N., Coffey, & Hersch, G. (1989). *Activity analysis handbook.* Thorofare, NJ: Slack Inc.

Langer, E., & Rodin, J. (1976). The effects of choice and enhanced personal responsibility for the aged: A field experiment in an institutional setting. *Journal of Personality and Social Psychology, 34*, 191–198.

Lauzon, P. (1987). *Music therapy: A handbook of activities for people with special needs.* Fredericton, New Brunswick, Canada: Author.

Lee, V. (1991). Language changes and Alzheimer's disease: A literature review. *Journal of Gerontological Nursing, 17*(1), 16–20.

Lewis-Long, M. (1989). *Realistic Alzheimer's activities.* Buffalo, NY: Potentials Development Inc.

Lilley, J., & Jackson, L. (1990). The value of activities: Establishing a foundation for cost-effectiveness—a review of the literature. *Activities, Adaptation and Aging, 14*(4), 5–20.

MacDonald, M. (1978). Environmental programming for the socially isolated aging. *The Gerontologist, 18*, 350–354.

MacDonald, M., & Butler, A. (1974). Reversal of helplessness: Introducing walking behavior in nursing home wheelchair residents using behavior modification procedures. *Journal of Gerontology, 29*, 97–101.

Madeira, K., & Goldman, A. (1989). Some aspects of sensory properties that relate to food habits and associated problems of elderly consumers. *Journal of Nutrition for the Elderly, 8*, 3–24.

McClannahan, L., & Risley, T. (1975a). Activities and materials for severely disabled geriatric patients. *Nursing Homes, 24*, 10–13.

McClannahan, L., & Risely, T. (1975b). Design of living environments for nursing home residents: Increasing participation in recreational activities. *Journal of Applied Behavior Analysis, 8*, 261–268.

McQuillen, D. (1985). Pet therapy: Initiating a program. *Canadian Journal of Occupational Therapy, 52*, 73–76.

Merchant, M., & Saxby, P. (1981, August). Reality orientation—a way forward. *Nursing Times*, 1442–1445.

Moehle, K., & Long, C. (1989). Models of aging and neuropsychological test performance decline with age. *Journal of Gerontology, 44*, 176–177.

Morris, J., & McManus, D. (1991). The Neurology of aging. Normal versus pathologic change. *Geriatrics, 46*, 47–54.

Mulcahy, N., & Rosa, N. (1981, July/August). Reality orientation in a general hospital. *Geriatric Nursing*, 264–268.

Nodhturft, V., & Sweeney, N. (1982). Reality orientation therapy for the institutionalized elderly. *Journal of Gerontological Nursing, 8*, 396–401.

Parker, C., & Somers, C. (1983, May/June). Reality orientation on a geropsychiatric unit. *Geriatric Nursing*, 163–165.

Peck, C. (1990). Discovery: An intergenerational education research program. Paper distributed by Third Age Life Centre, Oklahoma City, OK.

Pendergast, D., Calkins, E., Fisher, N., & Vickers, R. (1987). Muscle rehabilitation in nursing home residents with cognitive impairment: A pilot study. *American Journal of Alzheimer's Care and Related Disorders and Research, 2*(4), 20–25.

Post, S. (1986). If it isn't written it isn't done: How to formulate individual treatment plans. *Activities, Adaptation and Aging, 9*, 85–92.

Preston, T. (1973). When words fail. *American Journal of Nursing, 73*, 2064–2066.

Quattrochi-Tubin, S., & Jason, L. (1980). Enhancing social interactions and activity among the elderly through stimulus control. *Journal of Applied Behavior Analysis, 13*, 159–163.

Reeve, W., & Ivison, D. (1985). Use of environmental manipulation and classroom and modified informal reality orientation with institutionalized, confused elderly patients. *Age and Aging, 14*, 119–121.

Richman, L. (1969). Sensory training for geriatric patients. *The American Journal of Occupational Therapy, 22*, 254–257.

Robb, S., Boyd, M., & Pristash, C. (1980). A wine bottle, plant and puppy: Catalysts for social behavior. *Journal of Gerontological Nursing, 6*(12), 721–728.

Robb, S., & Stegman, C. (1983). Companion animals and elderly people: A challenge for evaluators of social support. *The Gerontologist, 23*, 277–282.

Rodegast, P., & Stanton, J. (1989). *Emmanuel's book II: The choice for love.* New York: Bantam Books.

Rodin, J., & Langer, E. (1980). Aging labels: The decline of control and the fall of self-esteem. *Journal of Social Issues, 36*, 12–29.

Rohling, M., Ellis, N., & Scogin, F. (1991). Automatic and effortful memory processes in elderly persons with organic brain pathology. *Journal of Gerontology, 46*(4), 137–143.

Romaniuk, N. (1983). The application of reminiscing to the clinical interview. *Clinical Gerontologist, 1*(3), 39–43.

Roper, J., Shapira, J., & Chang, B. (1991). Agitation in the demented patient: A framework for management. *Journal of Gerontological Nursing, 17*(3), 17–21.

Russell, R. (1990). Recreation and quality of life in old age. A causal analysis. *The Journal of Applied Gerontology, 9*, 77–90.

Ryan, D., Tainsh, S., Kolodny, V., Lendrum, B., & Fisher, R. (1988). Noise-making amongst the elderly in long term care. *The Gerontologist, 28*, 369–371.

Salthouse, T., Kausler, D., & Saults, J. (1988). Investigation of student status, background variables, and feasibility of standard tasks in cognitive aging research. *Psychology and Aging, 3*, 29–37.

Schiedermayer, D. (1988, July/August). The common clinical trilemma. In Alzheimer's: Reflections on tube feeding and antibiotics after a hosue call to Velma D. *American Journal of Alzheimer's Care and Related Disorders and Research*, 40–46.

Schwenk, M. (1979). Reality orientation for the institutionalized aged: Does it help? *The Gerontologist, 19*, 373–377.

Scogin, F., & Rohling, M. (1989). Cognitive processes, self-reports of memory functioning and mental health status in older adults. *Journal of Aging and Health, 1*, 507–520.

Scogin, F., & Bienias, J. (1988). A three year follow-up of older adult participants in a memory-skills training program. *Psychology and Aging, 4*, 334–337.

Sheridan, C. (1987). *Failure-free activities for the Alzheimer's patient.* Oakland, CA: Cottage Books.

Sherman, E. (1987). Reminiscence groups for community elderly. *The Gerontologist, 27*, 569–572.

Sullivan, S., & Lewin, M. (Eds.). (1988). *The economics and ethics of long-term care and disability.* Washington, DC: American Enterprise Institute for Public Policy Research.

Szekais, B. (1985). Using the milieu: Treatment-environment consistency. *The Gerontologist, 25*, 15–18.

VanBiervliet, A., Spangler, P., & Marshall, A. (1981). An ecobehavioral examination of a simple strategy for increasing meal-time language in residential facilities. *Journal of Applied Behavior Analysis, 14*, 293–305.

Voelkel, D. (1978). A study of reality orientation and resocialization groups with confused elderly. *Journal of Gerontological Nursing, 4*(3), 13–18.

Ward, H., Ramsdell, J., Jackson, J., Renvall, M., Swart, J., & Rockwell, E. (1990). Cognitive function testing in comprehensive geriatric assessment. *Journal of the American Geriatrics Society, 38*(10), 1088–1092.

Wells, C. (1979). Pseudodementia. *American Journal of Psychiatry, 136*, 895–900.

Williams, G. (1989). Management of depression in the elderly. *Primary Care, 16*(2), 451.

Williams, S. (1988). A proposal for a pet therapy program. Student paper. Dalhousie University School of Occupational Therapy, Halifax, Nova Scotia, Canada.

Wolfensberger, W. (1972). *The principles of normalization in human services.* Toronto: National Institute on Mental Retardation.

Woods, R. (1979). Reality orientation and staff attention: A controlled study. *British Journal of Psychiatry, 134,* 502–507.

Woods, R. (1983). Specificity of learning in reality-orientation sessions: A single case study. *Behavior Research and Therapy, 21,* 173–175.

Index

A

Abstract thought, 49
Accommodation, description of, 17
ACLFs. *See* Adult/geriatric congregate living facilities (ACLFs)
Acquired immunodeficiency syndrome (AIDS), dementia and, 41
Activities of daily living (ADL), 123–25. *See also specific activities*
  food-related, 129–33
  functional ability for, impairment in, 51–52
  grooming groups, 129
  handicrafts, 133–36
  horticultural, 136–48, *139, 141, 142, 143, 144, 146*
  independence in, 125–26
  meal groups, 126–29, *127, 129*
  sensory stimulation during, 298–99
Activity(ies). *See also* Food-related activities; Handicraft activities; Horticultural activities; Sensory stimulation activities; Therapeutic activities
  food-related, 129–33
  functional abilities for, 51–52
  in group therapy, 104–108, *107,* 111–12
  handicraft, 133–36
    projects for, 189–98
  horticultural, 136–48
    projects for, 199–206
  intergenerational, 148–50
  kinesthetic, 289–90
  resources for, 169–70
  self-directed, 294
  sensory stimulation and, 277
Activity plan, 115
Activity theory, 83–85
Acuity, description of, 17

Acute care hospitals, 356
AD. *See* Alzheimer's disease (AD)
Adaptation
  in group therapy, 101
  to activities, 111
  visual, to dark, 17
ADL. See Activities of daily living (ADL)
Administrative issues, 351
  analyzing the system service, 358–59.
  annotated bibliography on, 376–79
  change, anticipating and planning for, 375
  change agents, providers as, 375
  community-based service settings, 355–56
  data-based decision making, 359
  ethical and philosophical basis for services, 351–53
  health care systems, differences in Canadian and American, 353–55
  institution-based service settings, 356–57
  moral versus medical treatment, 352–53
  need, establishment of, 352
  organized effort, influencing policy through, 375–76
  political process, grass-roots effect on, 375
  program
    development of, 357–58, *358*
    evaluation of, 360–61
    implementation of, 359–60
  system factors, interplay of, *358*
ADRD. *See* Alzheimer's disease and related disorders (ADRD)
Adult day programs, 355–56
Adult/geriatric congregate living facilities (ACLFs), 356
Advanced stage of Alzheimer's disease, 39
  communication losses in, 63
Aggressive behavior, 119–20
Aging, normal
  advantages of, 7–8

Note: *italicized* numbers indicate items found in figures, tables, or exhibits.

S